Taking Sides: Clashing Views
in U.S. History, Volume 2,
Reconstruction - Present, 17e

Larry Madaras
James M. SoRelle

http://create.mheducation.com

ISBN-10: 1259677583   ISBN-13: 9781259677588

Contents

Detailed Table of Contents

Unit 1: The Gilded Age

Issue: Did Reconstruction Fail as a Result of Racism?
YES: George M. Frederickson, from *The Black Image in the White Mind: The Debate on Afro-American Character and Destiny, 1817–1914*, Harper & Row (1971)
NO: Heather Cox Richardson, from *The Death of Reconstruction: Race, Labor, and Politics in the Post-Civil War North, 1865–1901*, Harvard University Press (2001)

George M. Fredrickson concludes that racism, in the form of the doctrine of white supremacy, colored the thinking not only of southern whites but of most white northerners as well and produced only half-hearted efforts by the Radical Republicans in the postwar period to sustain a commitment to black equality. Heather Cox Richardson argues that the failure of Radical Reconstruction was primarily a consequence of a national commitment to a free-labor ideology that opposed the expanding central government that legislated rights to African Americans that other citizens had acquired through hard work.

Issue: Did a "New South" Emerge Following Reconstruction?
YES: Ronald D. Eller, from "A Magnificent Field for Capitalists," in *Miners, Millhands, and Mountaineers: Industrialization of the Appalachian South, 1880–1930*, University of Tennessee Press (1982)
NO: James Tice Moore, from "Redeemers Reconsidered: Change and Continuity in the Democratic South, 1870–1900," *Journal of Southern History* (1978)

Ronald D. Eller describes the post-Reconstruction entrepreneurial spirit that altered the traditional rural economy of the Mountain South through the introduction of the railroad and the development of coal, iron, and lumber industries in Appalachia. James Tice Moore challenges the view that the white, Democratic political elite that ruled the post-Reconstruction South abandoned antebellum rural traditions in favor of business and commerce and concludes that these agriculturally-oriented "Redeemers" represented a continuity of leadership from the Old South to the New.

Issue: Were Nineteenth-Century Entrepreneurs "Robber Barons"?
YES: Howard Zinn, from "Robber Barons and Rebels," in *A People's History of the United States: 1492 - Present*, Harper Collins (1999)
NO: John S. Gordon, from "Was There Ever Such a Business!" in *An Empire of Wealth: The Epic History of American Economic Power*, Harper Perennial (2004)

According to Howard Zinn, the new industrialists, such as John D. Rockefeller, Andrew Carnegie, and J. P. Morgan, adopted business practices that encouraged monopolies and used the powers of the government to prevent the masses from rebellion. John Steele Gordon argues that the nineteenth-century men of big business, such as John D. Rockefeller and Andrew Carnegie, developed through the oil and steel industries consumer products that improved the lifestyle of average Americans.

Issue: Were Anarchists Responsible for the Haymarket Riot?
YES: Timothy Messer-Kruse, from *The Haymarket Conspiracy: Transatlantic Anarchist Networks*, University of Illinois Press (2012)
NO: Paul Avrich, from *The Haymarket Tragedy*, Princeton University Press (1984)

Timothy Messer-Kruse challenges the traditional narrative of the Haymarket riot and concludes that the violence in Chicago on May 4, 1886, was the culmination of a thoroughly planned conspiracy by dedicated anarchists committed to the cause of violent revolution. Paul Avrich confirms that Chicago's anarchist leaders employed threatening rhetoric in response to the battle between workers and police at the McCormick Reaper Works that left two strikers dead on May 3, 1886, but he insists that the police, led by Inspector John Bonfield, precipitated the violence near Haymarket Square on May 4 by attempting to break up what had been a peaceful labor meeting.

Unit 2: Reform, War, and Depression

Issue: Did Southern White Christians Actively Support Efforts to Maintain Racial Segregation?
YES: Carolyn Renée Dupont, from "A Strange and Serious Christian Heresy: Massive Resistance and the Religious Defense of Segregation," in *Mississippi Praying: Southern White Evangelicals and the Civil Rights Movement, 1945-1975*, New York University Press (2013)
NO: David L. Chappell, from "Broken Churches, Broken Race: White Southern Religious Leadership and the Decline of White Supremacy," in *A Stone of Hope: Prophetic Religion and The Death of Jim Crow*, University of North Carolina Press (2004)

Carolyn Renée Dupont argues that in the post-*Brown* years of the 1950s and 1960s most white Mississippians, including Christian ministers and laypersons, zealously drew upon biblical texts, religious tracts, and sermons to craft a folk theology supporting massive resistance to racial segregation. David L. Chappell concludes that white southern religious leaders from the mainline Protestant denominations, preferring peace and social order, failed to provide sufficient support to enable segregationist politicians to mount a united front in defending the doctrine of white supremacy.

Issue: Did President Nixon Negotiate a "Peace With Honor" in Vietnam in 1973?
YES: Richard Nixon, from "The Vietnam Syndrome," in *The Real War*, Warner Books (1980)
NO: Jeffrey Kimball, from "Debunking Nixon's Myths of Vietnam," *The New England Journal of History* (2000)

Former President Richard Nixon believes that the South Vietnamese government would not have lost the war to North Vietnam in 1975 if Congress had not cut off aid. Jeffrey Kimball believes that the Nixon-Kissinger versions of the peace negotiations were designed to protect their reputations as diplomatic realists and misrepresented the truth that the failure to bomb North Vietnam into submission had produced a military stalemate by the middle of 1972 and political pressure from liberals and conservatives that forced the two men to negotiate the withdrawal of US troops by early 1973.

Issue: Has the Women's Movement of the 1970s Failed to Liberate American Women?
YES: F. Carolyn Graglia, from *Domestic Tranquility: A Brief against Feminism*, Spence Publishing (1998)
NO: Jo Freeman, from "The Revolution for Women in Law and Public Policy," in *Women: A Feminist Perspective*, McGraw-Hill Education (1995)

Writer and lecturer F. Carolyn Graglia argues that women should stay at home and practice the values of "true motherhood" because contemporary feminists have discredited marriage, devalued traditional homemaking, and encouraged sexual promiscuity. Jo Freeman claims that the feminist movement produced a revolution in law and public policy in the 1960s and 1970s that completed a drive to remove discriminatory laws regarding opportunities for women in the United States.

Issue: Were the 1980s a Decade of Affluence for the Middle Class?
YES: J. David Woodard, from "A Rising Tide," in *The America That Reagan Built*, Praeger (2006)
NO: Thomas Byrne Edsall, from "The Changing Shape of Power: A Realignment in Public Policy" in *The Rise and Fall of the New Deal Order, 1930-1980*, Princeton University Press (1989)

According to Professor J. David Woodard, supply-side economics unleashed a wave of entrepreneurial and technological innovation that transformed the economy and restored America's confidence in the Golden Age from 1983 to 1992. Political journalist Thomas B. Edsall argues that the Reagan revolution brought about a policy realignment that reversed the New Deal and redistributed political power and economic wealth to the top 20 percent of Americans.

Preface

Larry Madaras and James M. SoRelle, eds., *Taking Sides: Clashing Views in United States History. Volume 2: Reconstruction to the Present,* 17th ed. (Dubuque, Iowa: McGraw-Hill Education, 2016)

Since 1985, our aim has been to create an effective instrument to enhance classroom learning and to foster critical thinking in the subject area of U.S. history. Historical facts presented in a vacuum are of little value to the educational process. For students, whose search for historical truth often concentrates on *when* something happened rather than on *why*, and on specific events rather than on the *significance* of those events, *Taking Sides* is designed to offer an interesting and valuable departure. The understanding arrived at based on the evidence that emerges from the clash of views encourages the reader to view history as an *interpretive* discipline, not one of rote memorization. In this edition, we have continued our efforts to maintain a balance between traditional approaches to political, economic, and diplomatic topics on one hand and the new social history, which depicts a society that benefited from the presence of Native Americans, African Americans, women, and workers of various racial and ethnic backgrounds, on the other. The success of the past 16 editions of *Taking Sides: Clashing Views in United States History* has encouraged us to remain faithful to its original objectives and methods, but previous users of this reader will notice several changes in the format of this new edition.

Book Organization

As in previous editions, issues and their accompanying pairs of essays are arranged in chronological order and can be incorporated easily into any American history survey course. Each issue has an *Introduction*, which sets the stage for the debate that follows in the YES and NO selections and provides historical and methodological background to the problem that the issue examines. Each introduction has been expanded to focus more intentionally on *alternative perspectives* that are applicable to the question at hand in order to demonstrate that these issues contain a level of complexity that cannot be addressed fully in a simple Yes/No format. Additionally, each introduction is accompanied by a set of student-focused *Learning Outcomes* which are designed to highlight what knowledge the reader should take away

from reading and studying the issue. Also, at the end of each essay we have included a brief biographical sketch of each of the authors whose selections you have just read.

Following the essays, there are several features that are designed to generate further understanding of the issue question and the individual selections. First, there are several questions that relate to the learning outcomes and to the material in the preceding essays that are designed to stimulate *Critical Thinking and Reflection*. Second, *Is There Common Ground?* attempts to encourage students to think more deeply about the issue by highlighting points shared by scholars on the subject at hand and tying the readings to alternative perspectives within the debate. Third, *Additional Resources* offers a brief list of important books and/or journal articles relating to the issue. Also, Internet site addresses (URLs), which should prove useful as starting points for further research, have been provided on the *Internet References* page that accompanies each issue.

Acknowledgments   Many individuals have contributed to the successful completion of this edition. We appreciate the evaluations submitted to McGraw-Hill Contemporary Learning Series by those who have used *Taking Sides* in the classroom. Special thanks to those who responded with specific suggestions for past editions. We are particularly indebted to Maggie Cullen, Cindy SoRelle, the late Barry Crouch, Virginia Kirk, Joseph and Helen Mitchell, and Jean Soto, who shared their ideas for changes, pointed us toward potentially useful historical works, and provided significant editorial assistance. The staffs at the University of Tennessee–Knoxville Library, in particular Doug Engle and Christine Nassir, and the Interlibrary Loan Office at Moody Library at Baylor University provided essential assistance in the acquisition of source materials for our consideration of new issue topics. Lynn Wilder performed indispensable typing duties connected with this project. Finally, we are sincerely grateful for the commitment, encouragement, advice, and patience provided by Jill Meloy, senior product developer for the McGraw-Hill Create®/CLS, and the entire staff of McGraw-Hill Education.

Editors of This Volume

LARRY MADARAS is professor of history emeritus at Howard Community College in Columbia, Maryland. He received a BA from the College of Holy Cross in 1959 and an MA and PhD from New York University in 1961 and 1964, respectively. He has also taught at Spring Hill College, the University of South Alabama, and the University of Maryland at College Park. He has been a Fulbright Fellow and has held two fellowships from the National Endowment for the Humanities. He is the author of dozens of journal articles and book reviews, and also has edited another volume in this series, *Taking Sides: Clashing Views in United States History Since 1945*.

JAMES M. SORELLE is a professor of history, former chair, and current undergraduate program director in the Department of History at Baylor University in Waco, Texas. He received a BA and MA from the University of Houston in 1972 and 1974, respectively, and a PhD from Kent State University in 1980. In addition to introductory courses in United States and world history, he teaches advanced undergraduate classes in African American history, the American civil rights movement, and the 1960s, as well as a graduate seminar on the civil rights movement. He also has held a summer fellowship from the National Endowment for the Humanities. His scholarly articles have appeared in *Houston Review*, *Southwestern Historical Quarterly*, and *Black Dixie: Essays in Afro-Texan History and Culture in Houston* (Texas A&M University Press, 1992), edited by Howard Beeth and Cary D. Wintz. He also has contributed entries to *The New Handbook of Texas*, *The Oxford Companion to Politics of the World*, *Encyclopedia of African American Culture and History*, the *Encyclopedia of the Confederacy*, and the *Encyclopedia of African American History*.

Academic Advisory Board Members

Members of the Academic Advisory Board are instrumental in the final selection of articles for *Taking Sides* books. Their review of the articles for content, level, and appropriateness provides critical direction to the editors and staff. We think that you will find their careful consideration reflected in this book.

Guy Alain Aronoff
Humboldt State University

Tomas R. Bennett
Florida Hospital College of Health Sciences

Steven Berizzi
Norwalk Community College

Jeffrey Bloodworth
Gannon University

Jianyue Chen
Northeast Lakeview College

Gary Donato
Bentley University

Richard M. Filipink
Western Illinois University

Nichole Gotschall
Columbia Southern University

Aimee Harris-Johnson
El Paso Community College

Lisa Hill
Tuskegee University

Sandy Hoover
East Texas Baptist University

Laurie Kozakiewicz
University at Albany

Michael S. Mayer
University of Montana

Debra Meyers
Northern Kentucky University

Karl Rodabaugh
Winston-Salem State University

Scott Seagle
Chattanooga State Community College

Christy J. Snider
Berry College

Tamrala Swafford
Columbia Southern University

Joseph Thurman
Jefferson College

Joseph Villano
Barry University

Introduction

The Study of History

In a pluralistic society such as ours, the study of history is bound to be a complex process. How an event is interpreted depends not only on the existing evidence but also on the perspective of the interpreter. Consequently, understanding history presupposes the evaluation of information, a task that often leads to conflicting conclusions. An understanding of history, then, requires the acceptance of the idea of historical relativism. Relativism means the redefinition of our past is always possible and desirable. History shifts, changes, and grows with new and different evidence and interpretations. As is the case with the law and even with medicine, beliefs that were unquestioned 100 or 200 years ago have been discredited or discarded since.

Relativism, then, encourages revisionism. There is a maxim that "the past must remain useful to the present." Historian Carl Becker argued that every generation should examine history for itself, thus ensuring constant scrutiny of our collective experience through new perspectives. History, consequently, does not remain static, in part because historians cannot avoid being influenced by the times in which they live. Almost all historians commit themselves to revising the views of other historians by either disagreeing with earlier interpretations or creating new frameworks that pose different questions.

Schools of Thought

Five predominant schools of thought have emerged in American history since the first graduate seminars in history were given at the Johns Hopkins University in Baltimore, Maryland, in the 1870s. The *progressive* school dominated the professional field in the first half of the twentieth century. Influenced by the reform currents of populism, progressivism, and the New Deal, these historians explored the social and economic forces that energized America. The progressive scholars tended to view the past in terms of conflicts among groups, and they sympathized with the underdog.

The post–World War II period witnessed the emergence of a new group of historians who viewed the conflict thesis as overly simplistic. Writing against the backdrop of the Cold War, these *neoconservative* and *consensus* historians argued that Americans possess a shared set of values and that the areas of agreement within our nation's basic democratic and capitalistic framework are more important than areas of disagreement.

In the 1960s, however, the civil rights movement, women's liberation, and the student rebellion (with its condemnation of the war in Vietnam) fragmented the consensus of values upon which historians of the 1950s had centered their interpretations. This turmoil set the stage for the emergence of another group of scholars. *New Left* historians began to reinterpret the past once again. They emphasized the significance of conflict in American history, and they resurrected interest in those groups ignored by the consensus school. New Left history is still being written.

Since the 1970s, a fourth generation of scholars, however, focuses upon social history. Rather than focusing on politics and diplomacy, their primary concern is to discover what the lives of "ordinary Americans" were really like. These new social historians employ previously overlooked court and church documents, house deeds and tax records, letters and diaries, photographs, and census data to reconstruct the everyday lives of average Americans. Some employ new methodologies, such as quantification (enhanced by advanced computer technology) and oral history, whereas others borrow from the disciplines of political science, economics, sociology, anthropology, and psychology for their historical investigations.

At the same time social historians were rescuing the lives of average Americans, a fifth group of scholars emerged from the right of the political spectrum. Though marginalized by the historical profession, these "New Right" historians attack the liberal reform paradigm found in most U.S. history textbooks. Their political heroes are Calvin Coolidge and Ronald Reagan, not Woodrow Wilson and Franklin Roosevelt. Their economic models are Andrew Carnegie and John D. Rockefeller rather than railroad capitalist Jay Gould. These historians, like their compatriots in sociology, political science, and economics, espouse laissez-faire doctrine and denounce the liberal economist John Maynard Keynes. Some are libertarians economically and isolationists in diplomatic affairs, but most favor a muscular foreign policy not only in Europe but also in Asia and the Middle East.

The proliferation of historical approaches, which are reflected in the issues debated in this book, has had mixed results. On the one hand, historians have become so specialized in their respective time periods and methodological styles that it is difficult to synthesize the recent scholarship into a comprehensive text for the general reader. On the other hand, historians now know more about new questions or ones that previously were considered to be germane only to scholars in other social sciences. Although there is little agreement about the answers to these questions, the methods employed and the issues explored make the "new history" a very exciting field to study.

The topics that follow represent a variety of perspectives and approaches. Each of these controversial issues can be studied for its individual importance to American history. Taken as a group, they interact with one another to illustrate larger historical themes. When grouped thematically, the issues reveal continuing motifs in the development of American history.

Entrepreneurs, Laborers, Immigrants, African Americans, and Farm Workers

The dynamics of the modern economy are explored through investigations of the nineteenth-century entrepreneurs. Were these industrial leaders "robber barons," as portrayed by contemporary critics and many history texts? Or were they industrial statesmen and organizational geniuses? Radical historians view the new industrialists as robber barons who adopted business practices that encouraged monopolies and used the power of government to control the masses from rebellion. But business historians argue that men such as Rockefeller and Carnegie developed, through the oil and steel industries, consumer products that improved the lifestyle of average Americans.

In the wake of industrialization during the late 1800s, the rapid pace of change created new working conditions for the labor class. How did laborers react to these changes? Did they lose their autonomy in large corporations? Did they accept or reject the wage system? Were they pawns of the economic cycles of boom and bust, to be hired and fired at will? Did they look for an alternative to capitalism by engaging in strikes, establishing labor unions, or creating a socialist movement? To what extent did they resort to violence in an effort to realize their goals?

The vast majority of these factory workers came from the farms and cities of Europe. Massive immigration to the United States in the late nineteenth and early twentieth centuries introduced widespread changes in American society. Moreover, the presence of increasing

numbers of immigrants from Southern or Eastern Europe, many of them Catholics and Jews, seemed to threaten American-born citizens, most of whom were Protestant and of Northern or Western European ancestry. Asian immigrants, mainly from China or Japan, added to nativist fears. The Handlin thesis argues that the immigrants were alienated from their Old World cultures as they adjusted to an unfamiliar and often hostile environment. Others insist that immigrants never gave up the fight for their personal autonomy. They point out that many immigrants to the United States believed their stay in America would be temporary, a fact that limited their efforts at assimilation and reinforced ties to their original homelands, to which many of them returned once they had acquired some wealth.

One section of the country that was different from the rest in many respects was the American South. Following the end of the Civil War and Reconstruction, did a "New South" emerge or was there continuity with the "Old South." In the New South, many southerners labored as industrial workers in the textile, tobacco, furniture, lumber, and mining industries. Moreover, although most southerners remained farmers, their lives too were impacted by industrial forces in the region. Other scholars see more continuity than change in the post-Reconstruction South. They insist that the Democratic political leaders who replaced the Radical Republicans in the South did not abandon their antebellum rural traditions in favor of business and commerce. Instead, they promoted policies that supported the interests of farmers far more than those benefiting business-oriented elites.

Another region of importance in the post–Civil War era was the West, which became a central focus to historian Frederick Jackson Turner at the end of the nineteenth century. For generations, the "taming" of the "Wild West" was a central topic in U.S. history courses, and the frontier regions of the trans-Mississippi West have long been immersed in mythology and lore. For most students of the American past, this was a region inhabited by Native Americans and ruggedly individualistic farmers, cattlemen, and miners. More recently, "New West" scholars have recognized the presence of women on the frontier and have debated the degree to which female homesteaders and farmwives were able to adapt successfully to the strikingly new environments in which they found themselves.

With the end of slavery, one of the most controversial questions confronting those responsible for reconstructing the nation following the Civil War involved the future of African Americans. Perhaps no other period of American history has been subjected to more myths than has this postwar era. Even though most scholars today recognize that Reconstruction did not achieve its most enlightened economic and social goals, they differ in their explanations about the source of this failure. The South may have lost the Civil War but it won the historical battle in interpreting the failure of Reconstruction. White southern historians blamed the failure on the northern white carpetbaggers and their radical Republican allies in Congress for raping the South. The assumptions of these historians were twofold. First, African Americans were intellectually inferior to whites; second, the South should handle its own problems. Beginning in the 1950s, a more balanced approach to Reconstruction came from white northern scholars as well as African American historians who had been marginalized earlier by the professional historical associations. Explanations differ. Some stress the racism that permeated not only the South but the entire nation. Others emphasize the fact that the country was worn out by the war, and the U.S. Supreme Court, whose interpretations of the Thirteenth, Fourteenth, and Fifteenth Amendments sanctioned segregation and a laissez-faire ideology toward the economy, kept the national government's role in reconstructing the political, social, and economic structures in the South at minimum levels.

Most African Americans were denied full political and economic rights until the 1960s. The starting point of the civil rights movement is traditionally dated with the *Brown* case of 1954, which mandated desegregated schools, or the Montgomery boycott of the following year that challenged seating arrangements on local bus lines that disproportionately served black riders. Some have challenged this traditional chronology by asking whether or not World War II served as the true "watershed" for the efforts to roll back Jim Crow laws that most associate with the 1950s and 1960s. In his seminal article written in 1968, Richard M. Dalfiume points out the hypocrisy and paradox of fighting for democracy abroad while denying full citizenship rights to African Americans at home. Prior to Pearl Harbor, black leaders, such as labor leader A. Philip Randolph, threatened to march on the nation's capital unless the Roosevelt administration enforced equal employment opportunities in defense industries and took steps to desegregate American military forces. Randolph's approach clearly represented a commitment to black militancy that is more often associated with the direct action campaigns of Martin Luther King, Jr. Other historians question the degree to which African Americans practiced militant protest during the war. Recognizing evidence of mass protests by blacks during the 1930s, they note that once the United States entered the war in late 1941, most African American citizens and their leaders supported a united war effort to defeat the nation's enemies.

American Diplomacy in the Twentieth Century

As the United States developed a preeminent position in international affairs, the nation's politicians were forced to consider the proper relationship between their country and the rest of the world. To what extent, many asked, should the United States seek to expand its political, economic, and moral influence around the globe?

The United States became a major participant in two world wars in the twentieth century. At the end of World War I, President Woodrow Wilson attempted to enlarge the United States' role in world affairs by brokering the peace settlement and establishing the League of Nations to prevent the outbreak of another war. Ironically, the United States never joined the League, and historians have differed in their explanations as to why. Some focus on the political conflict between Wilson and his leading Republican opponent, Senator Henry Cabot Lodge. Some insist that the debilitating stroke the president suffered while campaigning in support of the Treaty of Versailles prevented him from being able to negotiate effectively with his Republican and isolationist opponents in the Senate. Still others blame Wilson for an ideological obstinacy that prevented him from being willing to accept any compromise to the League framework he had worked so hard to secure at the peace conference.

World War II brought the end of Nazi Germany and Imperial Japan and the opening of the Atomic Age. It also produced a rivalry between the United States and the Soviet Union that developed into what we know as the Cold War. Was this conflict inevitable? Was one nation more responsible than the other? Revisionists tend to blame the United States. President Truman, they say, was a parochial nationalist who did not understand Russian security needs and had a limited vision of foreign affairs that precluded minimal negotiations with the Russians. Most traditional Cold War historians believe that Joseph Stalin was the man primarily responsible for the Cold War.

The nuclear arms race produced the Cold War's greatest crisis in 1962 when Soviet Premier Nikita Khrushchev approved the construction and arming of offensive nuclear weapon sites on the island of Cuba, less than 100 miles from the shores of Miami, Florida. How did President John F. Kennedy fare in his handling of the Cuban missile crisis? Revisionists argue that Kennedy complicated the situation by adopting the tactic of military ultimatums recommended by his hastily organized decision-making committee of 14 experts, instead of seeking less volatile diplomatic solutions. Traditionalists, however, argue that sources uncovered over the past 20 years depict Kennedy as an anti-Communist Cold Warrior who nevertheless acted in a firm, rational, yet conciliatory manner toward his opposing head of state in resolving the missile crisis.

No discussion of American foreign policy is complete without some consideration of the Vietnam War. Was America's escalation inevitable in 1965? Did the U.S. government accomplish a "peace with honor" when it withdrew American troops from Vietnam in 1973 in exchange for the return of American POWs? Former President Richard Nixon believed that the South Vietnamese government would not have lost the civil war in 1975 had not the U.S. Congress cut off aid. Nixon's critics argue that he knew the Paris Peace Accords of 1973 were flawed, but he had intended to prevent the collapse of South Vietnam by bombing North Vietnamese targets. This plan was short-circuited, however, when Nixon was forced out of office in the wake of the Watergate scandal.

Political and Economic Changes

Historians have traditionally characterized the years from 1897 to 1917 as the Progressive Era. Whether the reformers of this period were successful in making significant alterations to the modern, urban-industrial society in their midst has been a subject of considerable debate through the years. Most historians recognize that there were several different approaches to reform in the early twentieth century. Good government reformers, for example, believed that getting rid of corrupt political machines by direct democratic reforms would change the United States for the better. Others thought cleaning up cities by abolishing liquor, child labor, compulsory schooling until age 16, factory inspection laws, and housing reforms would ameliorate harsh urban living. Finally, getting control over the power of the mega-corporations through regulatory agencies and real enforcement of antitrust laws would solve the major problems of urban-industrial America. But historians disagree whether these reforms worked. Progressives' harshest critics on the left believe that trying to impose a uniform set of values on a society which was no longer homogeneous because of massive immigration was doomed to failure. Other scholars are far more positive about the Progressives' ability to enact numerous reforms, especially at the national level, by enhancing the role of the federal government in addressing the

concerns of the American people in a rapidly growing urban-industrial society.

The Great Depression of the 1930s remains one of the most traumatic events in U.S. history. The characteristics of that decade are deeply etched in American folk memory, but the remedies that were applied to those social and economic ills—known collectively as the New Deal—are not easy to evaluate. Liberal historians contend that the economic stabilizers created by the New Deal programs prevented the recurrence of another Great Depression. New Right historians, on the other hand, criticize the New Deal from a twenty-first century conservative perspective. In this view, allegedly antibusiness New Deal agencies overregulated the economy and did not allow the free enterprise system to work out of the depression that FDR's programs prolonged.

The American people experienced a shock in the 1970s due to the normal expectations of constant growth. Rising oil prices, global economic competition, and double-digit interest and inflation rates created an economic recession and laid the groundwork for the economic policies associated with the "Reagan Revolution" in the 1980s. Did the decade of the 1980s produce an affluent American middle class? Some experts explain that supply-side economics unleashed a wave of entrepreneurial and technological innovation that transformed the American economy to the benefit of Middle America. Critics, however, insist that the economic realignments associated with President Reagan redistributed political power and economic wealth to the top 20 percent of Americans.

Social and Cultural Rebellions

Some writers believe that the decade of the 1920s represented a New Era of business prosperity that transformed the economy and ushered in a mass consumer culture with purchases of vacuum cleaners, electrical appliances, and automobiles, often financed through the installment plan. The decade was not without its seamier side, however. For example, the Ku Klux Klan proclaimed its commitment to "100 Percent Americanism" and emerged as the leading anti-Catholic, anti-immigrant, antiforeign group in the nation. Most writers take the traditional position that the Klan was a violent, reactionary organization that was unwilling to accept the cultural and social changes of the decade. Taking a more sympathetic view, new researchers see the Klan less as a nativist group and more as a pressure group. Exhibiting real concerns about the changing moral standards in their communities, many Klan members entered politics and attempted to enforce the older, Victorian moral standards that appeared to be under attack. As a consequence, the Klan of the twenties appeared to exhibit a commitment to the values of the majority of white American Protestants, but doubt remains as to how fully the majority of Americans were willing to embrace Klansmen as respectable advocates of mainstream society.

The 1950s brought about the return of the consumer culture which temporarily disappeared during the Great Depression and the World War II years. The population explosion that took place after World War II led to a youth culture which challenged the value system of their parents. Or did they? Did rock and roll music create new forms of rebellion that led to the 1960s civil rights, antiwar, and counterculture movements? Or did young people's style of rebellion differ even as they adhered to the basic conservative values of their parents?

The African American freedom struggle represented the most significant social movement of the 1950s and 1960s. While leaders, such as Dr. Martin Luther King, Jr., developed a nonviolent direct action campaign drawn from the experiences of Mohandas Gandhi and the moral and ethical framework of Christianity, the question remains as to how religion informed white southerners' approach to the desegregation campaigns of the civil rights era. For some, religious influences inspired a commitment to attack the Jim Crow system, but for many white southerners their responses to civil rights were influenced by ministers and lay leaders who interpreted their faith in such a way as to oppose efforts to tear down the walls of racial segregation.

A direct descendant of the civil rights movement was the Women's Liberation Movement of the 1970s. Did it help or harm women? Conservative women have argued that women should stay at home and practice the values of "true motherhood," noting that contemporary feminists have discredited marriage, devalued traditional homemaking, and encouraged sexual promiscuity. Feminist and activist scholars take a much more positive view of the women's movement for suffrage and liberation over the past century. Despite their class, racial, religious, ethnic, and regional differences, they argue that women in the twentieth-century United States experienced major transformations in their private and public lives and that those victories have extended globally into the twenty-first century.

Conclusion

The process of historical study should rely more on thinking than on memorizing data. Once the basics of who, what, when, and where are determined, historical thinking shifts to a higher gear. Explanation, analysis, evaluation, comparison, and contrast take command. These skills not only increase our knowledge of the past, but also provide general tools for the comprehension of all the topics about which human beings think.

The diversity of a pluralistic society, however, creates some obstacles to comprehending the past. The spectrum of differing opinions on any particular subject eliminates the possibility of quick and easy answers. In the final analysis, conclusions often are built through a synthesis of several different interpretations, but even then they may be partial and tentative.

The study of history in a pluralistic society allows each citizen the opportunity to reach independent conclusions about the past. Since most, if not all, historical issues affect the present and future, understanding the past becomes necessary if society is to progress. Many of today's problems have a direct connection with the past. Additionally, other contemporary issues may lack obvious direct antecedents, but historical investigation can provide illuminating analogies. At first, it may appear confusing to read and to think about opposing historical views, but the survival of our democratic society depends on such critical thinking by acute and discerning minds.

Larry Madaras
Emeritus, *Howard Community College*

James M. SoRelle
Baylor University

Unit 1

UNIT

The Gilded Age

*E*conomic expansion and the seemingly unlimited resources available in the postbellum United States offered great opportunities and created new political, social, and economic challenges. After an initial burst of freedom, African Americans were disfranchised and segregated from mainstream America and limited in their opportunities for full citizenship. As the United States became more heavily industrialized in the years following the Civil War, the need for cheap labor to run the machinery of the Industrial Revolution created an atmosphere for potential exploitation, which was intensified by the concentration of wealth in the hands of a few capitalists. Even the defeated South experienced the impact of industrialization, but questions remain as to how much the South remained tied to the political, economic, and social institutions of the Old South. In regions where industry thrived, the labor movement took root, with some elements calling for an overthrow of capitalism, whereas others sought to establish political power within the existing system. The formation of labor unions demanding rights for workers produced industrial warfare as management sought the support of the federal government to counter the efforts of strikers. Political freedom and economic opportunity provided incentives for immigration to the United States, but strains began to develop between immigrants and native-born workers. At the same time, thousands of Americans sought their opportunities in the trans-Mississippi West where they sought to earn their livelihoods in farming, herding, and mining.

Selected, Edited, and with Issue Framing Material by:
Larry Madaras, *Howard Community College*
and
James M. SoRelle, *Baylor University*

ISSUE

Did Reconstruction Fail as a Result of Racism?

YES: George M. Fredrickson, from *The Black Image in the White Mind: The Debate on Afro-American Character and Destiny, 1817–1914* (Harper & Row, 1971)

NO: Heather Cox Richardson, from *The Death of Reconstruction: Race, Labor, and Politics in the Post–Civil War North, 1865–1901* (Harvard University Press, 2001)

Learning Outcomes

After reading this issue, you will be able to:

- Explain several factors that prevented the Reconstruction process from achieving greater success.
- Analyze the political, economic, and social implications of the era of Reconstruction.
- Evaluate the role played by race in the reaction to the Reconstruction governments in the South following the Civil War.
- Define free labor ideology and explain its influence on Reconstruction.

ISSUE SUMMARY

YES: George M. Fredrickson concludes that racism, in the form of the doctrine of white supremacy, colored the thinking not only of southern whites but of most Northerners as well and produced only half-hearted efforts by the Radical Republicans in the postwar period to sustain a commitment to black equality.

NO: Heather Cox Richardson argues that the failure of Radical Reconstruction was primarily a consequence of a national commitment to a free labor ideology, which opposed an expanding central government that legislated rights to African Americans that other citizens had acquired through hard work.

Given the complex issues of the post–Civil War years, it is not surprising that the era of Reconstruction (1865–1877) is shrouded in controversy. For the better part of a century following the war, historians typically characterized Reconstruction as a total failure that had proved detrimental to all Americans—Northerners and Southerners, whites and blacks. According to this traditional interpretation, a vengeful Congress, dominated by Radical Republicans, imposed military rule upon the southern states. Carpetbaggers from the North, along with traitorous white scalawags and their black accomplices in the South, established coalition governments that rewrote state constitutions, raised taxes, looted state treasuries,

and disenfranchised former Confederates while extending the ballot to the freedmen. This era finally ended in 1877 when courageous southern white Democrats successfully "redeemed" their region from "Negro rule" by toppling the Republican state governments.

This portrait of Reconstruction dominated the historical profession until the 1960s. One reason for this is that white historians (both Northerners and Southerners) who wrote about this period operated from two basic assumptions: (1) the South was capable of solving its own problems without federal government interference; and (2) the former slaves were intellectually inferior to whites and incapable of running a government (much less one in which some whites would be their subordinates). African

American historians, such as W.E.B. Du Bois, wrote several essays and books that challenged this negative portrayal of Reconstruction, but their works seldom were taken seriously in the academic world and rarely were read by the general public. Still, these black historians foreshadowed the acceptance of revisionist interpretations of Reconstruction, which coincided with the successes of the civil rights movement (or "Second Reconstruction") in the 1960s.

Without ignoring obvious problems and limitations connected with this period, revisionist historians identified a number of accomplishments of the Republican state governments in the South and their supporters in Washington, D.C. For example, revisionists argued that the state constitutions that were written during Reconstruction were the most democratic documents that the South had seen up to that time. Also, although taxes increased in the southern states, the revenues generated by these levies financed the rebuilding and expansion of the South's railroad network, the creation of a number of social service institutions, and the establishment of a public school system that benefited African Americans as well as whites. At the federal level, Reconstruction achieved the ratification of the Fourteenth and Fifteenth Amendments, which extended significant privileges of citizenship (including the right to vote) to African Americans, both North and South. Revisionists also placed the charges of corruption leveled by traditionalists against the Republican regimes in the South in a more appropriate context by insisting that political corruption was a national malady. Although the leaders of the Republican state governments in the South engaged in a number of corrupt activities, they were no more guilty than several federal officeholders in the Grant administration, or the members of New York City's notorious Tweed Ring (a Democratic urban political machine), or even the southern white Democrats (the Redeemers) who replaced the Radical Republicans in positions of power in the former Confederate states. Finally, revisionist historians sharply attacked the notion that African Americans dominated the reconstructed governments of the South.

There can be little doubt that racism played some role in the failure of the Radical Republicans to realize their most ambitious goals for integrating African Americans into the mainstream of American society in the years following the Civil War. After all, white supremacy was a powerful doctrine. At the same time, we should not so cavalierly dismiss some of the more positive conclusions reached by that first generation of revisionist historians who built upon W.E.B. Du Bois' characterization of Reconstruction as a "splendid failure." For example, Kenneth Stampp's *The Era of Reconstruction, 1865–1877* (Alfred A.

Knopf, 1965) ends with the following statement: "The Fourteenth and Fifteenth Amendments, which could have been adopted only under the conditions of Radical Reconstruction, make the blunders of that era, tragic though they were, dwindle into insignificance. For if it was worth a few years of civil war to save the Union, it was worth a few years of Radical Reconstruction to give the American Negro the ultimate promise of equal civil and political rights." Eric Foner, too, recognizes something of a silver lining in the nation's post–Civil War reconstruction process. In *Reconstruction: America's Unfinished Revolution, 1863–1877* (Harper & Row, 1988), Foner claims that Reconstruction, while perhaps not all that radical, offered African Americans at least a temporary vision of a free society. Similarly, in *Nothing But Freedom: Emancipation and Its Legacy* (Louisiana State University Press, 1984), Foner advances his interpretation by comparing the treatment of ex-slaves in the United States with that of newly emancipated slaves in Haiti and the British West Indies. Only in the United States, he contends, were the freedmen given voting and economic rights. Although these rights had been stripped away from the majority of black Southerners by 1900, Reconstruction had, nevertheless, created a legacy of freedom that inspired succeeding generations of African Americans.

On the other hand, C. Vann Woodward, in "Reconstruction: A Counterfactual Playback," an essay in his thought-provoking *The Future of the Past* (Oxford University Press, 1988), challenges Foner's conclusions by insisting that former slaves were as poorly treated in the United States as they were in other countries. He also maintains that the confiscation of former plantations and the redistribution of land to the former slaves would have failed in the same way that the Homestead Act of 1862 failed to generate equal distribution of government lands to poor white settlers.

Thomas Holt's *Black over White: Negro Political Leadership in South Carolina During Reconstruction* (University of Illinois Press, 1977) is representative of state and local studies that employ modern social science methodology to yield new perspectives. While critical of white Republican leaders, Holt (who is African American) also blames the failure of Reconstruction in South Carolina on freeborn mulatto politicians, whose background distanced them economically, socially, and culturally from the masses of freedmen. Consequently, these political leaders failed to develop a clear and unifying ideology to challenge white South Carolinians who wanted to restore white supremacy.

In the selections that follow, George Fredrickson and Heather Cox Richardson present thought-provoking analyses of the influence racism played in the failure of

Reconstruction. In the first selection, Fredrickson contends that the doctrine of white supremacy that galvanized southern opposition to the political, economic, and social empowerment of African Americans after the war also dominated the thinking of white Northerners, including many Radical Republicans. As a consequence, racism prevented the success of efforts to incorporate African Americans fully into American society on an equitable basis.

Heather Cox Richardson offers a post-revisionist interpretation of the failure of Reconstruction and contends that the key barrier to postwar assistance for African Americans was the nation's commitment to a free labor ideology. Believing that social equality derived from economic success, most Americans opposed legislation, such as the Civil Rights Act of 1875, which appeared to provide special interest legislation solely for the benefit of the former slaves.

YES

George M. Fredrickson

The Black Image in the White Mind:
The Debate on Afro-American Character
and Destiny, 1817–1914

Race and Reconstruction

Once freed, the black population of the South constituted a new element that had to be incorporated somehow into the American social and political structure. Some Radical Republicans and veterans of the antislavery crusade regarded justice and equality for the freedmen as a fulfillment of national ideals and a desirable end in itself. For a larger number of loyal Northerners the question of Negro rights was, from first to last, clearly subordinate to the more fundamental aim of ensuring national hegemony for Northern political, social, and economic institutions. But even those who lacked an ideological commitment to black equality could not avoid the necessity of shaping a new status for the Southern blacks; for there they were in large numbers, capable of being either a help or a hindrance to the North's effort to restore the Union and secure the fruits of victory.

Before 1863 and 1864, Northern leaders had been able to discuss with full seriousness the possibility of abolishing slavery while at the same time avoiding the perplexing and politically dangerous task of incorporating the freed blacks into the life of the nation. President Lincoln and other moderate or conservative Republicans, feeling the pulse of a racist public opinion, had looked to the reduction or elimination of the black population through colonization or emigration as a way of approaching the racial homogeneity which they associated with guaranteed national unity and progress. By itself the Emancipation Proclamation had not destroyed such hopes, but events soon made the colonization schemes irrelevant and inappropriate. . . .

Whatever the motivation of Radical Reconstruction and however inadequate its programs, it was a serious effort, the first in American history, to incorporate Negroes into the body politic. As such, it inevitably called forth bitter opposition from hardcore racists, who attempted to discredit radical measures by using many of the same arguments developed as part of the proslavery argument in the prewar period.

The new cause was defined as "white supremacy"—which in practice allowed Southern whites to reduce the freedmen to an inferior caste, as they had attempted to do by enacting the "Black Codes" of 1865. To further this cause in 1868, [John] Van Evrie simply reissued his book *Negroes and Negro "Slavery"* with a topical introduction and under the new title *White Supremacy and Negro Subordination.* [Josiah] Nott also entered the Reconstruction controversy. In an 1866 pamphlet he reasserted the "scientific" case for inherent black inferiority as part of an attack on the Freedmen's Bureau and other Northern efforts to deal with the Southern race question. "If the whites and blacks be left alone face to face," he wrote, "they will soon learn to understand each other, and come to proper terms under the law of necessity."

Edward A. Pollard, a Richmond journalist and prewar fire-eater, also attacked Northern Reconstruction proposals on racial grounds. His book *The Lost Cause Regained,* published in 1868, contended that "the permanent, natural inferiority of the Negro was the true and *only* defense of slavery" and lamented the fact that the South had wasted its intellectual energy on other arguments. Before the war, Pollard had advocated a revival of the slave trade because it would deflate the pretensions of uppity house servants and town Negroes by submerging them in a flood of humble primitives; he now endorsed Van Evrie's thesis that white democracy depended on absolute black subordination, and concluded his discussion of Negro racial characteristics by asserting that the established "fact" of inferiority dictated "the true *status* of the Negro." Other propagandists of white supremacy, North and South, joined the fray. A writer named Lindley Spring attacked Radical Reconstruction in 1868 with a lengthy discourse on the benighted and savage record of blacks in Africa;

and a Dr. J. R. Hayes excoriated the proposed Fifteenth Amendment in 1869 with a rehash of all the biological "evidence" for Negro incapacity.

Inevitably, the pre-Adamite theory of Dr. Samuel A. Cartwright and Jefferson Davis was trotted out. In 1866 Governor Benjamin F. Perry of South Carolina made it the basis of a defense of white supremacy; and in 1867 a Nashville publisher named Buckner Payne, writing under the pseudonym "Ariel," revived a controversy among racists by expounding the doctrine at some length in a pamphlet entitled *The Negro: What Is His Ethnological Status?* Payne not only asserted that the Negro was "created before Adam and Eve" as "a *separate* and *distinct* species of the *genus homo,*" but also argued that it was because some of the sons of Adam intermarried with this inferior species, related, as it was, to the "higher orders of the monkey," that God had sent the flood as a punishment for human wrongdoing. Like almost all the racist respondents to Reconstruction, he contended that Negro equality would lead inevitably to amalgamation, and that miscegenation, in addition to resulting in the debasement of the white race, would bring on catastrophic divine intervention: "The states and people that favor this equality and amalgamation of the white and black races, *God will exterminate. . . .* A man can not commit so great an offense against his race, against his country, against his God, . . . as to give his daughter in marriage to a negro—a *beast. . . .*"

Most of the propagandists who attacked Radical measures on extreme racist grounds had a prewar record as apologists for slavery, but Hinton Rowan Helper attracted the greatest attention because of his fame or notoriety as an antebellum critic of slavery, As we have seen, Helper had never concealed his anti-Negro sentiments. A letter of 1861 summed up his philosophy: "A trio of unmitigated and demoralizing nuisances, constituting in the aggregate, a most foul and formidable obstacle to our high and mighty civilization in America are Negroes, Slavery, and Slaveholders. . . .

Death to Slavery!
Down with the Slaveholders!
Away with the Negroes!"

Having done justice to the first two imperatives in *The Impending Crisis,* Helper turned after the war to the third. His *Nojoque,* published in 1867, may have been the most virulent racist diatribe ever published in the United States. It contemplated with relish the time when "the negroes, and all the other swarthy races of mankind," have been "completely fossilized." To speed up the divinely ordained process of racial extermination, Helper proposed as immediate

steps the denial of all rights to Negroes and their complete separation from the whites. All this of course went in the teeth of the emerging Reconstruction policies of what had been Helper's own party, and throughout the book he excoriated "the Black Republicans" for departing from the attitudes of the prewar period, a time when Republicans had billed themselves as "the white man's party." His heroes were "White Republicans" like Secretary of State Seward and those few Republicans in the House and Senate who had remained loyal to President Johnson and joined the Democrats in efforts to prevent Federal action on behalf of Negro equality.

The active politicians—mostly Democrats—who opposed Radical Reconstruction were quite willing to resort to racist demagoguery, although they generally avoided the excesses of polemicists like Payne and Helper. President Johnson, for example, played subtly but unmistakably on racial fears in his veto messages of 1866; and later, in his third annual message to Congress, he put his views squarely on the line: ". . . it must be acknowledged that in the progress of nations negroes have shown less capacity for self-government than any other race of people. No independent government of any form has ever been successful in their hands. On the contrary whenever they have been left to their own devices they have shown an instant tendency to relapse into barbarism. . . . The great difference between the two races in physical, mental, and moral characteristics will prevent an amalgamation or fusion of them together in one homogeneous mass. . . . Of all the dangers which our nation has yet encountered, none are equal to those which must result from the success of the effort now making to Africanize the [Southern] half of our country." Equally blatant were the Northern Democratic Congressmen who made speeches against Radical measures which appealed directly to the prejudices of white workingmen. As Representative John W. Chanler of New York put it, in attacking an 1866 proposal to give the vote to Negroes in the District of Columbia: "White democracy makes war on every class, caste, and race which assails its sovereignty or would undermine the mastery of the white working man, be he ignorant or learned, strong or weak. Black democracy does not exist. The black race have never asserted and maintained their inalienable right to be a people, anywhere, or at any time."

In addition to such crude appeals to "white democracy," Democratic spokesmen in Congress provided detailed and pretentious discourses on the "ethnological" status of the Negro, drawn from writers like Nott and Van Evrie. The most notable of such efforts was the speech Representative James Brooks of New York delivered on December 18, 1867, in opposition to the First

Reconstruction Act. "You have deliberately framed a bill," he accused the Radicals, "to overthrow this white man's government of our fathers and to erect an African Government in its stead. . . . The negro is not the equal of the white man, much less his master; and this I can demonstrate anatomically, physiologically and psychologically too, if necessary. Volumes of scientific authority establish the fact. . . ." Brooks then proceeded "in the fewest words possible to set forth scientific facts." He discoursed at length on "the hair or wool of the negro," on "the skull, the brain, the neck, the foot, etc.," and on the perils of miscegenation. In considering the last topic, he conceded that "the mulatto with white blood in his veins often has the intelligence and capacity of a white man," but added that he could not consent to suffrage for mulattoes because to do so would violate the divine decree "that all are to be punished who indulge in a criminal admixture of races, so that beyond the third or fourth generation there could be no further mulatto progeny." Having covered black and brown physiology, Brooks went on in standard racist fashion to portray Negro history as a great emptiness.

In general such anti-Negro arguments were simply ignored by the proponents of Radical Reconstruction, who, by and large, tried to avoid the whole question of basic racial characteristics. But Brook's speech, perhaps the most thorough presentation of the racist creed ever offered in Congress, could not go unanswered. In a brief reply, Thaddeus Stevens dismissed Brook's views as contradicting the Biblical doctrine of the unity of mankind. Resorting to sarcasm and impugning Brook's loyalty, Stevens agreed that Negroes were indeed "barbarians," because they had "with their own right hands, in defense of liberty, stricken down thousands of the friends of the gentleman who has been enlightening us today." Disregarding Brooks's point about the "intelligence and capacity of mulattoes," Stevens proposed to match Frederick Douglass against Brooks in an oratorical contest. A more serious and extended reply to Brooks was made from the Republican side of the aisle by John D. Baldwin of Massachusetts. Baldwin's speech is significant because it clearly reveals both the strengths and weaknesses of the Radical position on race as a factor in Reconstruction.

In the first place, Baldwin contended, Brooks's argument was largely a *non sequitur;* for "the question presented in these discussions is not a question concerning the equality or the inequality of human races . . . it is a question concerning human rights. It calls on us to decide whether men shall be equal before the law and have equality in their relations to the Government of their country." Races, like individuals, might indeed differ in their capacities, but this should not affect their fundamental rights.

In reply to Brooks's claim that miscegenation would result from equality, Baldwin suggested that it was much more likely to result from degradation such as had occurred under slavery, a system which provided a "fatal facility" for "the mixture of races." As for Brooks's position on political rights, it meant in effect that all Negroes should be excluded from suffrage while "even the most ignorant and brutal white man" should be allowed to vote: "If he should propose to guard the ballot by some exclusion of ignorance or baseness, made without regard to race or class, candid men would listen to him and discuss that proposition." But Brooks was propounding, according to Baldwin, a concept of white privilege and "divine right" completely incompatible with the American egalitarian philosophy. Eventually Baldwin touched gingerly on the question of inherent racial differences and conceded the point that the races were not alike, but argued that "it is quite possible that we shall find it necessary to revise our conception of what constitutes the superiority of race." The prevailing conception, he noted, had resulted from an admiration for the ability to conquer and dominate; but were such aggressive qualities "really the highest, the most admirable development of human nature?" Pointing to the recent rise of a higher regard for the gentler, more peaceable virtues, Baldwin suggested "that each race and each distinct family of mankind has some peculiar gift of its own in which it is superior to others; and that an all-wise Creator may have designed that each race and family shall bring its own peculiar contribution to the final completeness of civilization. . . ." Although he did not discuss directly how the racial character of whites and Negroes differed, he was clearly invoking the romantic racialist conceptions that had long been popular among Radicals and abolitionists.

At first glance it would appear that Baldwin's speech constituted an adequate response to the racist critique of Radical Reconstruction, despite his avoidance of Brooks's specific physiological, anatomical, and historical arguments. It was indeed "rights" that the Radicals were attempting to legislate and not the identity of the races. But if, as Baldwin conceded, the races had differing "gifts"—with the whites holding a monopoly of the kind of qualities that led to dominance and conquest—then the competitive "test" of racial capabilities that the Radicals envisioned as resulting from their program would, to follow their own logic, lead inevitably to white domination, even without the support of discriminatory laws. Furthermore, their tendency to accept the concept of innate racial differences and their apparent repulsion to intermarriage were invitations to prejudice and discrimination on the part of those whites—presumably the over-whelming majority of Americans—who were less likely to respond to romantic appeals to racial benevolence than to draw traditional white-supremacist conclusions from any Radical admissions that blacks were "different" and, in some sense, unassimilable.

❧

A few Radicals and abolitionists had early and serious doubts about the efficacy and underlying assumptions of the Reconstruction Acts of 1867 and 1868. They suspected that quick readmission of Southern states into the Union under constitutions providing for Negro suffrage and the disfranchisement of prominent ex-Confederates would not by itself give blacks a reasonable opportunity to develop their full capacities and establish a position of genuine equality. Some understanding of this problem had been reflected in the land confiscation proposals of men like Thaddeus Stevens and Wendell Phillips. But it was the Radicals who worked for extended periods among the freedmen in the South who gained the fullest awareness of what needed to be done beyond what most Congressional proponents of Radical Reconstruction thought was necessary. Charles Stearns, an abolitionist who attempted to establish a co-operative plantation in Georgia as a step toward Negro landownership, attacked the notion that legal and political rights were all that was required to give the black man a fair, competitive position. In *The Black Man of the South and the Rebels,* published in 1872, Stearns denounced Greeley's philosophy of "root hog or die," arguing that even a hog could not root without a snout. In his view, provisions for land and education, far beyond anything that was then available to the blacks, were absolutely essential. Arguing that "the black man possesses all the natural powers that we possess," he pointed out that the blacks had not yet recovered from the degrading effects of slavery and were unable, even under Radical Reconstruction, to compete successfully or maintain their rights in the face of a bitterly hostile Southern white population.

Albion W. Tourgée, an idealistic "carpetbagger" who settled in North Carolina and became a judge under its Radical regime, was an eloquent and persistent spokesman for the same point of view. Tourgée, who eventually made his experiences and perceptions the basis of a series of novels, sensed from the beginning that the Radical program, as it finally emerged from Congress, constituted a halfhearted commitment to Negro equality which was doomed to fail in the long run. In a letter to the *National Anti-Slavery Standard* in October, 1867, he announced his opposition to the "Plan of Congress" that was taking shape. "No law, no constitution, no matter how cunningly framed," he wrote, "can shield the poor man of the South from the domination of that very aristocracy from which rebellion sprang, when once states are established here. Anarchy or oligarchy are the inevitable results of reconstruction. Serfdom or bloodshed must necessarily follow. The 'Plan of Congress,' so called, if adopted, would deliver the free men of the South, bound hand and foot to their old-time, natural enemies." The Southern Republican Party, Tourgée was saying, was composed largely of impoverished blacks and lower-class whites. Even if assured of temporary political dominance by the disfranchisement of ex-Confederates, these men would soon find themselves at the mercy of the large landowners, who were in a position to apply economic pressure and undo the reforms of Reconstruction. With rare realism, Tourgée argued in effect that political power could not be maintained on the basis of suffrage alone but must be bolstered by adequate economic and social power—and this was precisely what Southern Republicans lacked.

Tourgée's predictions of course came true. As the North looked on, manifesting an increasing reluctance to interfere—a growing desire to wash its hands of the whole matter—Southern white "redeemers" toppled one Radical government after another between 1870 and 1877 and established white-supremacist regimes. Southern Radicalism, supported largely by black votes and ruling through shifting and unstable alliances of Northern "carpetbaggers," Southern white "scalawags," and emergent black spokesmen, had no chance of withstanding the economic, political, and paramilitary opposition of the white majority. In his 1879 Reconstruction novel, *A Fool's Errand,* Tourgée provided an acute assessment of what the Northern leadership had done and why it failed to achieve its original objectives:

> After having forced a proud people to yield what they had for more than two centuries considered a right,—the right to hold the African race in bondage,—they proceeded to outrage a feeling as deep and fervent as the zeal of Islam or the exclusiveness of the Hindoo caste, by giving the ignorant, the unskilled and dependent race—a race which could not have lived a week without the support or charity of the dominant one—equality of political right. Not content with this, they went farther, and by erecting the rebellious territory into self-regulating and sovereign states, they abandoned these parties to fight out the question of predominance without the possibility of national interference, they said to the colored man in the language of one of the pseudo-philosophers of that day, 'Root, hog, or die!'

The Negro never had a chance in this struggle, as the entire novel makes clear. His ignorance and poverty made him no match for the white conservative forces.

What Tourgée and a few others—notably Representative George W. Julian of Indiana—would have preferred as a plan of reconstruction was a comparatively long-term military occupation or territorial rule of the South, which would have guaranteed "Regeneration before Reconstruction." This "territorial tutelage" would have lasted for an indeterminate period, perhaps as long as twenty or thirty years—long enough to give the North a chance to prepare the freedmen for citizenship through extensive programs of education and guidance, presumably including some form of economic assistance, while at the same time working for a diminution of the racial prejudice and "disloyalty" of the whites. But such an approach was rendered impossible both by pressures which impelled Republican politicians to seek readmission of loyalist-dominated Southern states to the Union in time for the election of 1868 and by the underlying social and racial attitudes that have been described. According to the dominant "self-help" ideology, no one, regardless of his antecedents, had a claim on society for economic security or special protection, or was entitled to a social status that he had not earned through independent struggle and hard work; the just penalty for laziness, inefficiency, or vice was severe social and economic deprivation, and it was becoming an open question at this time whether society's most abysmal "failures" should even retain their full right to participate in the political process. Having been provided with Federal laws and Constitutional amendments which supposedly guaranteed his legal equality, the black man was expected to make his own way and find his "true level"

with a minimum of interference and direct assistance. When the Reconstruction governments foundered, many in the North were quick to say that the blacks had had their fair chance, had demonstrated their present incapacity for self-government, and could justifiably be relegated, for the time being at least, to an inferior status.

Tourgée probably understood better than anyone how tenuous and conditional the Northern commitment to Negro equality had been. His book *An Appeal to Caesar*, published in 1884, contended that the Northern people "have always reflected the Southern idea of the negro in everything except as to his natural right to be free and to exercise the rights of the freedman. From the first [the North] seems to have been animated by the sneaking notion that after having used the negro to fight its battles, freed him as the natural result of a rebellion based on slavery, and enfranchised him to constitute a political foil to the ambition and disloyalty of his former master, it could at any time unload him upon the states where he chanced to dwell, wash its hands of all further responsibility in the matter, and leave him to live or die as chance might determine."

GEORGE M. FREDRICKSON is the Edgar E. Robinson Professor of U.S. History Emeritus at Stanford University and the preeminent American scholar on the history of race. He is the author of *The Inner Civil War: Northern Intellectuals and the Crisis of the Union* (Harper & Row, 1965); *White Supremacy: A Comparative Study of American and South African History* (Oxford University Press, 1981); and *Black Liberation: A Comparative History of Black Ideologies in the United States and South Africa* (Oxford University Press, 1995).

Heather Cox Richardson

 **NO**

The Death of Reconstruction: Race, Labor, and Politics in the Post–Civil War North, 1865–1901

Civil Rights and the Growth of the National Government, 1870–1883

Northern Republican disillusionment with African-American attitudes toward social issues compounded the Northern association of Southern freedmen with labor radicals who advocated confiscation of wealth. Taking place during and immediately after the South Carolina tax crisis, the civil rights debates of the 1870s seemed to confirm that African-Americans were turning increasingly to legislation to afford them the privileges for which other Americans had worked individually. Civil rights agitation did more than simply flesh out an existing sketch of disaffected black workers, however; it suggested that advocates of African-American rights were actively working to expand the national government to cater to those who rejected the free labor ideal.

❦

"Civil rights," in the immediate aftermath of the war, meant something different than it gradually came to mean over the next several years. *Harper's Weekly* distinguished between "natural rights" to life, liberty, and "the fruits of . . . honest labor," and "civil rights," which were critical to a freedperson's ability to function as a free worker. Civil rights, it explained, were "such rights as to sue, to give evidence, to inherit, buy, lease, sell, convey, and hold property, and others. Few intelligent persons in this country would now deny or forbid equality of natural and civil rights," it asserted in 1867. The 1866 Civil Rights Act, written by the man who had drafted the Thirteenth Amendment, Illinois senator Lyman Trumbull, was intended to secure to African-Americans "full and equal benefit of all laws and proceedings for the security of person and

property as is enjoyed by white citizens." It guaranteed only that the legal playing field would be level for all citizens; state legislatures could not enact legislation endangering a black person's right to his life or his land. By 1867, hoping to woo conservative Republican voters into the Democratic camp and to undercut the justification for black suffrage, even moderate Democrats claimed to be willing to back civil rights for African-Americans "with every token of sincerity . . . from a free and spontaneous sense of justice."

"Social" equality was a different thing—it was a result of a person's economic success rather than a condition for it. It was something to be earned by whites and blacks alike. Directly related to economic standing, a man's social standing rose as he prospered. A good social position also required that a person possess other attributes that the community valued. A place in upwardly mobile American society required religious observance and apparently moral behavior, as well as the habits of thrift and economy dictated by a plan for economic success. This gradual social elevation became a mirror of gradual economic elevation through hard work as a traditional free laborer.

Immediately after the Civil War, as Democrats insisted that black freedom would usher in social mixing between races and intermarriage, almost all Northern Republicans emphatically denied that emancipation was intended to have any effect on social issues and reiterated that African-Americans must rise in society only through the same hard effort that had brought other Americans to prominence. In 1867, a correspondent to the radical *Cincinnati Daily Gazette* from Louisiana painted a complimentary portrait of Louisiana African-Americans, then concluded that they had neither the expectation nor the desire for "social equality, that favorite bugbear." They would ridicule any attempt to break down social distinctions by legislation, knowing that the government could give them only political equality, the writer claimed, quoting his informants as saying, "Our own brains, our own conduct, is what we must depend upon for our future elevation; each one of us striving for himself and laboring to improve his mental and moral condition." Adding credence to the correspondent's representations, the Georgia Freedmen's Convention of 1866 resolved, "We do not in any respect desire social equality beyond the transactions of the ordinary business of life, inasmuch as we deem our own race, equal to all our wants of purely social enjoyment."

As the Republicans enacted legislation promoting the interests of African-Americans, however, racist Democrats insisted they were forcing social interaction to promote African-Americans artificially, at the expense of whites. When the Civil Rights Act of 1866 took effect, Democrats charged that the Republican concept of black equality before the law meant Republicans believed that blacks and whites were entirely equal. The *New York World* predicted interracial marriages; the *Columbus (Ohio) Crisis* insisted that a black orator in Richmond had told his black audience to "vote for the man who will bring you into his parlor, who will eat dinner with you, and who, if you want her, will let you marry his daughter." In 1868, *De Bow's Review* argued that negro suffrage meant that African-Americans would "next meet us at the marriage altar and in the burial vault," where they would "order the white ancestors' bones to be disinterred and removed elsewhere, and their own transferred into these hitherto held sacred white family sepulchers."

In response to Democratic attacks, in 1868 the *New York Times* reiterated that Republicans planned only for African-Americans to share the rights and opportunities of typical free laborers. It maintained that "reconstruction did not fly in the face of nature by attempting to impose social . . . equality," it simply established political and legal equality. These rights would eventually "obliterate" social prejudices as white men sought black votes. The next year the *Times* approvingly reported that abolitionist agitator Wendell Phillips had said that "the social equality of the black race will have to be worked out by their own exertion." Frederick Douglass put out the best idea, it continued later, namely: "Let the negro alone."

❧❧❧

Republican insistence that social equality would work itself out as freedpeople worked their way up to prosperity could not provide an answer for the overwhelming discrimination African-Americans faced. While many black and white Southerners accepted the established patterns of segregation, those practices meant that African-Americans'

public life was inferior to that of their white counterparts. Black people could not sit on juries in most of the South, they could not be certain of transportation on railroads or accommodation at inns, their schools were poor copies of white schools. In addition to creating a climate of constant harassment for African-Americans, discrimination, especially discrimination in schooling, seemed to hamper their ability to rise economically. The Fourteenth and Fifteenth Amendments had made all Americans equal before the law, but they could not guarantee equal access to transportation, accommodations, or schools, and while many ex-slaves accepted conditions as an improvement on the past and dismissed civil rights bills as impractical, those African-Americans who had worked hard to become members of the "better classes" deeply resented their exclusion from public facilities. "Education amounts to nothing, good behavior counts for nothing, even money cannot buy for a colored man or woman decent treatment and the comforts that white people claim and can obtain," complained Mississippi Sheriff John M. Brown. Prominent African-Americans called for legislation to counter the constant discrimination they faced.

African-American proponents of a new civil rights law to enforce nondiscrimination in public services had a champion in the former abolitionist Senator Charles Sumner of Massachusetts. An exceedingly prominent man, the tall, aloof Sumner was the nation's leading champion of African-American rights after the war and had advocated a civil rights measure supplementary to the Civil Rights Act of 1866 since May 1870, when he introduced to the Senate a bill (S. 916) making the federal government responsible for the enforcement of equal rights in public transportation, hotels, theaters, schools, churches, public cemeteries, and juries.

But Sumner's sponsorship of a civil rights bill immediately made more moderate congressmen wary of it; his enthusiasm for black rights frequently made him advocate measures that seemed to remove African-Americans from the free labor system and make them favored wards of a government that was expanding to serve them. Only two months after the ratification of the fifteenth Amendment had reassured moderate Republicans and Democrats alike that they had done everything possible to make all men equal in America, Sumner told the Senate that black men were not actually equal enough, but that his new bill would do the trick. When it passes, he said, "I [will] know nothing further to be done in the way of legislation for the security of equal rights in this Republic." . . .

❧❧❧

By 1874, most Republicans were ready to cut the freed-people's ties to the government in order to force African-Americans to fall back on their own resources and to protect the government from the machinations of demagogues pushing special-interest legislation. When Mississippi Republicans asked President Grant in January 1874 to use the administration to shore up their state organization, the *Philadelphia Inquirer* enthusiastically reported his refusal. Grant "remove[d] his segar from his mouth and enunciate[d] a great truth with startling emphasis," according to a writer for the newspaper. The president said it was "time for the Republican party to unload." The party could not continue to carry the "dead weight" of intrastate quarrels. Grant was sick and tired of it, he told listeners. "This nursing of monstrosities has nearly exhausted the life of the party. I am done with them, and they will have to take care of themselves." The *Philadelphia Inquirer* agreed that the federal government had to cease to support the Southern Republican organizations of freed-people and their demagogic leaders. The *New York Daily Tribune* approved Grant's similar hands-off policy in Texas, thrilled that "there [was] no longer any cause to apprehend that another State Government will be overturned by Federal bayonets."

Benjamin Butler's role as the House manager of the civil rights bill only hurt its chances, for he embodied the connection between freedpeople and a government in thrall to special interests. The symbol of the "corruption" of American government, Butler was popularly credited with strong-arming the House into recognizing the Louisiana representatives backed by the Kellogg government, which was generally believed to be an illegal creation of Louisiana's largely black Republican party, supported not by the people of the state but by federal officers. Honest men wanted to destroy "the principle which Mr. Butler and his followers represent," wrote the *New York Daily Tribune* and others. "The force in our politics of which he is the recognized exponent, and of which thousands of our politicians of less prominence are the creatures." "Butlerism" meant gaining power by promising an uneducated public patronage or legislation in their favor, and all but the stalwart Republicans and Democratic machine politicians hoped for the downfall of both Butler and what he represented.

Despite the fact that it was prosperous African-Americans who advocated the bill, it appeared to opponents that the civil rights bill was an extraordinary piece of unconstitutional legislation by which demagogues hoped to hold on to power in the South, and thus in the nation, by catering to the whims of disaffected African-Americans who were unwilling to work. The proposed law seemed to offer nothing to the nation but a trampled constitution, lazy freedpeople, and a growing government corrupted into a vehicle for catering to the undeserving.

The civil rights bill would probably never have passed the Senate had it not been for the sudden death of Charles Sumner on March 11, 1874. Before he died, Sumner charged fellow Massachusetts senator George F. Hoar to "take care of the civil-rights bill,—my bill, the civil-rights bill, don't let it fail." Even Republican enemies of the bill eulogized the "great man"; the *Chicago Tribune* reflected that "there is no man, friend or enemy, who does not pause to pay respect to the memory of Charles Sumner." African-Americans across the country mourned Sumner's death and called for the passage of his "last and grandest work," and on April 14, 1874, from the Committee on the Judiciary, Senator Frederick T. Frelinghuysen reported Sumner's civil rights bill protecting African-Americans from discrimination in public facilities, schools, and juries. The committee's amendments placed firmly in the national legal apparatus responsibility for overseeing violations of the proposed law. In caucus on May 8, some Republican senators objected to "certain features" of the bill but expressed a desire to act "harmoniously" on the measure. In the next caucus, the Republicans decided to support the bill without amendments.

After an all-night session of the Senate, a handful of African-American men in the galleries applauded as the Senate passed the bill on May 23, 1874, by a vote of twenty-nine to sixteen. Rumors circulated that the president had "some doubts about signing it" if it should pass the House, and many Republicans indicated they would not mind the loss of the bill. "Respect for the dead is incumbent on us all," snarled the *New York Times*, "—but legislation should be based on a careful and wise regard for the welfare of the living, not upon 'mandates,' real or fictitious, of the dead." Referring to the apparent African-American control of Southern governments, the *Times* asked whether the freedman "stands in need of protection from the white man, or the white man stands in need of protection from him." The House Judiciary Committee could not agree on its own civil rights measure and decided to replace its bill with the Senate's. The House then tabled the bill for the rest of the session, despite the continued urging of "leading colored men" that Benjamin Butler get it taken up and passed. . . .

The civil rights bill was rescued from oblivion only by Democratic wins in the 1874 elections. Republican congressmen's desire to consolidate Reconstruction before the Democrats arrived barely outweighed party members' fears that the measure was an attempt of corrupt politicians to harness the black vote by offering African-Americans extraordinary benefits that would undermine their willingness to work. When the lame-duck Congress reconvened in December 1874, House Republican leader Benjamin Butler tried to pass a bill protecting freedmen at the polls and an army appropriations bill to shore up stalwart Republicans in the South. Democrats filibustered. Butler was unable to get a suspension of the rules to maneuver around them as fifteen Republicans joined the opposition, worried that Butler's attempt to suspend the rules was simply a means "to get through a lot of jobbing measures under cover of Civil Rights and protection of the South." With his reputation as a special-interest broker, Butler had a terrible time getting the civil rights bill off the Speaker's table. Finally Republicans agreed to let Butler take it to the floor in late January.

The galleries were full as the House discussed the bill in early February. After omitting provisions for integrated schools, churches, and cemeteries, the House passed the bill on February 5 by a vote of 162 to 100. While African-Americans in favor of a civil rights bill were horrified at the sacrifice of the school clause, all but the most radical Republicans approved the omission. "The bill . . . is worthy [of] the support of every congressman who wishes to deal equitably with the citizens of the United States, white and black," wrote even the *Boston Evening Transcript*. "This measure simply provides for the education of the blacks, and does not force their children into association with white scholars," at the same time demanding that the schools be equal. "The Republicans can stand upon such a platform as that," the *Transcript* chided unwilling party members. "The great desire and solicitude of the people are to support 'civil rights' and so execute in good faith the constitutional pledges of the nation." After initial reluctance, the Senate passed the school amendment by a vote of 38 to 62, and despite Democratic plans to talk the bill to death, the Senate repassed the civil rights bill without further amendment on February 27, 1875, with Democrats in the opposition. Grant signed the civil rights bill into law on March 1, 1875.

While some radical papers like the *Boston Evening Transcript* defended the bill—wondering "[i]f the blacks and whites cannot shave and drink together . . . how can they remain tolerably peaceful in the same community?"—its passage drew fire from conservative and moderate Northern Republicans who still read into the measure a larger political story of the corruption of a growing government by those determined to advance through government support rather than through productive labor. The *New York Times* noted that Northern African-Americans were "quiet, inoffensive people who live for and to themselves, and have no desire to intrude where they are not welcome." In the South,

however, it continued, "there are many colored men and women who delight in 'scenes' and cheap notoriety." It was these people, the "negro politician, . . . the ignorant field hand, who, by his very brutality has forced his way into, and disgraces, public positions of honor and trust—men . . . who have no feeling and no sensibility," who would "take every opportunity of inflicting petty annoyances upon their former masters." The author concluded that the law would not be enforceable, and that "it is a great mistake to seek to impose new social customs on a people by act of Congress." Noticing the immediate efforts of Southerners to circumvent the law by giving up public licenses and legislating against public disturbances, the *San Francisco Daily Alta California* agreed that the act was likely to produce more trouble than equality, and reiterated that social equality must be earned rather than enforced by law.

The true way for African-Americans to achieve equality, Republicans argued, was to work. The *New York Times* approvingly quoted an African-American minister in the South who reiterated the idea that laborers must rise socially only as they acquired wealth and standing. The *Times* recorded his warning that "character, education, and wealth will determine their position, and all the laws in the world cannot give them a high position if they are not worthy of it." Even a correspondent for the staunchly Republican *Cincinnati Daily Gazette* reflected that "Sambo . . . can go to the hotels, ride in first-class cars, and enjoy a box in the theater. To what good is all this? . . . He needs now, to be let alone, and let work out his own destiny, aided only as his wants make him an object of charity. . . .

❧

In 1883, the U.S. Supreme Court considered five civil rights cases, one each from Tennessee, New York, Kansas, Missouri, and California. On October 15, 1883, the court decided that the Civil Rights Act of 1875 was unconstitutional because federal authority could overrule only state institutional discrimination, not private actions; Justice John Marshall Harlan of Kentucky cast the only dissenting vote. With the decision, Northern Republicans stated that they had never liked the law, because it removed African-Americans from the tenets of a free labor society, using the government to give them benefits for which others had to work. The *New York Times* declared that African-Americans "should be treated on their merits as individuals precisely as other citizens are treated in like circumstances" and admitted that there was, indeed, "a good deal of unjust prejudice against" them. But the *Times* remained skeptical that legislation could resolve the problem. Even newspapers like the *Hartford Courant*, which supported the law, said it did so only because it proved that Americans were sincere in their quest for equal rights. Three days later that newspaper mused that the law had been necessary only for "the reorganization of a disordered society," and that freedpeople no longer needed its protection. The *Philadelphia Daily Evening Bulletin* agreed that public sentiment had changed so dramatically that the law was now unnecessary. Even the radical African-American *Cleveland Gazette,* which mourned the court's decision, agreed that the law was a dead letter anyway. The *New York Times* welcomed the decision, going so far as to charge the law with keeping "alive a prejudice against the negroes . . . which without it would have gradually died out."

Instead of supporting the Civil Rights Act, Republicans reiterated the idea that right-thinking African-Americans wanted to succeed on their own. The *New York Times* applauded the public address of the Louisville, Kentucky National Convention of Colored Men that concentrated largely on the needs of Southern agricultural labor and referred not at all to civil rights. That the convention had pointedly rejected chairman Frederick Douglass's draft address, which had included support for civil rights legislation, made the *Times* conclude that most attendees were "opposed to the extreme views uttered by Mr. Douglass," and that the great African-American leader should retire, since his "role as a leader of his race is about played out."

Despite the *Times's* conclusion, African-Americans across the country protested the decision both as individuals and in mass meetings, reflecting, "It is a mercy that Charles Sumner is not alive to mourn for his cherished Civil Rights bill." At a mass meeting in Washington, D.C., Frederick Douglass admonished that the decision "had inflicted a heavy calamity on the 7,000,000 of colored people of this country, and had left them naked and defenceless against the action of a malignant, vulgar and pitiless prejudice." When the African Methodist Episcopal (AME) Church Conference of Western States, in session in Denver, discussed the decision, delegates made "incendiary" speeches and "[a] Bishop declared that if the negroes' rights were thus trampled upon a revolution would be the result." . . .

Republicans and Democrats agreed that the only way for African-Americans to garner more rights was to work to deserve them, as all others did in America's free labor system. The *Philadelphia Daily Evening Bulletin* repeated this view:

> [F]urther advancement depends chiefly upon themselves, on their earnest pursuit of education, on their progress in morality and religion,

on their thoughtful exercise of their duties as citizens, on their persistent practice of industry, on their self-reliance, and on their determination to exalt themselves, not as proscribed or despised Africans, but as American men clothed with the privileges of citizenship in the one great republic of the earth. They have it in their power to secure for themselves, by their own conduct, more really important "rights" than can be given to them by any formal legislation of Congress.

The Democratic *Hartford Weekly Times* agreed, and asserted that true black leaders, "not men like Fred Douglass, who are 'professional' colored men, and who have been agitating something and been paid for it all of their lives," approved of the decision. "They say there is no such thing as social equality among white men, and that the colored man cannot get it by law, but by the way he conducts himself."

Republican and Democratic newspapers highlighted those African-Americans who cheerfully told their neighbors "to acquire knowledge and wealth as the surest way of obtaining our rights." From Baltimore came the news that "Mr. John F. Cook, a colored man of character, who deservedly enjoys the respect of this entire community, who has held and administered with marked ability for years the responsible office of Collector of Taxes for the District of Columbia," told a reporter that he had no fears of white reprisals after the decision, expecting whites to accord to African-Americans "what legislation could never accomplish." "These are golden words, and if all men of his race were like Mr. Cook there would never be any trouble on this subject," concluded the Republican *Philadelphia Daily Evening Bulletin*.

Even many Northern Democrats painted their own picture of an egalitarian free labor society that had no need of a civil rights law. First they restated the idea that Republican efforts for African-Americans had simply been a ploy to control the government by marshalling the black vote. Trying to make new ties to African-American voters, the Democratic *San Francisco Examiner* emphasized that Republicans had only wanted to use the black vote to create a Republican empire and that the reversal showed that Republicanism no longer offered advantages to black citizens. A reporter noted that members of the black community had said that "it was about time to shake off the Republican yoke and act in politics as American citizens, not as chattels of a party who cared but for their votes."

While the rhetoric of the *San Francisco Examiner* repeated long-standing Democratic arguments, it also reinforced the idea that some hardworking African-Americans had indeed prospered in America, and that these upwardly mobile blacks were fully accepted even in Democratic circles. In San Francisco, the paper noted, "there are . . . many intelligent and educated men and women of African descent." Using the Republican pattern of according prosperous African-Americans names, descriptions, and their own words, it interviewed the Reverend Alexander Walters, whom it described respectfully as an educated and well-traveled young man, and happily printed both his assertion that in cities across the nation and "in the West . . . race prejudice has died out," and his prediction that the court's decision would drive black voters from the Republican party. Similarly, it quoted P. A. Bell, "the veteran editor of the *Elevator,* the organ of the colored people," as saying that in California—a Democratic state—"we people are treated just as well as if there were fifty Civil Rights bills."

With the overturning of the 1875 Civil Rights Act, mainstream Republicans and Democrats, black and white, agreed that there must be no extraordinary legislation on behalf of African-Americans, who had to work their way up in society like everyone else. Stalwart Republicans who advocated additional protection for black citizens were seen as either political demagogues who wanted the black vote to maintain their power or misguided reformers duped by stories of white atrocities against freedpeople. Northern black citizens who advocated civil rights legislation, like Frederick Douglass, were either scheming politicians who, like their white counterparts, needed the votes of uneducated African-Americans, or they were disaffected workers who believed in class struggle and wanted to control the government in order to destroy capital.

Southern blacks seemed to be the worst of all these types. They appeared to want to increase the government's power solely in order to be given what others had earned, and to do so, they were corrupting government by keeping scheming Republican politicos in office.

HEATHER COX RICHARDSON is a professor of history at the University of Massachusetts, Amherst. Her other books include *The Greatest Nation of the Earth: Republican Economic Policies during the Civil War* (Harvard University Press, 1997) and *West from Appomattox: The Reconstruction of America After the Civil War* (Yale University Press, 2007).

EXPLORING THE ISSUE

Did Reconstruction Fail as a Result of Racism?

Critical Thinking and Reflection

1. What were the main barriers to African Americans being accorded full civil and political rights after the Civil War?
2. In what way does an economic interpretation play a significant role in the essay by Heather Cox Richardson?
3. In what ways does a racial interpretation play a significant role in the selections by both Fredrickson and Richardson?

Is There Common Ground?

The question posed in this issue assumes that Reconstruction policy ended in failure. Certainly, many of the goals formulated by the Radical Republicans in Congress remained unfulfilled by the time the Compromise of 1877 removed federal troops from the South. If the goal of Reconstruction was to bring the former Confederate states back into the Union, however, that task was accomplished despite the fact that relations between the North and South remained uneasy. If the goal was to rebuild the South economically, positive steps were taken in that direction as well. And coinciding with the end of Reconstruction were the efforts by some white Southerners to demonstrate their willingness at reconciliation with the despised Yankees by attracting industrial and manufacturing interests to the "New" South as a means of diversifying the region's economy. In addition, state constitutions were democratized and public education was made available on a large scale for the first time.

For those few forward-thinking "Radicals" who envisioned a multiracial society in the South that extended full rights of citizenship to African Americans, many of whom had lived their entire lives in slavery until the end of the Civil War, failure was likely foreordained given the strength of the doctrine of white supremacy not only in the South but also nationally. Absent a firm economic foundation that could guarantee self-sufficiency, sustained access to the ballot box, and a broad-based commitment to equality of the races, African Americans in the South

possessed little protection from poverty, political powerlessness, and the privilege of whiteness. Quiet, small victories would have to be crafted from within segregated black communities, while African Americans held out hope for future enforcement of the Fourteenth and Fifteenth Amendments.

Create Central

www.mhhe.com/createcentral

Additional Resources

Richard Nelson Current, *Those Terrible Carpetbaggers: A Reinterpretation* (Oxford University Press, 1988).

W.E.B. Du Bois, *Black Reconstruction in America: An Essay Toward a History of the Part Which Black Folk Played in the Attempt to Reconstruct Democracy in America, 1860–1880* (New York: Harcourt, Brace, 1935).

Carol Faulkner, *Women's Radical Reconstruction: The Freedmen's Aid Movement* (University of Pennsylvania Press PA: 2004).

Leon F. Litwack, *Been in the Storm So Long: The Aftermath of Slavery* (New York: Alfred A. Knopf, 1980).

Forrest G. Wood, *The Era of Reconstruction, 1863–1877* (Arlington Heights, IL: Harlan Davidson, 1975).

Internet References . . .

America's Reconstruction: People and Politics After the Civil War

http://www.digitalhistory.uh.edu/exhibits/reconstruction/

Freedmen's Bureau Online

http://www.freedmensbureau.com/

Reconstruction

http://www.gilderlehrman.org/history-by-era/civil-war
-and-reconstruction-1861-1877/reconstruction

Selected, Edited, and with Issue Framing Material by:
Larry Madaras, *Howard Community College*
and
James M. SoRelle, *Baylor University*

ISSUE

Did a "New South" Emerge Following Reconstruction?

YES: Ronald D. Eller, from "A Magnificent Field for Capitalists," in *Miners, Millhands, and Mountaineers: Industrialization of the Appalachian South, 1880–1930* (University of Tennessee Press, 1982)

NO: James Tice Moore, from "Redeemers Reconsidered: Change and Continuity in the Democratic South, 1870–1900," *Journal of Southern History* (vol. 44, August 1978, pp. 357–378)

Learning Outcomes

After reading this issue, you will be able to:

- Define what scholars mean when they talk about a "New South" following the era of Reconstruction.
- Evaluate the extent to which the "New South" differed from the "Old South."
- Discuss the degree to which industrial processes were introduced into the southern economy after Reconstruction.
- Compare and contrast the characteristics of southern political leadership from the antebellum period to the late nineteenth century.
- Understand the concepts of "continuity" and "change" as they apply to historical processes in general and the realities of the post-Reconstruction South in particular.

ISSUE SUMMARY

YES: Ronald D. Eller describes the post-Reconstruction entrepreneurial spirit that altered the traditional rural economy of the Mountain South through the introduction of the railroad and the development of coal, iron, and lumber industries in Appalachia.

NO: James Tice Moore challenges the view that the white, Democratic political elite that ruled the post-Reconstruction South abandoned antebellum rural traditions in favor of business and commerce and concludes that these agriculturally oriented "Redeemers" actually represented a continuity of leadership from the Old South to the New South.

O ne of the critical questions confronting those empowered to restore the former Confederate states to the Union following the Civil War was "What would the New South be like?" This rather large question can be broken down into several more specific parts: (1) "Who would take the reins of leadership in the South now that the war was over?"; (2) "How would the southern economy differ, if at all, in light of the fact that the plantation system had been dealt a blow by the end of chattel slavery?"; and (3) "What would be the nature of race relations in the South in the wake of emancipation?" Over the course of the Reconstruction period, the Republican politicians who seized control of the southern state governments in the late 1860s sought to impose their image of America upon the vanquished South, but they confronted intense resistance from most white southerners, who railed against "Yankee oppression" and the imposition of "Negro rule." Most of the "radical Republican" governments fell quickly, and within a decade, conservative white Democrats had regained control of the South and were in a position to determine the economic and social meanings of the New South.

Prior to the Civil War, the southern economy had been based overwhelmingly on agricultural production dominated by the plantation-slave system. The South was not without its manufacturing operations, but as the sectional conflict began, the region lacked a sufficient industrial base to sustain a people at war. By the late 1870s, some influential white southerners realized that the economic future of the South, and their ultimate reconciliation with the North, depended upon their willingness to participate actively in the industrial expansion that was sweeping much of the nation north of the Mason-Dixon line. What would such a program entail? It would require the exploitation of the South's abundant natural resources of timber, coal, and iron; the establishment of local industries funded by local capital; the expansion of the southern railway system; the creation of new banks to extend credit; and the building of new towns as mercantile and industrial centers.

The proponents of the New South looked forward to the prospect that one day their region would support a business culture associated with cities, factories, and trade. Their supporting statements found robust voice in language that would have been unimaginable only a few years before, among a handful of southern newspaper editors who propagandized the goals of a diversified southern economy. Francis Dawson, editor of the *Charleston News and Courier,* wrote: "As for Charleston, the importation of about five hundred Yankees of the right stripe would put a new face on affairs, and make the whole place throb with life and vivid force." Henry Waterson of Louisville, Kentucky's *Courier-Journal,* proclaimed that the "ambition of the South is to out-Yankee the Yankee." The most outspoken proponent of a New South, however, was Henry Grady, editor of the *Atlanta Constitution.* Grady traveled widely to promote his vision of the New South, and in a speech to the New England Society of New York in 1886, he offered a message of regional reconciliation when he told his audience, "There was a South of slavery and secession—that South is dead. There is now a South of union and freedom—that South, thank God, is living, breathing, and growing every hour."

There was more than a rhetorical flourish to the idea of the New South; cotton textiles, iron and steel manufacturing, sulfur and phosphate production, and tobacco products made significant headway in diversifying the southern economy. For example, from 1880 to 1900, the number of spindles of cotton thread produced in the textile states of North and South Carolina, Georgia, and Alabama increased from 423,000 to 3,792,000. The capital invested in the textile industry alone increased from $17.4 million to $124.6 million, an increase of over 600 percent. Iron and steel manufacturing became major industries in the middle and lower South. This activity led Richard Edmonds, editor of the *Manufacturer's Record* to report that "the easy-going days of the South have passed away, never to return." On another occasion, he proclaimed that throughout the South one could hear "a continuous and unbroken strain of what has been termed 'the music of progress'—the whir of the spindle, the buzz of the saw, the roar of the furnace and the throb of the locomotive." By 1914, the New South had become industrialized in ways that few Americans could have imagined at the end of the Civil War. More importantly, this was permanent change, despite the fact that the great majority of southerners (and other Americans for that matter) continued to earn their livelihoods from the soil. This industrial growth marked the beginning of the South's integration into the nation.

The first generation of professionally trained historians, many of them native-born southerners, were, along with propagandists like Henry Grady, largely responsible for the pronouncement that a New South had emerged from the Civil War. For these scholars, the New South had reconciled with the North and become more urbanized and industrialized. Businessmen and manufacturers enjoyed a prominent place in southern society, but members of the antebellum planter aristocracy—the Bourbons—were most responsible for overthrowing the Reconstruction regimes and continued to wield significant economic and political power. This view of the post-Reconstruction Gilded Age remained largely intact until C. Vann Woodward published his monumental *The Origins of the New South,* 1877–1913 (Louisiana State University Press, 1951). Woodward argued vigorously for a New South that had broken the back of the antebellum planter class. The architects of the elimination of Republican rule in the 1870s were "Redeemers"—white, conservative, business-oriented Democrats who, in Woodward's view, tried but failed to close the gap between the North and the South in terms of industrial production. At the same time, Woodward's Redeemers oversaw corrupt governments that failed to respond to the real needs of the southern population, especially African Americans, and pursued economic policies that ultimately left the South as little more than a colony of northeastern corporate interests. In the years since 1951, virtually every book and essay written about the South in the period from 1877 to 1913 has been crafted as a response to the "Woodward thesis." This is certainly the case in the two selections that follow.

Ronald D. Eller recognizes Woodward's claim that southern industrialization did not match the exaggerated claims of many New South proponents, but he is convinced that the southern economy made impressive strides in numerous enterprises, such as railroads and extractive industries, that rose to national prominence with the aid of local and outside capitalization. Perhaps more importantly, this industrial activity touched the lives of thousands of Appalachian residents, providing opportunities for them that might not otherwise have existed.

James Tice Moore focuses his attack on Woodward's depiction of the Redeemers. Where Woodward finds discontinuity in leadership from the antebellum period, Moore insists that the South's post-Reconstruction political elite were neither subservient to business interests nor willing to abandon the region's antebellum rural traditions. Southern politicians, he concludes, depended upon rural constituencies, held the same types of occupations as antebellum leaders, and are best characterized as members of agriculturally oriented elite.

YES ⤶

Ronald D. Eller

A Magnificent Field for Capitalists

In the summer of 1888, Charles Dudley Warner, a New York journalist and coauthor with Mark Twain of *The Gilded Age,* made a journey along the Wilderness Road from Pineville to Cumberland Gap in eastern Kentucky. As was the fashion with northern journalists who ventured into the southern backcountry in the late nineteenth century, Warner published an account of his travels the following spring in *Harper's New Monthly Magazine.* This was not Warner's first trip to the mountains, nor was this his first effort to describe the region which Will Wallace Harvey had labeled "A Strange Land and Peculiar People." Four years earlier, after riding through the Blue Ridge country of southwest Virginia, east Tennessee, and western North Carolina, Warner had written a major travelogue entitled "On Horseback." The latter had established its author as one of the leading figures in the new literary "discovery" of Appalachia. His journey into eastern Kentucky in 1888 promised to provide more of the same local-color material that had interested his urban middle-class readers.

Leaving the railroad near Pineville, Warner and his party traveled the thirteen miles to Cumberland Gap by wagon and then, crossing into Virginia, rode horseback up the Powell River Valley to Big Stone Gap. The scenery along the way was much the same as that which Warner had found in the Blue Ridge. "The road had every variety of badness conceivable—loose stones, ledges of rock, boulders, sloughs, holes, mud, sand, deep fords." Settlements were few—only "occasional poor shanties" and "rugged little farms"—but the landscape was spectacular with "the great trees . . . frequent sparkling streams, and lovely mountain views." The ineffable beauty of this virgin land, however, hid a "primitive and to a considerable extent illiterate" population that had long been isolated from the moving world. Amid the splendors of the great forests and swift streams were depressing scenes of poverty, ignorance, and lawlessness. . . .

Yet, in contrast to his adventure in the Blue Ridge, Warner found much in eastern Kentucky to inspire hope for the region's future. The picturesque hills, which had so long secluded the natural beauty of the region and had isolated the mountaineers from the currents of modern life, had also guarded the treasures of the mountains—the rich stores of coal, timber, and iron ore. The Civil War had removed major obstacles to the exploitation of this vast supply of natural wealth, and recent "scientific investigation [had] made the mountain district . . . the object of the eager competition of both domestic and foreign capital." The entire country from the Breaks of the Big Sandy River to Big Creek Gap in the Cumberland Mountain was "on the eve of an astonishing development—one that will revolutionize eastern Kentucky, and powerfully affect the iron and coal markets of the country." This region of "clear, rapid streams, stuffed with coals, streaked with iron, abounding in limestone, and covered with superb forests . . . [appealed] as well to the imagination of the traveller as to the capitalist." As Warner observed; "I saw enough to comprehend why eager purchasers are buying the forests and the mining rights, why great companies, American and English, are planting themselves there and laying the foundations of cities, and why the gigantic railway corporations are straining every nerve to penetrate the mineral and forest heart of the region. . . It is a race for the prize."

And what of the mountaineers? The arrival of the "commercial spirit," Warner believed, would transform this benighted society. Other writers had found the mountain people to be a "worthless, good-for-nothing, irreclaimable" lot, but Warner was not so despondent about their future. "Railroads, trade, the sight of enterprise and industry, will do much with this material." Business and enterprise would bring law and order, sobriety, education, health care, and the other fruits of the modern age. Now that an industrializing America had need for the abundance of fuel that had been so long stored in the mountains, a new day was dawning for the mountaineers. Because of the vast developments about to occur in the Cumberlands, this land had become "one of the most important and interesting regions in the Union."

Warner was not alone in his optimism about the potential industrialization of the Appalachians. As early as the 1870s, politicians, businessmen, and journalists had begun to promote the wealth of the mountains in newspapers and boardrooms throughout the United States and Europe. The untapped treasures of the hill country, these individuals believed, offered innumerable possibilities for the accumulation of personal wealth. Nowhere in the eastern United States could one find the vital industrial elements of coal, iron ore, timber, and water in such vast quantities and so close to one another. Among many promoters in the South, the natural resources of the Appalachians offered not only the opportunity for the accumulation of great personal wealth but for the revitalization of southern society as well. Lying in the very heartland of the South, the mountains harbored the materials necessary for building a "new civilization"—a New South constructed from the ashes of the old, but patterned in a more modern industrial mold. In the years from 1870 to 1900, therefore, for both personal and social reasons, advertising the mountains became an important component of the New South creed.

Yet the promotion of industrial development of the Appalachians reflected more than just opportunism or the romantic visions of a defeated South. The coming of what Warner called "the commercial spirit" to the mountains was part of a larger drama taking place in the nation as a whole. Throughout most of the nineteenth century, the forces of modernization had largely bypassed the mountains while fundamentally restructuring the fabric of American life. In the years following the Civil War, those forces were rapidly moving the nation down the road toward urban-industrial maturity, and the abundant resources of Appalachia provided vital fuel for that final industrial drive. As technological developments increased the productive capacities of urban centers in the Northeast, South, and Midwest, capitalists began to turn to surrounding rural areas for the human and natural resources to undergird expansion. The exploitation of peripheral rural areas for the benefit of industrializing urban centers became a requisite of industrial growth, resulting in unequal economic development and prolonged social tension between urban and rural communities. Appalachia, being one of the most rural areas of eastern America and rich in natural resources, provided a stage upon which much of this great social drama was played out. In a rapidly industrializing society, the wealth of the Appalachians became a passkey to affluence and power. Indeed, "it was a race for the prize." . . .

The emergence of economic and intellectual interest in the Appalachians in the late nineteenth century marked the beginning of the decline of the stable, traditional society that had evolved in the mountains. Although major aspects of modernization were not to be felt in the region until after the turn of the century (and even later-in some remote areas), the years from 1880 to 1900 were among the most critical decades in the region's history. The penetration of the region during these years by outside speculators, land developers, and industrialists launched a revolution in land use and ownership that drastically altered the mountaineer's relationship to the land. As ownership and control of the land were transferred from the mountaineers to the spokesmen of the new industrial order, the fate of the region became irretrievably tied to that of the larger society. The selling of the mountains and the subsequent arrival of the railroads were, as Warner noted, the first stage in the remaking of mountain life.

The Selling of the Mountains

By the year in which Charles Dudley Warner made his journey into eastern Kentucky, the mineral and timber wealth of the Appalachians was already well known to American capitalists, . . . but it was not until the post-Civil War years that interest in the potential of these resources quickened. Throughout most of the antebellum period, the difficulties of transportation, the absence of any real market, and the deep agrarian biases of southern leaders had prevented the large-scale development of the mountain reserves. In the years immediately following the war, however, a sudden rush of activity in commerce, investment, and new technology focused increasing attention on the mountains as a source of materials to fuel the industrial revolution. Among a new generation of southern leaders, moreover, the road to wealth seemed no longer to lead to the plantation but rather to the coal and iron fields of the Appalachians.

The rise of the industrial spirit in the South after Reconstruction did not substantially alter the basic structure of southern society. The South remained primarily an agricultural region until well into the twentieth century. Yet, changes in the character and outlook of southern leadership did take place in these years, opening large areas of the South, especially the Appalachians, to exploitation by absentee investors. Whether or not southern leaders themselves benefited economically from the new commercial enterprises (and many did), their receptive attitude toward industrial development eased the way for the penetration of southern regions by northern capital. To that outspoken band of southerners who believed that the future of their region lay in commercial and industrial growth, the abundant resources of the Appalachians provided a major incentive for capital investment. Beginning in the 1870s and growing in intensity in the 1880s and 1890s, advocates of the New South creed ardently promoted the industrialization of the South and the development of the timber and mineral reserves of the southern mountains. If the South was to fulfil its destiny as a leading center of industry, they argued, it must exploit the "exhaustless treasures" of its mountains.

The New South creed was part of a national booster spirit that emerged in the late nineteenth century, and, like its larger counterpart, was predominantly an urban phenomenon. Its loudest proponents were members of the new middle class that had begun to rise in major southern cities. Proselytes of the creed could be found in most towns and many villages throughout the postwar South, but the industrial faith burned brightest in three cities of the Southeast: Atlanta, Louisville, and Richmond. Each had evolved as an important railroad center, had developed a large manufacturing base, and supported a powerful business community. Moreover, each was home to a leading newspaper whose pages became fliers for the dissemination of the faith.

The Richmond *Whig,* under the control of conservative politician and railroad president William Mahone, was without equal in its promotion of railroads, mining, timber, and iron manufacturing in the Virginias. General Mahone had acquired extensive railroad interests in southwest Virginia, and his newspaper became a major advocate of "new ways for the Old Dominion." Across the mountains in Louisville, the *Courier-Journal* and its fiery editor Henry Watterson—sometimes spokesman for the Louisville and Nashville Railroad—called for the industrial development of Kentucky and the attraction of "Eastern Capital" to that state's coal fields. But the most outspoken apostle of the new order was Henry Grady of the Atlanta *Constitution.* In his years with the *Constitution,* Grady developed a national reputation as the leading disciple of the New South creed. As orator and editor, he advertised the opportunities for investment in the South and encouraged southern businessmen to exploit the industrial potential of their region.

These three metropolitan newspapers combined to spread the gospel of industrialism throughout the South and much of the nation. A line drawn through the urban headquarters of each of these presses would form a triangle completely enclosing the heartland of the Appalachian South. It was only natural, therefore, that as these centers of modernization sought to expand their industrial bases, they turned to their own "internal periphery" and to the natural resources of the mountains. In the years after 1870, these and other New South papers brought increasing pressure to bear upon politicians and state officials to publicize this backcountry wealth.

Convincing southern state leaders of the need for publicity was relatively easy during the initial postwar years. In this era of social and economic depression, politicians from all parties were interested in improving business conditions. During the 1870s and 1880s, campaigns were launched in every southern Appalachian state aimed at attracting foreign immigration and commercial investment. State authorities established immigration bureaus and dispatched agents to New York and Europe to spread the word of southern opportunities. Exhibitions of state resources were creatively displayed at commercial conventions throughout America and Europe, and by the turn of the century geological surveys were being commissioned to detail the extent of the states' mineral wealth for the benefit of potential buyers. . . .

Notwithstanding the efforts of organized groups, the promotional activity that was most influential in the development of the mountains was that carried on by private speculators. Riding into the mountains in the years following the Civil War, these men surveyed iron and coal deposits, purchased land or mineral rights from local residents, and attempted to entice railroads and industrialists to the area. Many of these "mineral men"—or "mineral hunters," as mountain people called them—were ex-military officers who had served in the region during the Civil War and had become familiar with the untapped wealth of the land. Others were the paid agents of northern capitalists who sought to invest in the lucrative resource potential of the South. Together with a zealous band of local promoters, they prepared the way for the invasion of the larger corporations.

Among the earliest and most ardent promoters of coal and iron development in the southern mountains were two former Confederate officers, General John Daniel Imboden and Major Jedidiah Hotchkiss. As early as 1872, General Imboden was urging legislators and prominent citizens of Virginia to exploit the forgotten coal and iron fields of the Appalachians. "Within this imperial domain of Virginia," he told a Richmond gathering, "lie almost unknown to the outer world, and not fully appreciated by their owners," greater mineral deposits than could be found in all of England and which, if tapped, would "attract hither millions of money, and enterprising thousands of people to aid in the restoration of the 'Old Dominion' to a foremost rank amongst the States of the Union." Such developments, he argued, would make Richmond the southern rival of Pittsburgh and Philadelphia. . . .

The work of General Imboden, however, was surpassed by that of his friend, Major Jedidiah Hotchkiss, who might fairly be called the father of coal development in parts of southwest Virginia and southern West Virginia.

Long before the coming of the railroad, Hotchkiss was promoting the mineral wealth of the Flat Top Mountain region along the headwaters of the Bluestone, Elkhom, Big Sandy, and Guyandotte rivers. He was primarily responsible for attracting the Philadelphia capital that constructed the Norfolk and Western Railroad (N & W) and transformed the Flat Top area into one of the most productive coal fields in the world. . . .

In 1873, the owners of the Wilson Cary Nicholas grant, a Revolutionary war grant of 500,000 acres around Flat Top Mountain, hired Hotchkiss to make a survey and evaluation of their holdings. Hotchkiss in turn hired Captain Isaiah Welch, a fellow Confederate officer and noted geologist, to make a detailed examination of the property and report on timber and mineral deposits. Welch entered the tract along Laurel Creek in Tazewell County, Virginia, and quickly discovered a seam of coal thirteen feet thick, which was then being used to fuel a local blacksmith shop. Since this seam was "about twice the height of the highest seams then known," he continued to follow the outcroppings north into Mercer, McDowell, and Wyoming counties in West Virginia before returning home. Welch's report thoroughly confirmed the presence of valuable coal deposits in the Flat Top district and generated a flurry of interest in developing the area. Major Hotchkiss subsequently persuaded a group of Philadelphia capitalists headed by Thomas Graham to purchase "some of the best land in the territory" and to begin construction of a narrow-gauge railroad, but the business depression of the 1870s prevented the realization of these plans. . . .

A similar rush of interest in land speculation swept the mountains of Tennessee and North Carolina in these years, although the prize was primarily the virgin timber and purported iron deposits of the territory. Expectations for the development of iron in the mountains failed to mature, partly because of the low quality of the ore, but speculators in the late nineteenth century were convinced of the region's potential for iron production. Great iron centers had evolved to the north of the mountains in Pittsburgh and on the region's southern fringe in Birmingham. It seemed logical that East Tennessee, with its proximity to the new coal fields and its purported deposits of iron ore, would become one of the leading industrial centers of the South. As one developer maintained in 1889,

What we need to make East Tennessee the most prosperous and desirable section of the South is capital. That would be a panacea for our financial ills and would disarm poverty of its terrors.

It would put us on the high road to wealth. . . . We need hundreds of blazing furnaces distributed over this region, along the foothills of our mountains, lighting up their gorges and developing and utilizing the iron embedded in their bowels. . . . What a magnificent field for capitalists!

Spurred by the rise of the industrial spirit, two cities in East Tennessee, Knoxville and Chattanooga, became centers for speculative activity in the surrounding mountains. After the revival of the economy in 1880, northern financiers sent an army of agents into these urban centers to survey the possibilities for investment. One of the leading examples of this northern invasion was H.B. Wetzell, a native of Pennsylvania and former Michigan businessman who came to live in Knoxville in the early 1880s to investigate "the natural resources of the southern Appalachian region from West Virginia to Alabama." Finding that the region was "A Country of Infinite Wealth-Creating Possibilities," Wetzell stayed on for over a decade, traveling on foot and horseback throughout the mountains and buying timber and mineral properties for northern investors.

In eastern Kentucky, the pioneer coal prospector of these years was Richard M. Broas of New York City. An engineer and former captain in the Union Army, Broas had spent the postwar years searching for oil in Pennsylvania and for gold and silver in the Sierras. In 1881, he came to the Big Sandy Valley between West Virginia and Kentucky to examine coal lands for the "Walbridge interests" of Toledo, Ohio. Failing to discover coal at the mouth of the Tug and Levisa forks of Big Sandy, Broas was hired by Nathanial Stone Simkins of Massachusetts to push on up the river and examine lands in the Miller's Creek section of Pike County. There, and later in the valley of the Elkhorn, he found seams of coal with immense possibilities and began a ten-year effort to promote the development of the mineral lands of the Elkhorn district. Like Hotchkiss in southwest Virginia, Broas met with repeated rebuffs, but this did not prevent his acquiring options on large tracts of land and mineral rights in the area. Between 1887 and 1891, Broas purchased or leased thousands of acres of mineral property in Pike and Letcher counties. At the height of his buying venture, he employed about twenty surveyors and a number of title attorneys. Most of his mineral leases were purchased at one dollar per acre in tracts of from 100 to 400 acres, generally from poor, often illiterate farmers. . . .

Some buyers, moreover, like Richard M. Broas, offered to purchase only the minerals under the land, leaving the surface to the ownership and use (and tax liability) of the farmer. The land would be disturbed at some future date, but it was difficult for the mountaineer to envision the scale and impact of industrial change. These "broad form deeds," as they were known in eastern Kentucky, effectively transferred to the land agents all of the mineral wealth and the right to remove it by whatever means necessary, while leaving the farmer and his descendants with the semblance of land ownership. It was not until the railroads penetrated the district that those who had concluded such deals realized their mistake. Not only had they lost all rights to the minerals below the land, but they had also relinquished such other rights to the surface of the land as to limit its use for residential or agricultural purposes.

In this way, millions of acres of land and even greater quantities of timber and mineral rights passed out of the hands of mountain residents and into the control of absentee owners. Most mountain families sold their land voluntarily, but the negotiations were hardly between equals. The mountaineer had little knowledge of the value his natural resources had to distant industrial centers, nor was he able to comprehend the changes that would come to the mountains as a result of efforts to tap those resources. Despite its importance to mountain life and culture, land was often taken for granted by the mountaineers, for it had always been plentiful and ownership had never been a deterrent to common use. The prices paid by land agents during these early years varied greatly from state to state and according to the potential wealth of the property, but amounts generally ranged from twenty-five cents to three dollars per acre. Some mountaineers were reported to have sold entire mountains rich in coal and timber for a mule, a saddle horse, or a hog rifle. . . .

Despite the crucial role played by outside agents in the selling of the mountains, that played by local speculators was almost equally important. Especially after many residents began to question the integrity of outside interests, native middle-class entrepreneurs served as effective brokers for absentee investors and as energetic missionaries of the new industrial faith. Particularly in the larger villages and towns, the relatively small mountain middle class and landed elite actively promoted the development of Appalachian natural resources as a panacea for their own as well as the region's financial ills. Local merchants and lawyers speculated widely in timber and mineral lands and advertised the potential of mountain property in the leading business journals and newspapers. Often serving as agents of northern capitalists, such individuals quietly bought up land from their neighbors at nominal prices.

By 1900, the emergence of new urban centers within the region had brought about the concentration of many resident speculators and promoters in towns such as Charleston, Bluefield, Ashland, Paintsville, Bristol, and Asheville. These development centers (called "growth centers" by modern planners) served as convenient extensions of the eastern industrial core into the Appalachian heartland. In many ways, they functioned in the same exploitative relationship to their surrounding rural counties as did the larger metropolises of the South and Northeast to the region as a whole. Promoters of industrialization increasingly used these centers as bases of operation from which to launch their invasions of the outlying rural districts.

The mountains had always contained a small ruling class whose economic power and political influence were derived from longstanding ownership of large tracts of land. Having evolved over the years into a planter-lawyer-merchant class, these mountain elites had much in common with the wealthier planters of the lowland South. Many had remained loyal to the Confederacy and the Democratic party. After Reconstruction, they joined with other "Redeemer" or "Bourbon" Democrats in writing new state constitutions and enacting a new series of land laws. While these laws further confused the system of land registry in the mountains, they benefited many of the same lawyer-politicians, who specialized in litigation of disputed land titles. When outside capitalists sought to acquire land in the mountains in the 1870s and 1880s, resident lawyers grew rich on corporation retainers and through ownership of valuable real estate. During the next three decades, the new laws passed by "conservative" politicians not only contributed to the wealth of the mountain elite but facilitated, with the help of that elite, "the eventual transfer of titles and mineral rights from small proprietors to mining and lumber corporations.". . .

Early Industrial Developments, 1870–1900

To urban middle-class Americans of the late nineteenth century, nothing symbolized the progress of American civilization quite as much as the railroad. Not only had the great surge in railroad construction after the Civil War helped to create a modern market economy, but the iron horse itself seemed to embody the energy, force, and technology of the new order. In fact, the fanning out of railroads from urban centers was an integral part of the modernizing process, tying the natural and human resources of rural areas to the industrializing core. If the mountains were to fuel the advance of industrial capitalism, they too would have to be breeched by the iron horse. "Capitalists and speculators," wrote a western North Carolinian in 1889, "have but very little wish to visit and examine counties without a railroad." Those resident mountain speculators who were most successful in their efforts, therefore, were those who were able to attract the interest of railroad men.

The coming of railroads to the Appalachian South was almost as dramatic as the selling of the land itself. In 1870, only one railroad line penetrated the region, and it ran down the valleys of southwest Virginia and eastern Tennessee, connecting Norfolk with Knoxville. This valley line had little impact on the surrounding mountain communities. By 1900, however, four major railroads had extended branch lines into the heart of the region: the Chesapeake and Ohio (C&O) into southern West Virginia, the Norfolk and Western (N&W) into southwest Virginia, the Louisville and Nashville (L&N) into eastern Kentucky and eastern Tennessee, and the Southern into western North Carolina. . . .

The last major extension of the N&W during these feverish days of the railroad's growth was an extension into the Clinch Valley of southwest Virginia, where rich coal deposits had been discovered in Wise County along the Kentucky border. Construction of the Clinch Valley Branch began in 1887 on a line running from Bluefield, on the New River Division, to Norton, near the Kentucky state line, a distance of 103 miles. The tracks of the N&W reached Norton in 1891, along with those of the L&N Railroad, which had constructed a branch up the Powell River Valley from Cumberland Gap. About this time another line, the Virginia and Southwestern—originally backed by Massachusetts interests—was completed from Bristol to Appalachia, Virginia, just below Norton. The completion of these three lines opened up markets for Wise County coal in the Southeast, the West, and the eastern seaboard, and the rapid economic development that followed quickly turned Wise County into the leading coal-producing county in the state. In 1902, the coal production for Wise County totaled more than 2.4 million tons, three times that of any other county in Virginia.

The two largest developers of the Wise County fields were the Virginia Coal and Iron Company, a Pennsylvania firm, and the Virginia Iron, Coal and Coke Company, financed by New York capital. Together, these two companies controlled a majority of the coal and coke produced in the county. The older of the two firms was the Virginia Coal and Iron Company, founded in 1882 by Edward K. Hyndman, Judge John Leisenring, and others of the Connellsville, Pennsylvania, coal region. These men had been attracted to Wise County by General J.D. Imboden,

who had convinced them of the potential wealth of Virginia coal. With Imboden serving as their attorney and land agent, the Connellsville syndicate had purchased about 67,000 acres of coal lands on the headwaters of the Powell River, paying as little as 35 cents an acre for some tracts. In the late 1880s, other companies began to acquire land in the area, and a new town sprang up at Big Stone Gap, near the Virginia Coal and Iron Company properties. Shortly thereafter, the company hired Rufus A. Ayers to manage its development, and in 1890 the first coal openings were made and the first coke was produced at Stonega, near Big Stone Gap. Progress was slow until railroads reached the area, but by 1896 the company was producing over 7,000 tons of coal a month and operating more than five hundred coking ovens. . . .

Riding from Pineville to Middlesborough and Big Stone Gap in 1889, Charles Dudley Warner had stumbled upon the revolution that was transforming the mountains. Everywhere about him industrialists, speculators, railroad men, and coal barons were busy remaking the civilization and structure of mountain life. "It is my belief," he wrote, "that this central and hitherto neglected portion of the United States will soon become the theatre of vast and controlling industries." The "remarkable progress" that was taking place in the mountains, he added, would inevitably provide for this region a "prosperous" and "great future."

Unfortunately for Appalachia, only "Warner's first prediction was correct. By the turn of the century, the Appalachian South had become the economic colony of the urban Northeast, and Warner's "vast and controlling industries" had begun to sap the region of its mineral and timber wealth. As the resources of the mountains flowed wantonly out of the region, so did any hope for the independence and prosperity of the mountain people. The selling of the mountains, therefore, was only the first stage in the eventual modernization of Appalachia, but it marked the beginning of the process that would make miners and millhands out of the southern mountaineers.

Ronald D. Eller earned his PhD degree from the University of North Carolina-Chapel Hill and is currently Distinguished Professor of History at the University of Kentucky. A specialist on the Appalachian region, he served 15 years as the director of the Appalachian Center at Kentucky. His most recent book is the award-winning *Uneven Ground: Appalacia Since 1945* (University Press of Kentucky, 2008).

James Tice Moore    **NO**

Redeemers Reconsidered: Change and Continuity in the Democratic South, 1870–1900

The political leaders of the post-Reconstruction South have experienced a curious fate at the hands of historians. Variously known as "Bourbons," "Redeemers," or "New Departure Democrats" (*Redeemers* is used in this essay), these men were lionized by scholars well into the twentieth century—only to suffer a sharp decline in their reputations from the 1920s to the 1950s. The sources of their initial popularity are readily apparent, for they had expelled the hated carpetbag governments from the South, reestablished white supremacy on the wreckage of a defunct Radicalism, and put an end to the humiliating military occupation of the region. Reflecting this favorable climate, historians in the first four or five decades after Reconstruction rarely questioned the motives or personal integrity of the Democratic leaders. Instead, scholars generally contented themselves with eulogies on the Redeemers' Confederate war records, their heroism and sagacity in the struggles against "Negro rule," and their ties in blood and sentiment to the chivalric aristocracy of antebellum days.

Occasional criticisms crept into these early analyses, to be sure; students of the period sometimes suggested that the region's Gilded Age Democrats had been too parsimonious in their spending policies and too conservative in their political outlook, too resistant to new men and new ideas. Even so, historians excused these short-comings because of the politicians' service on the battlefields and in the legislative halls. Repeatedly hailed as the heirs and equals of the patriots of 1776, the Redeemers' place in history seemed assured. They were—in the eyes of scholars and public alike—the patrician saviors of their homeland, the natural leaders of the South.

This exalted image has not survived. Attacks on the post-Reconstruction leadership began to appear in the 1920s and became increasingly vitriolic for a generation. Inspired by Charles Austin Beard and other reformist

historians of the Progressive Era, scholars . . . emphasized the negative aspects of the Redeemer establishment, and an image of the Democratic elite took shape that was far different from the heroic vision of previous years.

Where an earlier generation had perceived courage, self-sacrifice, and a sincere devotion to good government, the revisionist historians of the 1930s and 1940s by and large saw only intolerance, avarice, and a shocking indifference to popular needs. Many historians examined long-forgotten Democratic financial scandals and conflicts of interest, and they attacked the Redeemers' inadequate funding for schools, asylums, and prisons. Most important of all, students of the period questioned the social and economic origins of the post-Reconstruction leadership. Rejecting the previous emphasis on the Redeemers' "good blood" and patrician heritage, hostile scholars described the Democratic politicians of the 1870s and 1880s as an essentially new class of money-hungry townsmen, as upstart capitalists who had muscled their way to prominence in the turbulent post-Civil War era. This revisionist trend culminated in the 1951 publication of C. Vann Woodward's *Origins of the New South,* a work which brilliantly synthesized the findings of the preceding decades.

According to Woodward, the collapse of the carpetbaggers neither restored the South's prewar leaders to office nor revitalized the region's traditional values and beliefs. The secessionist firebrands of the planter class never regained their old preeminence, and the powers of government gravitated inexorably into the hands of urban-oriented parvenus, men who had enjoyed little influence in the antebellum years. Railroad executives, corporation lawyers, and speculators of various kinds set the political tone in Professor Woodward's New South. Revisionist historians also emphasized the importance of erstwhile Whigs in the Democratic hierarchy, and Woodward exploited this theme with particular effectiveness.

He insisted that probusiness Whigs monopolized public offices in the Redeemer period, displacing the old-line adherents of Jefferson and Jackson. He described a Democratic elite that allegedly ignored the farmers' demands, lavished favors on the corporate interests, and aligned itself with northeastern capital on the great economic issues of the Gilded Age. In Woodward's opinion, therefore, the Redeemer hegemony represented fundamental, irreversible change. Parvenus presumably gained power over traditionalists, Whigs over Jacksonians, capitalists over agrarians. New men with new ideas clearly held sway in the revisionist South. . . .

In spite of its wide acceptance by historians, the revisionist appraisal, dominant for at least three decades, is now itself in need of revision. This claim is supported by the marked increase in historical research and writing on the Redeemer years since the publication of *Origins of the New South*. . . . This abundant new information should make possible a reassessment of the revisionist argument. Were the Democratic leaders in fact townsmen instead of farmers? Did parvenus take the place of aristocrats? Were old-line Jacksonians overshadowed by erstwhile Whigs? Did the Redeemers actually abandon antebellum traditions and favor industry and commerce at the expense of agriculture? The extent of change in the South's Gilded Age ruling class is obviously at issue, and this essay will attempt to gauge the strength of the contending forces of continuity and discontinuity, tradition and innovation.

As noted previously, revisionist scholars have concluded that the Redeemers were much more urban in occupation and attitude than were the prewar elite. Analysis of this claim suggests, however, that the evidence supporting it is too narrowly based to be conclusive. In 1922 Alex Mathews Arnett demonstrated that townsmen controlled the Georgia legislature and held almost all of the state's congressional seats in the 1870s and 1880s, but subsequent investigations have offered only the most tenuous proof of similar developments elsewhere. Revisionist arguments on this point have by and large been founded more on untested assumptions and sweeping generalizations than on substantive research.

C. Vann Woodward attempted to bolster the case for Redeemer urbanism, but his evidence was insufficient. Although Woodward cited examples of urban Democratic spokesmen throughout the region, including a number of governors and senators, he offered no systematic proof that these men were representative of the Redeemer leadership. On the contrary, much of the pertinent statistical data supports the concept of a continuing and potent agricultural influence. Publishing his findings in 1926, Francis Butler Simkins noted that farmers occupied most of the seats in South Carolina's legislature in the mid-1880s (several years before the upsurge of Tillmanite "agrarianism"), and Willie D. Halsell's 1945 analysis of Mississippi's "Bourbon" regime documented the predominance of rural lawmakers in that state as well. William Best Hesseltine in his 1950 survey of the post-Civil War careers of 656 former Confederate leaders—men whose activities shaped the economic and political life of the Gilded Age South—acknowledged that many of these prestigious individuals pursued new opportunities in the business world, but he also showed that the percentage of agriculturalists among them increased from 20 percent in the antebellum era to almost 30 percent after the war. The number of lawyers in the group, by contrast, actually declined, further indicating that the urban ascendancy over the countryside may have been less pronounced than historians have assumed. The argument that rural interests were eclipsed should be modified.

Approaching Redeemer urbanism from another direction, it is inaccurate to argue (as revisionists typically do) that the presence of a sizable group of lawyers or businessmen in a postwar southern legislature or congressional delegation constitutes *prima facie* evidence of a sharp break with antebellum or agrarian ideals, attitudes, or even personnel. Definitive statistical evidence on this point is lacking, but some of the "urban-oriented" Redeemer leaders may have emerged from the old plantation elite and borne its impress on their personal values and intellectual heritage. A planter or his son could move to the city and begin a new career with relative ease, but abandoning the ideological trappings of a lifetime was undoubtedly more difficult. Perhaps an even larger number of the postwar Democratic leaders lived in crossroads hamlets or courthouse towns. Although they were no longer planters, these Redeemer "urbanites" depended on rural constituencies for their livelihood and political preferment and were only little more independent of agricultural interests than the antebellum leadership had been. Such circumstances offer as great, if not greater, support for notions of continuity as for change in Gilded Age political patterns. To complicate the issue still further, Ralph Ancil Wooster has demonstrated that nonfarm occupational groups, especially lawyers, were already assuming dominant governmental roles in the upper South before the Civil War and held a smaller (though sizable) number of positions in the antebellum cotton states also. Developments in the 1870s and 1880s consequently represented, to some extent at least, a continuation of long-established trends. In other words, evidence concerning Redeemers' occupations does not appear adequate in and of itself to sustain the concept of a sharp break with the prewar regime. . . .

The revisionists' stress on the emergence of new men in the Redeemer leadership appears at first glance to contradict another, more vital tenet of their interpretation—their emphasis on the continuing importance of Old Whigs in the southern Democratic regimes of the 1870s and 1880s. The Whigs had been a vigorous political force in the antebellum South, battling the Democrats on relatively even terms for a generation before the Civil War. The presence of many erstwhile Whigs in the Gilded-Age Democratic ranks (their own party having collapsed in the 1850s) would seem, therefore, to provide yet another link between antebellum and postbellum days, another evidence of continuity with the past. Accentuating change, however, Woodward and like-minded scholars have contended that former Whigs not only survived into the New South era but actually achieved a dominant role in the politics of the period—successfully imposing their nationalistic, capitalistic views on their old-line Democratic rivals. This dramatic upsurge of Whigs and Whiggery, according to the Woodward appraisal, thus further differentiated the New South from the Old. . . .

Professor Woodward's revisionist interpretation of Redeemer origins is itself in need of revision. City dwellers, parvenus, and persistent Whigs undoubtedly participated in Democratic politics in the 1870s and 1880s, but there is little evidence that they were numerically dominant in the party councils. Indeed, historical scholarship for the past three decades strongly supports the opposite conclusion. Recent state studies for the most part suggest that traditionalist, agriculturally oriented elites grasped the New South as firmly as they had the Old. William James Cooper provided the most forceful statement of this viewpoint in his analysis of Wade Hampton's South Carolina, but support for it can be found in other works as well. Allen Johnston Going and William Warren Rogers stressed the influence of black-belt planters in Redeemer Alabama, and Roger L. Hart wrote about the return to power of a similar group in Tennessee at the start of the 1880s. C. Alwyn Barr, Jr., emphasized the preeminence of cotton farmers, cattlemen, and other rural interests in post-Reconstruction Texas. William Ivy Hair and Edward Charles Williamson noted the continuing power of old-line "Bourbons" in Louisiana and Florida respectively, and Willie D. Halsell documented the influence of agricultural representatives in Mississippi's Redeemer government, especially in the state legislature. Jack P. Maddex, Jr., broke with the prevailing trend by accentuating the capitalistic, entrepreneurial character of Virginia's ruling elite in the 1870s. But Allen Wesley Moger argued instead that antebellum attitudes and values permeated the Old Dominion's Conservative regime.

These developments were paralleled in the other states. Indeed, only in the case of Georgia has the revisionist interpretation been fully sustained. In that state, according to Judson Clements Ward, Jr., the corporate interests set the political tone and controlled the operations of the Democratic machine. Elsewhere in the Redeemer South, by contrast, Whiggish innovators apparently continued to function as subordinate elements or junior partners—just as they had before the Civil War. Such findings necessarily point to the need for a reassessment of other aspects of the revisionist interpretation. If traditionalist groups dominated most of the post-Reconstruction Democratic regimes, it seems unlikely that those governments actually adopted the one-sidedly prourban and pro-industrial approach to the region's problems that Woodward describes. A new appraisal of Redeemer economic policies is, therefore, essential to a more accurate reinterpretation of the period.

Revisionist historians have devoted considerable attention to Redeemer economic programs, and, as noted previously, their findings have done little to enhance the image of the South's Democratic regimes. Exposés of pro-business bias fill their pages, and the evidence they advance to support their accusations is impressive. Seeking to attract capital investments, five of the post-Reconstruction state governments granted tax exemptions to new manufacturing enterprises. Legislatures and state constitutional conventions granted monopolies to such companies as the infamous Louisiana State Lottery, and the convict-lease system provided cheap labor for ambitious entrepreneurs, especially for owners of railroads, mines, and lumber camps. Railroads, in particular, became prime beneficiaries of Redeemer largesse. Democratic regimes in North Carolina and Virginia sold state-owned railroad properties to private interests at bargain prices, and the governments of Texas and Florida encouraged the construction of new lines with massive grants of government land. Further exploiting this Redeemer generosity, speculators purchased millions of additional acres of timber and mineral lands from state and federal governments at extremely low prices. Such developments, according to the revisionists, constituted nothing less than a southern-style "great barbecue," a wholesale plundering of the region's resources by avaricious capitalists.

This indictment of Redeemer economic policies is damning in tone and, for the most part, convincing in its main thrust. The Democratic regimes undoubtedly made numerous errors in their quest for economic growth. They squandered resources with little or no thought for the future and frequently confused private greed with public good. Even so, the revisionist argument is misleading in several significant respects. For one thing, the Woodward school employs this evidence of probusiness activity to support the concept of a radical break between New South and antebellum attitudes toward economic growth—a highly questionable assumption. Working essentially within the interpretive framework established by Charles A. Beard, the revisionists view the Redeemer program as marking the ascendancy of industry over agriculture in the region, the collapse of pre–Civil War agrarianism before the onslaughts of triumphant capitalism. . . .

In addition to exaggerating the innovative character of the Redeemer program, the dominant Woodward interpretation of New South economic policies suffers from another significant defect: the revisionists' stress on Democratic favoritism toward business led them for the most part to neglect Redeemer attempts to exact concessions from the corporate interests, to tap their financial resources for the public benefit. The post-Reconstruction politicians' efforts along these lines are evident in their revenue policies. Railroad magnates and other businessmen made handsome profits from the convict-lease system, as noted previously, but they also had to pay hundreds of thousands of dollars into southern state treasuries each year in return for the privilege. Louisiana derived forty thousand dollars annually from lottery interests in compensation for gambling rights, and South Carolina reaped even greater profits from its abundant phosphate beds. Allowing private contractors to mine the rich deposits, the state siphoned off mineral royalties which amounted to over $250,000 a year by 1890. Public-land sales, even at bargain prices, provided another source of funds for the Democratic regimes. Florida's Redeemer administration obtained a million dollars from one such sale during the 1880s, while Texas officials employed half the state's land receipts to support the public school system.

Revenues from these sources, however trifling by modern standards, constituted major windfalls at a time when a typical southern state's budget ranged from one to two million dollars a year. Carrying this approach still further, the Democratic leaders also demonstrated a willingness to exact license fees, sales taxes, and property taxes from the business community. Although liberal in their treatment of new factories and the railroads (many of which continued to enjoy tax exemptions under their original antebellum charters), the Redeemers showed much less consideration for the mercantile and professional classes. Southern legislatures imposed a bewildering variety of levies on storekeepers, insurance agents, traveling salesmen, liquor dealers, expressmen, money lenders, and other urban occupational groups. The enactment of such measures suggests a significant conclusion:

the Redeemers were less subservient to business than has generally been assumed. They granted important concessions, but they expected those interests to pay part of the cost of providing public services.

The Democrats' pragmatic attitude toward businessmen was also expressed in their penchant for retracting privileges they had previously bestowed. The opportunism of South Carolina politicians in this respect is particularly notable. After witnessing the rapid expansion of the state's textile industry at the start of the 1880s, the Redeemers in 1885 repealed the tax exemption for new factories. Tax incentives in South Carolina rapidly gave way to tax levies. Southern Democrats also retreated from favoritism toward the railroads, especially after many of the lines fell under the control of Wall Street financiers during the depression of the 1870s. This northern takeover reignited old sectional antagonisms, and anti-railroad sentiment surged through the former Confederacy. Responding to this unrest, Redeemer legislatures passed laws requiring the rail corporations to maintain adequate depots, to fence their rights-of-way, and to compensate farmers for livestock killed by trains. Democratic regimes in Arkansas and Florida manifested the new hostility by defeating the rail lines in the courtroom, enabling them to raise the tax assessments on railroad property early in the 1880s—in the Florida case abolishing tax exemptions granted in 1855. Most important of all, the Redeemers joined with western politicians in pioneering the practice of governmental railroad regulation. Between 1877 and 1891 all the states of the former Confederacy except Arkansas and Louisiana established regulatory commissions of one sort or another. Significant rate cuts ensued, even though the commissions were frequently hampered by corporate intransigence and judicial conservatism. Not satisfied with these efforts, the region's Democrats played prominent roles in the struggle for federal railroad regulation as well. Texas Senator John H. Reagan led the fight to establish the Interstate Commerce Commission, and Alabama Redeemer Walter Lawrence Bragg, another champion of the regulatory cause, served as one of the original members of the new agency.

Paralleling these developments, moreover, Democratic attitudes toward the public lands underwent a similar transformation. Eager for economic growth, southerners had generally favored liberal land policies at the start of the Redeemer era. Northern lumber interests had bought timber tracts in the South in order to forestall potential competition, and other capitalists had purchased large acreages for purely speculative purposes, making no immediate effort to promote the region's prosperity. Misgivings arose about the land boom, and in 1888 southern congressmen led a successful movement to suspend cash sales of federal land, a maneuver which paved the way for reorganization of the entire public-land system along conservationist lines. Two Redeemers in Grover Cleveland's cabinet also worked to improve the management of natural resources. Secretary of the Interior Lucius Q. C. Lamar of Mississippi and Attorney General Augustus Hill Garland of Arkansas took action against illegal encroachments on the federal domain, and together they expelled speculators, ranchers, and railroads from an estimated 45,000,000 acres in the South and West. In land policies as well as railroad regulations, therefore, southern Democrats manifested an increasingly sophisticated attitude toward Gilded Age capitalism. Skepticism gradually supplanted gullibility; restrictions accompanied and sometimes overshadowed concessions.

Abounding in such ambiguities, the Redeemer economic program offered uncertain and tenuous encouragement for the entrepreneurial classes. Indeed, a case can be made that the Democratic elite provided more consistent and reliable support for farmers than for businessmen. Gathering most of their electoral strength from the countryside, Redeemer politicians generally reflected agrarian biases on such issues as debt scaling and railroad regulation, and their tax policies followed a similar pattern. As noted previously, they veered from one direction to another in their revenue demands on business. But they pursued a much more uniform and straightforward course with reference to property taxes—the exactions which fell most heavily on rural areas. Appalled by the high property levies of the Reconstruction years, Democratic leaders moved in the 1870s and 1880s to prevent the recurrence of such abuses. They wrote strict limits on property taxes into their state constitutions, severely curtailing the revenue-gathering authority of local as well as state governments. Southern legislatures accelerated this trend with numerous tax cuts, and the results were impressive. Mississippi set the pace for the entire region by slashing its state property levy from 14 mills in 1874 to 2.5 mills in 1882, a reduction of more than 80 percent. Alabama's less drastic adjustment from 7.5 mills in 1874 to 4 mills in 1889 was more typical, but substantial reductions occurred in state after state. These cuts, together with the South's traditionally low assessments of property values, offered massive tax savings for the agricultural population. The impact of these reforms was readily apparent, for millions of acres which had been forfeited for delinquent taxes during Reconstruction were reclaimed by farmers in the Redeemer era.

Applying political pressure through the Grange and Alliance, the rural interests derived many additional benefits from the Democratic regimes. Agricultural and mechanical colleges received increased funding, and the Redeemers established new land-grant schools in the Carolinas, Mississippi, and Virginia. Government-supported agricultural experiment stations proliferated as well. North Carolina pioneered the development of experimental farms in the 1870s, setting a pattern which the rest of the South followed during the next decade. Democratic legislatures provided another recognition of the farmers' importance by creating state departments of agriculture. Although hampered by inadequate budgets, these new agencies became increasingly innovative and efficient. By the 1880s state agriculture departments were inspecting commercial fertilizers, analyzing soil samples, conducting geological surveys, encouraging immigration, providing veterinary services, dispatching speakers to farm meetings, and collecting statistics on crop yields. In Alabama the Department of Agriculture eventually became the second most powerful agency in the state, enjoying an influence exceeded only by that of the governor.

Southern Democrats also demonstrated their support for farmers by sponsoring agricultural societies. Legislatures appropriated thousands of dollars each year to subsidize these groups (primarily to enable them to hold state fairs). Further belying the notion of the Redeemers' indifference to rural needs, the region's legislators passed hundreds of laws regarding the crop-lien system, the maintenance of fences and roads, and the conservation of fish and wildlife—all issues of concern to farm areas. These activities reflected an essential fact: the agriculturalists still constituted the most important interest group in the South, and they received due consideration from the Democratic elite.

The Redeemers' favoritism toward farmers also influenced developments at the national level, undermining another facet of the revisionist interpretation. According to Professor Woodward, investment-hungry southern congressmen generally subordinated the needs of their section and its people to the demands of the capitalistic, conservative Northeast. If this in fact was the case, the Democratic leaders manifested their subservience in an extremely curious way—by opposing the northern business interests on almost all the great economic issues of the Gilded Age. Southern crusades for federal railroad regulation and the conservation of the public domain have been noted previously, but the Redeemers assumed anticorporate stands in other national controversies as well. The great majority of the region's political leaders denounced protective tariffs and for decades battled to reinstitute the low duties of the antebellum years. Gaining particular prominence in these struggles, newspaper editor Henry Watterson of

Kentucky, together with Senator Lamar of Mississippi, formulated the famous "tariff for revenue only" pledge in the 1880 Democratic platform, and House Ways and Means Chairman Roger Quarles Mills of Texas led the unsuccessful congressional fight for tariff reform in 1888. . . .

The Redeemers' commitment to an increased money supply also led them to criticize the restrictive policies of the national banking system. They opposed the rechartering of many of the national banks in the 1880s, and they urged the repeal of the federal government's prohibitive tax on state bank notes. Far from endorsing the Hamiltonian financial structure which had emerged during the Civil War, as revisionist historians have maintained, the southern Democrats were instead among the more persistent critics of that structure. Only with reference to federal aid to internal improvements did they find themselves in harmony with the prevailing system. Having witnessed the destruction of their ports, railroads, and levees by federal power during the war years, southerners requested federal money for rebuilding them. Even on this issue, surprisingly enough, the Redeemers' stand placed them in opposition to northern sentiment. Northeastern congressmen—Democrats and Republicans alike—had turned against government-financed internal improvements after the scandals of the Grant era, and the southerners were only able to vote the funds for their projects with the help of the West. On issue after issue, therefore, the Redeemers took sides against, not with, the masters of capital.

These national developments, together with similar trends at the state level, clearly point up inadequacies in the revisionist interpretation of Redeemer origins and views. Parvenus, urbanites, and persistent Whigs made their way into the Democratic leadership during the post–Civil War years, as Woodward and others have argued, but these potentially innovative groups proved either unable or unwilling to alter the entrenched patterns of southern government. Traditionalist forces enjoyed too much strength in both the electorate and the party hierarchy to permit any wholesale departure from established practices and policies. As a result the southern Democrats neither abandoned the farmers nor embraced Whiggery in the aftermath of Reconstruction. Indeed, their economic programs were more congruent with the ideals of Jefferson, Jackson, or even Calhoun than with those of Clay or Webster. Although they promoted limited industrial growth, the Redeemers continued to acknowledge and reward the primacy of agriculture in their region's life. Although they accepted the defeat of secession and the collapse of the slave system, most of them also continued to regard the capitalistic North with a deep-seated antagonism. . . . In the decisive economic clashes of the Gilded Age, . . . the Redeemer South consistently joined forces with the other great agricultural section of the United States, the West. Such facts lend further support to the notion of continuity between the Old and New Souths. All things had not changed with Appomattox, much less with the Compromise of 1877.

James Tice Moore (1946–2009) was a professor of history and former department chair at Virginia Commonwealth University where he taught for 31 years. His scholarly works focused on the American South, especially Virginia and include *Two Paths to the New South: Virginia Debt Controversy, 1870–83* (University Press of Kentucky, 1974) and (with Edward Younger) *The Governors of Virginia* (University of Virginia Press, 1982).

EXPLORING THE ISSUE

Did a "New South" Emerge Following Reconstruction?

Critical Thinking and Reflection

1. Based on the YES and NO selections, what is meant by the term "New South"?
2. How did the political leadership of the post-Reconstruction South differ from that of the antebellum period?
3. What impact did industrial production have on the South in the last quarter of the nineteenth century?
4. Based on your understanding of the YES and NO selections, to what extent did the economic and political character of the post-Reconstruction South represent continuity with the antebellum period?

Is There Common Ground?

Although the Civil War and Reconstruction clearly produced changes in the South, scholarly debates continue as to the extent of this change. For example, despite the introduction of impressive industrial processes, the vast majority of southerners continued to depend upon farming for their livelihoods. Moreover, Woodward recognizes that the South's postwar industries were tied to raw materials and natural resources extracted from southern lands. Even Woodward's argument in support of the discontinuity between the antebellum South and the postwar South suggests that the distinctions were not always complete. Whether or not the post-Reconstruction political leaders of the New South were "Bourbons" or "Redeemers," they still were white, conservative Democrats. In addition, the attitudes of post-Reconstruction politicians toward urban-industrial growth differed from state to state, making generalizations about change more difficult.

Another important aspect of this question, one that is not addressed in the YES and NO selections, is the social change in the post-Civil War South. Specifically, how different were patterns of race relations once the war had ended and slavery had been abolished? On the one hand, efforts by some Radical Republicans to promote a truly egalitarian society resulted in a framework to extend citizenship rights to African Americans through the Civil Rights Acts of 1866 and 1875 and the Fourteenth and Fifteenth Amendments. These actions held out the promise of a dramatic departure from the antebellum slave statutes or the quasi-freedom of the Black Codes

in the immediate postwar South. On the other hand, the demise of the Reconstruction governments resulted in a general withdrawal of any commitment to advancing the status of black southerners and paved the way by the end of the century to firmly entrenched policies of peonage, political disfranchisement, and racial segregation. From the perspective of most black southerners, then, the prospect of fully participating in the benefits of American democracy seemed just as remote in 1900 as it had been in 1860.

Create Central

www.mhhe.com/createcentral

Additional Resources

Edward L. Ayers, *The Promise of the New South: Life After Reconstruction* (Oxford University Press, 1992).

James C. Cobb, *Industrialization and Southern Society, 1877–1984* (University Press of Kentucky, 1984).

Pete Daniel, *Breaking the Land: The Transformation of Cotton, Tobacco, and Rice Cultures Since 1880* (University of Illinois Press, 1985).

Paul Gaston, *The New South Creed: A Study in Southern Mythmaking* (Alfred A. Knopf, 1970).

Gavin Wright, *Old South, New South: Revolutions in the Southern Economy Since the Civil War* (Basic Books, 1986).

Internet References . . .

History of the United States:
Industrialization and Reform (1870–1916)

www.theusaonline.com/history/industrialization.htm

The New South

http://www.apstudynotes.org/us-history/topics
/the-new-south/

The South After the Civil War

www.cs.unm.edu/~sergiy/amhistory/ch21.html

Selected, Edited, and with Issue Framing Material by:
Larry Madaras, *Howard Community College*
and
James M. SoRelle, *Baylor University*

ISSUE

Were the Nineteenth-Century Entrepreneurs "Robber Barons"?

YES: Howard Zinn, from "Robber Barons and Rebels," in *A People's History of the United States: 1942–Present* (HarperCollins, 1999)

NO: John S. Gordon, from "Was There Ever Such a Business!" in *An Empire of Wealth: The Epic History of American Economic Power* (Harper Perennial, 2004)

Learning Outcomes

After reading this issue, you will be able to:

- Identify and explain the significance of the terms "robber baron," "entrepreneurial statesmen," and "organizational revolution."
- Critically analyze the strengths and weaknesses of the "entrepreneurial statesmen," "robber baron," and "organizational revolution" interpretations of the dominance of big business during the Gilded Age (1867–1900).
- Describe how the times we live in influence our interpretation of the rise of big business in the late nineteenth century.

ISSUE SUMMARY

YES: According to Howard Zinn, the new industrialists such as John D. Rockefeller, Andrew Carnegie, and J. P. Morgan adopted business practices that encouraged monopolies and used the powers of the government to control the masses from rebellion.

NO: John S. Gordon argues that the nineteenth-century men of big business such as John D. Rockefeller and Andrew Carnegie developed through the oil and steel industries' consumer products that improved the lifestyle of average Americans.

Between 1860 and 1914, the United States was transformed from a country of farms, small towns, and modest manufacturing concerns to a modern nation dominated by large cities and factories. During those years, the population tripled and the nation experienced astounding urban growth. A new proletariat emerged to provide the necessary labor for the country's developing factory system. In the period between the Civil War and World War I, the value of manufactured goods in the United States increased 12-fold, and the capital invested in industrial pursuits multiplied 22 times. In addition, the application of new machinery and scientific methods of agriculture produced abundant yields of wheat, corn, and other foodstuffs, despite the decline in the number of farmers.

Why did this industrial revolution occur in the United States during the last quarter of the nineteenth century? What factors contributed to the rapid pace of American industrialization? In answering these questions, historians often point to the first half of the 1800s and the significance of the "transportation revolution," which produced better roads, canals, and railroads to move people and goods more efficiently and cheaply from one point to another. Technological improvements such as the Bessemer process, refrigeration, electricity, and the telephone also made their mark in the nation's "machine age." Government cooperation with business, large-scale immigration from Europe and Asia, and the availability of foreign capital for industrial investments provided still other underpinnings for this industrial growth. Finally, American industrialization depended upon a number of individuals in the United States who were willing to organize and finance the nation's industrial base for the sake of anticipated profits. These, of course, were the entrepreneurs.

Regardless of how American entrepreneurs are perceived, there is no doubt that they constituted a powerful elite and were responsible for defining the character of society in the Gilded Age. For many Americans, these businessmen represented the logical culmination of the country's attachment to laissez-faire economics and rugged individualism. In fact, it was not unusual at all for the nation's leading industrialists to be depicted as the real-life models for the "rags-to-riches" theme epitomized in the self-help novels of Horatio Alger.

Closer examination of the lives of most of these entrepreneurs, however, reveals the mythical dimensions of this American idea. Simply put, the typical business executive of the late nineteenth century did not rise up from humble circumstances, a product of the American rural tradition or the immigrant experience, as frequently claimed. Rather, most of these big businessmen were of Anglo-Saxon origin and reared in a city by middle-class parents. According to one survey, over half of the leaders had attended college at a time when even the pursuit of a high school education was considered unusual. In other words, instead of having to pull themselves up by their own bootstraps from the bottom of the social heap, these individuals usually started their climb to success at the middle of the ladder or higher.

American public attitudes have reflected a schizophrenic quality with regard to the activities of the industrial leaders of the late nineteenth century. So much is this the case that the field of business history can be divided into three major interpretations: (1) the robber baron or anti-big business viewpoint; (2) the entrepreneurial statesman or pro-big business account; and (3) the organizational or bureaucratic functional framework, which deems the robber baron and entrepreneurial arguments irrelevant.

Although the "robber barons" stereotype emerged as early as the 1870s and was reinforced by the muckrakers of the Progressive Era (1897–1917) who were critical of the immoral methods used by businessmen such as J.J. Hill, John D. Rockefeller, and Andrew Carnegie to gain control over the railroads and the oil and steel processing industries, the book that did the most to fix the stereotype of the late nineteenth-century businessman as a predator was Matthew Josephson's *The Robber Barons: The Great American Capitalists, 1861–1901* (Harcourt Brace and World, 1934, 1962). Published in the midst of the Great Depression, Josephson admitted that large-scale production proved more efficient but concluded that the negative consequences far outweighed the positive. Some form of the "robber baron" interpretation continued to be found in high school and college texts through the 1960s. For example, New Left historians such as Gabriel Kolko in *The Triumph of Conservatism: A Reinterpretation of American History* (MacMillan, 1963) kept the interpretation alive as he blamed big business for the militarism, poverty, and racism, which still existed in the 1960s.

The Josephson interpretation did not go unchallenged. The Harvard Business School in the 1930s and writers such as the famous journalist and popular historian Allan Nevins, whose two-volume biography of John D. Rockefeller appeared in 1940 and was rewritten in 1953, stressed the oil mogul's positive attributes. Rockefeller was not a robber baron, maintained Nevins, but an entrepreneurial statesman who imposed upon American industry "a more rational and efficient pattern." Rockefeller and others like him were motivated not by wealth but by competition, achievement, and the "imposition of their will over a given environment." Through men like Rockefeller, the industries that developed in steel, oil, textiles, chemicals, and electricity gave the United States such a competitive advantage that the nation was able to win both world wars in the twentieth century.

The third school of business history was the organizational school. Led by Alfred D. Chandler, Jr., who almost single-handedly reshaped the way in which historians write about corporations, this view avoided the morality tale between robber barons and industrial statesmen and employed organizational theories of decision making borrowed from sociologists to stress how large-scale corporations in the United States vertically organized themselves with departments that stretched from production, accounting, marketing, sales, and distribution. Key to Chandler's view was the importance of the new national urban markets that had developed by 1900. The best place to start with Chandler is "The Beginning of 'Big Business' in American Industry," *Business History Review* (vol. 33, Spring 1959, pp. 1–31). See also *Strategy and Structure: Chapters in the History of American Industrial Enterprise* (MIT Press, 1962); *The Visible Hand: The Managerial Revolution in American Business* (Harvard University Press, 1977); and *Scale and Scope: The Dynamics of Industrial Capitalism* (Harvard University Press, 1990). Chandler's most important essays are collected in Thomas K. McCraw, ed., *The*

Essential Alfred Chandler: Essays Toward a Historical Theory of Big Business (Harvard Business School Press, 1988). For an assessment of Chandler's approach and contributions, see Louis Galambos, "The Emerging Organizational Synthesis in Modern American History," *Business History Review* (Autumn 1970), and Thomas K. McCraw, "The Challenge of Alfred D. Chandler, Jr.: Retrospect and Prospect," *Reviews in American History* (March 1987).

    Chandler's critics have complained that he ignored the role of the individual entrepreneur in developing particular industries. In "Entrepreneurial Persistence Through the Bureaucratic Age," *Business History Review* (vol. 51, Winter 1977, pp. 415–443), Professor Harold C. Livesay tries to reconcile an organizational and entrepreneurial approach via case studies of Andrew Carnegie, Michigan National Bank President Howard Stoddard, and Henry Ford II and his post–World War II revival of the Ford Motor Company. Two important articles examine the main currents in business history today. Maury Klein, "Coming Full Circle: The Study of Big Business Since 1950," *Enterprise and Society* (vol. 2, September 2001, pp. 425–460), contrasts the broader external approach pushed by Professors Thomas C. Cochran and William Miller, *The Age of Enterprise: A Social History of Industrial America,* revised

ed. (Harper & Row, 1961) with the internal bureaucratic approach of Chandler.

    The YES and NO selections reveal the divergence of scholarly opinion as it applies to the nineteenth-century entrepreneurs who came to epitomize both the success and excess of corporate capitalism in the United States. In the YES selection, the late radical historian Howard Zinn portrays the economic environment of late nineteenth-century America in the tradition of Matthew Josephson. In brief, the new industrialists such as oil magnate John D. Rockefeller, steel baron Andrew Carnegie, and the financier J. P. Morgan adopted business and banking practices that encouraged monopolies and used the powers of the government to control the masses from rebellion. In Zinn's view, the state militia, the courts, the churches, and even the education system, both colleges and high schools, were designed to produce executives for the corporations and workers for the factories.

    In the NO selection, independent scholar John Steele Gordon extols the virtues of the men of big business. He stresses the innovations in production and organization as well as the new technologies that entrepreneurs such as Rockefeller and Carnegie employed to improve the lifestyle of average Americans.

YES ↵

Howard Zinn

Robber Barons and Rebels

In the year 1877, the signals were given for the rest of the century: the blacks would be put back; the strikes of white workers would not be tolerated; the industrial and political elites of North and South would take hold of the country and organize the greatest march of economic growth in human history. They would do it with the aid of, and at the expense of, black labor, white labor, Chinese labor, European immigrant labor, female labor, rewarding them differently by race, sex, national origin, and social class, in such a way as to create separate levels of oppression—a skillful terracing to stabilize the pyramid of wealth.

Between the Civil War and 1900, steam and electricity replaced human muscle, iron replaced wood, and steel replaced iron (before the Bessemer process, iron was hardened into steel at the rate of 3 to 5 tons a day; now the same amount could be processed in 15 minutes). Machines could now drive steel tools. Oil could lubricate machines and light homes, streets, factories. People and goods could move by railroad, propelled by steam along steel rails; by 1900 there were 193,000 miles of railroad. The telephone, the typewriter, and the adding machine speeded up the work of business.

Machines changed farming. Before the Civil War it took 61 hours of labor to produce an acre of wheat. By 1900, it took 3 hours, 19 minutes. Manufactured ice enabled the transport of food over long distances, and the industry of meatpacking was born.

Steam drove textile mill spindles; it drove sewing machines. It came from coal. Pneumatic drills now drilled deeper into the earth for coal. In 1860, 14 million tons of coal were mined; by 1884 it was 100 million tons. More coal meant more steel, because coal furnaces converted iron into steel; by 1880 a million tons of steel were being produced; by 1910, 25 million tons. By now electricity was beginning to replace steam. Electrical wire needed copper, of which 30,000 tons were produced in 1880; 500,000 tons by 1910.

To accomplish all this required ingenious inventors of new processes and new machines, clever organizers and administrators of the new corporations, a country rich with land and minerals, and a huge supply of human beings to do the back-breaking, unhealthful, and dangerous work. Immigrants would come from Europe and China, to make the new labor force. Farmers unable to buy the new machinery or pay the new railroad rates would move to the cities. Between 1860 and 1914, New York grew from 850,000 to 4 million, Chicago from 110,000 to 2 million, Philadelphia from 650,000 to 1½ million.

In some cases the inventor himself became the organizer of businesses—like Thomas Edison, inventor of electrical devices. In other cases, the businessman compiled other people's inventions, like Gustavus Swift, a Chicago butcher who put together the ice-cooled railway car with the ice-cooled warehouse to make the first national meatpacking company in 1885. James Duke used a new cigarette-rolling machine that could roll, paste, and cut tubes of tobacco into 100,000 cigarettes a day; in 1890 he combined the four biggest cigarette producers to form the American Tobacco Company.

While some multimillionaires started in poverty, most did not. A study of the origins of 303 textile, railroad, and steel executives of the 1870s showed that 90 percent came from middle- or upper-class families. The Horatio Alger stories of "rags to riches" were true for a few men, but mostly a myth, and a useful myth for control.

Most of the fortune building was done legally, with the collaboration of the government and the courts. Sometimes the collaboration had to be paid for. Thomas Edison promised New Jersey politicians $1,000 each in return for favorable legislation. Daniel Drew and Jay Gould spent $1 million to bribe the New York legislature to legalize their issue of $8 million in "watered stock" (stock not representing real value) on the Erie Railroad.

The first transcontinental railroad was built with blood, sweat, politics and thievery, out of the meeting of the Union Pacific and Central Pacific railroads. The Central Pacific started on the West Coast going east; it spent $200,000 in Washington on bribes to get 9 million acres of free land and $24 million in bonds, and paid $79 million, an overpayment of $36 million, to a construction company which really was its own. The construction was done by three thousand Irish and ten thousand Chinese, over a period of four years, working for one or two dollars a day.

The Union Pacific started in Nebraska going west. It had been given 12 million acres of free land and $27 million in government bonds. It created the Credit Mobilier company and gave them $94 million for construction when the actual cost was $44 million. Shares were sold cheaply to Congressmen to prevent investigation. This was at the suggestion of Massachusetts Congressman Oakes Ames, a shovel manufacturer and director of Credit Mobilier, who said: "There is no difficulty in getting men to look after their own property." The Union Pacific used twenty thousand workers—war veterans and Irish immigrants, who laid 5 miles of track a day and died by the hundreds in the heat, the cold, and the battles with Indians opposing the invasion of their territory.

Both railroads used longer, twisting routes to get subsidies from towns they went through. In 1869, amid music and speeches, the two crooked lines met in Utah.

The wild fraud on the railroads led to more control of railroad finances by bankers, who wanted more stability—profit by law rather than by theft. By the 1890s, most of the country's railway mileage was concentrated in six huge systems. Four of these were completely or partially controlled by the House of Morgan, and two others by the bankers Kuhn, Loeb, and Company.

J. P. Morgan had started before the war, as the son of a banker who began selling stocks for the railroads for good commissions. During the Civil War he bought five thousand rifles for $3.50 each from an army arsenal, and sold them to a general in the field for $22 each. The rifles were defective and would shoot off the thumbs of the soldiers using them. A congressional committee noted this in the small print of an obscure report, but a federal judge upheld the deal as the fulfillment of a valid legal contract.

Morgan had escaped military service in the Civil War by paying $300 to a substitute. So did John D. Rockefeller, Andrew Carnegie, Philip Armour, Jay Gould, and James Mellon. Mellon's father had written to him that "a man may be a patriot without risking his own life or sacrificing his health. There are plenty of lives less valuable."

It was the firm of Drexel, Morgan and Company that was given a U.S. government contract to float a bond issue of $260 million. The government could have sold the bonds directly; it chose to pay the bankers $5 million in commission.

On January 2, 1889, as Gustavus Myers reports:

> . . . a circular marked "Private and Confidential" was issued by the three banking houses of Drexel, Morgan & Company, Brown Brothers & Company, and Kidder, Peabody & Company. The most painstaking care was exercised that this document should not find its way into the press or otherwise become public. . . . Why this fear? Because the circular was an invitation . . . to the great railroad magnates to assemble at Morgan's house, No. 219 Madison Avenue, there to form, in the phrase of the day, an iron-clad combination . . . a compact which would efface competition among certain railroads, and unite those interests in an agreement by which the people of the United States would be bled even more effectively than before.

There was a human cost to this exciting story of financial ingenuity. That year, 1889, records of the Interstate Commerce Commission showed that 22,000 railroad workers were killed or injured.

In 1895 the gold reserve of the United States was depleted, while twenty-six New York City banks had $129 million in gold in their vaults. A syndicate of bankers headed by J. P. Morgan & Company, August Belmont & Company, the National City Bank, and others offered to give the government gold in exchange for bonds. President Grover Cleveland agreed. The bankers immediately resold the bonds at higher prices, making $18 million profit.

A journalist wrote: "If a man wants to buy beef, he must go to the butcher. . . . If Mr. Cleveland wants much gold, he must go to the big banker."

While making his fortune, Morgan brought rationality and organization to the national economy. He kept the system stable. He said: "We do not want financial convulsions and have one thing one day and another thing another day." He linked railroads to one another, all of them to banks, banks to insurance companies. By 1900, he controlled 100,000 miles of railroad, half the country's mileage.

Three insurance companies dominated by the Morgan group had a billion dollars in assets. They had $50 million a year to invest—money given by ordinary people for their insurance policies. Louis Brandeis, describing this in his book *Other People's Money* (before he became a Supreme Court justice), wrote: "They control the people through the people's own money."

John D. Rockefeller started as a bookkeeper in Cleveland, became a merchant, accumulated money, and decided that, in the new industry of oil, who controlled the oil refineries controlled the industry. He bought his first oil refinery in 1862, and by 1870 set up Standard Oil Company of Ohio, made secret agreements with railroads to ship his oil with them if they gave him rebates—discounts—on their prices, and thus drove competitors out of business.

One independent refiner said: "If we did not sell out. . . we would be crushed out. . . . There was only one buyer on the market and we had to sell at their terms." Memos like this one passed among Standard Oil officials: "Wilkerson & Co. received car of oil Monday 13th. . . . Please turn another screw." A rival refinery in Buffalo was rocked by a small explosion arranged by Standard Oil officials with the refinery's chief mechanic.

The Standard Oil Company, by 1899, was a holding company which controlled the stock of many other companies. The capital was $110 million, the profit was $45 million a year, and John D. Rockefeller's fortune was estimated at $200 million. Before long he would move into iron, copper, coal, shipping, and banking (Chase Manhattan Bank). Profits would be $81 million a year, and the Rockefeller fortune would total two billion dollars.

Andrew Carnegie was a telegraph clerk at seventeen, then secretary to the head of the Pennsylvania Railroad, then a broker in Wall Street selling railroad bonds for huge commissions, and was soon a millionaire. He went to London in 1872, saw the new Bessemer method of producing steel, and returned to the United States to build a million-dollar steel plant. Foreign competition was kept out by a high tariff conveniently set by Congress, and by 1880 Carnegie was producing 10,000 tons of steel a month, making $1½ million a year in profit. By 1900 he was making $40 million a year, and that year, at a dinner party, he agreed to sell his steel company to J. P. Morgan. He scribbled the price on a note: $492,000,000.

Morgan then formed the U.S. Steel Corporation, combining Carnegie's corporation with others. He sold stocks and bonds for $1,300,000,000 (about 400 million more than the combined worth of the companies) and took a fee of 150 million for arranging the consolidation. How could dividends be paid to all those stockholders and bondholders? By making sure Congress passed tariffs keeping out foreign steel; by closing off competition and maintaining the price at $28 a ton; and by working 200,000 men twelve hours a day for wages that barely kept their families alive.

And so it went, in industry after industry—shrewd, efficient businessmen building empires, choking out competition, maintaining high prices, keeping wages low, using government subsidies. These industries were the first beneficiaries of the "welfare state." By the turn of the century, American Telephone and Telegraph had a monopoly of the nation's telephone system, International Harvester made 85 percent of all farm machinery, and in every other industry resources became concentrated, controlled. The banks had interests in so many of these monopolies as to create an interlocking network of powerful corporation directors, each of whom sat on the boards of many other corporations. According to a Senate report of the early twentieth century, Morgan at his peak sat on the board of forty-eight corporations; Rockefeller, thirty-seven corporations.

Meanwhile, the government of the United States was behaving almost exactly as Karl Marx described a capitalist state: pretending neutrality to maintain order, but serving the interests of the rich. Not that the rich agreed among themselves; they had disputes over policies. But the purpose of the state was to settle upper-class disputes peacefully, control lower-class rebellion, and adopt policies that would further the long-range stability of the system. The arrangement between Democrats and Republicans to elect Rutherford Hayes in 1877 set the tone. Whether Democrats or Republicans won, national policy would not change in any important way.

When Grover Cleveland, a Democrat, ran for President in 1884, the general impression in the country was that he opposed the power of monopolies and corporations, and that the Republican party, whose candidate was James Blaine, stood for the wealthy. But when Cleveland defeated Blaine, Jay Gould wired him: "I feel . . . that the vast business interests of the country will be entirely safe in your hands." And he was right.

One of Cleveland's chief advisers was William Whitney, a millionaire and corporation lawyer, who married into the Standard Oil fortune and was appointed Secretary of the Navy by Cleveland. He immediately set about to create a "steel navy," buying the steel at artificially high prices from Carnegie's plants. Cleveland himself assured industrialists that his election should not frighten them: "No harm shall come to any business interest as the result of administrative policy so long as I am President . . . a transfer of executive control from one party to another does not mean any serious disturbance of existing conditions."

The presidential election itself had avoided real issues; there was no clear understanding of which interests would gain and which would lose if certain policies were adopted. It took the usual form of election campaigns, concealing the basic similarity of the parties by dwelling on personalities, gossip, trivialities. Henry Adams, an astute literary commentator on that era, wrote to a friend about the election:

> We are here plunged in politics funnier than words can express. Very great issues are involved. . . . But the amusing thing is that no one talks about real interests. By common consent they agree to let these alone. We are afraid to discuss them. Instead of this the press is engaged in a most amusing dispute whether Mr. Cleveland had an illegitimate child and did or did not live with more than one mistress.

In 1887, with a huge surplus in the treasury, Cleveland vetoed a bill appropriating $100,000 to give relief to Texas farmers to help them buy seed grain during a drought. He said: "Federal aid in such cases . . . encourages the expectation of paternal care on the part of the government and weakens the sturdiness of our national character." But that same year, Cleveland used his gold surplus to pay off wealthy bondholders at $28 above the $100 value of each bond—a gift of $45 million.

The chief reform of the Cleveland administration gives away the secret of reform legislation in America. The Interstate Commerce Act of 1887 was supposed to regulate the railroads on behalf of the consumers. But Richard Olney, a lawyer for the Boston & Maine and other railroads, and soon to be Cleveland's Attorney General, told railroad officials who complained about the Interstate Commerce Commission that it would not be wise to abolish the Commission "from a railroad point of view." He explained:

> The Commission . . . is or can be made, of great use to the railroads. It satisfies the popular clamor for a government supervision of railroads, at the same time that that supervision is almost entirely nominal. . . . The part of wisdom is not to destroy the Commission, but to utilize it.

Cleveland himself, in his 1887 State of the Union message, had made a similar point, adding a warning: "Opportunity for safe, careful, and deliberate reform is now offered; and none of us should be unmindful of a time when an abused and irritated people . . . may insist upon a radical and sweeping rectification of their wrongs."

Republican Benjamin Harrison, who succeeded Cleveland as President from 1889 to 1893, was described by Matthew Josephson, in his colorful study of the post-Civil War years, *The Politicos:* "Benjamin Harrison had the exclusive distinction of having served the railway corporations in the dual capacity of lawyer and soldier. He prosecuted the strikers [of 1877] in the federal courts . . . and

he also organized and commanded a company of soldiers during the strike. . . ."

Harrison's term also saw a gesture toward reform. The Sherman Anti-Trust Act, passed in 1890, called itself "An Act to protect trade and commerce against unlawful restraints" and made it illegal to form a "combination or conspiracy" to restrain trade in interstate or foreign commerce. Senator John Sherman, author of the Act, explained the need to conciliate the critics of monopoly: "They had monopolies . . . of old, but never before such giants as in our day. You must heed their appeal or be ready for the socialist, the communist, the nihilist. Society is now disturbed by forces never felt before. . . ."

When Cleveland was elected President again in 1892, Andrew Carnegie, in Europe, received a letter from the manager of his steel plants, Henry Clay Frick: "I am very sorry for President Harrison, but I cannot see that our interests are going to be affected one way or the other by the change in administration." Cleveland, facing the agitation in the country caused by the panic and depression of 1893, used troops to break up "Coxey's Army," a demonstration of unemployed men who had come to Washington, and again to break up the national strike on the railroads the following year.

Meanwhile, the Supreme Court, despite its look of somber, black-robed fairness, was doing its bit for the ruling elite. How could it be independent, with its members chosen by the President and ratified by the Senate? How could it be neutral between rich and poor when its members were often former wealthy lawyers, and almost always came from the upper class? Early in the nineteenth century the Court laid the legal basis for a nationally regulated economy by establishing federal control over interstate commerce, and the legal basis for corporate capitalism by making the contract sacred.

In 1895 the Court interpreted the Sherman Act so as to make it harmless. It said a monopoly of sugar refining was a monopoly in manufacturing, not commerce, and so could not be regulated by Congress through the Sherman Act (*U.S. v. E. C. Knight Co.*). The Court also said the Sherman Act could be used against interstate strikes (the railway strike of 1894) because they were in restraint of trade. It also declared unconstitutional a small attempt by Congress to tax high incomes at a higher rate (*Pollock v. Farmers' Loan & Trust Company*). In later years it would refuse to break up the Standard Oil and American Tobacco monopolies, saying the Sherman Act barred only "unreasonable" combinations in restraint of trade.

A New York banker toasted the Supreme Court in 1895: "I give you, gentlemen, the Supreme Court of the United States—guardian of the dollar, defender of private property, enemy of spoliation, sheet anchor of the Republic."

Very soon after the Fourteenth Amendment became law, the Supreme Court began to demolish it as a protection for blacks, and to develop it as a protection for corporations. However, in 1877, a Supreme Court decision (*Munn v. Illinois*) approved state laws regulating the prices charged to farmers for the use of grain elevators. The grain elevator company argued it was a person being deprived of property, thus violating the Fourteenth Amendment's declaration "nor shall any State deprive any person of life, liberty, or property without due process of law." The Supreme Court disagreed, saying that grain elevators were not simply private property but were invested with "a public interest" and so could be regulated.

One year after that decision, the American Bar Association, organized by lawyers accustomed to serving the wealthy, began a national campaign of education to reverse the Court decision. Its presidents said, at different times: "If trusts are a defensive weapon of property interests against the communistic trend, they are desirable." And: "Monopoly is often a necessity and an advantage."

By 1886, they succeeded. State legislatures, under the pressure of aroused farmers, had passed laws to regulate the rates charged farmers by the railroads. The Supreme Court that year (*Wabash v. Illinois*) said states could not do this, that this was an intrusion on federal power. That year alone, the Court did away with 230 state laws that had been passed to regulate corporations.

By this time the Supreme Court had accepted the argument that corporations were "persons" and their money was property protected by the due process clause of the Fourteenth Amendment. Supposedly, the Amendment had been passed to protect Negro rights, but of the Fourteenth Amendment cases brought before the Supreme Court between 1890 and 1910, nineteen dealt with the Negro, 288 dealt with corporations.

The justices of the Supreme Court were not simply interpreters of the Constitution. They were men of certain backgrounds, of certain interests. One of them (Justice Samuel Miller) had said in 1875: "It is vain to contend with Judges who have been at the bar the advocates for forty years of railroad companies, and all forms of associated capital. . . ." In 1893, Supreme Court Justice David J. Brewer, addressing the New York State Bar Association, said:

> It is the unvarying law that the wealth of the community will be in the hands of the few. . . . The great majority of men are unwilling to endure that long self-denial and saving which makes accumulations possible . . . and hence it always

has been, and until human nature is remodeled always will be true, that the wealth of a nation is in the hands of a few, while the many subsist upon the proceeds of their daily toil.

This was not just a whim of the 1880s and 1890s—it went back to the Founding Fathers, who had learned their law in the era of *Blackstone's Commentaries,* which said: "So great is the regard of the law for private property, that it will not authorize the least violation of it; no, not even for the common good of the whole community."

Control in modern times requires more than force, more than law. It requires that a population dangerously concentrated in cities and factories, whose lives are filled with cause for rebellion, be taught that all is right as it is. And so, the schools, the churches, the popular literature taught that to be rich was a sign of superiority, to be poor a sign of personal failure, and that the only way upward for a poor person was to climb into the ranks of the rich by extraordinary effort and extraordinary luck.

In those years after the Civil War, a man named Russell Conwell, a graduate of Yale Law School, a minister, and author of best-selling books, gave the same lecture, "Acres of Diamonds," more than five thousand times to audiences across the country, reaching several million people in all. His message was that anyone could get rich if he tried hard enough, that everywhere, if people looked closely enough, were "acres of diamonds." A sampling:

> I say that you ought to get rich, and it is your duty to get rich. . . . The men who get rich may be the most honest men you find in the community. Let me say here clearly . . . ninety-eight out of one hundred of the rich men of America are honest. That is why they are rich. That is why they are trusted with money. That is why they carry on great enterprises and find plenty of people to work with them. It is because they are honest men. . . .
>
> I sympathize with the poor, but the number of poor who are to be sympathized with is very small. To sympathize with a man whom God has punished for his sins . . . is to do wrong . . . let us remember there is not a poor person in the United States who was not made poor by his own shortcomings. . . .

Conwell was a founder of Temple University. Rockefeller was a donor to colleges all over the country and helped found the University of Chicago. Huntington, of the Central Pacific, gave money to two Negro colleges, Hampton Institute and Tuskegee Institute. Carnegie gave money to colleges and to libraries. Johns Hopkins was founded by a millionaire merchant, and million-aires Cornelius Vanderbilt, Ezra Cornell, James Duke, and Leland Stanford created universities in their own names.

The rich, giving part of their enormous earnings in this way, became known as philanthropists. These educational institutions did not encourage dissent; they trained the middlemen in the American system—the teachers, doctors, lawyers, administrators, engineers, technicians, politicians—those who would be paid to keep the system going, to be loyal buffers against trouble.

In the meantime, the spread of public school education enabled the learning of writing, reading, and arithmetic for a whole generation of workers, skilled and semiskilled, who would be the literate or force of the new industrial age. It was important that these people learn obedience to authority. A journalist observer of the schools in the 1890s wrote: "The unkindly spirit of the teacher is strikingly apparent; the pupils, being completely subjugated to her will, are silent and motionless, the spiritual atmosphere of the classroom is damp and chilly."

Back in 1859, the desire of mill owners in the town of Lowell that their workers be educated was explained by the secretary of the Massachusetts Board of Education:

> The owners of factories are more concerned than other classes and interests in the intelligence of their laborers. When the latter are well-educated and the former are disposed to deal justly, controversies and strikes can never occur, nor can the minds of the masses be prejudiced by demagogues and controlled by temporary and factious considerations.

Joel Spring, in his book *Education and the Rise of the Corporate State,* says: "The development of a factory-like system in the nineteenth-century schoolroom was not accidental."

This continued into the twentieth century, when William Bagley's *Classroom Management* became a standard teacher training text, reprinted thirty times. Bagley said: "One who studies educational theory aright can see in the mechanical routine of the classroom the educative forces that are slowly transforming the child from a little savage into a creature of law and order, fit for the life of civilized society."

It was in the middle and late nineteenth century that high schools developed as aids to the industrial system, that history was widely required in the curriculum to foster patriotism. Loyalty oaths, teacher certification, and

the requirement of citizenship were introduced to control both the educational and the political quality of teachers. Also, in the latter part of the century, school officials—not teachers—were given control over textbooks. Laws passed by the states barred certain kinds of textbooks. Idaho and Montana, for instance, forbade textbooks propagating "political" doctrines, and the Dakota territory ruled that school libraries could not have "partisan political pamphlets or books."

Against this gigantic organization of knowledge and education for orthodoxy and obedience, there arose a literature of dissent and protest, which had to make its way from reader to reader against great obstacles. Henry George, a self-educated workingman from a poor Philadelphia family, who became a newspaperman and an economist, wrote a book that was published in 1879 and sold millions of copies, not only in the United States, but all over the world. His book *Progress and Poverty* argued that the basis of wealth was land, that this was becoming monopolized, and that a single tax on land, abolishing all others, would bring enough revenue to solve the problem of poverty and equalize wealth in the nation. Readers may not have been persuaded of his solutions, but they could see in their own lives the accuracy of his observations:

> It is true that wealth has been greatly increased, and that the average of comfort, leisure and refinement has been raised; but these gains are not general. In them the lowest class do not share. . . . This association of poverty with progress is the great enigma of our times. . . . There is a vague but general feeling of disappointment; an increased bitterness among the working classes; a widespread feeling of unrest and brooding revolution. . . . The civilized world is trembling on the verge of a great movement. Either it must be a leap upward, which will open the way to advances yet undreamed of, or it must be a plunge downward which will carry us back toward barbarism. . . .

A different kind of challenge to the economic and social system was given by Edward Bellamy, a lawyer and writer from western Massachusetts, who wrote, in simple, intriguing language, a novel called *Looking Backward,* in which the author fells asleep and wakes up in the year 2000, to find a socialistic society in which people work and live cooperatively. *Looking Backward,* which described socialism vividly, lovingly, sold a million copies in a few years, and over a hundred groups were organized around the country to try to make the dream come true.

It seemed that despite the strenuous efforts of government, business, the church, the schools, to control their thinking, millions of Americans were ready to consider harsh criticism of the existing system, to contemplate other possible ways of living. They were helped in this by the great movements of workers and farmers that swept the country in the 1880s and 1890s. These movements went beyond the scattered strikes and tenants' struggles of the period 1830–1877. . . . They were nationwide movements, more threatening than before to the ruling elite, more dangerously suggestive. It was a time when revolutionary organizations existed in major American cities, and revolutionary talk was in the air.

HOWARD ZINN was a civil rights protester and peace activist with a PhD from Columbia University. He taught for many years at Spelman College and Boston University, and was immensely popular with the students. He has written hundreds of articles, but *A People's History of the United States* (HarperCollins, 1980, 1999) has sold enough copies to make a millionaire out of a Socialist.

John S. Gordon  **NO**

Was There Ever Such a Business!

The industrial empires that were created by the robber barons appeared more and more threatening in their economic power as they merged into ever-larger companies. In the latter half of the 1890s, this trend toward consolidation accelerated. In 1897 there were 69 corporate mergers; in 1898 there were 303; the next year 1,208. Of the seventy-three "trusts" with capitalization of more than $10 million in 1900, two-thirds had been created in the previous three years.

In 1901 J. P. Morgan created the largest company of all, U.S. Steel, merging Andrew Carnegie's empire with several other steel companies to form a new company capitalized at $1.4 billion. The revenues of the federal government that year were a mere $586 million. The sheer size of the enterprise stunned the world. Even the *Wall Street Journal* confessed to "uneasiness over the magnitude of the affair," and wondered if the new corporation would mark "the high tide of industrial capitalism." A joke made the rounds where a teacher asks a little boy about who made the world. "God made the world in 4004 B.C.," he replied, "and it was reorganized in 1901 by J. P. Morgan."

But when Theodore Roosevelt entered the White House in September 1901, the laiseez-faire attitude of the federal government began to change. In 1904 the government announced that it would sue under the Sherman Antitrust Act—long thought a dead letter—to break up a new Morgan consolidation, the Northern Securities Corporation. Morgan hurried to Washington to get the matter straightened out.

"If we have done anything wrong," Morgan told the president, fully encapsulating his idea of how the commercial world should work, "send your man to my man and they can fix it up."

"That can't be done," Roosevelt replied.

"We don't want to fix it up," his attorney general, Philander Knox, explained. "We want to stop it."

From that point on, the federal government would be an active referee in the marketplace, trying—not always

successfully, to be sure—to balance the needs of efficiency and economies of scale against the threat of overweening power in organizations that owed allegiance only to their stockholders, not to society as a whole.

In 1907 the federal government took on the biggest "trust" of all, Standard Oil. The case reached the Supreme Court in 1910 and was decided the following year, when the Court ruled unanimously that Standard Oil was a combination in restraint of trade. It ordered Standard Oil broken up into more than thirty separate companies.

The liberal wing of American politics hailed the decision, needless to say, but in one of the great ironies of American economic history, the effect of the ruling on the greatest fortune in the world was only to increase it. In the two years after the breakup of Standard Oil, the stock in the successor companies doubled in value, making John D. Rockefeller twice as rich as he had been before.

Nothing so epitomized the economy of the late nineteenth-century Western world as steel. Its production became the measure of a country's industrial power, and its uses were almost without limit. Its influence in other sectors of the economy, such as railroads and real estate, was immense. But steel was hardly an invention of the time. Indeed, it has been around for at least three thousand years. What was new was the cost of producing it.

Pig iron, the first step in iron and steel production, is converted into bar iron by remelting it and mixing it with ground limestone to remove still more impurities. Cast iron is then created by pouring this into molds, producing such items as frying pans, cookstoves, and construction members. Cast iron was widely used in urban construction in the antebellum period, but it had serious drawbacks. Extremely strong in compression, cast iron makes excellent columns. But, because it is very brittle, it is weak in tension, making it unsuitable for beams. For them, wrought iron was needed.

Wrought iron is made by melting pig iron and stirring it repeatedly until it achieves a pasty consistency and most of the impurities have been volatilized. The laborers who worked these furnaces were known as puddlers and were both highly skilled and highly paid. After the metal is removed from the puddling furnace, it is subjected to pressure and rolled and folded over and over—in effect, it is kneaded like bread dough—until it develops the fibrous quality that makes wrought iron much less brittle than cast iron and thus moderately strong in tension. Wrought iron is quite soft compared to cast iron but it is also ductile, able to be drawn out and hammered into various shapes, just as copper can be.

Wrought iron, of course, was much more expensive to produce than cast iron but could be used for making beams, bridges, ships, and, most important to the nineteenth-century economy after 1830, railroad rails. The Industrial Revolution simply could not have moved into high gear without large quantities of wrought iron.

Steel, which is iron alloyed with just the right amount of carbon under suitable conditions, has the good qualities of both cast and wrought iron. It is extremely strong and hard, like cast iron, while it is also malleable and withstands shock like wrought iron. And it is far stronger in tension than either, and thus makes a superb building material.

But until the mid-nineteenth century, the only way to make steel was in small batches from wrought iron, mixing the iron with carbon and heating it for a period of days. Thus its use was limited to very high-value items such as sword blades, razors, and tools, where its ability to withstand shock and take and hold a sharp edge justified its high cost. At mid-century, roughly 250,000 tons of steel were being made by the old methods in Europe, and only about 10,000 tons in the United States.

Then, in 1856, an Englishman named Henry Bessemer (later Sir Henry) invented the Bessemer converter, which allowed steel to be made directly and quickly from pig iron. As so often happens in the history of technological development, the initial insight was the result of an accidental observation. Bessemer had developed a new type of artillery shell, but the cast-iron cannons of the day were not strong enough to handle it. He began experimenting in hopes of developing a stronger metal, and one day a gust of wind happened to hit some molten iron. The oxygen in the air, combining with the iron and carbon in the molten metal, raised the temperature of the metal and volatilized the impurities. Most of the carbon was driven off. What was left was steel.

Bessemer, realizing what had happened, immediately set about designing an industrial process that would duplicate what he had observed accidentally. His converter was a large vessel, about ten feet wide by twenty feet high, with trunnions so that its contents could be poured. It was made of steel and lined with firebrick. At the bottom, air could be blasted through holes in the firebrick into the "charge," as the mass of molten metal in the crucible was called, converting it to steel in a stupendous blast of flame and heat. With the Bessemer converter, ten to thirty tons of pig iron could be turned into steel every twelve to fifteen minutes in what is one of the most spectacular of all industrial processes.

The labor activist John A. Fitch wrote in 1910 that "there is a glamor about the making of steel. The very size of things—the immensity of the tools, the scale of production—grips the mind with an overwhelming sense of power. Blast furnaces, eighty, ninety, one hundred feet tall, gaunt and insatiable, are continually gaping to admit ton after ton of ore, fuel, and stone. Bessemer converters dazzle the eye with their leaping flames. Steel ingots at white heat, weighing thousands of pounds, are carried from place to place and tossed about like toys. . . . [C]ranes pick up steel rails or fifty-foot girders as jauntily as if their tons were ounces. These are the things that cast a spell over the visitor in these workshops of Vulcan."

One of the visitors to Henry Bessemer's steelworks in Sheffield, England, in 1872, was a young Scottish immigrant to America, Andrew Carnegie. He was mightily impressed—so impressed, in fact, that in the next thirty years he would ride the growing demand for steel to one of the greatest American fortunes.

Carnegie had been born in Dunfermline, a few miles northwest and across the Firth of Forth from Edinburgh, in 1835. His father was a hand weaver who owned his own loom, on which he made intricately patterned damask cloth. Dunfermline was a center of the damask trade, and skilled weavers such as William Carnegie could make a good living at it.

But the Industrial Revolution destroyed William Carnegie's livelihood. By the 1840s power looms could produce cloth such as damask much more cheaply than handlooms. While there had been 84,560 handloom weavers in Scotland in 1840, there would be only 25,000 ten years later. William Carnegie would not be one of them.

The elder Carnegie sank into despair, and his far tougher-minded wife took charge of the crisis. She had gotten a letter from her sister, who had immigrated to America, settling in Pittsburgh. "This country's far better for the working man," her sister wrote, "than the old one, & there is room enough & to spare, notwithstanding the thousands that flock to her borders." In 1847, when Andrew was twelve, the Carnegie family moved to Pittsburgh.

The Carnegies were in the first wave of one of the great movements of people in human history, known as the Atlantic migration. At first most of the immigrants came from the British Isles, especially Ireland after the onset of the Great Famine of the 1840s. Later Germany, Italy, and Eastern Europe provided immigrants in huge numbers, more than two million in 1900 alone.

In its size and significance the Atlantic migration was the equal of the barbarian movements in late classic times that helped bring the Roman Empire to an end. But while many of the barbarian tribes had been pushed by those behind them, the more than thirty million people who crossed the Atlantic to settle in America between 1820 and 1914 were largely pulled by the lure of economic opportunity.

Many, such as the land-starved Scandinavians who settled in the Upper Middle West, moved to rural areas and established farms. But most, at least at first, settled in the country's burgeoning cities, in the fast-spreading districts that came to be called slums (a word that came into use, in both Britain and America, about 1825). For the first time in American history, a substantial portion of the population was poor. But most of the new urban poor were not poor for long.

These slums, by modern standards, were terrible almost beyond imagination, with crime- and vermin-ridden, sunless apartments that often housed several people, sometimes several families, to a room and had only communal privies behind the buildings. In the 1900 census, when conditions in the slums had much improved from mid-century, one district in New York's Lower East Side had a population of more than fifty thousand but only about five hundred bathtubs.

Such housing, however, was no worse—and often better—than what the impoverished immigrants left behind in Europe, and as Mrs. Carnegie's sister—and millions like her—reported back home, the economic opportunities were far greater. The labor shortage so characteristic of the American economy since its earliest days had not abated. So the average stay for an immigrant family in the worst of the slums was less than fifteen years, before they were able to move to better housing in better neighborhoods and begin the climb into the American middle class.

The migration of people to the United States in search of economic opportunity has never ceased, although legal limits were placed on it beginning in the early 1920s. And this vast migration did far more than help provide the labor needed to power the American economy. It has given the United States the most ethnically diverse population of any country in the world. And because of that, it has provided the country with close personal connections with nearly every other country on the globe, an immense economic and political advantage.

The Carnegies moved into two rooms above a workshop that faced a muddy alleyway behind Mrs. Carnegie's sister's house in Allegheny City, a neighborhood of Pittsburgh. Mrs. Carnegie found work making shoes, and Mr. Carnegie worked in a cotton mill. Andrew got a job there as well, as a bobbin boy earning $1.20 a week for twelve-hour days, six days a week.

Needless to say, it didn't take the bright and ambitious Andrew Carnegie fifteen years to start up the ladder. By 1849 he had a job as a telegraph messenger boy, earning $2.50 a week. This gave him many opportunities to become familiar with Pittsburgh and its business establishment, and Carnegie made the most of them. Soon he was an operator, working the telegraph himself and able to interpret it by ear, writing down the messages directly. His salary was up to $25 a month.

In 1853, in a classic example of Louis Pasteur's dictum that chance favors the prepared mind, Thomas A. Scott, general superintendent of the Pennsylvania Railroad, a frequent visitor to the telegraph office where Carnegie worked, needed a telegraph operator of his own to help with the system being installed by the railroad. He chose Carnegie, not yet eighteen years old. By the time Carnegie was thirty-three, in 1868, he had an annual income of $50,000, thanks to the tutelage of Thomas Scott and numerous shrewd investments in railway sleeping cars, oil, telegraph lines, and iron manufacturing. But after his visit to Bessemer's works in Sheffield, he decided to concentrate on steel.

❧❦❧

It had been pure chance that had brought the Carnegie family to Pittsburgh, but its comparative advantages would make it the center of the American steel industry.

Set where the Allegheny and Monongahela rivers join to form the Ohio and provide easy transportation over a wide area, Pittsburgh had been founded, as so many cities west of the mountains were, as a trading post. Shortly after the Revolution, Pittsburgh began to exploit the abundant nearby sources of both iron ore and coal and specialize in manufacturing. While the rest of the country still relied on wood, coal became the dominant fuel in Pittsburgh, powering factories that were turning out glass, iron, and other energy-intensive products. As early as 1817, when the population was still only six thousand, there were 250 factories in operation, and the nascent city, with already typical American boosterism, was calling itself the "Birmingham of America." Because of the cheap coal, Pittsburgh exploited the steam engine long before it began to displace water power elsewhere, and most of its factories were steam-powered by 1830.

There was, however, a price to be paid for the cheap coal, which produces far more smoke than does wood. About 1820, when Pittsburgh was still a relatively small town, a visitor wrote that the smoke formed "a cloud which almost amounts to night and overspreads Pittsburgh with the appearance of gloom and melancholy." By the 1860s even Anthony Trollope, London-born and no stranger to coal smoke, was impressed with the pall. Looked down on from the surrounding hills, Trollope reported, some of the tops of the churches could be seen, "But the city itself is buried in a dense cloud. I was never more in love with smoke and dirt than when I stood here and watched the darkness of night close in upon the floating soot which hovered over the house-tops of the city." As the Industrial Revolution gathered strength, other American cities became polluted with coal smoke and soot, but none so badly as Pittsburgh.

The most important coal beds in the Pittsburgh area were those surrounding the town of Connellsville, about thirty miles southeast of the city. What made Connellsville coal special was that it was nearly perfect for converting into coke. Indeed it is the best coking coal in the world.

Coke is to coal exactly what charcoal is to wood: heated in the absence of air to drive off the impurities, it becomes pure carbon and burns at an even and easily adjusted temperature. And either charcoal or coke is indispensable to iron and steel production. As the iron industry in Pittsburgh grew, it turned more and more to coke, the production of which was far more easily industrialized than was charcoal.

By the time Andrew Carnegie was moving into steel, Henry Clay Frick, who had been born in West Overton, Pennsylvania, not far from Connellsville, in 1849, was moving into coke. Like Carnegie, Frick was a very hard-headed businessman and willing to take big risks for big rewards. And like Carnegie, he was a millionaire by the time he was thirty. Unlike Carnegie, however, he had little concern with public opinion or the great social issues of the day. Carnegie always wanted to be loved and admired by society at large. Frick was perfectly willing to settle for its respect. Unlike Carnegie, he rarely granted newspaper interviews and never wrote articles for publication.

By the 1880s the Carnegie Steel Company and the H. C. Frick Company dominated their respective industries, and Carnegie was by far Frick's biggest customer. In late 1881, while Frick was on his honeymoon in New York, Carnegie, who loved surprises, suddenly proposed a merger of their companies at a family lunch one day.

Frick, who had no inkling the proposal was coming, was stunned. So was Carnegie's ever-vigilant mother, now in her seventies. The silence that ensued was finally broken by what is perhaps the most famous instance of maternal concern in American business history.

"Ah, Andra," said Mrs. Carnegie in her broad Scots accent, "that's a very fine thing for Mr. Freek. But what do we get out of it?"

Needless to say, Carnegie had calculated closely what he would get out of it. First, the Carnegie Steel Company would get guaranteed supplies of coke at the best possible price; second, he would get the surpassing executive skills of Henry Clay Frick; and third, he would further the vertical integration of the steel industry in general and his company in particular.

Vertical integration simply means bringing under one corporation's control part or all of the stream of production from raw materials to distribution. It had been going on since the dawn of the Industrial Revolution (Francis Cabot Lowell had been the first to integrate spinning and weaving in a single building) but greatly accelerated in the last quarter of the nineteenth century as industrialists sought economies of scale as well as of speed to cut costs.

Carnegie and Frick shared a simple management philosophy: (1) Innovate constantly and invest heavily in the latest equipment and techniques to drive down operating costs. (2) Always be the low-cost producer so as to remain profitable in bad economic times. (3) Retain most of the profits in good times to take advantage of opportunities in bad times as less efficient competitors fail.

One such opportunity arose in 1889, by which time Frick was chairman of the Carnegie steel companies (Carnegie himself never held an executive position in the companies he controlled, but as the holder of a comfortable majority of the stock, he was always the man in charge). That year Frick snapped up the troubled Duquesne Steel Works, paying for it with $1 million in Carnegie company bonds due to mature in five years. By the time the bonds were paid off, the plant had paid for itself five times over.

Much of the technological advances that Carnegie was so quick to use came from Europe's older and more established steel industries, just as, nearly a century earlier, the American cloth industry had piggybacked on Britain's technological lead. As one of Carnegie's principal lieutenants, Captain W. M. Jones, explained to the British Iron and Steel Institute as early as 1881, "While your metallurgists as well as those of France and Germany, have been devoting their time and talents to the discovery of new processes, we have swallowed the information so generously tendered through the printed reports of the

Institute, and we have selfishly devoted ourselves to beating you in output."

And beat them they did. In 1867 only 1,643 tons of Bessemer steel was produced in the United States. Thirty years later, in 1897, the tonnage produced was 7,156,957, more than Britain and Germany combined. By the turn of the century the Carnegie Steel Company alone would outproduce Britain. It would also be immensely profitable. In 1899 the Carnegie Steel Company, the low-cost producer in the prosperous and heavily protected American market, made $21 million in profit. The following year profits doubled. No wonder Andrew Carnegie exclaimed at one point, "Was there ever such a business!"

And steel was also transforming the American urban landscape. When stone was the principal construction material of large buildings, they could not rise much above six stories, even after the elevator was perfected in the 1850s, because of the necessary thickness of the walls. It was church steeples that rose above their neighbors and punctuated the urban skyline. But as the price of steel declined steadily as the industry's efficiency rose—by the 1880s the far longer-lasting steel railroad rails cost less than the old wrought-iron rails—more and more buildings were built with steel skeletons and could soar to the sky. Between the 1880s and 1913 the record height for buildings was broken as often as every year as "skyscrapers" came to dominate American urban skylines in an awesome display of the power of steel. . . .

While the late-nineteenth-century American economy was increasingly built by and with steel, it was increasingly fueled by oil. In 1859, the year Edwin Drake drilled the first well, American production amounted to only 2,000 barrels. Ten years later it was 4.25 million and by 1900, American production would be nearly 60 million barrels. But while production rose steadily, the price of oil was chaotic, sinking as low as 10 cents a barrel—far below the cost of the barrel itself—and soaring as high as $13.75 during the 1860s. One reason for this was the vast number of refineries then in existence. Cleveland alone had more than thirty, many of them nickel-and-dime, ramshackle operations.

Many people, while happy to exploit the new oil business, were unwilling to make large financial commitments to it for fear that the oil would suddenly dry up. The field in northwestern Pennsylvania was very nearly the only one in the world until the 1870s, when the Baku field in what was then southern Russia opened up. There would be no major new field in the United States until the fabulous Spindletop field in Texas was first tapped in 1902.

But a firm named Rockefeller, Flagler, and Andrews, formed to exploit the burgeoning market for petroleum products, especially kerosene, took the gamble of building top-quality refineries. Like Carnegie, it intended to exploit being the low-cost producer, with all the advantages of that position. The firm also began buying up other refineries as the opportunity presented itself.

The firm realized that there was no controlling the price of crude oil but that it could control, at least partly, another important input into the price of petroleum products: transportation. It began negotiating aggressively with the railroads to give the firm rebates in return for guaranteeing high levels of traffic. It was this arrangement that often allowed the firm to undersell its competitors and still make handsome profits, further strengthening the firm's already formidable competitive position.

In 1870 one of the partners, Henry Flagler, convinced the others to change the firm from a partnership to a corporation, which would make it easier for the partners to continue to raise capital to finance their relentless expansion while retaining control. The new corporation, named Standard Oil, was capitalized at $1 million and owned at that time about 10 percent of the country's oil refining capacity. By 1880 it would control 80 percent of a much larger industry.

The expansion of Standard Oil became one of the iconic stories of latenineteenth-century America, as its stockholders became rich beyond imagination and its influence in the American economy spread ever wider. Indeed, the media reaction to Standard Oil and John D. Rockefeller in the Gilded Age is strikingly similar to the reaction to the triumph of Microsoft and Bill Gates a hundred years later. It is perhaps a coincidence that Rockefeller and Gates were just about the same age, their early forties, when they became household names and the living symbols of a new and, to some, threatening economic structure.

The image of Standard Oil that remains even today in the American folk memory was the product of a number of writers and editorial cartoonists who often had a political agenda to advance first and foremost. The most brilliant of these was Ida Tarbell, whose *History of the Standard Oil Company*, first published in *McClure's* magazine in 1902, vividly depicted a company ruthlessly expanding over the corporate bodies of its competitors, whose assets it gobbled up as it went.

That is by no means a wholly false picture, but it is a somewhat misleading one. For one thing, as the grip of Standard Oil relentlessly tightened on the oil industry, prices for petroleum products *declined* steadily, dropping by two-thirds over the course of the last three decades of the nineteenth century. It is simply a myth that monopolies will raise prices once they have the power to do so.

Monopolies, like everyone else, want to maximize their profits, not their prices. Lower prices, which increase demand, and increased efficiency, which cuts costs, is usually the best way to achieve the highest possible profits. What makes monopolies (and most of them today are government agencies, from motor vehicle bureaus to public schools) so economically evil is the fact that, without competitive pressure, they become highly risk-aversive—and therefore shy away from innovation—and notably indifferent to their customers' convenience.

Further, Standard Oil used its position as the country's largest refiner not only to extract the largest rebates from the railroads but also to induce them to deny rebates to refiners that Standard Oil wanted to acquire. It even sometimes forced railroads to give it secret rebates not only on its own oil, but on that shipped by its competitors as well, essentially a tax on competing with Standard Oil. (This is about as close as the "robber barons" ever came to behaving like, well, robber barons.) It thus effectively presented these refiners with Hobson's choice: they could agree to be acquired, at a price set by Standard Oil, or they could be driven into bankruptcy by high transportation costs.

The acquisition price set, however, was a fair one, arrived at by a formula developed by Henry Flagler, and consistently applied. Sometimes, especially if the owners of the refinery being acquired had executive talents that Standard wished to make use of, the price was a generous one. Further, the seller had the choice of receiving cash or Standard Oil stock. Those who chose the latter—and there were hundreds—became millionaires as they rode the stock of the Standard Oil Company to capitalist glory. Those who took the cash often ended up whining to Ida Tarbell.

None of this, of course, was illegal, and that was the real problem. In the late nineteenth century people such as Rockefeller, Flagler, Carnegie, and J. P. Morgan were creating at a breathtaking pace the modern corporate economy, and thus a wholly new economic universe. They were moving far faster than society could fashion, through the usually slow-moving political process, the rules needed to govern that new universe wisely and fairly. But that must always be the case in democratic capitalism, as individuals can always act far faster than can society as a whole. Until the rules were written—largely in the first decades of the twentieth century—it was a matter of (in the words of Sir Walter Scott)

The good old rule, the simple plan
That they should take who have the power
And they should keep who can.

Part of the problem is that there is a large, inherent inertia in any political system, and democracy is no exception. Politicians, after all, are in the reelection business, and it is often easier to do nothing than to offend one group or another. So while the American economy had changed profoundly since the mid-nineteenth century, the state incorporation laws, for instance, had not. As an Ohio corporation, Standard Oil was not allowed to own property in other states or to hold the stock of other corporations. As it quickly expanded throughout the Northeast, the country, and then across the globe, however, Standard Oil necessarily acquired property in other states and purchased other corporations.

The incorporation laws, largely written in an era before the railroads and telegraph had made a national economy possible, were no longer adequate to meet the needs of the new economy. To get around the outdated law, Henry Flager, as secretary of Standard Oil, had himself appointed as trustee to hold the property or stock that Standard Oil itself could not legally own. By the end of the 1870s, however, Standard owned dozens of properties and companies in other states, each, in theory, held by a trustee who was in some cases Flagler and in other cases other people. It was a hopelessly unwieldy corporate structure.

In all probability, it was Flagler—a superb executive—who found the solution. Instead of each subsidiary company having a single trustee, with these trustees scattered throughout the Standard Oil empire, the same three men, all at the Cleveland headquarters, were appointed trustees for all the subsidiary companies. In theory, they controlled all of Standard Oil's assets outside Ohio. In fact, of course, they did exactly what they were told.

Thus was born the business trust, a form that was quickly imitated by other companies that were becoming national in scope. The "trusts" would be one of the great bogeymen of American politics for the next hundred years, but, ironically, the actual trust form of organization devised by Henry Flagler lasted only until 1889. That year New Jersey—seeking a source of new tax revenue—became the first state to modernize its incorporation laws and bring them into conformity with the new economic realities. New Jersey now permitted holding companies and interstate activities, and companies flocked to incorporate there, as, later, they would flock to Delaware, to enjoy the benefits of a corporation-friendly legal climate. Standard Oil of New Jersey quickly became the center of the Rockefeller interests, and the Standard Oil Trust, in the legal sense, disappeared.

With the growth of American industry, the nature of American foreign trade changed drastically. The United States remained, as it remains today, a formidable exporter of agricultural and mineral products. Two new ones were even added in the post-Civil War era: petroleum and copper. But it also became a major exporter of manufactured goods that it had previously imported. In 1865 they had constituted only 22.78 percent of American exports. By the turn of the twentieth century they were 31.65 percent of a vastly larger trade. The percentage of world trade, meanwhile, that was American in origin doubled in these years to about 12 percent of total trade.

Nowhere was this more noticeable than in iron and steel products, the cutting edge of late-nineteenth-century technology. Before the Civil War the United States exported only $6 million worth of iron and steel manufactures a year. In 1900 it exported $121,914,000 worth of locomotives, engines, rails, electrical machinery, wire, pipes, metalworking machinery, boilers, and other goods. Even sewing machines and typewriters were being exported in quantity. . . .

This country has never developed an aristocracy, because the concept of primogeniture, with the eldest son inheriting the bulk of the fortune, never took hold. Thus great fortunes have always been quickly dispersed among heirs in only a few generations. The American super rich are therefore always nouveau riche and often act accordingly, giving new meaning in each generation to the phrase *conspicuous consumption*. In the Gilded Age, they married European titles, built vast summer cottages and winter retreats that cost millions but were occupied only a few weeks a year. . . .

John S. Gordon is a specialist in business and financial history whose articles have appeared in numerous prominent magazines and newspapers for the past 20 years. He is a contributing editor to *American Heritage* and since 1989 has written the "Business of America" column. His other books include *Hamilton's Blessing: The Extraordinary Life and Times of Our National Debt* (Walker, 1997), *The Great Game: The Emergence of Wall Street as a World Power, 1653–2000* (Scribner, 1999), and *A Thread Across the Ocean: The Heroic Story of the Transatlantic Cable* (Walker, 2002).

EXPLORING THE ISSUE

Were the Nineteenth-Century Entrepreneurs "Robber Barons"?

Critical Thinking and Reflection

1. Howard Zinn has been called a Marxist historian. What does this mean? How does his interpretation of the political and economic dynamics of nineteenth-century America fit a Marxist interpretation?
2. What is a "robber baron"? Describe and critically analyze Zinn's description of the monopolistic practices of the American businessmen John D. Rockefeller, J. P. Morgan, and Andrew Carnegie. Critically analyze how Zinn argues that the political system, religion, and education supported the monopolistic practices of the business elite.
3. Define vertical integration. Define horizontal integration. Explain how Rockefeller vertically integrated the oil industry. Explain how Carnegie integrated the steel industry.
4. What is more important in a successful business—organization or entrepreneurship? Critically discuss, using Rockefeller and Carnegie as examples.
5. Compare, contrast, and critically evaluate the interpretations of Zinn and Gordon toward the nineteenth-century men of big business. Were they "robber barons" or "industrial statesmen"? Is it possible to reconcile the two viewpoints? Does Zinn provide enough evidence that the political, economic, judicial, and social climate of opinion was stacked against the worker? Critically discuss.

Is There Common Ground?

Questions concerning the characterization of late-nineteenth century entrepreneurs seldom fail to elicit strong student reaction. On one hand, Zinn draws upon the Josephson antibusiness tradition of the 1930s and his own New Left radical outlook of the 1960s and 1970s, which blamed business for the racism, poverty, and militarism, which infected American society. On the other hand, John Steele Gordon emphasizes the technological benefits in lifestyle—better homes, heating, food, automobiles—that the nineteenth-century industrial statesmen brought to the United States. Who is more persuasive—Zinn or Gordon? Critics have faulted Zinn's interpretation as too one-sided and lacking an appreciation for the divisions between small and large businessmen and small and large farmers or the pressures put upon Congress, the Justice Department that staffed the Antitrust Division in charge of enforcing the Sherman Act, and the members of the Interstate Commerce Commission who were supposed to regulate the railroads. Critics of the entrepreneurial statesmen point of view have challenged Gordon's rosy picture of development and questioned whether management paid workers a living wage and provided a clean and safe working environment at the same time they produced

a creative and dynamic economy. Could a nation of pre-1880s small entrepreneurs competing with each other have produced the consumer-oriented society with its munificent lifestyle enjoyed by middle-class and upper-class Americans? Is monopoly or managed or mismanaged capitalism the best system?

Create Central

www.mhhe.com/createcentral

Additional Resources

Ron Chernow, *Titan: The Life of John D. Rockefeller, Sr.* (Random House, 1998).

Harold C. Livesay, *Americans Made: Men Who Shaped the American Economy* (Little, Brown, 1986).

Thomas K. McCraw, ed., *The Essential Alfred Chandler: Essays Toward a Historical Theory of Big Business* (Harvard University Press, 1988).

Jean Strouse, *Morgan: American Financier* (Harper Collins, 1999).

Richard White, *Railroaded: The Transcontinentals and the Making of Modern America* (Norton, 2012).

Internet References . . .

International Institute of Social History

www.socialhistory.org

John D. Rockefeller and the Standard Oil Company

www.micheloud.com/FXM/SO/rock.html

PBS.org

www.pbs.org/wgbh/amex/carnegie
/peopleevents/pande01.html

Selected, Edited, and with Issue Framing Material by:
Larry Madaras, *Howard Community College*
and
James M. SoRelle, *Baylor University*

ISSUE

Were Anarchists Responsible for the Haymarket Riot?

YES: **Timothy Messer-Kruse**, from *The Haymarket Conspiracy: Transatlantic Anarchist Networks*, University of Illinois Press (2012)

NO: **Paul Avrich**, from *The Haymarket Tragedy*, Princeton University Press (1984)

Learning Outcomes
After reading this issue, you will be able to:
• Understand the historical context and basic details of the Haymarket riot of 1886.
• Summarize attitudes in Chicago toward organized labor.
• Evaluate the relationship between anarchism and labor ideologies prevalent in the late 1800s.
• Assess the role that anarchists played in the Haymarket riot.
• Assess the role that law enforcement officials, the local media, and representatives of the business community played in the events preceding, during, and following the Haymarket riot.

ISSUE SUMMARY

YES: Timothy Messer-Kruse challenges the traditional narrative of the Haymarket riot and concludes that the violence in Chicago on May 4, 1886, was the culmination of a thoroughly planned conspiracy by dedicated anarchists committed to the cause of violent revolution.

NO: Paul Avrich confirms that Chicago's anarchist leaders employed threatening rhetoric in response to the battle between workers and police at the McCormick Reaper Works that left two strikers dead on May 3, 1886, but he insists that the police, led by Inspector John Bonfield, precipitated the violence near Haymarket Square on May 4 by attempting to break up what had been a peaceful labor meeting.

In 1880, the total labor force in the United States numbered over 17 million, of which approximately 25 percent (4.5 million) were industrial workers. Most of these industrial workers were unskilled, owned no property, and despite beliefs that the United States was a land of opportunity for anyone who was willing to work for a living, these laborers were likely to remain unskilled and propertyless for their entire lives. They typically earned little more than a dollar a day, and the workday was long by modern standards. Steel workers were employed in a 12-hour shift, 7 days a week. In 1890, American workers in all manufacturing industries averaged 60 hours a

week. Even though real wages increased over the course of the late nineteenth century, full employment was jeopardized by a wildly fluctuating economy that weathered severe depressions in the early 1870s and 1890s and which led to reduced hours, full layoffs, or cuts in pay for many employees. Wages could also be affected adversely by illness or injury on the job at a time when there was no workman's compensation, health insurance, or industrial accident insurance. American industrial workers labored at their own risk in a nation that led the world in the number of industrial accidents. In short, most workers possessed little bargaining power at all with their employers.

How did industrial workers respond to these conditions? Since most did not possess a strong sense of working class consciousness and because they continued to believe that the American Dream remained within their reach, they struggled on enduring the hardships that confronted them in the workplace. Some, however, sought to improve their lot by joining with fellow workers in labor organizations that they hoped would serve as a counterweight to the power of the companies that employed them. The two major labor unions that developed in the late nineteenth century were the Knights of Labor and the American Federation of Labor. Because of hostility toward workers' unions, the Knights of Labor functioned for twelve years as a secret organization. Between 1879 and 1886, the Knights of Labor grew from 10,000 to 700,000 members. Idealistic in many of its aims, the union supported social reforms such as equal pay for men and women, the prohibition of alcohol, and the abolition of convict and child labor. Economic reforms included the development of workers' cooperatives, public ownership of utilities, and an eight-hour workday.

In 1886, the American Federation of Labor (AFL), under the leadership of Samuel Gompers, succeeded the Knights of Labor as the foremost union in the United States. The AFL concentrated its efforts on organizing skilled workers, and Gompers pushed for practical reforms—better hours, wages, and working conditions. Unlike the Knights, the AFL avoided associations with political parties, workers' cooperatives, unskilled workers, immigrants, and women. Gompers was heavily criticized by his contemporaries, and later by historians, for his narrow craft unionism, but despite the depression of the 1890s, AFL membership increased from 190,000 to 500,000 by 1900, to 1,500,000 by 1904, and to 2,000,000 on the eve of World War I.

Despite this growth, only about 10 percent of the nation's workers joined labor unions, and those who did were staunchly opposed by powerful elements within American society. The national and local governments were in the hands of men who were sympathetic to the rise of big business and hostile to the attempts of workers to organize. Representatives of the business community almost uniformly sought to destroy the unions. According to one such leader, "Labor organizations are today the greatest menace to this government that exists. Their influence for disruption is far more dangerous to the perpetuation of our government in its purity and power than would be the hostile array on our borders of the army of the entire world combined." The result of this unrelenting opposition to efforts by workers to improve their circumstances through organization was a series of violent encounters between labor and management. Whether it was the railroad strike of 1877, the Homestead steel strike of 1892, or the Pullman car strike of 1894, the pattern of repression was always the same. Companies would cut wages, workers would go out on strike, scab workers would be brought in, fights would break out, corporate leaders would receive court injunctions, and the police and state and federal militia would assault the unionized workers and their supporters. After a strike was broken, workers would lose their jobs or would accept pay cuts and longer workdays.

For the past 35 years historians have been studying the social and cultural environment of the American working class. The approach is modeled after Edward P. Thompson's highly influential and sophisticated Marxist analysis *The Making of the English Working Class* (Vintage Books, 1966), which is the capstone of an earlier generation of British and French social historians. The late Herbert G. Gutman was the first to discuss American workers as a group separate from the organized union movement and deservedly is recognized as the father of the "new labor history" in the United States. In *Work, Culture and Society in Industrializing America* (Alfred A. Knopf, 1976) and *Power and Culture: Essays on the American Working Class* (Pantheon, 1987), Gutman laid the groundwork for a whole generation of scholars who have produced case studies of union and nonunion workers in both urban and rural areas of the United States. In addition, Gutman's chronological framework differed from that of more traditional American labor historians. For example, he abandoned the division of American history at the Civil War/Reconstruction fault line and proposed a three-fold chronological division for free, white workers: (1) the premodern early industrial period from 1815 to 1843; (2) the transition to capitalism, which encompassed the years from 1843 to 1893; and (3) the development of a full-blown industrial system, which took place from the late 1890s through World War I. Gutman also challenged the view that workers were helpless pawns of the owners and that they were forced to cave in every time a strike took place. He shows that on a local level in the 1880s, immigrant workers not only joined unions but also usually won their strikes with the aid of small shopkeepers and workers in other industries who often supported those who were out on strike. Gutman's influence on labor historians can be sampled in the following collections of articles: Daniel J. Leab and Richard B. Morris, eds., *The Labor History Reader* (University of Illinois Press, 1985); Charles Stephenson and Robert Asher, eds., *Life and Labor: Dimensions of American Working-Class History* (State University of New York Press, 1986); and Milton Cantor, ed., *American Working Class*

Culture: Explorations in American Labor and Social History (Greenwood 1979).

A different approach can be found in Carl Degler's *Out of Our Past: The Forces That Shaped America*, 3rd ed. (1984). Degler agrees with traditional labor historians that the American worker lacked a true working-class consciousness, believed in the promise of workers' social mobility, and accepted capitalism. But he reverses the radical-conservative dichotomy as applied to the conflict between the worker and the businessman. In his view, the real radicals were the industrialists who created a more mature system of capitalism. Labor merely fashioned a conservative response to the radical changes brought about by big business.

Although strikes and other labor conflicts occurred throughout the nation in the late nineteenth century, Chicago developed a reputation as the heart of labor activism. An industrial center that served as the major railroad hub for the nation, Carl Sandburg's "City of Big Shoulders" attracted thousands of prospective workers, both native and foreign-born, who came to Chicago to improve their circumstances. Most settled in bulging working-class neighborhoods that challenged the local government to provide adequate city services and which became a matter of concern to the "respectable" middle-class residents of the city. One local minister complained: "It is said that Chicago has more of the Communistic element in it than any other city in America. Look at your workingmen going out to some celebration. Look on the flag they carry and see the inscription, 'Our Children Cry for Bread'! A more Communistic power slogan was never put on a flag than that." These views were shared by the editors of local newspapers who responded to reports of labor upheaval by rallying to the defense of factory owners and condemning the radical nature of labor's demands. To be sure, there were an assortment of labor radicals, including socialists and anarchists, who resided in Chicago, and they were frequently the first to blame when conflicts erupted between labor and management. Such was the case in 1886 as workers attempted to generate pressure on employers to adopt the eight-hour day as an industry standard.

In the essays that follow, Timothy Messer-Kruse and Paul Avrich evaluate the role of the anarchist movement in the labor upheavals that culminated in violence on the evening of May 4, 1886. Both authors agree that labor advocates identified as "anarchists" were a forceful presence in Chicago, but Messer-Kruse challenges the traditional view of many labor historians who have characterized the Haymarket defendants as victims of an unwarranted assault by law enforcement officials and the judicial process that convicted them of conspiracy and murder. Messer-Kruse insists that a careful reading of the court record leaves no doubt that the defendants were part of an organized international revolutionary conspiracy that sought to topple American capitalism by violent means.

Paul Avrich, on the other hand, is more sympathetic to Albert Parsons, August Spies, and other advocates of the eight-hour workday who had gained reputations as critics of the capitalist system through the rhetoric of their public speeches and pronouncement in numerous labor newspapers. While a strike in Chicago on May 1, 1886 in support of the eight-hour standard had passed without rioting or disorder, violence between workers and law enforcement officials had erupted outside the McCormick Reaper Works two days later, precipitating the call for a meeting the following evening near Haymarket Square to air workers' grievances. According to Avrich, the violence that occurred that evening would have been avoided had local police not marched on the assembly to disperse what up to that time had been a peaceful event.

YES ⟵

Timothy Messer-Kruse

The Haymarket Conspiracy: Transatlantic Anarchist Networks

A few minutes after ten o'clock on Tuesday, May 4, 1886, in the midst of a national general strike for the eight-hour workday, nearly two hundred police officers poured out from the Desplaines Street station and marched the hundred yards to where Chicago's anarchists were holding a protest meeting. Captain William Ward stopped a few feet from where Samuel Fielden was just concluding his speech and loudly ordered the crowd to disperse. At that moment, someone partially sheltered by a stack of fish crates left on a nearby curb threw a round leaden bomb, slightly bigger than a softball, into the police ranks. The resulting explosion threw dozens of policemen to the ground, leading to the deaths of five cops. Gunfire erupted as police fired indiscriminately into the crowd and some protesters answered in kind. Two more policemen and at least three civilians were shot and killed.

The meeting had been called the day before in protest of the alleged police killing of six workers during a riot at the McCormick Reaper Works, one of the largest industrial establishments in the city. (In fact, two men had died as a result of wounds sustained in this incident.) Broadsides demanding "revenge" and calling on workers to arm themselves were hurriedly printed, and code words signaling the muster of radical armed groups were published in the *Arbeiter-Zeitung*, a German-language daily newspaper that had become the flagship of revolutionary anarchism in Chicago. A secret meeting of revolutionary militiamen was held in a basement room beneath a saloon known as Greif's Hall, and various plans for attacking police stations, cutting firemen's hoses, and aiding striking workers with force of arms were made.

What became known as the Haymarket Riot did not take place in the Haymarket, a widening of Randolph Street on Chicago's near west side, but commenced around the corner from Randolph on a narrow side street pierced with even narrower alleyways when anarchist editor and leader August Spies scrambled onto a freight wagon and addressed a modest crowd. Spies's presence aroused the suspicions of police bunkered in their station only one block away, as he had been speaking from the top of a boxcar the day before when a large portion of his audience suddenly attacked workers leaving the McCormick factory at the end of their shift.

It took only a few minutes for police to sweep Desplaines Street clear of all protesters, save those writhing on the ground, but it took them weeks to piece together a case that could make someone legally responsible for the tragedy. Orders were given to arrest all the men who had spoken from that wagon, and the following morning the police raided the offices of the *Arbeiter-Zeitung* and arrested all twenty-three editors, writers, printers, typesetters, and "devil boys" they found there. Jimmying open Spies's desk, they discovered receipts from an explosives company and two sticks of dynamite. More dynamite was found in a closet, and fuses and blasting caps were found in a trunk. Adolph Fischer, Spies's editorial assistant, was apprehended leaving the building armed with a revolver, a "dirk" knife, and a blasting cap. Over the next four weeks, dozens of buildings and homes were searched, and many anarchists and their associates were detained or arrested. . . .

For their part, the prosecution took full advantage of the public's nativism and anti-leftist bias. Prosecutors festooned the courtroom with anarchist and socialist flags and banners seized from workers' meeting halls. Incendiary passages from anarchist books and newspapers were read into the record. As the trial progressed, an arsenal of weapons was heaped on tables in front of the jury, including loaded bombs. Such lurid displays were hardly necessary, though, as during the six-week trial prosecutor Julius Grinnell brought in witnesses and metallurgical evidence establishing Lingg as the bomb maker as well as witnesses who identified Schnaubelt as the bomber and Spies and Fischer as his accomplices. An old toy-maker, George Engel, was fingered as the man who had proposed bombing police stations at the secret meeting. Two other anarchists, Michael Schwab and Oscar Neebe, were implicated by witnesses as having knowledge of some sort of violent action at the Haymarket meeting, though they were never directly connected to the bombing. [Albert] Parsons was shown to have attempted to purchase fifty pistols and was one of the speakers at the meeting, but beyond that little implicated him in the alleged plot.

Defense lawyers and witnesses described how the police charged into a peaceful meeting, guns drawn, and fired wildly in panic after the bomb exploded. The defense attempted to undermine the testimony of informants by getting them to admit they had been paid by the police, but the sums they admitted to were below what everyone in Chicago knew to be a decent bribe. In what might have been the greatest legal blunder of the age, the defense placed defendant August Spies on the stand, and he arrogantly admitted that the dynamite found in his desk was indeed his and that he kept a few bombs around his office for the purpose of frightening reporters and to "experiment" with.

The jury took little time to arrive at a guilty verdict, condemning all the men to death except for Oscar Neebe. The Illinois Supreme Court reaffirmed the verdict and dismissed defense claims that the jury had been illegally packed. When the U.S. Supreme Court refused to hear the case, pressure was turned on Illinois governor Richard Oglesby to commute the sentences of those who showed remorse for their actions. By this time a clemency movement had taken shape, based largely on several highly selective accounts of the trial that were published by friends of the condemned. Oglesby commuted the sentences of Schwab and Fielden, who wrote letters of confession, to life in prison. While the others held steadfast in their refusal to sign such letters, Louis Lingg was caught with four small dynamite bombs in his cell. Speculation was that they were to be used by four of the condemned men to cheat the hangman. Anarchist lawyers attempted to distance the other defendants from Lingg by petitioning the court to declare him legally insane. A few days later it was discovered that Lingg had managed to either squirrel away one last charge or have an accomplice smuggle another one into the jail; he had reclined on his cot and lit an explosive like a cigar, leading to his death a few hours later.

On November 11, 1887, Albert Parsons, August Spies, George Engel, and Adolph Fischer were hanged in the Cook County jail. A line of thousands of mourners followed their coffins to Waldheim Cemetery, where in 1893 a graceful monument to their martyrdom was erected. Four years earlier a larger and less elegant edifice was erected in Chicago's Haymarket Square to commemorate the heroism of the dead policemen. The same year that the anarchists' memorial was dedicated, Governor Peter Altgeld signed pardons for

the remaining three imprisoned anarchists languishing in Joliet Prison.

The Haymarket bombing and trial marked a pivotal moment in the history of American social movements. It sparked the nation's first "red scare," whose fury disrupted even moderately leftist movements for a generation. It drove the nation's labor unions onto a more conservative path than they had been heading before the bombing. It also began a tradition within the American left of memorializing the Haymarket defendants as martyrs to the cause of the eight-hour workday, free speech, and the cause of labor generally. . . .

In presuming the Haymarket anarchists' innocence, historians have had only to explain the tragic chain of events that led to the anarchists' martyrdom. Their jailhouse denials and post-bombing explanations were not only accepted uncritically but also became the lens through which the character of the anarchist movement was interpreted. When that lens is taken away, when the anarchist movement is chronicled according to what its members said and did over the course of years, rather than according to what they and their defenders claimed they had done when facing the noose, the whole story changes. From this new vantage point, one neglected question appears as the fundamental issue: did anarchist leaders plot a campaign of violent attacks to coincide with the general strike for the eight-hour workday that first weekend of May 1886?

Upon the answer to this question turns the whole history of the anarchist movement in America. If there was no organized conspiracy to attack the police in May 1886, then the relevant historical questions are those that are already fully answered by the many historians who have told the tale of the "Haymarket Tragedy" and the unjust execution of leaders of Chicago's labor movement. But if there was such a conspiracy, then the meaning of this radical moment is uncertain. . . .

From Eight Hours to Revolution

Though the Chicago River was frozen and May Day was still four months away as the new year began, it was obvious to Chicago's anarchists that the eight-hour-workday movement was catching fire. The Trades and Labor Assembly and its Eight-Hour League, ably led by barrel maker George Schilling, were active in all corners of the city and winning ground by the day. TLA organizers held their organizing meetings among Chicago's Polish workers, the Eight-Hour League drafted lengthy manifestos to manufacturers, and the TLA held an eight-hour-workday benefit soiree at Cavalry Armory. Around the same time,

Selected, Edited, and with Issue Framing Material by:
Larry Madaras, *Howard Community College*
and
James M. SoRelle, *Baylor University*

ISSUE

Were Late Nineteenth-Century Immigrants "Uprooted"?

YES: Oscar Handlin, from "The Shock of Alienation," in *The Uprooted: The Epic Story of the Great Migrations That Made the American People*, 2nd ed. (Little, Brown and Company, 1973)

NO: Mark Wyman, from "The America Trunk Comes Home," in *Round Trip to America: The Immigrants Return to Europe, 1880–1930* (Cornell University Press, 1993)

Learning Outcomes

After reading this issue, you will be able to:

- Describe the difficulties of immigrants relating both to their former homeland and to the United States.
- Evaluate the changing attitudes of native Americans toward immigrants during the nineteenth century.
- Assess the challenges attached to the assimilation of immigrants to American ways.
- Analyze the role of social workers in the lives of immigrants to the United States.
- Explain a broader range of short-term and long-range goals exhibited by those who immigrated to the United States between 1880 and 1930.

ISSUE SUMMARY

YES: Oscar Handlin asserts that immigrants to the United States in the late nineteenth century were alienated from the cultural traditions of the homeland they had left as well as from those of their adopted country.

NO: Mark Wyman argues that as many as four million immigrants to the United States between 1880 and 1930 viewed their trip as temporary and remained tied psychologically to their homeland to which they returned once they had accumulated enough wealth to enable them to improve their status back home.

Immigration has been one of the most powerful forces shaping the development of the United States since at least the early seventeenth century. In fact, it should not be overlooked that even the ancestors of the country's native population were migrants to this "New World" some 37,000 years ago. There can be little doubt that the United States is a nation of immigrants, a reality reinforced by the motto "E Pluribus Unum" (One from Many), which is used on the Great Seal of the United States and on several U.S. coins.

The history of immigration to the United States can be organized into four major periods of activity:

1607–1830, 1830–1890, 1890–1924, and 1968 to the present. During the first period, the seventeenth and eighteenth centuries, there were a growing number of European migrants who arrived in North America, mostly from the British Isles, as well as several million Africans who were forced to migrate to colonial America as a consequence of the Atlantic slave trade. Although increased numbers of non-English immigrants arrived in America in the eighteenth century, it was not until the nineteenth century that large numbers of immigrants from other northern and western European countries, as well as from China, arrived and created significant population diversity. Two European groups predominated during this second major period: as a result of the potato famine, large numbers of Irish Catholics emigrated in the 1850s; and, for a variety of religious, political, and economic reasons, so did many Germans. Chinese immigration increased, and these immigrants found work in low-paying service industries, such as laundries and restaurants, and as railroad construction workers.

The Industrial Revolution of the late nineteenth century sparked a third wave of immigration. Millions of the newcomers, attracted by the unskilled factory jobs that were becoming more abundant, began pouring into the United States. Migration was encouraged by various companies whose agents distributed handbills throughout Europe advertising the ready availability of good-paying jobs in America. This phase of immigration, however, represented something of a departure from previous ones as most of these "new immigrants" came from Southern and Eastern Europe. This flood continued until World War I, after which mounting xenophobia culminated in the passage by Congress in 1924 of the National Origins Act, which restricted the number of immigrants into the country to 150,000 annually, and which placed quotas on the numbers permitted from each foreign country. By 1882, Congress already had curtailed Asian immigration with the Chinese Exclusion Act, a measure that remained in effect until its repeal in 1943.

In the aftermath of World War II, restrictions were eased for several groups, especially those who survived the Nazi death camps or who sought asylum in the United States in the wake of the aggressive movement into Eastern Europe by the Soviet Union after the war. But many other restrictions were not lifted until the Immigration Reform Act of 1965, which set in motion a fourth phase of immigration history. In contrast to earlier migrations, the newest groups entering the United States in large numbers have come from Latin America, the Middle East, and South and Southeast Asia.

Efforts to curb immigration to the United States reflect an anxiety and ambivalence that many Americans have long held with regard to "foreigners." Anxious to benefit from the labor of these newcomers but still hesitant to accept the immigrants as full-fledged citizens entitled to the same rights and privileges as native residents, Americans have on a number of occasions discovered that they had an "immigrant problem." Harsh anti-immigrant sentiment based on prejudicial attitudes toward race, ethnicity, or religion has periodically boiled over into violence and calls for legislation to restrict immigration, as is the case today in response to fears of international terrorism and concerns over the presence of illegal aliens drawing upon the nation's resources.

These concerns are by no means unique to contemporary society. In 1890, Jacob Riis, a Danish immigrant who had arrived in the United States 20 years earlier, published an exposé of the living conditions of the poor, most of them immigrants, in New York City. Riis had served as a police reporter for the *New York Tribune* and in that capacity had gained an awareness of the squalid living conditions in the city's Lower East Side. His book, *How the Other Half Lives* replete with photographic evidence of slum conditions, pioneered in the form of investigative reporting that his friend Theodore Roosevelt labeled "muckraking." Primarily directed at middle-class audiences whose influence could possibly demand reform of New York's worst tenements, almost every reader of this classic today would cringe at the numerous stereotypical depictions of the subjects whose circumstances Riis hoped to improve. He described the Italian as a "born gambler"; of Eastern European Jews, he wrote, "Money is their God"; and he comments on the "sensuality and . . . lack of moral accountability" of African Americans living in Harlem. Riis's greatest hostility, however, was directed at the Chinese who, despite their "scrupulous neatness," would "rather gamble than eat any day" and who, he claimed, were guilty of luring young white women into opium dens, hooking them on drugs, and turning them to a life of prostitution.

The traditional welcome and appreciation for immigrants in American society became particularly harsh during difficult economic times. Not long after the publication of *How the Other Half Lives,* the American economy began to sink into the worst economic depression in the nation's history up to that time. The Panic of 1893 unleashed anxieties that produced a backlash against the millions of new immigrants who had poured into the United States during the previous decade. It was not unusual, as indicated in the quotation from Jacob Riis cited above, that this antagonism occasionally took the form of religious hostility. For example, the American Protective Association (APA), an anti-Catholic secret society established in 1887, became particularly active in the 1890s. Requiring its members never to employ, work for, or vote for a Catholic, the leaders of the APA in 1893 circulated a bogus document allegedly written by Pope Leo XIII imploring the Catholic faithful in the United States to begin preparations for an invasion of the United States by a papal army for the purpose of overthrowing the U.S. federal government and imposing Catholic rule over the nation. While the Pope's military force never showed up, the APA's actions stirred up significant hysteria in some parts of the country and produced a wave of anti-Catholicism, much of which was directed at recent Catholic immigrants.

What effect did these kinds of attitudes have on those who migrated to the United States in search of a life better than the one they experienced in their native lands? What happened to their Old World customs and traditions? How fully did immigrants assimilate into the new culture they encountered in the United States? Was the United States, in fact, a melting pot for immigrants, as some have suggested?

The first historian to give significant attention to the subject of immigration to the area that became the United States was Marcus Lee Hansen. A student of the noted American historian Frederick Jackson Turner, Hansen called for systematic research on the various aspects of the immigrant experience. In *The Atlantic Migration, 1607–1860* (Harvard University Press, 1940), Hansen, himself the son of immigrant parents, focused on the European conditions and forces that had stimulated early migration to America.

Oscar Handlin (1915–2011) was perhaps the most influential scholar of American immigration history. His doctoral dissertation, published as *Boston's Immigrants: A Study in Acculturation* (Harvard University Press, 1941) when he was only 26 years old, won the Dunning Prize from the American Historical Association as the best historical study by a young scholar. This was the first study of immigration to integrate sociological concepts within a historical framework, but a decade later, Handlin published *The Uprooted* (Little, Brown, 1951) in which he combined an interdisciplinary framework with a personal narrative of the immigrants' history. Although many historians criticized this approach, the book earned Handlin a Pulitzer Prize.

John Bodnar's *The Transplanted,* while offering a contrasting metaphor for the immigration experience to the United States, shares with Handlin's work an attempt to present a general account of that experience, to portray the immigrants in a sympathetic light, and to employ an interdisciplinary approach by borrowing concepts from the social sciences. Handlin and Bodnar, however, differ in their perspectives about America's ethnic past. Handlin viewed the immigrants as people who were removed from their particular Old World cultures and who assimilated into the New World value system within two generations. In contrast, Bodnar argues that some first-generation immigrants may have shed their traditional culture quickly upon arrival in the United States, but more continued to maintain a viable lifestyle in their adopted homeland that focused upon the family household and the neighboring ethnic community. "Not solely traditional, modern or working class," writes Bodnar of this immigrant experience, "it was a dynamic culture, constantly responding to changing needs and opportunities and grounded in a deep sense of pragmatism and mutual assistance."

In the YES and NO selections, Oscar Handlin argues that the immigrants were uprooted from their Old World cultures as they attempted to adjust to an unfamiliar and often hostile environment in the United States. Mark Wyman points out that many immigrants to the United States believed that their stay in America would be temporary, a fact that limited their efforts at assimilation and reinforced ties to their original homelands.

YES ↩

Oscar Handlin

The Shock of Alienation

. . . As the passing years widened the distance, the land the immigrants had left acquired charm and beauty. Present problems blurred those they had left unsolved behind; and in the haze of memory it seemed to these people they had formerly been free of present dissatisfactions. It was as if the Old World became a great mirror into which they looked to see right all that was wrong with the New. The landscape was prettier, the neighbors more friendly, and religion more efficacious; in the frequent crises when they reached the limits of their capacities, the wistful reflection came: *This would not have happened there.*

The real contacts were, however, disappointing. The requests—that back there a mass be said, or a wise one consulted, or a religious medal be sent over—those were gestures full of hope. But the responses were inadequate; like all else they shrank in the crossing. The immigrants wrote, but the replies, when they came, were dull, even trite in their mechanical phrases, or so it seemed to those who somehow expected these messages to evoke the emotions that had gone into their own painfully composed letters. Too often the eagerly attended envelopes proved to be only empty husks, the inner contents valueless. After the long wait before the postman came, the sheets of garbled writing were inevitably below expectations. There was a trying sameness to the complaints of hard times, to the repetitious petty quarrels; and before long there was impatience with the directness with which the formal greeting led into the everlasting requests for aid.

This last was a sore point with the immigrants. The friends and relatives who had stayed behind could not get it out of their heads that in America the streets were paved with gold. *Send me for a coat. . . . There is a piece of land here and if only you would send, we could buy it. . . . Our daughter could be married, but we have not enough for a dowry. . . . We are ashamed, everyone else gets . . . much more frequently than we.* Implicit in these solicitations was the judgment that the going-away had been a desertion, that unfulfilled obligations still remained, and that the village could claim assistance as a right from its departed members.

From the United States it seemed there was no comprehension, back there, of the difficulties of settlement. It was exasperating by sacrifices to scrape together the remittances and to receive in return a catalogue of new needs, as if there were not needs enough in the New World too. The immigrants never shook off the sense of obligation to help; but they did come to regard their Old Countrymen as the kind of people who depended on help. The trouble with the Europeans was, they could not stand on their own feet.

The cousin green off the boat earned the same negative appraisal. Though he be a product of the homeland, yet here he cut a pitiable figure; awkward manners, rude clothes, and a thoroughgoing ineptitude in the new situation were his most prominent characteristics. The older settler found the welcome almost frozen on his lips in the face of such backwardness.

In every real contact the grandeur of the village faded; it did not match the immigrants' vision of it and it did not stand up in a comparison with America. When the picture came, the assembled family looked at it beneath the light. This was indeed the church, but it had not been remembered so; and the depressing contrast took some of the joy out of remembering.

The photograph did not lie. There it was, a low building set against the dusty road, weather-beaten and making a candid display of its ill-repair. But the recollections did not lie either. As if it had been yesterday that they passed through those doors, they could recall the sense of spaciousness and elevation that sight of the structure had always aroused.

Both impressions were true, but irreconcilable. The mental image and the paper representation did not jibe because the one had been formed out of the standards and values of the Old Country, while the other was viewed in the light of the standards and values of the New. And it was the same with every other retrospective contact. Eagerly the immigrants continued to look back across the Atlantic in search of the satisfactions of fellowship. But the search was not rewarded. Having become Americans, they were no longer villagers. Though they might willingly assume the former obligations and recognize the former responsibilities, they could not recapture the former points of view or hold to the former judgments. They had seen too much, experienced too much to be again members of the community. It was a vain mission on which they continued to dispatch the letters; these people, once separated, would never belong again.

Their home now was a country in which they had not been born. Their place in society they had established for themselves through the hardships of crossing and settlement. The process had changed them, had altered the most intimate aspects of their lives. Every effort to cling to inherited ways of acting and thinking had led into a subtle adjustment by which those ways were given a new American form. No longer Europeans, could the immigrants then say that they belonged in America? The answer depended upon the conceptions held by other citizens of the United States of the character of the nation and of the role of the newcomers within it.

In the early nineteenth century, those already established on this side of the ocean regarded immigration as a positive good. When travel by sea became safe after the general peace of 1815 and the first fresh arrivals trickled in, there was a general disposition to welcome the movement. The favorable attitude persisted even when the tide mounted to the flood levels of the 1840s and 1850s. The man off the boat was then accepted without question or condition.

The approval of unlimited additions to the original population came easily to Americans who were conscious of the youth of their country. Standing at the edge of an immense continent, they were moved by the challenge of empty land almost endless in its extension. Here was room enough, and more, for all who would bend their energies to its exploitation. The shortage was of labor and not of acres; every pair of extra hands increased the value of the abundant resources and widened opportunities for everyone.

The youth of the nation also justified the indiscriminate admission of whatever foreigners came to these shores. There was high faith in the destiny of the Republic, assurance that its future history would justify the Revolution and the separation from Great Britain. The society

and the culture that would emerge in this territory would surpass those of the Old World because they would not slavishly imitate the outmoded forms and the anachronistic traditions that constricted men in Europe. The United States would move in new directions of its own because its people were a new people.

There was consequently a vigorous insistence that this country was not simply an English colony become independent. It was a nation unique in its origins, produced by the mixture of many different types out of which had come an altogether fresh amalgam, the American. The ebullient citizens who believed and argued that their language, their literature, their art, and their polity were distinctive and original also believed and argued that their population had not been derived from a single source but had rather acquired its peculiar characteristics from the blending of a variety of strains.

There was confidence that the process would continue. The national type had not been fixed by its given antecedents; it was emerging from the experience of life on a new continent. Since the quality of men was determined not by the conditions surrounding their birth, but by the environment within which they passed their lives, it was pointless to select among them. All would come with minds and spirits fresh for new impressions; and being in America would make Americans of them. Therefore it was best to admit freely everyone who wished to make a home here. The United States would then be a great smelting pot, great enough so that there was room for all who voluntarily entered; and the nation that would ultimately be cast from that crucible would be all the richer for the diversity of the elements that went into the molten mixture.

The legislation of most of the nineteenth century reflected this receptive attitude. The United States made no effort actively to induce anyone to immigrate, but neither did it put any bars in the way of their coming. Occasional laws in the four decades after 1819 set up shipping regulations in the hope of improving the conditions of the passage. In practice, the provisions that specified the minimum quantities of food and the maximum number of passengers each vessel could carry were easily evaded. Yet the intent of those statutes was to protect the travelers and to remove harsh conditions that might discourage the newcomers.

Nor were state laws any more restrictive in design. The seaports, troubled by the burdens of poor relief, secured the enactment of measures to safeguard their treasuries against such charges. Sometimes the form was a bond to guarantee that the immigrant would not become at once dependent upon public support; sometimes it was a small tax applied to defray the costs of charity. In either case there was no desire to limit entry into the country; and none of these steps had any discernible effect upon the volume of admissions.

Once landed, the newcomer found himself equal in condition to the natives. Within a short period he could be naturalized and acquire all the privileges of a citizen. In some places, indeed, he could vote before the oath in court so transformed his status. In the eyes of society, even earlier than in the eyes of the law, he was an American. . . .

❧

As the nineteenth century moved into its last quarter, a note of petulance crept into the comments of some Americans who thought about this aspect of the development of their culture. It was a long time now that the melting pot had been simmering, but the end product seemed no closer than before. The experience of life in the United States had not broken down the separateness of the elements mixed into it; each seemed to retain its own identity. Almost a half-century after the great immigration of Irish and Germans, these people had not become indistinguishable from other Americans; they were still recognizably Irish and German. Yet even then, newer waves of newcomers were beating against the Atlantic shore. Was there any prospect that all these multitudes would ever be assimilated, would ever be Americanized?

A generation earlier such questions would not have been asked. Americans of the first half of the century had assumed that any man who subjected himself to the American environment was being Americanized. Since the New World was ultimately to be occupied by a New Man, no mere derivative of any extant stock, but different from and superior to all, there had been no fixed standards of national character against which to measure the behavior of newcomers. The nationality of the new Republic had been supposed fluid, only just evolving; there had been room for infinite variation because diversity rather than uniformity had been normal.

The expression of doubts that some parts of the population might not become fully American implied the existence of a settled criterion of what was American. There had been a time when the society had recognized no distinction among citizens but that between the native and the foreign-born, and that distinction had carried no imputation of superiority or inferiority. Now there were attempts to distinguish among the natives between those who really belonged and those who did not, to separate out those who were born in the United States but whose immigrant parentage cut them off from the truly indigenous folk.

It was difficult to draw the line, however. The census differentiated after 1880 between natives and native-born of foreign parents. But that was an inadequate line of division; it provided no means of social recognition and offered no basis on which the *true Americans* could draw together, identify themselves as such.

Through these years there was a half-conscious quest among some Americans for a term that would describe those whose ancestors were in the United States before the great migrations. Where the New Englanders were, they called themselves Yankees, a word that often came to mean non-Irish or non-Canadian. But Yankee was simply a local designation and did not take in the whole of the old stock. In any case, there was no satisfaction to such a title. Its holders were one group among many, without any distinctive claim to Americanism, cut off from other desirable peoples prominent in the country's past. Only the discovery of common antecedents could eliminate the separations among the really American.

But to find a common denominator, it was necessary to go back a long way. Actually no single discovery was completely satisfactory. Some writers, in time, referred to the civilization of the United States as Anglo-Saxon. By projecting its origins back to early Britain, they implied that their own culture was always English in derivation, and made foreigners of the descendants of Irishmen and Germans, to say nothing of the later arrivals. Other men preferred a variant and achieved the same exclusion by referring to themselves as "the English-speaking people," a title which assumed there was a unity and uniqueness to the clan which settled the home island, the Dominions, and the United States. Still others relied upon a somewhat broader appellation. They talked of themselves as Teutonic and argued that what was distinctively American originated in the forests of Germany; in this view, only the folk whose ancestors had experienced the freedom of tribal self-government and the liberation of the Protestant Reformation were fully American.

These terms had absolutely no historical justification. They nevertheless achieved a wide currency in the thinking of the last decades of the nineteenth century. Whatever particular phrase might serve the purpose of a particular author or speaker, all expressed the conviction that some hereditary element had given form to American culture. The conclusion was inescapable: to be Americanized, the immigrants must conform to the American way of life completely defined in advance of their landing.

❧

There were two counts to the indictment that the immigrants were not so conforming. They were, first, accused of their poverty. Many benevolent citizens, distressed by the miserable conditions in the districts inhabited by the laboring people, were reluctant to believe that such social flaws were indigenous to the New World. It was tempting, rather, to ascribe them to the defects of the newcomers, to improvidence, slovenliness, and ignorance rather than to inability to earn a living wage.

Indeed to those whose homes were uptown the ghettos were altogether alien territory associated with filth and vice and crime. It did not seem possible that men could lead a decent existence in such quarters. The good vicar on a philanthropic tour was shocked by the moral dangers of the dark unlighted hallway. His mind rushed to the defense of the respectable young girl: *Whatever her wishes may be, she can do nothing—shame prevents her from crying out.* The intention of the reformer was to improve housing, but the summation nevertheless was, *You cannot make an American citizen out of a slum.*

The newcomers were also accused of congregating together in their own groups and of an unwillingness to mix with outsiders. The foreign-born flocked to the great cities and stubbornly refused to spread out as farmers over the countryside; that alone was offensive to a society which still retained an ideal of rusticity. But even the Germans in Wisconsin and the Scandinavians in Minnesota held aloofly to themselves. Everywhere, the strangers persisted in their strangeness and willfully stood apart from American life. A prominent educator sounded the warning: *Our task is to break up their settlements, to assimilate and amalgamate these people and to implant in them the Anglo-Saxon conception of righteousness, law, and order.*

It was no simple matter to meet this challenge. The older residents were quick to criticize the separateness of the immigrant but hesitant when he made a move to narrow the distance. The householders of Fifth Avenue or Beacon Street or Nob Hill could readily perceive the evils of the slums but they were not inclined to welcome as a neighbor the former denizen of the East Side or the North End or the Latin Quarter who had acquired the means to get away. Among Protestants there was much concern over the growth of Catholic, Jewish, and Orthodox religious organizations, but there was no eagerness at all to provoke a mass conversion that might crowd the earlier churches with a host of poor foreigners. When the population of its neighborhood changed, the parish was less likely to try to attract the newcomers than to close or sell its building and move to some other section.

Indeed there was a fundamental ambiguity to the thinking of those who talked about "assimilation" in these years. They had arrived at their own view that American culture was fixed, formed from its origins, by shutting out the great mass of immigrants who were not English or at least not Teutonic. Now it was expected that those excluded people would alter themselves to earn their portion in Americanism. That process could only come about by increasing the contacts between the older and the newer inhabitants, by sharing jobs, churches, residences. Yet in practice, the man who thought himself an Anglo-Saxon found proximity to the other folk just come to the United States uncomfortable and distasteful and, in his own life, sought to increase rather than to lessen the gap between his position and theirs.

There was an escape from the horns of this unpleasant dilemma. It was tempting to resolve the difficulty by arguing that the differences between Americans on the one hand and Italians or Jews or Poles on the other were so deep as to admit of no conciliation. If these other stocks were cut off by their own innate nature, by the qualities of their heredity, then the original breed was justified both in asserting the fixity of its own character and in holding off from contact with the aliens. . . .

The fear of everything alien instilled by the First World War brought to fullest flower the seeds of racist thinking. Three enormously popular books by an anthropologist, a eugenist, and a historian revealed to hundreds of thousands of horrified Nordics how their great race had been contaminated by contact with lesser breeds, dwarfed in stature, twisted in mentality, and ruthless in the pursuit of their own self-interest.

These ideas passed commonly in the language of the time. No doubt many Americans who spoke in the bitter terms of race used the words in a figurative sense or in some other way qualified their acceptance of the harsh doctrine. After all, they still recognized the validity of the American tradition of equal and open opportunities, of the Christian tradition of the brotherhood of man. Yet, if they were sometimes troubled by the contradiction, nevertheless enough of them believed fully the racist conceptions so that five million could become members of the Ku Klux Klan in the early 1920s. . . .

The activities of the Klan were an immediate threat to the immigrants and were resisted as such. But there was also a wider import to the movement. This was evidence, at last become visible, that the newcomers were among the excluded. The judgment at which the proponents of assimilation had only hinted, about which the racist thinkers had written obliquely, the Klan brought to the open. The hurt came from the fact that the mouthings of the Kleagle were not eccentricities, but only extreme statements of beliefs long on the margin of acceptance by many Americans. To the foreign-born this was demonstration of what they already suspected, that they would remain as alienated from the New World as they had become from the Old.

Much earlier the pressure of their separateness had begun to disturb the immigrants. As soon as the conception of Americanization had acquired the connotation of conformity with existing patterns, the whole way of group life of the newcomers was questioned. Their adjustment had depended upon their ability as individuals in a free society to adapt themselves to their environment through what forms they chose. The demand by their critics that the adjustment take a predetermined course seemed to question their right, as they were, to a place in American society.

Not that these people concerned themselves with theories of nationalism, but in practice the hostility of the "natives" provoked unsettling doubts about the propriety of the most innocent actions. The peasant who had become a Polish Falcon or a Son of Italy, in his own view, was acting as an American; this was not a step he could have taken at home. To subscribe to a newspaper was the act of a citizen of the New World, not of the Old, even if the journal was one of the thousand published by 1920 in languages other than English. When the immigrants heard their societies and their press described as un-American they could only conclude that they had somehow become involved in an existence that belonged neither in the old land nor in the new.

Yet the road of conformity was also barred to them. There were matters in which they wished to be like others, undistinguished from anyone else, but they never hit upon the means of becoming so. There was no pride in the surname, which in Europe had been little used, and many a new arrival was willing enough to make a change, suitable to the new country. But August Björkegren was not much better off when he called himself Burke, nor the Blumberg who became Kelly. The Lithuanians and Slovenes who moved into the Pennsylvania mining fields often endowed themselves with nomenclature of the older settlers, of the Irish and Italians there before them. In truth, these people found it difficult to know what were the "American" forms they were expected to take on.

What they did know was that they had not succeeded, that they had not established themselves to the extent that they could expect to be treated as if they belonged where they were.

If he was an alien, and poor, and in many ways helpless, still he was human, and it rankled when his dignity as a person was disregarded. He felt an undertone of acrimony in every contact with an official. Men in uniform always found him unworthy of respect; the bullying police made capital of his fear of the law; the postmen made sport of the foreign writing on his letters; the streetcar conductors laughed at his groping requests for directions. Always he was patronized as an object of charity, or almost so.

His particular enemies were the officials charged with his special oversight. When misfortune drove him to seek assistance or when government regulations brought them to inspect his home, he encountered the social workers, made ruthless in the disregard of his sentiments by the certainty of their own benevolent intentions. Confident of their personal and social superiority and armed with the ideology of the sociologists who had trained them, the emissaries of the public and private agencies were bent on improving the immigrant to a point at which he would no longer recognize himself.

The man who had dealings with the social workers was often sullen and unco-operative; he disliked the necessity of becoming a case, of revealing his dependence to strangers. He was also suspicious, feared there would be no understanding of his own way of life or of his problems; and he was resentful, because the powerful outsiders were judging him by superficial standards of their own. The starched young gentleman from the settlement house took stock from the middle of the kitchen. Were there framed pictures on the walls? Was there a piano, books? He made a note for the report: *This family is not yet Americanized; they are still eating Italian food.*

The services are valuable, but taking them is degrading. It is a fine thing to learn the language of the country; but one must be treated as a child to do so. *We keep saying all the time, This is a desk, this is a door. I know it is a desk and a door. What for keep saying it all the time? My teacher is a very nice young lady, very young. She does not understand what I want to talk about or know about.*

The most anguished conflicts come from the refusal of the immigrants to see the logic of their poverty. In the office it seems reasonable enough: people incapable of supporting themselves would be better off with someone to take care of them. It is more efficient to institutionalize the destitute than to allow them, with the aid of charity, to mismanage their homes. But the ignorant poor insist on clinging to their families, threaten suicide at the mention of the Society's refuge, or even of the hospital. What help the woman gets, she is still not satisfied. Back comes the ungrateful letter. *I don't ask you to put me in a poorhouse where I have to cry for my children. I don't ask you to put them*

in a home and eat somebody else's bread. I can't live here with-
out them. I am so sick for them. I could live at home and spare
good eats for them. What good did you give me to send me to
the poorhouse? You only want people to live like you but I will
not listen to you no more.

A few dedicated social workers, mostly women, learned to understand the values in the immigrants' own lives. In some states, as the second generation became prominent in politics, government agencies came to co-operate with and protect the newcomers. But these were rare exceptions. They scarcely softened the rule experience everywhere taught the foreign-born, that they were expected to do what they could not do—to live like others.

For the children it was not so difficult. They at least were natives and could learn how to conform; to them the settlement house was not always a threat, but some-times an opportunity. Indeed they could adopt entire the assumption that national character was long since fixed, only seek for their own group a special place within it. Some justified their Americanism by discovery of a colo-nial past; within the educated second generation there began a tortuous quest for eighteenth-century antecedents that might give them a portion in American civilization in its narrower connotation. Others sought to gain a sense of participation by separating themselves from later or lower elements in the population; they became involved in agi-tation against the Orientals, the Negroes, and the newest immigrants, as if thus to draw closer to the truly native. Either course implied a rejection of their parents who had themselves once been green off the boat and could boast of no New World antecedents.

The old folk knew then they would not come to belong, not through their own experience nor through their off-spring. The only adjustment they had been able to make to life in the United States had been one that involved the separateness of their group, one that increased their aware-ness of the differences between themselves and the rest of the society. In that adjustment they had always suffered from the consciousness they were strangers. The demand that they assimilate, that they surrender their separate-ness, condemned them always to be outsiders. In practice, the free structure of American life permitted them with few restraints to go their own way, but under the shadow of a consciousness that they would never belong. They had thus completed their alienation from the culture to which they had come, as from that which they had left.

OSCAR HANDLIN was the Carl M. Loeb professor of history at Harvard University in Cambridge, Massachusetts, where he has been teaching since 1941. A Pulitzer Prize–winning historian, he has written or edited more than 100 books, including *Liberty in Expansion* (Harper & Row, 1989), which he coauthored with Lilian Handlin, and *The Distortion of America,* 2nd ed. (Transaction Publishers, 1996).

Mark Wyman    **NO**

The America Trunk Comes Home

The Ubiquitous Remigrant

The emigrant who once boarded a ship for America was returning, and with him came the "America trunk" that had been loaded so carefully for the outgoing voyage. In Finland, this *American arkku* was filled when it came home with everything from glass dishes to locks from a baby's first haircut to such prized American objects as a phonograph player or double-bitted axe. Its contents were the talk of the neighborhood, valued for decades as mementos.

The America trunk is an apt symbol of both emigration and remigration, of immigrants coming to America and returning to their homelands. The symbol persists, for the trunk occupies hallowed positions today in homes of third-generation Americans who cling to an image of their ancestral saga; in many European homes, similarly, the chest that came back is still revered as a remnant, a piece of that dream which once drew an emigrant across the seas.

But there was more, much more, symbolized in the America trunk. Within its recesses were tools or clothes that carried memories of hard struggles abroad. It provided a continuing connection with America, and because the United States increasingly played a leading role in international affairs, remigrants would be called on to interpret that role. They became *americani* and "Yanks"; America's importance raised their importance. And the items they valued enough to carry back in trunks would provide clues to what America's impact would be: was it tools the returners brought? or books on political theory, nationalist aspirations, labor organization, new churches? Or were the contents of the America trunk to be used to impress neighbors, perhaps to be sold to help purchase a shop or an extra piece of land? Modern students of immigration who seek answers to such questions are no different than Charles Dickens, who gazed at the emigrants returning home to Europe on his ship in 1842 and admitted that he was "curious to know their histories, and with what expectations they had gone out to America, and on what errands they were going home, and what their circumstances were.". . .

The trunks were but one small part, like the tip of an iceberg, of the enormity of the movement of people, objects, and ideas back to Europe.

Percentage rates of return ranged from 30 to 40 percent for such groups as the Italians, down to 10 percent among the Irish. Using these as a rough guide, it is possible to estimate that the total return to Europe may have been as high as four million repatriated emigrants during the 1880–1930 era of mass immigration into North America.

Examined within individual countries, these massive totals mean that one in twenty residents of Italy was a returned emigrant at the time of World War I, and shortly thereafter in a Norwegian county of heavy emigration it was found that one-fourth of all males over age fifteen had lived at least two years in America. Such high numbers signify that for the next sixty years visitors to European villages would encounter former residents of Scranton or Cleveland or Detroit, happy to describe their American experiences, wanting to know how the baseball pennant race was shaping up. . . .

A More-Reachable America

The years 1880–1930 stand out in the immigrant experience. Europeans crossed to North America in ever-increasing numbers as major improvements appeared in transportation. For generations before, however, an extensive pattern of short-term, work-seeking migration had existed in most areas of Europe, from Macedonians heading out to jobs around the Mediterranean to Irishmen and women crossing to England and Scotland for farm work. These nearby treks continued into the era of mass transatlantic emigration, as was evident in Polish totals: at the peak of Polish emigration to the United States in 1912–13, 130,000 left for America—compared to 800,000 heading for seasonal work elsewhere in Europe. It is true that development of the oceangoing steamship, coupled with an increasing flow of news and publicity about American jobs, helped shift the destinations of many short-term migrants to the West, across the Atlantic. North and South America were becoming more closely fitted into the Atlantic economy and, if this meant that midwestern pork could now be packed for consumers in Germany, it also signified that Germans from those same consuming areas, and Poles, Italians, and Finns, could easily travel to find employment in those same U.S. packing plants.

These developments welded mass migration closely to the variations, booms, and busts of American industry. To these immigrants, America became basically the site of factory employment, gang labor on a railroad section, a job underground following a coal seam. One Italian could talk of his American experiences only in terms of trains, rails, and crossties, "as if all of America was nothing but a braid of tracks," a countryman reported.

As the trio of concerns of *journey, job hunt, and employment* became more predictable, less dangerous, the trip to America could then be viewed as something other than a lifetime change. Like short-term labor migration within Europe, it became a means to improve life at home, through earning enough to achieve a higher status or more solid position in the village. It was not so much the start of a new life as another step in the process of social mobility. These factors in turn dictated that life in the American "workshop" would be temporary for many.

. . . In all, it is impossible to know what percentage of immigrants planned to return home, but it is not reaching far beyond the evidence to estimate that a majority in the 1880–1930 period initially expected to turn their backs on life and labor overseas once they had accumulated some wealth. Various things caused most to change their minds: in the United States these included realizing that opportunities in America outstripped those at home, gaining a better job, becoming accustomed to a higher standard of living, the arrival of news from abroad that removed the necessity for return, or gradual Americanization through learning the language, acquiring American friends, falling in love with a local girl.

Sometimes the shifts in expectations could be traced through a progression of names, as in the case of a Lithuanian immigrant couple who lived in coal towns in Pennsylvania and Illinois, always planning to return to Lithuania until they moved on to Oklahoma and decided to settle down. Their first two children were born in 1896 and 1900, when they still expected to go back to Europe, and were accordingly named Gediminas and Juozas. The third arrived in 1912, when they had become Americans. They named him Edwin.

But until that decision was made, until the carefully plotted return plans were finally abandoned, then every act, every expenditure had to be undertaken with an eye toward repatriation. This fact dawned gradually on an American in 1903 as he traveled about Italy and found that returned emigrants were much different, better persons at home; they had lived in brutal conditions in the United States because of "a feeling among them that they were merely temporizing . . .; that they had come to America to make a few hundred dollars to send or take back to Italy; and that it did not make much difference what they ate, wore or did, just so long as they got the money and got back." Their day-to-day existence in the United States would not improve until they were "drawn into the real American life" and changed their minds about going back to Europe.

Dreams of the village were especially strong among such persons; their thoughts were directed eastward toward home, even while they lived and worked in the West. This longing made assimilation difficult, and ethnic identities were further maintained by life in immigrant enclaves, blocking or discouraging connections with American institutions. Such isolation drew the fire of many Americans and settled members of the Old Immigration. Angered at the spectacle of U.S. dollars being carried overseas, they were also appalled by living conditions among those expecting to return. Labor unions suffered from the influx of these low-wage immigrants who often rejected invitations to join their fight for better wages and conditions. For years the unions approached the newcomers from two directions, often at the same time: seeking to organize the aliens while attacking them as strikebreakers and cheap competition. And the continued exodus of remigrants added to the pressure on union leaders to side with the restrictionist movement. . . .

As these immigrants held back from identifying with their new country of residence, many became part of a subculture within their own immigrant culture; that is, the temporary immigrant did even less than other immigrants to learn English, adapt to American ways, join American organizations. This reluctance further stimulated nativist attacks, which reached a climax with the restriction legislation of the postwar 1920s. Remigrants were not the only cause of the nativist surge, but their lifestyles in America helped fuel the restrictionist drive and they became one of the nativists' easiest targets.

Praise and Scorn at Home

As they returned to Europe the remigrants found a mixed welcome. Constructing new-style houses of brick rather than wood, many wore fancy clothes and endeavored to climb the social ladder. But villagers often looked askance at these people who seemed all too often to be putting on airs. One critic was the father of later emigrant Stoyan Christowe, who observed the well-dressed remigrants parading around their Bulgarian village and spat out, "An ox is an ox even if you put golden horns on him."

Their stories were often too fantastic, too farfetched. Norwegians began referring to them as *Amerikaskroner*—"tall tales from America." One man recalled his uncle's return to Norway in 1929 and his strange revelations about the things he had seen: "He told us about the Christmas trees that went round and round, he talked about streetcars, he talked of electric lights, he told of huge buildings, skyscrapers, he told us how they built them, he talked about the communications, railroads that went to every corner in the land, he told us about an industrial society which was so different from what we knew that it was like a completely different world." Was it all believable? Perhaps not. More recently, a returned emigrant showed his Norwegian grade school pupils a U.S. postcard with a photograph of a giant Pacific Northwest log on a logging truck, the driver standing proudly on top. When he translated the postcard's legend, "Oregon Toothpick," one child retorted, "I've always heard that Americans have big mouths."

Their money was a reality that could not be denied, however. The cash carried home, together with the vast sums mailed back by those still toiling across the ocean, helped stabilize the economies of Europe and served as a stimulus for local booms. Business experience and connections became the most obvious gains from remigration in many districts, especially in Germany. Land, apartment houses, taverns, shops, and other firms were purchased by those coming home with "golden horns." For a time in Bydgoszcz, a Polish city in Pomerania, seventy agencies worked primarily to help remigrants obtain or sell properties. Two generations later the flow of retirees back from America would stimulate similar activities through their Social Security checks and factory pensions.

Most who returned in the 1880–1930 era went into agriculture, and this activity was at the center of much of the debate over their impact. Certainly agriculture was extremely backward in many areas; one estimate by returning Norwegians was that farming in Norway was fifty years behind that in the United States. But would returned emigrants be the ones to launch the required changes? Remigrants rushed to buy farmland, and large-scale commercialization of land became one of the most noted results of the vast emigration and return. But early evidence indicated that remigrants then continued or even expanded traditional and backward farming practices.

In contrast, areas such as Prussia and the English Midlands, where farm progress was extensive in the late nineteenth century, featured either the growth of larger land units with major investments of capital or the contrary development of smaller but more specialized farms that used the latest in farm technology and benefited from growing consumer demand. A student of the transformation of British agriculture notes increased farming complexity through use of artificial manures and new seeds and livestock breeds and adds that this "no doubt . . . also required flexibility of mind." But flexibility of mind regarding agricultural improvements may have been missing among many remigrants coming back to traditional farming in such areas as southern Italy or Poland. Few had worked on American farms, and this fact alone predicted that their impact on the Continent's agriculture would be minimal. Sporadic improvements and changes were widely publicized, but these were unusual, like the tomatoes planted by some Finns or the new flowers appearing in Polish gardens. Only in certain areas, such as parts of Scandinavia, could it be said that the remigrants were a definite mainstay of drives to modernize agriculture.

But in other occupations and situations, where emigrants had been able to learn American methods, improvements were obvious. To begin with, more vigorous work habits were widely noted. Also, many carried home sewing machines, which led to improvements in clothing, and holiday garb began to be worn more regularly. Homemaking benefited: when Irish women returned, they refused to continue traditional hearth cooking because it only permitted meat to be boiled; soon they installed grates or bought ranges. Personal hygiene improved, and a Hungarian report indicated that remigrants even kept their windows open at night, rejecting the traditional belief that night air held evils.

Many threw themselves into various campaigns for government change: Irish Home Rulers sought to throw off British control, Slovaks and Croatians pushed for separate nations, some Finns who had attended the Duluth Work People's College wanted to destroy capitalism. Others agitated for the development of public schools, and the remigrants' presence helped spread English through Gaelic-speaking areas of Ireland and in many other districts across Europe. Returned emigrants began to appear as members of village councils, school boards, even national legislatures; three of them became prime ministers, of Norway, Latvia, and Finland. . . .

Conclusions

In an examination of the remigrant from 1880 to 1930, before leaving Europe, at work in America, and after the return home, nine broad conclusions emerge:

1. The temporary immigrant was in truth far different from the immigrant who planned to stay. The expectations

of any immigrant were all-important in directing his or her job-seeking, assimilation, and adjustment to American life, and the immigrant who stepped onto American soil planning permanent residence saw these goals differently than did the short-term industrial migrant. The latter was basically a *sojourner*, defined by sociologists as a deviant form of the stranger, who remains psychologically in his homeland while living somewhere else, culturally isolated, tied physically but not mentally to a job. He may have changed his mind eventually, but until that point he lived the life of one who saw his future back in Europe.

Employment became the critical part of the remigrant's American existence. Like a New England girl arriving to work briefly in the Lowell mills in the 1830s, or a Turkish *Gastarbeiter* in Germany today, the temporary industrial migrant in the 1880–1930 period saw the world through different eyes than did (or does) the worker planning to remain. To ignore this fact and its implications is to miss a major facet of immigration's impact and an important explanation of immigrants' failure to assimilate despite lengthy residence abroad. Failing to take it into account would also make it difficult to understand why so many who returned home took up farming rather than the industrial occupations they had known overseas. If one task of the historian is to see the past from different angles, then following the contrary path of the temporary immigrant can provide an important new perspective.

2. The American immigration story becomes less unified, more diverse, when remigrants are considered within the broad picture of the peopling of a continent. There was little in common between the Bohemian family settling the Nebraska prairies in the 1890s and Bohemian men arriving for a year's work in a Chicago stockyard. Assimilation was soon forced on those farming in Nebraska; it was not even a remote goal of most of those lining up for their wages each fortnight in Chicago. One immigrant is not always equal to another—an obvious fact, but one made both more apparent and more significant when the remigrant experience is considered. . . .

3. There were many Americas contained within the broad vision of the United States by the 1880s, but America as the symbol of economic opportunity increasingly became uppermost for immigrants, especially those planning a temporary stay. Democracy was of little importance to a sojourner dreaming of adding to his piece of earth in the Mezzogiorno. When economic opportunity and democracy were seen as two branches of the same trunk, however, one could buttress the other in forming an image of the nation. But a remigrant who had witnessed few examples of democracy in his twelve-hour days in a steel mill would consider America in a different light

than would another new resident escaping from religious unrest and finding herself in the competitive free-for-all of U.S. church denominations. Economic opportunity became the representative American symbol to millions.

4. The basis of American nativism was not opposition to return migration, but it gained several major arguments in the course of reacting to temporary immigrants. Nativists began to erupt in anger as thousands and thousands of short-term residents avoided assimilation and escaped abroad with their American earnings. The exodus goaded many Americans into ever stronger condemnations of immigration in general, and the identification of European remigrants with Chinese sojourners became complete. This provided an opening for earlier, permanent immigrants to condemn later arrivals and to become in effect immigrant nativists. Anti-foreign sentiment among U.S. labor groups leaned especially hard on the temporary immigrant.

5. The striving for status—to hold onto a vanishing position, or even to climb higher—emerges as one of the main forces behind remigration as well as emigration. Remigrants often left Europe to seek a higher status at home; they did not seek a permanent existence and better status in America. The New World may have represented a horn of plenty, but its wealth would be more useful back in Europe. Basic subsistence could be met, and after that the possibility of becoming landowners of importance in the village. Immigrants knew enough about life in the United States to understand the saying, "America for the oxen, Europe for the peasant." It was in Europe, not America, that the opportunity to reach a new level of existence waited.

6. The remigrant's importance in stimulating further immigration may have eclipsed even that of the much-maligned steamship agent. A large-scale exodus developed mainly from European areas where there had been an earlier emigration, which had produced a return flow of successes with money to purchase land and to construct "American houses." These acts promoted America with more impact than did handbills posted on village walls. There is also evidence of what might be called "emigration families," providing members from each generation who spent time in the United States and then returned, their tales handed down to stimulate others to try America later. The process was then repeated, generation after generation, and the remigrant ancestors became long-term role models. Their example competed with the emigrant letter as the chief propagandist of emigration. And the picture of America as a horn of plenty became indelibly fastened on a people who grew up hearing American stories around the winter hearth.

7. The return flow must be counted as a major reason that Europe's enormous exodus to America did not result in a net loss for the home society. Some form of general decline might have been expected for a continent that lost 36 million of its most active and future-oriented citizens to the United States from 1820 to 1975. The same could have been predicted for other regions that sent their people to America; one might even apply it to Mexico and the Caribbean nations today. But instead of causing a deterioration, the era of mass emigration proved overall to be one of general advance and progress for the people of many nations. This pattern continues. Certainly many things, tangible and intangible, have contributed to this result, but one is the extensive return flow of people, money, and ideas. As a Polish priest concluded from his study of the emigration from Miejsce parish in 1883, the returns from America meant that the exodus was "not a loss but a gain for this province." It could be said for most of Europe.

The Continent benefited as well from the return of organizational and political skills, as men and women of all ideologies and aspirations came back to launch labor unions and community organizations and to become involved in political affairs. Churches were challenged and new philosophies began to circulate. When Finland and Latvia achieved independence amid scenes of enormous chaos, leadership in each new country fell to those already experienced in labor and political struggles in America. Norway also chose a remigrant as its prime minister to lead the country through the dark days of depression and World War II. Many others coming back occupied government posts in municipalities as well as in national regimes.

The remigrants brought change in many forms. New words were carried home: modern Finnish has been enriched by many remigrant words and phrases, according to recent studies. Beyond this, many of those returning to Europe displayed an openness, an attitude that shook off the old and helped transform the peasant world. And remigration contributed further to a mingling of cultures which encouraged change as well as helping bring a gradual integration of the cultures of Europe and America.

The United States is more than just people transferred from Europe; Europe is guided by more than influences from America. But the two-way exchange was one crucial factor in the historical development of both, and the remigrant helped in both directions, a continuing link between two cultures.

8. American "exceptionalism," the view that the American experience has been unique and that developments in the United States were basically different from those elsewhere, is dealt a further blow by the remigration

story. The United States was not a land where every immigrant came to stay; it was a country seen by many foreigners as a means rather than an end. As such, the American immigration pageant contained many scenes known elsewhere, for temporary stays as well as permanent moves have long been part of human migrations.

Parallels are numerous. Just as was often the case in the United States, temporary migrants were unpopular in the Ruhr, where German unions fought Poles, employers put aliens in the dirtiest jobs, and officials sought their removal. Swiss workers assaulted Italians in 1896, the government meanwhile blocked their naturalization, and welfare groups refused to give aid. This was nativism run wild. Riots erupted against Italian workers in France from the 1880s on; in 1893, fifty Italians were killed and 150 wounded during an attack by French miners at the Aigues-Mortes salt-works. There was physical violence in the United States, but as in Europe the opposition to those planning to return usually took other forms: unions sought their dismissal, politicians argued for bans on their employment, and editorial writers aimed darts at those who carried off national wealth. . . .

9. Finally, the story of the returned immigrant brings the historian face to face with the importance of human feelings, human emotions, in world events. Scholars often stress impersonal forces when discussing developments involving masses of people. But the fact that several million immigrants could turn around and leave a land with a higher standard of living and all the glitter of modernization, to cross the ocean again and return to a backward peasant village, with its distinctive culture and traditions, stands as supreme testimony to the pull of kin and home.

The Psalmist cried, "How shall we sing the Lord's song in a strange land?" And the longing to be within the family circle, in the familiar pathways and fields of home, has always been part of the human condition. The human heart must be given equal rank here with cold economic statistics and the pleadings of steamship agents. For the sense of being lost, away from moorings, left thousands of immigrants with the feeling that nothing seemed right in the New World—not holidays, not religious rites, not even the summer sunrise. They like the Psalmist felt lost in a strange land. The Swedish novelist of emigration, Vilhelm Moberg, reflected on these feelings in his autobiographical novel *A Time on Earth:*

> Man must have a root in the world; he must belong somewhere. He cannot abandon the land where he was born and adopt another country as his birthplace. Prattle about old and new mother countries is prattle only, and a lie. Either I have a

country of my own, or I have not. Mother country is singular, never plural.

The country you knew as child and young man was the country you left. That was your fate; you could never find another homeland.

In the final analysis, the story of the returned immigrants is a record of the endurance of home and family ties. It provides further evidence that, for many, immigration demonstrated the strength and unity of the family—both in going to America and in returning—rather than the family's weakening or destruction. For it was to rejoin their people, to walk again on their own land, to sit in the parish church once more, that the temporary immigrants repacked their America trunks and booked passage again, this time for home. The journey to America had been round-trip. And as they had helped shape life in the United States, its world of work, its image of itself and of foreigners, now they would affect the lives of their own families, their villages, their homelands. It would be a different future on both continents because of the returned immigrants.

Mark Wyman is a professor of history at Illinois State University and the author of *Round-Trip to America: The Immigrant Returns to Europe, 1880–1930* (Cornell University Press, 1993).

EXPLORING THE ISSUE

Were Late Nineteenth-Century Immigrants "Uprooted"?

Critical Thinking and Reflection

1. Compare and contrast the YES and NO selections by Handlin and Wyman in terms of the way that immigrants identified with their native homelands and their adopted country.
2. Based upon your reading of the YES and NO selections, what problems did immigrants to the United States face in assimilating to American ways?
3. Given your understanding of the immigrant experience in the United States, to what extent is it appropriate to describe late nineteenth-century American society as a "melting pot"?
4. What does Mark Wyman's NO selection suggest about the geographical mobility of immigrants in the United States?
5. Why does Wyman believe that the portrait he paints of the immigrant experience challenges the notion of American exceptionalism?
6. Identify and summarize the nine conclusions that emerge from Wyman's argument.

Is There Common Ground?

It is very difficult for a country recognized and defined as a "nation of immigrants" not to appreciate the contributions made to the historical development of the nation by peoples who have migrated from other lands. Nevertheless, the ongoing debate over illegal aliens and national immigration policy threatens to undermine that reality. One wonders if a similar debate might have taken place among native Americans five centuries ago as Europeans began disembarking from their ships to plant colonies in what they considered to be a vast New World wilderness.

The newest immigrants to America have always occupied the position of "outsider," "foreigner," or "other" in the eyes of those claiming to be "native." All of those immigrants left something behind, but unless they were coerced by capture, as was the case with Africans and some indentured servants, or came as children with little voice in the matter, they made a conscious decision to leave their homeland in search of economic opportunity, political or religious freedom, or adventure—in short, a better life. They often faced hardship, a sense of alienation, and/or prejudice in one form or another. Still, most endured, and remained rooted themselves in the soil of their adopted

society and at some point made the transition from alien to citizen. For some Americans, that immigrant experience occurred centuries ago; for others, it has just begun.

Create Central

www.mhhe.com/createcentral

Additional Resources

John Higham, *Strangers in the Land: Patterns of American Nativism, 1860–1925* (Rutgers University Press, 1955).

Maldwyn Allen Jones, *American Immigration* (University of Chicago Press, 1960).

Thomas Kessner, *The Golden Door: Italian and Jewish Immigrant Mobility in New York City, 1880–1915* (Oxford University Press, 1977).

Humbert Nelli, *Italians in Chicago, 1880–1930: A Study of Ethnic Mobility* (Oxford University Press, 1970).

Ronald Takaki, *Strangers from a Distant Shore: A History of Asian Americans* (Little, Brown, 1989).

Internet References . . .

American Family Immigration History Center

www.ellisisland.org

Destination America

www.pbs.org/destinationamerica/usim_wy.html

Immigration and Industrialization in the Nineteenth Century

www.angelfire.com/ns/immigration/

International Channel

www.i-channel.com

U.S. Immigration, 1880–1914

teacher.scholastic.com/researchtools
/researchstarters/immigration/

Selected, Edited, and with Issue Framing Material by:
Larry Madaras, *Howard Community College*
and
James M. SoRelle, *Baylor University*

ISSUE

Did Women Adapt Favorably to Life in the American West in the Late Nineteenth Century?

YES: **Glenda Riley**, from "Women, Adaptation, and Change," Harlan Davidson (1992)

NO: **Christine Stansell**, from "Women on the Great Plains 1865–1890," *Women's Studies* (1976)

Learning Outcomes
After reading this issue, you will be able to:
• Briefly define the Turner thesis.
• Critically evaluate the positive and negative aspects of the Turner thesis.
• Critically evaluate applying the Turner thesis (although absent) to frontier women.
• Critically evaluate the three images of frontier women in American Literature.
• List some of the new sources and critically evaluate how they can be used to explain how women adapted to frontier life.

ISSUE SUMMARY

YES: Glenda Riley argues that in spite of enduring harsh environmental, political, and personal conditions on the Great Plains, women created rich and varied social lives through the development of strong support networks.

NO: Christine Stansell contends that women on the Great Plains were torn from their eastern roots, isolated in their home environment, and separated from friends and relatives. She concludes that they consequently endured lonely lives and loveless marriages.

In 1893 young historian Frederick Jackson Turner (1861–1932) delivered an address before the American Historical Association entitled "The Significance of the Frontier in American History." Turner's essay not only sent him from Wisconsin to Harvard University, it became one of the most important essays ever written in American history. According to Turner's thesis, American civilization was different from European civilization because the continent contained an abundance of land that was settled in four waves of migration from 1607 through 1890. During this process the European heritage was shed and the American characteristics of individualism, mobility, nationalism, and democracy developed.

This frontier theory of American history did not go unchallenged. Some historians argued that Turner's definition of the frontier was too vague and imprecise; he underestimated the cultural forces that came to the West from Europe and the eastern states; he neglected the forces of urbanization and industrialization in opening the West; he placed an undue emphasis on sectional developments and neglected class struggles for power; and finally, his provincial view of American history prolonged the isolationist views of a nation that had become involved in world affairs in the twentieth century. By the time Turner died, his thesis had been widely discredited. Historians continued to write about the West, but new fields and new theories were competing for attention.

they faced was fire. She added that her father immediately turned all stock loose in the face of an oncoming fire because the animals instinctively headed for the safety of the river valley, while her mother placed her in the middle of the garden on the presumption that fire would not "pass into the ploughed land." Other women described the deafening noise and blinding smoke of the fires that threatened their families and homes.

In addition, many women claimed that the Plains climate plagued them and interfered with their work. Destructive storms and blizzards were a constant threat, while summer heat and winter cold were regular annoyances. A Norwegian woman confronted her cold kitchen each winter morning dressed in overshoes, heavy clothing, and a warm head-scarf. Another woman simply wrote in her journal, "the snow falls upon my book while I write by the stove."

Ever-present insects and animals also challenged women at every turn. Grasshoppers not only demolished crops, but could destroy homes and household goods as well. The "hoppers" gnawed their way through clothing, bedding, woodwork, furniture, mosquito netting, and stocks of food. Bliss Isely of Kansas claimed that she could remember the grasshopper "catastrophe" of 1874 in vivid detail for many years after its occurrence. As she raced down the road trying to outrun the "glistening white cloud" of grasshoppers thundering down from the sky, she worried about the baby in her arms. When the grasshoppers struck, they ate her garden to the ground, devoured fly netting, and chewed a hole in her black silk shawl. "We set ourselves to live through a hungry winter," she remembered. In the months that followed, she "learned to cook wheat and potatoes in every way possible." She made coffee from roasted wheat and boiled wheat kernels like rice for her children. Another Kansas woman who survived the grasshopper attack bitterly declared that Kansas had been "the state of cyclones, the state of cranks, the state of mortgages—and now grasshopper fame had come!"

Political Upheaval

As if the physical environment wasn't enough to discourage even the hardiest and most determined women, another problem, political conflict, beset them as well. The ongoing argument over slavery especially affected the Kansas Territory when in 1856 an outbreak of violence between free-staters and proslavery factions erupted. "Border ruffians" added to the chaos by crossing frequently into "Bleeding Kansas" from Missouri in an attempt to impose slavery on the territory by force.

Sara Robinson of Lawrence felt terrorized by frequent "street broils" and saw her husband imprisoned during what she termed the "reign of terror" in Kansas. Another Kansas woman lamented that there was no respite between this convulsive episode and the Civil War, which plucked men out of homes for military service. Women not only lost the labor and income of their men, but they feared the theft of food and children and the threat of rape for themselves and their daughters at the hands of raiders, thieves, and other outlaws made bold by the absence of men. In addition, the departure of men caused the burden of families, farms, and businesses to fall on the shoulders of already beleaguered women.

The disputes that followed in the wake of the Civil War continued to disrupt women's lives. The period of Reconstruction between 1865 and 1877 included, for example, the chaotic entry of Exodusters (former slaves) into Kansas and other Plains states. In turn, prejudice against Exodusters created difficulties for African American women who had hoped they were migrating to a more hospitable region than the American South. Also during this period, economic unrest and dissatisfaction with federal and state government policies resulted in Populist agitation through the Plains during the 1880s and 1890s. By 1900, it seemed to many women that their lives had been entangled in a long series of political upheavals.

Personal Conflict

Women experienced personal conflict as well. Prejudice against Catholics, Jews, and people of other faiths led to intolerance at best and violence at worst. Ethnic and racial groups also received their share of distressing treatment. African American, Asian, and Mexican women were expected to work in the most menial, low-paid jobs, were barred from shops and other businesses, and were personally treated with disdain by many other migrants. This situation was especially difficult for women because they were frequently told that they were to be the arbitrators of society, yet they felt helpless to right this situation. Women also wanted desperately to shield their children from such treatment.

Some women also faced trouble within their own homes. Anecdotal evidence demonstrates that some husbands were domineering, demanding, and physically or verbally abusive. A young Jewish woman whose father had insisted that his family migrate to North Dakota remembered continual strife between her mother and father. "How can one bring the close, intimate life of the Russian *shtetl* to the vast open wilderness of the prairie?" she asked. But her mother tried. According to her daughter, "she rose early and cooked and baked and washed and scrubbed and sewed. She prayed and observed the fast days and holidays by making special dishes." Yet she also regretted and complained. Unable to understand her sorrow or offer her some much-needed sympathy, her husband argued and remonstrated. One day, much to his daughter's relief, he ran from the house storming and raging. Jumping into a buggy and seizing the reins, he shouted, "Goodbye, goodbye—I am leaving. This is more than human flesh can bear. . . . This is the end. I can take no more. It is beyond enduring. Goodbye, goodbye." When he soon returned, her joy dissipated: "My father had not kept his promise to go away and leave us in peace. He had returned. We were all trapped."

On the Plains, and throughout the West, thousands of women deserted such husbands or sought relief in divorce courts. Census figures indicate that western women sought and received a higher proportion of divorces than women in other regions of the country. Whether economic opportunities encouraged this proclivity to divorce or whether western women had a spirit that sought independence is as yet unclear.

Given the many difficulties that beset women, a reasonable person might ask why they stayed on the Plains. In fact, many did not stay. They and their families returned to former homes or moved onward to try life in another western region or town. After spending two years in Kansas, Helen Carpenter was delighted to become a new bride about to migrate to California. In 1857, Carpenter began her trail journal by going "back in fancy" over the two years she had spent in Kansas. She recalled the initial "weary journey of three weeks on a river boat" when all the children fell ill. Then, she wrote, it was "the struggle to get a roof over our heads . . . then followed days of longing for youthful companions . . . and before the summer waned, the entire community was stricken with fever and ague." Just as she finally made some friends and established something of a social life, "such pleasures were cut short by border troubles and an army of 'Border Ruffians' . . . who invaded the neighborhood, with no regard for life or property." She admitted that Kansas was "beautiful country" with its tall grass and lush wildflowers, but added that "the violent thunderstorms are enough to wreck the nerves of Hercules and the rattlesnakes are as thick as the leaves on the trees, and lastly 'but not leastly,' the fever and ague are corded up ever ready for use." Given the nature of her memories, it is not surprising that Carpenter concluded, "in consideration of what we have undergone physically and mentally, I can bid Kansas Good Bye without a regret." Another Kansas woman whose family left the region said that her father had taken

sick and that her "Auntie wanted to get away from a place always hideous in her eyes."

Fortunately, not all women felt so strongly about the drawbacks of their environment. Many women had already experienced a demanding life and, as Laura Ingalls Wilder put it, they saw the rigors of the Plains as "a natural part of life." They hung on because they had hope for the future, or according to one migrant, because they didn't expect the hard times to last. Often, their optimism was rewarded, and conditions did improve. Innovative technology gradually conquered the arid Plains, and economic booms occasionally appeared. A Nebraska woman of the early 1900s summed up her triumph in a pithy way when she wrote, "we built our frame house and was thru with our old leaky sod house. . . . We now had churches, schools, Telephones, Rural Mail."

Still we must ask: did the women who remained on the Plains suffer disillusionment and despair, growing old and ill before their time? Did they blame their menfolk who had seen economic opportunity in the Plains for their misfortunes? The answer is "yes": many women who stayed on the Plains did so with resentment and hostility. Their writings tell of crushing work loads, frequent births, illnesses and deaths, recurring depression, loneliness, homesickness, and fear. A common complaint was the absence of other women; Plains women also longed for family members who had stayed at home. A Wyoming woman even claimed that the wind literally drove her crazy and that she could no longer bear to spend long winters on a remote ranch with no other women.

Some women's lamentations were unrelenting, but others gradually included more pleasant observations. They noted that other people, including women, soon moved in and that often members of their own families joined them. Gradually, the depression of many hostile women ebbed and was replaced by a sense of affection for their new homes. Even the Wyoming woman who feared for her own mental stability later maintained that "those years on the Plains were hard years but I grew to like the West and now I would not like to live any other place."

Numerous women did blame men for their circumstances. But it is often difficult to determine which women had fair cause to lay blame. Because women were hesitant to record personal troubles in journals or letters sent back home, it is not always clear how responsible men were for women's difficulties. Certainly, sad stories do exist of men who verbally or physically abused women or who were alcoholic, lazy, financially inept, or generally irresponsible. In the patriarchal family structure of the time, men were often slow to recognize the importance of women's labor, allow women a voice in family decisions, and extend understanding for women's concerns. As early as 1862, the U.S. Commissioner of Agriculture's annual report suggested that the supposedly prevalent insanity of plainswomen resulted more from the harsh treatment doled out by their own men than from the Plains climate, family finances, or infant mortality. In following years, newspaper reports of wife-beating or journal accounts of alcoholic husbands gave credence to his assertion.

Here again, the negative testimony is balanced by other accounts. Countless women wrote about the energy, responsibility, support, community participation, and kindness of fathers, brothers, husbands, and sons. Women spoke of men's "cheerful spirits," patience, thoughtfulness, sympathy, and companionship. Army wives Ada Vogdes and Elizabeth Custer both felt that the hardships of their lives as women in western forts were greatly offset by the courtesy and consideration of their husbands, other officers, and enlisted men. More important, a considerable number of plucky women faced challenges with creativity, energy, optimism, and motivation. They battled the circumstances of their environment by confronting the necessities of each day while maintaining hope for a better future. They met political upheaval and violence with religious faith and a commitment to help establish order. And they endured conflict with family members, neighbors, and members of other cultural groups by persevering and seeking the companionship of others, especially other women.

A Kansan of the 1880s, Flora Moorman Heston, is one example of a woman who confronted poverty, hard work, loneliness, and other problems with buoyant spirits. In a letter home, she maintained that "we have the best prospect of prosperity we ever had and believe it was right for us to come here." She added that "I have a great deal more leasure [sic] time than I used to have It dont take near the work to keep one room that it does a big house." Like women in the Midwest, Southwest, and Far West, plainswomen relied on their inner strength and kept a positive outlook. Although these qualities are often forgotten in conventional descriptions of the darker side of Plains living, they did indeed exist.

How Women Adapted

Most women who ventured to the Plains states were highly motivated. They sought wealth, health, a more promising future for their children, lower taxes, and end to slavery, less prejudice or more freedom from governmental control. During the hard times and disasters, their hopes sustained them. When their fathers, brothers, or husbands talked of moving elsewhere, they often reminded the men of the particular dream that had brought them to the Plains in the first place. Others relied upon religious faith, or clung to their belief that they were civilizing a raw region, or some other commitment to keep them strong in the face of adversity.

Many women migrants created rich and varied social lives out of limited opportunities. They relieved their own isolation by writing in cherished journals or penning letters to friends and family. A young Nebraska woman who lamented the lack of women in the neighborhood wrote daily in her journal. "What should I do without my journal!" she exclaimed on one of its pages. Yet, as time passed, her entries became less frequent while her apologies to her neglected journal increased.

Women also turned to the books and newspapers they had brought with them, borrowed from others, or had purchased with hoarded butter-and-egg money. Bliss Isely explained that even when she and her husband could "not afford a shotgun and ammunition to kill rabbits" they subscribed to newspapers and bought books. She made it a personal rule that "no matter how late at night it was or how tired [she] was, never to go to bed without reading a few minutes from the Bible and some other book." Other women wrote of their longing for more books, of feeling settled when their books were unpacked, and of borrowing books from others. Faye Cashatt Lewis poignantly wrote: "Finishing the last book we borrowed from the Smiths, and having it too stormy for several days to walk the mile and a half to return it and get more, was a frequent and painful experience. Seeing the end of my book approaching was like eating the last bite of food on my plate, still hungry, and no more food in sight."

Music also provided solace and sociability. Frequently women insisted upon bringing guitars, pianos, and miniature parlor organs to the Plains. Despite the fact that Ada Vogdes and her husband were transported from fort to fort in army ambulances with limited space, she clung to her guitar. In her journal, she frequently mentioned the pleasure that playing that guitar and singing along brought to her and others. Vogdes, like many others, also depended upon mail to keep her amused and sane. When a snowstorm stopped the mail for two long weeks, Vogdes proclaimed that she could not wait much longer. To many women, the arrival of the mail provided a lifeline to home and family and brought news of the larger world through magazines, journals, ethnic and other newspapers, and books.

The coming of the railroad had great social implications. Not only did railroad companies bring additional people, but they sponsored fairs and celebrations and provided ties with other regions of the country. An Indian agent's wife in Montana wrote that "the coming of the Northern Pacific Railroad in 1883 brought us in closer touch with civilization, with kin and friends, with medical and military aid, but put an end to the old idyllic days." In 1907, a Wyoming woman was delighted to see the railroad come into her area and claimed that its very existence alleviated her depression. She explained that with "no trees and few buildings" to hamper her view of passing trains, she felt that she kept "in touch with the outside pretty well."

Women also became effective instigators and organizers of a huge variety of social events including taffy pulls, oyster suppers, quilting bees, dinners, picnics, box suppers, church "socials," weddings and chivarees, spelling bees, dances, theatricals, song fests, puppet shows, and readings. Perhaps most important were the celebration of such special holidays as Thanksgiving, Hanukkah, Christmas, and the Fourth of July. The menus concocted by women on special occasions often confounded other women. After a particularly splendid dinner, one woman wrote, "however she got up such a variety puzzled me, as she cooks by the fireplace and does her baking in a small covered skillet."

A third way in which women adapted was in their belief that they were family and cultural conservators. Women often derived great satisfaction and a sense of significance by establishing "real" homes for their families, preserving traditional values, folkways, and mores, passing on family and ethnic traditions, contributing to local schools and churches, and establishing women's organizations. Many would have probably agreed with the poetic woman who said of them, "Without their gentle touch, this land/Would still be wilderness." Certainly, women spent a good deal of time and energy recording and relating their cultural activities.

In this role, women placed a great deal of emphasis on material goods. They preserved, but also used, family treasures. Some insisted on fabric rather than oilcloth table coverings, served holiday eggnog to cowhands in silver goblets, and used their best silver and chinaware whenever the occasion arose. Years after coming to the Plains, Faye Lewis still proudly displayed her mother's Haviland china. She explained that "Father had urged strongly that this china be sold, but the thought was so heartbreaking to mother that he relented and helped her pack it." Lewis perceptively saw that her mother's china was "more than a set of dishes to her, more than usefulness, or even beauty. They were a tangible link, a reminder, that there

are refinements of living difficult to perpetuate . . . perhaps in danger of being forgotten." Certainly Mary Ronan felt this way. On an isolated Indian reservation in Montana, she still regularly set her dinner table with tablecloths and ivory napkin rings. She explained that "heavy, satiny damask" cloths gave her "exquisite satisfaction" although her children did not like them. She added that she had "one beautiful set of dishes" but used them only on "gala occasions."

Rituals such as the celebration of Christmas were also important. In the early years, the Christmas trees in many Plains homes were scraggly, ornaments few and homemade, and Christmas dinner far from lavish. But as their situations improved financially, women provided more festive trees, elaborate presents, and special foods. They placed trees decorated with nuts, candy, popcorn balls, strings of cranberries, wax candles, and homemade decorations in schools and churches. They then surrounded the trees with gifts for family and friends as well as presents for poor children who might otherwise be deprived of a Christmas celebration. Often music, singing, speeches, and prayers preceded the arrival of a local man dressed as Santa Claus."

It is important to note that women contributed to a diversity of cultural patterns because of their own mixed ethnic and racial stock. European, Native American, African American, Mexican, and Asian women who desired to preserve their own rich heritages subscribed to a variety of newspapers and magazines in their own languages, continued to wear traditional clothing, practiced their customary holiday rituals, and added their own words, foods, and perspectives to the evolving society. A Norwegian woman in Nebraska continued to speak Norwegian in her home, sent her children to parochial school, and cooked Norwegian food. African American women were another group who added their folkways to the cultural blend, especially after the Civil War when significant numbers of them migrated to Plains states as Exodusters.

Jewish women were yet another group who brought their own culture to the Plains. Although many Jewish settlers first came to the Plains as members of agricultural communities, particularly under the auspices of the Jewish Colonization Association and the Hebrew Emigrant Aid Society, they soon relocated in such cities as Omaha, Nebraska, and Grand Forks, North Dakota. Here they established businesses and communities that could support rabbis and supply other religious needs. This relocation was important to many Jewish women who despaired of their inability to provide their children with religious education and keep a kosher home when separated from a sizable Jewish community.

A fourth, and crucial, factor that aided many women in their adaptation to life on the Plains was their ability to bond with other women and to create what we would today call supportive networks. On the Plains, as elsewhere, women turned to each other for company, encouragement, information, and help in times of need. Women's longing for female companionship is clearly revealed by their laments about the lack of other women. One of only three known women migrants in a remote region of North Dakota stated simply, "Naturally I was very lonely for women friends."

Consequently, women frequently overcame barriers of age, ethnicity, social class, and race in forming friendships. Arriving in Oklahoma Territory in the early 1900s, Leola Lehman formed an extremely close friendship with a Native American woman whom she described as "one of the best women" she had known in her lifetime. A Kansas woman similarly characterized an African American woman who was first a domestic, then a confidante and friend, as "devoted, kind-hearted, hard-working." Still other women told how they found a way around language barriers in order to gain companionship from women of other races and cultures.

Typically, women began a friendship with a call or chat. Lehman was hanging out her wash when the Indian woman who became her friend quietly appeared and softly explained, "I came to see you. . . . I thought you might be lonesome." The company of other women was especially important in male-dominated military forts, where a woman began receiving calls upon arrival. Ada Vogdes recorded her gratitude for being whisked off by another officer's wife the moment she first arrived at Fort Laramie. Her journal overflowed with mention of calls, rides, and other outings with women friends. When her closest friends left the fort, Vogdes described herself as feeling "forsaken and forlorn" and overwhelmed by an aching heart. Some years later, Fanny McGillycuddy at Fort Robinson in South Dakota also logged calls and visits with other women and noted their great importance to her.

Women also established friendships, gave each other information and support and passed on technical information, often through quilting bees and sewing circles. Bliss Isely remembered that as a young woman she was always invited to the "sewings and quiltings" held by the married women in her neighborhood. On one occasion, she invited them in return and was pleased that "they remained throughout the day." Isely felt that these events gave her invaluable training in much-needed domestic

skills and that the women had "a good time helping each other" with their work.

Older women lavished new brides with maternal attention and were often very generous in sharing their time, energy, and skills with the novice. In 1869 the *Bozeman Chronicle* quoted a recent bride as saying, "In all there were just fourteen women in the town in 1869, but they all vied with each other to help us and make us welcome." This hospitality even included much-needed cooking lessons for the seventeen-year-old wife. A decade later, another bride arriving in Miles City, Montana, recalled that she met with a similar welcome: "Ladies called. . . . I wasn't at all lonely."

Women were also quick to offer their services to other women in times of childbirth, illness, and death. Such aid in time of need created strong bonds between women that often stretched beyond racial, ethnic, and class lines. In 1871, the *Nebraska Farmer* quoted a settler who claimed that such women acted "without a thought of reward" and that their mutual aid transformed women into "unbreakable friends." During the early 1880s, a Jewish woman in North Dakota explained that when a woman was about to give birth she would send her children "to the neighbors to stay for the time" so that she "could have rest and quiet the first few days, the only rest many of these women ever knew." She added that "the rest of us would take home the washing, bake the bread, make the butter, etc." Other women said that in time of illness or death they would take turns watching the patient, prepare medicines, bring food, prepare a body with herbs, sew burial clothes, organize a funeral, and supply food. The crucial nature of another woman's assistance in time of physical need was perhaps best expressed by Nannie Alderson, a Montana ranch wife during the 1880s. When she was ill, male family members and ranch hands strongly urged her to call a doctor from Miles City. Her reply: "I don't want a doctor. I want a woman!" When the men surrounding her failed to understand her need, they again pressed her to call a doctor. She sent for a neighbor woman instead. After her recovery, she justified her action by saying, "I simply kept quiet and let her wait on men, and I recovered without any complications whatever."

As the number of women increased in an area, women began to join together in the public arena as well as in private. They formed a myriad of social, educational, and reform associations. Women's literary clubs studied books and started libraries. Temperance societies—the most famous of which was the national Women's Christian Temperance Union—attempted to help control the evil of alcoholism that was so damaging to women and children who were economically dependent upon men. And woman suffrage groups fought for the right to vote. Nebraskan Clara Bewick Colby, suffragist and editor of. *The Woman's Tribune,* noted again and again that the Plains states were particularly fertile ground for suffrage reform.

Plainswomen split, however, on the issue of suffrage. Nebraskan Luna Kellie explained that she "had been taught that it was unwomanly to concern oneself with politics and that only the worst class of women would ever vote if they had a chance." But when a tax reform proposed to cut the length of the school term, Kellie, a mother of several small children, "saw for the first time that a woman might be interested in politics and want a vote." With her father's and husband's help, she promoted a campaign that resulted in woman suffrage in local school elections. Kellie's husband urged her to continue her efforts to obtain women's right to vote in general elections. In 1888, one Kansas women placed a cap bearing presidential candidate Belva Lockwood's name on her daughters head. Still, many women opposed the suffrage cause, maintaining that the vote should belong to men only. These women believed that women should focus on their homes and families rather than on making political decisions. Some of these women even organized anti-suffrage associations.

But advocates of woman suffrage were not so easily deterred. After the National Woman Suffrage Association was organized in 1869 (the same year that Wyoming Territory granted women the right to vote), Elizabeth Cady Stanton and Susan B. Anthony traveled through the West promoting suffrage. Stanton thought that Wyoming was a "blessed land . . . where woman is the political equal of man." Although Esther Morris is usually given credit for bringing woman suffrage to Wyoming Territory and was later called the Mother of Woman Suffrage, some people dispute the centrality of her role. Evidently, many women worked to convince the Democratic legislature to adopt a Women's Rights Bill in December 1869 and persuaded Republican governor John A. Campbell to sign the bill on December 10, 1869.

In addition to suffrage organizations, thousands of other women's clubs and associations existed, including hospital auxiliaries, housekeepers' societies, current events clubs, musical groups, tourist clubs, world peace groups, Red Cross units, and Women's Relief Corps chapters. By the 1880s, so many organizations existed that one Wyoming woman termed the era "the golden age of women's clubs." One leading Oklahoma clubwoman established or led over forty associations during her life.

Unfortunately, much of the sharing that had existed during the early days of a region now began to dissipate. Many women's clubs were segregated; women of color formed their own groups and fought for suffrage or reforms in their own way. For instance, African American women worked energetically within their own communities to provide medical care, playgrounds, and better educational facilities.

Some men's organizations also invited women (usually only white women, however) to join their membership and support their causes. A few even expanded their platforms to include women's issues. As a result, women joined the Patrons of Husbandry (the Grange), the Farmers' Alliance, and the Populist party. Annie La Porte Diggs of Kansas, for example, was an active Populist speaker and writer known for her religious liberalism. Of course, the most famous Populist woman orator was Mary Elizabeth Lease, a woman who was admitted to the Kansas bar in 1885 and who gave in 1890 over 160 speeches in support of the Populist cause. She became famous for her admonition 10 farmers to "raise less corn and more hell" and was dubbed by the media "Mary Yellin'." So many other women spoke from wagons and platforms, carried banners, and marched in parades that political humorist Joseph Billings wrote, "Wimmin is everywhere."

Women also began to run for office on the Populist ticket. They had long held elected positions on local, county, and state school boards so the idea was not totally unacceptable to many women and men. In 1892, Ella Knowles, a Montana lawyer who in 1889 successfully lobbied for a statute allowing women to practice law in the state, ran unsuccessfully for attorney general. She was, however, appointed to a four-year term as assistant attorney general, and during the mid 1890s was a delegate to Populist conventions and a member of the Populist National Committee. During this period, Olive Pickering Rankin served as the only woman on the school board in Missoula, Montana. She was also the mother of Jeanette Rankin, the first woman to serve in the U.S. Congress and the person who introduced the "Anthony Amendment" for woman suffrage into the U.S. House of Representatives.

Many men also supported women in other areas of life. Cases of supportive, helpful, sympathetic men who offered a helping hand and a listening ear when needed abounded in all communities. Faye Cashatt Lewis, whose mother so plaintively complained that the great trouble with North Dakota was that "there is nothing to make a shadow," claimed that her father was her mother's "saving support" throughout her various travails. Lewis said that her mother "could never have felt lost while he was by her side." Children too offered assistance, company, and comfort to the older women of a family. While the men were gone in the fields, working in a shop, practicing a profession, or making trips, children were often women's solace, friends, and helpers. According to Lewis, she and her siblings were not only her mother's assistants, but her friends and confidantes as well.

The ability of many women to concentrate on their hopes and dreams, create and enjoy socializing, serve as cultural conservators, and form strong bonds with others—both female and male—helped them triumph over the innumerable demands of the West. Although the Plains was an especially difficult environment for women, they were not generally disoriented, depressed, or in disarray. Rather, the majority of them managed to maintain homes and families, carry out domestic functions, and perpetuate the many values associated with the home. While depression, insanity, or bitterness characterized some women's lives, many more were able to respond to the challenges and hardships involved in Plains living in ways that insured survival and often brought contentment and satisfaction as well.

GLENDA L. RILEY is the Alexander M. Brackin Professor Emerita of History at Ball State University, where she taught from 1991 to 2003. She served as president of the Western Historical Association and is the author of 23 books and numerous articles, including *Women and Nature: Saving the "Wild" West* (University of Nebraska Press, 1999), *Taking Land, Breaking Land: Women Colonizing the American West and Kenya, 1840–1940* (University of New Mexico Press, 2003), and *Confronting Race: Women and Indians on the Frontier* (University of New Mexico Press, 2004).

Christine Stansell    **NO**

Women on the Great Plains 1865–1890

In 1841, Catharine Beecher proudly attested to the power of her sex by quoting some of Tocqueville's observations on the position of American women. On his tour of 1831, Tocqueville had found Americans to be remarkably egalitarian in dividing social power between the sexes. In his opinion, their ability to institute democratic equality stemmed from a clearcut division of work and responsibilities: "in no country has such constant care been taken . . . to trace two clearly distinct lines of action for the two sexes, and to make them keep pace with the other, but in two pathways which are always different." In theory, men and women controlled separate "spheres" of life: women held sway in the home, while men attended to economic and political matters. Women were not unaware of the inequities in a trade-off between ascendancy in the domestic sphere and participation in society as a whole. Attached to the metaphorical bargain struck between the sexes was a clause ensuring that women, through "home influence," could also affect the course of nation-building. For Miss Beecher, domesticity was also imperial power: "to American women, more than to any others on earth, is committed the exalted privilege of extending over the world those blessed influences, which are to renovate degraded man, and 'clothe all climes with beauty.'"

Yet despite Beecher's assertions to the contrary, by 1841 one masculine "line of action" was diverging dangerously from female influences. Increasing numbers of men were following a pathway which led them across the Mississippi to a land devoid of American women and American homes. In the twenty-odd years since the Santa Fe trade opened the Far West to American businessmen, only men, seeking profits in furs or trading, had gone beyond the western farmlands of the Mississippi Valley; no women participated in the first stages of American expansion. Consequently, by 1841 the West was in one sense a geographical incarnation of the masculine sphere, altogether untouched by "home influence." Although in theory American development preserved a heterosexually

balanced democracy, in actuality, the West, new arena of political and economic growth, had become a man's world.

In 1841, the first Americans intending to settle in the trans-Mississippi region rather than only trap or trade began to migrate over the great overland road to the coast. For the first time, women were present in the caravans, and in the next decades, thousands of women in families followed. Their wagon trains generally carried about one-half men, one-half women and children: a population with the capacity to reinstate a heterosexual culture. Only during the Gold Rush years, 1849–1852, were most of the emigrants once again male. Many of the forty-niners, however, chose to return East rather than to settle. In the aftermath or the Rush, the numerical balance of men and women was restored. By 1860, the sex ratio in frontier counties, including those settled on the Great Plains, was no different from the average sex ratio in the East.

Despite the heterosexual demography, however, the West in the years after 1840 still appeared to be masculine terrain. Everywhere, emigrants and travellers saw "such lots of men, but very few ladies and children." In mining camps, "representatives of the gentler sex were so conspicuous by their absence that in one camp a lady's bonnet and boots were exhibited for one dollar a look." Similarly, "the Great Plains in the early period was strictly a man's country." Even later, historians agree that "the Far West had a great preponderance of men over women," and that the absence of "mothers and wives to provide moral anchorage to the large male population" was a primary cause or its social ills. What accounts for the disparity between these observations and the bare facts of demography? In many frontier regions, women failed to reinstitute their own sphere. Without a cultural base of their own, they disappeared behind the masculine preoccupations and social structure which dominated the West. Despite their numbers, women were often invisible, not only in the first two decades of family settlement but in successive phases as well.

In this essay, I try to sketch out some ways of understanding how the fact of this masculine imperium affected women's experience in the great trans-Mississippi migrations. The following pages are in no way a monograph but rather a collection of suggestions which I have developed through reading and teaching about the West, and which I hope will encourage others to begin investigating this neglected area. Western migration constituted a critical rite of passage in nineteenth-century culture; its impact still reverbates a century later in our own "Western" novels, movies, and television serials, Women's relationship to this key area of the "American experience" has remained submerged and unquestioned. There are only a few secondary books on women in the West, and the two best-known works are simplistic and sentimental. Few writers or scholars have attempted to look at frontier women in the light of the newer interpretations of women's history which have evolved over the last four years. There are a wealth of questions to investigate and a wealth of sources to use. To demonstrate how new analyses can illuminate conventional teaching and lecture material, I have chosen one clearly defined area of "pioneer experience," settlers on the Great Plains from 1865–1890. The half-dozen books I use here are nearly all published and readily available.

Until after the Civil War, emigrants usually travelled over the Great Plains without a thought of stopping. Explorers, farmers, and travellers agreed that the dry grasslands of the "Great American Desert"—the Dakotas, western Kansas and western Nebraska—were not suitable for lucrative cultivation. In the late 60's, however, western land-grant railroads attempting to boost profits from passenger fares and land sales by promoting settlement in the region launched an advertising campaign in America and Europe which portrayed the Plains as a new Eden of verdant grasslands, rich soil, and plenteous streams. The railroad propaganda influenced a shift in public opinion, but technological advances in wheat-growing and steadily expanding urban markets for crops were far more significant in attracting settlers from Europe and the Mississippi Valley to the region. Emigrants came to take advantage of opportunities for more land, more crops, and more profits.

Who decided to move to the new lands? In the prevailing American notions of family relations, decisions about breadwinning and family finances were more or less in the hands of the male. Of course, removal to the Plains was a significant matter, and it is doubtful that many husbands and fathers made a unilateral decision to pull up stakes. Unfortunately, no large body of evidence about the choice to migrate to the Plains has been found or, at least, utilized in scholarly studies. I have sampled,

however, some of the more than seven hundred diaries of men and women travelling to California and Oregon twenty years earlier. These indicate that the man usually initiated a plan to emigrate, made the final decision, and to a greater or lesser degree imposed it on his family. Men's involvement with self-advancement in the working world provided them with a logical and obvious rationale for going West.

The everyday concerns of "woman's sphere," however, did not provide women with many reasons to move. In the system that Tocqueville praised and Beecher vaunted, women's work, social responsibilities, and very identities were based almost entirely in the home. Domesticity involved professionalized housekeeping, solicitous childrearing, and an assiduous maintenance of a proper moral and religious character in the family. Clearly, women could keep house better, literally and metaphorically, in "civilized" parts, where churches, kinfolk, and women friends supported them. The West held no promise of a happier family life or a more salutary moral atmosphere. On the contrary, it was notoriously destructive to those institutions and values which women held dear.

The Plains region was an especially arid prospect for the transplantation of womanly values. Lonely and crude frontier conditions prevailed into the 90's; in some areas, the sparse population actually declined with time: "following the great boom of the 80's, when the tide of migration began to recede, central Dakota and western Nebraska and Kansas presented anything but a land of occupied farms." The loneliness which women endured "must have been such as to crush the soul," according to one historian of the region. Another asserts that "without a doubt" the burden of the adverse conditions of Plains life—the aridity, treelessness, heat, perpetual wind, and deadening cold—fell upon the women. Almost without exception, others concur: "although the life of the frontier farmer was difficult special sympathy should go to his wife" . . . "it is certain that many stayed until the prairie broke them in spirit or body while others fled from the monotonous terror of it." An observer who visited the Plains in the 50's found life there to be "peculiarly severe upon women and oxen." The duration as well as the severity of cultural disruption which Plains women experienced was perhaps without parallel in the history of nineteenth-century frontiers.

First of all, emigrant women did not move into homes like the ones they had left behind, but into sod huts, tarpaper shacks, and dugouts. Seldom as temporary as they planned to be, these crude structures still existed as late as the nineties. Most settlers lived in one room "soddies" for six or seven years: if luck left a little cash, they might move into a wooden shack. Thus a farmer's wife often spent years trying to keep clean a house made of dirt. The effort became especially disheartening in rainstorms, when leaking walls splattered mud over bed-clothes and dishes: "in those trying times the mud floors were too swampy to walk upon and wives could cook only with an umbrella held over the stove; after they were over every stitch of clothing must be hung out to dry." Dry weather gave no respite from dirt, since dust and straw incessantly sifted down from the walls. Housekeeping as a profession in the sense that Catharine Beecher promul-gated it was impossible under such circumstances. Soddies were so badly insulated that during the winter, water froze away from the stove. In summer, the paucity of light and air could be stifling.

Often there was simply no money available to build a decent house. Drought, grasshoppers, or unseasonable rains destroyed many of the harvests of the 80's and 90's. Even good crops did not necessarily change a family's living conditions, since debts and mortgages which had accrued during hard times could swallow up any profits. But in any case, home improvements were a low prior-ity, and families often remained in soddies or shacks even when there was cash or credit to finance a frame house. The farmer usually earmarked his profits for reinvestment into the money-making outlay of better seeds, new stock, machinery, and tools. Farm machinery came first, labor-saving devices for women last: "there was a tendency for the new homesteader to buy new machinery to till broad acres and build new barns to house more stock and grain, while his wife went about the drudgery of household life in the old way in a little drab dwelling overshadowed by the splendour of machine farming." Washers and sewing machines graced some farms in the 80's, but "for the most part . . . the machine age did not greatly help woman. She continued to operate the churn, carry water, and run the washing machine—if she were fortunate enough to have one—and do her other work without the aid of horse power which her more fortunate husband began to apply in his harvesting, threshing, and planting."

Against such odds, women were unable to recreate the kinds of houses they had left. Nor could they rein-state the home as a venerated institution. A sod house was only a makeshift shelter; no effort of the will or imagina-tion could fashion it into what one of its greatest defend-ers eulogized as "the fairest garden in the wide field of endeavour and achievement." There were other losses as well. Many feminine social activities in more settled farm communities revolved around the church, but with the exception of the European immigrant enclaves, churches were scarce on the Plains. At best, religious observance was

makeshift; at worst, it was non-existent. Although "it is not to be supposed that only the ungodly came west," one historian noted, "there seemed to exist in some parts of the new settlements a spirit of apathy if not actual hostility toward religion." Circuit-riders and evangelical freelancers drew crowds during droughts and depressions, but during normal times, everyday piety was rare. Few families read the Bible, sang hymns, or prayed together: "when people heard that a family was religious, it was thought that the head of the household must be a minister."

Women were also unable to reconstitute the network of female friendships which had been an accustomed and sustaining part of daily life "back home." Long prairie winters kept everyone housebound for much of the year. During summers and warmer weather, however, men travelled to town to buy supplies and negotiate loans, and rode to nearby claims to deliver mail, borrow tools, or share news. "As soon as the storms let up, the men could get away from the isolation," wrote Mari Sandoz, Nebraska writer and daughter of a homesteader: "But not their women. They had only the wind and the cold and the problems of clothing, shelter, food, and fuel." On ordi-nary days men could escape, at least temporarily, "into the fields, the woods, or perhaps to the nearest saloon where there was warmth and companionship," but women had almost no excuses to leave. Neighbors lived too far apart to make casual visiting practicable; besides, a farmer could seldom spare a wagon team from field work to take a woman calling. Hamlin Garland, who moved to the Plains as a young boy, remembered that women visited less than in Wisconsin, his former home, since "the work on the new farms was never-ending": "I doubt if the women—any of them—got out into the fields or meadows long enough to enjoy the birds and the breezes."

In most respects, the patterns of life rarely accom-modated women's needs. Plains society paid little mind to women, yet women were essential, not incidental, to its functioning. Without female labor, cash-crop agriculture could never have developed. A man could not farm alone, and hired help was almost impossible to come by. Ordinar-ily, a farmer could count only on his wife and children as extra hands. On the homestead, women's responsibilities as a farmhand, not as a homemaker or a mother, were of first priority. Women still cooked, sewed, and washed, but they also herded livestock and toted water for irrigation.

The ambitious farmer's need for the labor power of women and children often lent a utilitarian quality to relations between men and women. For the single set-tler, marriage was, at least in part, a matter of efficiency. Courtships were typically brief and frank. Molly Dorsey Sanford, a young unmarried homesteader in Nebraska territory, recorded in her diary over half a dozen proposals in a few years. Most of her suitors were strangers. One transient liked her cooking, another heard about a "hull lot of girls" at the Dorsey farm and came to try his luck, and an old man on the steamboat going to Nebraska proposed after an hour's acquaintance. Jules Sandoz, father of Mari Sandoz, married four times. Three wives fled before he found a woman who resigned herself to the emotionless regimen of his farm. Stolid and resilient, the fourth, Mari's mother, lived to a taciturn old age, but her daughter could not forget others of her mother's generation who had not survived their hasty marriages: "after her arrival the wife found that her husband seldom mentioned her in his letters or manuscripts save in connection with calamity. She sickened and left her work undone . . . so the pioneer could not plow or build or hunt. If his luck was exceedingly bad, she died and left him his home without a housekeeper until she could be replaced." With characteristic ambivalence, Sandoz added, "at first this seems a calloused, even a brutal attitude, but it was not so intended."

Instrumentality could also characterize other family relations. Jules Sandoz "never spoke well of anyone who might make his words an excuse for less prompt jumping when he commanded. This included his wife and children." Garland described himself and his fellows as "a Spartan lot. We did not believe in letting our wives and children know they were an important part of our contentment." Jules' wife "considered praise of her children as suspect as self praise would be." Preoccupied by her chores, she maintained only minimal relationships with her family and assigned the care of the younger children to Mari, the oldest daughter.

In the domestic ideology of the family, careful and attentive child-rearing was especially important. Unlike the stoic Mrs. Sandoz, the American women who emigrated were often openly disturbed and troubled by a situation in which mothering was only peripheral to a day's work, and keenly felt the absence of cultural support for correct child-rearing. Mrs. Dorsey, the mother of diarist Molly Sanford, continually worried that her children, exiled from civilization, would turn into barbarians. In towns like Indianapolis, the family's home, schools, churches, and mothers worked in concert. In Nebraska, a mother could count on few aids. The day the Dorseys reached their claim, Molly wrote, "Mother hardly enters into ecstasies . . . she no doubt realizes what it is to bring a young rising family away from the world . . . if the country would only fill up, if there were only schools or churches or even some society. We do not see women at all. All men, single, or bachelors, and one gets tired

of them." Molly occasionally responded to her mother's anxiety by searching herself and her siblings for signs of mental degeneration, but Mrs. Dorsey's fears were never warranted. The children grew up healthy and dutiful: in Molly's words, "the wild outdoor life strengthens our physical faculties, and the privations, our power of endurance." To her confident appraisal, however, she appended a cautionary note in her mother's mode: "so that we do not degenerate mentally, it is all right; Heaven help us." Mrs. Dorsey, however, could seldom be reassured. When a snake bit one of the children, "Poor Mother was perfectly prostrated . . . she sometimes feels wicked to think she is so far away from all help with her family." On her mother's fortieth birthday, Molly wrote, "I fear she is a little blue today. I do try so hard to keep cheerful. I don't know as it is hard work to keep myself so, but it is hard with her. She knows now that the children ought to be in school. We will have to do the teaching ourselves." Without help from the old networks of kin and institutions, a mother could not be assured of success in fending off the dangers of nook, in which for the night we might be guarded."

As Mrs. Dorsey saw her ideas of child-rearing atrophy, she also witnessed a general attenuation of the womanliness which had been central to her own identity and sense of importance in the world. Her daughters particularly taxed her investment in an outmoded conception of womanhood. Molly, for instance, was pleased with her facility in learning traditionally male skills. "So it seems I can put my hand to almost anything," she wrote with pride after helping her father roof the house. Mrs. Dorsey regarded her daughter's expanding capacities in a different light. When Molly disguised herself as a man to do some chores, "it was very funny to all but Mother, who fears I am losing all the dignity I ever possessed." Molly was repentant but defensive: "I know I am getting demoralized, but I should be more so, to mope around and have no fun."

Mrs. Dorsey's partial failure to transmit her own values of womanhood to her daughter is emblematic of many difficulties of the first generation of woman settlers. Women could not keep their daughters out of men's clothes, their children in shoes, their family Bibles in use, or their houses clean; at every step, they failed to make manifest their traditions, values, and collective sensibility. It was perhaps the resistance of the Plains to the slightest feminine modification rather than the land itself which contributed to the legend of woman's fear of the empty prairies: "literature is filled with women's fear and distrust of the Plains . . . if one may judge by fiction, one must conclude that the Plains exerted a peculiarly appalling effect on women." The heroine of Rolvaag's *Giants in the Earth* echoed the experience of real women in her question to herself: "how will human beings he able to endure this place? . . . Why, there isn't even a thing that one can *hide behind*!" The desolation even affected women who passed through on their way to the coast. Sarah Royce remembered shrinking from the "chilling prospect" of her first night on the Plains on the Overland Trail: "surely there would he a few trees or a sheltering hillside. . . . No, only the level prairie. . . . Nothing indicated a place for us—a cozy nook, in which for the night we might be guarded."

Fright was not a rarity on the Plains. Both men and women knew the fear of droughts, blizzards, and accidental death. Yet the reported frequency of madness and suicide among women is one indication that Dick may have been right in his contention that "the real burden . . . fell upon the wife and mother." Men's responsibilities required them to act upon their fears. If a blizzard hung in the air, they brought the cattle in; if crops failed, they renegotiated the mortgages and planned for the next season. In contrast, women could often do nothing in the face of calamity. "If hardships came," Sandoz wrote, "the women faced it at home. The results were tersely told by the items in the newspapers of the day. Only sheriff sales seem to have been more numerous than the items telling of trips to the insane asylum."

Men made themselves known in the acres of furrows they ploughed up from the grassland. Women, lacking the opportunities of a home, had few ways to make either the land or their neighbors aware of their presence. The inability of women to leave a mark on their surroundings is a persistent theme in Sandoz's memoirs. When Mari was a

child, a woman killed herself and her three children with gopher poison and a filed down case knife. The neighbors agreed that "she had been plodding and silent for a long time," and a woman friend added sorrowfully, "If she could 'a had even a geranium, but in that cold shell of a shack. . . ." In Sandoz's memory, the women of her mother's generation are shadows, "silent . . . always there, in the dark corner near the stove."

I have emphasized only one side of woman's experience on the Plains. For many, the years brought better times, better houses, and even neighbors. A second generation came to maturity: some were daughters like the strong farm women of Willa Cather's novels who managed to reclaim the land that had crushed their mothers. Yet the dark side of the lives of the first women on the Plains cannot he denied. Workers in an enterprise often not of their own making, their labor was essential to the farm, their womanhood irrelevant. Hamlin Garland's *Main Travelled Roads*, written in part as a condemnation of "the futility of women's life on a farm," elicited this response from his mother: "you might have said more but I'm glad you didn't. Farmer's wives have enough to bear as it is."

Christine Stansell earned her PhD in American studies at Yale University and is the Stein-Freiler Distinguished Service Professor Emerita in United States History at the University of Chicago. She is the author of *City of Women: Sex and Class in New York City, 1789–1860* (University of Illinois Press, 1986) and *The Feminist Promise, 1792 to the Present* (Random House, 2010.)

EXPLORING THE ISSUE

Did Women Adapt Favorably to Life in the American West in the Late Nineteenth Century?

Critical Thinking and Reflection

1. Explain what women feared they would lose when they migrated west. According to Stansell, did these fears come true? Critically analyze Stansell's portrait of women's lives on the Great Plains.
2. List the three major drawbacks women on the Great Plains faced. List four ways in which women overcame the obstacles and developed quality lifestyles, as discussed by Riley. Compare the negatives and positives, and critically analyze.
3. Riley gives some examples of the multicultural frontier. When did women begin to segregate themselves along class and social lines? Why?
4. Critically discuss how women got involved in the politics of the West.

Is There Common Ground?

Both Stansell and Riley admit that women in the Great Plains faced considerable hardships in the latter half of the nineteenth century. Both would agree that the first generation of women migrants faced considerable obstacles in trying to recreate a home environment which middle-class women had established in cities by the 1850s where they maintained a clean physical environment with strong moral values. Stansell gives one example where a mother is upset because her daughter dressed like a man and was able to perform many necessary or so-called masculine farm chores.

Riley moves beyond Stansell and sees second generation women recreating the eastern environment with the establishment of magazines, newspapers, churches and the Women's Christian Temperance union to prohibit liquor and its harmful effects on the family. She also finds that in the 1880s white women often formed friendships with minorities—Afro-Americans, Mexicans, Native Americans—until the late 1890s, when these groups self-segregated themselves

Additional Resources

Susan Armitage and Elizabeth Jameson, eds., *The Women's West* (University of Oklahoma Press, 1987)

Richard W. Etulain, *The Life and Legends of Calamity Jane* (University of Oklahoma Press, 2014)

Elizabeth Jameson and Sheila McManus, eds., *One Step over the Line: Toward a History of Women in the North American West* (University of Alberta Press, 2008)

Lillian Schlissel, Vicki L. Ruiz, and Janice Monk, eds., *Western Women: Their Land, Their Lives* (University of New Mexico Press, 1988)

Special Issue on Western Women, *Journal of the West* 21 (April, 1982)

Richard White, "Western History [A Historiographical Essay]," in Eric Foner, ed., *American History* (Temple University Press, 1997)

Internet References . . .

(Gene) Autry National Center

http://www.autrynationalcenter.org

GO WEST, YOUNG WOMAN—Sight and Sound

http://search.proquest.com/docview
/871364951?accountid=14766

Ken Burns' History of the American West

https://www.pbs.org/weta/thewest
/program/episodes

UNIT

Reform, War, and Depression

*T*he maturing of the industrial system, a major economic depression, agrarian unrest, and labor violence all came to a head in 1898 with the Spanish-American War. The progressives brought about major domestic reforms to ameliorate the worst abuses of rapid industrial growth and urbanization.

Progressive-era presidents advanced a proactive foreign policy, but the nation's role as a mediator of global conflicts was pushed to the limit when Woodrow Wilson tried and failed to get the United States to join the League of Nations at the end of World War I.

The end of the war brought on the "new era" of the 1920s, marked by political conservatism in the political arena, economic prosperity and the rise of a consumer culture, and what some have labeled a "revolution of morals and manners." Within this rapidly changing environment a new Ku Klux Klan appeared. There is controversy over whether the Klan created a climate of lawlessness in the 1920s or was primarily a mainstream organization committed to traditional white, middle-class, Protestant values.

The rise of a more activist federal government accelerated with the Great Depression. In the midst of widespread unemployment, Franklin D. Roosevelt was elected on a promise to give Americans a "New Deal." Every sector of the economy was affected by the proliferation of the alphabet soup New Deal agencies, and historians continue to debate whether the New Deal measures ameliorated or prolonged the Great Depression.

The emergence of a conservative Congress and the impending world war killed the New Deal by 1939. With the fall of France to the Germans in 1940, FDR tried to abandon the traditional foreign policy of isolationism by aiding allies in Europe and Asia without involvement in the war. The effort failed, and on December 7, 1941, the Japanese attacked Pearl Harbor. At home, African Americans connected the struggle for democracy abroad to their own efforts to secure full citizenship rights in their own country. The war framed a debate over the status of blacks in the United States, whereas the end of the war, through the introduction of weapons of mass destruction, not only introduced the world to the Atomic Age, but also produced a controversy involving the moral efficacy of deploying such weapons.

Selected, Edited, and with Issue Framing Material by:
Larry Madaras, *Howard Community College*
and
James M. SoRelle, *Baylor University*

ISSUE

Did the Progressives Succeed?

YES: Neil A. Wynn, from "The Progressive Era: American Society, 1900–1914," Holmes & Meier Publishers (1986)

NO: Richard M. Abrams, from "The Failure of Progressivism," Little, Brown (1971)

Learning Outcomes

After reading this issue, you will be able to:

- Define progressivism.
- List the supporters and opponents of progressivism.
- List the successes and failures of progressivism.
- Distinguish between a progressive reformer and a progressive socialist.
- Critically evaluate progressivism's impact on today's society.

ISSUE SUMMARY

YES: Neil Wynn argues that the progressives were a diverse group of reformers who confronted and ameliorated the worst abuses that emerged in urban-industrial America during the early 1900s.

NO: Professor of history Richard Abrams maintains that progressivism was a failure because it tried to impose a uniform set of values upon a culturally diverse people and never seriously confronted the inequalities that still exist in American society.

Progressivism is a word used by historians to define the reform currents in the years between the end of the Spanish-American War and America's entrance into the Great War in Europe in 1917. The so-called progressive movement had been in operation for several decades before the label was first used in the 1912 electoral campaigns. Former President Theodore Roosevelt ran as a third-party candidate in the 1912 election on the Progressive party ticket, but in truth the party had no real organization outside of the imposing figure of Theodore Roosevelt. Therefore, as a label, "progressivism" was rarely used as a term of self-identification for its supporters. Even after 1912, it was more frequently used by journalists and historians to distinguish the reformers of the period from socialists and old-fashioned conservatives.

The 1890s was a crucial decade for many Americans. From 1893 until almost the turn of the century, the nation went through a terrible economic depression. With the forces of industrialization, urbanization, and immigration wreaking havoc upon the traditional political, social, and economic structures of American life, changes were demanded. The reformers responded in a variety of ways. The proponents of good government believed that democracy was threatened because the cities were ruled by corrupt political machines while the state legislatures were dominated by corporate interests. The cure was to purify democracy and place government directly in the hands of the people through such devices as the initiative, referendum, recall, and the direct election of local school board officials, judges, and U.S. senators.

Social justice proponents saw the problem from a different perspective. Settlement workers moved into cities and tried to change the urban environment. They pushed for sanitation improvements, tenement house reforms, factory inspection laws, regulation of the hours and wages of women, and the abolition of child labor.

A third group of reformers considered the major problem to be the trusts. They argued for controls over the power of big business and for the preservation of the free enterprise system. Progressives disagreed on whether the issue was size or conduct and on whether the remedy was trust-busting or the regulation of big business. But none could deny the basic question: How was the relationship between big business and the U.S. government to be defined?

How successful was the progressive movement? What triggered the reform impulse? Who were its leaders? How much support did it attract? More important, did the laws that resulted from the various movements fulfill the intentions of its leaders and supporters?

Historians have generally been sympathetic to the aims and achievements of the progressive historians. Many, like Charles Beard and Frederick Jackson Turner, came from the Midwest and lived in model progressive states like Wisconsin. Their view of history was based on a conflict between groups competing for power, so it was easy for them to portray progressivism as a struggle between the people and entrenched interests.

It was not until after World War II that a more complex view of progressivism emerged. Richard Hofstadter's *Age of Reform* (Alfred A. Knopf, 1955) was exceptionally critical of the reformist view of history as well as of the reformers in general. Born of a mixed marriage with a Jewish immigrant mother and raised in Buffalo and New York City, the Columbia University professor argued that progressivism was a moral crusade undertaken by white Anglo-Saxon Protestant (WASP) families in an effort to restore older Protestant and individualistic values and to regain political power and status. Both Hofstadter's "status revolution" theory of progressivism and his profile of the typical progressive have been heavily criticized by historians. Nevertheless, he changed the dimensions of the debate and made progressivism appear to be a much more complex issue than had previously been thought.

Most of the writing on progressivism for the past 20 years has centered around the "organizational" model. Writers of this school have stressed the role of the "expert" and the ideals of scientific management as basic to an understanding of the progressive era. This fascination with how the city manager plan worked in Dayton or railroad regulation in Wisconsin or the public

schools laws in New York City makes sense to a generation surrounded by bureaucracies on all sides. Two books that deserve careful reading are Robert Wiebe's *The Search for Order, 1877–1920* (Hill & Wang, 1967) and the wonderful collection of essays by Samuel P. Hays, *American Political History as Social Analysis* (University of Tennessee Press, 1980), which brings together two decades' worth of articles from diverse journals that were seminal in exploring ethnocultural approaches to politics within the organizational model.

In a highly influential article written for the *American Quarterly* in spring 1970, Professor Peter G. Filene proclaimed "An Obituary for the 'Progressive Movement.'" After an extensive review of the literature, Filene concluded that since historians cannot agree on its programs, values, geographical location, members, and supporters, there was no such thing as a progressive movement. Few historians were bold enough to write progressivism out of the pantheon of American reform movements. But Filene put the proponents of the early twentieth-century reform movement on the defensive. Students who want to see how professional historians directly confronted Filene in their refusal to attend the funeral of the progressive movement should read the essays by John D. Buenker, John C. Burnham, and Robert M. Crunden in *Progressivism* (Schenkman, 1977).

Three works provide an indispensable review of the literature of progressivism in the 1980s. Link and McCormick's *Progressivism* (Harland Davidson, 1983) deserves to be read in its entirety for its comprehensive yet concise coverage. More scholarly but still readable are the essays on the new political history in McCormick's *The Party Period and Public Policy: American Politics from the Age of Jackson to the Progressive Era* (Oxford University Press, 1986). The more advanced student should consult Daniel T. Rodgers, "In Search of Progressivism," *Reviews in American History* (December 1982). While admitting that progressives shared no common creed or values, Rodgers nevertheless feels that they were able "to articulate their discontents and their social visions" around three distinct clusters of ideas: "the first was the rhetoric of anti-monopolism, the second was an emphasis on social bonds and the social nature of human beings, and the third was the language of social efficiency."

In the first selection, Professor Neil A. Wynn views progressivism from the point of view of the reformers and ranks it as a qualified success. In his definition, progressives were a diverse group of middle-class reformers who constantly formed shifting coalitions in order to pass the numerous reforms. Some thought political reforms were the keys to preserving democracy while others focused on social reforms such as the elimination of child labor, the regulation of hours and working conditions, and the establishment of a minimum wage. The progressives were also ambivalent in their attitude toward big business. A handful believed that business monopolies were inevitable. Therefore regulation of monopolies was the cure. But most progressives wanted business monopolies eliminated with the enforcement and strengthening of the antitrust laws. In the presidential election of 1912, candidates Theodore Roosevelt and Woodrow Wilson debated whether size or conduct was the defining issue regarding whether large business combinations should be broken up.

Wynn stresses three areas of the progressive movement which Abrams neglects. First was their reliance on social science experts. Through the use of the studies by sociologists, economists, and political scientists the progressives could document their successes and failures. They were able to distinguish between the passage of legislation and its actual results. The progressives were the first reformers to document their failures.

Second, the progressives were motivated by evangelical Christianity. Progressives were often inspired by the Protestant ministers and churches which established the Social Gospel movement to clean up the cities. Women reformers such as Jane Addams' Hall House in Chicago and the Henry Street Settlement House in New York City led the movements to clean up the cities.

Progressives were also motivated by the investigative journalists known as the muckrakers, a term negatively coined by President Theodore Roosevelt. These journalists, featured in a new book by Doris Kearns Goodwin, *The Bully Pulpit: Theodore Roosevelt, William Howard Taft and the Golden Age of Journalism* (Simon & Schuster, 2013), discovered a lot of muck to be raked. Every facet of American industrial society was examined—the Standard Oil Company, the U.S. Senate, municipal governments, and finally *The Jungle*, a novel about the meat packing industry in Chicago, which forced President Theodore Roosevelt to push the passage of the Meat Inspection Act.

So the question remains, did the progressive movement succeed or fail? In the second selection, Richard M. Abrams views the movement in very negative terms. He distinguishes the progressives from other reformers of the era such as the Populists, the Socialists, the mainstream labor unions, and the corporate reorganization movement. He then argues that the progressive movement failed because it tried to impose a uniform set of middle-class traditional Protestant moral values upon a nation that was growing more culturally diverse, and that the reformers supported movements that brought about no actual changes or only superficial ones at best. The real inequities in American society, says Abrams, were never really addressed.

By 1910, says Abrams, xenophobic racism and nativism had blended with reform movements in the Far West and South. Restrictions limiting "coolie labor" and laws preventing African-Americans from voting pushed the reformers to become more interested in controlling the behavior patterns of the working classes. Anti-Catholicism was also spreading, probably because of the large number of immigrants coming in from Southern and Eastern Europe. The more diverse the population the harder it was to achieve a consensus of old fashioned moral values. The Americanization and prohibition movements were speeded up by the United States' entrance into World War I. Since the German-Americans were the major beer brewers, the supporters of the Anti-Saloon League were able to push through Congress the Eighteenth Amendment prohibiting "the manufacture, sale or transportation of intoxicating liquors within, the importation . . . into or the exportation . . . from the United States." Many states forbade teaching the German language in the schools while grocery stores sold liberty burgers instead of hamburgers.

Abrams is particularly harsh in his criticism of the political and economic reforms of the period. Direct election of senators and legislators didn't prevent the wealthy from dominating the legislatures. The initiative and the referendum are devices used primarily by special interest groups to promote their agendas. Laws controlling the practices of the railroads didn't change the general rate structure until the 1940s. Farmers could mortgage their homes but they were still dependent upon bankers, middlemen, and the international market to make money. The Federal Reserve Act of 1913 didn't prevent the Depression of 1929 and the modification and strengthening of the Sherman Antitrust Act and the Federal Trade Commission have not seriously stopped the mergers of billion-dollar corporations.

Both authors admit that on occasion the progressives were insensitive to the needs of the immigrants regarding prohibition and child labor, the latter of which was essential to the family income. But Wynn stressed the role of women reformers in the social justice movement where they pushed for laws restricting the hours children and women should be allowed to work; settlement houses to improve sanitary conditions for immigrant women; voting rights for women in order to outlaw prostitution, gambling, and most importantly the prohibition of alcohol and drugs.

Perhaps Link and McCormick go too far in arguing the progressive movement outstrips the later New Deal and Great Society reform movements. Say Link and McCormick: "The problems with which the progressives struggled have, by and large, continued to challenge Americans ever since. And, although the assumptions and techniques of progressivism no longer command the confidence which early twentieth century Americans had in them, no equal body of reforms has ever been adopted in their place."

YES

Neil A. Wynn

The Progressive Era:
American Society, 1900–1914

The Progressive movement covered a wide political and social spectrum and encompassed a diversity of aims. . . . As historians have pointed out, the movement varied from region to region, city to city. In some areas it was middle class; in others, it was almost upper class. Ranging from California to New York, through Wisconsin, Iowa, and Illinois, the Progressives had a diversity of aims. While some groups wished to prevent extremism and violence by reforming society and removing the root causes of strife and disorder through social justice, others were more concerned with social control and the preservation of existing institutions and beliefs. For some, concern with efficiency was seen in terms of human values and social welfare; for others it was seen in economic relations and political pragmatism. As a consequence, progressivism was to include social workers, town planners, urban managers, trade unionists, businessmen, church leaders, politicians, and representatives of both sexes. The one thing almost all had in common was the faith in society's ability to resolve major problems satisfactorily through political action. This belief led Progressives to look increasingly to government and resulted in the gradual spread of the movement from the state and local level up to the national level, culminating in the adoption of Progressive policies by both Republican and Democratic parties and their presidential candidates in the elections of 1912.

Whatever the problems about its motivation and composition, there is little doubt that progressivism began in the cities. It was concern for the plight of the urban poor that led to the formation of Charity Organization Societies, beginning in 1877, to oversee and coordinate the distribution of relief in order to maximize benefits and to minimize corruption and waste. Closely related to this was a sense of disquiet occasioned by the perception of a moral and religious decline in the cities, and a desire to bring moral uplift to the urban poor. The result was a religious revival in the shape of the Social Gospel movement and

the development of the concept of Christian responsibility for the welfare of society. Both found expression in the growth of urban missionary work, the YMCA, and the Salvation Army: by 1900, for example, the Salvation Army had over three thousand officers and some seven hundred congregations, and the number of city mission houses had reached three thousand by 1920. The Charity Organizations, while not so directly concerned with religious matters, were motivated by "the assumption that the urban poor had degenerated morally because the circumstances of city life had cut them off from the elevating influence of their moral betters." Much of their work was, therefore, in the form of individual visits to the homes of the poor in an attempt to establish links between the lower classes and their so-called social betters.

To some extent these aims were shared by members of the Settlement House movement, which grew in late nineteenth-century America. However, the emphasis in the settlements was more on creating an environment in which the poor could achieve their own salvation, both in practical and moral terms, and in which social barriers could be broken down through the interaction of representatives of the different classes. This idea of a meeting point for different social groups in a mutually rewarding setting originated in England and was introduced to America in 1886. It spread rapidly across the country, and by 1916 there were some four hundred houses in different cities, the best-known being Jane Addams's Hull House in Chicago, Lillian Wald's Henry Street Settlement in New York, and Robert A. Woods's South End House in Boston. The stress in these and other settlements was on awareness and education, but they also attempted to tackle basic problems facing the poorer city inhabitants. Thus they often provided accommodation and food for the needy, care for children of working mothers, health and civic education programs, plus classes in English as well as those on cultural or artistic topics. At the same time, of course, the settlements provided an opportunity for members of the middle classes to take part in worthwhile labor and to gain experience of the lives of the less fortunate sections of the community.

The social workers' efforts to improve local urban neighborhoods soon led them into other areas of concern. In order to achieve better city management, urban redevelopment, housing programs, and legislation to cover areas of social welfare, working conditions of women and children, and general labor matters, they began to call for political action. The desire for more responsive legislatures led in turn to demands for further democratization of the political system. At the municipal level this included the adoption of the referendum, the initiative, and the recall; at the state level it embraced direct primaries and the direct election of senators, and the extension of the franchise to include women. By 1916 more than twenty states had enacted the referendum, thirty-seven had direct primaries, and thirteen permitted women the vote. The direct election of senators was secured with the passage of the Seventeenth Amendment in 1913 and was implemented in the congressional elections of November 1914.

Concern for democracy, efficiency, scientific and rational management, and a fairer and more humane order extended not just to the problems of the city, but also to the economic sphere. The Progressives' attack on corruption, exploitation, and suffering led them to challenge the power and influence of the industrial monopolies, and to call for government controls. However, not all Progressives could be labeled antibusiness. Many accepted big business as the logical and natural outcome of beneficial economic developments, which had to be accepted as part of progress—if only in a modified form with governmental checks. Some businessmen were themselves party to the call for government regulation and rationalization in the industrial sector in order to bring stability and reduce unnecessary and harmful competition. However, like other groups involved in the Progressive movement, such businessmen were often divided on aims and methods, and along regional and ideological lines. The National Civic Federation (1900), representing corporate leaders, could be at odds with the smaller businessmen represented in the National Association of Manufacturers; eastern bankers could differ with those in the West and South; and western shippers could be sharply critical of eastern railroad men. Not even on the subject of labor relations was there unanimity of opinion among the industrialists: the National Civic Federation hoped to achieve stability through cooperation with labor and the adoption of programs of welfare capitalism, and to that end included labor leaders like [Samuel] Gompers among its members; the National Association of Manufacturers, on the other hand, steadfastly refused to contemplate union recognition.

Labor's own position within the Progressive camp was itself ambiguous. The AFL traditionally concentrated on narrow economic objectives rather than on broad programs of political reform, and although the challenge from more radical organizations forced it into the political arena, the AFL resisted legislation that might undermine its authority in the economic sphere. Thus laws that strengthened the rights of workers were welcomed, but those that threatened government regulation of unions or that perhaps would make unions seem unnecessary, were not. Although Gompers and his colleagues supported some social welfare legislation, they still insisted that conditions could best be improved through collective bargaining on the shop floor rather than by political programs: increased wages and regular employment would enable individual workers to provide for the welfare of their families without government aid. . . . In order to protect and enhance the position of its members, the AFL was intent both on obtaining a greater share of the national wealth from the industrialists and ensuring that its workers' position was not undermined by immigrant labor. As a consequence, the AFL was one of a number of groups that, increasingly in the late nineteenth century, advocated immigration controls. . . .

A "problem" often associated with immigration, and a concern of some Progressives, was that of drink. Prohibition, described by one historian as "the linch pin of modern reform," revealed the moralistic side of the reform movement—the wish to *make* people good if they could not control their own worst desires. However, the Prohibitionists could not be characterized just as moral or religious bigots, nor as cranks: they had considerable public support, and, like nativism, Prohibition was a powerful force by the early 1900s. Initially, the Prohibitionist movements, the Women's Christian Temperance Union (1874) and the Anti-Saloon League (1893), both had their greatest following in southern and midwestern states, but they had some backing in eastern states, particularly the more rural type such as Vermont, Maine, and New Hampshire, and urban reformers often blamed drink for causing poverty and social decay in the cities. Nonetheless, the fight for Prohibition tended to be between rural and urban areas, and between native- and foreign-born Americans. In 1905 only Maine, Kansas, Nebraska, and North Dakota were "dry" states, but by 1914, following a state-by-state campaign led by the Anti-Saloon League, fourteen states had voted in favor of Prohibition.

Like Prohibition, prostitution and vice were issues that revealed a mixture of influences among the reformers, ranging from a genuine concern for the poor, religious and moral outrage tinged with repressive puritanism, and anti-immigrant feeling. Prostitution clearly involved exploitation of the poorer classes, and it also posed a threat to public health; but for many it was indicative too of the physical and moral decline, and hypocrisy, of the cities and their new, foreign, populations. Muckraking exposés of prostitution and the white slave trade led to the setting up of investigatory vice commissions across the nation (over 100 between 1902 and 1916), the formation of organizations like the National Vigilance Society (1911) and the American Social Hygiene Association (1913), and the passage of the famous Mann Act in 1910, which made it a federal offense to cross state lines with a woman for immoral purposes.

Prominent among all movements for reform, including those of prohibition and vice, were women. The Women's Christian Temperance Union was actively involved not just in the campaign against alcohol, but also in those for penal reform, labor legislation, and female suffrage. Leading settlement house workers like Jane Addams and Lillian Wald were described as "heroines in a new crusade against want, illiteracy, disease and crime," and they and others like Florence Kelley and Julia Lathrop were concerned with child welfare, regulation of women's work, peace organizations, and suffrage. Florence Kelley, a former worker in Hull House, moved from Illinois's State Bureau of Labor Statistics to become secretary of the National Consumer League in 1899 and remained in that post for thirty-two years. With Lillian Wald, the director of the Henry Street Settlement in New York, Kelley helped to found the National Child Labor Committee in 1906, which led to the White House Conference on Children in 1909 and the establishment of the Children's Bureau in the Department of Labor in 1912. Julia Lathrop, another product of Hull House, became head of the Children's Bureau. Jane Addams and Hull House were clearly inspirations for many of the early social workers, women and men alike, and this was acknowledged in 1909 when Addams became the first woman president of the National Conference of Charities and Corrections (later to become the National Conference of Social Work). But as well as her welfare concerns, Jane Addams was also involved in the range of reform, from local politics through to the international peace movement and the women's suffrage campaign. In 1911, she became vice-president of the National American Women's Suffrage Association (NAWSA) and was involved in the struggle for suffrage until it was finally achieved in 1920.

Suffrage was an issue that united many women in the years before the war. The women's movement had its origins in the abolitionism and general reform ferment of the 1840s, but had languished after an internal rift following the Civil War. The coming together of the two sections, the Woman Suffrage Association and the National Woman's Suffrage Association, to form NAWSA in 1893 was the start of a revitalized campaign, which, like the British suffrage struggle, came to a peak from about 1910 to 1920. Led first by Anna Howard Shaw (1904–15) and then by Carrie Chapman Catt (and, as mentioned, with Jane Addams as vice-president from 1911), NAWSA increased its membership from one hundred thousand in 1915 to 2 million by 1917. By 1914, following a state-by-state battle, eleven states had granted women the right to vote. However, despite the inclusion of suffrage planks in the platforms of both major parties, Congress still failed to vote in favor of the suffrage amendment to the Constitution (the Susan B. Anthony Amendment, named after the suffrage campaigner, who died in 1906). Faced by strong resistance from southerners, who feared federal intervention in voting because of the racial question; from brewing interests because of female support for Prohibition; from businessmen, who opposed regulation of child and female labor; from machine politicians, who resisted the reforming impulse of women; and from those who generally resisted change, more militant and impatient women, led by Alice Paul, formed the Congressional Union in 1913, an organization modeled on the example of the Pankhursts' Social and Political Union in England. On the eve of the European war, American politicians, like their British counterparts, were increasingly confronted by women demanding recognition and the right to vote.

The growth of the suffrage movement and the prominent part played by women in the Progressive movement as a whole, was a reflection of the changes that had occurred in women's position in society since the 1860s—changes that encouraged commentators to write of a "New Woman" as early as the 1890s. Changes in legal status, recognizing women's family rights and the right to own property, were matched by some economic progress. In 1870 less than 15 percent of women over the age of sixteen worked outside the home; by 1910 24 percent, or 8 million women, worked, and they constituted over 20 percent of the labor force. The great majority, however, were employed either in domestic service or in "traditional" areas of female employment such as textiles, the garment trade, shoe manufacture, and food production—in other words, cooking, sewing, and making clothes. Nonetheless, the increase in employment of women did lead to some organization and the formation of the National Women's Trade Union League in 1903. But while the NWTUL was concerned with working conditions and wages and was involved in organizing the militant strikes in the textile industries of Baltimore, Chicago, Philadelphia, and New York in 1909 and 1913, the suffrage movement was to a large extent a separate campaign that drew its following primarily from the growing middle class of women, the college-educated and white-collar workers.

The number of women at college doubled between 1880 and 1900 as more and more colleges opened their doors to female students. Many of the female graduates then found employment as schoolteachers, and others, as we have seen, worked in the settlement houses. By 1890, 250,000 women were teaching, and some 70 percent of Settlement House residents were women. Although these were often the only outlets for the talents of qualified women, new opportunities were increasingly opening up as industry grew and as jobs were created by the advent of the telegraph, telephone, and typewriter. In 1870 less than 3 percent of all clerical workers were women; by 1910 women accounted for almost 38 percent. The number of female telephone operators rose from 15,000 in 1900 to 88,000 in 1910, and by 1917 almost 99 percent of the 140,000 operators were women.

Even with these changes, few married women worked outside of the home (only about 10 percent in 1910), and the mid-nineteenth-century image of the "ideal woman" concerned only with domestic matters still persisted. But even women confined to the home were becoming more active in society at large, and they found a voice through women's clubs and societies, which created the General Federation of Women's Clubs in 1889. By 1910 the federation had a membership of over one million, and it joined with other organizations in calling for child labor legislation, Prohibition, and women's suffrage. . . .

Whatever their social background or motivation, it is clear that women and their organizations not only shared many of the concerns of male reformers, but also did much to shape the movement that was to dominate national politics by 1912. In 1912 the Progressive influence was evident in both major parties and their platforms, and in the presence of Socialist and Prohibitionist presidential candidates. However, the clearest reflection of the reform impulse was in the formation of the separate Progressive party from among insurgent Republicans led first by Robert M. La Follette, and then by Theodore Roosevelt. But before that point was reached the Progressives had already achieved much at both the local and national level, and in doing so had created the base for a national political organization.

From about 1900 on, reformers took control in a number of city and state governments. La Follette was a leading example, turning Wisconsin into what Roosevelt described as a "laboratory of democracy," which was copied from Oregon and California through to Minnesota, Iowa, Ohio, New Jersey, New York, and many other states. As governor from 1900, and then as senator from 1906, La Follette could claim responsibility for the democratization of state politics in Wisconsin, the improvement of government and civil service organization, the reform of the education system, the introduction of child and female labor laws, and public health and pure food laws, the regulation and control of the railroads, and the implementation of income tax and inheritance tax. Similar programs were enacted elsewhere, and by 1914 over twenty-five states had some form of workmen's compensation provision, and over forty had child labor laws or laws regulating women's work. A number of states had pension schemes of one sort or another (although most mainly had widow's pensions), and, following the British example of 1911, consideration was being given to proposals for unemployment insurance in a number of states. Reform was not confined to state level—"Scarcely a major city in the nation escaped the municipal reform wave." From San Francisco to Galveston, from Cleveland and Toledo to New York, city managers were introduced, civil service departments were shaken up and improved, and new departments were established to deal with urban developments, parks, police, fire, water, safety, and public hygiene. It was in eastern city government as an assemblyman and as police commissioner of New York City, that Theodore Roosevelt was to gain his political experience before becoming assistant secretary of the navy and then governor of New York in 1898.

. . . Roosevelt was nominated as the vice-presidential candidate by Republican party managers in order to limit his influence. However, the gamble misfired, and, following the assassination of President McKinley by an anarchist in Buffalo, Roosevelt, "that damned cowboy," according to party organizer Mark Hanna, became president in 1901. Reelected in his own right with a landslide majority in 1904, Roosevelt was to provide the Progressive movement with a national leader and to begin the program of federal reform.

From the start, the ebullient Roosevelt made it clear that he would be an active president who intended to assert executive authority, particularly in the industrial and economic sphere. He was responsible for the revitalization of the Sherman Anti-trust Act of 1890, and in 1902 he encouraged his attorney general to file a suit against the newly formed combination of railroads owned by Morgan, Rockefeller, and others, the Northern Securities Company. As a result, the company was ordered to dissolve in 1904. This attack on excessive business monopoly continued with a further forty-three suits against other trusts, and, in a related act of 1903, Roosevelt established the Department of Commerce and Labor, with The Bureau of Corporations to investigate business organization and practice. The Elkins Act of 1903 and the Hepburn Act of 1906 forbade certain practices on the railroads, such as hidden rebates, and increased the power of the Interstate Commerce Commission to regulate charges. These various pieces of legislation, together with the Pure Food and Drug Act and the Meat Inspection Act of 1906 (the latter inspired in part by [Upton] Sinclair's *The Jungle*), did much to create Roosevelt's "trust-busting," antibusiness reputation. In reality, however, these measures were not as far-reaching as some Progressives like La Follette would have wished. In most cases the final acts were compromises, with limitations in their administration, requirements, and penalties. They were, though, important precedents, and they were indicative of a new approach to government and to business.

Equally important precedents were set in the area of land conservation and labor policy. Roosevelt, an avid naturalist and at heart a westerner, supported his chief forester, Gifford Pinchot, in withdrawing millions of acres from possible private use and exploitation in order to conserve and develop the nation's natural resources. Land reclamation and irrigation programs were introduced with the Newlands Act of 1904, and conservation was brought fully to the public's attention with the White House Conference of 1908. Once again, the achievements of Congress were few, but as a publicist Roosevelt directed attention and provided leadership in a vital aspect of the country's life. This was also the case with his intervention in the mining dispute of 1902 when, acting in the public interest as he saw it, Roosevelt intervened, as no previous president had ever done, to bring the conflict to a conclusion. In this case Roosevelt appeared sympathetic to the workers—the miners won a 10 percent raise—but this did not stop the mine owners and other employers denying union recognition, nor did it prevent the Supreme Court decisions in 1905 and 1908 that respectively invalidated maximum-hour laws and allowed the Sherman Anti-trust Act to be applied to unions. However, in his final annual address in 1908 Roosevelt pointed to these and other areas in which legislation was still required. He then went off to hunt lions in Africa. When he returned to the presidential campaign trail as the candidate of the Progressive party four years later, it was on a platform that included equal suffrage, legislation to prevent industrial accidents, to reduce working hours, prohibit child labor and women's night work, to provide for minimum wages, and to introduce social insurance, as well as further regulation of the corporations. . . .

The election of 1912 was remarkable because all parties could claim to be for some degree of reform, but the division in the Republican party ensured the election of the Democratic candidate, Woodrow Wilson. Although himself a "reformer" while governor of New Jersey, there were considerable differences between Wilson's brand of progressivism and that of Roosevelt. Roosevelt increasingly accepted business monopoly as a feature of modern life, but he stressed the positive role of a strong federal government acting as a regulating or countervailing force. Influenced by Herbert Croly's *Promise of American Life* (1909), Roosevelt described his philosophy as a "New Nationalism" of "government supervision . . . of all corporations," with the president acting as "the steward of the public welfare." In his campaign he clearly moved toward the idea of a protective welfare state. Woodrow Wilson's "New Freedom" was much more conservative. As a southerner, the new president was strongly influenced by states' rights; as a staunch Presbyterian he expected men to be governed by moral law. In principle, Wilson wished to restore the laissez-faire system in which men were free from *both* the domination of the trusts *and* from government controls, and in which all men were free to compete equally. He was, he said, for "the men who are on the make rather than the men who are already made."

The first act of the New Freedom was the massive reduction of protective tariffs in 1913 and the replacement of lost revenue with the introduction of an income tax. The Federal Reserve Act the same year prevented the buildup of a bank trust and provided for federal regulation without a central national bank. The Farm Loan Act of 1916 provided long-term loans at low cost and met a long-held demand of the Populists to counter exploitive banking. Regulation of business continued too: more than eighty antitrust suits were launched, and the Clayton Anti-trust Act of 1914 specified those business practices regarded as unfair. The creation of the Federal Trade Commission in 1914 enabled the investigation of business and the examination of some two thousand malpractice complaints. However, the powers of the commission were limited by the appointment of weak officials, and fewer than four hundred cease-and-desist orders were issued as the body increasingly became "a counsellor and friend of the business world," rather than its adversary. In 1916, to ensure Progressive support in an election year, Wilson moved left and began to implement some of the Progressive party's proposals for social reform. That year witnessed the passage, with presidential support, of the Child Labor Bill, the Workmen's Compensation Act (for federal civil servants), and the Adamson Eight Hour Act (establishing the eight-hour day for rail workers engaged in interstate commerce, and so averting a threatened national strike). According to leading historian, Arthur Link, Wilson and the Democrats had enacted every important plank of the Progressive platform of 1912 by the end of the year, and, as the president and American people became preoccupied with foreign affairs, the drive for reform came to a halt.

Although "presidential progressivism" may have ended, the movement for reform was to continue for some time at the lower levels. Main concerns of progressivism—women's suffrage, Prohibition, immigration, the "problem" of the cities—were to find their resolution either during the war years or in their immediate aftermath, and new concerns and issues were also to arise. Nonetheless, for a variety of reasons the movement did change after 1917, and an assessment of its achievements before America entered the world war is in order.

Progressivism's prewar accomplishments are, of course, the subject of some historical debate. Certainly, when compared with developments in Britain or Germany, where the foundations of modern welfare states had been laid in the form of national insurance plans, old-age pensions, educational reform, and progressive taxation schemes, then American reform had not gone very far. In fact, the legislation passed may have served to satisfy the popular demand for reform, but in reality it left basic social and economic patterns largely unchanged. Class relationships were hardly altered, the distribution of wealth remained uneven, workers' organizations were hardly more secure, nor had the power of business been much affected, as the Ludlow massacre of 1914 clearly revealed. The reasons for these shortcomings are not hard to find: the federal system of government and effects of different regional interests; the division of political authority given the checks and balances of the American system; the entrenched power of conservative political and economic elites in Congress and in the Supreme Court; the racial and ethnic divisions of the population; and above all, the persistence of values based on individualism and independence. . . .

Judged against that context, and in terms of the early twentieth century rather than more recent times, then progressivism was not necessarily a failure. Even the most deep-seated of American values had been modified to some extent. The tensions introduced by rapid industrial and urban development and the clear evidence of physical, economic, and social change had forced the American people to act in order to preserve traditional institutions and standards. The result was the revitalization of government at all levels and the acceptance of an enlarged role for central government, and particularly for the national executive, in an attempt to ensure a more efficient and equitable society. By 1916 Roosevelt and Wilson had both successively shifted the balance of political power in favor of the presidency and, emphasizing the paramount importance of the public rather than the individual good, had committed government to a positive interventionist policy. If the rich were not stripped of their wealth, they were at least made aware of the poor and forced to accept some responsibility for them; if industrialists could still combine to wield enormous power and influence, competition was now at least partially regulated, and the employers had to consider the rights and welfare of both their workers and consumers; if men still exercised all economic and political power, women now insisted on being heard and were accorded some recognition; if politics was still dominated by an elite, there were new groups to be reckoned with, and there was a greater public accountability and the opportunity for general political involvement. Although this might not add up to the revolution some historians have claimed took place in this period, it was by no means insignificant.

Neil A. Wynn is a professor of twentieth-century American history at the University of Gloucestershire. He also is the author of *The Afro-American and the Second World War* (Holmes & Meier, 1976, 1993) and is coeditor of *Transatlantic Roots Music: Folk, Blues, and National Identity* (University Press of Mississippi, 2012).

Richard M. Abrams

 **NO**

The Failure of Progressivism

Our first task is definitional, because clearly it would be possible to beg the whole question of "failure" by means of semantical niceties. I have no intention of being caught in that kind of critics' trap. I hope to establish that there was a distinctive major reform movement that took place during most of the first two decades of this century, that it had a mostly coherent set of characteristics and long-term objectives, and that, measured by its own criteria—not criteria I should wish, through hindsight and preference, to impose on it—it fell drastically short of its chief goals.

One can, of course, define a reform movement so broadly that merely to acknowledge that we are where we are and that we enjoy some advantages over where we were would be to prove the "success" of the movement. In many respects, Arthur Link does this sort of thing, both in his and William B. Catton's popular textbook, *American Epoch,* and in his article, "What Happened to the Progressive Movement in the 1920s?" In the latter, Link defines "progressivism" as a movement that "began convulsively in the 1890s and waxed and waned afterward to our own time, to insure the survival of democracy in the United States by the enlargement of governmental power to control and offset the power of private economic groups over the nation's institutions and life." Such a definition may be useful to classify data gathered to show the liberal sources of the enlargement of governmental power since the 1890s; but such data would not be finely classified enough to tell us much about the *non*-liberal sources of governmental power (which were numerous and important), about the distinctive styles of different generations of reformers concerned with a liberal society, or even about vital distinctions among divergent reform groups in the era that contemporaries and the conventional historical wisdom have designated as progressive. . . .

Now, without going any further into the problem of historians' definitions which are too broad or too narrow—there is no space here for such an effort—I shall attempt a definition of my own, beginning with the problem that contemporaries set themselves to solve and that gave the era its cognomen, "progressive." That problem was *progress*—or more specifically, how American society was to continue to enjoy the fruits of material progress without the accompanying assault upon human dignity and the erosion of the conventional values and moral assumptions on which the social order appeared to rest. . . .

To put it briefly and yet more specifically, a very large body of men and women entered into reform activities at the end of the nineteenth century to translate "the national credo" (as Henry May calls it) into a general program for social action. Their actions, according to Richard Hofstadter, were "founded upon the indigenous Yankee-Protestant political tradition [that] assumed and demanded the constant disinterested activity of the citizen in public affairs, argued that political life ought to be run, to a greater degree than it was, in accordance with general principles and abstract laws apart from and superior to personal needs, and expressed a common feeling that government should be in good part an effort to moralize the lives of individuals while economic life should be intimately related to the stimulation and development of individual character."

The most consistently important reform impulse, among many reform impulses, during the progressive era grew directly from these considerations. It is this reform thrust that we should properly call "the progressive movement." We should distinguish it carefully from reform movements in the era committed primarily to other considerations.

The progressive movement drew its strength from the old mugwump reform impulse, civil service reform, female emancipationists, prohibitionists, the social gospel, the settlement-house movement, some national expansionists, some world peace advocates, conservation advocates, technical efficiency experts, and a wide variety of intellectuals who helped cut through the stifling, obstructionist smokescreen of systematized ignorance. It gained powerful allies from many disadvantaged business interests that appealed to politics to redress unfavorable trade positions; from some ascendant business interests seeking institutional protection; from publishers who discovered the promotional value of exposes; and from politicians-on-the-make who sought issues with which to dislodge long-lived incumbents from their place. Objectively it focused on or expressed (1) a concern for responsive, honest, and efficient government, on the local and state levels especially; (2) recognition of the obligations of society—particularly of an affluent society—to its underprivileged; (3) a desire for more rational use of the nation's resources and economic energies; (4) a rejection, on at least intellectual grounds, of certain social principles that had long obstructed social remedies for what had traditionally been regarded as irremediable evils, such as poverty; and, above all, (5) a concern for the maintenance or restoration of a consensus on what conventionally had been regarded as *fixed moral* principles. "The first and central faith in the national credo," writes Professor May, "was, as it always had been, the reality, certainty, and eternity of moral values. . . . A few thought and said that ultimate values and goals were unnecessary, but in most cases this meant that they believed so deeply in a consensus on these matters that they could not imagine a serious challenge." Progressives shared this faith with most of the rest of the country, but they also conceived of themselves, with a grand sense of stewardship, as its heralds, and its agents.

The progressive movement was (and is) distinguishable from other contemporary reform movements not only by its devotion to social conditions regarded, by those within it as well as by much of the generality, as *normative,* but also by its definition of what forces threatened that order. More specifically, progressivism directed its shafts at five principal enemies, each in its own way representing reform:

1. The *socialist reform movement*—because, despite socialism's usually praiseworthy concern for human dignity, it represented the subordination of the rights of private property and of individualistic options to objectives that often explicitly threatened common religious beliefs and conventional standards of justice and excellence.
2. The corporate reorganization of American business, which I should call the *corporate reform movement* (its consequence has, after all, been called "the corporate revolution")—because it challenged the traditional relationship of ownership and control of private property, because it represented a shift from production to profits in the entrepreneurial definition of efficiency, because it threatened the proprietary small-business character of the American social structure, because it had already demonstrated a capacity for highly concentrated and socially irresponsible power, and because it sanctioned practices that strained the limits of conventionality and even legality.
3. *The labor union movement*—because despite the virtues of unionized labor as a source of countervailing force against the corporations and as a basis for a more orderly labor force, unionism (like corporate capitalism and socialism) suggested a reduction of individualistic options (at least for wage-earners and especially for small employers), and a demand for a partnership with business management in the decision-making process by a class that convention excluded from such a role.
4. *Agrarian radicalism,* and populism in particular—because it, too, represented (at least in appearance) the insurgency of a class conventionally believed to be properly excluded from a policy-making role in the society, a class graphically represented by the "Pitchfork" Bens and "Sockless" Jerrys, the "Cyclone" Davises and "Alfalfa" Bills, the wool hat brigade and the rednecks.
5. *The ethnic movement*—the demand for specific political and social recognition of ethnic or ex-national affiliations—because accession to the demand meant acknowledgment of the fragmentation of American society as well as a retreat from official standards of integrity, honesty, and efficiency in government in favor of standards based on personal loyalty, partisanship, and sectarian provincialism.

Probably no two progressives opposed all of these forces with equal animus, and most had a noteworthy sympathy for one or more of them. . . .

So much for what progressivism was not. Let me sum it up by noting that what it rejected and sought to oppose necessarily says much about what it was—perhaps even more than can be ascertained by the more direct approach.

My thesis is that progressivism failed. It failed in what it—or what those who shaped it—conceived to be its principal objective. And that was, over and above everything else, to restore or maintain the conventional consensus on a particular view of the universe, a particular set of values, and a particular constellation of behavioral modes in the country's commerce, its industry, its social relations, and its politics. Such a view, such values, such modes were challenged by the influx of diverse religious and ethnic elements into the nation's social and intellectual stream, by the overwhelming economic success and power of the corporate form of business organization, by the subordination of the work-ethic bound up within the old proprietary and craft enterprise system, and by the increasing centrality of a growing proportion of low-income, unskilled, wage-earning classes in the nation's economy and social structure. Ironically, the *coup de grâce* would be struck by the emergence of a philosophical and scientific rationale for the existence of cultural diversity within a single social system, a rationale that largely grew out of the very intellectual ferment to which progressivism so substantially contributed.

Progressivism sought to save the old view, and the old values and modes, by educating the immigrants and the poor so as to facilitate their acceptance of and absorption into the Anglo-American mode of life, or by excluding the "unassimilable" altogether; by instituting antitrust legislation or, at the least, by imposing regulations upon corporate practices in order to preserve a minimal base for small proprietary business enterprise; by making legislative accommodations to the newly important wage-earning classes—accommodations that might provide some measure of wealth and income redistribution, on-the-job safety, occupational security, and the like—so as to forestall a forcible transfer of policy-making power away from the groups that had conventionally exercised that power; and by broadening the political selection process, through direct elections, direct nominations, and direct legislation, in order to reduce tensions caused unnecessarily by excessively narrow and provincial cliques of policymakers. When the economic and political reforms failed to restore the consensus by giving the previously unprivileged an ostensible stake in it, progressive energies turned increasingly toward using the force of the state to proscribe or restrict specifically opprobrious modes of social behavior, such as gaming habits, drinking habits, sexual habits, and Sabbatarian habits. In the ultimate resort, with the proliferation of sedition and criminal syndicalist laws, it sought to constrict political discourse itself. And (except perhaps for the disintegration of the socialist movement) *that* failed, too.

One measure of progressivism's failure lies in the xenophobic racism that reappeared on a large scale even by 1910. In many parts of the country, for example, in the far west and the south, racism and nativism had been fully blended with reform movements even at the height of progressive activities there. The alleged threats of "coolie labor" to American living standards, and of "venal" immigrant and Negro voting to republican institutions

generally, underlay the alliance of racism and reform in this period. By and large, however, for the early progressive era the alliance was conspicuous only in the south and on the west coast. By 1910, signs of heightening ethnic animosities, most notably anti-Catholicism, began appearing in other areas of the country as well. As John Higham has written, "It is hard to explain the rebirth of anti-Catholic ferment [at this time] except as an outlet for expectations which progressivism raised and then failed to fulfill." The failure here was in part the inability of reform to deliver a meaningful share of the social surplus to the groups left out of the general national progress, and in part the inability of reform to achieve its objective of assimilation and consensus.

The growing ethnic animus, moreover, operated to compound the difficulty of achieving assimilation. By the second decade of the century, the objects of the antagonism were beginning to adopt a frankly assertive posture. The World War, and the ethnic cleavages it accentuated and aggravated, represented only the final blow to the assimilationist idea; "hyphenate" tendencies had already been growing during the years before 1914. It had only been in 1905 that the Louisville-born and secular-minded Louis Brandeis had branded as "disloyal" all who "keep alive" their differences of origin or religion. By 1912, by now a victim of anti-Semitism and aware of a rising hostility toward Jews in the country, Brandeis had become an active Zionist; before a Jewish audience in 1913, he remarked how "practical experience" had convinced him that "to be good Americans, we must be better Jews, and to be better Jews, we must become Zionists."

Similarly, American Negroes also began to adopt a more aggressive public stance after having been subdued for more than a decade by antiblack violence and the accommodationist tactics suggested in 1895 by Booker T. Washington. As early as 1905, many black leaders had broken with Washington in founding the Niagara Movement for a more vigorous assertion of Negro demands for equality. But most historians seem to agree that it was probably the Springfield race riot of 1908 that ended illusions that black people could gain an equitable share in the rewards of American culture by accommodationist or assimilationist methods. The organization of the NAACP in 1909 gave substantive force for the first time to the three-year-old Niagara Movement. The year 1915 symbolically concluded the demise of accommodationism. That year, the Negro-baiting movie, "The Birth of a Nation," played to massive, enthusiastic audiences that included notably the president of the United States and the chief justice of the Supreme Court; the KKK was revived; and Booker T. Washington died. The next year, black nationalist Marcus Garvey arrived in New York from Jamaica.

Meanwhile, scientific knowledge about race and culture was undergoing a crucial revision. At least in small part stimulated by a keen self-consciousness of his own "outsider" status in American culture, the German-Jewish immigrant Franz Boas was pioneering in the new anthropological concept of "cultures," based on the idea that human behavioral traits are conditioned by historical traditions. The new view of culture was in time to undermine completely the prevailing evolutionary view that ethnic differences must mean racial inequality. The significance of Boas's work after 1910, and that of his students A. L. Kroeber and Clyde Kluckhohn in particular, rests on the fact that the racist thought of the progressive era had founded its intellectual rationale on the monistic, evolutionary view of culture; and indeed much of the progressives' anxiety over the threatened demise of "the American culture" had been founded on that view.

Other intellectual developments as well had for a long time been whittling away at the notion that American society had to stand or fall on the unimpaired coherence of its cultural consensus. Yet the new work in anthropology, law, philosophy, physics, psychology, and literature only unwittingly undermined that assumption. Rather, it was only as the ethnic hostilities grew, and especially as the power of the state came increasingly to be invoked against dissenting groups whose ethnic "peculiarities" provided an excuse for repression, that the new intelligence came to be developed. "The world has thought that it must have its culture and its political unity coincide," wrote Randolph Bourne in 1916 while chauvinism, nativism, and antiradicalism were mounting; now it was seeing that cultural diversity might yet be the salvation of the liberal society—that it might even serve to provide the necessary countervailing force to the power of the state that private property had once served (in the schema of Locke, Harrington, and Smith) before the interests of private property became so highly concentrated and so well blended with the state itself.

The telltale sign of progressivism's failure was the violent crusade against dissent that took place in the closing years of the Wilson administration. It is too easy to ascribe the literal hysteria of the postwar years to the dislocations of the War alone. Incidents of violent repression of labor and radical activities had been growing remarkably, often in step with xenophobic outbreaks, for several years before America's intervention in the War. To quote Professor Higham once more. "The seemingly

unpropitious circumstances under which antiradicalism and anti-Catholicism came to life [after 1910] make their renewal a subject of moment." It seems clear that they both arose out of the sources of the reform ferment itself. When reform failed to enlarge the consensus, or to make it more relevant to the needs of the still disadvantaged and disaffected, and when in fact reform seemed to be encouraging more radical challenges to the social order, the old anxieties of the 1890s returned.

The postwar hysteria represented a reaction to a confluence of anxiety-laden developments, including the high cost of living, the physical and social dislocations of war mobilization and the recruitment of women and Negroes into war production jobs in the big northern cities, the Bolshevik Revolution, a series of labor strikes, and a flood of radical literature that exaggerated the capabilities of radical action. "One Hundred Per Cent Americanism" seemed the only effective way of meeting all these challenges at once. As Stanley Coben has written, making use of recent psychological studies and anthropological work on cultural "revitalization movements"; "Citizens who joined the crusade for one hundred per cent Americanism sought, primarily, a unifying forte which would halt the apparent disintegration of their culture. . . . The slight evidence of danger from radical organizations aroused such wild fear only because Americans had already encountered other threats to cultural stability."

Now, certainly during the progressive era a lot of reform legislation was passed, much that contributed genuinely to a more liberal society, though more that contributed to the more absolutistic moral objectives of progressivism. Progressivism indeed had real, lasting effects for the blunting of the sharper edges of self-interest in American life, and for the reduction of the harsher cruelties suffered by the society's underprivileged. These achievements deserve emphasis, not least because they derived directly from the progressive habit of looking to standards of conventional morality and human decency for the solution of diverse social conflicts. But the deeper nature of the problem confronting American society required more than the invocation of conventional standards; the conventions themselves were at stake, especially as they bore upon the allocation of privileges and rewards. Because most of the progressives never confronted that problem, in a way their efforts were doomed to failure.

In sum, the overall effect of the period's legislation is not so impressive. For example, all the popular government measures put together have not conspicuously raised the quality of American political life. Direct nominations and elections have tended to make political campaigns so expensive as to reduce the number of eligible candidates for public office to (1) the independently wealthy; (2) the ideologues, especially on the right, who can raise the needed campaign money from independently wealthy ideologues like themselves, or from the organizations set up to promote a particular ideology; and (3) party hacks who pay off their debt to the party treasury by whistle-stopping and chicken dinner speeches. Direct legislation through the Initiative and Referendum device has made cities and states prey to the best-financed and organized special-interest group pressures, as have so-called nonpartisan elections. Which is not to say that things are worse than before, but only that they are not conspicuously better. The popular government measures did have the effect of shaking up the established political organizations of the day, and that may well have been their only real purpose.

But as Arthur Link has said, in his text, *The American Epoch,* the popular government measures "were merely instruments to facilitate the capture of political machinery. . . . They must be judged for what they accomplished or failed to accomplish on the higher level of substantive reform." Without disparaging the long list of reform measures that passed during the progressive era, the question remains whether all the "substantive reforms" together accomplished what the progressives wanted them to accomplish.

Certain social and economic advantages were indeed shuffled about, but this must be regarded as a short-term achievement for special groups at best. Certain commercial interests, for example, achieved greater political leverage in railroad policy-making than they had had in 1900 through measures such as the Hepburn and Mann-Elkins Acts—though it was not until the 1940s that any real change occurred in the general rate structure, as some broad regional interests had been demanding at the beginning of the century. Warehouse, farm credits, and land-bank acts gave the diminishing numbers of farm owners enhanced opportunities to mortgage their property, and some business groups had persuaded the federal government to use national revenues to educate farmers on how to increase their productivity (Smith-Lever Act, 1914); but most farmers remained as dependent as ever upon forces beyond their control—the bankers, the middlemen, the international market. The FTC, and the Tariff Commission established in 1916, extended the principle of using government agencies to adjudicate intra-industrial conflicts ostensibly in the national interest, but these agencies would develop a lamentable tendency of deferring to and even confirming rather than moderating the power of each industry's dominant interests.

The Federal Reserve Act made the currency more flexible, and that certainly made more sense than the old system, as even the bankers agreed. But depositers would be as prey to defaulting banks as they had been in the days of the Pharaoh—bank deposit insurance somehow was "socialism" to even the best of men in this generation. And despite Woodrow Wilson's brave promise to end the banker's stifling hold on innovative small business, one searches in vain for some provision in the FRA designed specifically to encourage small or new businesses. In fact, the only constraints on the bankers' power that emerged from the era came primarily from the ability of the larger corporations to finance their own expansion out of capital surpluses they had accumulated from extortionate profits during the War.

A major change almost occurred during the war years when organized labor and the principle of collective bargaining received official recognition and a handful of labor leaders was taken, temporarily, into policy-making councils (e.g., in the War Labor Board). But actually, as already indicated, such a development, if it had been made permanent, would have represented a defeat, not a triumph, for progressivism. The progressives may have fought for improved labor conditions, but they jealously fought against the enlargement of union power. It was no aberration that once the need for wartime productive efficiency evaporated, leading progressives such as A. Mitchell Palmer, Miles Poindexter, and Woodrow Wilson himself helped civic and employer organizations to bludgeon the labor movement into disunity and docility. (It is possible, I suppose, to argue that such progressives were simply inconsistent, but if we understand progressivism in the terms I have outlined above I think the consistency is more evident.) Nevertheless, a double irony is worth noting with respect to progressivism's objectives and the wartime labor developments. On the one hand, the progressives' hostility to labor unions defeated their own objectives of (1) counterbalancing the power of collectivized capital (i.e., corporations), and (2) enhancing workers' share of the nation's wealth. On the other hand, under wartime duress, the progressives did grant concessions to organized labor (e.g., the Adamson Eight-Hour Railway Labor Act, as well as the WLB) that would later serve as precedents for the very "collectivization" of the economic situation that they were dedicated to oppose.

Meanwhile, the distribution of advantages in the society did not change much at all. In some cases, from the progressive reformers' viewpoint at least, it may even have changed for the worse. According to the figures of the National Industrial Conference Board, even income was as badly distributed at the end of the era as before. In 1921, the highest 10 percent of income recipients received 38 percent of total personal income, and that figure was only 34 percent in 1910. (Since the share of the top 5 percent of income recipients probably declined in the 1910–20 period, the figures for the top 10 percent group suggest a certain improvement in income distribution at the top. But the fact that the share of the lowest 60 percent also declined in that period, from 35 percent to 30 percent, confirms the view that no meaningful improvement can be shown.) Maldistribution was to grow worse until after 1929.

American farmers on the whole and in particular seemed to suffer increasing disadvantages. Farm life was one of the institutional bulwarks of the mode of life the progressives ostensibly cherished. "The farmer who owns his land" averred Gifford Pinchot, "is still the backbone of the Nation; and one of the things we want most is more of him, . . . [for] he is the first of home-makers." If only in the sense that there were relatively fewer farmers in the total population at the end of the progressive era, one would have to say farm life in the United States had suffered. But, moreover, fewer owned their own farms. The number of farm tenants increased by 21 percent from 1900 to 1920; 38.1 percent of all farm operators in 1921 were tenants; and the figures look even worse when one notices that tenancy *declined* in the most *impoverished* areas during this period, suggesting that the family farm was surviving mostly in the more marginal agricultural areas. Finally, although agriculture had enjoyed some of its most prosperous years in history in the 1910–20 period, the 21 percent of the nation's gainfully employed who were in agriculture in 1919 (a peak year) earned only 16 percent of the national income.

While progressivism failed to restore vitality to American farming, it failed also to stop the vigorous ascendancy of corporate capitalism, the most conspicuous challenge to conventional values and modes that the society faced at the beginning of the era. The corporation had drastically undermined the very basis of the traditional rationale that had supported the nation's freewheeling system of resource allocation and had underwritten the permissiveness of the laws governing economic activities in the nineteenth century. The new capitalism bypassed the privately owned proprietary firm, it featured a separation of ownership and control, it subordinated the profit motive to varied and variable other objectives such as empire-building, and, in many of the techniques developed by financial brokers and investment bankers, it appeared to create a great gulf between the making of money and the producing of useful goods and services. Through a remarkable series of judicial sophistries, this nonconventional form of business enterprise had become, in law, a person, and had won privileges and liberties once entrusted only to men, who were presumed to be conditioned and restrained by the moral qualities that inhere in human nature. Although gaining legal dispensations from an obliging Supreme Court, the corporation could claim no theoretical legitimacy beyond the fact of its power and its apparent inextricable entanglement in the business order that had produced America's seemingly unbounded material success.

Although much has been written about the supposed continuing vitality of small proprietary business enterprise in the United States, there is no gainsaying the continued ascendancy of the big corporation nor the fact that it still lacks legitimation. The fact that in the last sixty years the number of small proprietary businesses has grown at a rate that slightly exceeds the rate of population growth says little about the character of small business enterprise today as compared with that of the era of the American industrial revolution; it does nothing to disparage the apprehensions expressed in the antitrust campaigns of the progressives. To focus on the vast numbers of automobile dealers and gasoline service station owners, for example, is to miss completely their truly humble dependence upon the very few giant automobile and oil companies, a foretold dependence that was the very point of progressives' anticorporation, antitrust sentiments. The progressive movement must indeed be credited with placing real restraints upon monopolistic tendencies in the United States, for most statistics indicate that at least until the 1950s business concentration showed no substantial increase from the turn of the century (though it may be pertinent to note that concentration ratios did increase significantly in the decade immediately following the progressive era). But the statistics of concentration remain impressive—just as they were when John Moody wrote *The Truth About the Trusts* in 1904 and Louis Brandeis followed it with *Other People's Money* in 1914. That two hundred corporations (many of them interrelated) held almost one-quarter of all business assets, and more than 40 percent of all corporate assets in the country in 1948; that the fifty largest manufacturing corporations held 35 percent of all industrial assets in 1948, and 38 percent by 1962; and that a mere twenty-eight corporations or one one-thousandth of a percentage of all nonfinancial firms in 1956 employed 10 percent of all those employed in the nonfinancial industries, should be sufficient statistical support for the apprehensions of the progressive era—*just as it is testimony to the failure of the progressive movement to achieve anything substantial to alter the situation.*

Perhaps the crowning failure of progressivism was the American role in World War I. It is true that many progressives opposed America's intervention, but it is also true that a great many more supported it. The failure in progressivism lies not in the decision to intervene but in the futility of intervention measured by progressive expectations. It is . . . clear from the biographical masterwork on Wilson that Arthur Link [completed] that nothing was quite so important in shaping the Wilson policies toward Germany as Wilson's commitment to the Anglo-American system of values by which he defined "civilization." Wilson's decision to intervene ultimately rested . . . not only on his unwillingness to see England defeated but on his desire to make certain that America would have a major decision-making role at the peace table—where it could help shape the world according to the same principles of stewardship that guided the Wilsonian program at home. . . .

The inability of progressive reform to solve the problems of a society driven by industrial alienation, by the community-dissolving experience of the industrial process, by the convention-defying influence of massive immigration, by the faith-shattering impact of modern science, and the by consensus-destroying effect of rival nationalisms at war, helps us to understand the estrangement from all causes and social purpose that seems to have characterized the generation of Americans that came out of the War era. . . .

For younger men, such as F. Scott Fitzgerald, who were just emerging from college, it seemed that they had come on the scene "with all gods dead, with all wars fought, with all faiths shaken." For progressives, the god that was dead was the one that had made them "stewards" of the people; the faith that was shaken was what had given them the criteria upon which they could confidently assert their definition of the "general interest"; and the war (to end all wars) that had been fought—to make the world safe for democracy—had been a mockery, an exercise in futility, a grand illusion, especially because even the object no longer had the hallowed shimmer they thought they had perceived.

RICHARD M. ABRAMS is a professor of history emeritus and associate director of international and area studies at the University of California, Berkeley, where he has been teaching for 47 years. He has been a Fulbright professor in both London and Moscow and has taught and lectured in many countries throughout the world, including China, Austria, Norway, Italy, Japan, Germany, and Australia. He has published numerous articles in history, business, and law journals, and he is the editor of *The Shaping of Twentieth Century America: Interpretive Essays*, 2nd ed. (Little, Brown, 1971) and the author of *The Burdens of Progress* (Scott, Foresman, 1978). His most recent book is *America Transformed: Sixty Years of Revolutionary Change, 1941–2001* (Cambridge University Press, 2006).

EXPLORING THE ISSUE

Did the Progressives Succeed?

Critical Thinking and Reflection

1. State in one or two sentences Abrams' definition of progressivism. Discuss who joined the movement, what the reformers' philosophical principles were, and who the movement's five principal enemies were.
2. Critically examine those areas where Abrams says progressivism blunted "the sharper edges of self-interest in American life, and the harsher cruelties suffered by the society's underprivileged."
3. Critically analyze the reasons why the progressives failed to achieve their goals, according to both Wynn and Abrams. In your answer consider:
   a. The progressives relied on natural science and social science reforms.
   b. The progressives had deep ambivalence about industrialism and its consequences.
   c. The progressives never came to grips with the real conflicts of American society.
4. In the introductory essay to the issue, Professor Wynn among others argues that the problems faced by the progressives have continued to challenge Americans. Discuss what they mean by this. Do you agree? Why, or why not?
5. Compare and contrast the successes of progressivism (Wynn) with its failures (Abrams). Point out areas where the authors are in agreement and areas where they totally disagree.

Is There Common Ground?

In spite of their differences, both Abrams's and Wynn's interpretations make concessions to their respective critics. Wynn, for example, admits that the intended reforms did not necessarily produce the desired results. Furthermore, the authors concede that many reformers were insensitive to the cultural values of the lower classes and attempted to impose middle-class Protestant ways on the urban masses. Nevertheless, Wynn argues that in spite of the failure to curb the growth of big business, the progressive reforms did ameliorate the worst abuses of the new urban industrial society. Although the progressives failed to solve all the major problems of their times, they did set the agenda that still challenges the reformers of today.

Abrams also makes a concession to his critics when he admits that "progressivism had real lasting effects for the blunting of the sharper edges of self-interest in American life, and for the reduction of the harsher cruelties suffered by the society's underprivileged." Yet the thrust of his argument is that the progressive reformers accomplished little of value. While Abrams probably agrees with Wynn that the progressives were the first group to confront the problems of modern America, he considers their intended reforms inadequate by their very nature. Wynn believes that Americans were unable to achieve the foundations of the welfare state accomplished by Great Britain or Germany because of the entrenched power of the conservative elites, the federal system of government, the racial and ethnic divisions of the population, a conservative labor movement, "and above all the persistence of values based on individualism and independence."

Additional Resources

Steven J. Diner, *A Very Different Age: Americans of the Progressive Era* (Hill and Wang, 1998)

Glenda Elizabeth Gilmore, ed., *Who Were the Progressives?* (Bedford/St. Martin's, 2002)

Lewis L. Gould, *America in the Progressive Era* (Routledge, 2001)

Michael McGeer, *A Fierce Discontent: The Rise and Fall of the Progressive Movement in America* (Oxford University Press, 2003)

Robert H. Wiebe, *The Search for Order: 1877–1920* (Hill and Wang, 1967)

Internet References . . .

Gilded Age and Progressive Era Resources

www.2.tntech.edu/history/gilprog.html

Theodore Roosevelt Association

www.theodoreroosevelt.org

Woodrow Wilson Presidential Library

www.woodrowwilson.org

Selected, Edited, and with Issue Framing Material by:
Larry Madaras, *Howard Community College*
and
James M. SoRelle, *Baylor University*

ISSUE

Was Woodrow Wilson Responsible for the Failure of the United States to Join the League of Nations?

YES: **Thomas A. Bailey**, from "Woodrow Wilson Wouldn't Yield," in Alexander De Conde and Armin Rappaport, eds., *Essays Diplomatic and Undiplomatic of Thomas A. Bailey* (Appleton-Century-Crofts, 1969)

NO: **William G. Carleton**, from "A New Look at Woodrow Wilson," *The Virginia Quarterly Review* (Autumn 1962)

Learning Outcomes

After reading this issue, you will be able to:

- Discuss how Woodrow Wilson performed in various presidential roles.
- Distinguish between the realist approach and the idealist approach to foreign policy and evaluate whether Wilson was a realist or idealist.
- Determine whether Wilson was either psychologically or physically impaired during the treaty fight in the Senate.
- Conclude whether Wilson or Senator Henry Cabot Lodge killed the Treaty of Versailles.
- Determine whether Wilson was ahead of his times and American public opinion during the treaty fight.

ISSUE SUMMARY

YES: Thomas A. Bailey argues that a physically infirm Woodrow Wilson was unable to make the necessary compromises with the U. S. Senate to join the League of Nations and convince America that the United States should play a major role in world affairs.

NO: The late William G. Carleton believed that Woodrow Wilson understood better than any of his contemporaries the role that the United States would play in world affairs.

The presidential polls of Arthur Schlesinger in 1948 and 1962 as well as the 1983 Murray-Blessing poll have ranked Woodrow Wilson among the top 10 presidents. William Carleton considers him the greatest twentieth-century president, only two notches below Jefferson and Lincoln. Yet, among his biographers, Wilson has been treated ungenerously. They carp at him for being naïve, overly idealistic, and too inflexible. It appears that Wilson's biographers respect the man but do not like the person.

Wilson's own introspective personality may be partly to blame. He was, along with Jefferson and to some extent

Theodore Roosevelt, America's most intellectual president. He spent nearly 20 years as a history and political science teacher and scholar at Bryn Mawr, Wesleyan, and at his alma mater Princeton University. While his multivolume *History of the United States* appears dated as it gathers dust on musty library shelves, his PhD dissertation on Congressional Government, written as a graduate student at Johns Hopkins, remains a classic statement of the weakness of leadership in the American constitutional system.

There is one other reason why Wilson has been so critically analyzed by his biographers. Certainly, no president before or since has had less formal political experience than Wilson. Apparently, academic work does not constitute the proper training for the presidency. Yet, in addition to working many years as a college professor and a short stint as a lawyer, Wilson served eight distinguished years as the president of Princeton University. He turned it into one of the outstanding universities in the country. He introduced the preceptorial system, widely copied today, which supplemented course lectures with discussion conferences led by young instructors. He took the lead in reorganizing the university's curriculum. He lost two key battles. The alumni became upset when he tried to replace the class-ridden eating clubs with his "Quadrangle Plan," which would have established smaller colleges within the university system. What historians most remember about his Princeton career, however, was his losing fight with the Board of Trustees and Dean Andrew West concerning the location and eventual control over the new graduate school. Wilson resigned when it was decided to build a separate campus for the graduate school.

Shortly after Wilson left Princeton in 1910, he ran for governor of New Jersey and won his only political office before he became the president. As a governor, he gained control over the state Democratic Party and pushed through the legislature a litany of progressive measures—a primary elections law, a corrupt practices act, workmen's compensation, utilities regulation, school reforms, and an enabling act that allowed certain cities to adopt the commission form of government. When he was nominated on the 46th ballot at the Democratic convention in 1912, Wilson had enlarged the power of the governor's office in New Jersey and foreshadowed the way in which he would manage the presidency.

If one uses the standard categories of the late Professor Clinton Rossiter, Wilson ranks very high as a textbook president. No one, with the exception of Franklin Roosevelt and perhaps Ronald Reagan, performed the ceremonial role of the presidency as well as Wilson. His speeches rang with oratorical brilliance and substance. No wonder he abandoned the practice of Jefferson and his successors by delivering the president's annual State of the Union address to Congress in person rather than in writing.

During his first four years, he also fashioned a legislative program rivaled only by FDR's later "New Deal." The "New Freedom" pulled together conservative and progressive, rural and urban, as well as southern and northern Democrats in passing such measures as the Underwood-Simmons Tariff, the first bill to significantly lower tariff rates since the Civil War, and the Owens-Keating Child Labor Act. It was through Wilson's adroit maneuvering that the Federal Reserve System was established. This banking measure, the most significant in American history,

established the major agency that regulates money supply in the country today. Finally, President Wilson revealed his flexibility when he abandoned his initial policy of rigid and indiscriminate trust busting for one of regulating big business through the creation of the Federal Trade Commission.

More controversial were Wilson's presidential roles as commander-in-chief of the armed forces and chief diplomat. Some have argued that Wilson did not pay enough attention to strategic issues in the war, whereas other writers said he merged the proper dose of force and diplomacy. Thomas A. Bailey's *Woodrow Wilson and the Lost Peace* (Macmillan, 1944) and *Woodrow Wilson and the Great Betrayal* (Macmillan, 1945) were written as guidance for President Franklin Roosevelt to avoid the mistakes that Wilson made at home and abroad in his failure to gain ratification of the Treaty of Versailles. Specifically, Bailey blamed Wilson for failing to compromise with Republican senator Henry Cabot Lodge. Similarly, Wilson was the target of diplomat George F. Kennan whose chapter in *American Diplomacy, 1900–1950* (Mentor Books, 1951) protested vehemently about the "legalistic-moralistic" streak that he believed permeated Wilson's foreign policy. Scholars have criticized the realist approach to Wilson for a number of reasons. Some say that it is "unrealistic" to expect an American president to ask for a declaration of war to defend abstract principles such as the balance of power or the American national interest. Presidents and other elected officials must have a moral reason if they expect the American public to support a foreign war in which American servicemen might be killed. More recently, former Secretary of State Henry Kissinger, in his scholarly history *Diplomacy* (Simon & Schuster, 1994), insisted that Wilson was excessively moralistic and naïve in telling the American people that they were entering the war to "bring peace and safety to all nations and make the world itself at last free." Other realistic critics included influential journalist Walter Lippman and political scientists Robert Endicott Osgood and Hans Morgenthau. Osgood's study *Ideals and Self-Interest in American Foreign Relations* (University of Chicago Press, 1953) established the realist/idealist dichotomy later utilized by former Secretary of State Henry Kissinger in his scholarly history of *Diplomacy* (Simon & Schuster, 1994).

Many recent historians agree with David F. Trask that Wilson developed realistic and clearly articulated goals and coordinated his larger diplomatic aims with the use of force better than any other wartime U.S. president. See his essay "Woodrow Wilson and the Reconciliation of Force and Diplomacy, 1917–1918," *Naval War College Review* (January/February 1975). John Milton Cooper, Jr., in *The Warrior and the Priest: Woodrow Wilson and Theodore Roosevelt* (Harvard University Press, 1984), presents Wilson as the realist and Theodore Roosevelt as the idealist. Arthur S. Link, coeditor of the *Papers of Woodrow Wilson,* 60 vols. (Princeton, 1966–1993), gives a blow-by-blow response to Kennan in revised lectures given at Johns Hopkins University in *Woodrow Wilson: Revolution, War and Peace* (Harlan Davidson, 1979), nicely summarized in "The Higher Realism of Woodrow Wilson," in a book of essays with the same title (Vanderbilt University Press, 1971). Kennan himself acknowledged that his earlier criticism of Wilson had to be viewed within the context of the Cold War. "I now view Wilson," he wrote in 1991, "as a man who, like so many other people of broad vision and acute sensitivities, was ahead of his time, and did not live long enough to know what great and commanding relevance his ideas would acquire before this century was out." See "Comments on the Paper, Entitled 'Kennan Versus Wilson'" by Thomas J. Knock in John Milton Cooper et al., eds., *The Wilson Era: Essays in Honor of Arthur S. Link* (Harlan Davidson, 1991).

Wilson's health has received serious scrutiny from scholars. In the early 1930s, Sigmund Freud and William C. Bullitt, a former diplomat, wrote a scathing and highly inaccurate biography of Thomas Woodrow Wilson (Houghton Mifflin, 1967) published posthumously in 1967. The book was poorly received and scathingly reviewed by Arthur S. Link, "The Case for Woodrow Wilson," in *The Higher Realism of Woodrow Wilson and Other Essays.* The major controversy seems to be those who stress psychological difficulties—see Alexander and Juliette George, *Woodrow Wilson and Colonial House: A Personality Study* (Dover Press, 1956, 1964)—versus medical illnesses—see Edwin A. Weinstein, *Woodrow Wilson: A Medical and Psychological Biography* (Princeton University, 1981). For the best summaries of the controversy, see Thomas T. Lewis, "Alternative Psychological Interpretations of Woodrow Wilson," *Mid-America* (vol. 45, 1983), and Lloyd E. Ambrosius, "Woodrow Wilson's Health and the Treaty Fight, 1919–1920," *The International History Review* (February 1987). Phyllis Lee Levin, *Edith and Woodrow: The White House Years* (Scribners, 2001), and Robert J. Maddox, "Mrs. Wilson and the Presidency," *American History* (February 1973), makes the case that we have already had America's first woman president.

The four best bibliographies of Wilson are as follows: the introduction to Lloyd E. Ambrosius's *Wilsonianism: Woodrow Wilson and His Legacy in American Foreign Relations* (Palgrave Macmillan, 2002), which is a collection of his articles from the leading realist Wilsonian scholar. John A. Thompson, a British scholar, has an up-to-date analysis of the Wilson scholarship in *Woodrow Wilson* (Pearson Macmillan, 2002), a short, scholarly sympathetic

study in the "Profiles in Power" series designed for student use. Advanced undergraduates should consult David Steigarwald, "The Reclamation of Woodrow Wilson," *Diplomatic History* (Winter 1999). Political Science majors should consult Francis J. Gavin, "The Wilsonian Legacy in the Twentieth Century," *Orbis* (Fall 1997).

Thomas Bailey claims that Wilson made mistakes at home that affected his foreign policies. For example, by attempting to politicize the war issue by asking voters to elect a Democratic Congress in the off-year elections in 1918, voters responded by restoring the Republicans to power in the Senate. Wilson also failed to name any prominent Republicans to the peace delegation he took to Paris. This was the first time a president was going outside the United States to conduct foreign affairs. Had he brought any prominent Senate Republicans with him, including Henry Cabot Lodge, he might have successfully negotiated a treaty acceptable to Senate ratification. During the negotiations at Paris, Wilson was forced to compromise on issues of self-determination for settling territorial disputes, parceling out "mandates" to the winners over former German clinical possessions, and saddling Germany with a high reparations bill. Bailey mentions but does not dwell on the attempts by Senator Lodge to privately negotiate a compromise treaty with the Democrats. Might the real villain have been the irreconcilable isolationist Senator William Borah who threatened to remove Lodge as Senate majority leader? Was Lodge afraid that an open fight with Borah could have split the Republican Party as had occurred in 1912 when ex-President Theodore Roosevelt walked out of the convention and ran as a third-party candidate? Wilson, who hated the sound of Lodge's name, had also privately worked out his own set of reservations with Democratic Senate minority leader Gilbert M. Hitchcock. Bailey maintains the compromise reservations differed only slightly in degree from those of Senator Lodge. If this was the case, would Wilson have been better off staying at home and negotiating a compromise with the Senate instead of delivering emotional appeals to the American public on the ill-fated tour where he suffered a paralyzing stroke to the left side of his body?

The late William G. Carleton presents an impassioned defense of both Wilson's policies at Versailles as well as their implications for the future of American foreign policy. Carleton responds to the two main charges historians continue to level against Wilson: his inability to compromise and his naïve idealism. In contrast to Bailey, Carleton excoriates Lodge, as the chairman of the Senate Foreign Relations Committee, for adding "nationally self-centered" reservations that he knew would emasculate the League of Nations and most likely cause other nations to add reservations to the Treaty of Versailles. Wilson, says Carleton, was

Was Woodrow Wilson Responsible for the Failure of the United States to Join the League of Nations? by Madaras and SoRelle

145

a true realist when he rejected the Lodge reservations. In his article, Carleton advanced many of the arguments that historians Trask, Link, and Kennan later used in defending Wilson's "higher realism." Rejecting the view of Wilson as a naïve idealist, Carleton maintains: "He recognized the emergence of the anti-imperialist revolutions . . . the importance of social politics in the international relations of the future . . . the implications for future world politics of the technological revolutions in war, of total war, and of the disintegration of the old balance of power."

YES ⬅

Thomas A. Bailey

Woodrow Wilson Wouldn't Yield

"As a friend of the President . . . I solemnly declare to him this morning: If you want to kill your own child [League of Nations] because the Senate straightens out its crooked limbs, you must take the responsibility and accept the verdict of history."

—Senator Henry F. Ashurst, in Senate, 1920

I

The story of America's rejection of the League of Nations revolves largely around the personality and character of Thomas Woodrow Wilson.

Born in Virginia and reared in Yankee-gutted Georgia and the Carolinas, Wilson early developed a burning hatred of war and a passionate attachment to the Confederate-embraced principle of self-determination for minority peoples. From the writings of Thomas Jefferson he derived much of his democratic idealism and his invincible faith in the judgment of the masses, if properly informed. From his stiff-backed Scotch-Presbyterian forebears, he inherited a high degree of inflexibility; from his father, a dedicated Presbyterian minister, he learned a stern moral code that would tolerate no compromise with wrong—as defined by Woodrow Wilson.

As a leading academician who had first failed at law, he betrayed a contempt for "money-grubbing" lawyers, many of whom sat in the Senate, and an arrogance toward lesser intellects, including those of the "pygmy-minded" senators. As a devout Christian keenly aware of the wickedness of this world, he emerged as a fighting reformer, whether as president of Princeton, governor of New Jersey, or President of the United States.

As a war leader, Wilson was superb. Holding aloft the torch of idealism in one hand and the flaming sword of righteousness in the other, he aroused the masses to a holy crusade. We would fight a war to end wars; we would make the world safe for democracy. The phrase was not a mockery then. The American people, with an amazing display of self-sacrifice, supported the war effort unswervingly.

The noblest expression of Wilson's idealism was his Fourteen Points address to Congress in January, 1918. It compressed his war aims into punchy, placard-like paragraphs, expressly designed for propaganda purposes. It appealed tremendously to oppressed peoples everywhere by promising such goals as the end of secret treaties, freedom of the seas, the removal of economic barriers, a reduction of arms burdens, a fair adjustment of colonial claims, and self-determination for oppressed minorities. In Poland, university men would meet on the streets of Warsaw, clasp hands, and soulfully utter one word, "Wilson." In remote regions of Italy peasants burned candles before poster portraits of the mighty new prophet arisen in the West.

The fourteenth and capstone point was a league of nations, designed to avert future wars. The basic idea was not original with Wilson; numerous thinkers, including Frenchmen and Britons, had been working on the concept long before he embraced it. Even Henry Cabot Lodge, the Republican senator from Massachusetts, had already spoken publicly in favor of *a* league of nations. But the more he heard about the Wilsonian League of Nations, the more critical of it he became.

A knowledge of the Wilson–Lodge feud is basic to an understanding of the tragedy that unfolded. Tall, slender, aristocratically bewhiskered, Dr. Henry Cabot Lodge (Ph.D., Harvard), had published a number of books and had been known as "the scholar in politics" before the appearance of Dr. Woodrow Wilson (Ph.D., Johns Hopkins). The Presbyterian professor had gone further in both scholarship and politics than the Boston Brahmin, whose mind was once described as resembling the soil of his native New England: "naturally barren but highly cultivated." Wilson and Lodge, two stubborn men, developed a mutual antipathy which soon turned into freezing hatred.

From *Essays Diplomatic and Undiplomatic of Thomas A. Bailey* (Appleton-Century-Crofts, 1969); original to *American Heritage*, June 1957, pp. 20–25, 105–106. Copyright © 1957 by American Heritage Publishing Co. Reprinted by permission.

II

The German armies, reeling under the blows of the Allies, were ready to surrender November, 1918. The formal armistice terms stipulated that Germany was to be guaranteed a peace based on the Fourteen Points, with two reservations concerning freedom of the seas and reparations.

Meanwhile the American people had keyed themselves up for the long-awaited march on Berlin; eager voices clamored to hang the Kaiser. Thus the sudden end of the shooting left inflamed patriots with a sense of frustration and letdown that boded ill for Wilson's policies. The red-faced Theodore Roosevelt, Lodge's intimate of long standing, cried that peace should be dictated by the chatter of machine guns and not "the clicking of typewriters."

Wilson now towered at the dizzy pinnacle of his popularity and power. He had emerged as the moral arbiter of the world and the hope of all peoples for a better tomorrow. But regrettably his wartime sureness of touch began to desert him, and he made a series of costly fumbles. He was so preoccupied with reordering the world, someone has said, that he reminded one of the baseball player who knocks the ball into the bleachers and then forgets to touch home plate.

First came his tactlessly direct appeal for a Democratic Congress in October, 1918. The voters trooped to the polls the next month and, by a narrow margin, returned a Republican Congress. Wilson had not only goaded his partisan foes to fresh outbursts of fury, but he had unnecessarily staked his prestige on the outcome—and lost. When the Allied leaders met at the Paris peace table, he was the only one not entitled to be there—on the European basis of a parliamentary majority.

Wilson next announced that he was sailing for France, presumably to use his still enormous prestige to fashion an enduring peace. At that time no President had ever gone abroad, and Republicans condemned the decision as evidence of a dangerous Messiah complex—of a desire, as former President Taft put it, "to hog the whole show."

The naming of the remaining four men to the peace delegation caused partisans further anguish. Only one, Henry White, was a Republican, and he was a minor figure at that. The Republicans, now the majority party, complained that they had been good enough to die on the battlefield; they ought to have at least an equal voice at the peace table. Nor were any United States senators included, even though they would have a final whack at the treaty. Wilson did not have much respect for the "bungalow-minded" senators, and if he took one, the logical choice would be Henry Cabot Lodge. There were already enough feuds brewing at Paris without taking one along.

Doubtless some of the Big Business Republicans were out to "get" the President who had been responsible for the hated reformist legislation of 1913–14. If he managed to put over the League of Nations, his prestige would soar to new heights. He might even arrange—unspeakable thought!—to be elected again and again and again. Much of the partisan smog that finally suffocated the League would have been cleared away if Wilson had publicly declared, as he was urged to do, that in no circumstances would he run again. But he spurned such counsel, partly because he was actually receptive to the idea of a third term.

III

The American President, hysterically hailed by European crowds as "Voovro Veelson," came to the Paris peace table in January, 1919, to meet with Lloyd George of Britain, Clemenceau of France, and Orlando of Italy. To his dismay, he soon discovered that they were far more interested in imperialism than in idealism. When they sought to carve up the territorial booty without regard for the colonials, contrary to the Fourteen Points, the stern-jawed Presbyterian moralist interposed a ringing veto. The end result was the mandate system—a compromise between idealism and imperialism that turned out to be more imperialistic than idealistic.

Wilson's overriding concern was the League of Nations. He feared that if he did not get it completed and embedded in the treaty, the imperialistic powers might sidetrack it. Working at an incredible pace after hours, Wilson headed the commission that drafted the League Covenant in ten meetings and some thirty hours. He then persuaded the conference not only to approve the hastily constructed Covenant but to incorporate it bodily in the peace treaty. In support of his adopted brain child he spoke so movingly on one occasion that even the hard-boiled reporters forgot to take notes.

Wilson now had to return hurriedly to the United States to sign bills and take care of other pressing business. Shortly after his arrival the mounting Republican opposition in the Senate flared up angrily. On March 4, 1919, 39 senators or senators-elect—more than enough to defeat the treaty—published a round robin to the effect that they would not approve the League in its existing form. This meant that Wilson had to return to Paris, hat in hand, and there weaken his position by having to seek modifications.

Stung to the quick, he struck back at his senatorial foes in an indiscreet speech in New York just before his departure. He boasted that when he brought the treaty back from Paris, the League Covenant would not only be tied in but so thoroughly tied in that it could not be cut out without killing the entire pact. The Senate, he assumed, would not dare to kill the treaty of peace outright.

IV

At Paris the battle was now joined in deadly earnest. Clemenceau, the French realist, had little use for Wilson, the American idealist. "God gave us the ten commandments and we broke them," he reportedly sneered. "Wilson gave us the Fourteen Points—we shall see." Clemenceau's most disruptive demand was for the German Rhineland; but Wilson, the champion of self-determination, would never consent to handing several million Germans over to the tender mercies of the French. After a furious struggle, during which Wilson was stricken with influenza, Clemenceau was finally persuaded to yield the Rhineland and other demands in return for a security treaty. Under it, Britain and America agreed to come to the aid of France in the event of another unprovoked aggression. The United States Senate shortsightedly pigeonholed the pact, and France was left with neither the Rhineland nor security.

Two other deadlocks almost broke up the conference. Italy claimed the Adriatic port of Fiume, an area inhabited chiefly by Yugoslavs. In his battle for self-determination, Wilson dramatically appealed over the head of the Italian delegation to the Italian people, whereupon the delegates went home in a huff to receive popular endorsement. The final adjustment was a hollow victory for self-determination.

The politely bowing Japanese now stepped forward to press their economic claims to China's Shantung, which they had captured from the Germans early in the war. But to submit 30,000,000 Chinese to the influence of the Japanese would be another glaring violation of self-determination. The Japanese threatened to bolt the conference, as the Italians had already done, with consequent jeopardy to the League. In the end, Wilson reluctantly consented to a compromise that left the Japanese temporarily in possession of Shantung.

The Treaty of Versailles, as finally signed in June, 1919, included only about four of the Fourteen Points essentially intact. The Germans, with considerable justification, gave vent to loud cries of betrayal. But the iron hand of circumstance had forced Wilson to compromise away many of his points in order to salvage his fourteenth point, the League of Nations, which he hoped would iron out the injustices that had crept into the treaty. He was like the mother who throws her younger children to the pursuing wolves in order to save her sturdy first born son.

V

Bitter opposition to the completed treaty had already begun to form in America. Tens of thousands of homesick and disillusioned soldiers were pouring home, determined to let Europe "stew in its own juice." The wartime idealism, inevitably doomed to slump, was now plunging to alarming depths. The beloved Allies had apparently turned out to be greedy imperialists. The war to make the world safe for democracy had obviously fallen dismally short of the goal. And at the end of the war to end wars there were about twenty conflicts of varying intensity being waged all over the globe.

The critics increased their clamor. Various foreign groups, including the Irish-Americans and the Italian-Americans, were complaining that the interests of the "old country" had been neglected. Professional liberals, notaby the editors of the *New Republic,* were denouncing the treaty as too harsh. The illiberals, far more numerous, were denouncing it as not harsh enough. The Britain-haters, like the buzz-saw Senator James Reed of Missouri and the acid-penned William R. Hearst, were proclaiming that the British had emerged with undue influence. Such ultra-nationalists as the isolationist Senator William E. Borah of Idaho were insisting that the flag of no superstate should be hoisted above the glorious Stars and Stripes.

When the treaty came back from Paris, with the League firmly riveted in, Senator Lodge despaired of stopping it. "What are you going to do? It's hopeless," he complained to Borah. "All the newspapers in my state are for it." The best that he could hope for was to add a few reservations. The Republicans had been given little opportunity to help write the treaty in Paris; they now felt that they were entitled to do a little rewriting in Washington.

Lodge deliberately adopted the technique of delay. As chairman of the powerful Senate Committee on Foreign Relations, he consumed two weeks by reading aloud the entire pact of 264 pages, even though it had already been printed. He then held time-consuming public hearings, during which persons with unpronounceable foreign names aired their grievances against the pact.

Lodge finally adopted the strategy of tacking reservations onto the treaty, and he was able to achieve his goal because of the peculiar composition of the Senate. There were 49 Republicans and 47 Democrats. The Republicans consisted of about twenty "strong reservationists" like Lodge, about twelve "mild reservationists" like future Secretary of State Kellogg, and about a dozen "irreconcilables." This last group was headed by Senator Borah and the no less isolationist Senator Hiram Johnson of California, a fiery spellbinder.

The Lodge reservations finally broke the back of the treaty. They were all added by a simple majority vote, even though the entire pact would have to be approved by a two-thirds vote. The dozen or so Republican mild reservationists were not happy over the strong Lodge reservations, and if Wilson had deferred sufficiently to these men, he might have persuaded them to vote with the Democrats. Had they done so, the Lodge reservations could have all been voted down, and a milder version, perhaps acceptable to Wilson, could have been substituted.

VI

As the hot summer of 1919 wore on, Wilson became increasingly impatient with the deadlock in the Senate. Finally he decided to take his case to the country, as he had so often done in response to his ingrained "appeal habit." He had never been robust, and his friends urged him not to risk breaking himself down in a strenuous barnstorming campaign. But Wilson, having made up his mind, was unyielding. He had sent American boys into battle in a war to end wars; why should he not risk his life in a battle for a League to end wars?

Wilson's spectacular tour met with limited enthusiasm in the Middle West, the home of several million German-Americans. After him, like baying bloodhounds, trailed Senators Borah and Johnson, sometimes speaking in the same halls a day or so later, to the accompaniment of cries of "Impeach him, impeach him!" But on the Pacific Coast and in the Rocky Mountain area the enthusiasm for Wilson and the League was overwhelming. The high point—and the breaking point—of the trip came at Pueblo, Colorado, where Wilson, with tears streaming down his cheeks, pleaded for his beloved League of Nations.

That night Wilson's weary body rebelled. He was whisked back to Washington, where he suffered a stroke that paralyzed the left side of his body. For weeks he lay in bed, a desperately sick man. The Democrats, who had no first-rate leader in the Senate, were left rudderless. With the wisdom of hindsight, we may say that Wilson might better have stayed in Washington, providing the necessary leadership and compromising with the opposition, insofar as compromise was possible. A good deal of compromise had already gone into the treaty, and a little more might have saved it.

Senator Lodge, cold and decisive, was now in the driver's seat. His Fourteen Reservations, a sardonic parallel to Wilson's Fourteen Points, had been whipped into shape. Most of them now seem either irrelevant, inconsequential, or unnecessary; some of them merely reaffirmed principles and policies, including the Monroe Doctrine, already guaranteed by the treaty or by the Constitution.

But Wilson, who hated the sound of Lodge's name, would have no part of the Lodge reservations. They would, he insisted, emasculate the entire treaty. Yet the curious fact is that he had privately worked out his own set of reservations with the Democratic leader in the Senate, Gilbert M. Hitchcock, and these differed only in slight degree from those of Senator Lodge.

VII

As the hour approached for the crucial vote in the Senate, it appeared that public opinion had evidently veered considerably. Although confused by the angry debate, it still favored the treaty—but with some safeguarding reservations. A stubborn Wilson was unwilling to accept this disheartening fact, or perhaps he was not made aware of it. Mrs. Wilson, backed by the President's personal physician, Dr. Cary Grayson, kept vigil at his bedside to warn the few visitors that disagreeable news might shock the invalid into a relapse.

In this highly unfavorable atmosphere, Senator Hitchcock had two conferences with Wilson on the eve of the Senate ballot. He suggested compromise on a certain point, but Wilson shot back, "Let Lodge compromise!" Hitchcock conceded that the Senator would have to give ground but suggested that the White House might also hold out the olive branch. "Let Lodge hold out the olive branch," came the stern reply. On this inflexible note, and with Mrs. Wilson's anxiety mounting, the interview ended.

The Senate was ready for final action on November 19, 1919. At the critical moment Wilson sent a fateful letter to the Democratic minority in the Senate, urging them to vote down the treaty with the hated Lodge reservations so that a true ratification could be achieved. The Democrats, with more than the necessary one-third veto, heeded the voice of their crippled leader and rejected the treaty with reservations. The Republicans, with more than the necessary one-third veto, rejected the treaty without reservations.

The country was shocked by this exhibition of legislative paralysis. About four-fifths of the senators professed to favor the treaty in some form, yet they were unable to agree on anything. An aroused public opinion forced the Senate to reconsider, and Lodge secretly entered into negotiations with the Democrats in an effort to work out acceptable reservations. He was making promising progress when Senator Borah got wind of his maneuvers through an anonymous telephone call. The leading irreconcilables hastily summoned a council of war, hauled Lodge before them, and bluntly accused him of treachery. Deeply disturbed, the Massachusetts Senator said: "Well, I suppose I'll have to resign as majority leader."

"No, by God!" burst out Borah. "You won't have a chance to resign! On Monday, I'll move for the election of a new majority leader and give the reasons for my action." Faced with an upheaval within his party such as had insured Wilson's election in 1912, Lodge agreed to drop his backstage negotiations.

VIII

The second-chance vote in the Senate came on March 19, 1920. Wilson again directed his loyal Democratic following to reject the treaty, disfigured as it was by the Lodge reservations. But by this time there was no other form in which the pact could possibly be ratified. Twenty-one realistic Democrats turned their backs on Wilson and voted Yea; 23 loyal Democrats, mostly from the rock-ribbed South, joined with the irreconcilables to do the bidding of the White House. The treaty, though commanding a simple majority this time of 49 Yeas to 35 Nays, failed of the necessary two-thirds vote.

Wilson, struggling desperately against the Lodge reservation trap, had already called upon the nation, in a "solemn referendum," to give him a vote in favor of the League in the forthcoming Presidential election of 1920. His hope was that he could then get the treaty approved without reservations. But this course was plainly futile. Even if all the anti-League senators up for reelection in 1920 had been replaced by the pro-League senators, Wilson would still have lacked the necessary two-thirds majority for an unreserved treaty.

The American people were never given a chance to express their views directly on the League of Nations. All they could do was vote either for the voluble Democratic candidate, Cox, who stood for the League, or the stuffed-shirt Republican candidate, Harding, who wobbled all over the evasive Republican platform. If the electorate had been given an opportunity to express itself, a powerful majority probably would have favored the world organization, with at least some reservations. But wearied of Wilsonism, idealism, and self-denial, and confused by the wordy fight over the treaty, the voters rose up and swept Harding into the White House on a tidal wave of votes. The winner had been more anti-League than pro-League, and his prodigious plurality of 7,000,000 votes condemned the League to death in America.

IX

What caused this costly failure of American statesmanship?

Wilson's physical collapse intensified his native stubbornness. A judicious compromise here and there no doubt would have secured Senate approval of the treaty, though of course with qualifications. Wilson believed that in any event the Allies would reject the Lodge reservations. The probabilities are that the Allies would have worked out some kind of acceptance, so dire was their need of America's economic support, but Wilson never gave them a chance to act.

Senator Lodge was also inflexible, but prior to the second rejection he was evidently trying to get the treaty through—on his own terms. As majority leader of the Republicans, his primary task was to avoid another fatal split in his party. Wilson's primary task was to get the pact approved. From a narrowly political point of view, the Republicans had little to gain by engineering ratification of a Democratic treaty.

The two-thirds rule in the Senate, often singled out as the culprit, is of little relevance. Wilson almost certainly would have pigeonholed the treaty, as he threatened, if it had passed with the Lodge reservations appended.

Wilson's insistence that the League be wedded to the treaty actually contributed to the final defeat of both. Either would have had a better chance if it had not been burdened by the enemies of the other. The United Nations, one should note, was set up in 1945 independently of any peace treaty.

Finally, the American public in 1919–20 was not yet ready for the onerous new world responsibilities that had suddenly been forced upon it. The isolationist tradition was still potent, and it was fortified by postwar disillusionment. If the sovereign people had cried out for the League with one voice, they almost certainly would have had their way. A treaty without reservations, or with a few reservations acceptable to Wilson, doubtless would have slipped through the Senate. But the American people were one war short of accepting that leadership in a world organization for peace which, as Wilson's vision perceived, had become a necessity for the safety and the welfare of mankind.

The blame for this failure of statesmanship cannot fall solely on the excessive partisanship of both parties, the shortsighted outlook of Lodge, or the rigidity of a sick and ill-informed President. Much of the responsibility must be placed at the door of a provincial population anxious to escape overseas responsibilities while basking in the sunshine of normalcy and prosperity.

THOMAS A. BAILEY (1902–1983) taught for nearly 50 years at Stanford University and was America's leading diplomatic historian. His major works include a two-volume exegesis titled *Woodrow Wilson's World War One Diplomacy* and the popular *A Diplomatic History of the American People* that went through ten editions.

William G. Carleton

NO

A New Look at Woodrow Wilson

All high-placed statesmen crave historical immortality. Woodrow Wilson craved it more than most. Thus far the fates have not been kind to Wilson; there is a reluctance to admit him to as great a place in history as he will have.

Congress has just gotten around to planning a national memorial for Wilson, several years after it had done this for Theodore Roosevelt and Franklin D. Roosevelt. Wilson is gradually being accepted as one of the nation's five or six greatest Presidents. However, the heroic mold of the man on the large stage of world history is still generally unrecognized.

There is a uniquely carping, hypercritical approach to Wilson. Much more than other historical figures he is being judged by personality traits, many of them distorted or even fancied. Wilson is not being measured by the yardstick used for other famous characters of history. There is a double standard at work here.

What are the common errors and misrepresentations with respect to Wilson? In what ways is he being judged more rigorously? What are the reasons for this? Why will Wilson eventually achieve giant stature in world history?

⁂

There are two criticisms of Wilson that go to the heart of his fame and place in history. One is an alleged inflexibility and intransigence, an inability to compromise. The other is that he had no real understanding of world politics, that he was a naïve idealist. Neither is true.

If Wilson were indeed as stubborn and adamant as he is often portrayed he would have been a bungler at his work, for the practice and art of politics consist in a feeling for the possible, a sense of timing, a capacity for give-and-take compromise. In reality, Wilson's leadership of his party and the legislative accomplishments

of his first term were magnificent. His performance was brilliantly characterized by the very qualities he is said to have lacked: flexibility, accommodation, a sense of timing, and a willingness to compromise. In the struggles to win the Federal Reserve Act, the Clayton Anti-Trust Law, the Federal Trade Commission, and other major measures of his domestic program, Wilson repeatedly mediated between the agrarian liberals and the conservatives of his party, moving now a little to the left, now to the right, now back to the left. He learned by experience, cast aside pride of opinion, accepted and maneuvered for regulatory commissions after having warned of their danger during the campaign of 1912, and constantly acted as a catalyst of the opposing factions of his party and of shifting opinion.

The cautious way Wilson led the country to military preparedness and to war demonstrated resiliency and a sense of timing of a high order. At the Paris Conference Wilson impressed thoughtful observers with his skill as a negotiator; many European diplomats were surprised that an "amateur" could do so well. Here the criticism is not that Wilson was without compromise but that he compromised too much.

Actually, the charge that Wilson was incapable of compromise must stand or fall on his conduct during the fight in the Senate over the ratification of the League of Nations, particularly his refusal to give the word to the Democratic Senators from the South to vote for the Treaty with the Lodge Reservations, which, it is claimed, would have assured ratification. Wilson, say the critics, murdered his own brain child. It is Wilson, and not Lodge, who has now become the villain of this high tragedy.

Now, would a Wilsonian call to the Southerners to change their position have resulted in ratification? Can we really be sure? In order to give Southerners time to readjust to a new position, the call from the White House would have had to have been made several weeks before that final vote. During that time what would have prevented Lodge from hobbling the League with still more

From *The Virginia Quarterly Review,* vol. 38, no. 4 (Autumn 1962), pp. 545–566. Copyright © 1962 by University of Virginia. Reprinted by permission.

reservations? Would the mild reservationists, all Republicans, have prevented this? The record shows, I think, that in the final analysis the mild reservationists could always be bamboozled by Lodge in the name of party loyalty. As the fight on the League had progressed, the reservations had become more numerous and more crippling. Wilson, it seems, had come to feel that there simply was no appeasing Lodge.

During the Peace Conference, in response to the Senatorial Round Robin engineered by Lodge, Wilson had reopened the whole League question and obtained the inclusion of American "safeguards" he felt would satisfy Lodge. This had been done at great cost, for it had forced Wilson to abandon his position as a negotiator above the battles for national advantages and to become a suppliant for national concessions. This had resulted in his having to yield points in other parts of the Treaty to national-minded delegations from other countries. When Wilson returned from Paris with the completed Treaty, Lodge had "raised the ante," the Lodge Reservations requiring the consent of other signatory nations were attached to the Treaty, and these had multiplied and become more restrictive in nature as the months went by. Would not then a "final" yielding by Wilson have resulted in even stiffer reservations being added? Was not Lodge using the Reservations to effect not ratification but rejection, knowing that there was a point beyond which Wilson could not yield?

Wilson seems honestly to have believed that the Lodge Reservations emasculated the League. Those who read them for the first time will be surprised, I think, to discover how nationally self-centered they were. If taken seriously, they surely must have impaired the functioning of the League. However, Wilson was never opposed to clarifying or interpreting reservations which would not require the consent of the other signatories. Indeed, he himself wrote the Hitchcock Reservations.

Even had the League with the Lodge Reservations been ratified, how certain can we really be that this would have meant American entrance into the League? Under the Lodge Reservations, every signatory nation had to accept them before the United States could become a member. Would all the signatories have accepted every one of the fifteen Lodge Reservations? The United States had no monopoly on chauvinism, and would not other nations have interposed reservations of their own as a condition to their acceptance of the Lodge Reservations?

At Paris, Wilson had personally experienced great difficulty getting his own mild "reservations" incorporated into the Covenant. Now, at this late date, would Britain have accepted the Lodge Reservation on Irish

self-determination? In all probability. Would Japan have accepted the Reservation on Shantung? This is more doubtful. Would the Latin American states have accepted the stronger Reservation on the Monroe Doctrine? This is also doubtful. Chile had already shown concern, and little Costa Rica had the temerity to ask for a definition of the Doctrine. Would the British Dominions have accepted the Reservation calling for one vote for the British Empire or six votes for the United States? Even Lord Grey, who earlier had predicted that the signatories would accept the Lodge Reservations, found that he could not guarantee acceptance by the Dominions, and Canada's President of the Privy Council and Acting Secretary for External Affairs, Newton W. Rowell, declared that if this Reservation were accepted by the other powers Canada would withdraw from the League.

By the spring of 1920, Wilson seems to have believed that making the League of Nations the issue in the campaign of 1920 would afford a better opportunity for American participation in an effective League than would further concessions to Lodge. To Wilson, converting the Presidential election into a solemn referendum on the League was a reality. For months, because of his illness, he had lived secluded in the White House, and the memories of his highly emotional reception in New York on his return from Paris and of the enthusiasm of the Western audiences during his last speaking trip burned vividly bright. He still believed that the American people, if given the chance, would vote for the League without emasculating reservations. Does this, then, make Wilson naïve? It is well to remember that in the spring of 1920 not even the most sanguine Republican envisaged the Republican sweep that would develop in the fall of that year.

If the strategy of Wilson in the spring of 1920 was of debatable wisdom, the motives of Lodge can no longer be open to doubt. After the landslide of 1920, which gave the Republicans the Presidency and an overwhelming majority in a Senate dominated by Lodge in foreign policy, the Treaty was never resurrected. The Lodge Reservations, representing months of gruelling legislative labor, were cavalierly jettisoned, and a separate peace was made with Germany.

What, then, becomes of the stock charge that Wilson was intolerant of opposition and incapable of bending? If the truth of this accusation must rest on Wilson's attitude during the Treaty fight, and I think it must, for he showed remarkable adaptability in other phases of his Presidency, then it must fall. The situation surrounding the Treaty fight was intricately tangled, and there is certainly as much evidence on the side of Wilson's forbearance as on the side of his obstinacy.

Was Woodrow Wilson Responsible for the Failure of the United States to Join the League of Nations? by Madaras and SoRelle

153

A far more serious charge against Wilson is that he had no realistic understanding of world politics, that he was an impractical idealist whose policies intensified rather than alleviated international problems. Now what American statesman of the period understood world politics better than Wilson—or indeed in any way as well as he? Elihu Root, with his arid legalism? Philander Knox, with his dollar diplomacy? Theodore Roosevelt or Henry Cabot Lodge? Roosevelt and Lodge had some feel for power politics, and they understood the traditional balance of power, at least until their emotions for a dictated Allied victory got the better of their judgment: but was either of them aware of the implications for world politics of the technological revolution in war and the disintegration of the old balance of power? And were not both of them blind to a new force in world politics just then rising to a place of importance—the anti-imperialist revolutions, which even before World War I were getting under way with the Mexican Revolution and the Chinese Revolution of Sun Yat-sen?

Wilson is charged with having no understanding of the balance of power, but who among world statesmen of the twentieth century better sated the classic doctrine of the traditional balance of power than Wilson in his famous Peace Without Victory speech? And was it not Theodore Roosevelt who derided him for stating it? With perfectly straight faces Wilson critics, and a good many historians, tell us that TR, who wanted to march to Berlin and saddle Germany with a harsh peace, and FDR, who sponsored unconditional surrender, "understood" the balance of power, but that Wilson, who fought to salvage a power balance by preserving Germany from partition, was a simple-simon in world politics—an illustration of the double standard at work in evaluating Wilson's place in history.

Wilson not only understood the old, but with amazing clarity he saw the new, elements in world politics. He recognized the emergence of the anti-imperialist revolutions and the importance of social politics in the international relations of the future. He recognized, too, the implications for future world politics of the technological revolution in war, of total war, and of the disintegration of the old balance of power—for World War I had decisively weakened the effective brakes on Japan in Asia, disrupted the Turkish Empire in the Middle East and the Austro-Hungarian Empire in Europe, and removed Russia as a make-weight for the foreseeable future. Wilson believed that a truncated Germany and an attempted French hegemony would only add to the chaos, but he saw too that merely preserving Germany as a power unit would not restore the old balance of power. To Wilson, even in its prime the traditional balance of power had worked only indifferently and collective security would have been preferable, but in his mind the revolutionary changes in the world of 1919 made a collective-security system indispensable.

Just what is realism in world politics? Is it not the ability to use purposefully many factors, even theoretically contradictory ones, and to use them not singly and consecutively but interdependently and simultaneously, shifting the emphasis as conditions change? If so, was not Wilson a very great realist in world politics? He used the old balance-of-power factors, as evidenced by his fight to save Germany as a power unit and his sponsoring of a tripartite alliance of the United States, Britain, and France to guarantee France from any German aggression until such time as collective security would become effective. But he labored to introduce into international relations the new collective-security factors to supplement and gradually supersede in importance the older factors, now increasingly outmoded by historical developments. To label as doctrinaire idealist one who envisaged world politics in so broad and flexible a way is to pervert the meaning of words. . . .

❧

Ranking the Presidents has become a popular game, and even Presidents like to play it, notably Truman and Kennedy. In my own evaluation, I place Wilson along with Jefferson and Lincoln as the nation's three greatest Presidents, which makes Wilson our greatest twentieth-century President. If rated solely on the basis of long-range impact on international relations, Wilson is the most influential of all our Presidents.

What are the achievements which entitle Wilson to so high a place? Let us consider the major ones, although of course some of these are more important than others.

. . . [B]etter than any responsible statesman of his day, Wilson understood and sympathized with the anti-imperialist revolutions and their aspirations for basic internal reforms. He withdrew American support for the Bankers' Consortium in China, and the United States under Wilson was the first of the great powers to recognize the Revolution of Sun Yat-sen. Early in his term he had to wrestle with the Mexican Revolution. He saw the need for social reform; avoided the general war with Mexico that many American investors, Catholics, and professional patriots wanted; and by refusing to recognize the counter-revolution of Huerta and cutting Huerta off from trade and arms while allowing the flow of arms to Carranza, Villa, and Zapata, he made possible the overthrow of the counter-revolution and the triumph of the Revolution. What merciless criticism was heaped on Wilson for insisting that Latin Americans should be positively encouraged to institute reforms and develop democratic practices. Yet today Americans applaud their government's denial of Alliance-for-Progress funds to Latin American countries which refuse to undertake fundamental economic and social reforms and flout democracy.

. . . [C]onfronted with the stupendous and completely novel challenge of having to mobilize not only America's military strength but also its civilian resources and energies in America's first total war, the Wilson Administration set up a huge network of administrative agencies, exemplifying the highest imagination and creativity in the art of practical administration. FDR, in his New Deal and in his World War II agencies, was to borrow heavily from the Wilson innovations.

. . . Wilson's Fourteen Points and his other peace aims constituted war propaganda of perhaps unparalleled brilliance. They thrilled the world. They gave high purpose to the peoples of the Allied countries and stirred their war efforts. Directed over the heads of the governments to the enemy peoples themselves, they produced unrest, helped bring about the revolutions that overthrew the Sultan, the Hapsburgs, and the Hohenzollerns, and hastened the end of the war.

. . . [T]he Treaty of Versailles, of which Wilson was the chief architect, was a better peace than it would have been (considering, among other things, the imperialist secret treaties of the Allies) because of Wilson's labors for a just peace. The League of Nations was founded, and this was to be the forerunner of the United Nations. To the League was assigned the work of general disarmament. The mandate system of the League, designed to prepare colonial peoples for self-government and national independence, was a revolutionary step away from the old imperialism. The aspirations of many peoples in Europe for national independence were fulfilled. (If the disruption of the Austro-Hungarian Empire helped destroy the old balance of power, it must be said that in this particular situation Wilson's doctrine of national autonomy only exploited an existing fact in the interest of Allied victory, and even had there been no Wilsonian self-determination the nationalities of this area were already so well developed that they could not have been denied independence after the defeat of the Hapsburgs. Wilson's self-determination was to be a far more *creative* force among the colonial peoples than among the Europeans.) The Treaty restrained the chauvinism of the Italians, though not as much as

Wilson would have liked. It prevented the truncating of Germany by preserving to her the Left Bank of the Rhine. The war-guilt clause and the enormous reparations saddled on Germany were mistakes, but Wilson succeeded in confining German responsibility to civilian damage and the expenses of Allied military pensions rather than the whole cost of the war; and had the United States ratified the Treaty and participated in post-war world affairs, as Wilson expected, the United States would have been in a position to join Britain in scaling down the actual reparations bill and in preventing any such adventure as the French seizure of the Ruhr in 1923, from which flowed Germany's disastrous inflation and the ugly forces of German nihilism. (There is poignancy in the broken Wilson's coming out of retirement momentarily in 1923 to denounce France for making "waste paper" of the Treaty of Versailles.) Finally, if Shantung was Wilson's Yalta, he paid the kind of price FDR paid and for precisely the same reason—the collapse of the balance of power in the immediate area involved.

. . . [T]he chief claim of Wilson to a superlative place in history—and it will not be denied him merely because he was turned down by the United States Senate—is that he, more than any other, formulated and articulated the ideology which was the polestar of the Western democracies in World War I, in World War II, and in the decades of Cold War against the Communists. Today, well past the middle of the twentieth century, the long-time program of America is still a Wilsonian program: international collective security, disarmament, the lowering of economic barriers between nations (as in America's support for the developing West European community today), anti-colonialism, self-determination of nations, and democratic social politics as an alternative to Communism. And this was the program critics of Wilson called "anachronistic," a mere "throw-back" to nineteenth-century liberalism!

America today is still grappling with the same world problems Wilson grappled with in 1917, 1918, and 1919, and the programs and policies designed to meet them are still largely Wilsonian. But events since Wilson's time have made his solutions more and more prophetic and urgent. The sweep of the anti-imperialist revolutions propels us to wider self-determination and social politics. The elimination of space, the increasing interdependence of the world, the further disintegration of the balance of power in World War II, and the nuclear revolution in war compel us to more effective collective security and to arms control supervised by an agency of the United Nations.

There will be more unwillingness to identify Wilson with social politics abroad than with the other policies

Was Woodrow Wilson Responsible for the Failure of the United States to Join the League of Nations? by Madaras and SoRelle

155

with which he is more clearly identified. Historians like to quote George L. Record's letter to Wilson in which he told Wilson that there was no longer any glory in merely standing for political democracy, that political democracy had arrived, that the great issues of the future would revolve around economic and social democracy. But Wilson stood in no need of advice on this score. Earlier than any other responsible statesman, Wilson had seen the significance of the Chinese Revolution of Sun Yat-sen and of the Mexican Revolution, and he had officially encouraged both. Wilson believed that economic and social reform was implicit in the doctrine of self-determination, especially when applied to the colonial peoples. He recognized, too, that the Bolshevist Revolution had given economic and social reform a new urgency in all parts of the world. He was also well aware that those who most opposed his program for a world settlement were the conservative and imperialist elements in Western Europe and Japan, that socialist and labor groups were his most effective supporters. He pondered deeply how closely and openly he could work with labor and socialist parties in Europe without cutting off necessary support at home. (This—how to use social democracy and the democratic left to counter Communism abroad and still carry American opinion—was to be a central problem for every discerning American statesman after 1945.) Months before he had received Record's letter, Wilson himself had expressed almost the same views as Record. In a long conversation with Professor Stockton Axson at the White House, Wilson acknowledged that his best support was coming from labor people, that they were in touch with world movements and were international-minded, that government ownership of some basic resources and industries was coming, even in the United States, and that it was by a program of social democracy that Communism could be defeated.

In 1918 two gigantic figures—Wilson and Lenin—faced each other and articulated the contesting ideologies which would shake the world during the century. Since then, the lesser leaders who have succeeded them have added little to the ideology of either side. We are now far enough into the century to see in what direction the world is headed, provided there is no third world war. It is not headed for Communist domination. It is not headed for an American hegemony. And it is not headed for a duality with half the world Communist and the other half capitalist. Instead, it is headed for a new pluralism. The emerging new national societies are adjusting their new industrialism to their own conditions and cultures; and their developing economies will be varying mixtures of privatism, collectivism, and welfarism. Even the Communist states differ from one another in conditions, cultures, stages of revolutionary development, and degrees of Marxist "orthodoxy" or "revisionism." And today, all national states, old and new, Communist and non-Communist, join the United Nations as a matter of course.

There will be "victory" for neither "side," but instead a world which has been historically affected by both. Lenin's international proletarian state failed to materialize, but the evolving economies of the underdeveloped peoples are being influenced by his collectivism. However, the facts that most of the emerging economies are mixed ones, that they are working themselves out within autonomous national frameworks, and that the multiplying national states are operating internationally through the United Nations all point to a world which will be closer to the vision of Wilson than to that of Lenin. For this reason Wilson is likely to become a world figure of heroic proportions, with an acknowledged impact on world history more direct and far-reaching than that of any other American.

WILLIAM G. CARLETON (1903–1982) was a professor emeritus at the University of Florida and author of the widely used textbook, *The Revolution in American Foreign Policy*.

EXPLORING THE ISSUE

Was Woodrow Wilson Responsible for the Failure of the United States to Join the League of Nations?

Critical Thinking and Reflection

1. Compare and contrast the roles of President Wilson and Senator Lodge in bringing about the defeat of the Treaty of Versailles in the Senate. Who should bear responsibility for this failure?
2. Given Bailey's interpretation, do you think Wilson would have compromised on the treaty with Senator Lodge had he not suffered a severe stroke? Discuss.
3. Critically analyze how Carleton defends Wilson from the charges of (1) inflexibility and (2) naïve optimism. Do you agree or disagree with these criticisms? Why?
4. Evaluate whether Wilson was a realist or an idealist.
5. Compare and contrast the interpretations of Bailey and Carleton regarding Wilson's approach to foreign policy.

Is There Common Ground?

Both Carleton and Bailey make strong cases for their points of view. Carleton blames the Republicans, in particular the chairman of the Senate Foreign Relations Committee, Henry Cabot Lodge, for stalling votes on the treaty by reading its provisions to an empty Senate for nearly two weeks. He also rejects the Freudian interpretation, which argues that Wilson was incapable of compromise.

Bailey, on the other hand, blames Wilson more than Lodge for killing the treaty and the opportunity for the United States to enter and influence the League of Nations. Had Wilson not been physically damaged by his stroke, he might have struck a deal with Republicans as he had done previously in passing his New Freedom legislative program. Perhaps Bailey best hits the mark when he argues that Wilson was ahead of his times, and the American people were not willing to overthrow their traditional isolationist views to join an international League of Nations. Carleton also agrees that Wilson was ahead of his time. Maybe it was impossible for the United States to have joined the League of Nations at this time.

Create Central

www.mhhe.com/createcentral

Additional Resources

Lloyd E. Ambrosius, "Woodrow Wilson's Health and the Treaty Fight," *Wilsonianism: Woodrow Wilson and His Legacy in American Foreign Relations* (Palgrave Macmillan, 2002).

John M. Cooper, *Breaking the Heart of the World* (Cambridge University Press, 2001).

Arthur S. Link, "The Case for Woodrow Wilson," in *The Higher Realism of Woodrow Wilson* (Vanderbilt University Press, 1971).

Arthur S. Link, *Woodrow Wilson: Revolution, War, and Peace* (Johns Hopkins University Press, 1979).

John A. Thompson, *Woodrow Wilson* (Pearson Education, 2002).

Internet References . . .

The Treaty of Versailles and the League of Nations

> www.ushistory.org/us/45d.asp

U.S. Department of State

> http://history.state.gove/milestones/1914-1920/WWI

Wilson—A Portrait: League of Nations

> www.pbs.org/wgbh/amex/wilson/portrait/wp
> _league.html

Wilson Embarks on Tour to Promote League of Nations

> www.history.com/this-day-in-history/wilson-embarks
> -on-tour-to-promote-league-of-nations

Selected, Edited, and with Issue Framing Material by:
Larry Madaras, *Howard Community College*
and
James M. SoRelle, *Baylor University*

ISSUE

Was the Ku Klux Klan of the 1920s a Mainstream Organization?

YES: Shawn Lay, from "The Second Invisible Empire and Toward a New Historical Appraisal of the Klu Klux Klan of the 1920s," in *The Invisible Empire in the West: Toward a New Historical Appraisal of the Ku Klux Klan of the 1920s* (University of Illinois Press, 1992)

NO: Thomas R. Pegram, from *One Hundred Percent American: The Rebirth and Decline of the Ku Klux Klan in the 1920s* (Rowman & Littlefield Publishers)

Learning Outcomes

After reading this issue, you will be able to:

- Identify the origin and major goals of the Ku Klux Klan in the 1920s.
- Understand how the Ku Klux Klan of the 1920s differed from Klan organizations during Reconstruction and in the mid-twentieth century.
- Understand how scholarly views of the Klan have changed over time.
- Discuss the importance of religion in Klan ideology and activities.
- Evaluate the reasons for the decline of the Klan in the 1920s.

ISSUE SUMMARY

YES: Shawn Lay rejects the view of the Ku Klux Klan (KKK) as a radical fringe group comprised of marginal men and instead characterizes the KKK of the 1920s as a mainstream, grassroots organization that promoted traditional values of law, order, and social morality that appealed to Americans across the nation.

NO: Thomas Pegram, on the other hand, recognizes that Klansmen were often average members of their communities, but this did not prevent most Americans from denouncing the organization's commitment to white supremacy, xenophobia, religious intolerance, and violence as contradictory to the values of a pluralistic society.

There have been three Ku Klux Klans in American history: (1) the Reconstruction-era Klan, which arose in the South at the end of the Civil War and whose primary purpose was to prevent newly emancipated African Americans from voting and attaining social and economic equality with whites; (2) the 1920s Klan, which had national appeal and emerged out of disillusionment with the aftermath of U.S. intervention in World War I and the changing social, economic, and cultural values that had transformed the United States as a result of the Industrial Revolution; and (3) the modern Klan, which arose after World War II in the rural areas of the Deep South and (like the Reconstruction Klan) sought to prevent blacks from attaining citizenship rights guaranteed by the passage of civil rights legislation in the 1950s and 1960s.

The Ku Klux Klan that rose to prominence in the 1920s was founded in 1915 by William J. Simmons, a Methodist circuit preacher, and a group of his followers. For its first five years this new organization consisted of a few thousand members in local "klaverns" scattered throughout Georgia and Alabama, but on June 7, 1920, Simmons signed a contract with Edward Clarke and Elizabeth Tyler, two clever salespersons who engineered some of the most remarkable organizing and mass marketing techniques to attract tens of thousands of new members to the Klan over the course of the next year. By October 1921, some 85,000 men had joined the KKK. At its height in the mid-1920s, Klan membership nationally was estimated at somewhere between 3 and 5 million, constituting approximately one out of every five Protestant males in the United States. The 1920s Klan differed greatly from its earlier and later organizational iterations in terms of its wide-ranging geographical and political influence. It was not merely a southern movement but rather enjoyed broad appeal in all parts of the country, with major strongholds in the Southwest and Midwest. Politically, Klan members dominated state legislatures in Oklahoma, Texas, and Indiana, and city councils in El Paso, Texas, Denver, Colorado, Anaheim, California, and Tillamook, Oregon. The Klan of the 1920s was the most politically powerful right-wing movement of the decade.

While the members of the 1920s Klan continued to adhere to a doctrine of white supremacy and opposed equal rights for African Americans, they focused many of their attacks upon Catholic and Jewish residents who had come to the United States as part of the "new immigration" between 1870 and 1910. Klansmen seemed particularly to dislike Roman Catholics, who constituted 36 percent of the nation's population in 1920. Klansmen accused Catholics of placing loyalty to the pope over loyalty to the United States and characterized them as "un-American." If Catholics gained political control, the Klan asserted, separation of church and state would be abolished, and freedoms of speech, press, and religious worship would be eradicated. In large part, these views were a product of a wave of xenophobia that swept the United States following World War I. America's participation in the war had ended in public disillusionment. The U.S. Senate reflected the public's suspicion of all things foreign by refusing to ratify the Treaty of Versailles or join Woodrow Wilson's League of Nations. Antiforeign sentiments were also reflected in reforms passed in 1921 and 1924, which severely curtailed immigration from southern and eastern Europe and completely excluded Japanese and other Asians.

Historians have offered a variety of explanations for the resurgence of the Ku Klux Klan in the 1920s. Scholars in the 1920s generally agreed that growing Klan membership derived from small-town residents who responded irrationally to the dramatic economic and social changes that affected them as a result of rapid industrialization and urbanization. These views were largely adopted by Richard Hofstadter in *The Age of Reform: From Bryan to F.D.R.* (Alfred A. Knopf, 1955) in which he argued that the Klan represented a "status revolt" among "relatively unprosperous and uncultivated native white Protestants" who were distressed that their traditional way of life was being replaced by the forces of modernity. This position was largely adopted by David H. Bennett in *The Party of Fear: From Nativist Movements to the New Right in American History* (University of North Carolina Press, 1988). Challenges to this traditional interpretation appeared in the 1960s in studies by Charles Alexander and Kenneth Jackson. In *The Ku Klux Klan in the Southwest* (University of Kentucky Press, 1966), Alexander agreed with earlier scholars that the Klan of the 1920s was a vigilante organization, but he portrayed the KKK as an accepted mainstream association that focused its attacks not so much on members of racial or religious minorities but rather on offenders of their community's Victorian moral code. Jackson's *The Ku Klux Klan in the City, 1915–1930* (Oxford University Press, 1967) revised the traditional narrative of the Klan by arguing that the organization was centered in large cities, not in small towns or rural areas, and that historians had exaggerated the level of violence meted out by Klansmen.

Recent scholarship on the 1920s draws upon the insights of Alexander, Jackson, and others to focus on the Klan's grassroots political participation. In these newer studies, Klansmen are viewed less as extremists and more as political pressure groups whose aims were to gain control of various local and state governmental offices. Robert Alan Goldberg's *Hooded Empire: The Ku Klux Klan in Colorado* (University of Illinois Press, 1982) concludes that Klan members in Colorado were drawn largely from civic activists who sought peaceful political reforms. Similarly, Leonard J. Moore, in *Citizen Klansmen: The Ku Klux Klan in Indiana, 1921–1928* (University of North Carolina Press, 1991), focuses upon perhaps the strongest Klan operation in the nation during the 1920s and concludes that Hoosier State Klansmen represented a cross-section of white Protestant society and constituted a popular social movement, not an extremist vigilante organization. These revisionist views have been challenged by Nancy MacLean in *Behind the Mask of Chivalry: The Making of the Second Ku Klux Klan* (Oxford University Press, 1994). MacLean returns the Klan story to the South (Athens, Georgia) and emphasizes the violent activities of the Klan while characterizing its membership as typical white middle-class Protestant males who hoped to assert their hierarchical dominace in American society.

Was the Klan of the 1920s a mainstream organization? Shawn Lay describes the Ku Klux Klan of the 1920s as a vast social, political, and folk movement whose program was deeply embedded in mainstream values shared by a majority of white Protestants, including opponents of the

Klan. By denying that the KKK was a racial fringe group comprised of marginal men, he challenges the traditional view that the Klan's activities lay outside the major currents of American political and social life.

Thomas Pegram has provided a valuable synthesis of Klan scholarship, which suggests that while Klan members shared certain values with mainstream American Protestant society, such as racism, anti-Semitism, and anti-Catholicism, their use of violence, their internal political conflicts, and their difficulty in adhering to their own stated moral values prevented the Klan from being widely accepted by the vast majority of Americans who found the group's commitment to secrecy and vigilantism particularly objectionable and incendiary.

YES ↵

Shawn Lay

The Second Invisible Empire

Even in our time of apparent widespread historical illiteracy, few Americans have not heard of the Ku Klux Klan and formed strong opinions about this controversial organization Many would agree that no single group more starkly demonstrates the endurance of dark social forces in the United States—racism, religious bigotry, extralegal vigilantism, moral authoritarianism—than the Klan, a hooded secret order now well into its second century of existence. As one popular writer has termed it, the KKK is commonly viewed as a persistent social virus thriving during periods of exceptional discord, tension, and intolerance. This appraisal, however, obscures the fact that the Klan has not been a monolithic movement throughout its history. Although linked by a common name and a commitment to secrecy, the major episodes of mass Klan activity have been characterized by distinctive organizational features, recruiting patterns, and sociopolitical agendas. . . .

More than seventy years ago, between the eras of the Klans of the first and second Reconstructions, an even more distinctive, and historically significant, Invisible Empire appeared—the Knights of the Ku Klux Klan (Inc.). While its earlier and later namesakes were either confined almost exclusively to the South or were relatively small in size, this organization demonstrated great appeal among mainstream elements across the nation, attracting millions of members at the height of its power in the 1920s. Simultaneously a vast social, political, and folk movement, the Klan of the twenties, more than any other manifestation of the hooded order, succeeded in significantly influencing national life for a period, establishing the white-robed Klansman as one of the enduring symbols of a critical decade in American development. . . .

[T]he great KKK movement of the twenties originated in Georgia, founded by William Joseph Simmons, a thirty-five-year-old Spanish-American War veteran and former Methodist circuit rider. Simmons, as historians of the Klan have been fond of pointing out, hardly seemed a likely candidate to head a successful enterprise of any type. Chronic ineptitude had characterized his career as

a minister, resulting in a formal suspension by Methodist church authorities in 1912, and a drinking problem undermined what little ability he possessed for long-term planning. Yet, Simmons did have certain assets, including an impressive physical appearance, an ability for effective public speaking, and an amiable personality. After his dismissal from the clergy, Simmons embarked on a career as a professional "fraternalist," soliciting recruits for men's societies such as the Woodmen of the World (which assigned him the honorary rank of "Colonel," a title he would proudly use the rest of his life). The former minister's personal skills served him well in the fraternal world of the South and he eventually rose to the position of district manager for the Woodmen in Atlanta. This moderate bout of success encouraged Simmons in a longstanding ambition to found a men's order of his own. As he envisioned it, the organization would be the grandest of patriotic fraternities, a banding together of true Americans that would "destroy from the hearts of men the Mason and Dixon line and build thereupon a great American solidarity."

After an accident placed him in the hospital for a three-month stay, Colonel Simmons had time to develop detailed plans for his fraternal society. Drawing upon the colorful tales he had heard about the Reconstruction Klan, and recognizing that the public mood was auspicious, Simmons decided to create a Klan of his own, albeit an essentially fraternal one. In the days that followed, the Colonel devised an elaborate Masonically inspired ritual for the order and designed the eerie hoods and robes that would become so notorious; he also laid out an elaborate chain of command for the new Invisible Empire, ranging from an Imperial Wizard at the top of the hierarchy to the various klaliffs, kludds, kligrapps, klabees, kladds, and klexters who would manage the affairs of the organization's various local chapters (dubbed klaverns). By the time of his release from the hospital, all that remained for Simmons to do was to persuade others to join the revived Klan, a task for which his earlier fraternal work had left him well prepared.

The Colonel energetically applied himself to finding members for his new order and by October 1915 had recruited thirty-four Georgians, who successfully petitioned their state for an official charter. On a cold and windy Thanksgiving evening a month later, Simmons and fifteen others of the group ascended Stone Mountain outside Atlanta, ignited a large cross at the peak's summit, and declared the rebirth of the Invisible Empire. This and similar publicity efforts, often in association with Atlanta showings of *The Birth of a Nation,* intensified local interest in the Klan and by the end of the year Atlanta Klan No. 1 was in operation. During the first months of its existence, the new KKK scarcely resembled the original order. Although formally committed to the principles of Protestantism, Americanism, and white supremacy, Klansmen demonstrated little interest in social or political affairs, preferring to occupy their time with fraternal ritualism. The advent of American participation in World War I thrust the Klan into a broader role, however, as the organization became involved with the Citizens' Bureau of Investigation, a volunteer home-front vigilante group. Appointed as "secret-service men" by Imperial Wizard Simmons, Klansmen harassed those they perceived to be slackers, enemy aliens, or immoral women. As spirited as these activities were, they nevertheless drew little special attention to the Klan during a period when many of the nation's citizens were participating in vigilantism of one kind or another. As a southwestern newspaper editor observed in 1918, "In a hundred American communities the Ku Klux Klan is riding again . . . , not by that name, but in that spirit."

Despite its increased activity during the war, the Klan's membership remained small, numbering only a few thousand by the end of 1919, almost all of whom resided in Georgia and Alabama. Chronic financial problems threatened even this modest growth, particularly after a leading Klan officer embezzled several thousand dollars in precious initiation fees. In 1920, however, the KKK's fortunes improved dramatically, following Colonel Simmon's decision to acquire the services of the Southern Publicity Association, a small advertising agency headed by Edward Young Clarke and Elizabeth Tyler. Efficient business managers who realized the Klan's potential had barely been exploited, Clarke and Tyler completely reorganized the secret society's finances and membership procurement procedures, floating large new loans and hiring hundreds of full-time recruiters (kleagles). In short order, Klan representatives were visiting communities across the South, touting the order's commitment to pure Americanism and the defense of traditional standards of law, order, and social morality.

Relatively little is known about the precise manner in which these professional organizers went about setting up fledgling klaverns, but evidently the majority of initial contacts took place in fraternal lodges, particularly those of the various Masonic orders. Fraternal connections gave the kleagles valuable access to prominent men, including elected officials, whose recruitment enhanced the organization's prestige and general appeal. But the Invisible Empire's interaction with leading civic elements was exceedingly complex and varied from community to community. Depending on the local set of circumstances, the Klan might support, oppose, or ignore a particular group. Essentially the Klan was a chameleon during this early organizational stage, adjusting its sales pitch in light of the local context and the dictates of opportunism.

Benefiting from its adaptability, the revitalized Ku Klux Klan dramatically demonstrated its popular appeal throughout vast regions of the southern United States in 1920 and early 1921, garnering tens of thousands of eager recruits, mostly in Texas, Louisiana, and Oklahoma. The KKK simultaneously provided evidence of some of the darker impulses of its members, as an outbreak of violent extralegal vigilantism accompanied the spread of the Invisible Empire. While blacks did not escape the secret order's ire, the bulk of the violence focused upon perceived moral offenders who were white.

This upsurge in vigilante activity soon attracted the attention of the national press, which began to detail alleged Klan outrages in an attempt to alert the country to a mounting danger. Leading the way was the Pulitzer-owned *New York World,* which extensively investigated the organization in mid-1921 and then released a sensational expose of Klan-sponsored violence. At the same time, major publications such as *Literary Digest, Outlook,* and *Independent* started to feature numerous articles dedicated to uncovering the pernicious appeal and activities of the revived KKK. The alarm generated by this media coverage prodded the Congressional House Rules Committee into holding hearings in October 1921 to determine whether there were grounds for a federal investigation. While evidence presented in the hearings indicated that the Invisible Empire was far from the pristine group it claimed to be, no major irregularities came to light, and Imperial Wizard Simmons emerged from hostile questioning in surprisingly good form. In subsequent months, Congress failed to take any further action concerning the Klan, and to many Americans it appeared that the order had received at least a degree of official approval. Apparently among those convinced was President Warren G. Harding, who entered the ranks of the Invisible Empire in a special ceremony held in the Green Room of the White House.

The publicity produced by the *World's* widely syndicated expose and the subsequent Klan hearings assisted the Invisible Empire in escaping its sectional confines and becoming a bonafide national movement. By early 1922, local Klan chapters—which would include tens of thousands in Chicago alone—were gathering strength in the Midwest, and Ku Kluxing continued at a furious pace up and down the Pacific coast; the order likewise began to make impressive inroads in Pennsylvania and parts of New York and New England, even setting up a klavern at Harvard University. It now appeared a definite possibility that the Ku Klux Klan might establish itself as a major and enduring influence in American society.

This tremendous and sudden success naturally delighted Imperial officials but also fostered a belief within the upper echelons of the hierarchy that the Klan required better leadership. Gradually, throughout 1922, a politically ambitious coeterie of prominent Klansmen wrested control of the order from Colonel Simmons, who was being variously condemned for heavy drinking, financial ineptitude, and an unswerving defense of Edward Young Clarke and Elizabeth Tyler in the aftermath of a morals scandal. Replacing Simmons as Imperial Wizard was Hiram Wesley Evans, a successful Dallas dentist who would head the KKK for the remainder of the 1920s. Evans's ascendency signaled the advent of intensive Klan involvement in politics, and he dreamed of forging the hooded order into "a great militant political organization." Such an aspiration, however, had to contend with the relative independence of the Klan's hundreds of widely scattered local chapters. Although on paper the Invisible Empire seemed tightly structured along quasi-military lines, the chain of command served little purpose other than to funnel funds back to Imperial headquarters in Atlanta, Once established, klaverns received only minimal central direction. Most of the national Klan experience, therefore, would be played out in numerous community-level KKK episodes, in which local conditions would profoundly shape the goals, activities, and membership of the Invisible Empire.

A central core of beliefs, of course, held the Klan together. As the organization's constitution and other Imperial documents indicate Klansmen advocated "pure Americanism" and "the faithful maintenance of White Supremacy." The Klan viewed with suspicion those who owed "allegiance of any nature or degree to any foreign Government, nation, institution, sect, ruler, person, or people," and proudly asserted that Anglo-Saxons were "the only race that has ever proved its ability and supremacy and its determination to progress under any and all conditions and handicaps." The order also advocated strict enforcement of the law, particularly the various prohibition statutes. Yet, the appeal of this program—which was well-grounded in mainstream views that the vast majority of white Protestants probably shared to one degree or another—did not insure a uniform level of success for the Klan across the nation. In neither Mississippi nor South Carolina, overwhelmingly Protestant states with powerful racist and vigilante traditions, did the Klan establish itself as a major force, while the order thrived in more "progressive" locales such as Oregon, Michigan, and Ohio. In Tennessee, the KKK prospered in Memphis and Knoxville but quickly died in Nashville, surely not an exceptional bastion of liberal enlightenment in the 1920s. In Orange County, California, the communities of Anaheim, Fullerton, Brea, and La Habra proved very receptive to the Invisible Empire's appeal, but the hooded order never developed an enduring following in the nearby towns of Orange and Santa Ana. Thus, almost inevitably, one is drawn to the community level in order to assess the sources of the Klan's popularity or lack thereof. Indeed, few topics in the American past more clearly demonstrate the validity of the famous dictum that "all history is ultimately local history" than the Ku Klux Klan of the 1920s. . . .

Toward a New Historical Appraisal of the Ku Klux Klan of the 1920s

During the latter half of the 1920s, the Ku Klux Klan rapidly faded as a significant factor in American social and political life. Part of this decline can be attributed to the sordid revelations concerning Indiana Klan leader David C. Stephenson during his sensational murder trial in 1925, but . . . the hooded order had already lost much of its appeal. . . . Here and there, groups of ardent Klansmen continued to meet well into the 1930s, but their impact and influence were minimal.

Nearly seventy years after it spread across the nation like a prairie wildfire, the Ku Klux Klan of the 1920s largely remains a historical enigma. Only a relative handful of local klaverns (almost all in urban areas) have been closely examined, and even for these chapters many questions have not been answered. We anticipate, however, that the state of Klan studies will greatly improve in the near future, particularly as historians make use of the 1920 manuscript census. In the hope of encouraging and advancing this process, we submit the following observations and suggestions.

The rise and fall of the Ku Klux Klan constituted an exceedingly complex social and political phenomenon, involving millions of individuals in many different types of communities spread across a large nation. Although much additional research remains to be done, we have discovered that many of the accepted explanations for the growth of so-called intolerance in this period are of limited usefulness. Most notably, we have not detected a struggle between cosmopolitan urban forces and declining rural and small-town elements at the heart of western Klan experiences. No doubt, the Invisible Empire developed a considerable rural following in the West and elsewhere, but the extent and nature of the hooded order's attractiveness in nonurban areas and among country people who had recently moved to the city have yet to be adequately explored. Perhaps future Klan historians will be able to demonstrate how the KKK's social agenda reflected distinct rural influences; for the present, however, we sense that the Invisible Empire's appeal cut across urban and rural lines without much difficulty and that it would be a serious mistake for students of the KKK to be uncritically committed to the concept of urban-rural conflict in the 1920s. . . .

If the recruiting pattern of western Klans holds true for other regions (and recent work on the KKK in Indiana and western New York suggests that it does), then it is clear that the Invisible Empire succeeded in attracting balanced support across the Protestant religious spectrum, including that of Episcopalians and German-American Lutherans—groups viewed by the ethno culturalists as having often been at political odds with evangelical Protestants. Thus, the nature of the KKK's membership may demonstrate that by the 1920s Protestant-Catholic ethnocentrism had replaced pietist-liturgical conflict as the most important influence shaping American politics. The order's widespread appeal among Protestants additionally indicates that the Klan should not be viewed as being composed largely of religious fundamentalists. Although many Klansmen paid homage to the "old-time religion" and rejected the thinking of religious "modernists" in the 1920s, the vast majority did not belong to fundamentalist sects; rather they were members of traditional evangelical and nonevangelical Protestant denomination or did not formally affiliate with a particular church. The non-fundamentalist composition of the Klan is supported by a recent evaluation of 12,000 Klansmen in Indianapolis that discovered that a lower percentage of fundamentalist church members joined the Invisible Empire than any other Protestant group in that community. The Klan is best seen, therefore, as an organization with strong and direct links to mainstream Protestant society.

If the 1920s KKK does not readily conform to explanatory schemas based on urban-rural conflict, intra-Protestant ethnocultural conflict, or religious extremism, then there are numerous other promising means for assessing this movement. Once a sufficient number of case studies from a variety of regions have been produced, the national Klan experience should be compared and contrasted with other episodes of social and political activism in American history, such as Populism, the various crusades of the Progressive era, and even the civil rights, antiwar, and woman's rights movements of the 1960s and 1970s. Through the careful exploitation of social science theory, election returns, and manuscript census data, scholars will determine to what extent the KKK represented a traditional form of grass-roots insurgency. Such analysis will surely have to consider the profound organizational developments that took place in the 1920s, particularly the intensified effort of political and business elites to order communities in accordance with their desire for stability, efficiency, economic growth, and the maintenance of power. . . .

[T]he Klan was often at odds with established community leaders and regularly attempted to pose as the champion of the "common people." Whether this indicated that the Invisible Empire largely (if indirectly) served as a means of expressing class discontent is debatable. . . .

Beyond its political and social activism, other aspects of the second Klan merit extensive examination. The Klan's role as a fraternal group needs additional investigation, particularly in light of the new and provocative scholarship that has been produced on secret men's societies in the nineteenth century. As Nancy K. MacLean has recently demonstrated, gender analysis can be utilized to learn more about the men and women who supported the KKK. The techniques of collective biography, psychological analysis, and oral history should also be effective in uncovering the influences that led Americans into the Klan. Indeed, given the large membership, geographic expansiveness, and general complexity of the Invisible Empire, the research possibilities for political, social, intellectual, religious, and cultural historians and other scholars are practically limitless. . . .

The Knights of the Ku Klux Klan (Inc.) was not a fanatical fringe group composed of marginal men. The order drew its membership from a generally balanced cross section of the white male Protestant population, with the exception of the extreme upper and lower tiers of the socioeconomic hierarchy. In the context of early twentieth-century American society, the great bulk of Klansmen were not aberrationally racist, religiously bigoted, or socially alienated, although they were more likely to openly express and act upon their views. With a few exceptions, members of the hooded order avoided violent vigilantism.

The Klan demonstrated a multifaceted appeal, but discontent over local issues primarily fueled the organization's spectacular rise. The immediate postwar period was a time of dramatic expansion and brought problems associated with law enforcement, social morality, political control, labor relations, and the allocation of community resources. These difficulties placed great strains upon established leaders and created sizeable blocs of discontented citizens, many of whom turned to the Klan as a means of challenging the policies of dominant decision makers. This does not mean, however, that the KKK should be viewed as a uniformly antielite movement. The precise dynamics of Klan-elite interaction varied from community to community, and . . . certain bankers, businessmen, government officials, doctors, lawyers, ministers, and newspaper editors were among those who donned white hoods and robes in the twenties.

Whatever their social or economic standing, a commitment to civic activism united members of the order. Through the medium of the Klan, citizens discussed local problems, formulated plans of action, and vigorously pursued their social and political agendas. Although the focus of Klan activism varied according to specific community circumstances, the KKK typically espoused stricter law enforcement (especially of the prohibition statutes), open and honest government, improved social morality, and Protestant control of the schools. This hardly constituted a novel or radical program: such goals had been advocated by mainstream Protestant elements throughout the nineteenth and early twentieth centuries. For the most part, Klansmen concentrated their efforts within the political arena, although some klaverns initiated boycotts of non-Protestant businesses and occasionally attempted to regulate social conditions.

Initially, the Ku Klux Klan functioned quite well as a medium of corrective civic action. The group's zealous Protestantism, ethnic militancy, and superpatriotism attracted a dedicated core of loyalists, and a policy of absolute secrecy hindered preemptive measures by the order's opponents. Operating largely behind the scenes, the Klan was free to exploit the electorate's concerns over community problems (concerns that most Klansmen sincerely shared) and make considerable political headway. Once it had achieved a degree of electoral success, however, the Klan typically foundered. The organization failed to establish an enduring political base, demonstrated little skill in administrative or legislative matters, and allowed its enemies to take the initiative. Probably more than anything else, the Klan suffered from its practice of hooded secrecy, which left the order and its political operatives vulnerable to charges of being part of a clandestine conspiracy against the American tradition of open and democratic government. Thus, ironically, the very

secrecy that had assisted the Klan in political mobilization eventually became its Achilles' heel.

Political setbacks, the fading of the order's fraternal allure, internecine feuding, and growing public antipathy all contributed to the Invisible Empire's rapid decline. When they realized that their organization had little hope of changing or improving local society, Klansmen departed in droves, evidence of the spirit of civic activism that had guided most of the membership. In some locales, pockets of diehard Klansmen held firm, but this was often because they yet hoped to make a political comeback.

It would be a mistake to view the Klan's gradual downfall as a victory of enlightened liberalism over the forces of reaction and intolerance. Many of the KKK's most dedicated foes endorsed patently racist policies, held disparaging views of Catholics and Jews, engaged in corrupt political practices, and, like the Klan, conspired in secret. In certain communities, prominent anti-Klansmen opposed the order not so much on the basis of its ideology as its potential for challenging the dominance of entrenched political and economic interests. This is not to say, however, that a historical debt of gratitude is not owed to the anti-KKK forces. Unopposed, the Ku Klux Klan certainly possessed the potential to evolve into an agency of intolerant oppression.

We realize that our portrait of the typical Klansman as a mainstream, grass-roots community activist may not retain its validity in all communities; in fact, we anticipate that future scholars will discover remarkable variety among klaverns across the nation. Yet, it is clear that the biased stereotype of the Invisible Empire as an irrational movement that lay outside the major currents of American political and social life must for the most part be discarded. Not only does this traditional view unfairly depict the millions of average citizens who joined or supported the Klan, but it obscures the racism and bigotry that have traditionally pervaded United States society. Far from being a historical aberration, the Ku Klux Klan reflected the hopes, fears, and guiding values of much of the American public in the 1920s.

SHAWN LAY received his PhD from Vanderbilt University and has taught at Coker College in Hartsville, South Carolina, since 1996. He currently serves as a professor of history and is chair of the department of history, philosophy, and religion. His other books include *War, Revolution, and the Ku Klux Klan: A Study of Intolerance in a Border City* (Texas Western Press, 1985) and *Hooded Knights on the Niagara: The Ku Klux Klan in Buffalo, New York* (New York University Press, 1995).

Thomas R. Pegram  **NO**

One Hundred Percent American: The Rebirth and Decline of the Ku Klux Klan in the 1920s

To most contemporary Americans, the Ku Klux Klan of the 1920s is a curious artifact from a bygone age. The pointed hoods, nonsensical terminology, and bigoted ideology of the Invisible Empire appeared anachronistic even in the 1920s as the United States absorbed immigrants from around the globe and began the slow process of reconciling American democracy with racial, ethnic, and cultural pluralism. Today, in a nation presided over by a president from a mixed-race background, the preoccupations of the Klan seem even more remote. The sharp racial and ethnic divisions that in the Klan's worldview determined fitness for citizenship and separated authentic American identity from alien allegiances contrast markedly with a more diverse and open public culture. Contemporary Klansmen are despised as violent troublemakers skulking on the margins of society. Yet even from our vantage point in the early twenty-first century, the Klan phenomenon of the New Era—as Americans called the years after World War I—has relevance.

The American profile is now broader than the native-born Protestant characteristics defended by the Invisible Empire, but disagreement over the nature of American identity persists into our time. Distracted opponents of President Barack Obama insist that he is not a true American eligible to hold the nation's highest office. Others strain to curtail unregulated immigration, complaining that the flow of undocumented newcomers undermines the rule of law and endangers the economic interests and cultural rights of Americans. Catholics and Jews, the special targets of the New Era Klan, now reside comfortably within the American mainstream, but a substantial number of Americans consider another religious tradition, Islam, to be incompatible with the social and political institutions of the nation. All these contemporary issues are contested, but so too were the disputes of the 1920s in which the Invisible Empire engaged. . . .

Scholarly opinion of the New Era Klan has shifted considerably over the last generation. Beginning in the 1980s and accelerating in the 1990s, historians reconsidered the image of the 1920s Invisible Empire as a violent, racially oppressive fringe movement populated by the rootless and defeated stragglers left behind by the nation's march to modernity. Building on earlier insights from Charles C. Alexander and Kenneth Jackson, scholars such as Leonard Moore and Shawn Lay deemphasized the national Klan organization and instead paid close attention to local manifestations of the Klan movement, often in Midwestern or Pacific Coast communities. A series of Klan community studies revealed the degree to which the Invisible Empire flourished at the grassroots level, reflecting a sense of American identity and civic engagement that was shared by many white Protestant Americans in the aftermath of World War I. Fraternal fellowship, community-building, reform of local government, and close attention to public schools, law enforcement, and proper moral comportment distinguished these Klansmen from the night-riding Ku Kluxers of earlier historiography.

The proponents of this populist or civic interpretation of the New Era Klan presented vigilantism as a minor theme in the grassroots Klan movement, confined chiefly to violence-prone regions of the South and Southwest. The unmistakable hooded emphasis on white supremacy, anti-Catholicism, and Protestant cultural chauvinism approximated broader patterns of intolerance that beset the United States in the 1920s. In short, the new interpretation of the Klan stressed how representative and mainstream were the attributes of the hooded order. In this view, the Klan phenomenon also was most authentic and vigorous as a social movement at the klavern, or local club, level. The national Klan's drive for political influence and mainstream acceptance, spearheaded by Imperial Wizard Hiram W. Evans, vainly sought to reproduce the civic accomplishments of local Klans on state and federal levels.

The last generation of Klan studies has clarified the interior life of local Klans and the civic activism that motivated many knights. But taken as a whole, the new Klan literature is incomplete. The violence and exclusionary politics that compelled attention to the Invisible Empire seem at odds with the citizen Klansmen highlighted in recent local studies. No general history of the 1920s Klan phenomenon reflects the new research and perspectives on the Klan movement. Nor is there an updated analysis of the movement that brings the fullness of the Klan experience from that period into balance. Ties of belief and a commitment to bold action linked the moral vigilantism of Southwestern knights with the school board politics and voluntary prohibition enforcement that occupied Midwestern Klansman. . . . [This essay] recognizes the diversity of the Klan movement while charting the shared patterns that determined the organization's rise and fall. [It] situates the Klan within mainstream developments in American postwar life but also explains why the Klan failed to achieve mainstream status in the 1920s.

I have tried to rethink the history of the 1920s Klan by drawing on the rich inventory of theses, dissertations, articles, and focused studies of local or state Klans that have accumulated since the revival of Klan scholarship. The recent unpublished literature, which has been underused by historians, has been an especially important resource in this study. I have also sought to contextualize the New Era Klan movement in the light of new studies of race, ethnicity, political culture, social reform, and governance that have enriched the historical understanding of the post–World War I United States. Revisiting the documentary record of the Klan and the contemporary analysis of the movement provided by insightful New Era journalists helps connect the scattered Klan community studies into a more comprehensive examination of the hooded order's expansion, operations, and collapse. I have tried to supply more thorough analyses of community formation among Klansmen, the power of racial identity and anti-Catholicism in the hooded movement, and such topics as education reform, prohibition enforcement, violence, and political organization than are now available. Close attention to these issues also illuminates the tension between local Klans and the national organization that provoked the sudden and rapid decline of the Invisible Empire at mid-decade.

I hope this [essay] will also advance discussion of the Klan movement's flirtation with the American mainstream of the New Era. The hooded empire clearly was not an anomalous development in the 1920s. It shared many of the same patterns and influences that distinguished American society in the wake of World War I.

The collective weight of the new Klan community studies further emphasizes the representative qualities of 1920s Klansmen. Yet the Klan movement only approached the American mainstream of the 1920s, which was increasingly pluralistic if still not fully participatory.

Ku Kluxers never comfortably occupied the mainstream because the Invisible Empire aroused bitter contemporary opposition and denunciation. Anti-Klan sentiment extended beyond the groups specifically targeted by the Invisible Empire to the white Protestant establishment itself. Immediate and sustained criticism of the organization's secrecy, masks, and vigilantism was evident throughout the New Era. Several states took action to banish the Klan or passed anti-mask laws to break up its public events. Even in an age when assumptions of white supremacy, unembarrassed ethnic chauvinism, and religious intolerance toward Catholics and Jews were commonplace, the Klan's expression of these themes was deemed incendiary and objectionable. Nor were the Klan's public policy positions accepted as uncomplicated contributions to public life. Its civic stances in support of public schools and law enforcement were clearly tainted with anti-Catholicism and suspicion of immigrants. Local Klans frequently incorporated into their school reform proposals the demand that Catholic teachers and administrators be fired from public schools.

To consider the Klan a mainstream interest group defending beleaguered Protestant social and cultural standards, therefore, is to drain the contemporary controversy from the Invisible Empire. The new Klan historians have done a service in placing the revived Klan squarely at the center of the social, cultural, and political turbulence of what the historian David J. Goldberg has termed the discontented America of the 1920s. In its assertion of what it saw as embattled American values, the hooded order incorporated reform themes from the populist and progressive traditions, as well as patterns of bigotry and repression that had deep roots in American society. And in areas with thin minority populations, such as Indiana and Oklahoma, where white Protestant domination was assured, the Klan was more likely to be regarded, at least temporarily, as a legitimate participant in civic discourse.

But it is an overstatement to characterize the second Klan as a mainstream proponent of culturally based reform. The 1920s Klan interacted with the mainstream and attracted the short-term loyalty of many ordinary Americans, but it was not, even when judged by its own intention to wield stealthy influence, a mainstream organization. One historian of the Klan, David A. Horowitz, has reflected the ambiguous position of the Invisible Empire in 1920s society by describing "the normality of extremism" evident in the "widespread legitimacy and pervasive appeal" of a masked, secret society that nevertheless lost members nearly as quickly as it recruited them. In the end, however, Ku Klux extremism overwhelmed the community-based features of hooded fellowship, white Protestant identity, and local activism that had attracted many knights to the organization. Persistent violence committed by and against Klansmen, the arrogance and misbehavior of hooded leaders, and an ill-considered grab at political power drove disaffected knights out of the organization halfway through the 1920s. But it is an indication of the Klan's significance as a social movement and of the discordant cultural negotiations of the postwar period that so many average citizens were compelled to articulate their understanding of Americanism through such an extraordinary and flawed instrument. . . .

Historians and the Klan

The contradictions of Klan movement—its mixture of the common-place and the extreme, its civic expression and violent outbreaks, the depth of its appeal and its rapid, spectacular dissolution—have made the 1920s Ku Klux Klan a particularly difficult puzzle for historians. Beyond the inherent interpretive problems in evaluating a complicated social movement, the secrecy and disingenuousness of the self-styled Invisible Empire created an imbalance in the documentary record of the second Klan. Klansmen (usually) hid their identity in public behind masks and were instructed to deny their membership in the order when questioned about it. Membership lists were kept strictly confidential, and individual klaverns closely guarded their minute books. Enemies of the Klan periodically stole and published Klan membership lists to undermine the hooded order (indeed, the Chicago-based journal *Tolerance* devoted itself to revealing the identities of secret Ku Kluxers), but, while helpful in recovering portions of the Klan's vital statistics, these sources were usually incomplete and frequently inaccurate. For instance, *Tolerance* mistakenly listed William Wrigley Jr., the sportsman and chewing gum magnate, as a Klansman and printed numerous corrections of similar errors concerning lesser known individuals.

On the other hand, the leaders and official representatives of the hooded order, Imperial Wizard Hiram Evans in particular, freely identified themselves, gave interviews, wrote articles in the popular press about the Klan's beliefs and political positions, and directed at least a portion of their official duties to the public sphere. The Klan also published its own magazines and newspapers, such as the official journal from Atlanta, the *Kourier,* or Indiana's *Fiery Cross.* Some of these publications, especially newspapers, provided glimpses of local concerns and conditions in the grassroots of Klandom, but the heavy hand of grand dragons or the imperial hierarchy was usually evident. An overrepresentation of elite sources on the Klan movement was therefore available to contemporary observers. Key facts such as membership figures relied on Klan statements, usually inflated, or fairly broad estimates by informed outsiders. Insights into the inner workings of Klandom came from investigative journalists, revelations by estranged Klansmen, testimony obtained in the course of efforts undertaken by several states to revoke Klan charters, government hearings, or legal documents and depositions produced by the many lawsuits and occasional criminal proceedings that punctuated the active history of the 1920s Klan. Taken together, these records were rich and revelatory but not comprehensive. They also highlighted national Klan concerns over local issues, the perspectives of leaders over the perception of ordinary knights, and the impact of Klan misdeeds over routine behavior.

Although much of the journalistic coverage of the Klan in the 1920s was discerning, the absence of local records led the first serious studies of the second Klan to miss some essential features of the movement. Beginning with John M. Mecklin's 1924 analysis, *The Ku Klux Klan: A Study of the American Mind,* and carrying into the 1960s, scholars and popular writers depicted the Klan movement as an irrational rebuke of modernity by undereducated, economically marginal bigots, religious zealots, and dupes willing to be manipulated by the Klan's cynical, mendacious leaders. It was, in this view, a movement of country parsons and small-town malcontents who were out of step with the dynamism of twentieth-century urban America. As Mecklin put it, even though the Klan drew on common themes and prejudices rooted in the historical experience of the United States, the hooded order was "a refuge for mediocre men, if not weaklings," attracted from the "more or less ignorant and unthinking middle class" of back-roads America. These followers supposedly found in the elaborate ceremonies and simplistic crusades of the Invisible Empire relief from "the drabness of village and small town life" and the "monotonous and unimaginative round" of their daily existence. Emphasis was also placed on the Klan's Southern roots and its violent repression of African Americans, Jews, and Catholics, often in contrast to more tolerant, urbane sentiments expressed by the Klan's critics. Rather than explaining the Klan as a product of 1920s America, assembled from its current fears and aspirations, the initial historical portrait of the second Klan characterized the Invisible Empire as an anachronistic holdover from the nineteenth century, at odds with its own society.

An inescapable ideological context after World War II also framed historical considerations of the Klan. In the wake of the wreckage produced by nationalistic, racially charged mass movements of the 1930s and 1940s, and the repressive atmosphere of McCarthyism in the early Cold War, American scholars regarded popular movements from the Klan to the late nineteenth-century populist rebellion with suspicion as pathways to intolerance, anti-intellectualism, and even dictatorship. After all, Evans himself described the Klan as representing "a movement of the plain people, very weak in the matter of culture, intellectual support, and trained leadership." Some journalists in the 1920s argued that the Klan was a prototype for American fascism, a claim later taken up by the historians Robert Moats Miller and, most recently, Nancy MacLean. Others who had witnessed in the early 1950s the disturbing, seemingly credulous, popular support for Joseph McCarthy's reckless charges of disloyalty against unoffending Americans found it reasonable to conclude that "relatively unprosperous and uncultivated" folk had been seduced by the Klan's insistence that alien values imperiled Protestant cultural and political ascendancy in the 1920s. The perspective from a later social movement, the campaign for civil rights, also influenced impressions of the second Klan. In many Southern states, civil rights activism was met by yet another incarnation of the Ku Klux Klan, which functioned as the terroristic wing of the massive resistance to desegregation and voting rights that erupted among white Southerners. The shadow of that crudely violent and racist Klan revival further distorted considerations of the 1920s Klan phenomenon. Influenced by the evidence of intolerance, racism, and violence that marred the public record of the 1920s Klan, hampered by the absence of thorough membership records, and reflecting the low regard for mass movements among intellectuals, a generation of scholars concluded that the second Klan was a violence-prone fringe movement populated by outcasts and losers on the margins of the white Protestant population of the New Era.

By the 1960s, however, historians began to challenge some of the central assumptions about the 1920s Klan. By refocusing attention from the national Klan hierarchy to the particular locations where the hooded order flourished, historians developed a keener appreciation of the context, variety, and depth of the Klan movement. The small-town and village base of the Ku Klux enthusiasm was effectively refuted by Kenneth Jackson's *The Ku Klux Klan in the City*. Jackson documented the centrality of the urban Klan in the 1920s. Not only did about half the membership of the Invisible Empire reside in cities, but the concentration of Klansmen in some cities (up to fifty thousand in

Chicago, thirty-eight thousand in Indianapolis, thirty-five thousand in Detroit and in greater Philadelphia, twenty-three thousand in Denver, and twenty-two thousand in Portland, Oregon), along with the location of realm headquarters in urban centers, made the urban-based Klan especially influential. Moreover, Jackson argued that many Klansmen resided in transitional urban neighborhoods, where they came into conflict with aspiring immigrants, black migrants, Catholics, and Jews moving into those contested areas. Whereas the village-based interpretation of the Klan emphasized the abstract, essentially ideological, clash between small-town Klansmen and minority groups they rarely encountered, the daily friction between urban Klansmen and their "alien" neighbors situated the Klan more concretely in the contested cultural landscape of the 1920s. Historians became more careful to point out, as Robert Moats Miller exemplifies, that the Klan "tapped rather than created Negrophobia and anti-Catholicism, so it did not so much inspire as reflect a pervasive Anglo-Saxon racism." The Klan movement also came into focus as a more diverse phenomenon, encompassing both urban and small-town experiences.

Regional studies of the Klan also demonstrated greater complexity and variation on the matter of the hooded order's violence. Charles Alexander in *The Ku Klux Klan in the Southwest* examined the first great hotbed of Klan expansion in the 1920s, the states of Louisiana, Texas, Oklahoma, and Arkansas, from which the first alarms concerning the violent character of the second Klan emerged. Alexander chronicled ample evidence of vigilantism and brutality on the part of Southwestern Klansmen, but he found most of it not to be directed in any sustained pattern against blacks, Catholics, Jews, or immigrants. Rather, it was aimed at fellow white Protestants. Violations of anti-vice laws (mainly bootlegging, gambling, and prostitution) and transgressions against traditional moral standards (adultery, abdication of family responsibilities, defiance of parents, and sexual attachments across racial or ethnic lines) prompted intimidating visits from masked Klansmen, painful and humiliating punishment, and demands for reformed behavior or immediate departure from the community. Alexander's research underlined the significance of the moral crisis perceived by Klansmen and the varied uses of violence in the Klan's quest for white Protestant hegemony. In contrast to the Southwestern experience, Norman Weaver's pioneering 1954 analysis of the Midwestern realms of Indiana, Ohio, Wisconsin, and Michigan found no significant record of violence or physical intimidation in one of the Invisible Empire's principal strongholds.

Historians also had begun assembling evidence that brought into question the prevailing assumptions about rank-and-file Klansmen. The increasing availability in archives of state and local Klan membership information and a few klavern minute-books, though geographically scattered and incomplete, allowed scholars to move beyond conjecture and compile statistical analyses of Klan membership. In keeping with the growing interpretive emphasis on the second Klan's representative rather than marginal status in 1920s society, scholars found Klansmen to fit the overall demographic, occupational, and religious patterns of their communities, especially among white Protestants. In most locales, few members from the highest or lowest economic strata joined the Klan. The most thorough recent study concluded that Ku Kluxers were "less likely to hold unskilled jobs and more likely to be in service jobs or [to be] professionals" than were non-Klansmen. Moreover, the study found that hooded knights were slightly better educated than their typical fellow citizens and more likely to be married. By most accepted economic and social measurements, Klansmen were better characterized by their stability than by marginal status.

Historians' revaluation of the 1920s Ku Klux Klan was also influenced by the emergence of social history as a major disciplinary force in the 1970s. Moving beyond the traditional narratives and sources that featured elite decision-makers, social history investigated the viewpoints and agency of ordinary people. It sought out sources—tax records, church files, rosters of voluntary associations, and court documents—and used quantitative methods that allowed the reconstruction of "history from the bottom up," with an emphasis on local conditions and everyday experience. The characteristic form of social history investigation was the community study, an intensive analysis of associational networks, economic relationships, governance, belief systems, behavioral patterns, and forces of conflict and comity that made up the structure of life at the grassroots level. These were the sorts of documents and approaches that a new generation of historians of the Klan movement would use to get inside the Invisible Empire. Significantly, the social history perspective also approached popular movements with respect and sought to understand the beliefs and behavior of ordinary Americans in their own terms before subjecting them to critical analysis. In contrast to the 1950s historians who distrusted popular social movements as illiberal and repressive, the academic atmosphere has more recently been open to careful consideration of the Klan movement as an expression of popular belief, despite its racial exclusivity and intolerant worldview.

New sources and a new approach to historical scholarship produced in the 1980s and 1990s a series of focused studies on individual Klan communities that have very nearly turned the traditional interpretation of the 1920s Klan on its head. Close examinations of grassroots Klan activism in Anaheim, California; El Paso, Texas; Buffalo, New York; small communities in Oregon and northeastern Ohio; and, most important, the bellwether Klan states of Colorado and Indiana, concluded that the popular Klan of the 1920s, while diverse, was more of a civic exponent of white Protestant social values than a repressive hate group. The most outspoken advocate of this "populist" interpretation of the Klan, Leonard Moore, fittingly titled his thorough examination of the Indiana Klan *Citizen Klansmen*. Acknowledging the sordid behavior and intolerant rhetoric of the Klan hierarchy, Moore emphasized the civic activism of Hoosier knights. Spurning violence and largely ignoring Indiana's small minority population, the Invisible Empire, according to Moore, "became a kind of interest group for average white Protestants who believed that their values should be dominant in their community." Up to one-third of white native-born Protestant men in Indiana joined the hooded order, representing all Protestant liturgical traditions, including German Lutherans, other than the nonpolitical fundamentalist sects.

Elsewhere the new Klan community studies revealed some evidence of violence and intolerance, but, for the most part, local Klansmen were engaged in civic campaigns to enforce prohibition, improve public schools, demand better performance from elected officials, and even repair local infrastructure against the resistance of business elites and entrenched political rings. These Klansmen resembled their white Protestant neighbors, except for the hooded knights' greater engagement in civic organizations, community-building, elections, and public life in general. The second Klan became, according to Moore, "a means through which average citizens could resist elite political domination and attempt to make local and even state governments more responsive to popular interests." As befitted populists, local Klansmen were often embroiled in policy conflicts with powerful local interests. "Do you know that you have been at the mercy of a political ring for nearly a quarter of a century?" Colorado knights informed their Fremont County neighbors in 1924. "Do you know that the leaders of the Independent Party [then challenging the Klan insurgency] have been that ring? They have had their hands on the public money all that period, have had court procedures in their hands and have managed the affairs of county and city alike. Politically, they have owned Fremont County, body and soul." In Salt Lake City the small Klan movement criticized the political dominance of Mormon religious authorities. Borrowing the language of the 1890s populists, some Klansmen referred, to themselves as the "plain people" battling for the values held by most ordinary Americans. The restrictive racial and religious identification of the Klan made its white Protestant nationalism an exclusive form of populism, but Moore argued that the grassroots Klan phenomenon was still more of a mainstream movement in 1920s America than it was a product of fringe beliefs and violent extremism.

While accepting portions of the populist interpretation, other historians have criticized key elements of it. Many historians of the Southern realms, for example, continue to insist on the centrality of violence and racism in the 1920s Klan. Violence was an accepted and "pervasive part of Klan activity in Alabama," concluded Glenn Feldman, even as an essential feature of moral regulation. Moreover, "the revival of the KKK in Alabama coincided with a dramatic increase in mob violence, especially violence directed at the published enemies of the Klan—blacks, Catholics, jews, immigrants, and the offenders of a variety of moral and community sensibilities." So extensive was Klan violence in Alabama that its brutal image undermined the often progressive initiatives of the Invisible Empire and disrupted the hooded order's political challenge against the state's dominant planters and industrialists. Basing her conclusions on a close investigation of an Athens, Georgia, klavern, Nancy MacLean argues that Southern Klansmen developed a more sinister brand of mass mobilization: reactionary populism. Determined to uphold their racial, class, and gender privileges, Klansmen mounted a popular movement to reassert control over independent women and refractory African Americans; to protect white small property holders and middling merchants from chain stores, banks, and other forms of concentrated capital; and to choke off dangerous class consciousness on the part of workers. As the representatives of white Protestant hegemony, Klansmen acted violently, according to MacLean, "because they believed they had a *right* to use" violence. Patriarchal, racist reaction and not reform, in her view, motivated the Klan movement and therefore made the hooded order the closest American analogue to fascism rather than a popular democratic movement such as the People's Party of the 1890s.

Most of the populist Klan historians fault MacLean for extrapolating beyond the limits of her evidence. They also emphasize that the largest and most dynamic area of Klandom lay outside the violent South, thus diminishing the significance of her findings for the overall Klan movement of the 1920s. Yet even if MacLean is vulnerable to

the specific complaints of her fellow historians, it remains true that the breadth, sophistication, and analytical boldness of *Behind the Mask of Chivalry* make her study the best-known and most influential single book on the 1920s Klan. Thus the historical debate on the New Era Ku Klux movement is stuck in an unresolved minor key. MacLean's sweeping interpretation is contested by most specialists in the field while remaining influential in the wider scholarly community. On the other hand, the populist community studies have cast doubt on the salience of bigotry and violence in the Klan movement at the grassroots level—but have not adequately incorporated the undeniable presence of violence, racist beliefs, and anti-Catholic activism into a balanced appraisal of the Klan phenomenon.

The latest examination of the 1920s Klan, Rory McVeigh's *The Rise of the Ku Klux Klan,* reflects the concerns with social movement mobilization, theoretical development, and national patterns that have characterized most sociological investigations of the hooded order. Such inquiries have their place in the scholarly search for meaning. Historical understanding, however, requires attention to specificity, acknowledgment of the peculiar uniqueness of historical context, the willingness to accept contradictions, and the patience to discern patterns in a myriad of local variations. The New Era Klan movement was a complex and fragile undertaking, distinctive in its local manifestations yet subject to the influence of national figures and distant events. Klansmen were often average members of their communities, but their membership in the Invisible Empire just as often provoked fierce controversy. Ultimately most Americans in the 1920s found the Klan incompatible with order, civility, and improvement in a pluralistic democracy. For some, deep regret accompanied the discovery. The task of the historian is to examine the context and circumstances that led different groups of people to that realization.

THOMAS R. PEGRAM earned his PhD in American civilization from Brandeis University and has taught at Loyola University Maryland since 1990 where he is currently a professor of history. His other books include *Partisans and Progressives: Private Interest and Public Policy in Illinois, 1870–1922* (University of Illinois Press, 1992) and *Battling Demon Rum: The Struggle for a Dry America, 1900–1933* (Ivan R. Dee, 1998).

EXPLORING THE ISSUE

Was the Ku Klux Klan of the 1920s a Mainstream Organization?

Critical Thinking and Reflection

1. What factors contributed to the resurgence of the Ku Klux Klan in the 1920s?
2. How did the Klan of the 1920s differ, if at all, from the Klan of the Reconstruction era?
3. In what ways are the interpretations of Shawn Lay and Thomas Pegram similar? How do they differ?

Is There Common Ground?

The Ku Klux Klan of the 1920s owed its meteoric rise to two key events in 1915: (1) the release of D.W. Griffith's highly popular, though historically distorted motion picture, *Birth of a Nation*, based on Thomas Dixon's racist novel *The Clansman,* which glorified the actions of the Reconstruction-era Klan in overthrowing Radical Republican rule in the South; and (2) the 1915 lynching of Leo Frank, a Jewish businessman in Atlanta, Georgia, whose execution sentence for allegedly raping and murdering a 13-year-old female employee had been commuted by the governor because the evidence used to convict Frank appeared in fact to indicate his innocence. Together these events sparked the emergence of a new Klan organization that reached its height in 1925 and that not only targeted African Americans but added Roman Catholics, Jews, supporters of labor unions, and opponents of prohibition to their lengthening list of opponents of "One Hundred Percent Americanism."

While Klan harassment, beatings, and murders certainly corroborate the traditional interpretation of this organization as an extremist group, it is not altogether clear that many of the attitudes expressed in the rhetoric and publications of the KKK differed all that much from significant segments of the mainstream population in the United States. The fact that the vast majority of American citizens did not join the KKK in the 1920s does not mean that they did not share many of the attitudes articulated by Klansmen regarding the dangers posed by blacks, foreigners, radicals, and violators of Victorian moral codes. These attitudes were pervasive in a nation wrestling with dramatic economic, social, and cultural changes associated with the "New Era" of post–World War I America,

especially (though not exclusively) among white Anglo Saxon Protestants. The U.S. government had contributed to a growing level of intolerance both during and after the war through the anti-German proganda of the Committee on Public Information (the Creel Committee), passage by Congress of the Espionage and Sedition Acts, as well as the National Origins Act in 1924, and the Justice Department's anti-labor, anti-Communist Palmer raids. Under these circumstances, it is perhaps not surprising that some Americans reacted aggressively if not violently to the changing realities of a modern, industrialized, urban nation.

Create Central

www.mhhe.com/createcentral

Additional Resources

Kathleen M. Blee, *Women of the Klan: Racism and Gender in the 1920s* (University of California Press, 1991).

David M. Chalmers, *Hooded Americanism: The History of the Ku Klux Klan*, 3rd ed. (Duke University Press, 1987).

Stanley Coben, *Rebellion Against Victorianism: The Impetus for Cultural Change in 1920s America* (Oxford University Press, 1991).

Rory McVeigh, *The Rise of the Ku Klux Klan: Right-Wing Movements and National Politics* (University of Minnesota Press, 2009).

Wyn Craig Wade, *The Fiery Cross: The Ku Klux Klan in America* (Oxford University Press, 1987).

Internet References . . .

Between the Wars: The Klan Rides Again

chnm.gmu.edu/courses/hist409/klan.html

The Ku Klux Klan

ehistory.osu.edu/osu/mmh/clash/imm_kkk
/kkkpages.html

The KKK in the 1920s

www1.assumption.edu/ahc/1920s
/Eugenics/Klan.html

**The Ku Klux Klan in Washington State,
1920s**

depts.washinton.edu/civilr/kkk_intro.html

The Roaring 20s

http://www.besthistorysites.net/index.php
/american-history/1900/roaring-20s

Selected, Edited, and with Issue Framing Material by:
Larry Madaras, *Howard Community College*
and
James M. SoRelle, *Baylor University*

ISSUE

Did the New Deal Prolong the Great Depression?

YES: **Gary Dean Best**, from *Pride, Prejudice, and Politics: Roosevelt versus Recovery, 1933–1938*, Praeger (1990)

NO: **David M. Kennedy**, from "What the New Deal Did," *Political Science Quarterly* (2009)

Learning Outcomes

After reading this issue, you will be able to:

- Describe the major programs of the New Deal.
- Analyze the major arguments supporting the positive aspects of the New Deal.
- Describe Keynesian economics.
- Analyze the major free-market critiques of the New Deal.
- Critically discuss whether World War II brought about the nation's economic recovery.
- Distinguish between the short-term and long-term effects of the New Deal's recovery program.

ISSUE SUMMARY

YES: Professor of history Gary Dean Best argues that Roosevelt established an antibusiness environment with the creation of the New Deal regulatory programs, which retarded the nation's economic recovery from the Great Depression until World War II.

NO: David M. Kennedy argues that while the New Deal programs did not end the Great Depression in the 1930s, many of those programs in banking, housing, and social welfare made life less risky for most Americans today.

The catastrophe triggered by the 1929 Wall Street debacle crippled the American economy, deflated the optimistic future most Americans assumed to be their birthright, and ripped apart the values by which the country's businesses, farms, and governments were run. During the next decade, the inertia of the Great Depression stifled their attempts to make ends meet.

The world depression of the 1930s began in the United States. The United States had suffered periodic economic setbacks—in 1873, 1893, 1907, and 1920—but those slumps had been limited and temporary. The omnipotence of American productivity, the ebullient American spirit, and the self-deluding thought "it can't happen here" blocked out any consideration of an economic collapse that might devastate the capitalist economy and threaten U.S. democratic government.

All aspects of American society trembled from successive jolts; there were 4 million unemployed people in 1930 and 9 million more by 1932. Those who had not lost their jobs took pay cuts or worked for scrip. There was no security for those whose savings were lost forever when banks failed or stocks declined.

Manufacturing halted, industry shut down, and farmers destroyed wheat, corn, and milk rather than sell them at a loss. Worse, there were millions of homeless Americans—refugees from the cities roaming the nation on freight trains, victims of the drought or the Dust Bowl seeking a new life farther west, and hobo children estranged from their parents.

Business and government leaders alike seemed immobilized by the economic giant that had fallen to its knees. Herbert Hoover, the incumbent president at the start of the Great Depression, attempted some relief programs. They were ineffective, however, considering the magnitude of the unemployment, hunger, and distress. Hoover's attempts at voluntary cooperation between business and labor to avoid layoffs or pay increases broke down by the severity of the depression in mid-1931. Still, Hoover went further than previous presidents in using the power of the federal government to make loans to ailing businesses, railroads, banks, and farmers, but they were too small and too late.

As governor of New York, Franklin D. Roosevelt (FDR, who was elected president in 1932) had introduced some relief measures, such as industrial welfare and a comprehensive system of unemployment remedies, to alleviate the social and economic problems facing the citizens of the state. Yet his campaign did little to reassure his critics that he was more than a rich man who wanted to be the president. In light of later developments, Roosevelt may have been the only presidential candidate to deliver more programs than he actually promised.

The New Deal attempted to jump-start the economy with dozens of recovery and relief measures. On inauguration day, FDR told the nation "the only thing we have to fear is fear itself." He declared a "bank holiday," and Congress passed the Emergency Banking Act, which pumped Federal Reserve notes into the major banks and stopped the wave of bank failures. Later banking acts separated commercial and investment institutions, and the Federal Deposit Insurance Corporation (FDIC) guaranteed people's savings from a loss of up to $2,500 in member banks. A number of relief agencies were set up that provided work for youth and able-bodied men on various state and local building projects. Finally, the Tennessee Valley Administration (TVA) was created to provide electricity in rural areas not serviced by private power companies.

In 1935 the Supreme Court ended the First New Deal by declaring both the Agriculture Adjustment and National Recovery Act unconstitutional. In response to critics on the left who felt that the New Deal was favoring the large banks, big agriculture, and big business, FDR shifted his approach in 1935. The Second New Deal created the Works Project Administration (WPA), which became the nation's largest employer in its eight years of operation. Congress passed Social Security, and the government guaranteed monthly stipends for the aged, unemployed, and dependent children. Labor pressured the administration for a collective bargaining bill, and the Wagner Act established a National Labor Relations Board to supervise industry-wide elections. The steel, coal, automobile, and some garment industries were unionized as membership tripled from 3 million in 1933 to 9 million in 1939.

Roosevelt was beloved by the average Americans. "He understands that my boss is a son-of-a-bitch," said one person to a pollster. In 1936, he was reelected by the largest popular majority in history, attaining 60 percent of the popular vote and carrying 46 of 48 states.

By the summer of 1937, the economy had almost recovered to 1929 levels. But Roosevelt, himself, never a Keynesian, cut spending in order to cut the deficit. The "Roosevelt recession" followed with 1.6 million WPA workers losing their jobs as well as 4 million others: industrial production dropped by more than 34 percent. With economic conditions reverting back to 1932 levels, Roosevelt asked Congress for an additional $5 billion for public works and relief programs in April 1938. Later in the year, the administration passed the Fair Labor Standards Act, which set up a 40-hour work week, a national minimum wage, and severely restricted child labor.

By the late 1930s, however, the New Deal, for all practical purposes, was over. Several factors hurt Roosevelt politically and stymied further domestic reform: (1) Roosevelt's attempt to expand the size of the Supreme Court in order to have the opportunity to nominate liberal justices made him appear devious; (2) his campaign in the South against anti–New Deal Democrats backfired and, along with the Court-packing scheme, produced a sizable conservative coalition of southern Democrats and Republicans that blocked progressive legislation; and (3) the outbreak of World War II in Europe in 1939 diverted the president's attention to foreign affairs.

The following selections debate whether or not the New Deal prolonged the Great Depression. Professor Gary Dean Best argues that with its swollen government agencies, promotion of cartels, confiscatory taxes, and dubious antitrust laws, the New Deal prolonged the depression. He argues that most historians, whom he calls "court historians," were sympathetic to the policies and programs of the New Deal, yet they admit that it was World War II and not FDR's programs that brought about the recovery. Compared with the rest of the world by 1938, 12 of the 15 major nations in the world had lower unemployment rates than the United States. According to Best, FDR's landslide reelection can be attributed to the massive handouts of the relief and recovery programs such as the Public Works Administration (PWA) and the Works Project Administration (WPA) as well as the failure of Republican opponent Alf Landon to counter with his own program. Finally, Best attributes the recovery after 1938 to the election of a more conservative Congress and the staffing of the World War II government agencies with pro-business personnel.

Best's critique is based on the arguments used by Roosevelt's Republican opponents in the 1930s as well as the conservative assumptions of the well-known free-market advocates Milton Friedman and Anna Jacobson Schwartz, who argue in *A Monetary History of the United States, 1867–1960* (Princeton University Press, 1963) that the Great Depression was a government failure brought on primarily by Federal Reserve policies that abruptly cut the money supply. This view runs counter to those of Peter Temin, *Did Monetary Forces Cause the Depression?* (Norton, 1976); Michael A. Bernstein, *The Great Depression: Delayed Recovery and Economic Change in America* (Cambridge University Press, 1987); and the lively account of John Kenneth Galbraith, *The Great Crash* (Houghton Mifflin, 1955), which argues that the crash exposed various structural weaknesses in the economy that caused the economic crisis.

Best's major failing is his ability to view the human side of the New Deal. By concentrating on the strengths and weaknesses of a business recovery, he seems to forget that the New Deal was much more than the sum total of a number of economic statistics. Since that time, people have come to expect the national government to manage the economy responsibly.

Written during the fall of 2008 when bank and mortgages houses were about to collapse on Wall Street, Professor David M. Kennedy, in the second essay, reminds us of the responses President Franklin D. Roosevelt and his advisers made during the 1930s Great Depression. Kennedy, who authored the Pulitzer Prize winning book *Freedom from Fear*, abandoned the traditional liberal framework suggested by the late Arthur Schlesinger, Jr., in his three volumes on the New Deal. Schlesinger divided the New Deal into two phases. Part One (1933–1934) emphasized economic recovery from the top down by saving the banks, big business, and big agriculture. After the Supreme Court declared unconstitutional the National Recovery Act and the Agricultural Adjustment Acts in 1935, Roosevelt shifted to a bottom-up economic approach where money would be spent on average individuals through collective bargaining (Wagner Act), a massive public works program (WPA), and a social welfare retirement program for the elderly (Social Security Act of 1935). The expectation was that consumer spending would create more jobs in the long run.

Professor Kennedy abandons the First and Second New Deal approach and sets up his own paradigm. He distinguishes between programs to solve the immediate crisis and those which would reshape flaws in the economic system, which Kennedy labels a "risk-reduced managed capitalism." He admits that it was World War II and not the New Deal programs that forced the nation to engage in massive federal spending and unbalanced budgets which were politically unfeasible in peacetime. The unemployment rate, which was 25 percent in 1933, still averaged 17 percent in the 1930s. World War II brought the rate down to 4 percent.

In Kennedy's view, the most important aspects of the New Deal were those pieces of legislation that have provided for the long-term security of the American people. In short, "The New Deal provided more assurance to bank depositors (FDIC), more reliable information to investors (SEC), more safety to lenders (FHA), more stability to relations between capital and labor (NLRB), more predictable wages to the most vulnerable works (FLSA), and a safety net for the unemployed and elderly (Social Security)." In short, FDR's main goal was not short-term economic recovery, but long-term structural reform. Whether FDR foresaw the results of these programs may be debated, but certainly the country is a much more economically secure nation than it was in the 1930s.

YES ↩   Gary Dean Best

Pride, Prejudice and Politics: Roosevelt versus Recovery, 1933–1938

This book had its genesis in the fact that I have for a long time felt uncomfortable with the standard works written about Franklin Delano Roosevelt and the New Deal, and with the influence those works have exerted on others writing about and teaching U.S. history. Although I approach the subject from a very different perspective, Paul K. Conkin's preface to the second edition of *The New Deal* (1975) expressed many of my own misgivings about writings on the subject. Conkin wrote that "pervading even the most scholarly revelations was a monotonous, often almost reflexive, and in my estimation a very smug or superficial valuative perspective—approval, even glowing approval, of most enduring New Deal policies, or at least of the underlying goals that a sympathetic observer could always find behind policies and programs."

Studies of the New Deal such as Conkin described seemed to me to be examples of a genre relatively rare in U.S. historiography—that of "court histories." . . .

But, like most historians teaching courses dealing with the Roosevelt period, I was captive to the published works unless I was willing and able to devote the time to pursue extensive research in the period myself. After some years that became possible, and this book is the result.

My principal problem with Roosevelt and the New Deal was not over his specific reforms or his social programs, but with the failure of the United States to recover from the depression during the eight peacetime years that he and his policies governed the nation. I consider that failure tragic, not only for the 14.6 percent of the labor force that remained unemployed as late as 1940, and for the millions of others who subsisted on government welfare because of the prolonged depression, but also because of the image that the depression-plagued United States projected to the world at a crucial time in international affairs. In the late 1930s and early 1940s, when U.S. economic strength might have given pause to potential aggressors in the world, our economic weakness furnished encouragement to them instead.

From the standpoint, then, not only of our domestic history, but also of the tragic events and results of World War II, it has seemed to me that Roosevelt's failure to generate economic recovery during this critical period deserved more attention than historians have given it.

Most historians of the New Deal period leave the impression that the failure of the United States to recover during those eight years resulted from Roosevelt's unwillingness to embrace Keynesian spending. According to this thesis, recovery came during World War II because the war at last forced Roosevelt to spend at the level required all along for recovery. This, however, seemed to me more an advocacy of Keynes' theories by the historians involved than an explanation for the U.S. failure to recover during those years. Great Britain, for example, managed to recover by the late 1930s without recourse to deficit spending. By that time the United States was, by contrast, near the bottom of the list of industrial nations as measured in progress toward recovery, with most others having reached the predepression levels and many having exceeded them. The recovered countries represented a variety of economic systems, from state ownership to private enterprise. The common denominator in their success was not a reliance on deficit spending, but rather the stimulus they furnished to industrial enterprise.

What went wrong in the United States? Simplistic answers such as the reference to Keynesianism seemed to me only a means of avoiding a real answer to the question. A wise president, entering the White House in the midst of a crippling depression, should do everything possible to stimulate enterprise. In a free economy, economic recovery means *business* recovery. It follows, therefore, that a wise chief executive should do everything possible to create the conditions and psychology most conducive to business recovery—to encourage business to expand production, and lenders and investors to furnish the financing and capital that are required. An administration seeking economic recovery will do as little as possible that might inhibit recovery, will weigh all its actions with the necessity for economic recovery in mind, and will consult with competent business and financial leaders, as well as economists, to determine the best policies to follow. Such a president will seek to promote cooperation between the federal government and business, rather than conflict, and will seek to introduce as much consistency and stability as possible into government economic policies so that businessmen and investors can plan ahead. While obviously the destitute must be cared for, ultimately the most humane contribution a liberal government can make to the victims of a depression is the restoration of prosperity and the reemployment of the idle in genuine jobs.

In measuring the Roosevelt policies and programs during the New Deal years against such standards, I was struck by the air of unreality that hung over Washington in general and the White House in particular during this period. Business and financial leaders who questioned the wisdom of New Deal policies were disregarded and deprecated because of their "greed" and "self-interest," while economists and business academicians who persisted in calling attention to the collision between New Deal policies and simple economic realities were dismissed for their "orthodoxy." As one "orthodox" economist pointed out early in the New Deal years,

> economic realism . . . insists that policies aiming to promote recovery will, in fact, retard recovery if and where they fail to take into account correctly of stubborn facts in the existing economic situation and of the arithmetic of business as it must be carried out in the economic situation we are trying to revive. The antithesis of this economic realism is the vaguely hopeful or optimistic idealism in the field of economic policy, as such, which feels that good intentions, enough cleverness, and the right appeal to the emotions of the people ought to insure good results in spite of inconvenient facts.

Those "inconvenient facts" dogged the New Deal throughout these years, only to be stubbornly resisted by a president whose pride, prejudices, and politics would rarely permit an accommodation with them.

Most studies of the New Deal years approach the period largely from the perspective of the New Dealers themselves. Critics and opponents of Roosevelt's policies and programs are given scant attention in such works except to point up the "reactionary" and "unenlightened" opposition with which Roosevelt was forced to contend in seeking to provide Americans with "a more abundant life." The few studies that have concentrated on critics and opponents of the New Deal in the business community have been by unsympathetic historians who have tended to distort the opposition to fit the caricature drawn by the New Dealers, so that they offer little to explain the impact of Roosevelt's policies in delaying recovery from the depression.

The issue of *why* businessmen and bankers were so critical of the New Deal has been for too long swept under the rug, together with the question of *how* Roosevelt and his advisers could possibly expect to produce an economic recovery while a state of war existed between his administration and the employers and investors who, alone, could produce such a recovery. Even a Keynesian response to economic depression is ultimately dependent on the positive reactions of businessmen and investors for its success, as Keynes well knew, and those reactions were not likely to be as widespread as necessary under such a state of warfare between government and business. Businessmen, bankers, and investors may have been "greedy" and "self-interested." They may have been guilty of wrong perceptions and unfounded fears. But they are also the ones, in a free economy, upon whose decisions and actions economic recovery must depend. To understand their opposition to the New Deal requires an immersion in the public and private comments of critics of Roosevelt's policies. The degree and nature of business, banking, and investor concern about the direction and consequences of New Deal policies can be gleaned from the hundreds of banking and business periodicals representative of every branch of U.S. business and finance in the 1930s, and from the letters and diaries of the New Deal's business and other critics during the decade.

❧⟐❧

Statistics are useful in understanding the history of any period, but particularly periods of economic growth or depression. Statistics for the Roosevelt years may easily be found in *Historical Statistics of the United States* published by the Bureau of the Census, U.S. Department of Commerce (1975). Some of the trauma of the depression years may be inferred from the fact that the population of the United States grew by over 17 million between 1920 and 1930, but by only about half of that (8.9 million) between 1930 and 1940.

Historical Statistics gives the figures . . . for unemployment, 1929–1940. These figures are, however, only estimates. The federal government did not monitor the number of unemployed during those years. Even so, these figures are shocking, indicating as they do that even after the war had begun in Europe, with the increased orders that it provided for U.S. mines, factories, and farms, unemployment remained at 14.6 percent.

One characteristic of the depression, to which attention was frequently called during the Roosevelt years, was the contrast between its effects on the durable goods and consumer goods industries. Between 1929 and 1933, expenditures on personal durable goods dropped by nearly 50 percent, and in 1938 they were still nearly 25 percent below the 1929 figures. Producers' durable goods suffered even more, falling by nearly two-thirds between 1929 and 1933, and remaining more than 50 percent below the 1929 figure in 1938. At the same time, expenditures on nondurable, or consumer, goods showed much less effect. Between 1929 and 1933 they fell only about 14.5 percent, and by 1938 they exceeded the 1929 level. These figures indicate that the worst effects of the depression, and resultant unemployment, were being felt in the durable goods industries. Roosevelt's policies, however, served mainly to stimulate the consumer goods industries where the depression and unemployment were far less seriously felt.

One consequence of Roosevelt's policies can be seen in the U.S. balance of trade during the New Deal years. By a variety of devices, Roosevelt drove up the prices of U.S. industrial and agricultural products, making it difficult for these goods to compete in the world market, and opening U.S. markets to cheaper foreign products. . . . With the exception of a $41 million deficit in 1888, these were the only deficits in U.S. trade for a century, from the 1870s to the 1970s.

. . . [W]hile suicides during the Roosevelt years remained about the same as during the Hoover years, the death rate by "accidental falls" increased significantly. In fact, according to *Historical Statistics*, the death rate by "accidental falls" was higher in the period 1934–1938 than at any other time between 1910 and 1970 (the years for which figures are given).

Interestingly, the number of persons arrested grew steadily during the depression years. In 1938 nearly twice as many (554,000) were arrested as in 1932 (278,000), and the number continued to increase until 1941. And, while the number of telephones declined after 1930 and did not regain the 1930 level until 1939, the number of households with radios increased steadily during the depression years. And Americans continued to travel. Even in the lowest year, 1933, 300,000 Americans visited foreign countries (down from 517,000 in 1929), while the number visiting national parks, monuments, and such, steadily increased during the depression—in 1938 nearly five times as many (16,331,000) did so as in 1929 (3,248,000).

Comparisons of the recovery of the United States with that of other nations may be found in the volumes of the League of Nations' *World Economic Survey* for the depression years. [A] table (from the volume of 1938/39) shows comparisons of unemployment rates. From this it can be seen that in 1929 the United States had the lowest unemployment rate of the countries listed; by 1932 the United States was midway on the list, with seven nations reporting higher unemployment rates and seven reporting lower unemployment. By mid-1938, however, after over five years of the New Deal, only three nations had higher unemployment rates, while twelve had lower unemployment. The United States, then, had lost ground in comparison with the other nations between 1932 and 1938.

The *World Economic Survey* for 1937/38 compared the levels of industrial production for 23 nations in 1937, expressed as a percentage of their industrial production in 1929. . . . It must be remembered that the figures for the United States reflect the level of industrial production reached just before the collapse of the economy later that year. Of the 22 other nations listed, 19 showed a higher rate of recovery in industrial production than the United States, while only 3 lagged behind. One of these, France, had followed policies similar to those of the New Deal in the United States. As the *World Economic Survey* put it, both the Roosevelt administration and the Blum government in France had "adopted far-reaching social and economic policies which combined recovery measures with measures of social reform." It added: "The consequent doubt regarding the prospects of profit and the uneasy relations between businessmen and the Government have in the opinion of many, been an important factor in delaying recovery," and the two countries had, "unlike the United Kingdom and Germany," failed to "regain the 1929 level of employment and production." The *World Economic Survey* the following year (1939) pointed out that industrial production in the United States had fallen from 92.2 to 65 by June 1938, and hovered between *77* and 85 throughout 1939. Thus, by the end of 1938 the U.S. record was even sorrier than revealed by the [data].

∾⊚⊱

Every survey of American historians consistently finds Franklin Delano Roosevelt ranked as one of this nation's greatest presidents. Certainly, exposure to even a sampling of the literature on Roosevelt and the New Deal can lead one to no other conclusion. Conventional wisdom has it that Roosevelt was an opportune choice to lead the United States through the midst of the Great Depression, that his cheerful and buoyant disposition uplifted the American spirit in the midst of despair and perhaps even forestalled a radical change in the direction of American politics toward the right or the left. Roosevelt's landslide reelection victory in 1936, and the congressional successes in 1934, are cited as evidence of the popularity of both the president and the New Deal among the American people. Polls by both Gallup and the Democratic National Committee early in the 1936 campaign, however, give a very different picture, and suggest that the electoral victories can be as accurately accounted for in terms of the vast outpourings of federal money in 1934 and 1936, and the inability or unwillingness of Landon to offer a genuine alternative to the New Deal in the latter year. To this must be added the fact that after early 1936 two of the most unpopular New Deal programs—the NRA and the AAA—had been removed as issues by the Supreme Court.

Conventional wisdom, in fact, suffers many setbacks when the Roosevelt years are examined from any other perspective than through a pro-New Deal Prism—from the banking crisis of 1933 and the first inaugural address, through the reasons for the renewed downturn in 1937, to the end of the New Deal in 1937–1938. The American present has been ill-served by the inaccurate picture that has too often been presented of this chapter in the American past by biographers and historians. Roosevelt's achievements in alleviating the hardship of the depression are deservedly well known, his responsibility for prolonging the hardship is not. His role in providing long-overdue and sorely needed social and economic legislation is in every high school American history textbook, but the costs for the United States of his eight-year-long war against business recovery are mentioned in none.

Such textbooks (and those in college, too) frequently contain a chapter on the Great Depression, followed by one on the New Deal, the implication being that somewhere early in the second of the chapters the depression was ended by Roosevelt's policies. Only careful reading reveals that despite Roosevelt's immense labors to feed the unemployed, only modest recovery from the lowest depths of the depression was attained before the outbreak of World War II. Roosevelt, readers are told, was too old-fashioned, too conservative, to embrace the massive compensatory spending and unbalanced budgets that might have produced a Keynesian recovery sooner. But World War II, the books tell us, made such spending necessary and the recovery that might have occurred earlier was at last achieved.

Generations of Americans have been brought up on this version of the New Deal years. Other presidential administrations have been reevaluated over the years, and have risen or fallen in grace as a result, but not the Roosevelt administration. The conventional wisdom concerning the Roosevelt administration remains the product of the "court historians," assessments of the New Deal period that could not have been better written by the New Dealers themselves. The facts, however, are considerably at variance with this conventional wisdom concerning the course of the depression, the reasons for the delay of recovery, and the causes of the recovery when it came, finally, during World War II.

From the uncertainty among businessmen and investors about the new president-elect that aborted a promising upturn in the fall of 1932, to the panic over the prospect of inflationary policies that was a major factor in the banking crisis that virtually paralyzed the nation's economy by the date of his inauguration, Roosevelt's entry into the White House was not an auspicious beginning toward recovery. The prejudices that were to guide the policies and programs of the New Deal for the next six years were revealed in Roosevelt's inaugural address, although the message was largely overlooked until it had become more apparent in the actions of the administration later. It was an attitude of hostility toward business and finance, of contempt for the profit motive of capitalism, and of willingness to foment class antagonism for political benefit. This was not an attitude that was conducive to business recovery, and the programs and policies that would flow from those prejudices would prove, in fact, to be destructive of the possibility of recovery.

There followed the "hundred days," when Roosevelt rammed through Congress a variety of legislation that only depressed business confidence more. The new laws were served up on attractive platters, with tempting descriptions—truth in securities, aid for the farmer, industrial self-regulation—but when the covers were removed the contents were neither attractive nor did they match the labels. By broad grants of power to the executive branch of the government, the legislation passed regulation of the U.S. economy into the hands of New Dealers whose aim was not to promote recovery but to carry out their own agendas for radical change of the economic system even at the expense of delaying recovery. Thus, truth in securities turned to paralysis of the securities markets, aid for the farmer became a war against profits by processors of agricultural goods, and industrial self-regulation became government control and labor-management strife. International economic cooperation as a device for ending the depression was abandoned for an isolationist approach, and throughout 1933 the threat of inflation added further uncertainty for businessmen and investors.

The grant of such unprecedented peacetime authority to an American president aroused concern, but these after all were only "emergency" powers, to be given up once recovery was on its way. Or were they? Gradually the evidence accumulated that the Tugwells and the Brandeisians intended to institutionalize the "emergency" powers as permanent features of American economic life. By the end of 1933, opposition to the New Deal was already sizable. Business alternated between the paralysis of uncertainty and a modest "recovery" born of purchases and production inspired by fear of higher costs owing to inflation and the effects of the AAA and NRA. The implementation of the latter two agencies in the fall of 1933 brought a renewed downturn that improved only slightly during the winter and spring. A renewed legislative onslaught by the New Deal in the 1934 Congress, combined with labor strife encouraged by the provisions of the NIRA, brought a new collapse of the economy in the fall of 1934, which lowered economic indices once again to near the lowest levels they had reached in the depression.

The pattern had been established. The war against business and finance was under way, and there would be neither retreat nor cessation. Roosevelt's pride and prejudices, and the perceived political advantages to be gained from the war, dictated that his administration must ever be on the offensive and never in retreat. But the administration suffered defeats, nevertheless, and embarrassment. The Supreme Court proved a formidable foe, striking down both the NRA and the AAA. Dire predictions from the administration about the implications for the economy of the loss of the NRA proved embarrassing when the economy began to show gradual improvement after its departure. But defeat did not mean retreat. Under the goading of Felix Frankfurter and his disciples, Roosevelt became even more extreme in his verbal and legislative assault against business. Their attempts to cooperate with the Roosevelt administration having been spurned, businessmen and bankers awakened to the existence of the war being waged upon them and moved into opposition. Roosevelt gloried in their opposition and escalated the war against them in the 1936 reelection campaign.

Reelected in 1936 on a tidal wave of government spending, and against a lackluster Republican campaigner who offered no alternative to the New Deal, Roosevelt appeared at the apogee of his power and prestige. His triumph was, however, to be short-lived, despite an enhanced Democratic majority in Congress. A combination of factors was about to bring the New Deal war against business to a stalemate and eventual retreat. One of these was his ill-advised attempt to pack the Supreme Court with subservient justices, which aroused so much opposition even in his own party that he lost control of the Democrat-controlled Congress. More important, perhaps, was the growing economic crisis that the Roosevelt administration faced in 1937, largely as a result of its own

past policies. The massive spending of 1936, including the payment of the veterans' bonus, had generated a speculative recovery during that year from concern about inflationary consequences. Fears of a "boom" were increased as a result of the millions of dollars in dividends, bonuses, and pay raises dispensed by businesses late in 1936 as a result of the undistributed profits tax. The pay raises, especially, were passed on in the form of higher prices, as were the social security taxes that were imposed on businesses beginning with 1937. Labor disturbances, encouraged by the Wagner Labor Act and the Roosevelt alliance with John L. Lewis' Congress of Industrial Organizations in the 1936 campaign, added further to the wage-price spiral that threatened as 1937 unfolded. Massive liquidations of low-interest government bonds, and sagging prices of the bonds, fueled concern among bankers and economists, and within the Treasury, that a "boom" would imperil the credit of the federal government and the solvency of the nation's banks whose portfolios consisted mainly of low-interest government bonds.

In considering the two principal options for cooling the "boom"—raising interest rates or cutting federal spending—the Roosevelt administration chose to move toward a balanced budget. It was a cruel dilemma that the New Dealers faced. All knew that the economy had not yet recovered from the depression, yet they were faced with the necessity to apply brakes to an economy that was becoming overheated as a consequence of their policies. Moreover, the reduction in consumer purchasing power caused by the cuts in federal spending was occurring at the same time that purchasing power was already being eroded as a result of the higher prices that worried the administration. Private industry, it should have been obvious, could not "take up the slack," since the Roosevelt administration had done nothing to prepare for the transition from government to private spending that John Maynard Keynes and others had warned them was necessary. The New Dealers had been far too busy waging war against business to allow it the opportunity to prepare for any such transition.

In fact, far from confronting the emergency of 1937 by making long-overdue attempts to cooperate with business in generating recovery, Roosevelt was busy pressing a new legislative assault against them. Denied passage of his legislative package by Congress during its regular 1937 session, Roosevelt called a special session for November despite evidence that the economy had begun a new downturn. Even the collapse of the stock market, within days after his announcement of the special session, and the growing unemployment that soon followed, did not deter Roosevelt from his determination to drive the legislative assault through it. With the nation in the grips of a full-blown economic collapse, Roosevelt offered nothing to the special session but the package of antibusiness legislation it had turned down in the regular session. Once again he was rebuffed by Congress. The nation drifted, its economic indices falling, with its president unwilling to admit the severity of the situation or unable to come to grips with what it said about the bankruptcy of the New Deal policies and programs.

By early 1938, Roosevelt was faced with problems similar to those he had faced when he first entered the White House five years earlier, but without the political capital he had possessed earlier. In 1933 the Hoover administration could be blamed for the depression. In 1938 the American people blamed the Roosevelt administration for retarding recovery. Five years of failure could not be brushed aside. Five years of warfare against business and disregard of criticism and offers of cooperation had converted supporters of 1933 into cynics or opponents by 1938. Even now, however, pride, prejudice, and politics dominated Roosevelt, making it impossible for him to extend the needed olive branch to business. The best that he could offer in 1938 was a renewal of federal spending and more of the same New Deal that had brought the nation renewed misery. In the 1938 congressional session he continued to press for passage of the antibusiness legislation that had been rejected by both sessions of 1937.

But Congress was no longer the pliant body it had been in 1933, and in the 1938 congressional elections the people's reaction was registered when the Republicans gained 81 new seats in the House and 8 in the Senate—far more than even the most optimistic Republican had predicted. If the message was lost on Roosevelt, it was obvious to some in his administration, notably his new Secretary of Commerce Harry Hopkins and his Secretary of the Treasury Henry Morgenthau. Two of the earliest business-baiters in the circle of Roosevelt advisers, they now recognized the bankruptcy of that course and the necessity for the administration to at last strive for recovery by removing the obstacles to normal and profitable business operation that the New Deal had erected. This was not what Roosevelt wanted to hear, nor was it what his Frankfurter disciples wanted him to hear. These latter knew, as Hopkins and Morgenthau had learned earlier, just which Rooseveltian buttons could be pushed to trigger his antibusiness prejudices and spite. A battle raged within the New Deal between the Frankfurter radicals and the "new conservatives," Hopkins and Morgenthau, amid growing public suspicion that the former were not interested in economic recovery.

It was not a fair battle. Hopkins and Morgenthau knew how to play the game, including use of the press, and had too many allies. They did not hesitate to talk bluntly to Roosevelt, perhaps the bluntest talk he had heard since the death of Louis McHenry Howe. Moreover, Roosevelt could afford the loss of a Corcoran and/or a Cohen, against whom there was already a great deal of congressional opposition, but a break with both Hopkins and Morgenthau would have been devastating for an administration already on the defensive. Gradually the Frankfurter radicals moved into eclipse, along with their policies, to be replaced increasingly by recovery and preparedness advocates, including many from the business and financial world.

Conventional wisdom has it that the massive government spending of World War II finally brought a Keynesian recovery from the depression. Of more significance, in comparisons of the prewar and wartime economic policies of the Roosevelt administration, is the fact that the war against business that characterized the former was abandoned in the latter. Both the attitude and policies of the Roosevelt administration toward business during the New Deal years were reversed when the president found new, foreign enemies to engage his attention and energies. Antibusiness advisers were replaced by businessmen, pro-labor policies became pro-business policies, cooperation replaced confrontation in relations between the federal government and business, and even the increased spending of the war years "trickled down" rather than "bubbling up." Probably no American president since, perhaps, Thomas Jefferson ever so thoroughly repudiated the early policies of his administration as Roosevelt did between 1939 and 1942. This, and not the emphasis on spending alone, is the lesson that needs to be learned from Roosevelt's experience with the depression, and of the legacy of the New Deal economic policies.

The judgment of historians concerning Roosevelt's presidential stature is curiously at odds with that of contemporary observers. One wonders how scholars of the Roosevelt presidency are able so blithely to ignore the negative assessments of journalists, for example, of the stature of Raymond Clapper, Walter Lippmann, Dorothy Thompson, and Arthur Krock, to name only a few. Can their observations concerning Roosevelt's pettiness and spitefulness, their criticism of the obstacles to recovery created by his anticapitalist bias, and their genuine concern over his apparent grasp for dictatorial power be dismissed so cavalierly? Is there any other example in U.S. history of an incumbent president running for reelection against the open opposition of the two previous nominees of his own party? Will a public opinion poll ever again find 45 percent of its respondents foreseeing the likelihood of dictatorship arising from a president's policies? Will a future president ever act in such a fashion that the question will again even suggest itself to a pollster? One certainly hopes not.

Perhaps the positive assessment of Roosevelt by American historians rests upon a perceived liberalism of his administration. If so, one must wonder at their definition of liberalism. Surely a president who would pit class against class for political purposes, who was fundamentally hostile to the very basis of a free economy, who believed that his ends could justify very illiberal means, who was intolerant of criticism and critics, and who grasped for dictatorial power does not merit description as a liberal. Nor are the results of the Gallup poll mentioned above consistent with the actions of a liberal president. If the perception is based on Roosevelt's support for the less fortunate "one-third" of the nation, and his program of social legislation, then historians need to be reminded that such actions do not, in themselves, add up to liberalism, they having been used by an assortment of political realists and demagogues—of the left and the right—to gain and hold power.

There were certainly positive contributions under the New Deal, but they may not have outweighed the negative aspects of the period. The weight of the negative aspects would, moreover, have been much heavier except for the existence of a free and alert press, and for the actions of the Supreme Court and Congress in nullifying, modifying, and rejecting many of the New Deal measures. When one examines the full range of New Deal proposals and considers the implications of their passage in the original form, the outline emerges of a form of government alien to any definition of liberalism except that of the New Dealers themselves. Historians need to weigh more thoroughly and objectively the implications for the United States if Roosevelt's programs had been fully implemented. They need also to assess the costs in human misery of the delay in recovery, and of reduced U.S. influence abroad at a critical time in world affairs owing to its economic prostration. We can only speculate concerning the possible alteration of events from 1937 onward had the United States faced the world with the economic strength and military potential it might have displayed had wiser economic policies prevailed from 1933 to 1938. There is, in short, much about Roosevelt and the New Deal that historians need to reevaluate.

GARY DEAN BEST (1936–2010) was professor of history at the University of Hawaii at Hilo. He was a former fellow of the American Historical Association and of the National Endowment for the Humanities, and he was a Fulbright Scholar in Japan from 1974 to 1975. He also is the author of *The Nickel and Dime Decade: American Popular Culture during the 1930s* (1993).

David M. Kennedy

What the New Deal Did

The United States now confronts a cascading economic crisis. Venerable banking houses collapse, once-mighty industries teeter on the brink of oblivion, and unemployment mounts. The air thickens with recollections of the Great Depression of the 1930s, and with comparisons between Barack Obama and Franklin D. Roosevelt.

So what was the Great Depression, and what did FDR do about it? The short answer is that the Great Depression was a rare political opportunity, and Roosevelt made the most of it, to the nation's lasting benefit. A longer answer would acknowledge that the Great Depression was a catastrophic economic crisis that Roosevelt failed to resolve, at least not until World War II came along, some eight years after he assumed office. A still longer answer would recognize the connection between FDR's short-term economic policy failure and the New Deal's long-term political success. Much misunderstanding surrounds these matters.

"At the heart of the New Deal," the distinguished historian Richard Hofstadter once wrote, "there was not a philosophy but a temperament." As a writer in *The New York Times* put it not long ago, "F.D.R. threw a bunch of policies against the wall, and the ones that stuck became the New Deal."

That view of the New Deal—as a kind of unprincipled, harum-scarum frenzy of random, incoherent policies that failed to slay the Depression demon—has become deeply embedded in our national folklore. It is badly mistaken. If we are to understand the Great Depression's relevance to our own time, it is imperative to understand the relationship between the economic crisis of the 1930s and that decade's signature political legacy, the New Deal.

Into the years of the New Deal was crowded more social and institutional change than in virtually any comparable compass of time in the nation's past. Change is always controversial. Change on the scale the New Deal wrought has proved interminably controversial. Debate about the New Deal's historical significance, its ideological identity, and its political, social, and economic consequences has ground on for three quarters of a century.

Roosevelt's reforms have become a perpetual touchstone of American political argument, a talisman invoked by all parties to legitimate or condemn as the occasion requires, an emblem and barometer of American attitudes toward government itself. So just what, exactly, *did* the New Deal do?

It might be well to begin by recognizing what the New Deal did not do. It fell pathetically short of achieving full economic recovery. Roosevelt's programs made a substantial dent in the 25 percent unemployment rate of 1933, but unemployment averaged 17 percent throughout the 1930s and never went below 14 percent until World War II occasioned massive federal spending and effectively wrote finis to the Depression Decade. Among the reasons that the New Deal failed to overcome the Depression and World War II did was the simple fact that the war made intellectually conceivable and politically possible deficit spending on a level that was neither dreamed nor attempted before the war came. The biggest New Deal deficit was some $4.2 billion in 1936, largely because of the veterans' "Bonus Bill," which passed, not incidentally, over Roosevelt's veto. No New Deal deficit reached 6 percent of GNP. In 1943, by contrast, the federal deficit was $53 billion, more than an order of magnitude larger than in 1936, and as a share of GNP nearly six times the largest New Deal deficit, at 28 percent.

What is more, much mythology and heated rhetoric notwithstanding, the New Deal did not substantially redistribute the national income. America's income profile in 1940 closely resembled that of 1930, and for that matter 1920. The falling economic tide of the Depression lowered all boats, but by and large they held their relative positions. What little income levelling there was resulted more from Depression-diminished returns to investments, rather than redistributive tax policies. True, the so-called "wealth tax," or "soak-the-rich" tax, that Roosevelt pushed through Congress in 1935 imposed a 79 percent marginal tax rate on incomes over $5 million; but that rate applied to but a single taxpayer in all the United States—John D. Rockefeller. The basic rate remained 4 percent, and even that applied to a decided minority of Americans. Until the war-time Revenue Acts hugely expanded federal tax collections, fewer than one American household in twenty paid any income tax at all. A Depression-era couple with an income of $4,000 would have been in the top tenth of all income receivers; if they had two children, they would have paid a federal income tax of $16 in 1936. A similar family making $12,000—placing them in the richest 1 percent of households—would have paid $600.

Nor, with essentially minor exceptions like the Tennessee Valley Authority's (TVA) electric-power business, did the New Deal challenge the fundamental tenet of capitalism, private ownership of the means of production. In contrast with the pattern in virtually all other industrial societies, whether communist, socialist, or capitalist, no significant state-owned enterprises emerged in New Deal America.

It is also frequently said that the New Deal conformed to no pre-existing ideological agenda, that it never produced a spokesman, not even Franklin Roosevelt, who was able systematically to lay out the New Deal's social and economic philosophy. Then and later, critics have charged that so many inconsistent impulses contended under the tent of Roosevelt's New Deal that to seek for system and coherence was to pursue a fool's errand. That accusation has echoed repeatedly in assessments that stress the New Deal's mongrel intellectual pedigree, its improbably plural constituent base, its political pragmatism, its abundant promiscuities, inconsistencies, contradictions, inconstancies, and failures. What unity of plan or purpose, one might ask, was to be found in an administration that at various times tinkered with inflation and with price-controls, with deficit spending and budget-balancing, cartelization and trust-busting, the promotion of consumption and the intimidation of investment, farm-acreage reduction and land reclamation, public employment projects and forced removals from the labor pool? "Economically," one historian concludes with some justice, "the New Deal had been opportunistic in the grand manner."

And yet, illumined by the stern-lantern of history, the New Deal can be seen to have left in place a set of institutional arrangements that constituted a more coherent pattern than is dreamt of in many philosophies. That pattern can be summarized in a single word: security.

It is fitting that the New Deal's most durable and consequential reform bears that very word in its title: the Social *Security* Act of 1935. A measure of security was the New Deal's gift to millions of Americans—farmers and workers, immigrants and blue-bloods, children and the elderly, as well as countless industrialists, bankers,

merchants, mortgage-lenders, and homebuyers, not to mention enormous tracts of forest, prairie, and mountain.

Forget about the colorful creations of the decidedly frenzied and much ballyhooed Hundred Days, like the Civilian Conservation Corps and the National Industrial Recovery Act. Most of them were short-lived and ultimately inconsequential. But all of the New Deal reforms that endured—The Federal Deposit Insurance Corporation, the Securities and Exchange Commission, the Federal Housing Administration, the National Labor Relations Board, the Fair Labor Standards Act, and above all the Social Security Act—had a common cardinal purpose: not simply to end the immediate crisis of the Depression, but to make life less risky and more predictable, to temper for generations thereafter what FDR repeatedly called the "hazards and vicissitudes" of life.

The New Deal provided more assurance to bank depositors (FDIC), more reliable information to investors (SEC), more safety to lenders (FHA), more stability to relations between capital and labor (NLRB), more predictable wages to the most vulnerable workers (FLSA), and a safety net for both the unemployed and the elderly (Social Security). Those innovations transformed the American economic and social landscape. They profoundly shaped the fates of Americans born long after the Depression crisis had passed. With the exception of FDIC, none of them dates from 1933. Had economic health been miraculously restored in the fabled Hundred Days, a swift return to business as usual might well have meant politics as usual as well, and none of those landmark reforms would have come to pass. Indeed, there would have been no New Deal as we know it.

To be sure, Roosevelt sought to enlarge the national state as the principal instrument of the security and stability that he hoped to impart to American life. But legend to the contrary, much of the security that the New Deal threaded into the fabric of American society was often stitched with a remarkably delicate hand, not simply imposed by the fist of the imperious state. And with the notable exceptions of agricultural subsidies and old-age pensions, it was not usually purchased with the taxpayers' dollars.

*

Nowhere was the artful design of the New Deal's security program more evident than in the financial sector. At the tip of Manhattan Island, south of the street laid out along the line where the first Dutch settlers built their wall to defend against marauding Indians, beats the very heart of American capitalism. Deep in the urban canyons of the old Dutch city sits the New York Stock Exchange, whence had come the first herald of the Depression's onset. As the great crash of 1929 reverberated through the financial system, annihilating billions of dollars in asset values and forcing bank closures, it raised a mighty cry for the reform of "Wall Street," a site that early and late has been beleaguered by threatening hordes incensed at its supposedly inordinate power. The New Deal heeded that cry. Among its first initiatives was the reform of the American financial sector, including the banks and the securities markets. What did it accomplish?

Faced with effectively complete collapse of the banking system in 1933, the New Deal confronted a choice. On the one hand, it could try to nationalize the system, or perhaps create a new government bank that would threaten eventually to drive all private banks out of business. On the other hand, it could accede to the long-standing requests of the major money-center banks—especially those headquartered around Wall Street—to relax restrictions on branch and interstate banking, allow mergers and consolidations, and thereby facilitate the emergence of a highly concentrated private banking industry, with just a few dozen powerful institutions to carry on the nation's banking business. That, in fact, was the pattern in most other industrialized countries. But the New Deal did neither. Instead, it left the astonishingly plural and localized American banking system in place, while inducing one important structural change and introducing one key new institution.

The structural change, mandated by the Glass-Steagall Banking Act of 1933, was to separate investment banks from commercial banks, thus securing depositors' savings against the risks of being used for highly speculative purposes. The same Act created a new entity, the Federal Bank Deposit Insurance Corporation (FBDIC, later simply FDIC). Guaranteeing individual bank deposits up to $5,000 (later raised), and funded by minimal subscriptions from Federal Reserve member institutions, the FDIC forever liberated banks and depositors from the fearful psychology of bank "runs" or panics. These two simple measures did not impose an oppressively elaborate new regulatory apparatus on American banking, nor did they levy appreciable costs on either taxpayers or member banks. But they did inject unprecedented stability into the American banking system. Bank failures, which had occurred at the rate of hundreds per year even before the Depression's descent, numbered fewer than 10 per year in the several decades after 1933.

If speculation and lack of depositor confidence had been the major problems of the banking system, the cardinal affliction of the closely related securities industry

had been ignorance. Pervasive, systemic ignorance blanketed Wall Street like a perpetual North Atlantic fog before the New Deal, badly impeding the efficient operation of the securities markets and leaving them vulnerable to all kinds of abuses. Wall Street before the 1930s was a strikingly information-starved environment. Many firms whose securities were publicly traded published no regular reports, or reports whose data were so arbitrarily selected and capriciously audited as to be worse than useless. It was this circumstance that had conferred such awesome power on a handful of investment bankers like J.P. Morgan, because they commanded a virtual monopoly of the information necessary to making sound financial decisions. Especially in the secondary markets where reliable information was all but impossible for the average investor to come by, opportunities abounded for insider manipulation and wildcat speculation. "It's easy to make money in this market," the canny speculator Joseph P. Kennedy had confided to a partner in the palmy days of the 1920s. "We'd better get in before they pass a law against it."

The New Deal did pass a law against it, and assigned Joseph P. Kennedy to implement that law, a choice often compared to putting the fox in the henhouse, or setting a thief to catch a thief. In 1934 Kennedy became the first chairman of the new Securities Exchange Commission, one of just four new regulatory bodies established by the supposedly regulation-mad New Deal. The SEC's powers derived from statutes so patently needed but so intricately technical that Texas Congressman Sam Rayburn admitted he did not know whether the legislation "passed so readily because it was so damned good or so damned incomprehensible." Yet some years later, Rayburn acknowledged that the SEC, thanks in part to the start it got from Kennedy, was "the strongest Commission in the government." A study of the federal bureaucracy overseen by Herbert Hoover called the SEC "an outstanding example of the independent commission at its best."

For all the complexity of its enabling legislation, the power of the SEC resided principally in just two provisions, both of them ingeniously simple. The first mandated disclosure of detailed information, such as balance sheets, profit and loss statements, and the names and compensation of corporate officers, about firms whose securities were publicly traded. The second required verification of that information by independent auditors using standardized accounting procedures. At a stroke, those measures ended the monopoly of the Morgans and their like on investment information. Wall Street was now saturated with data that were relevant, accessible, and comparable across firms and transactions. The SEC's regulations unarguably imposed new reporting requirements on businesses. They also gave a huge boost to the status of the accounting profession. But they hardly constituted a wholesale assault on the theory or practice of free-market capitalism. All to the contrary, the SEC's regulations dramatically improved the economic efficiency of the financial markets by making buy and sell decisions well-informed decisions, provided that the contracting parties consulted the data now so copiously available. This was less the reform than it was the rationalization of capitalism, along the lines of capitalism's own claims about how free markets were supposed to work. To be sure, a later generation's financial prestidigitation eluded the SEC's capacity responsibly and effectively to exercise its regulatory functions; but that sorry development supported an argument for updating and upgrading the Commission, not for challenging its essential rationale.

The New Deal's housing policies provide perhaps the best example of its techniques for stabilizing a major economic sector by introducing new elements of information and reliability—and offer another lesson in what can happen when government agencies fail to keep pace with changes in the private sector. By its very nature, the potential demand for housing was then and later large, widespread, and capable of generating significant employment in countless localities. John Maynard Keynes was not alone in recognizing that housing was a sector with enormous promise for invigorating the Depression-era economy. Well before Keynes urged Roosevelt to put his eggs in the housing basket, Herbert Hoover had patronized the Better Homes for America Movement in the 1920s. In 1931, as new home construction plunged by 95 percent from its pre-1929 levels, he had convened a national presidential conference on Home Building and Home Ownership. Its very title, especially the latter phrase, advertised Hoover's preferred approach to the housing issue.

As in the banking sector, the New Deal faced a choice in the housing field. It could take Keynes's advice and get behind proposals from congressional liberals like Robert Wagner for large-scale, European-style public housing programs. Or it could follow Hoover's lead and seek measures to stimulate private home building and individual home ownership. Despite its experimentation with government-built model communities like the so-called Greenbelt Towns (of which only three were built), and its occasional obeisance to public housing programs (as in the modestly funded Wagner-Steagall National Housing Act of 1937), the New Deal essentially adopted—and significantly advanced—Hoover's approach. Two new agencies implemented the New Deal's housing program, the Home Owners' Loan Corporation and the Federal Housing Administration, later supplemented by the

Federal National Mortgage Association (Fannie Mae) in 1938, the Veterans' Administration's housing program after World War II, and the Federal Home Loan Mortgage Corporation (Freddie Mac) in 1970.

The HOLC began in 1933 as an emergency agency with two objectives: to protect defaulting homeowners against foreclosure and to improve lending institutions' balance sheets by re-financing shaky mortgages. With much publicity, the HOLC stopped the avalanche of defaults in 1933. But its lasting legacy was a quieter affair. Just as the SEC introduced standardized accounting practices into the securities industry, the HOLC, to facilitate its nation-wide lending operations, encouraged uniform national appraisal methods throughout the real estate industry. Its successor, the FHA, created in 1934 to insure long-term mortgages in much the manner that the FDIC insured bank deposits, took the next logical step and defined national standards of home construction. The creation of Fannie Mae completed the New Deal's housing program apparatus. Fannie Mae furnished lending institutions with a mechanism for reselling their mortgages, thus increasing the lenders' liquidity and making more money available for subsequent rounds of construction. Taken together, the standardization of appraisal methods and construction criteria, along with the mortgage insurance and re-sale facilities the New Deal put in place, removed much of the risk from home-lending.

The FHA and Fannie Mae themselves neither built houses nor loaned money. Nor did they manage to stimulate much new construction in the 1930s. But they arranged an institutional landscape in which unprecedented amounts of private capital could flow into the home construction industry in the post-World War II years. The New Deal's housing policies, cleverly commingling public and private institutions, demonstrated that political economy need not be a zero-sum game, in which the expansion of state power automatically spelled the shrinkage of private prerogatives. Once the war was over, this New Deal "reform" proved not to have checked or intimidated capital so much as to have liberated it. And eventually it revolutionized the way Americans lived.

Before the New Deal, only about four Americans in ten lived in their own homes. Homeowners in the 1920s typically paid full cash or very large down payments for their houses, usually not less than 30 percent. The standard mortgage was offered by a local institution with a highly limited service area, had only a five to ten year maturity, bore interest as high as 8 percent, and required a large "balloon" payment, or refinancing, at its termination. Not surprisingly, under such conditions a majority of Americans were renters.

scholars lamented its incompleteness, its alleged political timidity, and its supposedly premature demise. But what needs emphasis, in the final accounting, is not what the New Deal failed to do, but how it managed to do so much in the uniquely plastic moment of the mid-1930s. That brief span of years, it is now clear, constituted one of only a handful of episodes in American history when substantial and lasting social change has occurred—when the country was, in measurable degree, remade. The American political system, after all, was purpose-built in the eighteenth century to prevent its easy manipulation from the national capital, to bind governments down from mischief, as Jefferson said, by the chains of the Constitution, especially by the notoriously constraining system of checks and balances. It is hardly surprising, therefore, that political stasis defines the "normal" American condition. Against that backdrop, what stands out about the New Deal are not its limitations and its temerity, but the boldness of its vision and the consequent sweep of its ultimate achievement.

For all his alleged inscrutability, Franklin Roosevelt's social vision was clear enough. "We are going to make a country," he once said to Secretary of Labor Frances Perkins, "in which no one is left out." In that unadorned sentence Roosevelt spoke volumes about the New Deal's lasting historical meaning. Like his rambling, comfortable, and unpretentious old home on the bluff above the Hudson River, Roosevelt's New Deal was a welcoming mansion of many rooms, a place where millions of his fellow citizens could find at last a measure of the security that the patrician Roosevelts enjoyed as their birthright.

Perhaps the New Deal's greatest achievement was its accommodation of the maturing immigrant communities that had milled uneasily on the margins of American society for a generation and more before the 1930s. In bringing them into the Democratic Party and closer to the mainstream of national life, the New Deal, even without fully intending to do so, also made room for an almost wholly new institution, the industrial union. To tens of millions of rural Americans, the New Deal offered the modern comforts of electricity, schools, and roads, as a well as unaccustomed financial stability. To the elderly and the unemployed it extended the promise of income security, and the salvaged dignity that went with it.

To black Americans the New Deal offered jobs with the CCC, WPA, and PWA, and, perhaps as importantly, the compliment of respect from at least some federal officials. The time had not come for direct federal action to challenge Jim Crow and put right at last the crimes of slavery and segregation, but more than a few New Dealers made clear where their sympathies lay, and quietly prepared

for a better future. Urged on by Eleanor Roosevelt, the President brought African-Americans into the government in small but unprecedented numbers. By the mid-1930s they gathered periodically as an informal "black cabinet," guided often by the redoubtable Mary McLeod Bethune. Roosevelt also appointed the first black federal judge, William Hastie. Several New Deal Departments and agencies, including especially Ickes' Interior Department and Aubrey Williams' National Youth Administration, placed advisers for "Negro affairs" on their staffs.

In the yeasty atmosphere of Roosevelt's New Deal, scores of social experiments flourished. Not all of them were successful, not all of them destined to last, but all shared the common purpose of building a country from whose basic benefits and privileges no one was excluded. The Resettlement Administration laid out model communities for displaced farmers and refugees from the shattered industrial cities, though only a handful of those social experiments survived, and they soon lost their distinctive, utopian character. The Farm Security Administration maintained migrant labor camps that sheltered thousands of families like John Steinbeck's Joads. The Tennessee Valley Authority brought electricity, and with it, industry, to the chronically depressed Upper South. The Bonneville Power Authority made a start on doing the same for the Columbia River Basin in the long-isolated Pacific Northwest. The New Deal also extended the hand of recognition to Native Americans. The Indian Reorganization Act of 1934—the so-called Indian New Deal—ended the half-century-old policy of forced assimilation and alienation of tribal lands. The new law encouraged tribes to establish their own self-governing bodies and to preserve their ancestral traditions. Though some Indians denounced this policy as a "back-to-the-blanket" measure that sought to make museum pieces out of Native Americans, the Act accurately reflected the New Deal's consistently inclusionary ethos.

The New Deal also succored the indigent and patronized the arts. It built roads and bridges and hospitals. It even sought a kind of security for the land itself, adding some 12 million acres of national parklands, including Olympic National Park in Washington State, Isle Royal in Lake Superior, the Everglades in Florida, and King's Canyon in California. It planted trees and fought erosion. It erected mammoth dams—Grand Coulee and Bonneville on the Columbia, Shasta on the Sacramento, Fort Peck on the Missouri—that were river-tamers and nature-busters, to be sure, but job-makers and region-builders, too.

Above all, the New Deal gave to countless Americans who had never had much of it a sense of security, and with it a sense of having a stake in their country. And it did it all without shredding the American Constitution or sundering the American people. At a time when despair and alienation were prostrating other peoples under the heel of dictatorship, that was no small accomplishment.

The columnist Dorothy Thompson summed up Franklin Roosevelt's achievements at the end of the Depression decade, in 1940:

> We have behind us eight terrible years of a crisis we have shared with all countries. Here we are, and our basic institutions are still intact, our people relatively prosperous, and most important of all, our society relatively affectionate. No rift has made an unbridgeable schism between us. The working classes are not clamoring for [Communist Party boss] Mr. Browder and the industrialists are not demanding a Man on Horseback. No country in the world is so well off.

In the last analysis, Franklin Roosevelt faithfully discharged his duties, in John Maynard Keynes's words of 1933, as "the trustee for those in every country" who believed in social peace and in democracy. He did mend the evils of the Depression by reasoned experiment within the framework of the existing social system. He did prevent a naked confrontation between orthodoxy and revolution. The priceless value of that achievement, surely as much as the columns of ciphers that recorded national income and production, must be reckoned in any final accounting of what the New Deal did.

The New Deal powerfully revitalized American life in the second half of the twentieth century. It built a platform for sustained economic growth, spread the benefits of prosperity widely, made more people more secure than they had ever been, and helped set the stage for the civil rights movement that brought at least a measure of long-delayed social justice for African-Americans. Yet as the century waned and a new generation came to power, national attitudes toward risk, security, and the role of government shifted consequentially. "Government is not the solution to our problem," Ronald Reagan declared. "Government is the problem." The policies that flowed from that political theology did not fully dismantle the New Deal, but they badly compromised the capacity of government to adapt to the rapidly changing character of the global post-industrial economy. As a new generation of political leaders peer into the maw of another monstrous economic calamity, they would do well to remember the enduring relevance of the New Deal: that government has not only a right, but an obligation, to make a country in which no one is left out, and in which all can live in safety and security.

David M. Kennedy is the Donald J. McLachlan Professor of History Emeritus at Stanford University. He received his PhD in American studies from Yale University and is the author of *Over Here: The First World War and American Society* (1980) and *Freedom from Fear: The American People in Depression and War, 1929–1945* (1999).

Selected, Edited, and with Issue Framing Material by:
Larry Madaras, *Howard Community College*
and
James M. SoRelle, *Baylor University*

ISSUE

Was the World War II Era a Watershed for the Civil Rights Movement?

YES: James A. Nuechterlein, from "The Politics of Civil Rights: The FEPC, 1941–46," *Prologue: The Journal of the National Archives* (1978)

NO: Harvard Sitkoff, from "African American Militancy in the World War II South: Another Perspective," University Press of Mississippi (1997)

Learning Outcomes

After reading this issue, you will be able to:

- Explain what historians mean when they speak of a "watershed" event.
- Discuss the concept of the "long civil rights movement."
- Analyze the impact of World War II on the African American freedom struggle.
- Identify the key leaders and organizations that worked during the war to advance the cause of civil rights for black Americans.
- Describe the attitudes of African Americans toward the U.S. involvement in World War II.
- Understand the relationship between the U.S. federal government and civil rights initiatives during World War II.

ISSUE SUMMARY

YES: James A. Nuechterlein insists that the efforts to improve employment opportunities for African Americans during World War II, as exemplified by the establishment of the Fair Employment Practices Commission (1941–1946), marked the beginning of the modern civil rights movement in the United States and set the stage for broader civil rights successes in the 1950s and 1960s.

NO: Harvard Sitkoff challenges the "watershed" interpretation by pointing out that, after Pearl Harbor, militant African American protest against racial discrimination was limited by the constraints imposed on the nation at war, the dwindling resources for sustained confrontation, and the genuinely patriotic response by black Americans to dangers faced by the nation.

Historians have long sought to identify and write about specific moments in the past that produced a major shift in the political, economic, social, or diplomatic fortunes of a particular nation or group of people. As a result, extensive scholarship has been devoted to "revolutions," "turning points," and "sea changes," following which conditions were markedly different from what they had been previously. These "watershed" events that mark a change of course from the past can be positive or negative, depending upon one's point of view, and U.S. history is filled with them: the American Revolution, the Civil War, the Great War (World War I), the Great Depression, World War II, the Cold War, and 9/11.

For students of the modern American civil rights movement, there are several events that appear to serve the purpose of a watershed moment: the U.S. Supreme Court's landmark decision in the Brown case that overturned

Plessy v. Ferguson and set the stage for the dismantling of legally supported racial segregation; Rosa Parks' refusal to relinquish her seat on a Montgomery city bus in December 1955, which precipitated a year-long boycott and served as a springboard to Dr. Martin Luther King's rise to national prominence; the actions of four African American college students in Greensboro, North Carolina, who had grown weary of a contradictory Jim Crow system that allowed them to purchase products in a Woolworth's store but not sit down at the lunch counter for service in the rear of the same establishment. Each of these events altered the trajectory of African American activism in important ways and cleared the path for what many scholars characterize as the most successful social movement in American history.

Over the course of the past two decades, however, historians have begun to take a broader look at the African American freedom struggle and to identify significant precursors to the movement that many previously had placed within the chronological time frame of 1954–1968. For example, see Jacqueline Dowd Hall, "The Long Civil Rights Movement and the Political Uses of the Past," *Journal of American History* 91 (March 2005): 1233–1263, who argues for a much earlier starting point for the civil rights struggle and insists that the search for watershed events must be moved back farther in the twentieth century. In the hands of such scholars, the key historical moments came in the World War II, as the United States and its Allies combatted a fascist dictatorship firmly committed to an ideology of extermination; or during the Great Depression as Franklin Roosevelt's New Deal produced a much larger role for government to play in the lives of the American people; or as a consequence of the Wilson administration's effort to make the world safe for democracy while maintaining strict segregation of the races in his own nation. Still others claim that it is not unreasonable to push back the timeline of the civil rights movement to cover the intense antilynching efforts of Ida B. Wells-Barnett or to the Reconstruction period with its efforts to establish citizenship rights for African Americans who, while freed from the bonds of slavery at war's end, remained captive to Chief Justice Roger Taney's dictum in the *Dred Scott* case (1857) that peoples of African descent possessed no rights that whites were bound by law to respect.

The story of the United States' involvement in World War II involves much more than a delineation of military engagements in Europe and the Pacific. The war occurred on the heels of a devastating depression and helped to turn the economy around with nearly full production and employment. The war possessed significant social implications for many Americans, including women and ethnic and racial minorities, a subject that has received general scholarly attention from prominent historians Richard Polenberg, *War and Society: The United States, 1941–1945* (J. B. Lippincott, 1972); John Morton Blum, *V Was for Victory: Politics and American Culture during World War II* (Harcourt Brace Jovanovich, 1976); and Allan M. Winkler, *Home Front U.S.A.: America during World War II*, 2nd ed. (Harlan Davidson, 2000). The present issue examines the impact of World War II on efforts by black Americans to demonstrate their loyalty to the United States while at the same time insisting upon the same citizenship rights accorded white Americans. It builds upon the pioneering efforts of Richard Dalfiume, whose "The 'Forgotten Years' of the Negro Revolution," *Journal of American History* 55 (June 1968): 99–106, argued that scholars had overlooked World War II as a period in which African Americans aggressively combined patriotism and a challenge to Jim Crow. During these "forgotten years," Dalfiume argued, civil rights organizations such as the National Association for the Advancement of Colored People (NAACP) and A. Philip Randolph's March on Washington Movement (MOWM) applied pressure on the Roosevelt administration to eliminate discrimination in the military and in defense industry hiring practices. In doing so, mass militancy became a major strategy among blacks during the war and sowed the seeds for the civil rights revolution of the postwar period.

In the selections that follow, James Nuechterlein and Harvard Sitkoff debate the degree to which World War II deserves to be considered a watershed event in the history of the American civil rights movement. Nuechterlein subscribes to the interpretation introduced by Dalfiume and focuses upon the battle to combat employment discrimination in the nation's defense industries that led to the establishment of the Fair Employment Practices Commission (FEPC) via Franklin Roosevelt's Executive Order 8802 in 1941. According to Nuechterlein, FDR's decision was generated by A. Philip Randolph's threat to employ direct action strategies, including a march by 100,000 African Americans on the nation's capital. The debate over FEPC, he concludes, produced shifts in political power and strategy within the Democratic Party and provided models for the activism that would drive the modern civil rights movement of the 1950s and 1960s.

Harvard Sitkoff, who interestingly once had been a proponent of the conclusions reached by Dalfiume and Nuechterlein, now questions the validity of the "watershed" interpretation. He makes a clear distinction between the views expressed by African Americans before Pearl Harbor and the ideas they articulated after December 7, 1941, and concludes that black militancy declined sharply following the attack on the American fleet in Hawaii. Even African American Communists, he reports, softened their attacks on American racism during the war. According to Sitkoff, the types of black militancy that were evident prior to the Pearl Harbor attack were now inhibited by the constraints imposed by a nation at war, dwindling resources for sustained protest, and the patriotic response by blacks to the dangers faced by the United States.

YES ↵   James A. Nuechterlein

The Politics of Civil Rights: The FEPC, 1941–46

It is now clear that the period of World War II marked the beginning of the modern civil rights movement in the United States. The most important event in that early development was the creation in 1941 by Franklin D. Roosevelt of the President's Committee on Fair Employment Practices. The history of the FEPC from its birth to its death in 1946 involved conflicts over political power and strategy within both major political parties but especially among the Democrats. The Roosevelt and Truman administrations were keenly sensitive to the party implications of the issue, while the congressional struggles over the FEPC, though involving the Republicans to some degree, essentially reflected shifts of strength and influence within the Democratic party. Those shifts heralded the later emergence of civil rights as the primary domestic political issue of postwar America. This essay builds on earlier studies of the FEPC by focusing in detail on the political aspects of the struggle, with particular reference to the conflicts within and between the parties in Congress. It attempts to illuminate, amplify, and specify a pattern of historical change in the politics of civil rights during this period that has frequently been asserted generally.

By 1940, Negroes had become one of the most dependable voting blocs supporting the Democratic party. Politically and economically the appeal of the New Deal to the nation's "forgotten men" carried special significance for blacks, and although the Roosevelt administration avoided a frontal assault on discrimination before 1941, its legislative and administrative programs directed at the problems of the poor included, perforce, benefits for Negroes. Responding to these programs, Negroes in increasing numbers forsook their traditional Republican affiliation and became an important component of the Roosevelt coalition.

For blacks, economic progress was circumscribed by racial barriers, and returning prosperity highlighted their struggle. The preparedness program of 1940-41 brought the economic recovery that had always eluded the New Deal; unemployment dropped sharply under the demand of manpower for defense. Yet, for reasons beyond inadequate education and training, Negro reemployment continued to lag. Discrimination prevailed not only in corporations and in labor unions but also in the very government agencies charged with responsibility for managing manpower for the defense effort.

The government's apparent acquiescence in discrimination, evidenced also by continuing racial segregation in the armed forces, brought despair and bitterness to the black community. Protests from Negro organizations produced, at best, sporadic and inconclusive results. Government defense agencies regularly issued orders forbidding discrimination by defense contractors but the orders were just as regularly ignored.

Roosevelt, while not unsympathetic to Negro aspirations, had never placed civil rights high on his list of political priorities. Acutely aware that he had to depend on Southern Democratic congressmen to enact essential programs, he had remained cautiously noncommittal during the various struggles in the 1930s to pass federal antilynching legislation. By mid-1941, however, the pressures for action against job discrimination became more powerful, as substantial numbers of white liberals joined the newly militant Negro spokesmen in their protests.

The president put increasing pressure for action on William Knudsen and Sidney Hillman, co-chairmen of the Office of Production Management. Hillman, especially, continually urged government contractors not to discriminate, but the administration feared to use sanctions and urgings alone brought minimal results. Even government industrial training program administrators practiced discrimination, despite legal provisions to the contrary.

Where liberal protest and government suasion failed, organized pressure groups finally succeeded. The man most responsible for creating the FEPC was A. Philip Randolph, founder in 1925 of the Brotherhood of Sleeping Car Porters, American Federation of Labor, the most influential Negro body in organized labor. Having participated with other Negro leaders in several fruitless attempts to promote government action against discrimination in civilian and military affairs, Randolph decided late in 1940 that more direct action was required. To that end, in February 1941 he created the March on Washington Movement, an all-black organization dedicated to eliminating racial bias in war industries, labor unions, government agencies, and the armed forces.

Randolph established the movement's Negroes-only policy for three reasons: to prevent infiltration by white Communists, to stimulate black pride and self-confidence, and to attract the large numbers of lower-class blacks necessary for it to succeed. The MOWM planned a series of massive rallies in major cities to focus attention on the problems of Negroes; should these fail to stimulate action, the organization threatened to stage a mass march on the nation's capital. To be credible, such a threat required evidence of broad and active support, and Randolph hoped for the kind of grassroots Negro enthusiasm that the middle-class, biracial National Association for the Advancement of Colored People and the Urban League had never enjoyed.

Throughout the first half of 1941, the MOWM organized rallies and put increased political pressure on the administration, setting July 1 as the date for its climactic march on Washington. Randolph may well have been unable to produce the massive march he predicted, but Roosevelt evidently decided that the threat could not be discounted. When new directives against discrimination from the Office of Production Management failed either to bring results or to appease Negro leaders, FDR assigned Fiorello LaGuardia, mayor of New York and director of civil defense, to negotiate with black spokesmen. At a White House conference held June 18, Negroes pressed upon Roosevelt and other administration leaders their demands for a government agency to combat discrimination in employment.

In a meeting that LaGuardia termed "a fine example of democracy at work," the Negroes won a clear, if not unqualified, victory. A week later, on June 25, Roosevelt issued Executive Order 8802 creating the President's Committee on Fair Employment Practices. For the first time since Reconstruction, an official government agency became responsible for safeguarding black rights. The victory was especially notable since many liberals, convinced by mid-1941 that domestic concerns must be subordinated to crushing fascism abroad, had given only peripheral attention to Negro demands. Furthermore, Roosevelt knew that in creating the FEPC he risked losing the Southern congressional support so urgently needed in the areas of preparedness and foreign policy.

Yet the defense effort had given blacks new leverage with the administration. Production for defense demanded full use of manpower regardless of race; the nation quite literally could not afford to exclude blacks from jobs. Also, the ideological struggle against Hitler required closer correspondence between democratic dogma and social reality in terms of equality of races. The creation of the FEPC persuaded Randolph to "postpone" indefinitely the march on Washington, thereby saving the administration a major embarrassment at home and abroad. Political pressure was important as well: Negro leaders did not have to remind the president that the votes of their followers were an increasingly important factor in Democratic support.

Significantly, blacks had gained the victory on their own. They had bargained and won by operating as a pragmatic, determined pressure group. What they learned in 1941 they applied throughout the war years; as in World War I they supported the defense and war efforts, but contrary to the practice in 1917, they insisted that the demands of national unity must not preclude the expansion of Negro rights. They persisted in reminding the public of the implications for race relations of a war fought in the name of democratic ideals. Though they ultimately failed, and though the FEPC finally became another war casualty, they initiated a process that would, at another day, begin to give economic, political, and social substance to black equality.

Frustration marked the five-year history of the FEPC. Assigned the task of ending discrimination "in the employment of workers in defense industries or government because of race, creed, color, or national origin," it never received the power commensurate with that mandate. Throughout its career, the committee lacked the needed authority and adequate budget and personnel resources; these weaknesses, in turn, reflected inadequate political support from the Roosevelt administration and from Congress. Created only under duress, ignored by the general public and government officials alike, the FEPC struggled doggedly against prejudice among its enemies and indifference among those who claimed to be its friends.

The wording of the enforcement clause in Executive Order 8802 indicated the timidity of the administration's approach:

> The Committee shall receive and investigate complaints of this order and shall take appropriate steps to redress grievances which it finds to be valid. The Committee shall also recommend to the several departments and agencies of the government of the United States and to the President all measures which may be deemed by it necessary or proper to effectuate the provisions of this order.

To be effective, then, the FEPC needed full cooperation from the major government agencies involved in the defense effort. When corporations or labor unions refused to comply with nondiscrimination orders, the committee requested that the supervising agencies cancel or not renew any contracts with offenders. Some agencies complied with these requests; but most did not. In July 1942, for example, the United States Employment Service issued a directive to its field offices permitting them to discriminate in referring workers if employers insisted on it.

The absence of coercive power required the committee to rely mainly on publicity to fulfill its objectives. To this end, it conducted a series of public hearings in major employment centers during late 1941 and early 1942. The committee claimed, perhaps optimistically, that these hearings resulted in marked increases in the number of Negroes employed in defense projects.

The hearings were of uncertain value politically. Predictably, they antagonized the FEPC's opponents while failing to satisfy its friends fully. The reaction in Birmingham, Alabama, was typical: Negroes and some white liberals resented the committee's acceptance of social segregation; the city's commissioner of public safety, Eugene "Bull" Connor, on the other hand, warned Roosevelt that federal agencies were attempting "to destroy segregation and bring about amalgamation of the races." Only a quick countermand by the president, Connor said, could prevent "the annihilation of the Democratic Party" in the South.

The FEPC encountered continuing problems related to its own staff and also to its position within the executive branch. The original six-man committee reflected careful efforts by Roosevelt to achieve racial and ideological balance. Mark Ethridge, vice president and general manager of the Louisville *Courier-Journal,* became the first chairman, and the committee selected Lawrence W. Cramer, former governor of the Virgin Islands, as executive secretary. Ethridge, representing moderate Southern opinion, interpreted Executive Order 8802 in terms of the manpower needs of the war effort, not as a social document intended to put an end to racial segregation. Harassed from the outset by both Southern racists and Northern liberals, Ethridge resigned from the chairmanship early in 1942, although the president persuaded him to remain on the committee under the new chairman, Malcolm MacLean, president of the Hampton Institute. Under MacLean, the committee hoped to expand its scope and authority. It asked the president for broader enforcement power as well as a budget large enough to establish a dozen regional offices.

Though he at first appeared sympathetic, Roosevelt soon acted to weaken, rather than strengthen, the committee. Originally established in the Labor Division of the Office of Production Management and responsible only to the president, the FEPC was moved to the War Production Board after the OPM was abolished in January 1942, although it retained its independent status. Political pressure from Southern congressmen, heightened after the Birmingham hearings of June 1942, convinced many officials in the administration of the need for closer control of the agency's activities. Bowing to that pressure, the president, without consulting with committee members, transferred the FEPC to the War Manpower Commission on July 30, 1942, placing the agency under the supervision and control of Paul V. McNutt, WMC director.

The shift shocked committee members. Chairman MacLean loyally declared that he would obey orders, but warned, "All hell will break loose" among minority groups. Roosevelt responded characteristically by directing his secretary, Marvin McIntyre, to "get McLean [sic] and McNutt into the office together and have them talk over this whole thing;" he was sure that the dispute involved "a lot of smoke and very little fire."

The president was wrong. Over the next several months the FEPC and the WMC attempted without success to establish a mutually satisfactory working relationship. FEPC officials fought against being absorbed into the existing antidiscrimination agencies of the WMC, while McNutt, determined to keep the committee under close control, refused to approve a budget for the FEPC until it accepted his supervision. As negotiations dragged on, black protests over the transfer became increasingly bitter, despite White House assurances that the move would strengthen the committee. Walter White of the NAACP curtly wrote McNutt: "Abolition of the Committee altogether would be a more honest and honorable act in that Negroes and other minorities would then be under no illusions" that the administration intended to fight discrimination in war industries or in the federal government.

significant achievement of the Negro press during this crisis, in our estimation," bragged African American publishers in 1944, "lies in the fact that the Negro newspapers have brought home to the Negro people of America that this is their war and not merely 'a white man's war.'"

However much the great majority of African Americans desired the end of racial discrimination and segregation in American life, only a minority thought that their fight for rights should take precedence over defeating Germany and Japan, and far fewer flirted with militant protests that might be considered harmful to the war effort. Thus A. Philip Randolph's March-on-Washington Movement, generally depicted as the epitome of mass black militancy during the war, truly held center-stage in the Negro community only for a few months in 1941, before American entry into the war, and then gradually withered away. Shunned as "unpatriotic" by many of the mainstream Negro organizations and newspapers that had earlier supported it, Randolph's group labored in vain to rebut accusations of employing the "most dangerous demagoguery on record" and of "Marching Against the War Effort." Polls in the Negro press during 1942. revealed a steady diminution of black support for a March on Washington to demand a redress of grievances. When Randolph called for mass marches on city halls in 1942, no blacks marched. When he called for a week of non-violent civil disobedience and non-cooperation to protest Jim Crow school and transportation systems in 1943, a poll indicated that more than 70 percent of African Americans opposed the campaign, and no blacks engaged in such activities. And when he called upon the masses to come to his "We Are Americans, Too!" conference in Chicago in the summer of 1943, virtually no blacks other than members of his Sleeping Car Porters union attended. By then, as Randolph admitted, the March-on-Washington Movement was "without funds." Unable to pay the rent for an office or for the services of an executive secretary, the organization existed only on paper.

Asa Philip Randolph's brief shining moment had passed quickly. The March-on-Washington Movement ended with Randolph having never led a wartime mass march or a civil disobedience campaign. When he described the program of his organization in Rayford Logan's *What the Negro Wants* (1944), Randolph barely discussed mass militant protests. Instead, most of his essay was devoted to attacking American Communists, to explaining why racial change in the South must be gradual and piecemeal, and to advocating race relations committees that would take the necessary measures to prevent or stop race riots. Quite at odds with the image of the wartime Randolph in most current accounts, his wartime agenda for the March-on-Washington Movement in fact differed little from that of the NAACP. Randolph, moreover, devoted the greatest amount of his time and energy during the war to criticizing discrimination within the American Federation of Labor and heading the National Council for a Permanent Fair Employment Practices Commission, a traditional legislative lobby which never advocated mobilizing the masses and which was controlled by an elite group of mainly white New York socialists and labor leaders. Penning the moribund March-on-Washington Movement's epitaph in 1945, Adam Clayton Powell, Jr., described it as an "organization with a name that it does not live up to, an announced program that it does not stick to, and a philosophy contrary to the mood of the times." Its former headquarters in Harlem had already been converted into a bookshop.

The Congress of Racial Equality suffered much the same fate as the March-on-Washington Movement during the war, but it did so in relative obscurity. The white media barely mentioned it, and the Negro press did so even less. A tiny interracial, primarily white, elite group of pacifist and socialist followers of A. J. Muste, CORE mainly engaged in efforts to counter discrimination in places of public accommodation and recreation in northern cities where those practices were already illegal. It did little to try to desegregate schools and housing, or to expand job opportunities for African Americans, or to influence civil rights legislation, and its wartime efforts proved negligible. Because its dozen or so local chapters took to heart the reconciliatory aspects of Gandhian non-violence, the vital importance of changing the consciousness of those engaged in racist practices, few of its Christian pacifist members went beyond negotiations to direct action in the streets. CORE's hopes of becoming a mass, broad-based movement lingered as only a dream during the war, and blacks at Howard University and in St. Louis who, independent of each other, thought they were inventing the sit-in in 1944, did not even know that CORE, too, sought to employ the tactics of the CIO's famous "sit-down" strikes to the fight against Jim Crow. Faced with public apathy, unstable chapters, and a budget of less than $100 a month for its national office, CORE did not even contemplate entering the upper South until 1947, when eight blacks and eight whites decided to test the compliance with the Supreme Court's 1946 ruling in the Irene Morgan case, declaring segregation in interstate carriers unconstitutional. Even then, CORE would not try to establish a chapter in the South for another decade.

The NAACP, on the other hand, saw its membership grow from 50,556 and 355 branches in 1940 to over half a million and more than a thousand branches in 1946.

Yet, it essentially remained middle-class in orientation and bureaucratic in structure, abhoring radical tactics and adhering to a legalistic approach that did not countenance collective action. This was especially so in the South, the site of three-quarters of the new wartime branches. None of the southern branches sanctioned confrontations, direct action, or extra-legal tactics. Ella Baker, who visited local chapters of the NAACP throughout the wartime South, first as an assistant field secretary of the Association and then as its national director of branches, never ceased hectoring the national office that most of those branches were little more than social clubs with no interest whatsoever in pursuing local protests. Thurgood Marshall also chafed at the reluctance of the southern branch officers to attack Jim Crow, and their tendency to devote themselves solely to teacher-salary equalization suits. Such suits "aroused little excitement, even in the Deep South," maintains George B. Tindall: "The tedious pace, the limited results, the manifest equity of the claim" muted white alarm. And that suited the NAACP's southern leadership of black academics, businessmen, and ministers just fine. The issue of inequitable salaries for Negro public school teachers would remain their top priority even in the immediate postwar years. The pursuit of traditional objectives by restrained tactics remained the hallmark of the Association in the South. As they had in the 1930s, the wartime southern branches lobbied and litigated against the poll tax, the white primary, and lynching, and requested a more equitable share of educational facilities and funds.

Continuity also characterized the work of the seven southern affiliates of the National Urban League. They held firm to their social work orientation and to their reliance on negotiations to expand employment, recreational, and housing opportunities for African Americans. Such matters as African American juvenile delinquency and family disorganization took precedence over the fight for equal rights. Their wariness toward demonstrations and protests reflected their fear of losing funding from the Community Chest and local philanthropies, their faith in being able to make progress by working in conventional channels, and their hostility toward the NAACP—which they viewed as a competitor for financial contributions. Confrontation and disruption, even harsh talk, did not fit the Urban League's pursuit of gradual and limited racial change. When Benjamin Bell, the newly appointed executive secretary of the Urban League in Memphis, angered white politicians and businessmen by denouncing Jim Crow, the national office quickly replaced him with someone more compliant.

Much as southern black leaders did not support direct action protests or forthright attacks on segregation during the war, the editorials of southern Negro newspapers rarely echoed the demands for racial equality of those in the North. Several African American newspapers in the South followed the wartime lead of the Savannah *Tribune* in discontinuing the practice of reprinting editorials from northern black newspapers. Most of the southern Negro press had never done so, and they continued, as did most southern black church and community leaders during the war, to stay on the sidelines of the civil rights struggle, to advocate upright behavior and individual economic advancement within the existing order, and to preach paternalism and "civility." Even when calling for "fair play" or an end to disfranchisement, they did so in a manner that posed no clear and present danger to white supremacy. Lest criticism be construed as unpatriotic, they accentuated African American loyalty and contributions to the war effort above all else. Surveying the Negro press in Mississippi during the war, Julius Thompson concluded: "Submission to the system was the watchword."

. . . African American Communists soft-pedaled their censure of racism in the United States during the war. Executing an about-face from the period of the Nazi-Soviet Pact, when they took the lead in exposing Jim Crow in the armed forces, the Communists opposed efforts by blacks to embarrass the military after Germany invaded the Soviet Union in June 1941. They even sought to prevent African American legal challenges against discrimination from coming before the courts. The party's wartime policy was to do nothing that might erode the unity necessary for prosecuting the war. Ben Davis vigorously denounced both the March-on-Washington Movement and the NAACP for placing the interests of blacks above the needs for "national unity, maximum war production, and the highest possible morale in the armed forces." Having opposed civil disobedience by blacks and mass protests against racism, and defended the military against its civil rights critics, Davis confessed after the war that he had "often lost sight of" the black liberation struggle. Communist leader and social scientist John Williamson later concurred. "Neglect of the problems of the Negro people," Williamson wrote, "and the cessation of organizing efforts in the South undoubtedly slowed the pace of the freedom movement which arose later.

As did most black Communists, Georgian Angelo Herndon and his *Negro Quarterly* followed Earl Browder's wartime policy of refraining from public censure of Jim Crow. Its articles and editorials downplayed racial militancy, emphasized the need for patriotic unity, dispelled the "dangerous fallacy" that this is "a white man's war," and subordinated all racial issues to victory over fascist aggression. Similarly, chapters of the National Negro Congress metamorphosed into Negro Labor Victory Committees;

UNIT

The Cold War and Beyond

World War II ended in 1945, but the peace that everyone had hoped for never came. In 1949, China came under communist control, the Russians developed an atomic bomb, and communist subversion by high-level officials in the State and Treasury Departments of the U.S. government was uncovered. By 1950 a "Cold War" between the Western powers and the Russians was in full swing, and American soldiers were fighting a hot war in Korea to "contain" communist expansion. In September 1962, the Soviets attempted to bring offensive missile sites onto the island of Cuba. By the end of the crisis, President Kennedy and Premier Nikita Khrushchev had developed a respect for one another, but not without bringing the world to the brink of nuclear war. Another hot spot was Southeast Asia, where President Lyndon B. Johnson (LBJ) escalated America's participation in the Vietnam War in 1965. President Nixon negotiated a peace in January 1973 to bring troops home, but 16 months later the South Vietnamese government surrendered to the communists.

From 1950 to 1974, most white American families were economically well off. Many veterans had attended college under the G.I. bill, moved to the suburbs, and worked in white-collar jobs. The nuclear family was frozen in a state described by one historian as "domestic containment." Ideally, dad went to work, mom stayed home, and the kids went to school. But fissures developed in the 1950s that affected African Americans who were segregated from the suburbs and most white-collar jobs; women who questioned the role of stay-at-home mom; and children who felt alienated from the cultural values of their family. The first sign was the emergence of rock and roll and its white icon Elvis Presley. Was the music revolt the traditional acting out of children against their parents, or did it reflect a real change in values that would culminate in political protests and the establishment of a counterculture in the 1960s?

Over the course of the 1960s, the United States experienced challenges to traditional institutions and values from African Americans who successfully fought for civil and voting rights; students opposing the Vietnam War; young adults forming communes and engaging in "counterculture" values; and women's liberation, which extended well into the 1970s.

Lyndon Johnson waged his Great Society, although the War on Poverty had mixed results. The costs of the Great Society and the endless war in Vietnam created economic problems for LBJ's successors. In the 1970s, Presidents Nixon, Ford, and Carter were unable to manage an economy whose major problem was to balance the trade-off between low levels of unemployment and acceptable levels of inflation. The economy of the 1980s, however, exploded with new high-tech jobs and created a growing gap not only between the rich and the poor but also between the wealthy and the American middle class.

By the opening of the twenty-first century, in the wake of the collapse of the Soviet Union and the end of the Cold War, the United States had emerged as the only true superpower. At the same time, democratic political aspirations and a desire for market economies had spread throughout much of the developing world.

Selected, Edited, and with Issue Framing Material by:
Larry Madaras, *Howard Community College*
and
James M. SoRelle, *Baylor University*

ISSUE

Was President Truman Responsible for the Cold War?

YES: Walter LaFeber, from *America, Russia, and the Cold War, 1945–2000*, 9th ed. (McGraw-Hill, 2002)

NO: John Lewis Gaddis, from "The Origins of the Cold War: 1945–1953," in *Russia, the Soviet Union, and the United States: An Interpretive History*, 2nd ed. (McGraw-Hill, 1990)

Learning Outcomes

After reading this issue, you will be able to:

- List the major events leading to the Cold War from 1945 to 1950.
- Identify and give the significance of the following terms: "atomic diplomacy" and "containment."
- Assess President Truman's role as a "parochial nationalist."
- Evaluate Stalin's responsibility for the Cold War.
- Compare and contrast the orthodox and revisionist interpretations as to who caused the Cold War.

ISSUE SUMMARY

YES: Walter LaFeber argues that the Truman administration exaggerated the Soviet threat after World War II because the United States had expansionist political and economic global needs.

NO: John Lewis Gaddis argues that the power vacuum that existed in Europe at the end of World War II exaggerated and made almost inevitable a clash between the democratic, capitalist United States and the totalitarian, communist USSR and that Joseph Stalin, unwilling to accept any diplomatic compromises, was primarily responsible for the Cold War.

Less than a month before the war ended in Europe the most powerful man in the world, President Franklin Delano Roosevelt, died suddenly from a brain embolism. A nervous, impetuous, and inexperienced Vice President Harry S Truman became the president. Historians disagree whether Truman reversed Roosevelt's relationship with Soviet leader Joseph Stalin or whether the similarities in policy were negated by Truman's blunt negotiating style compared with FDR's suave, calm approach. But disagreements emerged over issues such as control over the atomic bomb, Germany, Poland, and the economic reconstruction of Europe.

The question of Germany was paramount. During the war it was agreed that Germany would be divided temporarily into zones of occupation with the United States, Great Britain, and the newly liberated France controlling the western half of Germany, whereas the Russians would take charge of the eastern half. Berlin, which was 90 miles inside of the Russian zone, would also be divided into zones of occupation. Arguments developed over boundaries, reparations, and transfers of industrial equipment and agricultural foodstuffs between zones. In May 1946, the Americans began treating the western zones as a separate economic unit because the Russians were transferring the food from their zone back to the Soviet Union. In September 1946, Secretary of State James Byrnes announced that the Americans would continue to occupy their half of Germany indefinitely with military troops. By 1948, a separate democratic West German government was established. The Russians protested by blocking ground access to the western zones of Berlin, but the Americans continued to supply the West Berliners with supplies through an airlift. After 10 months, because of the bad publicity, the Russians abandoned the Berlin blockade and created a separate, communist East German government.

Roosevelt and Winston Churchill had conceded Russian control over Eastern Europe during the World War II conferences. The question was how much control. Stalin was not going to allow anticommunist governments to be established in these countries. He had no understanding of how free elections were held. Consequently, when the Cold War intensified in 1947 and 1948, Russian-dominated communist governments were established in Hungary, Poland, and Czechoslovakia.

In February 1946, Stalin delivered a major speech declaring the incompatibility of the two systems of communism and capitalism. The next month, Churchill, now a retired politician, delivered his famous speech at a commencement ceremony at Westminster College in Fulton, Missouri, with the Truman administration's consent, in which he complained about the "iron curtain" that Russia was imposing on Eastern Europe. At the same time, George Kennan, a bright multi-linguist American diplomat who spent years in Germany and Russia and who would become the head of Truman's policy planning staff, wrote a series of telegrams and articles which set the tone for the specific policies the Truman administration would undertake. Kennan had coined the phrase "containment," a word that would be used to describe America's foreign policy from Truman to the first President Bush. Containment would assume various meanings and would be extended to other areas of the globe besides Europe in ways Kennan claims were a misuse of what his original intentions were. Nevertheless the Truman administration moved to stop further Russian expansionism.

In 1947, a series of steps were undertaken both to "contain" Russian expansionism and to rebuild the economies of Europe. On March 12, Truman took the advice of Senator Arthur Vandenberg to "scare the hell out of the American people." In an address before a Republican-controlled Congress, the President argued in somewhat inflated rhetoric that "it must be the policy of the United States to support free peoples who are resisting attempted subjugation by armed minorities or by outside pressures." In the same speech, in what became known as the "Truman Doctrine," the president requested and received $400 million in economic and military assistance to Greece and Turkey. Almost as an afterthought, American military personnel were sent to oversee the reconstruction effort,

a precedent that would later be used to send advisers to Vietnam.

In June 1947, Secretary of State George C. Marshall announced a plan to provide economic assistance to all European nations. This included the Soviet Union, which rejected the offer and formed its own economic recovery group. In April 1948, Congress approved the creation of the Economic Cooperation Administration, the agency that would administer the program. The Marshall Plan would be remembered as America's most successful foreign aid program, in which $17 billion was channeled to the Western European nations. By 1950, industrial production had increased 64 percent since the end of the war, whereas the communist parties declined in membership and influence.

When did the Cold War begin? Was it inevitable? Should one side or the other take most of the blame for the anxiety and occasional hysteria that this conflict created?

Revisionist historians of the Cold War are critical of American foreign policy. In his essay "Another Such Victory: President Truman, American Foreign Policy, and the Cold War," *Diplomatic History* (Spring, 1999), Arnold Offner takes issue with President Truman's recent biographers Robert H. Ferrell, *Harry S. Truman: A Life* (University of Missouri Press, 1994), Alonzo L. Hamby, *Man of the People: A Life of Harry S Truman* (Oxford, 1995), and especially David McCullough's *Truman* (Simon & Schuster, 1992), all of whom rank Truman among the near-great presidents. Offner describes Truman as a "parochial nationalist" whose outlook on foreign policy was ethnocentric and who made rash and quick decisions to cover his insecurities. Offner also accuses the Truman administration with practicing "atomic diplomacy" at the end of the war, when the United States was the sole possessor of the A-bomb, to make the Russians more manageable in Europe.

In his book *We Now Know: Rethinking Cold War History* (Oxford University Press, 1997), John Gaddis argues more strongly than he has in his previous works that Stalin was primarily responsible for the Cold War. Based upon newly discovered, partially opened Soviet archival materials, Gaddis describes Stalin, Khrushchev, and even Chairman Mao as prisoners of a peculiar world view: "Aging Ponce de Leons in search of an ideological fountain of youth."

Professor Gaddis accepts the fact that Truman was insecure. He also believes that throughout 1945 up to early 1946, the Truman administration was responding to the political and economic uncertainties of the post–World War II environment. Although the United States took the lead in creating the World Bank and the International Monetary Fund to supply money for rebuilding Europe's destroyed infrastructure, these institutions were woefully inadequate to the task. It was also unclear whether the United States was going to reenter a recession, as had occurred at the end of the World War I. Gaddis insists that the United States created its Western European empire by invitation through the implementation of the Truman Doctrine, the Marshall Plan, the rebuilding of West Germany, and the formation of NATO. On the other hand, Russia created its empire by force. Starting in Romania in 1945 and in Poland and Hungary in 1947 and ending with the takeover in Czechoslovakia in 1948, the Russians imposed totalitarian governments on its citizens.

Students who wish to study the Cold War in greater detail should consult *Containment: Documents on American Policy and Strategy, 1945–1950* edited by Thomas H. Etzold and John Lewis Gaddis (Columbia University Press, 1978). Another comprehensive work is Melvyn P. Leffler, *A Preponderance of Power: National Security, the Truman Administration, and the Cold War* (Stanford University Press, 1992). The two best readers to excerpt the various viewpoints on the Cold War are Thomas G. Paterson and Robert J. McMahon, eds., *The Origins of the Cold War*, 3rd ed. (D.C. Heath, 1991) and David Reynolds' edited series of essays *The Origins of the Cold War: International Perspectives* (Yale University Press, 1994).

Walter LaFeber's selection in this issue contains most of the arguments advanced by the revisionist critics of America's Cold War policies, Truman's diplomatic style was blunt and impetuous; and he tended to oversimplify complex issues into black and white alternatives. He believes that the Truman administration exaggerated the Russian threat to the balance of power in Europe. It is not clear whether this was a deliberate miscalculation or whether the Truman administration misperceived the

motive behind the "iron curtain" that Russia drew around Eastern Europe. The author maintains that Stalin was more concerned with Russia's security needs than with world conquest.

John Gaddis's selection in the second reading is much less critical than LaFeber's of America's postwar policy. Gaddis believes that the United States and Russia would inevitably clash once the common enemy—Hitler—was defeated because the two countries had fundamentally different political and economic systems. He maintains that for nearly two years there was confusion and uncertainty in the United States' foreign policy in Europe. Truman, he says, did not reverse Roosevelt's policy. His manner was more blunt and, consequently, he showed less patience in dealing with Stalin. Gaddis acknowledges revisionist criticisms that the Americans misperceived Stalin's attempts to control Eastern Europe. The Soviet premier used expansionist rhetoric when he was primarily concerned with protecting Russia from another invasion. By early 1946, both sides were pursuing policies that would lead to an impasse. Still, Gaddis places most of the blame for the Cold War on Stalin, an authoritarian imperialist who "equated world revolution with the expanding influence of the Soviet state." In contrast, according to Gaddis, Truman was constrained by the democratic electoral system of checks and balances and a Republican-controlled Congress from 1946 to 1948, but Stalin had no such constraints. He purged all his real and potential revolutionary opponents in the 1930s and late 1940s and pursued foreign policy objectives as a romantic revolutionary. In summary, according to Gaddis, if Mikhail Gorbachev had been the Soviet leader in 1945, there might have been alternate paths to the Cold War, but with Stalin in charge, "there was going to be a cold war whatever the West did."

YES ↵

Walter LaFeber

America, Russia, and the Cold War, 1945–2000

. . . **T**ruman entered the White House [as a] highly inse-cure man. ("I felt like the moon, the stars, and all the plan-ets had fallen on me," he told reporters.) And he held the world's most responsible job in a world that was changing radically. Truman tried to compensate for his insecurity in several ways. First, he was extremely jealous of his presi-dential powers and deeply suspicious of anyone who chal-lenged those powers. Truman made decisions rapidly not only because that was his character but also because he determined "the buck stopped" at his desk. There would be no more sloppy administration or strong, freewheeling bureaucrats as in FDR's later years.

Second, and more dangerously, Truman was deter-mined that these decisions would not be tagged as "appeasement." He would be as tough as the toughest. After only twenty-four hours in the White House, the new President confidently informed his secretary of state, "We must stand up to the Russians," and he implied "We had been too easy with them." In foreign-policy discussions during the next two weeks, Truman interrupted his advis-ers to assure them he would certainly be "tough."

His determination was reinforced when he listened most closely to such advisers as Harriman, Leahy, and Secretary of the Navy James Forrestal, who urged him to take a hard line. Warning of a "barbarian invasion of Europe," Harriman declared that postwar cooperation with the Soviets, especially economically, must depend on their agreement to open Poland and Eastern Europe. In a deci-sive meeting on April 23, Secretary of War Henry Stimson argued with Harriman. Stimson declared that peace must never be threatened by an issue such as Poland, for free elec-tions there were impossible, Russia held total control, and Stalin was "not likely to yield . . . in substance." Stimson was not an amateur; he had been a respected Wall Street lawyer and distinguished public servant for forty years, including a term as Herbert Hoover's secretary of state.

But Truman dismissed Stimson's advice, accepted Harriman's, and later that day berated Soviet Foreign Min-ister Molotov "in words of one syllable" for breaking the Yalta agreement on Poland. Truman demanded that the Soviets agree to a "new" (not merely "reorganized") Polish government. An astonished Molotov replied, "I have never been talked to like that in my life." "Carry out your agree-ments," Truman supposedly retorted, "and you won't get talked to like that."

The next day Stalin rejected Truman's demand by observing that it was contrary to the Yalta agreement. The dictator noted that "Poland borders with the Soviet Union, what [sic] cannot be said of Great Britain and the United States." After all, Stalin continued, the Soviets do not "lay claim to interference" in Belgium and Greece where the Americans and British made decisions without consulting the Russians. . . .

Stimson had been correct. Truman's toughness had only stiffened Russian determination to control Poland.

An "iron fence" was falling around Eastern Europe, Churchill blurted out to Stalin in mid-1945. "All fairy-tales," the Soviet leader blandly replied. But it was partly true. The crises over Rumania and Poland only raised higher the fence around those two nations. In other areas, however, the Soviet approach varied. A Russian-sponsored election in Hungary produced a noncommunist govern-ment. In Bulgaria the Soviet-conducted elections satis-fied British observers, if not Americans. Stalin agreed to an independent, noncommunist regime in Finland if the Finns would follow a foreign policy friendly to Russia. An "iron fence" by no means encircled all of Eastern Europe. There was still room to bargain if each side wished to avoid a confrontation over the remaining areas.

But the bargaining room was limited. Stalin's doc-trine and his determination that Russia would not again be invaded from the west greatly narrowed his diplomatic options. So too did the tremendous devastation of the war. Rapid rebuilding under communism required security, required access to resources in Eastern and Central Europe, and continued tight control over the Russian people. The experience of war was indelible. Russians viewed almost everything in their lives through their "searing experience of World War II," as one psychologist has phrased it. The conflict had destroyed 1700 towns and 70,000 villages and left 25 million homeless. Twenty million died; 600,000 starved to death at the single siege of Leningrad. . . .

Some scholars have examined Stalin's acts of 1928–1945, pronounced them the work of a "paranoid," and concluded that the United States had no chance to avoid a cold war since it was dealing with a man who was mentally ill. That interpretation neatly avoids confronting the complex causes of the Cold War but is wholly insufficient to explain, those causes. However Stalin acted inside Russia, where he had total control, in his foreign policy during 1941–1946 he displayed a realism, a careful calculation of forces, and a diplomatic finesse that undercut any attempt to explain away his actions as paranoid. If he and other Soviets were suspicious of the West, they were realistic, not paranoid: the West had poured thousands of troops into Russia between 1917 and 1920, refused to cooperate with the Soviets during the 1930s, tried to turn Hitler against Stalin in 1938, reneged on promises about the second front, and in 1945 tried to penetrate areas Stalin deemed crucial to Soviet security.

American diplomats who frequently saw Stalin understood this background. In January 1945 Harriman told the State Department, "The overriding consideration in Soviet foreign policy is the preoccupation with 'security,' as Moscow sees it." The problem was that Americans did not see "security" the same way. They believed their security required an open world, including an open Eastern Europe. . . .

By mid-1945 Stalin's policies were brutally consistent, while Truman's were confused. The confusion became obvious when the United States, opposed to a sphere of interest in Europe, strengthened its own sphere in the Western Hemisphere. Unlike its policies elsewhere, however, the State Department did not use economic weapons. The economic relationship with Latin America and Canada could simply be assumed. . . .

But Latin America was not neglected politically. A young assistant secretary of state for Latin American affairs, Nelson Rockefeller, and Senator Arthur Vandenberg (Republican from Michigan) devised the political means to keep the Americas solidly within Washington's sphere. Their instrument was Article 51 of the U.N. Charter.

This provision was largely formulated by Rockefeller and Vandenberg at the San Francisco conference that founded the United Nations in the spring of 1945. The article allowed for collective self-defense through special regional organizations to be created outside the United Nations but within the principles of the charter. In this way, regional organizations would escape Russian vetoes

in the Security Council. The United States could control its own sphere without Soviet interference. . . .

The obvious confusion in that approach was pinpointed by Secretary of War Stimson when he condemned Americans who were "anxious to hang on to exaggerated views of the Monroe Doctrine [in the Western Hemisphere] and at the same time butt into every question that comes up in Central Europe." Almost alone, Stimson argued for an alternative policy. Through bilateral U.S.-U.S.S.R. negotiations (and not negotiations within the United Nations, where the Russians would be defensive and disagreeable because the Americans controlled a majority), Stimson hoped each side could agree that the other should have its own security spheres. But as he had lost the argument over Poland, so Stimson lost this argument. Truman was prepared to bargain very little. He might not get 100 percent, the President told advisers, but he would get 85 percent. Even in Rumania, where the Russians were particularly sensitive, the State Department secretly determined in August 1945, "It is our intention to attain a position of equality with the Russians." When, however, the Americans pressed, the Soviets only tightened their control of Rumania. . . .

Although Truman did not obtain his "85 percent" at Potsdam, en route home he received the news that a weapon of unimaginable power, the atomic bomb, had obliterated Hiroshima, Japan, on August 6. Eighty thousand had died. This was some 20,000 fewer than had been killed by a massive American fire bombing of Tokyo earlier in the year, but it was the newly opened secret of nature embodied in a single bomb that was overwhelming. Roosevelt had initiated the atomic project in 1941. He had decided at least by 1944 not to share information about the bomb with the Soviets, even though he knew Stalin had learned about the project. By the summer of 1945 this approach, and the growing Soviet-American confrontation in Eastern Europe, led Truman and Byrnes to discuss securing "further *quid pro quos*" in Rumania, Poland, and Asia from Stalin before the Russians could share the secret of atomic energy. . . .

Stimson, about to retire from the War Department, made one final attempt to stop an East-West confrontation. In a September 11 memorandum to Truman, Stimson prophesied "that it would not be possible to use our possession of the atomic bomb as a direct lever to produce the change" desired inside Eastern Europe. If Soviet-American negotiations continue with "this weapon rather ostentatiously on our hip, their suspicions and their distrust of our purposes and motives will increase." He again urged direct, bilateral talks with Stalin to formulate control of the bomb and to write a general peace settlement. Stimson's advice was especially notable because several months before he himself had hoped to use the bomb to pry the Soviets out of Eastern Europe. Now he had changed his mind.

Truman again turned Stimson's advice aside. A month later the President delivered a speech larded with references to America's monopoly of atomic power, then attacked Russia's grip on Eastern Europe. Molotov quickly replied that peace could not be reconciled with an armaments race advocated by "zealous partisans of the imperialist policy." In this connection, he added, "We should mention the discovery of . . . the atomic bomb."

With every utterance and every act, the wartime alliance further disintegrated. . . .

During early 1946 Stalin and Churchill issued their declarations of Cold War. In an election speech of February 9, the Soviet dictator announced that Marxist-Leninist dogma remained valid, for "the unevenness of development of the capitalist countries" could lead to "violent disturbance" and the consequent splitting of the "capitalist world into two hostile camps and war between them." War was inevitable as long as capitalism existed. The Soviet people must prepare themselves for a replay of the 1930s by developing basic industry instead of consumer goods and, in all, making enormous sacrifices demanded in "three more Five-Year Plans, I should think, if not more." There would be no peace, internally or externally. These words profoundly affected Washington. Supreme Court Justice William Douglas, one of the reigning American liberals, believed that Stalin's speech meant "The Declaration of World War III." *The New York Times* front-page story of the speech began by declaring that Stalin believed "the stage is set" for war.

Winston Churchill delivered his views at Fulton, Missouri, on March 5. The former prime minister exalted American power with the plea that his listeners recognize that "God has willed" the United States, not "some Communist or neo-Fascist state" to have atomic bombs. To utilize the "breathing space" provided by these weapons, Churchill asked for "a fraternal association of the English-speaking peoples" operating under the principles of the United Nations, but not inside that organization, to reorder the world. This unilateral policy must be undertaken because "from Stettin in the Baltic to Trieste in the Adriatic, an iron curtain has descended across the Continent" allowing "police government" to rule Eastern Europe. The Soviets, he emphasized, did not want war: "What they desire is the fruits of war and the indefinite expansion of their power and doctrines."

The "iron curtain" phrase made the speech famous. But, as Churchill himself observed, the "crux" of the message lay in the proposal that the Anglo-Americans, outside the United Nations and with the support of atomic weaponry (the title of the address was "The Sinews of Peace"), create "a unity in Europe from which no nation should be permanently outcast." The Soviets perceived this as a direct challenge to their power in Eastern Europe. Within a week Stalin attacked Churchill and his "friends" in America, whom he claimed resembled Hitler by holding a "racial theory" that those who spoke the English language "should rule over the remaining nations of the world." This, Stalin warned, is "a set-up for war, a call to war with the Soviet Union."

Within a short period after the Churchill speech, Stalin launched a series of policies which, in retrospect, marks the spring and summer of 1946 as a milestone in the Cold War. During these weeks the Soviets, after having worked for a loan during the previous fifteen months, finally concluded that Washington had no interest in loaning them $1 billion, or any other amount. They refused to become a member of the World Bank and the International Monetary Fund. These rejections ended the American hope to use the lure of the dollar to make the Soviets retreat in Eastern Europe and join the capitalist-controlled bank and IMF.

Actually there had never been reason to hope. Control of their border areas was worth more to the Russians than $1 billion, or even $10 billion. . . .

Truman's difficulties came into the open during the autumn of 1946, when he was attacked by liberals for being too militaristic and by conservatives for his economic policies.

The liberal attack was led by Henry Agard Wallace, a great secretary of agriculture during the early New Deal, Vice President from 1941–1945, maneuvered out of the vice-presidential nomination in 1944 so that Harry Truman could be FDR's running mate, and finally secretary of commerce in 1945. Here he devoted himself to the cause of what he liked to call the "Common Man," by extending increased loans to small businessmen and, above all, enlarging the economic pie by increasing foreign trade. Wallace soon discovered that Truman threatened to clog the trade channels to Russia, Eastern Europe, perhaps even China, with his militant attitude toward the Soviets.

At a political rally in New York on September 12, 1946, Wallace delivered a speech, cleared personally, and too rapidly, by Truman. The address focused on the necessity of a political understanding with Russia. This, Wallace declared, would require guaranteeing Soviet security in Eastern Europe. He hoped the capitalist and communist systems could compete "on a friendly basis" and "gradually become more alike." Wallace, however, added one proviso for his happy ending: in this competition "we must insist on an open door for trade throughout the world. . . . We cannot permit the door to be closed against our trade in Eastern Europe any more than we can in China." At that moment Byrnes and Vandenberg were in Paris, painfully and unsuccessfully trying to negotiate peace treaties with Molotov. They immediately demanded Wallace's resignation. On September 20, Truman complied. . . .

On March 12,1947, President Truman finally issued his own declaration of Cold War. Dramatically presenting the Truman Doctrine to Congress, he asked Americans to join in a global commitment against communism. The nation responded. A quarter of a century later, Senator J. William Fulbright declared, "More by far than any other factor anti-communism of the Truman Doctrine has been the guiding spirit of American foreign policy since World War II.". . .

The Truman Doctrine was a milestone in American history for at least four reasons. First, it marked the point at which Truman used the American fear of communism both at home and abroad to convince Americans they must embark upon a Cold War foreign policy. This consensus would not break apart for a quarter of a century. Second, . . . Congress was giving the President great powers to wage this Cold War as he saw fit. Truman's personal popularity began spiraling upward after his speech. Third, for the first time in the postwar era, Americans massively intervened in another nation's civil war. Intervention was justified on the basis of anticommunism. In the future, Americans would intervene in similar wars for supposedly the same reason and with less happy results. . . .

Finally, and perhaps most important, Truman used the doctrine to justify a gigantic aid program to prevent a collapse of the European and American economies. Later such programs were expanded globally. The President's arguments about the need to fight communism now became confusing, for the Western economies would have been in grave difficulties whether or not communism existed. The complicated problems of reconstruction and U.S. dependence on world trade were not well understood by Americans, but they easily comprehended anticommunism. So Americans embarked upon the Cold War for the good reasons given in the Truman Doctrine, which they understood, and for real reasons, which they did not understand. . . .

The President's program evolved naturally into the Marshall Plan. Although the speech did not limit American effort, Secretary of State Marshall did by concentrating the administration's attention on Europe. Returning badly shaken from a Foreign Ministers conference in Moscow, the secretary of state insisted in a nationwide broadcast that Western Europe required immediate help. "The patient is sinking," he declared, "while the doctors deliberate." Personal conversations with Stalin had convinced Marshall that the Russians believed Europe would collapse. Assuming that the United States must lead in restoring Europe, Marshall appointed a policy-planning staff under the direction of George Kennan to draw up guidelines. . . .

Building on this premise, round-the-clock conferences in May 1947 began to fashion the main features of the Marshall Plan. The all important question became how to handle the Russians. Ostensibly, Marshall accepted Kennan's advice to "play it straight" by inviting the Soviet bloc. In reality the State Department made Russian participation improbable by demanding that economic records of each nation be open for scrutiny. For good measure Kennan also suggested that the Soviets' devastated economy, weakened by war and at that moment suffering from drought and famine, participate in the plan by shipping Soviet goods to Europe. Apparently no one in the State Department wanted the Soviets included. Russian participation would vastly multiply the costs of the program and eliminate any hope of its acceptance by a purse-watching Republican Congress, now increasingly convinced by Truman that communists had to be fought, not fed. . . .

The European request for a four-year program of $17 billion of American aid now had to run the gauntlet of a Republican Congress, which was dividing its attention between slashing the budget and attacking Truman, both in anticipation of the presidential election only a year away. In committee hearings in late 1947 and early 1948, the executive presented its case. Only large amounts of government money which could restore basic facilities, provide convertibility of local currency into dollars, and end the dollar shortage would stimulate private investors to rebuild Europe, administration witnesses argued. . . .

The Marshall Plan now appears to have signaled not the beginning but the end of an era. It marked the last phase in the administration's use of economic tactics as the primary means of tying together the Western world. The plan's approach . . . soon evolved into military alliances. Truman proved to be correct in saying that the Truman Doctrine and the Marshall Plan "are two halves of the same walnut." Americans willingly acquiesced as the military aspects of the doctrine developed into quite the larger part. . . .

The military and personal costs of the Truman Doctrine. . . . were higher than expected. And the cost became more apparent as Truman and J. Edgar Hoover (director of the Federal Bureau of Investigation) carried out the President's Security Loyalty program. Their

European economic crisis if nothing was done to alleviate it. And action was taken, with such energy and dispatch that the fifteen weeks between late February and early June, 1947, have come to be regarded as a great moment in the history of American diplomacy, a rare instance in which "the government of the United States operat[ed] at its very finest, efficiently and effectively."

Such plaudits may be too generous. Certainly the language Truman used to justify aid to Greece and Turkey ("at the present moment in world history nearly every nation must choose between alternative ways of life. . . . I believe that it must be the policy of the United States to support free peoples who are resisting attempted subjugation by armed minorities or by outside pressures") represented a projection of rhetoric far beyond either the administration's intentions or capabilities. Whatever its usefulness in prying funds out of a parsimonious Congress, the sweeping language of the "Truman Doctrine" would cause problems later on as the president and his foreign policy advisers sought to clarify distinctions between vital and peripheral interests in the world. That such distinctions were important became apparent with the announcement in June, 1947, of the Marshall Plan, an ambitious initiative that reflected, far more than did the Truman Doctrine, the careful calibration of ends to means characteristic of the administration's policy during this period.

The European Recovery Program, to use its official title, proposed spending some $17 billion for economic assistance to the non-communist nations of Europe over the next four years. (Aid was offered to the Soviet Union and its East European satellites as well, but with the expectation, which proved to be correct, that Moscow would turn it down.) It was a plan directed, not against Soviet military attack, a contingency United States officials considered remote, but against the economic malaise that had sapped self-confidence among European allies, rendering them vulnerable to internal communist takeovers. It involved no direct military commitments; rather, its architects assumed, much as had advocates of the "arsenal of democracy" concept before World War II, that the United States could most efficiently help restore the balance of power in Europe by contributing its technology and raw materials, but not its manpower. . . .

III

Despite its limited character, the vigor of the American response to Soviet postwar probes apparently caught Stalin by surprise. His response was to try to strengthen further the security of his own regime, first by increasing safeguards against Western influences inside the Soviet Union;

second, by tightening control over Russia's East European satellites; and finally by working to ensure central direction of the international communist movement. By a perverse kind of logic, each of these moves backfired, as did a much earlier Soviet initiative whose existence only came to light at this point—the establishment, in the United States during the 1930s, of a major espionage network directed from Moscow. The result, in each of these cases, was to produce consequences that only made it more difficult for Stalin to obtain the kind of security he sought. . . .

Meanwhile, attempts to resolve the question of divided Germany had produced no results, despite protracted and tedious negotiations. In February, 1948, the three Western occupying powers, plus the Benelux countries, met in London and decided to move toward formation of an independent West German state. Stalin's response, after initial hesitation, was to impose a blockade on land access to Berlin, which the World War II settlement had left a hundred miles inside the Soviet zone. The Berlin crisis brought the United States and the Soviet Union as close to war as they would come during the early postwar years. Truman was determined that Western forces would stay in the beleaguered city, however untenable their military position there, and to reinforce this policy he ostentatiously transferred to British bases three squadrons of B-29 bombers. No atomic bombs accompanied these planes, nor were they even equipped to carry them. But this visible reminder of American nuclear superiority may well have deterred the Russians from interfering with air access to Berlin, and through this means the United States and its allies were able to keep their sectors of the city supplied for almost a year. Stalin finally agreed to lift the blockade in May, 1949, but not before repeating the dubious distinction he had achieved in the Russo-Finnish War a decade earlier: of appearing to be brutal and incompetent at the same time.

The Berlin blockade had two important consequences, both of which were detrimental from the Soviet point of view. It provided the impetus necessary to transform the Western Union into the North Atlantic Treaty Organization, a defensive alliance linking the United States, Canada, and ten Western European nations, established in April, 1949. Simultaneously, the blockade lessened prospects for a settlement of the German problem in collaboration with the Russians; the result was to accelerate implementation of the London program, a goal accomplished with the formation, in September, 1949, of the Federal Republic of Germany.

Stalin's efforts to tighten control over communists outside the Soviet Union also produced unintended consequences. In apparent reaction to the Marshall Plan, he authorized in September, 1947, the revival of a central directorate for the international communist movement, this time to be known as the Cominform. It is unlikely that Stalin had anything more in mind than to make international communism a more reliable instrument of Soviet foreign policy, but the effect in the West was to confirm lurking suspicions that his objective had always been world revolution. As Elbridge Durbrow, the American *chargé d'affaires* in Moscow, put it, the move was "patently a declaration of political and economic war against the U.S. and everything the U.S. stands for in world affairs."

Establishment of the Cominform substantially weakened the position of communist parties in Western Europe, whose success, up to that point, had been based largely on their ability to convince followers of their nationalist rather than internationalist credentials. Even worse, from the Soviet point of view, the effort to enforce ideological uniformity provoked an open split with Tito's Yugoslavia, heretofore the Kremlin's most reliable satellite. In Washington, the State Department's Policy Planning Staff immediately saw the importance of this development:

> For the first time in history we may now have within the international community a communist state. . . . independent of Moscow. . . . A new factor of fundamental and profound significance has been introduced into the world communist movement by the demonstration that the Kremlin can be successfully defied by one of its own minions.

Winning support from within the government and from Congress for a policy of actually aiding a communist regime took time, but by 1949 the United States was supporting Tito's position in the United Nations and providing economic assistance. After the outbreak of the Korean War, military aid would follow as well. Stalin's effort to impose monolithic unity had the ironic effect of producing the first visible crack in the monolith—an error of which the United States was quick to take advantage.

Yet another of Stalin's errors—this one made years earlier—came to light only at this point. There had long been rumors, and even some fragmentary evidence, of a Soviet espionage network operating within the United States, but Washington officials had not taken this information seriously nor had it been thoroughly investigated prior to the end of World War II. That situation changed, though, with the defection of Soviet code-clerk Igor Gouzenko in Ottawa shortly after V-J Day, together with the almost simultaneous confession of Elizabeth Bentley, an American who claimed to have been running spies for the Soviet KGB since 1940. These revelations suggested not only that Russians had been trying to steal atomic bomb secrets, but that an entire network of Soviet agents had been created during the 1930s for the purpose of infiltrating government agencies and conveying sensitive information to Moscow. The Truman administration responded by quietly removing suspected individuals from official positions and strengthening its security checks, but by 1948 the Congress had launched a series of sensational public hearings into the matter during which several highly-placed former officials—notably Harry Dexter White of the Treasury Department and Alger Hiss of the State Department—were accused of having committed espionage. White died before formal charges could be brought, but Hiss was convicted early in 1950 of having lied about his earlier communist connections; there quickly followed the arrests of British scientist Klaus Fuchs, who confessed to having transmitted atomic bomb information to the Russians while working on the wartime Manhattan Project, and of Julius and Ethel Rosenberg, who were eventually executed for the same crime in 1953. . . .

It might be argued that there was nothing unusual in all of this: espionage, after all, has a long and colorful history in relations between great powers. But there is, as yet, no evidence that the Americans or the British attempted to spy on the Russians in any substantial way during World War II; despite their success in breaking German and Japanese codes, they appear to have refrained from attempting a similar coup against the Russians, for fear of compromising the wartime alliance. The fact that Stalin felt no comparable inhibitions is revealing, both about his own mentality and about his expectations for cooperation after the war. It also causes one to wonder what the Russians gained from their elaborate espionage activities in Britain and the United States, as balanced against what they lost. For although Fuchs's treason may have accelerated the Soviet atomic bomb project by about a year, and although the Russians . . . may well have picked up sensitive inside information about the size of the American atomic stockpile, the cost to the Russians of their indulgence in espionage, once it became known in the West, was considerable. If Stalin ever hoped to win the trust of Western statesmen—and there is some reason to think he did—then this evidence of his own failure to reciprocate a wartime trust extended to him could only have defeated that purpose.

Through his own policies, therefore, Stalin brought about many of the things he most feared: an American commitment to defend Western Europe; a revived West German state, closely tied to his adversaries; the beginnings of fragmentation within the international communist movement; and a conviction on the part of Western leaders that, because the Soviet Union could not be trusted, negotiations with it on the resolution of out-standing differences could only be approached with the greatest caution and from positions of strength, if they were to take place at all. It was a sobering demonstration of the consequences that can follow from a chronic inability to anticipate the impact of one's own actions; it also pro-vides evidence for the view that one of the West's major—if unappreciated—assets during the early Cold War was the persistent ineptitude of the Soviet dictator himself.

JOHN LEWIS GADDIS is the Robert A. Lovett Professor of History at Yale University in New Haven, Connecticut. He has also been distinguished professor of history at Ohio University, where he founded the Contemporary His-tory Institute, and he has held visiting appointments at the United States Naval War College, the University of Helsinki, Princeton University, and Oxford University. He is the author of many books.

EXPLORING THE ISSUE

Was President Truman Responsible for the Cold War?

Critical Thinking and Reflection

1. Define "containment" as a policy. How did it originate? How did the Truman administration use it? Why was diplomat George F. Kennan critical of its long-term application?

2. Critically examine what Gaddis means by arguing that the United States created an "empire by invitation" in Europe after World War II. Also examine what LaFeber means when he argues that Truman was a "parochial nationalist." How did Truman's perception of the world affect the decisions he made during the years from 1945 to 1950?

3. Compare and contrast and critically evaluate the interpretation of the Cold War of Gaddis and LaFeber in regards to the following:
   a. The Munich analogy
   b. New strategic thinking (atomic diplomacy; containment)
   c. America's global interests
   d. Russia's global interests
   e. A combination of America's and Russia's military and economic power 1945–1950
   f. The lend-lease controversy
   g. Atomic diplomacy (threats or sincere arms control offers)
   h. Iran and Middle East issues
   i. Truman Doctrine
   j. Marshall Plan
   k. Korean War
   l. Truman's personality
   m. Stalin's personality

4. Do you think that if FDR had lived into 1948 that the Cold War could have been avoided? Was the Cold War the fault of Truman's "parochial nationalist" outlook?

5. Do you agree or disagree with Gaddis, who argues that the Cold War was inevitable because of Stalin's personality? Critically evaluate.

Is There Common Ground?

Both sides have hardened their positions in assessing blame for the Cold War. Revisionists believe that Americans did not recognize the legitimate concerns of the Soviet Union regarding its security. Understanding that Russia had suffered enormous casualties on the eastern front in World War II, the United States should have granted more concessions for Russian territorial control over Eastern Europe in order to prevent a third invasion from France or Germany through that weakened frontier. Meanwhile, after attempts to negotiate the Yalta agreements laid down by his predecessor FDR, President Truman recognized how difficult it would be to work with Stalin. There is a tendency among many Americans to lay blame for the

Cold War at the feet of the Soviet Union whose leaders were captive to communist ideology. What is ignored is the degree to which the United States was equally driven by a competing ideology of democracy and free market capitalism. Consequently, both sides viewed each other as a threat.

Additional Resources

John Lewis Gaddis, *The Cold War: A New History* (The Penguin Press, 2005).

Melvyn P. Leffler and David S. Painter, eds., *Origins of the Cold War: An International History* (Routledge, 1994).

Ralph Levering et al., *Debating the Origins of the Cold War: American and Russian Perspectives* (Rowman and Littlefield, 2002).

Wilson D. Miscamble, C.S.C., *From Roosevelt to Truman: Potsdam, Hiroshima and the Cold War* (Cambridge, 2007).

Ellen Schrecker, ed., *Cold War Triumphalism* (The New Press, 2004).

Internet References . . .

Central Intelligence Agency (CIA) Electronic Reading Room

www.foia.cia.gov/

CWIHP: Cold War International History Project

http://legacy.wilsoncenter.org/coldwarfiles/index.html

Harry S Truman Library

http://www.trumanlibrary.org/library.htm

Selected, Edited, and with Issue Framing Material by:
Larry Madaras, *Howard Community College*
and
James M. SoRelle, *Baylor University*

ISSUE

Was Rock and Roll Responsible for Dismantling America's Traditional Family, Sexual, and Racial Customs in the 1950s and 1960s?

YES: Jody Pennington, from "Don't Knock the Rock: Race, Business, and Society in the Rise of Rock and Roll," in Dale Carter, ed., *Cracking the Ike Age: Aspects of Fifties America* (Aarhus University Press, 1992)

NO: J. Ronald Oakley, from *God's Country: America in the Fifties* (Dembner Books, 1986, 1990)

Learning Outcomes
After reading this issue, you will be able to:
• Describe the origin of the term "rock and roll."   • Describe the roots of rock and roll music.   • Describe the revolutionary, evolutionary, and conservative aspects of 1950s' rock and roll music.   • Critically evaluate the controversy surrounding the effects of rock and roll music on society's values in the 1950s and 1960s.

ISSUE SUMMARY

YES: Jody Pennington believes that the emergence of rock and roll in the 1950s along with new forms of consumerism expressed "the inner conflict between conservative and rebellious forces for high school teenagers who wanted to rebel against their parents yet still grow up to be them."

NO: J. Ronald Oakley argues that although the lifestyles of youth departed from their parents, their basic ideas and attitudes mirrored the conservatism of the affluent age in which they grew up.

Most Americans assume that rock and roll has dominated American popular music since the 1950s, but this is not true. The phrase "rhythm and blues" was coined by the first white rock and roll Cleveland disc jockey Alan Freed who, when he went national, was pushed by a lawsuit in 1954 to abandon the name of his show from "The Moondog House" to "Rock 'n' Roll Party." An African American euphemism for sexual intercourse, "rock 'n' roll" had appeared as early as 1922 in a blues song and was constantly used by black singers into the early 1950s. It is not clear whether DJ Freed consciously made the name

change to cultivate a broader audience, but that is precisely what happened. The phrase caught on, and Freed and station WINS secured a copyright for it.

Rock and roll was a fashion of rhythm and blues, black gospel, and country-western music. It combined black and white music, which explains why so many of the early rock singers came from the South and recorded their hit songs in New Orleans or Memphis. Between 1953 and 1955, the first true rockers—Fats Domino, Chuck Berry, and Little Richard—were African Americans. Fats Domino came from New Orleans, sang from his piano, and sold over 65 million records between 1949 and 1960, including "Ain't That a Shame," "I'm Walking," and "Blueberry Hill." Even more influential because of his electric guitar riffs, body and leg gyrations, and songs full of wit and clever wordplay, Chuck Berry's lifestyle (he did two stints in prison) and songs ("Maybellene," "Johnny B. Good," and "Roll Over Beethoven") influenced two generations of rockers, including sixties British rock bands the Beatles and the Rolling Stones. Another rocker, Little Richard, known as "the Georgia Peach," became famous as much for his flamboyant style of dress with his towering hair and multicolored clothes that reflected a teasing sexuality. He created a string of hits—"Tutti Frutti," "Long Tall Sally," and "Good Golly Miss Molly,"—which were recorded as cover records by white artists such as Pat Boone. Best known today for his Geico commercial, Little Richard scared the hell out of white middle-class American parents.

Even more threatening from these parents' perspective, however, was Elvis Presley, the "King of Rock and Roll," and the most influential pop icon in the history of the United States. But Elvis was not the inventor of rock and roll. His voice was average and his songs (written by others) were often mediocre, but his rugged good looks and his sexy gyrations on the stage threw young girls into spasms. Most importantly, he was white. More than 30 years after his death, Elvis still defines the age of rock and roll, and his music remains popular with sales of his recordings numbering over a billion.

Presley was the first star to take advantage of the new teenage consumer market. By the middle 1950s there were 16.5 million teenagers, half in high school and the other half in college or the work force, who possessed a lot of disposable income, available via allowances or part-time jobs. Suburban teenagers had their own rooms replete with radios and record players. "By the end of 1957," says Glenn Altschuler, "seventy-eight Elvis Presley items had grossed $55 million." Presley helped promote the products, making personal appearances in department stores.

There is little argument that a new generation of teenagers had emerged in the fifties. Historians can trace the adolescent generations back to the early twentieth century. The gap between parent and child always existed, but the new value system that set apart the two generations might have occurred earlier had the Great Depression and World War II not intervened. Television shows were geared to the very young and the parents. Radio had lost its nightly sitcoms to television and switched to news and music formats. Teenagers were tired of their parents' sentimental croon and swoon ballads, which did not address their feelings. New DJs emerged, who played the

rock and roll songs for teenagers who sat in their rooms pretending to do their homework.

Between 1958 and 1963, rock and roll as a distinct form of music nearly disappeared. There were several reasons for this. First were the congressional investigations of 1959–61 into payoffs to DJs to push certain records on their shows. "Payola" ruined the careers of a number of rock DJs, including Alan Freed, who lost his two major jobs in New York, was hounded by the IRS for back taxes, and succumbed to alcoholism in 1965. But Dick Clark of American Bandstand fame was protected by the music establishment even though he became a multimillionaire with interests in a number of record companies whose songs he featured on his own show.

Second, "payola McCarthyism" receded in the early sixties as a result of rock and roll being fused into the mainstream of American popular music. Religious leaders appeared less worried about rock's perversion of the country's sexual moral values, southerners lost the fear of rock's racial mongrelization, and American parents no longer associated rock music with subversives, communists, and other radicals. How could they, when Elvis Presley cut his hair, was drafted into the Army, and sang ballads and religious songs that were often integrated into his two dozen forgettable movies? By the time Presley's manager finished reshaping the King's image, Elvis looked more like Pat Boone, the sanitized pop idol. At the same time, Dick Clark turned his Philadelphia-based show, American Bandstand, into an afternoon phenomenon that featured well-groomed teenagers dancing to the latest songs.

In 1963, serious rock was replaced by folk music. Greenwich Village, in the heart of downtown New York City, was its epicenter, Bob Dylan became its troubadour by writing new folk songs instead of retreading old ones, and the group Peter, Paul, and Mary popularized the music into commercial success. At the same time, folk music provided anthems for the civil rights and antiwar protest movements.

Meanwhile, a sixties rock revival came from two sources. First was the British invasion, symbolized by the arrival of the Beatles in 1963, followed by other groups, such as the Rolling Stones, who traced their roots to the early guitar riffs of Chuck Berry. Having come from working-class backgrounds in Liverpool, the Beatles grew up in an environment that challenged authority and poked fun at some of the hypocrisy of middle-class values. Their later songs influenced the protest movements in the United States.

A second source of revival for protest rock music came from the counterculture movement in San Francisco. Bands such as the Grateful Dead and Jefferson Airplane brought "underground" rock to the forefront. Soon, even the Beatles were imitating the San Francisco underground with their classic album, "Sgt. Pepper's Lonely Hearts Club Band," with a style that, according to one writer, combined "a peculiar blend of radical political rhetoric, of allusions to the drug culture, and of the excited sense of imminent, apocalyptic liberation."

Two events in 1969 symbolized the high and low points of sixties rock. In August, 500,000 people converged on a farm in upstate New York for a three-day rock festival. Woodstock became a legendary symbol. There was a scant political protest. Music was the common bond that united people sitting in the rain-filled mud, sharing food and drugs while drowning out the fears of participating in an endless war. In December, all the good will of Woodstock was destroyed at a free Rolling Stones concert in Altamont, California. Four people died, one of whom was clubbed, stabbed, and kicked to death by the Hell's Angles, hired as body guards for the Stones on the advice of the Grateful Dead.

Would the sixties "new left" and counterculture movements have taken place without the emergence of rock and roll in the 1950s? Did rock help to reshape America's values, or was it all one big commercial hustle?

The two best overviews of the early history of rock and roll are Glenn C. Altschuler, *All Shook Up: How Rock and Roll Changed America* (Oxford University Press, 2003) and James Miller, *Flowers in the Dustbin: The Rise of Rock and Roll, 1947–1977* (Simon & Schuster, 1999). Excellent overviews of the 1950s include Douglas T. Miller and Marion Nowak, *The Fifties: The Way We Really Were* (Doubleday, 1975); David Halberstam, *The Fifties* (Villard, 1993); and William L. O'Neill, *American High: The Years of Confidence,* *1945–1960* (Simon & Schuster, 1986). For the decade of the 1960s, see William O'Neill's *Coming Apart: An Informal History of the 1960s* (Times Books, 1971); David Farber, *The Age of Great Dreams: America in the 1960s* (Hill & Wang, 1994); and Terry H. Anderson, *The Movement and the Sixties: Protest in America from Greensboro to Wounded Knee* (Oxford University Press, 1995). David Marcus examines the impact of the 1950s and 1960s upon present-day politics and pop culture in *Happy Days and Wonder Years: The Fifties and Sixties in Contemporary Cultural Politics* (Rutgers University Press, 2004).

In the first selection, Jody Pennington believes that the emergence of rock and roll in the 1950s along with new forms of consumerism expressed "the inner conflict between conservative and rebellious forces for high school teenagers who wanted to rebel against their parents yet still grow up to be them." According to one book reviewer, Pennington has written in 20 plus pages the best and most reliable synthesis . . . on the relationship of rock 'n' roll music to the body politic. He carefully covers every aspect of the popular music business in the fifties, analyzing the crucial role played by the 'indies' (the independent record companies), the impact of technology on market distribution (45s and LPs quickly replaced the old 78s), as well as the way radio and the record business had to compete against the suddenly ubiquitous television for control of the family entertainment medium.

In the second selection, J. Ronald Oakley disagrees. "Although their lifestyle had departed from the conventions of their elders," Oakley believed, "their basic ideas and attitudes were still the conservative ones that mirrored the conservatism of the affluent age in which they grew up."

YES

Jody Pennington

Don't Knock the Rock: Race, Business, and Society in the Rise of Rock and Roll

Forty Miles of Bad Road

From the beginning, rock 'n' roll was geared for movement, for dancing: it sounded best in a car, cruising down the highway or cutting down the boulevard. You could buy the record and play it at home above the din of parents yelling 'turn that crap down!' or 'you call that music?' But that was never the same as hearing it suddenly on the car radio (even if for the tenth time in the same day) when some cool disc jockey dropped the needle in the groove. The music was everywhere: blaring out of every apartment, a radio in every car, turned on all the time. In 1956, the year rock 'n' roll peaked, it was the perfect accompaniment for bombing around in a '49 Ford or a new '55 Chevy: raked and flamed, decked and lowered, chopped and channeled with fins and tails on a Saturday night; burning rubber zero to sixty to the first red light and then on to the next, looking for another chump with overhead cams, a 4.56 rear end to cut out.

Cars and kids came together in the 1950s, and rock 'n' roll was best man at the wedding. This was the latest generation of American Huck Finns running from routine and convention. Their rivers were the roads, highways, boulevards, avenues, and streets of America's big cities and small towns. Their rafts were their cars, and their Nigger Jim was the latest hit on the radio. The night was all beginning and without end.

Mobility meant escape: from the rigidity of home, from high school, from authority. Suburban mothers abhorred deviant behavior in their children and had little patience with wild rock 'n' rollers who threatened their own interests or the creeds and symbols they cherished. Dad wanted stability and order on the home front so he could go about his daily bread-winning tasks. Parents restrained their kids with 'restriction', a form of Levittown house arrest meant to quash any interest in music, dancing, motorcycles, souped-up cars, violence, and sex.

Rock 'n' roll reflected the interests and needs of its young public; it moved them. This raucous new music appeared in young people's lives at the crucial intersection of the dependency of puberty and the autonomy of the post-teen years. To millions at this age, sitting with the family around the tube watching Milton Berle or Sid Caesar was a drag. Instead they kept to themselves in their own rooms, listening to the hi-fi or radio, with posters of Little Richard, Elvis, and Buddy Holly on the wall; or they went to concerts or dated or hung out with friends at diners and juke joints. Whatever they did, they got away from parents; wherever they went, rock 'n' roll was there: reinforcing and enhancing the sensation of independence. Mom and Dad stayed home, secure in their own opinions, values, and standards of conduct. They knew bikers, greasers, and rock 'n' rollers who flouted them were ignorant or wicked.

The attitudes embodied by the music were rebellious and provocative. That in itself was nothing new. Jitterbuggers in the 1930s had had their music labeled 'syncopated savagery'. Now as parents, twenty years later, these former savages were shocked at how seriously their offspring took rock 'n' roll. Parents saw in rock 'n' roll a destructive force, not just a symptom of awkward adolescence. Partly because the kids of the postwar era had wealth like none before them, however, the generational conflict sharpened as never before. As Greil Marcus would later write: 'it's a sad fact that most of those over thirty cannot be a part of it [rock 'n' roll], and it cannot be a part of them.' Who, then, were these parents, these over-thirty enemies of rock 'n' roll?

Squaresville

Following their victory over fascist Germany and Japan, returning vets felt like national heroes. It was now time to earn a little money, have a family, and prosper. Commuting along the paved highways of the golden fifties in MG-TCs, ex-GIs basked perkily in the suburban afterglow of battlefield heroism. The world was theirs for the conquering: a promotion here, a new house there; a barbecue grill, 2.5 kids who would some day go to college, a wife at home enjoying—or enduring—what Betty Friedan would later call the feminine mystique. Heroes made good neighbors: conservative, a bit artificial, and stiff. Jumpy at the mention of Alger Hiss and Whittaker Chambers, communist spies and Congressional committees, good Americans wore loyalty oaths on their sleeves . . .

High school: educational institution and model of life. A world all its own, filled with pep rallies and glee clubs, dress codes and demerits, school papers and assembly programs, field trips and drill teams; a complex of hall passes and phi-deltas, cheerleaders and team spirit, Big-Man-on-Campus and jocks, clicks and outsiders; a realm where one dressed for success in letter jackets, chinos, and penny loafers. Students were groomed to compete in the toughest of schools: popularity. You were either neat or gross, peachy keen or spastic. Lose in this game and you were a creep, a turkey, a *nothing*.

In many small towns and city neighborhoods, school was the focus of students' social lives. They were whipped into enthusiastic abandon by the marching band and wooed by the majorettes at the Friday night football games in the fall under stadium lights or wowed by the cheerleaders at basketball games. There were hockey games, track meets, and the wrestling team, as well as a plethora of cultural activities, from car washes and banquets to brownie sells and parades. To cap it off there were the high school balls: Homecoming, the sock hops, and the Senior Prom, the culmination of four exciting, memorable years. Amidst all this there was still time for classes. Governed by the conservative norms and mores of the middle class, these were simulations of 'real life' designed to transfigure zitty-faced kids into government or company employees, replicas of what William H. Whyte's 1956 volume dubbed *The Organization Man*. Character was molded by disciplinary measures like restrictions and demerits, but the emphasis was always on the individual. American high schools in the 1950s churned out good citizens: members of the Key Club or the Beta Club, trained in the habits of good citizenship; good employees: members of VICA, prepared to enter the world of work, or DECCA, the future marketing leaders of America; and good wives: members of the Future Home-makers of America, a credit to their sex. Still bolstered by the legacy of McCarthyism, moreover, schools had little problem dishing out their version of the 'American Way'. More than any other age-group, teenagers felt under pressure to conform and to become achievers in a society preoccupied with belonging and success.

Off campus, teenagers were flooded with enticements to consume. If they turned on the television or the radio, flipped through a magazine, or went to the movies, they found themselves barraged with endless images of a stimulating world, one which appeared as the virtual antithesis of high school's drab halls, lockers, and desks. Hedonism beckoned, and teenagers from middle-class families responded with indulgence: girls filled their hope chests with the basics for a good marriage; boys filled the tanks of their cars. They bought radios, cameras, hoola-hoops, frisbees, pogo sticks, television sets, swim suits, clothes, i.d. bracelets, deo, 'greasy kid stuff'—anything that brought them pleasure.

Rock 'n' roll hit this world like a bomb. The ultimate safety valve, the ultimate escape for anyone destined for a nine-to-five office job, it was music for the moment (it barely lasted longer). For two or three minutes anybody could be a rebel: speed the car up, hang an arm out the window, cop an attitude, moon a cop, *anything*. The best tracks could obliterate time, creating a world you could vanish into, lose yourself in, and then return from with the help of the disc jockey's patter. Maybe the nine-to-five world could serve as a means to an end: consumption. But it couldn't give life a purpose.

Rock 'n' roll fit perfectly into the conflict between the new patterns of the consumer society and the traditional Puritan work ethic of abstinence and industriousness. For these well-to-do teenagers the day was divided between the two worlds: in the classroom teachers propagated the traditional values; in their free time teenagers lived a life of impulse shopping. Just as the stop-and-jerk pace of Chuck Berry's 'Sweet Little Sixteen' swings the young girl from pretty young wild thing to Daddy's little girl, so their lives oscillated between obedience and indulgence. Through the works of writers like Jerry Leiber and Mike Stoller (who wrote 'Hound Dog' and 'Jailhouse Rock' for Elvis Presley, and all the Coasters' hits); Felice and Boudleaux Bryant (who penned hits for the Everly Brothers); and especially rock 'n' roll poet laureate Chuck Berry, rock 'n' roll spoke to these teenagers: it dealt with their problems and frustrations, their dancing and dates, their likes, dislikes, and obsessions.

That'll Be the Day

As much medium as message, rock 'n' roll was one of the first strokes of cultural self-awareness to blossom in the 1950s. Maybe the lyrics were sometimes as trite or nonsensical as Tin Pan Alley's, maybe white kids had problems understanding the singing, but rock 'n' roll—with its solid backbeat and driving eighth-note rhythm—fit the pace and rhythm of a world which had grown modern during the war and which was now coming to grips with its modernity: coast-to-coast broadcasts, transatlantic jet flights, super highways, fast cars, transistors, the Bomb, roller derbies, instant coffee, Sputnik, desegregation, *Playboy,* the rat race, frisbees, and Sugar Ray Robinson. Let Mom and Pop Suburbia condemn the noise and the meaningless babble, let them fox-trot and cha-cha to Frank Sinatra and Rosemary Clooney: what a slow burn! For Junior, it was slow dancing with a rise in his Levis and a tale to take back to the guys: get much?

From the start rock 'n' roll had its prophets of doom: 'it'll never last' went the wisdom of schmaltz, and it seemed sound enough. This was, after all, *Leave it to Beaver-land:* fads came, fads went. In fact, rock 'n' roll never dominated the charts or musical tastes. As Charlie Gillet points out in *The Sound of the City,* even during its heyday 'from 1955 through 1959, just under half of the top ten hits . . . could be classified as rock 'n' roll'. During those years, according to Serge Denisoff, rock 'n' roll 'did not constitute all of popular music, and even in the heyday of Elvis Presley not all teenagers were into his music, as many rock histories seem to imply'. Nonetheless rock 'n' roll endured. It was exclusive and well-guarded, with a strong sense of awareness that the music was something special; it was almost elitist in its sense of being reserved for those hip enough to *dig it.* Rock 'n' roll was a fever, a craze; and a lot of kids in the 1950s were on the edge of a fighting mood: 'Your ass is grass! Get bent! You're cruisin' for a bruisin'! Don't give me any grief.' Rock 'n' roll caught the mood—'Blue Suede Shoes', 'That'll be the Day', 'Too Much Monkey Business', 'Hound Dog', 'Rip it Up'. Chuck Berry summed up the new generation's disdain for the older: 'Roll Over Beethoven.'

Rock 'n' roll alone did not induce the new teenage behavioral patterns in the 1950s. Prosperity, new forms of distribution, the portable radio, and television made their presence felt. Still, something in the music sparked fires where cinders glowed. Rock 'n' roll was the matrix inside which middle-class teenagers played out fantasies of rebellion within the context of family, home, and future career. With rock 'n' roll's distribution through radio, television, and film, these kids became the standard image of teenagers' lives and values for the entire social spectrum. With the appearance of Elvis, *they*—white, American, middle-class teenagers—could dream of performing the music as well. Elvis expressed the inner conflict between conservative and rebellious forces for high school teenagers who wanted to rebel against their parents yet still grow up to be them.

Graceland

If rock 'n' roll was the dominant music of white teenagers during the second half of the 1950s, then the key was the King: Elvis Presley. An outsider and a success, he summed

up and incarnated the contradictions of the teenager's world. He was one of them: white and young. He had rejected the adult world and sneered his way to the pinnacle of stardom. Elvis not only got the Cadillac; Elvis was bigger and better than a Cadillac. In his music, in his stage act, in his voice, he demanded—and got—respect. As Peter Wicke puts it, he 'embodied the uncertain and consuming desire of American high school teenagers in the fifties, the desire somehow to escape the oppressive ordinariness which surrounded them without having to pay the bitter price of conformity. His quick success seemed to be the proof that, in principle, escape was possible'.

For parents and high school principals in an era when these words still meant something, Elvis Presley was sinful and wicked. He set a bad example. He was a hood, with his long sideburns, ducktail haircut, and curled upper lip. His blatant sexuality, aggressiveness, and bumping and grinding troubled adults. Inside the music industry, though, Elvis was King. From late April 1956, when 'Heartbreak Hotel' dethroned Nelson Riddle's 'Lisbon Antigua' and Les Baxter's 'The Poor People of Paris' at the top of the charts (remaining there for eight weeks), to his late March 1958 induction into the U.S. Army, Elvis ruled the hit parade. He had the number one single in no less than fifty-five out of one hundred and four weeks: 'I Want You, I Need You, I Love You'; 'Don't Be Cruel' and 'Hound Dog' (eleven weeks at number one); 'Love Me Tender' (five weeks); 'Too Much' (three weeks); 'All Shook Up' (nine weeks); 'Teddy Bear' and 'Jailhouse Rock' (seven weeks); and 'Don't' (five weeks).

Although his manager, 'Colonel' Tom Parker, and his record label, RCA, orchestrated his ascent to the top of the pop world, Elvis himself ultimately deserves credit. He had the charisma, the style, the personality, the voice, and (in contrast to Jerry Lee Lewis, who still hasn't lost his rough edges) he could adapt. Elvis had it all. As Greil Marcus would write: 'The version of the American dream that is Elvis's performance is blown up again and again, to contain more history, more people, more music, more hopes; the air gets thin but the bubble does not burst, nor will it ever. This is America when it has outstripped itself, in all of its extravagance.'. . .

The poverty and rural attitudes that were a part of life in the postwar South influenced the course of rock 'n' roll's development. Although the population of the Deep South had shifted during the twentieth century from ninety per cent rural to more than fifty per cent urban, transplanted bumpkins like the Presleys, who had themselves only recently moved to Memphis from Tupelo, Mississippi, stayed 'country'. They did so, moreover, in spite of an increase in their standard of living. (The

New Deal and World War Two had been important stimuli to economic growth in the South, but by the 1950s the region's average per capita income was still only half that of the national average). Like country truck driver Elvis, rock 'n' roll reflected this migration from the farm to the city. Elvis's first single had a blues number on the A-side and a country song on the flip side. Bill Haley had his roots in Texas and Oklahoma country swing in the tradition of Bob Wills. Jerry Lee (as well as Elvis and the other Sun label stars) had his roots in country swing and white gospel. The Everly Brothers had theirs in bluegrass and the country duet singing of Charlie and Ira Louvin and the Delmore Brothers.

Both the R&B and the country elements of rock 'n' roll have origins in the folk music traditions of the outsiders and outcasts of twentieth century America: on the one hand, the African-Americans who picked the cotton; on the other, the so-called 'white trash' who worked it through the cotton mills. The folk blues, typically in a first-person voice, express the experience of African-Americans living in the South during the first half of the twentieth century. The vocabulary is minimal and filled with images of traveling and country roads, field workers and prisoners. Although the dialect and diction are slightly different, the lyrics of country music deal with the realities of rural and city life in the South and the West, again in simple, straightforward language that incorporates the colloquialisms of these regions. Images of truck stops and sunsets, honky-tonks and fields, gamblers and drinkers, cheating and working tell the sentimental stories of taxing, emotional circumstances. The lyrics, sentiments, and, frequently, religious undertones common to both country blues and country and western reflected the inanity of segregation: Southerners of any race had more in common with each other than with anyone from other regions of the USA. Both forms feature expressive vocals: on the one hand, the sharp, nasal sound of country; on the other, the minor pentatonic sound of the blues. An original American sound was heard in the meeting of the two: first in minstrels and then in the songs of Stephen Foster, who was influenced not only by the minstrels but by the music of the African-American churches as well. Generations later, rock 'n' roll would emerge as a sort of electrified Stephen Foster in the unlikely form of Bill Haley.

Although both blues and country had long been commercialized when they merged in the guise of rock 'n' roll, Decca was taking a chance on Haley. And while the label enjoyed great success—at his first session with Decca, Haley recorded both 'Rock Around the Clock' and 'Shake, Rattle and Roll'— taking chances was not the norm for the majors. Their standard operating procedure had long been to churn out 'cover versions' of songs that had already been recorded by someone else. In the 1950s, however, the majors gave cover versions a new twist. Just as in the 1920s Paul Whiteman's orchestra had set out, in his words, to 'make a lady' of hot jazz, so thirty years later the industry recast R&B in an all-white form: performed by whites (such as Steve Lawrence, Andy Williams, Pat Boone, or the Fontane Sisters), recorded by whites, sold by whites, bought by whites, and profited from by whites. (Otherwise rejecting African-American music, the majors would at best record so-called 'black sepias' like Nat King Cole, who appealed to the white mainstream with sentimental, melodramatic crooning.)

As part of this tactic, the majors thus recorded white artists covering R&B tunes originally cut by African-American artists for the independent lablels or 'indies'. These white versions were arranged and perfomed to sound like banal pop music, with a unique beat but always in a simple 'sing-along' form that would be music to white ears. Working on assumptions derived from European classical music traditions, producers like Mitch Miller considered their cover versions to be an improvement on the originals, which they thought sounded like primitive jungle music: harsh, low-down, and dirty. Such assumptions were broadly shared by the white record-buying public. In mainstream America, Bill Haley was thought of as having introduced a new music, a new rhythm; hardly anyone bothered to mention that 'his sound came from the music of the black population, a people whose "great sense of rhythm" had always been admired, but who, white America insisted, otherwise had nothing non-physical to contribute'.

A Choice of Colors

Cultural interaction between African-Americans and the white majority was never strictly a matter of black *or* white. An irreducible component of Southern culture was the mutual influence of the races upon one another. At shows in towns like Macon, Georgia, white kids would sneak in (behind the backs of their parents and white authorities) and slip upstairs to see the African-American kids down on the floor. At first, the white kids would just sit and watch. In the end, however, they were bound to come down and dance. When some young white performers—like Jerry Lee Lewis, sneaking into the 'nigra' clubs in Ferriday, Louisiana, with his cousin Jimmy Lee Swaggart to hear artists like B.B. King—took the music at face value, they helped transform popular music and thereby American youth culture.

Sometimes these Southern rockers covered R&B hits, but more often they brought elements of R&B into their own tunes. Instead of adapting African-American styles to white tastes, they tried to imitate the originals as closely as they could, as when Elvis covered Big Mama Thornton's 'Hound Dog'. Perhaps the swing disappeared in these white attempts at R&B: simplified in rock 'n' roll to a more rigid, basic rhythm under the influence of Hank Williams and the hard-driving style of country pickers like Merle Travis, Joe Maphis, and James Burton. Still, rock 'n' roll was noisy and aggressive because these musicians had been singing and playing that way all along. The rock 'n' roll played by their native sons, rockabilly, frightened white Southerners most. Long in touch with African-American music, these musicians had sufficient spirit to sell records in the R&B, country, and pop markets. Since they were white, moreover, they could get away with it to such a degree that by 1956 even genuine R&B records started to gain acceptance in the mainstream pop market, much to the horror of many white Southerners.

It was no surprise, therefore, that 'the most extreme and bizarre expressions of antagonism towards rock 'n' roll tended to take place in the South. In April 1956, the *New York Times* reported several attempts by white Southern church groups to have rock 'n' roll suppressed. The whole movement towards rock 'n' roll, the church groups revealed, was part of a plot by the NAACP to corrupt white Southern youth'. A stepchild of R&B, the music was known dismissively in the South during those years as 'nigger music'. Rock 'n' roll was music played by and for *niggers* (African-American or white): Little Richard, Fats Domino, and Chuck Berry; Elvis Presley, Jerry Lee Lewis, Carl Perkins, and Buddy Holly. Renegade rednecks in the best Southern tradition, the white rock 'n' rollers were the very stuff of Southern nightmares. For although white Southerners deemed African-Americans rarely capable of attaining the same level of rectitude, white descent into blackness had to be averted. For decades Southern whites had drawn arms against an unseen enemy, evincing a distrust of both mulattoes (who *looked* white) and whites who behaved 'black'. Whites who, like the Southern rock 'n' rollers, strayed too close to African-Americans were known as 'white niggers': genetically white but 'black' in their behavior. The music they played, rock 'n' roll, which sounded like R&B, was the 'jungle music' of burr-heads, blue-skins, tar-pots, spies, jigaboos, darkies, and shines.

The white South's image of African-Americans in the 1950s was much as it had been since the turn of the century. Generations had grown up believing Booker T. Washington to have spoken for all African-Americans and spoken the truth: that they were content to 'cast down

their buckets' where they were, chop cotton, lay rails, and work, work, work until Saturday night. By the 1950s, Booker T. was long dead, but in white minds Sambo continued to shuffle contentedly along, bucket in hand. Even while insisting that 'our Nigras are good Nigras', white Southerners had nonetheless devised dogmas and institutions that assured the greatest possible distance between the races. Known collectively as Jim Crow, these had consisted of both legal and extralegal means designed to keep African-Americans in their place and to compel them to behave 'properly' in the presence of whites. The legal measures—the poll tax, stiff residency requirements, literacy tests, and 'grandfather clauses'—kept African-Americans away from the polls and thus ensured the stability of a caste system which governed all aspects of African-American life. Extralegal steps helped guarantee the invisibility of most African-Americans and made those who were visible the Sambos whites needed to see: gullible children in grown-up bodies who slapped their knees, jumped, and turned, and whom whites could allow to run free within their own world without constant guidance after work on Saturday—as long as they showed up at work on Monday morning.

The white South's ability to sustain the system was, of course, challenged on a city bus in Montgomery, Alabama, on 1 December 1955, when Rosa Parks refused to yield her seat to a white man. Although it took years to secure its greatest gains (after Montgomery there was a lull), with Martin Luther King, Jr. more than rising to the occasion the civil rights movement was in the ascendant.

From the Station to the Train

By the time of the civil rights movement, another movement, primarily geographical and cultural rather than social and political, had long since begun: the exodus of millions of African-Americans from the countryside to the nation's cities. Prompted partly by the decline and subsequent mechanization of Southern agriculture, partly by the attraction of often military-spawned jobs, and partly by the dream of a better life beyond Jim Crow, this vast folk migration took hundreds of thousands to Northern industrial cities like New York, Chicago, and Detroit and, to a lesser degree, Southern cities like Memphis and New Orleans. Between 1860 and 1960 the African-American share of the total Southern population dwindled from almost fifty per cent to twenty-nine per cent.

Musical forms born and raised in the South—the blues, jazz, gospel, R&B, and soul—also traveled. On the road, gospel waited alongside the blues in bus depots; jazz and R&B rode together on trains. The movement to the cities helped turn the blue note electric, and African-American radio stations pumped it out. By the early 1950s, R&B stations dotted the urban landscape. Fans had only to turn their tuning knobs to hear the dance blues of singers like Amos Milburn, Roy Brown, Fats Domino, and Lloyd Price, and the 'hot' style of disc jockeys like Hamp Swain in Macon, Georgia, Zenas 'Big Daddy' Sears and 'Jockey Jack' Gibson in Atlanta, and 'Sugar Daddy' in Birmingham. Meanwhile, Alan Freed at WINS in New York set a precedent for white disc jockeys playing R&B; those who followed his lead included Al Benson in Chicago, Hunter Hancock in Los Angeles, and 'Poppa Stoppa' in New Orleans.

These and other artists and disc jockeys gave a voice to a nation of wanderers looking for home: a tricky concept, as James Brown once pointed out, for a people who had been told to move along for a century and a half. Newly-urbanized African-Americans faced a world very different from the one they had known before, but when it came to the question of color, they found themselves on familiar ground. Not surprisingly, when confronted by the racial prejudice of the North and West, they survived just as they and their predecessors had done in the South: by building up their community, families, clubs, and churches. Whether in the North or South, then, home was cut off from white society. White people may have heard R&B as it made its way across the air waves. What their ears didn't hear, what their eyes didn't see, what they wanted neither to hear nor to see, was the distinct *community* which it addressed, a largely self-contained world created by American apartheid: the chitlin' circuit. . . .

Gospel music spoke for and sustained a distinct community, retaining collective and communal features which expressed something of the suppression which so many in that community had experienced. It also helped to transform that community. It did so partly through its influence on rhythm and blues.

Boogie at Midnight

Cacophonous vocals shouted explicit lyrics; loud saxophones, pianos, and guitars honked, rolled, and wailed while drums banged out the heavy rhythm; delirious artists expressed emotions and ideas which exhilarated their audience. Until 1949, when Jerry Wexler gave it the more sophisticated name 'rhythm and blues' while writing for *Billboard*, the white music industry branded all this 'race music'. The lines between urban blues and R&B were tenuous (as are all popular musical categories), and the early R&B charts looked like a blues who's-who: John Lee Hooker's 'Boogie Chillen', Lonnie Johnson's 'Tomorrow Night', shouter Wynonie Harris's 'Good Rockin' Tonight',

as well as tunes by Howlin' Wolf, Charles Brown, Muddy Waters, Bull Moose Jackson, and Ivory Joe Hunter.

R&B was updated and mellowed as the influence of gospel smoothed over its rougher edges. Technology played a crucial part. Although different radio stations programmed specific genres, listeners were not so constrained; as a result gospel singles crossed over to the R&B charts: in 1950, for example, the Five Blind Boys' 'Our Father' was chasing Wynonie Harris's 'I Like My Baby's Pudding' up the charts. Quartet singing, long a crossover area for artists like the Mills Brothers and the Ink Spots, was the springboard for the 'bird groups' (the Ravens and the Orioles), who in turn inspired groups like the Clovers and the Dominoes. Founded in 1950 by Billy Ward, the Dominoes built their sound around the gospel-style vocals of Clyde McPhatter. Race restricted the success of songs like 'Do Something for Me' and 'Have Mercy Baby' to the R&B charts, until the appearance of rock 'n' roll enabled an R&B group, Frankie Lymon and the Teenagers, to hit the charts for sixteen weeks in 1956, peaking at number six, with 'Why Do Fools Fall in Love?' The original did better than the cover versions by the Diamonds and Gale Storm. The Platters, who had charted in 1955 with 'Only You' released three Top Ten pop and R&B hits in 1956. Many of the R&B acts that followed went on to become rock 'n' roll, rather than soul, stars. Imperial artist Fats Domino rode 'Blueberry Hill' and 'I'm in Love Again' into the Top Ten. Two other 'R&B' artists, Chuck Berry and Little Richard, hit the charts with 'Maybellene', 'School Days', and 'Sweet Little Sixteen'; and 'Tutti-Frutti', 'Long Tall Sally', and 'Rip it Up', respectively.

White listeners started to develop a better feeling for the music: they heard R&B differently. As it became familiar, it became acceptable on its own terms. In its initial cross over into white culture, R&B attracted a cult following among college and high school students. Its rhythm and forbidden thrills, though still contrasting sharply with the milquetoast sounds of Perry Como and company, had been made more palatable by gospel. White R&B fans could now accept the real thing, not covers.

Even though more and more people came to prefer R&B, the majors could not and did not start promoting the product; they seemed scarcely aware of the market. The indies—often using singers with regional appeal in a regional market—detected the trend more quickly. Largely through their efforts, some juke boxes began stocking R&B records, while white dance bands started to incorporate R&B hits in their sets. Whether through the efforts of the majors or the indies, singers and musicians like Chuck Berry, Bo Diddley, and Little Richard found themselves able to play African-American music *as* African-American music: no crooning sepia nonsense. Racial barriers were dissolving as sons of slaves and sons of Pilgrims broke sonic barriers to create the sound of rebellion and deliverance: rock 'n' roll.

Whatever their race, these artists were dependent upon the various media to get their music to the widest possible audience. The people who played rock 'n' roll could not have known they were making history, but they did know they were on to something new, something that broke with musical traditions. These early rock 'n' rollers were no navel-gazers: they were carnival sideshow entertainers with a product to sell and a get-rich-quick scheme: a number one record. The world of rock 'n' roll was not only a cultural and social expression but also a commercial network of musical commodities—singles and albums—which had to be recorded, distributed, and promoted.

Have You Heard the News?

The music industry has survived despite the appearance of successive new media that at one time or another seemed capable of subjugating it. Radio initially made the need to buy records appear obsolete—until swing music became so popular in the 1930s that a rush on records ensued. Later, television appeared to threaten the industry. Again, however, it endured (most recently by becoming a part of television through MTV). Recorded music has survived because of its unique ability to create an emotional bond between the listener and recorded sound. Everything else—the technology, the marketing, the profits—have resulted from that bond and its basic power.

During and after World War Two, the record industry, radio, and television all experienced changes that together radically altered the modes of musical production: new recording techniques and small-group recording budgets; new companies and a redefinition of the target audience; reductions in record prices; and a new affiliation with broadcast radio. The shift from 78 revolutions per minute to the $33^1/_3$ and 45 rpm speeds, a change in the sizes of records, the substitution of shellac by vinyl, and television's influence on radio station programming—each had an impact on the industry. Although its story cannot be reduced solely to technical innovations, rock 'n' roll did evolve out of and along with the technology of these media. What was new about rock 'n' roll was its relationship with the means of mass communication: record, radio, television, and film. American rock 'n' roll depended on the existence of these media and accepted them without compromise as a condition of artistic creativity.

This Year's Model

Notable technological improvements associated with the introduction of magnetic tape resulted in recording techniques which were not only inexpensive but which made both overdubbing (with remarkably improved microphones) and the correcting of mistakes possible. One pioneer was guitarist Les Paul, who by 1947 had started making 'sound-on-sound' recordings. Real multitrack recording was first used in 1954. Employing just two tracks, it was far from today's sixty-four track digital studios; the basic principle of studio music production—sound-on-sound—nevertheless remains unaltered. Multitrack technology was to influence both the sound and the structure of rock music, since a producer could now assemble the music from individually recorded parts in a final mix instead of reproducing a single take of a song: records no longer needed to be exact copies of live performances, rendering the large rooms previously employed for recording big band orchestras unnecessary. . . .

When the majors finally realized that rock 'n' roll was here to stay, they restructured their A&R departments and hired men who had a better feel for the sound and who understood the new standards. From this point on, the A&R men from the majors picked from the same flock of producers, song writers, arrangers, and session men as the indies.

The most conspicuous technological innovation triggered the 'Battle of the Speeds'. By 1948 CBS engineer Peter Goldmark had perfected the high fidelity long-playing record (LP), which reduced the playing speed from 78 to $33^1/_3$ rpm. With their low noise characteristics and extended duration, LPs transformed not only recording studios and the contents of records themselves, but also the industry's hierarchy, as Columbia first stole the lead on RCA only to see the latter respond with 45 rpm singles. The ascent of rock 'n' roll paralleled that of the 45 rpm single (along with the portable radio). Until the emergence of rock 'n' roll, and especially Elvis Presley, the 45 rpm single's role in popular music had been minimal. Aimed at the new teenage market and priced within reach of teenagers' pocket money, however, its popularity rose quickly.

Until rock 'n' roll appeared in the 1950s, radio programming had changed very little since the 1930s, when the friendly, conversational microphone styles of Al Jarvis at KFWB in Los Angeles, Martin Block at WNEW in New York, and Arthur Godfrey had first raised announcers to the status of 'personalities', who received as much attention from their listeners as the music they played. Jarvis pioneered the 'Make Believe Ballroom' format, which simulated the atmosphere of a ballroom through the use of real or contrived conversations with the performers and dancers. Block's use of this framework would engender *Your Hit Parade* and *Lucky Lager Dance Time*. Godfrey's irreverent style helped make the radio disc jockey someone not to be treated lightly; his early morning show attracted many listeners and thus numerous sponsors. Such sponsorship represented a commercialization of radio that would have profound consequences. When the American Tobacco Company started sponsoring *The Lucky Strike Hit Parade* nationwide, records began to be ranked according to their popularity. Air play became the most effective type of direct marketing. By the end of World War Two most singers, musicians, record companies, and sheet music publishers had become aware of the interaction between sales and air play. Record sales and taste trends increasingly engendered and reflected one another: each at once parasite on and host for the other; both having a symbiotic relationship with the charts (particularly *Billboard's*). A song could become a hit because a lot of people liked it and bought the record, and a lot of people liked a song and bought the record because it was a hit.

Since television during the 1950s rapidly took over the family entertainment role once held by radio, and since programs like *Monitor* (a weekend program of interviews, satire, and news features) proved failures, radio programming other than news broadcasts returned to the hands of station owners, who responded to the challenge of television by converting their stations to a 'Top-Forty' format in order to survive. Top-Forty programs shaped teenagers' perceptions of rock 'n' roll: music was ranked, and hits were important. Cheap, battery-driven portable radios made possible by transistor technology came on the market in 1954. Rock 'n' roll developed within a technological milieu increasingly beyond parental control. Teenagers' relative independence in deciding what they liked and what they wanted to listen to resulted in an age-specific audience, and rock 'n' roll developed on its audience's terms. . . . Between 1954 and 1959 the record industry increased its sales from $213,000,000 to $603,000,000. A large proportion of the increase in sales accrued to the indies, who made their break into the market by providing assorted kinds of rock 'n' roll. After the majors had dropped their 'race' and 'new jazz' artists during World War Two, the indies had moved into the 'race' market and begun recording rhythm and blues. In 1954 they extended their market to white kids as they developed distribution networks sufficient to give them as good a chance of having a hit with a new record as any of the majors; once they saw the possibilities of profit in rock 'n' roll, they recorded almost anybody singing almost anything and put all their energy and money into promoting

those records that seemed to stand a chance. The independents doubled their number of Top Ten hits between 1955 and 1956, then doubled them again by 1957. They succeeded in spotting and responding to the grassroots signs of rock 'n' roll's popularity partly because, unlike the majors, the indies often signed singers with regional or local appeal. . . . Although lacking the sales figures, budgets, and distribution facilities of the major music publishers, record companies, and radio networks, the indies nevertheless changed the direction of popular music and the structure of the record industry.

The indies had produced twice as many hits by the end of the decade as the majors, yet the struggle for survival never eased up. Few would survive the 1960s. Plagued by competition from bootleggers (who pirated copies of their hits) and always fighting to collect from their distributors, indie labels still had to pay 'consultancy fees' to disc jockeys, and the monthly overheads of staff and offices, on top of the costs of pressings. Sometimes their wisest move was to license a likely hit to larger companies like Mercury, ABC, or Dot (all of whom formed fruitful relationships with independent producers).

Through their influence over distribution networks, the majors effectively controlled most record stores, juke boxes, sheet music sales, and radio airplay. Slow to realize the closing of the American racial gap which accompanied and followed World War Two, the majors thus adopted a conservative strategy, deploying their sizeable resources to fight for the success of their established performers, mostly older artists from the dance band era still under five year contracts. The singers who operated under such contracts had to be musical chameleons and appeal to just about anyone (unlike rock 'n' roll madmen like Little Richard and Jerry Lee Lewis who were, by contrast, anything but malleable). The majors used their contract singers for the cover versions recorded, released, and promoted hot on the tail of R&B hits. The majors did renovate their commercial policy by releasing singles more quickly, while strengthening their promotion work by marketing from coast to coast. Confident in their market domination, however, they underestimated the ways in which a few radio disc jockeys who appreciated the power of rhythm and blues (such as Danny 'Cat Man' Stiles, Hal Jackson, and George 'Hound Dog' Lorenz) could penetrate the cracks of segregation and discrimination by playing it to anyone who would listen.

The majors slowly came to understand teenage record buyers, drop their traditional sales categories of popular music and rhythm and blues, and call anything that appealed to teenage record buyers 'rock 'n' roll'. When the majors finally acted, rock 'n' roll devolved into teenybopper music, designed for and chiefly bought by people between the ages of nine and twenty four, who determined what the record charts looked like by the manner in which they spent their own or their parents' money. When some seventeen-year-old Peggy Sue bought the latest hit single by the King, she cared little about the technology or money that had gone into its production and had little interest in knowing that she was dancing to a product made to be marketed and consumed for profit. She simply bought a record she *liked*. Her reasons for picking this particular record were, of course, influenced by many things—her age, gender, race, and social background as well as the forces of advertising and peer group pressure—which may have had little to do with the song itself. Later, as she grew older, the music would nevertheless bring back memories of those halcyon days and the experiences she and her friends had shared with a rock 'n' roll backdrop.

As the music industry itself matured, styles would change: from heavy to folk, from country to soft, from bubble gum to disco, from glitter to glam; all, however, were variations on the basic rock 'n' roll theme, products of industry attempts to sustain old or develop new markets, while kids tried to find a new sound that fit their world and their experiences. Musicians starting out as kids looking for new sounds came into the industry and developed new styles in the lacuna between the industry's creating and following trends. As a result, the various genres of rock music through the ages—and especially the records that came with them—had (and continue to have) one thing in common: what James Von Schilling has called the ability to 'capture in time a unique combination of music, performance, and artistry and then enable us to make this "timepiece" part of our personal experience'.

Afterword: Funeral Dirge American Pie

Legend has it that rock 'n' roll died. Estimates of the precise date differ, but most agree that at some point in the late 1950s rock 'n' roll passed away, only to be reborn as 'rock' in 1964 when the Beatles arrived in New York and Dylan went electric. . . .

Jody Pennington is an associate professor in the department of aesthetics and communication at the University of Aarhus in Denmark. He is the author of *Sex in American Film* (Praeger, 2007), and in 2008 served as president of the Denmark Association of American Studies.

J. Ronald Oakley

God's Country: America in the Fifties

Generation in a Spotlight

As the 1950s opened, America's adolescents were basically a conservative, unrebellious lot. Although the word *teenager* had come into widespread circulation in the 1940s to describe this distinct age group mired in the limbo between puberty and adulthood, the teenagers of the early fifties had not yet developed a distinct subculture. They had few rights and little money of their own, wore basically the same kind of clothing their parents wore, watched the same television shows, went to the same movies, used the same slang, and listened to the same romantic music sung by Perry Como, Frank Sinatra, and other middle-aged or nearly middle-aged artists. Their idols were Joe DiMaggio, General MacArthur, and other prominent members of the older generation. In spite of what they learned from older kids and from the underground pornography that circulated on school playgrounds, they were amazingly naive about sex, believing well into their high school years that French kissing could cause pregnancy or that the douche, coitus interruptus, and chance could effectively prevent it. Heavy petting was the limit for most couples, and for those who went "all the way" there were often strong guilt feelings and, for the girl at least, the risk of a bad reputation. Rebellion against authority, insofar as it occurred, consisted primarily of harmless pranks against unpopular adult neighbors or teachers, occasional vandalism (especially on Halloween night), smoking cigarettes or drinking beer, and the decades-old practice of mooning. Although most families had the inevitable clashes of opinion between parents and offspring, there were few signs of a "generation gap" or of rebellion against the conventions of the adult world.

But all of this began to change in the early fifties, and by the middle of the decade the appearance of a distinct youth subculture was causing parents and the media to agonize over the scandalous behavior and rebellious nature of the nation's young people. The causes of the emergence of this subculture are not hard to find. One was the demographic revolution of the postwar years that was increasing the influence of the young by producing so many of them in such a short period of time. Another was the affluence of the period, an affluence shared with the young through allowances from their parents or through part-time jobs. As teenagers acquired their own money, they were able to pursue their own life-style, and now American business and advertisers geared up to promote and exploit a gigantic youth consumer market featuring products designed especially for them. Then there were the effects of progressive education and Spockian child-rearing practices, for while neither was quite as permissive or indulgent toward the young as the critics claimed, they did emphasize the treatment of adolescents as unique people who should be given the freedom to develop their own personality and talents. Another factor was television and movies, which had the power to raise up new fads, new heroes, and new values and to spread them to young people from New York to Los Angeles. And finally, there was rock 'n' roll, which grew from several strains in American music and emerged at mid-decade as the theme song of the youth rebellion and as a major molder and reflector of their values.

One of the earliest landmarks in the history of the youth rebellion came in 1951 with the publication of J. D. Salinger's *The Catcher in the Rye*. Infinitely more complex than most of its young readers or older detractors perceived, this novel featured the actions and thoughts of one Holden Caulfield, a sixteen-year-old veteran of several private schools, who roams around New York City in his own private rebellion from home and school. In colloquial language laced with obscenities absent from most novels of the day, Holden tells the reader of his rejection of the phoniness and corruption of the adult world, of how parents, teachers, ministers, actors, nightclub pianists and singers, old grads, and others lie to themselves and to the young about what the world is really like. *The Catcher in the Rye* was popular throughout the fifties with high school and college students, for while young people might not understand all that Salinger was trying to say, they did identify with his cynical rejection of the adult world and adult values. The book was made even more popular by the attempts of school boards, libraries, and

by Dean's own miraculous resurrection. Several records appeared—"Tribute to James Dean," "The Ballad of James Dean," "His Name Was Dean." "The Story of James Dean," "Jimmy Jimmy," and "We'll Never Forget You." Dozens of biographies and other literary tributes were rushed to the market, along with the inevitable movie, *The James Dean Story*. When the wreckage of his car was put on display in Los Angeles, over 800,000 people paid to view it. The adulation swept teens all across America and even in Europe. In England, a young man legally changed his name to James Dean, copied his clothing and mannerisms, went to America twice to visit the real Dean's family and grave, and claimed to have seen *Rebel Without a Cause* over 400 times. As *Look* magazine observed, the subject of this almost psychopathic adulation was "a 24-year old who did not live long enough to find out what he had done and was in too much of a hurry to find out who he was."

Along with *The Wild One,* a 1954 film starring Marlon Brando as the leader of a motorcycle gang, *The Blackboard Jungle* and the films of James Dean helped to spawn a series of films aimed specifically at young people. In addition to the films of Elvis Presley and other teen idols, the second half of the fifties saw a spate of second-rate rock movies—*Rock Around the Clock, Don't Knock the Rock, Rock Pretty Baby, Rock Around the World,* and *Let's Rock*—and a series of shallow, trashy movies about young people and delinquency, such as *Girls in Prison, Eighteen and Anxious, Reform School Girl, Hot Rod Rumble,* and *High School Confidential.* For better or worse—mostly worse—teenagers were getting their own movies as well as their own music.

In 1955 teenagers had their music, their movies, their idols—dead and alive—but as yet they had no one who combined all three of these and served as a focal point for their growing consciousness as a subculture. But he was waiting in the wings, for in that year a young performer with a regional reputation was making records and gaining a wide following among teenagers, especially young girls, with live performances in southern cities that were often punctuated by desperate attempts by the police to prevent these screaming fans from rushing the stage to tear off his clothes. He was a James Dean fan, who had seen *Rebel Without a Cause* several times, could recite the script by heart, and had been wearing tight pants, leather jackets, and a ducktail haircut with long sideburns for several years. In 1956 he would burst on the national entertainment stage and proceed to become one of the most popular and influential musical performers of all time, rivaling Rudy Vallee, Bing Crosby, Frank Sinatra, and other singers before him. His name was Elvis Presley, and he was destined to claim the title of King of Rock 'n' Roll. . . .

Record sales soared with the coming of rock 'n' roll. Aided by the affluence of the time, the invention of the 45 rpm and 33$\frac{1}{3}$ rpm records, and the introduction of high fidelity, record sales had steadily climbed from 109 million in 1945 to 189 million in 1950 and to 219 million in 1953, then with the arrival of rock 'n' roll rose to 277 million in 1955 and to 600 million in 1960. In 1956 alone, RCA Victor sold over 13.5 million Elvis Presley singles and 3.75 million Presley albums. By 1957, the new 45s and 33$\frac{1}{3}$s had driven the 78s out of production. Teenagers bought most of the inexpensive and convenient 45s and most of the long-playing rock 'n' roll albums, whereas adults bought most of the long-playing albums of traditional popular music, jazz, and classical music. While in 1950 the average record buyer was likely to be in his early twenties, by 1958, 70 percent of all the records sold in the United States were purchased by teenagers. Most of the popular singles were purchased by girls between the ages of thirteen and nineteen, the group most receptive, as one critic said, to "little wide-eyed wishes for ideal love and perfect lovers, little songs of frustration at not finding them." Thanks to these revolutions in the musical world, record sales, which had stood at only $7.5 million in 1940, had risen to a healthy $521 million in 1960.

Why was rock 'n' roll so popular? One of the reasons, of course, was that it was written and performed by young people and was centered upon what was important to them: love, going steady, jealousy, high school, sex, dancing, clothing, automobiles, and all the other joys and problems of being young. The lyrics were just as silly, sentimental, and idealistic as the music of the crooners of the first half of the decade, but it was written just for the young and the singing styles, beat, electrical amplification, and volume of the music was much more dynamic than that of the earlier period. Teens were attracted to its celebration of sexuality, expressed in the more explicit lyrics, driving tempo, movements of the rock 'n' roll performers, and in new dances at high school hops and private parties. Perhaps Jeff Greenfield, a member of this first generation of rock 'n' roll fans, expressed it best in his No *Peace, No Place.* "Each night, sprawled on my bed on Manhattan's Upper West Side, I would listen to the world that Alan Freed created. To a twelve- or thirteen-year-old, it was a world of unbearable sexuality and celebration: a world of citizens under sixteen, in a constant state of joy or sweet sorrow. . . . New to sexual sensations, driven by the impulses that every new adolescent generation knows, we were the first to have a music rooted in uncoated sexuality." And very importantly, rock 'n' roll gave young people a sense of cohesion, of unity, all across the nation. It was *their* music, written for them and for them only, about their world,

Was Rock and Roll Responsible for Dismantling America's Traditional Customs in the 1950s and 1960s? by Madaras and SoRelle

249

a world that adults could not share and did not understand. As such, it was one of the major harbingers of the generation gap.

It was not long after teenagers acquired their own music and movies that they also acquired their own television show. *American Bandstand* began as a local television show in Philadelphia in 1952, and in August of 1957 it premiered as a network show on ABC over sixty-seven stations across the country, from 3:00 to 4:30 in the afternoon, with twenty-six-year-old Dick Clark as the host. The first network show featured songs by Jerry Lee Lewis, the Coasters, and other top rock 'n' roll artists, and guest star Billy Williams singing "I'm Gonna Sit Right Down and Write Myself a Letter." Some of the early reviews of the show were not complimentary. According to *Billboard,* "The bulk of the ninety minutes was devoted to colorless juveniles trudging through early American dances like the Lindy and the Box Step to recorded tunes of the day. If this is the wholesome answer to the 'detractors' of rock 'n' roll, bring on the rotating pelvises." But by the end of 1958 the show was reaching over 20 million viewers over 105 stations, and had spawned dozens of imitations on local stations. This was a show about teens, and its consistent high rating and longevity proved that they liked it, regardless of what adults said about it.

American Bandstand had a great influence on popular music and on America's teenagers. Clark's good looks, neat clothing, and civilized manner helped reassure American parents that rock 'n' roll was not a barbarian invasion that was turning the young into juvenile delinquents. All the dancers on the show in the fifties were white, adhered to a strict dress code (coats and ties for boys, dresses and skirts and blouses for girls, and no jeans, T-shirts, or tight sweaters), and followed a strict language code that even prohibited the use of the term "going steady." One of Clark's most embarrassing moments on the show came when a young girl told him that the pin she was wearing was a "virgin pin." Stars with unsavory reputations were not allowed on the show, so when the news of Jerry Lee Lewis's marriage to his thirteen-year-old cousin broke, Clark joined other disc jockeys and promotors across the country in canceling all future appearances of the pioneer rock 'n' roll star. The show also featured the biggest stars of the day and helped launch the careers of Connie Francis, Fabian, Frankie Avalon, and several other singers. The new dances performed on the show—such as "the stroll," "the shake," and "the walk"—were soon copied all across the country. Teenagers everywhere also imitated the slang and the dress of this very influential show and bought the records its regulars danced to. The success of this dance show brought popularity and wealth to its host, who

freely admitted that "I dance very poorly," yet became a millionaire by the age of thirty.

The rise of rock 'n' roll, teen movies, teen television shows, and teen magazines helped create the teen idol. Many of the idols were singers, like Elvis Presley, Rick Nelson, Frankie Avalon, Bobby Darin, Fabian, Pat Boone, Connie Francis, and Annette Funicello. Others were movie or television actors, like James Dean and Marlon Brando, though, of course, many of the singers also went on to movie careers which might be called, at best, undistinguished. Most of the idols were teenagers themselves or in their twenties, and it is important to note here that while earlier generations had tended to create idols much older than themselves—like Bing Crosby, Perry Como, and Clark Gable—the teenagers of the late fifties made idols of people from their own generation. And although clean-cut starts like Ricky Nelson or Frankie Avalon were chosen as idols, many young people also idolized Brando and Dean, who seemed so much like them in their agonizing over the problems of life. The inclination of the young to idolize those who portrayed problem youth was puzzling and disturbing to parents who wanted their children to grow up to be clean-cut, middle-class kids who went to church, obeyed their parents and other authorities, drank nothing harder than a soft drink, had no sexual experience before marriage, saved and studied for college, hung around soda shops rather than pool rooms, and after college went into a respectable career with a good income and a secure future. In short, they wanted their children to be like Pat Boone.

Born in Jacksonville, Florida, in 1934, Boone rose to fame while still a college student by winning first place on Ted Mack's *Original Amateur Hour* and *Arthur Godfrey's Talent Scouts* in 1954. He became a regular on Godfrey's morning show, and then began a career as a singer, movie star (*Bernadine* and *April Love,* both in 1957), and television star with his own show (*Pat Boone Chevy Showroom*). Many of his recordings were covers of original black songs like "Tutti-Frutti" and "Ain't That a Shame," and traditional romantic tunes such as "Friendly Persuasion," "April Love," and "Love Letters in the Sand." Boone was an all-American boy, a dedicated Christian and family man who had not been spoiled by his success, although at the age of twenty-four he was already popular and wealthy, earning $750,000 annually. He had an attractive wife, four pretty daughters, a baccalaureate degree from Columbia University, a love of milk and ice cream, and a severe distaste for strong drink, tobacco, and anything else immoral. He attracted wide publicity in 1958 when he refused to kiss Shirley Jones in the movie *April Love,* saying that "I've always been taught that when you get married, you forget about kissing other women." However, after talking it over with his wife, he agreed to do the kissing scene, although "she would prefer to keep that part of our lives solely to ourselves." This old-fashioned wholesomeness enabled him to hit the best-seller list in 1958 with *Twist Twelve and Twenty,* a moral and social guide for teenagers that reflected Boone's conservative view of sex and his deeply religious outlook on life. Some teenagers found Boone hopelessly "square," but many others admired his moral rectitude. He was immensely popular in the fifties, perhaps second only to Elvis.

In spite of the existence of clean-cut white performers like Pat Boone, much of the adult world was against the new rock 'n' roll. Many musicians and music critics condemned it on musical grounds, disliking its primitive beat, electrical amplification, witless and repetitive lyrics, loudness, and screams. But most adults opposed it for other reasons. Many objected to its suggestive lyrics and claimed that it fomented rebellion against parents and other authorities, bred immorality, inflamed teenagers to riot, and was unchristian and unpatriotic. They agreed with Frank Sinatra, who called it "the martial music of every sideburned delinquent on the face of the earth." Others objected to its racial background and content, even claiming, as many southerners did, that rock 'n' roll was a plot jointly sponsored by the Kremlin and the NAACP, and that rock musicians and disc jockeys were dope addicts, communists, integrationists, atheists, and sex fiends. To many whites, North and South, it was "nigger music," and as such was designed to tear down the barriers of segregation and bring about sexual promiscuity, intermarriage, and a decline in the morals of young whites.

The fears of parents and other adults were fed by the isolated incidents of rioting that accompanied rock 'n' roll concerts in Boston, Washington, D.C., and several other cities. As a result of these headline-getting events, rock 'n' roll concerts were banned in many cities or else accompanied by heavy police security and strict regulations as to what the performers could do or say on stage. In many cities, city councils and other local groups also tried to ban rock 'n' roll from record stores or jukeboxes. In San Antonio, Texas, the city council even went so far as to ban the music from the jukeboxes of public swimming pools, claiming that it "attracted undesirable elements given to practicing their gyrations in abbreviated bathing suits." A disc jockey in Buffalo was fired when he played an Elvis Presley record, and across the country disc jockeys were similarly punished for playing the new music or were pressured into boycotting it. Some disc jockeys broke rock 'n' roll records on the air, while radio station WLEV in Erie, Pennsylvania, loaded over 7,000 rock 'n' roll records

into a rented hearse and led a funeral procession to Erie Harbor, where the records were "buried at sea." Ministers preached against it, claiming, like the Rev. John Carroll in Boston, that the music corrupted young people and that "rock and roll inflames and excites youth like jungle tom-toms readying warriors for battle," and many churches held public burnings of rock 'n' roll records. Some were even willing to resort to the ugliest kinds of violence to try to stem the advance of rock music. On April 23, 1956, in Birmingham, Alabama, where the White Citizens' Council had succeeded in removing all rock 'n' roll records from jukeboxes, five men connected with the council rushed the stage of the city auditorium and assaulted black ballad singer Nat King Cole, who was badly bruised before the police stopped the attack.

The debate over rock 'n' roll continued through the end of the decade, carried on in the press, over radio and television, in teachers' meetings, pulpits, and city council meeting rooms. By 1960 the debate had begun to die down, with parents coming to see that the music was not going to fade away, that it had not made delinquents of their children, and that all the other dire predictions had not come to pass, either. Some even began to admit grudgingly that they liked some of it, though they wished that it were not played so loudly. Some of the older professional musicians had also come to defend it—Benny Goodman, Sammy Kaye, Paul Whiteman, and Duke Ellington had kind words for the new music from the very beginning, and Whiteman and Kaye publicly recalled that most new musical forms, including their own swing music, had been condemned when it first appeared. And in the May 1959 issue of *Harper's,* critic Arnold Shaw noted that "perhaps it should be added (although it should be self-evident) that just as hot jazz of the twenties (then anathema to our grandparents) did not destroy our parents, and swing (anathema to our parents) did not destroy us, it is quite unlikely that rock 'n' roll will destroy our children."

The spectacular rise of rock 'n' roll should not obscure the fact that the older music continued to thrive. In 1957, when rock 'n' roll claimed seven of the top ten records of the year, the number one song was "Tammy," recorded by both Debbie Reynolds and the Ames Brothers, and Perry Como remained a favorite of young and old throughout the decade. In a 1956 poll by *Woman's Home Companion,* teenage boys and girls chose Como as the best male vocalist, with Presley, Boone, and Sinatra trailing behind. Johnny Mathis, Paul Anka, Pat Boone, Bobby Darin, the Everly Brothers, and many other teen idols also continued to sing fairly traditional love songs, and in the late fifties, building on a tradition established early in the decade by the Weavers, the Kingston Trio brought a revival of folk music to college students with a touch of rock and protest in songs like "Tom Dooley," "Tijuana Jail," and "A Worried Man," paving the way for the folk music explosion in the early 1960s. Rock music dominated from 1956 to 1960, but it did not completely push the older music aside.

In addition to obtaining their own music, movies, television shows, and idols, teenagers of the fifties also acquired their own fashions, and here they followed the trend toward casual dress that was characterizing the rest of society. The favorite dress of high school boys was denim jeans with rolled-up cuffs, sport shirts, baggy pegged pants, pleated rogue trousers with a white side stripe, slacks with buckles in the back, V-neck sweaters, button-down striped shirts, blazers, white bucks, and loafers. In 1955 they also joined older males on college campuses and executive offices in the pink revolution, donning pink shirts, pink striped or polka dot ties, and colonel string ties. Hair styles ranged from the popular flat top or crew cut to the Apache or ducktail (banned at some high schools). "Greasers" of course shunned the Ivy League and pink attire as too effeminate, sticking to their T-shirts (often with sleeves rolled up to hold a cigarette pack), jeans, leather jackets, and ducktails. For girls, the fashions ranged from rolled-up jeans to casual blouses or men's shirts, full dresses with crinolines, skirts and sweaters, blazers, occasional experiments with the tube dress and sack dress and other disasters foisted upon older women by fashion designers, short shorts (with rolled-up cuffs) that got progressively shorter as the decade wore on, two-piece bathing suits (few were bold enough to wear the bikini, imported from France in the late forties), brown and white saddle shoes and loafers, and hair styles from the poodle to the ponytail. Couples who were going steady wore one another's class rings, identification tags, and necklaces or bracelets, and often adopted a unisex look by wearing matching sweaters, blazers, and shirts.

Like the generations before them, the teenagers of the fifties also had their slang. Much of it was concerned, of course, with the great passion of teens, cars. Cars were *wheels,* tires were *skins,* racing from a standing start was called a *drag,* the bumper was *nerf-bar,* a special kind of exhaust system was called *duals,* and a car specially modified for more engine power was a *hot rod* or *souped up car* or *bomb.* A drive-in movie was a *passion pit,* anything or anyone considered dull was a *drag,* and a really dull person was a *square* or a *nosebleed.* An admirable or poised individual or anything worthy of admiration or approval was *cool* or *neat* or *smooth,* someone who panicked or lost his *cool* was accused of *clutching,* and people admonished not to worry were told to *hang loose.* Teenagers also borrowed lingo from the jazz and beatnik world, such as *dig, hip, cat,*

bread, and *chick.* A cutting, sarcastic laugh at someone's bad joke was expressed by a *hardeeharhar.* And teenagers also shared the jargon of the rest of society—*big deal, the royal screw or royal shaft, up the creek without a paddle, forty lashes with a wet noodle, wild, wicked, crazy, classy, horny, BMOC, looking for action, bad news, out to lunch, gross, fink, loser, creep, dumb cluck, doing the deed, going all the way, or coming across.* Many of these colloquialisms were borrowed from earlier generations, sometimes with modifications in meaning, while some had been regionalisms that now became national through the great homogenizing power of television.

By the mid-1950s there were 16.5 million teenagers in the United States. About half of them were crowding the nation's secondary schools, while the rest had entered college or the work world. Wherever they were, they had become, as Gereon Zimmerman would write in *Look* magazine, a "Generation in a Searchlight," a constant subject of media attention and a constant source of anxiety for their parents and the rest of the adult world. As Zimmerman observed, "No other generation has had so such attention, so much admonition, so many statistics."

Zimmerman might also have added that no other young generation had had so much money. One of the most revolutionary aspects of the teenage generation was its effects on the American economy, for by the midfifties teenagers made up a very lucrative consumer market for American manufacturers. By mid-decade teenagers of this affluent era were viewing as necessities goods that their parents, reared during the depression, still saw as luxuries, such as automobiles, televisions, record players, cameras, and the like. By the midfifties, teenagers were buying 43 percent of all records, 44 percent of all cameras, 39 percent of all new radios, 9 percent of all new cars, and 53 percent of movie tickets. By 1959, the amount of money spent on teenagers by themselves and by their parents had reached the staggering total of $10 billion a year. Teenagers were spending around $75 million annually on single popular records, $40 million on lipstick, $25 million on deodorant, $9 million on home permanents, and over $837 million on school clothes for teenage girls. Many teenagers had their own charge accounts at local stores and charge cards issued especially for them, such as Starlet Charge Account, Campus Deb Account, and the 14 to 21 Club. Like their parents, teenagers were being led by the affluence and advertising of the age to desire an ever-increasing diet of consumer goods and services and to buy them even if they had to charge them against future earnings.

Many adults had a distorted image of this affluent young generation, focusing too much on its delinquency, rock 'n' roll, unconventional hair styles and clothing, and dating and sexual practices. Only a very small percentage were delinquents or problem-ridden adolescents. Most were reasonably well-groomed, well-behaved, and active in school and extracurricular functions. Most were interested in sports, automobiles, movies, rock 'n' roll, dating, dancing, hobbies, radio, and television. Their major worries were the typical problems of youth in an affluent age: problems with their parents, their popularity with other teens, their looks and complexions, proper dating behavior, sex, first dates, first kisses, love, bad breath, body odors, posture, body build, friends, schoolwork, college, future careers, money, religion, and the draft.

These teenagers that parents worried so much about were remarkably conservative. Survey after survey of young people in the fifties found that over half of them—and sometimes even larger percentages—believed that censorship of printed materials and movies was justified, that politics was beyond their understanding and was just a dirty game, that most people did not have the ability to make important decisions about what was good for them, that masturbation was shameful and perhaps harmful, that women should not hold public office, and that the theory of evolution was suspect and even dangerous. Like their parents, they were also very religious as a group, tending to believe in the divine inspiration of the Bible, heaven and hell, and a God who answered the prayers of the faithful. They were suspicious of radical groups and were willing to deny them the right to assemble in meetings and to disseminate their ideas, and they saw nothing wrong with denying accused criminals basic constitutional rights, such as the right to know their accuser, to be free from unreasonable search or seizure of their property, or to refuse to testify against themselves. Teenagers were also very conformist: They were very concerned about what their friends thought of their dress, behavior, and ideas, and they tried very hard to be part of the group and not be labeled an oddball or individualist. In short, in this age of corporation man, the country also had corporation teen.

Most teens were also conservative in their approach to dating, sex, and marriage. Religious views, social and peer pressure, and fear of pregnancy all combined to create this conservatism and to ensure that most teens kept their virginity until marriage or at least until the early college years, though heavy petting was certainly prevalent among couples who were engaged or "going steady," a practice reflecting society's emphasis on monogamy. These conservative attitudes toward sexual behavior were reinforced by the authorities teenagers looked to for guidance—parents, teachers, ministers, advice to the lovelorn columnists like Dear· Abby and Ann Landers (both of whom began their columns in the midfifties), and books on teenage etiquette by Allen Ludden, Pat Boone, and *Seventeen* magazine. In his book for young men, *Plain Talk for Men Under 21,* Ludden devoted an entire chapter to such things as "That Good Night Kiss"—discussing whether to, how to, and the significance of it if you did. And in the very popular *The Seventeen Book of Young Living* (1957), Enid Haupt, the editor and publisher of *Seventeen* magazine, advised young girls to "keep your first and all your romances on a beyond reproach level" and to save themselves for the one right man in their lives. Acknowledging that "it isn't easy to say no to a persuasive and charming boy," she offered one answer for all potentially compromising situations: "'No, please take me home. Now.'"

The conservatism of the young would continue over into the college-age population, where it would remain entrenched for the rest of the fifties. The decade witnessed a boom in higher education, as rising prosperity, G.I. benefits, increasing governmental and private financial aid, fear of the draft, and a growing cultural emphasis on higher education all contributed to a great increase in the number of college students, faculty, programs, and buildings. The boom occurred at all levels—undergraduate, graduate, professional, and in the burgeoning junior- and community-college movement. The number of students, which had stood at 1.5 million in 1940 and 2.3 million in 1950, steadily rose in the decade and reached 3.6 million in 1960, and while the population of the country grew by 8 percent in the decade, the college population grew by 40 percent. By the end of the decade, almost 40 percent of the eighteen-to-twenty-one-year-old age group was attending some institution of higher education.

The conservatism of the college students of the 1950s led them to be called the Silent Generation. Why was it so silent? One of the most important reasons was that it mirrored the conservatism of the society at large, a society caught up in the materialistic and Cold War mentality of the decade. Like their elders, students were seeking the good life rather than the examined one, and as the Great Fear spread to the campuses, many were afraid of acquiring a radical reputation that might jeopardize their scholarships and their future careers in private industry, government service, or the military. Many were veterans, and their military experience, especially for those who had served in Korea, had tended to confirm their conservatism. Many others were in college in order to evade or at least defer the draft, and did not want to do or say anything that might endanger their deferred status. And finally, most students were white and drawn from the middle and upper-middle classes of society. The doors of higher education were still closed to most minority groups and to the economically and socially disadvantaged—groups who might have brought questioning or even radical attitudes into the field of higher education had they been part of it. It is not surprising then that most college students were hardworking, conservative, and career-oriented, truly deserving of their Silent Generation label.

The conservatism of the college generation prevailed throughout the decade. In a study of the college generation in 1951, *Time* magazine noted that "the most startling thing about the younger generation is its silence. . . . It does not issue manifestoes, make speeches, or carry posters." Most students, *Time* found, were worried about the Korean War and its effects on their plans for careers and marriage, but they pushed these fears into the background and concentrated on earning good grades and landing a good job. They were serious and hardworking, in rebellion against nothing, and had no real heroes or villains. Born during the depression years, they were primarily interested in a good job and security, and they did not want to do or say anything that would jeopardize these goals. "Today's generation," *Time* concluded, "either through fear, passivity, or conviction, is ready to conform."

Soon after the end of the Korean War, *Newsweek* studied college students in seven institutions, and its findings were little different from those of *Time* two years before. In "U.S. Campus Kids of 1953: Unkiddable and Unbeatable," *Newsweek* reported that students were hardworking, ambitious conformists who looked forward to secure jobs and a happy married life. Going steady was more popular than ever before, a sign of the period's emphasis on marriage and of young people's desire for the security that a going-steady relationship brought. Most students, *Newsweek* found, were not very interested in politics or international affairs, and they avoided being linked with unpopular causes. One Vassar girl told the magazine, "We're a cautious generation. We aren't buying any ideas we're not sure of." Another said that "you want to be popular, so naturally you don't express any screwy ideas. To be popular you have to conform." And a Princeton senior said that "the world doesn't owe me a living—but it owes me a job." *Newsweek* also saw a renewed interest in religion, as reflected in increasing enrollments in religion courses and frequent "religious emphasis weeks." The magazine found much to admire in the hardworking materialistic class of 1953, although it did concede that "they might seem dull in comparison with less troubled eras."

Similar collegiate characteristics were reported in a 1955 study by David Riesman, who found that students were ambitious, very sure of what they wanted to do, but also very unadventurous—they wanted secure positions in big companies and were already concerned about retirement plans. As one Princeton senior saw it,

"Why struggle on my own, when I can enjoy the big psychological income of being a member of a big outfit?" Most males had already decided that they wanted middle-management jobs—they did not want to rise to the presidential or vice-presidential level because that would require too much drive, take time away from their family life and leisure time, and force them to live in a big city. Most had already decided upon the kind of girl they would marry, how many kids they would have, and which civic clubs and other organizations they would join—and they would be joiners, for they liked the gregarious life and knew it would help their careers. They wanted educated wives who would be intellectually stimulating, yet they wanted them to be dutiful and obedient and to stay at home and raise the kids. Many said they wanted as many as four or five kids, because they felt that a large family would bring happiness, security, contentment. One Harvard senior said that "I'd like six kids. I don't know why I say that—it seems like a minimum production goal." They did not know or care much about politics, but they did like Ike and said that they would probably be Republicans because corporation life dictated that they should be.

These attitudes still seemed to prevail in 1957, when *The Nation* surveyed college and university professors about what their students were reading and thinking. Most reported that their students still read the standard authors—Hemingway, Wolfe, Lawrence, Orwell, Huxley, Faulkner, and Steinbeck—but shied away from fiction or nonfiction that dealt with economic, social, or political protest. One professor lamented that "the only young novelist I have heard praised vociferously is J. D. Salinger, for his discovery of childhood," and complained that "when a liberal and speculative voice is heard in the classroom, it is more likely than not to be the professor's, despite whatever caution the years may have taught him." The director of the Writing Program at Stanford University claimed that students were "hard to smoke out. Sometimes a professor is baited into protest by the rows and circles of their closed, watchful, apparently apathetic faces, and says in effect, 'My God, *feel* something! Get enthusiastic about something, plunge, go boom, look alive!'" A Yale English professor complained that "the present campus indifference to either politics or reform or rebellion is monumental." And most agreed with a University of Michigan professor's claim that to the student of 1957, "college has ceased to be a brightly lighted stage where he discovers who he is. It is rather a processing-chamber where, with touching submissiveness, he accepts the remarks of lecturers and the hard sentences of textbooks as directives that will lead him to a job."

What did the members of the Silent Generation do when they were not studying, planning what company they intended to find a safe niche in, deciding what kind of mate they would marry or how many kids they would have, or planning for retirement? They played sports, drank beer, ate pizzas and hamburgers, went to football games and movies, participated in panty raids, dated, dreamed of the opposite sex, read novels and magazines, watched television, and listened to recordings of jazz, classical music, or the popular crooners of the day. For most, the hottest issues on campus were what to do about a losing football coach or who should be elected homecoming queen or student body president. Both sexes wore conservative preppy clothes, and at many coeducational institutions women were forbidden to wear jeans or shorts to class. Those who could afford to joined one of the fast-growing number of fraternities or sororities in order to party, find identity and security, and form friendships that might later be useful in the business world they hoped to enter after graduation. College students were, indeed, an unrebellious lot.

By the late fifties America's teenagers had acquired a distinct subculture of their own. They had their own money, music, movies, television shows, idols, clothing, and slang. In contrast to previous generations, they were more affluent, better educated, talked more openly about sex, had greater mobility through the widespread ownership of automobiles by their parents or themselves, demanded and received more personal freedom, had more conflicts with their parents, and were the subject of more media and parental concern. But they were not yet in rebellion, for although their life-style had departed from the conventions of their elders, their basic ideas and attitudes were still the conservative ones that mirrored the conservatism of the affluent age in which they grew up.

Still, their parents were worried. As *Look* magazine reported in 1958 in an article entitled "What Parents Say About Teenagers," "many parents are in a state of confusion or despair about their teenagers. And they don't exactly know what to do about it. They would like to sit down with their children and talk over their mutual problems, but often this desire is thwarted by the teenagers themselves." The much-heralded generation gap was coming into view. In the next decade, when the junior high and senior high school students of the fifties crowded the colleges, marched in civil rights demonstrations, protested the Vietnam War, and engaged in unconventional sexual and drug practices, it would take on the temper of a revolution.

J.RONALD OAKLEY was a professor of history at Davidson County Community in Greensboro, North Carolina. He is also the author of *Baseball's Last Golden Age, 1946–1960: The National Pastime in a Period of Glory and Change* (McFarland, 1994).

Was Rock and Roll Responsible for Dismantling America's Traditional Customs in the 1950s and 1960s? by Madaras and SoRelle

255

EXPLORING THE ISSUE

Was Rock and Roll Responsible for Dismantling America's Traditional Family, Sexual, and Racial Customs in the 1950s and 1960s?

Critical Thinking and Reflection

1. Critically evaluate the controversy surrounding the effects of rock and roll music on society's values in the 1950s and 1960s.
2. Describe cover records. Explain how these records reflected the racial values of white Americans in the 1950s.
3. Compare and contrast the two major disc jockeys of rock and roll in the 1950s—Alan Freed and Dick Clark. Why was Freed driven to alcoholism and an early death while Clark sustained a successful career into the twenty-first century?
4. Explain why Elvis Presley was the key rock and roll figure of the 1950s? Could rock and roll have taken off and existed as the main form of popular music from the mid-1950s to the present without Elvis?
5. Discuss whether rock and roll influences the concerns and values of today's youth? Explain and compare with the concerns and values of the previous six decades of values.

Is There Common Ground?

Most historians agree on the basic facts surrounding the origins of rock and roll. They may disagree on details such as who were the first singers identified with rock and roll, but clearly by the mid-fifties a group of southern singers like Jerry Lee Lewis, Chuck Berry, and Elvis Presley fused rhythm and blues, country western and black gospel into a new form of music. The disagreement centers around the social impact of this music and whether local leaders and governmental authorities overreacted to rock and roll music by breaking up rock concerts and pressuring disc jockeys to stop playing rock music on the radio. Were the adolescents of the 1950s merely a younger generation in a traditional rebellion against the authority of their parents? Or was this generation in the process of breaking down the traditional norms of the family leading to the counterculture and political revolts of the 1960s?

Create Central

www.mhhe.com/createcentral

Additional Resources

Matthew F. Delmont, *The Nicest Kids in Town: American Bandstand, Rock 'n' Roll, and the Struggle for Civil Rights in 1950s Philadelphia* (University of California Press, 2012).

Peter Guralnick, *Last Train to Memphis: The Rise of Elvis Presley* (Back Bay Books, 1994).

John A. Jackson, *Big Beat Heat: Alan Freed and the Early Years of Rock & Roll* (Schirmer Books, 1991).

John A. Jackson, *American Bandstand: Dick Clark and the Making of a Rock 'n' Roll Empire* (Oxford University Press, 1998).

Sean Wilenz, *Bob Dylan in America* (Doubleday, 2010).

Internet References . . .

Rock and Roll Museum—Cleveland

www.Cleveland.com/rockhall

Rock & Roll Music—YouTube

www.youtube.com/watch?v=lH8lrcvdlD8

Rock and Roll Music—Listen Free at Last.fm

www.last.fm/tag/rock%20and%20roll

Selected, Edited, and with Issue Framing Material by:
Larry Madaras, *Howard Community College*
and
James M. SoRelle, *Baylor University*

ISSUE

Did President John F. Kennedy Cause the Cuban Missile Crisis?

YES: Thomas G. Paterson, from "When Fear Ruled: Rethinking the Cuban Missile Crisis," *New England Journal of History* (vol. 52, Fall 1995)

NO: Robert Weisbrot, from *Maximum Danger: Kennedy, the Missiles, and the Crisis of American Confidence* (Ivan R. Dee, 2001)

Learning Outcomes

After reading this issue, you will be able to:

- Understand Premier Khrushchev's reasons for putting Soviet missiles in Cuba in the summer of 1962.
- Understand President Kennedy's response to the missiles placed in Cuba.
- Understand the traditional and revisionist interpretations of the Cuban missile crisis.
- Understand the impact of the newly declassified documents—such as minutes of the meetings and conferences between former American and Soviet officials—in changing our perceptions about decision making in the Oval Office.
- Understand the impact of the concepts of "crisis management" and "nation building" in the formation of our foreign/policy.

ISSUE SUMMARY

YES: Professor Thomas G. Paterson believes that President Kennedy, even though he moderated the American response and compromised in the end, helped precipitate the Cuban missile crisis by his support for both the failed Bay of Pigs invasion in April 1961 and the continued attempts by the CIA to assassinate Fidel Castro.

NO: Historian Robert Weisbrot argues that the new sources uncovered in the past 20 years portray Kennedy as a president who had not only absorbed the values of his time as an anti-Communist cold warrior but who nevertheless acted as a rational leader and was conciliatory toward the Soviet Union in resolving the Cuban missile crisis.

In 1959, the political situation in Cuba changed drastically when Fulgencio Batista y Zaldi'var was overthrown by a 34-year-old revolutionary named Fidel Castro, who led a guerilla band in the Sierra Maestra mountain range. Unlike his predecessors, Castro refused to be a lackey for American political and business interests. The new left-wing dictator seized control of American oil refineries and ordered a number of diplomats at the U.S. embassy in Havana to leave the country. President Dwight D. Eisenhower was furious and responded shortly before he left office by imposing economic sanctions on the island and breaking diplomatic ties.

Eisenhower's successor, John F. Kennedy, supported an invasion of Cuba by a group of disaffected anti-Castro Cuban exiles that had been planned by the previous administration to foster the overthrow of Castro. The April 1961 Bay of Pigs invasion was a disaster as Castro's army routed the invaders, killing many and imprisoning others. The Kennedy administration responded by securing

Cuba's removal from the Organization of American States (OAS) in early 1962, imposed an economic embargo on the island, and carried out threatening military maneuvers in the Caribbean.

The isolation and possibility of a second invasion of this Caribbean communist client state probably influenced Soviet Premier Nikita Khrushchev to take a more proactive stance to defend Cuba. In the summer of 1962, he sent troops and conventional weapons to the island; by September 1962, missile launching pads had been installed. President Kennedy confronted criticism from Republicans, such as Senator Kenneth Keating of New York, who charged that the Russians were bringing not only troops but also nuclear weapons to Cuba. At first, Kennedy was concerned with the political implications of the charges for the 1962 congressional races, and on September 11, 1962, he assured reporters that the Cuban military buildup was primarily defensive in nature.

President Kennedy was probably caught off-guard with Khrushchev's bold actions in Cuba in the fall of 1962. Did Khrushchev want to compensate for the Russian "missile gap"? Did he want to trade Russia's withdrawal from Cuba with the American withdrawal from Berlin? Did Khrushchev wish to provide Cuba with military protection from another U.S. invasion? Forty years later, with much more evidence available from the Cuban and Russian participants in these events, Khrushchev's motives are still the subject of debate. President Kennedy, like most policymakers, had to make his decision to blockade Cuba on the basis of the best available information at the time.

The situation changed drastically on the morning of October 16, 1962, when National Security Council adviser McGeorge Bundy informed the president that photographs from U-2 reconnaissance flights over Cuba revealed that the Russians were building launching pads for 1,000-mile medium-range missiles as well as 2,200-mile intermediate-range missiles. The president kept the news quiet. He ordered more U-2 flights to take pictures and had Bundy assemble a select group of advisers who became known as the Executive Committee of the National Security Council (Ex-Comm). For six days and nights, the president favored a blockade, or what he called a "quarantine," of the island. On October 22, 1962, Kennedy revealed his plans for the quarantine over national television.

Mark J. White has succinctly summarized the resolution of the Cuban missile crisis in the introduction to his edited collection of documents entitled *The Kennedys and Cuba: The Declassified Documentary History* (Ivan R. Dee, 1999). "During the second week of the crisis," writes White, "from JFK's October 22 address to the achievement of a settlement six days later, Kennedy and Khrushchev initially fired off messages to each other, defending their own positions and assailing their adversary's. But a series of developments from October 26 to 28 suddenly brought the crisis to an end." Khrushchev offered to remove the missiles if the American president promised not to invade Cuba and removed the Jupiter missiles that the United States had installed along the Soviet border in Turkey. Kennedy publically promised not to invade Cuba and privately agreed to withdraw the missiles in Turkey, an arrangement that satisfied Khrushchev and brought an end to the most dangerous episode of the entire Cold War era.

Was President Kennedy responsible for the Cuban missile crisis? Professor Thomas Paterson, one of the best known revisionist diplomatic historians, has authored numerous books and articles critical of America's Cold War policies in Europe and Cuba, and is quite critical of what he sees as JFK's fumbling efforts to resolve the crisis via diplomacy. First he challenges the "Camelot image" of Kennedy as the hero who avoided nuclear war by negotiating a settlement with the Russians to take the missiles out of Cuba, thereby avoiding a military confrontation. In Paterson's view, Kennedy's reckless personal behavior was also carried out in his professional life. The president, according to Paterson, was looking for a way to manage the crisis. Rejecting the choices of Eisenhower, who wavered between threats of nuclear retaliation or doing nothing, Kennedy believed a third way, involving the use of "special forces" like the Green Berets, might alter the balance of power in the attempt to "nation build" third-world countries to favor the western way over the communist alternative. (The reader is not far off the mark if he perceives similar policies being pursued in Iraq and Afghanistan today.) Paterson admits that the Khrushchev–Castro decision to place missiles in Cuba "ranks as one of the most dangerous in the Cold War." Yet, he blames the policies of the Eisenhower–Kennedy administrations for this decision. As Paterson writes, "Had there been no exile expeditions at the Bay of Pigs, no destructive covert activities, no assassination plots, no military maneuvers and plans, and no economic and diplomatic steps to harass, isolate and destroy the Castro government, there would not have been a Cuban missile crisis." Was Kennedy's response a triumph of effective crisis management? Not in Paterson's view. "In the end," he says, "the two superpowers, frantic to avoid nuclear war and scared by the prospects of doomsday, stumbled toward a settlement."

In the NO selection, Professor Robert Weisbrot rejects both the earlier portraits of Kennedy partisans that JFK was an "effective crisis manager" and the assessments of critics who discern in the president's foreign policy "a dismal amalgam of anti-communist hysteria, reckless posturing, and a disturbing gleeful crisis orientation." Relying on new evidence made available over the past 20 years, such as the declassified Ex-Comm conversations and the transcripts of several conferences involving Soviet and American scholars and former officials (including Cuba's Castro), Weisbrot sees Kennedy not as a cold warrior but as a rational leader who defused the crisis. Concluding that Kennedy was neither the lone crisis hero as his chief speech writer Ted Sorenson portrayed him in *The Kennedy Legacy* (Macmillan, 1969) nor a macho anti-communist counterrevolutionary as many revisionists have insisted, Weisbrot credits a number of other participants for softening the crisis. Secretary of State Dean Rusk, for example, was not the "silent Buddha" as portrayed in the writings of earlier Kennedy admirers. It was Rusk who revealed that Kennedy's fall-back plan was to have U.N. Secretary General U. Thant propose a swap of missiles in Turkey and Cuba. It was Llewellyn Thompson, the former ambassador to the Soviet Union, and not Robert Kennedy who suggested accepting Khrushchev's tacit proposals and not the harsher terms of his public demands. Then there was Kennedy's National Security Adviser McGeorge Bundy who acknowledged: "The most important part of crisis management is not to have a crisis, because there's no telling what will happen once you're in one." Scott D. Sagan's, *Limits of Safety: Organizations, Accidents and Nuclear Weapons* (Princeton University, 1985), lists a number of potential disasters, which Professor Weisbrot recounts, that occurred during the Cuban missile crisis, some of which even President Kennedy was not aware. The real failure of crisis management occurred later, Weisbrot believes, when the Kennedy–Johnson team, full of exuberance over their success in Cuba, believed they could manage similar crises in Southeast Asia.

YES ⤶

Thomas G. Paterson

When Fear Ruled: Rethinking the Cuban Missile Crisis

Nikita Khrushchev cried and then rushed to the American Embassy in Moscow to sign the book of condolence. Fidel Castro remarked, again and again, "This is bad news," and then turned silent. In Bremen, Germany, a "sea of flowers" engulfed the U.S. consulate, and in Nice, France, construction crews stopped working. A Czech citizen asked: "Who will lead us now?" Europeans were left, said one of them, "Like children in the darkness."

"He glittered when he lived," wrote one of John F. Kennedy's admiring assistants and biographers, Arthur M. Schlesinger, Jr. "Everyone around him thought he had the Midas touch and could not lose." "It can be said of him," eulogized one editorial, "that he did not fear the weather, and did not trim his sails, but instead challenged the wind itself . . . to cause it to blow more softly and more kindly over the world and its people." "The man was magic," a congressman recalled, "He lit up a room. He walked in, and the air was lighter, the light was brighter."

In a time of wrenching turmoil at home and abroad, President John F. Kennedy, for people everywhere, represented hope, youthful energy, courage, determination, compassion, and innovative leadership. He envisioned a new order to pry America out of its doldrums, to get it moving again, as he so often put it. He had won popular approval from the American people and he had touched people abroad, becoming for many a legitimate hero. His wit, eloquent oratory, self-confident style, athleticism, and handsome looks captivated a generation seeking the light at the end of the tunnel. "Though I never met him, I knew him just the same," went the words of a song by the musical group, The Byrds. "He was a friend of mine."

Some thirty years after Kennedy's death, such words still resonate among Americans who feel the anguish of dashed hopes—their slain leader losing his chance to make a difference, taking with him the promise of a better future. Yet, now, we also have more perspective on the tumultuous decade of the sixties. We have had the terrible experience of Vietnam, many frightening Cold War

confrontations, and the Watergate and Iron-Contra scandals to make us more skeptical of our leaders and more searching in our assessments. Most important, we now have what must undergird any careful account of the Kennedy era—declassified documents from the Kennedy Library in Boston, the Central Intelligence Agency, and East German and Soviet archives, among others. The massive documentary record, although incomplete, has generated scholarly studies that peel back the layers of once hidden stories, expose complexities, separate image from reality, and compel us to contend with a less satisfying past than the one we would prefer and have imagined. The positive images Kennedy's advisers so skillfully broadcast—the cosmetic cream of celebration that covered his blemishes—have not altogether disappeared but they have faded. We have more balance, more insight, more evidence. Our portrait of John F. Kennedy has become necessarily less flattering. Such is the nature of always evolving historical research and interpretation, although we can take no comfort from it.

We now have an unadorned Kennedy, a whole Kennedy, a very human Kennedy, whose character, judgment, and accomplishments have been called into question. The demythologizing of John F. Kennedy, for example, includes a reconsideration of the image of the family man. Although Kennedy genuinely loved his children, he was a brazen, reckless womanizer who named the women he wanted for sex and usually got them, including Hollywood starlets and Judith Campbell Exner, mistress to crime bosses as well as to the President. This is the stuff of sensationalism, of course, but these sexual indiscretions also endangered national security, his presidency, and his health. Kennedy, moreover, was gravely ill. Had the voting public known the extent of his ailments in 1960—especially his Addison's disease and severe back pain, for which he took injections of concoctions of amphetamines, steroids, calcium, and vitamins administered by a discredited doctor—had the public known, they may not have taken the risk of sending him to the White House. His reputation as a writer has also encountered the test of evidence. His book, *Profiles in Courage,* published in 1955, for which he took personal credit and won a Pulitzer Prize, was actually written for him by an aide and a university professor.

The 1960 presidential candidate who criticizing the Eisenhower Administration for permitting the Soviets to gain missile superiority—the famed charge of a "missile gap"—became the President who learned that the United States held overwhelming nuclear supremacy—yet he nonetheless tremendously expanded the American nuclear arsenal. CIA officers, believing that they were carrying out presidential instructions, tried to assassinate Cuba's Fidel Castro and send sabotage teams to destroy life and property on the island. For a President who said that Americans should "never fear to negotiate," Kennedy seemed more enamored with military than with diplomatic means: defense expenditures increased thirteen percent in the Kennedy years, counter-insurgency training and warfare accelerated, and U.S. intervention in Vietnam deepened.

Given the disparity between image and reality and the inevitable reinterpretation that new documentation and distance from events stimulate, it is not surprising that ambiguity now marks Kennedy scholarship. He appears as both confrontationist and conciliator, hawk and dove, decisive leader and hesitant improviser, hyperbolic politician and prudent diplomat, poor crisis preventer but good crisis manager, idealist and pragmatist, glorious hero and flawed man of dubious character. On the one hand he sponsored the Peace Corps, and on the other he attended personally to the equipment needs of the Green Berets. On the one hand he called for an appreciation of Third World nationalism, and on the other he intervened in Vietnam and Cuba to try to squash nationalist movements he found unacceptable. He said that the United States respected neutralism, yet he strove to persuade important neutrals such as India, Indonesia, and Egypt to shed their non-alignment for alliance with the United States in the Cold War.

Kennedy preached democracy, but sent military aid to oppressive Latin American regimes, and the Alliance for Progress did not meet its goals because it shored up elites, who took the money for their own purposes. He said he knew that the Sino-Soviet split compelled a new policy toward the People's Republic of China, but he spoke often about a monolithic Communism and rejected options to improve relations with the PRC. On the one hand he created the Arms Control and Disarmament Agency, and on the other expanded the number of American intercontinental ballistic missiles from some 60 to more than 420. On the one hand, seeing Eastern Europe as the "Achilles heel of the Soviet empire" and discarding John Foster

Dulles' provocative and failed policy of "liberation," he strove for improved relations with Soviet Russia's neighbors. But on the other he signed a trade bill that denied most-favored-nation treatment to Yugoslavia. On the one hand he called for a new Atlantic community, and on the other he refused to share decision-making power with increasingly disgruntled Western European allies.

Some analysts have argued that had Kennedy lived and won reelection in 1964, he would have withdrawn from Vietnam and transformed the Cold War from confrontation to peace and disarmament. Some Kennedy-watchers have emphasized that the President was evolving as a leader; that is, through education imposed by crises, Kennedy grew and began to temper his ardent Cold War anti-Communism, learning the limits of American power. "The heart of the Kennedy legend," the journalist James Reston has aptly noted, "is what might have been." We can never be sure about what Kennedy might have done, but we do know what he *did*. And that is were we must focus our attention—on the Kennedy *record*. Was it "stunningly successful," as one writer has claimed, or was it something quite less—high on image, but mixed if not low on results?

The centerpiece in the Kennedy record is his handling of the Cuban missile crisis. His role in this disturbing crisis—the closest the United States and the Soviet Union ever came to nuclear war—has especially undergone scrutiny in the last few years. Recent international conferences, featuring Kennedy-era decisionmakers, and the declassification of documents in Russia, Cuba, and the United States give us a new, more textured view of Kennedy and the missile crisis. It may be true, as Secretary of State Dean Rusk remembered, that "President Kennedy had ice water in his veins," but serious doubts have emerged about whether this event ranks as his "finest hour."

This dangerous moment in world history should not be championed as a supreme display of crisis management, calculated control, and statesmanship, but rather explored as a case of near misses that scared the crisis managers on both sides into a settlement because, in the words of National Security Affairs Adviser McGeorge Bundy, the crisis was "so near to spinning out of control."

New evidence also prompts us to investigate the Cuban missile crisis not as a simple good guys–bad guys drama foisted on the United States by an aggressive Soviet Union and crazed Castroite Cuba, but as a crisis for which Kennedy policies must bear some responsibility. This article plumbs the origins of the crisis, Kennedy's management of it, and the outcome, the "narrow squeak" that it was.

Those hair-trigger days of October 1962, stand out in the drama of the Cold War. Before that quaking month, the Soviets had boldly and recklessly placed medium-range missiles in Cuba—missiles that could carry nuclear warheads and destroy American cities. On October 14, an American U-2 spy-plane snapped photographs which revealed the construction of several missile sites. Determined to force the missiles from Cuba, Kennedy soon convened a council of wise men called the Executive Committee or ExComm. ExComm considered four policy options: "talk them out," "squeeze them out," "shoot them out," or "buy them out." Ultimately the committee advised the president to surround Cuba with a naval blockade as the best means to resolve the crisis. Kennedy went on television the evening of October 22 to explain the crisis and the U.S. response.

An international war of nerves soon began. More than sixty American ships went on patrol to enforce the blockade. The Strategic Air Command went on nuclear alert, moving upward to Defense Condition (DEFCON) 2 for the first time ever—the next level being deployment. B-52 bombers, packed with nuclear weapons, stood ready, while soldiers and equipment moved to the southeastern United States to prepare for an invasion of Cuba. Thousands of road maps of the island were distributed to anxious troops. Nail-biting days followed as Soviet ships steamed toward the U. S. armada. Grabbing a few hours of sleep on cots in their offices and expecting doomsday, Kennedy's advisers wondered if they would ever see their families again. And then, finally, with great relief, on October 28, Khrushchev appealed for restraint and the Americans and Soviets settled. In return for a Kennedy pledge not to invade Cuba and to withdraw U.S. Jupiter missiles from Turkey, Khrushchev promised to "dismantle," "crate, and return" his SS-4 missiles to the Soviet Union, and he fulfilled his pledge.

Kennedy's handling of the crisis, Arthur Schlesinger had effusively written, constituted a "combination of toughness and restraint, of will, nerve and wisdom, so brilliantly controlled, so matchlessly calibrated." "We've won a great victory," Kennedy himself told congressional leaders. In private, the President crowed to friends, "I cut his balls off."

"We have been had," growled Admiral George Anderson, in a quite different view. The no invasion pledge, complained Cuban exiles, "was another Bay of Pigs for us." "It's the greatest defeat in our history," snapped General Curtis LeMay. These statements about "victory" and "defeat" actually set the question too narrowly. A more revealing question is this: How did we get into the crisis in the first place?

Cuba and the United States had been snarling at one another ever since Fidel Castro came to power in early 1959 and vowed to reduce U.S. power on the island. While Cuba accelerated a bitterly anti-American revolution, the Eisenhower Administration imposed economic sanctions and initiated covert CIA actions. A defiant Castro moved Cuba steadily toward Communism and military alliance with the Soviet Union. Just before Kennedy's inauguration, President Eisenhower broke diplomatic relations with Cuba. Kennedy soon accelerated a multitrack program of covert, economic, diplomatic, and propagandistic elements designed to bring Castro down. Secretary of Defense Robert McNamara later remarked: "If I had been in Moscow or Havana at that time [of 1961–1962], I would have believed the Americans were preparing for an invasion."

Essential to understanding the frightening missile crisis of fall 1962, in fact, is the relationship between U.S. activities and Soviet/Cuban decisions. The time of events is critical, and there is no doubt that Castro saw Cuba's acceptance of the missiles as the formation of a military alliance with the Soviet Union, similar to membership in the Warsaw Pact. In May 1962, the Soviets and Cubans first discussed the idea of placing nuclear-tipped missiles on the island; in early July, during a trip by Raul Castro to Moscow, a draft agreement was initialed; in late August, during a trip by Che Guevara to Moscow, the final touches were put on the accord.

What was the United States doing during those critical months before August? By 1962, more than two hundred anti-Castro Cuban exile organizations operated in the United States. After the failed Bay of Pigs invasion of early 1961, Cuban exiles chafed at the bit in Florida, eager to avenge their losses. Many of them banded together under the leadership of Jose Miro Cardona, the former prime minister. Miro Cardona met with President Kennedy in Washington on April 10, 1962, and the Cuban exile left the meeting persuaded that Kennedy intended to use U. S. armed forces against Cuba. Indeed, after Miro Cardona returned to Miami, he and his Revolutionary Council began to identify recruits for a Cuban unit in the U.S. military.

If Havana worried about such maneuverings, it grew apprehensive too about the alliance between the exile groups and the CIA, whose commitment to the destruction of the Castro regime knew few bounds. Hit-and-run saboteurs burned cane fields and blew up oil depots and transportation facilities. In May, one group attacked a Cuban patrol boat off the northern coast of the island. The Revolutionary Student Directorate, another exile organization, used two boats to attack Cuba in August. Alpha 66 attacked Cuba on numerous occasions, as did other CIA saboteurs. CIA officers and "assets" were at the same time plotting to assassinate Fidel Castro.

Some of these activities came under the wing of Operation Mongoose, the covert effort engineered by Attorney

General Robert Kennedy to disrupt the Cuban economy and stir unrest on the island. As General Maxwell Taylor recalled, after the Bay of Pigs "a new urgency" was injected into "Kennedy's concern for counterinsurgency. . . ." Robert Kennedy told counterinsurgency specialist Colonel Edward Lansdale that the Bay of Pigs "insult needed to be redressed rather quickly."

Intensified economic coercion joined covert activities. The Kennedy Administration, in February 1962, banned most imports of Cuban products. Washington also pressed its NATO allies to support the "economic isolation" of Cuba. Soon Cuba was forced to pay higher freight costs, enlarge its foreign debt, and suffer factory shutdowns due to the lack of spare parts once [bought] in the United States. The effect on Cuba was not what Washington intended: more political centralization and repression, more state management, closer ties to the Soviet Union.

In early 1962, as well, Kennedy officials engineered the eviction of Cuba from the Organization of American States. The expulsion registered loudly in Havana, which interpreted it as "political preparation for an invasion."

At about the same time, the American military planning and activities, some public, some secret, demonstrated U.S. determination to cripple the Castro government. Mongoose director Lansdale noted in a top secret memorandum to the President that he designed his schemes to "help the people of Cuba overthrow the Communist regime from within Cuba. . . ." And if the revolt proved successful, the United States would have to sustain it. That is, he said, the United States would likely have to "respond promptly with military force. . . ." Indeed, "the basic plan requires complete and efficient support of the [U.S.] military." The chairman of the Joint Chiefs of Staff, General Taylor, explained in the spring of 1962 that "indigenous resources" would carry out the Operation Mongoose plan to overthrow the Cuban government, but, he added, the plan "recognizes that final success will require decisive U.S. military intervention." Because the scheme also required close cooperation with Cuban exiles, it is likely that Castro's spies picked up from the leaky Cuban community in Miami at least vague suggestions that the U. S. military was plotting action against Cuba. As CIA agents liked to joke, there were three ways to transmit information rapidly: telegraph, telephone, and tell-a-Cuban.

Actual American military maneuvers heightened Cuban fears. One well publicized U.S. exercise, staged during April—also in 1962—included 40,000 troops and an amphibious landing on a small island near Puerto Rico. Some aggressive American politicians, throughout 1962, were calling for the real thing: an invasion of Cuba. In the summer of 1962, finally, the U. S. Army began a program to create Spanish-speaking units; the Cuban exiles who signed up had as their "primary" goal, as they put it, a "return to Cuba" to battle the Castro government.

By late spring/summer 1962, then, at the very time that Havana and Moscow were contemplating defensive measures that included medium-range missiles, Cuba felt besieged from several quarters. Havana was eager for protection. The Soviet Union had become its trading partner; and the Soviets, after the Bay of Pigs, had begun military shipments that ultimately included small arms, howitzers, armored personnel carriers, patrol boats, tanks, MIG jet fighters, and surface-to-air missiles. Yet all of this weaponry, it seemed, had not deterred the United States. And, given the failure of Kennedy's multitrack program to unseat the Cuban leader, "were we right or wrong to fear direct invasion" next, asked Fidel Castro. As he said in July 1962, shortly after striking the missile-deployment agreement with the Soviets: "We must prepare ourselves for that direct invasion." He welcomed the Soviet missiles to deter the United States. And the Soviet Union grabbed at any opportunity to notch up its position in the nuclear arms race.

The Khrushchev-Castro decision to place missiles in Cuba ranks as one of the most dangerous in the Cold War. Yet had there been no exile expedition at the Bay of Pigs, no destructive covert activities, no assassination plots, no military maneuvers and plans, and no economic and diplomatic steps to harass, isolate and destroy the Castro government, there would not have been a Cuban missile crisis. "We'd carried out the Bay of Pigs operation, never intending to use American military force—but the Kremlin didn't know that," a pensive Robert McNamara recalled some twenty-five years after the event. "We were running covert operations against Castro" [and] "people in the Pentagon were even talking about a first strike [nuclear policy]. . . . So the Soviets may well have believed we were seeking Castro's overthrow *plus* a first strike capability." The former Defense Secretary concluded: "This may have led them to do what they did in Cuba."

To stress only the global dimension—Soviet–American competition, as is commonly done, is to slight the local or regional sources of the conflict. As somebody put it, we have looked too much at the international climate and too little at the local weather. To slight the local conditions is to miss the central point that Premier Nikita Khrushchev would never have had the opportunity to install dangerous missiles in the Caribbean if the United States had not been attempting to actively to overthrow the Cuban government.

If Kennedy's war against Cuba helped initiate the crisis, Kennedy must also bear responsibility for how the crisis unfolded so dangerously—how the crisis began to spin out of control. Kennedyites prided themselves on a calculated, well managed foreign policy; they believed that they could control events through the rational use of force and wise deciphering of the intentions and capabilities of friends and foes alike.

The sources for such confidence in "control" were many. First, the popularity of the concept of "control accounting" or "management control" in business and government, popularized by think tanks such as the RAND Corporation and personified in Secretary McNamara, who believed that numbers told much if not all and that almost everything could be reduced to fine-tuned plans and balances—including a "balance of terror."

Second, the Kennedy people admired a strong presidency. Critical of Dwight Eisenhower for weak leadership in the 1950s, the Kennedyites extolled a strong, activist executive who would generate policy, command the bureaucracy, and lead Congress—in short, a chief executive in firm control.

Third, at work were popular Clausewitzian notions of disciplined war—that "war in all its phases must be rationally guided by meaningful political purposes." Yet another source of the control mentality was the "can-do" style of the Kennedy team and its exaggerated sense of U.S. power and the American ability to right a world gone wrong, to remake other societies, to face down adversaries. The United States, McGeorge Bundy once remarked, "was the locomotive at the head of mankind, and the rest of the world [was] the caboose." Arthur Schlesinger captured the mood this way: "Euphoria reigned; we thought for a moment that the world was plastic and the future unlimited."

Last, Kennedy officials had a faddish fascination with anti-revolutionary, counter-insurgency doctrines, modernization theories, and covert methods, which suggested that the application of limited power could produce desired results; that violence could be managed; and that through nation-building, the United States could guide countries toward peace and prosperity, if not replicate itself abroad and win allies."

In the early 1960s, this faith in control did not go unchallenged within the administration. Schlesinger himself grew alarmed by the Administration's fervent embrace of counterinsurgency. As he wrote later, it became a "mode of warfarer . . . which nourished an American belief in the capacity and right to intervene in foreign lands, and which was both corrupting in method and futile in effect." Ambassador Adlai Stevenson remarked to a friend that "they've got the damndest bunch of boy commandos running around [here] . . . [that] you ever saw." Under Secretary of State George Ball never warmed to what he called the "high priests, who talked a strange, sacerdotal language" with "a quaintly Madison Avenue ring." He criticized the nation-building ideas of Walt Rostow as a "most presumptuous undertaking," for Ball doubted that "American professors could make bricks without the straw of experience and with indifferent and infinitely various kinds of clay." This calls to mind Sam Rayburn's remark after Vice President Johnson came back from a White House meeting thoroughly excited about the brainpower of Kennedy's young assistants: "Well, Lyndon," Rayburn said, "they may be every bit as intelligent as you say, but I'd feel a whole lot better about them if just one of them had run for sheriff once."

As it turned out, the world was not malleable, events could not be predicted or controlled with pinpoint accuracy, and the rather heady people in the Kennedy entourage proved fallible. Recent studies of the Berlin crisis, for example, reveal just how difficult it is to control local leaders or commanders, be they General Lucius Clay in West Germany or Walter Ulbricht in East Germany. Clausewitz himself had warned about "uncertainty." The "general unreliability of all information," he wrote, "presents a special problem"—"all action takes place . . . in a kind of twilight, which, like fog or moonlight, often tends to make things seem grotesque and larger than they really are."

Still, the control mentality dominated the Kennedy Administration. Exploration of its place during the missile crisis helps scholars test the question of crisis management. What emerges from the mounds of documents is not so much an enviable exercise in crisis management, but rather a study in near misses, imperfect instructions, confusions, miscalculations, and exhaustion. These negative traits gained life because President Kennedy, at the start, ruled out negotiations with either the Soviet Union or Cuba. He decided to inform the Soviets of U.S. policy through a television address rather than through diplomatic channels. The stiff arming of diplomacy seriously raised the level of danger.

Some ExComm participants recommended that negotiations be tried first. In the beginning, McGeorge Bundy urged consideration not only of military plans but of a "political track" or diplomacy. But Kennedy showed little interest in negotiations. When McNamara mentioned that diplomacy might precede military action, for example, the President immediately switched the discussion to another question: How long would it take to get air strikes organized? Conspicuously absent from the first meeting of the crisis was a serious probing of Soviet and Cuban motivation or any reflection on how U.S. actions may have helped trigger the crisis. At the second ExComm meeting of October 16, Secretary of State Dean Rusk argued against the surprise air strike that General Taylor had bluntly advocated. Rusk recommended instead "a direct message

served this carrot on a stick, adding that either the Soviets must remove the missiles promptly or the Americans would do so. The next morning Khrushchev publicly acceded to these terms.

In the heady aftermath of the crisis, President Kennedy saluted the Soviet premier for his "statesmanlike" decision and privately cautioned aides that there should be "no boasting, no gloating, not even a claim of victory. We had won by enabling Khrushchev to avoid complete humiliation—we should not humiliate him now." Robert Kennedy recalled, "What guided all [the president's] deliberations was an effort not to disgrace Khrushchev," to leave the Soviets a path of graceful retreat.

For a nation emerging from a week of terror of the missile crisis, Henry Pachter wrote in the book *Collision Course,* the "style" and "art" of Kennedy's leadership had "restored America's confidence in her own power." Sorensen, haggard from two weeks of stress and fatigue, recalled pondering the president's achievement as he leafed through a copy of *Profiles in Courage* and read the introductory quotation from Burke's eulogy of Charles James Fox: "He may live long, he may do much. But here is the summit. He never can exceed what he does this day."

2. Revisionist Histories: Reckless Kennedy Machismo

Whether or not history moves in cycles, historians typically do, and by the 1970s the once-standard odes to President Kennedy had given way to hard-edged, often hostile studies. As portrayed by the new histories, the "brief shining moment" of Kennedy's Camelot was illumined by nothing more magical than the beacons of modern public relations. From his youth Kennedy had flaunted a reckless self-indulgence encouraged by the family's founding tyrant, Joseph P. Kennedy, who imparted to his male children his own ambition, opportunism, and a shameless *machismo* toward women. A succession of affairs unencumbered by emotional involvement; publication of an intelligent but amateurish senior thesis courtesy of family friends; embellishment of a war record marked by heroism but also by some unexplained lapses in leadership; and reception of a Pulitzer Prize for *Profiles in Courage,* written in significant part by his aide, Sorensen, all reflected a pursuit of expedience more than excellence.

Critics found that Kennedy's performance as president confirmed and extended rather than overcame this pattern of flamboyant mediocrity. They discerned in his conduct of foreign policy a dismal amalgam of anti-Communist hysteria, reckless posturing, and a disturbingly gleeful crisis orientation. The results were accordingly grim, ranging from the early disaster at the Bay of Pigs to the placement—or misplacement—of more than fifteen thousand U.S. military personnel in Vietnam by the time of Kennedy's death. Scarcely learning from his early mistakes, Kennedy ignored legitimate Cuban concerns for defense against American intervention and needlessly flirted with the apocalypse in order to force the removal of missiles that scarcely affected the world military balance. To judge from their skeptical recounting, this harrowing superpower confrontation might better be termed the "misled crisis," for it stemmed from Kennedy's perception of a threat to his personal and political prestige rather than (as Americans were misinformed) to the nation's security.

No crisis existed, then, until Kennedy himself created one by forgoing private diplomacy for a public ultimatum and blockade. Considering that the United States had already planned to remove its obsolete missiles from Turkey, Kennedy should have heeded Adlai Stevenson's advice to propose immediately a trade of bases, rather than rush into a confrontation whose outcome he could neither foresee nor fully control. Instead, "From the first, he sought unconditional surrender and he never deviated from that objective." "He took an unpardonable mortal risk without just cause," Richard J. Walton wrote. "He threatened the lives of millions for appearances' sake."

The prime historical mystery to the revisionists was why any American president would needlessly play Russian roulette in the nuclear age. Critics conceded that the president may have felt "substantial political pressures" over Cuba but blamed him for having largely created those pressures with shrill, alarmist speeches. "He had been too specific about what the United States would and would not tolerate in Cuba, and his statements reduced his options," Louise FitzSimons wrote. Garry Wills also saw Kennedy as a prisoner of his own superheated rhetoric about Khrushchev, Communists, and missiles, which aroused a false sense of crisis; "If he was chained to a necessity for acting, he forged the chains himself. . . . Having fooled the people in order to lead them, Kennedy was forced to serve the folly he had induced."

Revisionist writers detected a sad consistency in Kennedy's anti-Communist hyperbole, so that the missile crisis appeared to be a logical by-product of his style rather than simply a grisly aberration. During his bid for the presidency in 1960 Kennedy had stirred voters by charging his Republican opponent, Vice President Richard Nixon, with failing to "stand up to Castro" and to Khrushchev, or to prevent a potentially lethal "missile gap" with the Soviets (in fact Americans had a vast lead). Such ideological zeal remained evident in the Ex Comm, where, David Detzer claimed, Kennedy was "more Cold Warrior" than many, "worrying about America's reputation (and maybe his own) for toughness. . . ."

Scholars in the rising genre of psychohistory traced the nation's "perilous path" in the missile crisis to "the neuroticism of Kennedy's machismo." According to Nancy Gager Clinch, the president viewed the Cuban missiles "as a personal challenge to [his] courage and status," and "In the Kennedy lexicon of manliness, not being 'chicken' was a primary value." This interpretation radiated to other fields: Sidney Lens, in his study of the military-industrial complex, found in Kennedy's "willingness to gamble with the idea of nuclear war . . . a loss of touch with reality, almost a suicidal impulse."

The more judicious of the new historians, like Richard J. Walton, tempered their personal indictments by depicting the president as "an entirely conventional Cold Warrior." Still, in addition to "his fervent anti-communism, and his acceptance of the basic assumptions of American postwar foreign policy," "the *machismo* quality in Kennedy's character" pushed him to embark on "an anti-communist crusade much more dangerous than any policy Eisenhower ever permitted." Burdened by both personal flaws and political pressures, Kennedy failed during the missile crisis to keep American policy from exhibiting, in his own words, "a collective death-wish for the world."

Like traditional historians of the missile crisis, the revisionists identified a hero, but it was the Soviet premier, Nikita Khrushchev, who withdrew the missiles at risk to his prestige. "Had Khrushchev not done so, there might well have been no later historians to exalt Kennedy," for then Kennedy and his aides, so set on victory at any cost, "would burn the world to a cinder." In effect the new histories inverted the earlier images of Kennedy as a sentry for international order standing firm against a ruthless Soviet Union. To the revisionists, Kennedy's belligerence itself posed the chief threat of global annihilation, and only the belated prudence of his counterpart in the Kremlin salvaged the peace.

3. New Evidence, Old Myths

For more than two decades after the missile crisis, scholarship churned along these two interpretive poles, grinding ever finer a limited cache of primary sources. Denied access to most records of the Ex Comm meetings, historians continued to rely on memoirs by several of President Kennedy's aides. As for the Soviets, a commentator for *Izvestia* later lamented that their press "treated the episode with socialist surrealism," refusing even to concede Khrushchev's placement of nuclear weapons in Cuba. "The word 'missiles' never appeared in the newspapers, though later, in

the Kennedy-Khrushchev letters, the phrase 'weapons the United States considers offensive' was used."

As late as 1982 a writer surveying the historical literature could reasonably assert, "There are no new facts about the Kennedys, only new attitudes." Seldom has an insight aged more rapidly or spectacularly. Beginning in the mid-to-late eighties the volcanic flow of information and inquiry in the era of *glasnost* enabled several conferences on the missile crisis in which Soviet and American scholars and former officials shared facts and feelings long guarded like vital national secrets. These exchanges, coinciding with the declassification of various Ex Comm conversations, overturned much of what both traditional and revisionist scholars had long believed, extending even to shared assumptions about the basic facts of the crisis.

The entire twenty-five-year debate over whether Kennedy was warranted in not pledging to withdraw the Turkish missiles was abruptly exposed as based on a faulty record of events. In 1987 former Secretary of State Dean Rusk revealed that Kennedy had secretly prepared a fallback plan to have UN Secretary General U Thant propose a mutual dismantling of missiles in Cuba and Turkey. This would have let the president appear to comply only with a UN request rather than a Soviet demand. Whether Kennedy would have resorted to this gambit is uncertain, but clearly he had been seeking ways to defuse the risk of war.

Kennedy's back-channel efforts to end the crisis went further still. At a conference in Moscow in 1989, the former Soviet ambassador to the United States, Anatoly Dobrynin, recalled an explicit American agreement to withdraw the missiles from Turkey, not simply a vague expression of hope that this might eventually occur. Robert Kennedy had asked him not to draw up any formal exchange of letters, saying it was important not to publicize the accord, for it could show the administration to be purveying a falsehood to the American public. Sorensen deepened the panelists' astonishment by confirming that Robert Kennedy's diaries, which formed the basis of the posthumously published book *Thirteen Days,* were indeed explicit on this part of the deal. But at the time it was still a secret even on the American side, except for the president and a few officials within the Ex Comm. Sorensen explained that in preparing *Thirteen Days* for publication, "I took it upon myself to edit that out of his diaries."

As a result of Sorensen's editing discretion, Kennedy's conciliatory policy on the Turkish missiles was distorted by histories of the crisis into a symbol of either his valiant resolve or his confrontational bent. Similarly historians had long emphasized the imminent danger of a U.S. attack on the Cuban missile sites, whether to highlight the president's grave choices or to further indict him for war-mongering. Yet McNamara insisted in 1987, "There was no way we were going to war on Monday or Tuesday [October 29 or 30]. No way!" McNamara had suggested in the Ex Comm an intermediate step of tightening the quarantine to include petroleum, oil, and lubricants, and felt "very certain" that the president would have preferred this step to authorizing an attack.

Some of the new evidence is considerably less flattering to President Kennedy's image as a peacemaker. Records of the first day of Ex Comm meetings, October 16, show both John and Robert Kennedy inclined, with most other participants, to a quick air strike. The president's vaunted containment of the risks of war also appears less reassuring than in the idealized portrayals of early histories and memoirs. The perennial boast that he only modestly opened a Pandora's box of nuclear dangers lost much of its luster as scholars inventoried what had nearly escaped. The president never learned that U.S. destroyers might have crippled a Soviet submarine with depth charges near the quarantine line, an episode that could have triggered a wider naval clash. Kennedy also did not know of a series of false nuclear alerts that, in combination with the Strategic Air Command's heightened combat readiness, DEFCON (Defense Condition) 2, posed risks of inadvertent escalation.

Still more alarming, on October 27 a U.S. reconnaissance pilot strayed into Soviet territory, a violation that Khrushchev indignantly likened to a preparation for a preemptive nuclear strike. "There's always some son of a bitch who doesn't get the word," the president said on learning of this provocation. Kennedy would have been still more displeased had he known that because of the heightened military alert, U.S. fighter planes scrambling to protect the lost pilot from Russian MiGs were armed not with conventional weapons but with nuclear missiles. Scott D. Sagan, whose resourceful study *The Limits of Safety* discloses various military miscues and malfunctions during the crisis that might have led to a wider conflict, concludes that while "President Kennedy may well have been prudent," he lacked "unchallenged final control over U.S. nuclear weapons."

Nor did the danger of unwanted escalation stem entirely from U.S. nuclear forces. According to Anatoli Gribkov, who headed operational planning for the Soviet armed forces in 1962, the Russians had placed in Cuba not only medium-range missiles but also twelve *Luna* tactical missiles with nuclear warheads designed for ground combat support. Had Kennedy ordered an invasion, the Soviet commander in Cuba, General Issa Pliyev, in the event he lost contact with Moscow, had authority to fire the *Lunas* at the American landing force. On hearing this

in 1992, a stunned McNamara exclaimed, "No one should believe that a U.S. force could have been attacked by tactical nuclear warheads without the U.S. responding with nuclear warheads. And where would it have ended? In utter disaster."

Even Ex Comm veterans who had long exalted the Kennedy administration's "rational crisis management" have renounced the very notion as romantic—and dangerous. President Kennedy's National Security Adviser, McGeorge Bundy, acknowledged, "The most important part of crisis management is not to have a crisis, because there's no telling what will happen once you're in one." McNamara agreed, "'Managing' crises is the wrong term; you don't 'manage' them because you *can't*. . . ." On the twenty-fifth anniversary of the missile crisis, Sorensen, Kennedy's loyal aide and biographer, termed the confrontation "unwise, unwarranted and unnecessary."

The new scholarship has further chipped at the Kennedys' larger-than-life image by crediting the much maligned foreign policy establishment with contributions hitherto unknown or attributed wholly to the president and his brother. Secretary of State Dean Rusk, belying later charges that he was ineffectual in the Ex Comm and nearing a breakdown, originated the contingency plan to have UN Secretary General U Thant request the withdrawal of missiles in both Turkey and Cuba. With the president's approval, Rusk prepared Andrew Cordier, the president of Columbia University and a former UN parliamentarian, to approach U Thant. Had Khrushchev not accepted an earlier American offer, Rusk's idea might have served as the basis for a settlement under UN auspices.

The administration's celebrated "acceptance" of Khrushchev's tacit proposals on October 26 rather than his sterner public demands the next day—a ploy once credited to Robert Kennedy alone—in fact had a complex patrimony, Llewellyn Thompson, the former ambassador to the Soviet Union, whom Robert Kennedy's memoir credits generously but generally for "uncannily accurate" advice that was "surpassed by none," may have first suggested the outlines of this strategy. Bundy, Assistant Secretary of State for Latin American Affairs Edwin Martin, and others also offered variations on this gambit in informal discussions. Robert Kennedy formally proposed the idea in an Ex Comm meeting and drafted a response with Sorensen. But the view that this was his exclusive brainchild—a view nurtured by his own seemingly definitive account— underscores that memoirs seldom reveal an author's limitations other than a selective memory.

The very machinery of government, long viewed as a cumbersome, bumbling foil to a dynamic chief executive, now appears to have been a responsive (if not fully respected) partner. Contrary to early accounts, the failure to remove American missiles from Turkey before the crisis did not stem from unwitting bureaucratic sabotage of a presidential directive. Rather, Kennedy himself had acquiesced in the delay to avoid embarrassing a Turkish government that had only recently hinged its prestige on accepting the missiles. The president may well have been dismayed by their continued presence, but he was in no way surprised by it in the Ex Comm meetings. Rusk dismissed reports of the president's alleged betrayal by a lazy State Department, saying, "He never expressed any irritation to me because he had been fully briefed by me on that situation."

These and other discoveries all augur a far richer, more precise understanding of Kennedy's role in the missile crisis. But they have yet to produce an interpretive framework to encompass them. Should historians conclude that the president was less militant than once thought because he sanctioned a trade of missile bases? Or more militant because he initially leaned toward bombing Cuba? Does he now appear more adept at crisis management, given his elaborate fallback plans for a possible settlement through the UN? Or simply lucky to survive his own ignorance of swaggering American officers, false nuclear alerts, and nuclear-equipped Soviet forces in Cuba? Was the president more dependent on the Ex Comm in light of contributions by unsung heroes such as Llewellyn Thompson? Or did he treat the Ex Comm as having limited relevance, as in his concealment from most members of the private deal on the Turkish missiles? On these and other issues, the additions to our knowledge have been individually striking but cumulatively chaotic.

A way to make sense of these seemingly disparate and even conflicting pieces of evidence is to view President Kennedy as a moderate leader in a militant age. His vision at all times extended beyond the Ex Comm's deliberations, encompassing the formidable national consensus that the Soviet base in Cuba should be challenged militarily. Honing his policies on the grindstone of political necessity, Kennedy ordered a blockade of the island and considered still bolder action because he knew that Soviet leaders and the American public alike would otherwise view him as fatally irresolute. Yet within his circumscribed political setting, he proved more willing than most Americans, both in and outside his circle of advisers, to limit bellicose displays and to offer the Russians timely, if covert, concessions.

Despite a growing awareness of Kennedy's political constraints, the revisionist image of a man driven by both insecurity and arrogance to rash policies has proven extraordinarily resilient. Thomas G. Peterson, who

incisively recounts the covert war against Castro waged by two administrations, judges Kennedy's brand of cold war leadership more dangerous than Eisenhower's. "Driven by a desire for power," Paterson writes, "Kennedy personalized issues, converting them into tests of will." Far from simply continuing "his predecessor's anti-Castro policies," Kennedy "significantly increased the pressures against the upstart island" out of an obsession with Castro. "He thus helped generate major crises, including the October 1962 missile crisis. Kennedy inherited the Cuban problem—and he made it worse."

In *The Dark Side of Camelot* (1997) the award-winning journalist Seymour Hersh cranks up to full strength the assault on Kennedy's character that had stamped revisionist writings of the 1970s. Contrasting Khrushchev's "common sense and dread of nuclear war" with Kennedy's "fanaticism" during the missile crisis, Hersh concludes: "For the first time in his presidency, Kennedy publicly brought his personal recklessness, and his belief that the normal rules of conduct did not apply to him, to his foreign policy. . . . The Kennedy brothers brought the world to the edge of war in their attempts to turn the dispute into a political asset."

Textbooks too have incorporated into their "objective" look at American history the notion that Kennedy's belligerence is the key to understanding his foreign policy. In a leading work, *Promises to Keep: The United States Since World War II* (1999), Paul Boyer finds that "Kennedy's approach to Cold War leadership differed markedly from Eisenhower's. Shaped by an intensely competitive family and a hard-driving father whom he both admired and feared, he eagerly sought to prove his toughness to the Soviet adversary."

The focus on Kennedy's supposed confrontational bent to explain his policies reaches its fullest—and most problematic—development in the aptly titled study by Thomas C. Reeves, *A Question of Character*. Reeves's Kennedy was "deficient in integrity, compassion, and temperance," defects that clearly influenced his Cuban policy, from the decision [in 1961] to ignore the moral and legal objections to an invasion, and through the creation of Operation Mongoose." During the missile crisis too, "Kennedy at times seemed unduly militant, and his aggressive and competitive instincts led him to grant the [diplomatic] initiative to the Soviets at critical points where more skilled diplomacy might have avoided it." Reeves dismisses claims that the president sought never to "challenge the other side needlessly," with the comment, "Neither, of course, were the Kennedys prepared to accept anything short of victory." Faced with the mounting evidence of Kennedy's prudence, Reeves allows that the president's "personal agony over the conflict, his several efforts to avoid bloodshed, and his willingness to make a trade of Turkish for Cuban missiles, revealed a deeper concern for the nation and the world than many who knew him well might have suspected." But little else leavens Reeves's generally dour portrait of a president whose personal failings compounded the risks of war. Like other revisionist scholars, Reeves dutifully ingests the new scholarship on the missile crisis but cannot easily digest it.

The hazards of treating presidential character as the Rosetta stone to make sense of policies in the missile crisis should by now give pause to even the most confirmed of Kennedy's admirers or detractors. The emergence of contributions by Rusk, Thompson, Bundy, Martin, and other establishment figures has made it more difficult to portray the Kennedys as lonely titans striding across the political stage with ideas and policies uniquely their own. And, granted that Kennedy was "the key decisionmaker," he nonetheless acted within tightly defined parameters that had little to do with the character of the chief executive.

The amplified record of decision-making has also recast or removed issues that long galvanized and framed debates over Kennedy's character. Interpretations of the president's supposedly tough policy on the Jupiter missiles now appear to have rested on accounts that, by embellishment and concealment alike, exaggerated his brinkmanship. The puncturing of those distortions should deflate as well the images of Kennedy as either a surpassingly valiant leader or a Neanderthal cold warrior.

Traditional historians, it is now clear, both sanitized and romanticized the historical record in portraying President Kennedy as an ideal fusion of hawkish resolve and dovish reserve, who forced out the Cuban missiles without making needless concessions or taking heedless risks. In fact Kennedy resolved the crisis not simply through toughness and diplomatic legerdemain but by pledging to remove the missiles from Turkey, a deal he publicly spurned and his partisans long proudly but wrongly denied. And while Kennedy's defenders lauded his rejection of calls for air strikes and invasion, they overlooked the provocation of his actual policies, including the plots against Castro, the push for ever greater American nuclear superiority, and, of course, the blockade of Cuba.

The historical record is even more resistant to revisionist portraits of a president whose psychological deformities impelled him to risk peace for the sake of personal glory or catharsis. These accounts were from the first suspect, whether in drawing tortured connections between Kennedy's womanizing and his foreign policy or deriding him for sharing the beliefs of his own generation rather than a later one. They simply collapse under the weight of evidence that, during the gravest crisis of the cold war, Kennedy repeatedly proved more prudent than many aides, both civilian and military. As he told his brother Robert on October 26, "If anybody is around to write after this, they are going to understand that we made every effort to find peace and every effort to give our adversary room to move. I am not going to push the Russians an inch beyond what is necessary."

Ernest May and Philip Zelikow, editors of an invaluable annotated record of the Ex Comm sessions, marvel that "[Kennedy] seems more alive to the possibilities and consequences of each new development than anyone else." On October 27, with pressure mounting for decisive action, the president "is the only one in the room who is determined not to go to war over obsolete missiles in Turkey." May and Zelikow acknowledge Kennedy's partial responsibility for this superpower clash but deem it "fortunate" that "[he] was the president charged with managing the crisis."

The most telling dismissal of revisionist rhetoric comes from Kennedy's adversaries themselves. Shortly after the crisis ended, Khrushchev admitted to an American journalist, "Kennedy did just what I would have done if I had been in the White House instead of the Kremlin." In his memoirs the former Soviet leader lamented Kennedy's death as "a great loss," for "he was gifted with the ability to resolve international conflicts by negotiation, as the whole world learned during the so-called Cuban crisis. Regardless of his youth he was a real statesman." As for those "clever people" who "will tell you that Kennedy was to blame for the tensions which might have resulted in war," Khrushchev said, "You have to keep in mind the era in which we live." Castro, for his part, believed Kennedy "acted as he did partly to save Khrushchev, out of fear that any successor would be tougher."

The misrepresentations of Kennedy's leadership go deeper than the debates over whether he was heroic or merely reckless, idealistic or expedient, poised or impulsive. Scholars have so focused on Kennedy's style, aura, temperament, and character as to slight, if not obscure, the crucial framework of national values that he necessarily accommodated and largely shared. The missile crisis, as much as anything, is the story of how Kennedy faithfully reflected a remarkable consensus in political institutions and public opinion regarding America's role as Free World champion in the nuclear age.

Contrary to the impression left by Kennedy's partisans, the Executive Committee he formed to advise him during the missile crisis was never a sealed laboratory for reinventing American policy. Nor was it, as the revisionists later had it, a forum for venting personal demons at public expense. Rather, like any leader in a democracy, Kennedy self-consciously labored under constraints imposed by public opinion, the Congress, the military, the CIA, and a host of civilian constituencies. To argue that he could or should have disdained these pressures is to imply a preference for philosopher kings over accountable presidents. Whatever the appeal of such arguments, they leave little room for either the ideal or the reality of American democracy.

Americans in the early sixties overwhelmingly regarded the prospect of missiles in Cuba as intolerably threatening and judged leaders by their firmness against Soviet encroachments. Whoever occupied the Oval Office would therefore have faced intense pressures to demand removal of the missiles, direct low-level military action against Cuba, and avoid apparent concessions to the Russians. Buffeted by partisan sniping, public opinion, and the force of inherited policies, President Kennedy pursued all of these options. Throughout he sought to minimize confrontation with the Soviet Union to a degree consistent with his political survival.

Accounting for the full political weight of entrenched national attitudes can help resolve the central paradox of Kennedy's policies during the missile crisis, which reflected elements of both recklessness and restraint. Considered against the background of his times, Kennedy appears a rational leader, conciliatory and even empathetic towards his counterpart in the Kremlin. Yet he also represented a political culture marked by fear and bluster, qualities stoked by an uncontrolled arms race and Manichen visions of the East-West divide. To ask which was the "real" Kennedy is to speak of a chimera: a leader somehow extricable from his era.

Kennedy embodied the anti–Soviet, anti-Communist values—and obsessions–of his day, though with more skepticism and caution than most contemporaries. His relative detachment from cold war dogmas was not enough to avoid a crisis caused by mutual misjudgments. Still, it allowed for a crucial modicum of flexibility and restraint that helped keep this crisis from spiraling toward war.

It may be tempting to conclude that Kennedy's avoidance of a wider conflict warrants cynicism rather than celebration, as the bare minimum one should expect of any sane leader in the nuclear age. Yet the obstacles to military restraint between states are no less daunting simply because the dangers are so great. Whatever Kennedy's missteps, he proved—together with Soviet Premier Khrushchev—that leaders can resist the lures of unchecked escalation even while mired in a climate of mutual suspicion, fear, and hostility. This achievement may yet gain new luster as nuclear weapons spread to other nations steeped in their own bitter rivalries, a development auguring two, three, many missile crises to come.

ROBERT WEISBROT is a professor of history at Colby College in Waterville, Maine, where he is also on the advisory committee for the African American Studies Program. He is the author of *From the Founding of the Southern Christian Leadership Conference to the Assassination of Malcolm X* (1957–65) (Chelsea House, 1994).

EXPLORING THE ISSUE

Did President John F. Kennedy Cause the Cuban Missile Crisis?

Critical Thinking and Reflection

1. Critically analyze the disparity between the image of President Kennedy's foreign policy versus the reality.
2. Critically analyze the strengths and weaknesses of the new sources about the Cuban missile crisis—such as declassified government memos, transcriptions of the Ex-Comm meetings, and transcriptions of several conferences held in Moscow and Havana where participants and their children recalled the roles they played during the crisis.
3. Compare and contrast the traditional view, the revisionist view, and the post-revisionist view of the roles of Kennedy and Khrushchev in resolving the Cuban missile crisis.
4. Compare and contrast and critically evaluate the interpretations of Paterson and Weisbrot as to the causes and solutions of the Cuban missile crisis.

Is There Common Ground?

All writers agree on the timing of the events. Khrushchev started the crisis in the summer of 1962 when Russian ships brought offensive Intercontinental Ballistic Missiles (IBMs) to the island. Kennedy responded in a nontraditional way in the beginning by announcing over radio and television that the United States was establishing a "quarantine" or "blockade" around the island. After several attempts at back door diplomacy with Robert Kennedy, the Attorney General and the President's brother, pledging not to invade Cuba and privately to withdraw obsolete missiles in Turkey and Italy within the next six months, Khrushchev's negotiator agreed to take the missiles out of Cuba immediately.

The basic question asked is which national leader was most responsible for bringing the post–World War II superpowers to the brink of nuclear war. Both Kennedy and Khrushchev wanted to work out a compromise. Both were pressured by hard liners on their respective advising committees. Suppose the Russian ships crossed the blockade line and refused to turn back? Did the Russian commander have the right to start a war without checking with Khrushchev? If the United States had invaded Cuba, how much damage would American ships have suffered? If troop losses mounted because the CIA underestimated the number of Russian soldiers and ICBMs on the island, would the war have escalated to a full-scale nuclear one?

Two random incidents occurred, which might have led to war had more belligerent leaders other than the two Ks been in power. First, on October 27 a U-2 was shot down over Cuba by a surface-to-air missile. Who did it? Cubans? Russians? Kennedy decided to bypass his own committee and have his brother go behind the scenes to negotiate

with Khrushchev's aide. Meanwhile, Khrushchev ignored a U-2 flight whose pilot accidentally overflew the northeastern portion of the Soviet Union and was rescued by American planes without incident.

Managing a crisis such as the showdown in Cuba demonstrates that there is a lot of luck to keep events from spinning out of control. The reader need only study America's crisis over the Pearl Harbor attack, the escalation of the Vietnam War, and the 9/11 attacks, which led to the war on terror to realize the value of peacefully resolving the Cuban missile crisis.

Create Central

www.mhhe.com/createcentral

Additional Resources

Michael Dobbs, *One Minute to Midnight: Kennedy, Khrushchev, and Castro on the Brink of Nuclear War* (Alfred A. Knopf, 2008).

Aleksandr Fursenko and Timothy Naftali, *"One Hell of a Gamble": Khrushchev, Castro, and Kennedy, 1958–1964* (W.W. Norton, 1997).

Ernest R. May and Philip D. Zelikow, eds., *The Kennedy Tapes: Inside the White House During the Cuban Missile Crisis* (Harvard University Press, 1997).

James A. Nathan, ed., *The Cuban Missile Crisis Revisited* (St. Martin's Press, 1997).

Sheldon M. Stern, *The Cuban Missile Crisis in American Memory: Myths Versus Reality* (Stanford University Press, 2012).

Internet References . . .

Cold War: Cuban Missile Crisis

www.loc.gov/exhibits/archives/colc.html

Cuban Missile Crisis

www.history.com/topics/cold-war
/cuban-missile-crisis

Cuban Missile Crisis

www.jfklibrary.org/JFK/JFK-in-History
/Cuban-Missile-Crisis.aspx

The Cuban Missile Crisis, 1962: The 40th Anniversary

www2.gwu.edu/~nsarchiv/nsa/cuba_mis_cri
/moment.htm

The Cuban Missile Crisis, October 1962

https://history.state.gov/milestones/1961-1968
/cuban-missile-crisis

Selected, Edited, and with Issue Framing Material by:
Larry Madaras, *Howard Community College*
and
James M. SoRelle, *Baylor University*

ISSUE

Did Southern White Christians Actively Support Efforts to Maintain Racial Segregation?

YES: Carolyn Renée Dupont, from "A Strange and Serious Christian Heresy: Massive Resistance and the Religious Defense of Segregation," New York University Press (2013)

NO: David L. Chappell, from "Broken Churches, Broken Race: White Southern Religious Leadership and the Decline of White Supremacy," University of North Carolina Press (2004)

Learning Outcomes

After reading this issue, you will be able to:

- Understand the role religion played both in support of and in opposition to the desegregation movement.
- Evaluate the ways in which white southerners employed theological arguments to support racial segregation.
- Discuss the response of southern white ministers and laity to the goals of the civil rights movement.
- Assess the connection between religion and politics in reaction to desegregation campaigns in the South.
- Analyze the apparent contradiction between adherence to Christian principles and attitudes toward racial equality among many white southerners.

ISSUE SUMMARY

YES: Carolyn Renée Dupont argues that in the post-*Brown* years of the 1950s and 1960s most white Mississippians, including Christian ministers and laypersons, zealously drew upon biblical texts, religious tracts, and sermons to craft a folk theology supporting massive resistance to racial segregation.

NO: David L. Chappell concludes that white southern religious leaders from the mainline Protestant denominations, preferring peace and social order, failed to provide sufficient support to enable segregationist politicians to mount a united front in defending the doctrine of white supremacy.

On May 17, 1954, the U.S. Supreme Court announced the results of its deliberation in the case of *Brown v. Board of Education of Topeka et al.* In a unanimous decision engineered by new Chief Justice Earl Warren, the Court paved the way for the collapse of a legally supported racial segregation system that had dominated black-white relations in the United States since the *Plessy v. Ferguson* case of 1896.

The *Brown* ruling represented a significant victory for the National Association for the Advancement of Colored People (NAACP), the nation's leading civil rights organization, which had spearheaded a legal action campaign for four decades that had produced constitutional victories in the areas of housing, transportation, and voting, as well as education, in an effort to restore enforcement of the Fourteenth and Fifteenth Amendments in matters regarding race. Most African Americans saw the *Brown* decision as a vital step in finally eliminating separate and unequal facilities throughout the country and realizing the democratic promise of life in the United States. In contrast, the Warren Court's decision sent shock waves through the white South, and even as local school board representatives publicly announced that they would comply with the Court's ruling, back-channel efforts were quickly underway to block biracial schools. Unintentionally aided by the Supreme Court's refusal to establish a definite time frame by which desegregation of public schools should take place, many white southerners interpreted the Court's dictum to act "with all deliberate speed" to mean "never." Following the lead of a group of over one hundred southern congressmen who signed "The Southern Manifesto" that charged the Warren Court with abuse of power and pledged resistance to the enforcement of *Brown*, southern politicians at the local and state level, business leaders who formed White Citizens' Councils, and members of a reinvigorated Ku Klux Klan all joined to resist implementation of the *Brown* decision, claiming that they were only protecting traditional regional mores from the intrusive arm of the federal government.

In the face of this program of "massive resistance," many African Americans came to the conclusion that the NAACP's legal strategy was insufficient to guarantee genuine change in the realm of civil rights. The time seemed to be ripe for a new approach and a broader focus beyond public school desegregation. In 1955, the arrest of Rosa Parks and the subsequent bus boycott in Montgomery, Alabama, appeared to offer a powerful new weapon in the form of nonviolent direct action. Although most closely associated with the leadership approach of Dr. Martin Luther King, Jr., who rose to national prominence from his leadership role in the Montgomery campaign, direct action had long been an instrument for change in the black community. Black residents had employed this strategy in several American cities in the first decade of the twentieth century to oppose segregated seating on municipal streetcars; labor leader A. Philip Randolph had threatened the Roosevelt administration with direct action protests in 1941 in an effort to end racially discriminatory hiring practices in the nation's defense industries and segregation in the armed services; and the Congress of Racial Equality, organized in 1942, had conducted numerous nonviolent challenges to Jim Crow in the 1940s and 1950s. Beginning in 1960, African American college students, joined by their peers at all-white colleges and universities, sparked wide national attention to direct action and passive resistance through sit-in demonstrations that succeeded in desegregating lunch counters and restaurants

in over 200 southern communities. For his own part, Martin Luther King depended on nonviolent direct action to carry the day in his campaign to desegregate downtown facilities in Birmingham, Alabama, to lobby for federal action leading to the Civil Rights Act of 1964, and to stimulate broad support for political empowerment though voter registration drives in Selma, Alabama, and passage of the Voting Rights Act in 1965.

The literature on the civil rights movement is extensive. August Meier, Elliott Rudwick, and Francis L. Broderick, eds., *Black Protest Thought in the Twentieth Century*, 2nd ed. (Bobbs-Merrill, 1971) present a collection of documents that places the activities of the 1950s and 1960s in a larger framework. The reflections of many of the participants of the movement are included in Howell Raines, *My Soul Is Rested: The Story of the Civil Rights Movement in the Deep South* (G. P. Putnam, 1977). August Meier's contemporary assessment, "On the Role of Martin Luther King," *Crisis* (1965), in many ways remains the most insightful analysis of King's leadership. More detailed studies include David J. Garrow's Pulitzer Prize winning *Bearing the Cross: Martin Luther King, Jr., and the Southern Christian Leadership Conference* (William Morrow, 1986); and Harvard Sitkoff, *King: Pilgrimage to the Mountaintop* (Hill and Wang, 2008). Taylor Branch's award-winning trilogy *America in the King Years* (Simon & Schuster, 1988, 1998, 2006) is a wonderful read. For an understanding of the major civil rights organizations in the 1960s, see August Meier and Elliott Rudwick, *CORE: A Study in the Civil Rights Movement, 1942–1968* (Oxford University Press, 1973), Clayborne Carson, *In Struggle: SNCC and the Black Awakening of the 1960s* (Harvard University Press, 1981), Adam Fairclough, *To Redeem the Soul of America: The Southern Christian Leadership Conference and Martin Luther King, Jr.* (University of Georgia Press, 1987), and Patricia Sullivan, *Lift Every Voice: The NAACP and the Making of the Civil Rights Movement* (New Press, 2009). Finally, the texture of the civil rights movement is captured brilliantly in Henry Hampton's documentary series *Eyes on the Prize*.

The issue under consideration examines the role of religion in the modern civil rights movement. On the one hand, there is little doubt that religion, especially in the form of the Christian church, played an indisputable role in the efforts of African Americans to win full equality through their freedom struggle. As Aldon Morris has insisted in *The Origins of the Civil Rights Movement: Black Communities Organizing for Change* (Free Press, 1984), "The black church functioned as the institutional center of the modern civil rights movement. Churches provided the movement with an organized mass base; a leadership of clergymen largely economically independent of the larger white society and skilled in the art of managing people and resources; an institutionalized financial base through which protest was financed; and meeting places where the masses planned tactics and strategies and collectively committed themselves to the struggle." Martin Luther King, Jr.'s leadership reinforces the importance of this connection between religion and social struggle and is evident in virtually all of his sermons, speeches, and writings. For King, the strategy of nonviolent direct action was as much a way of life as his Christian witness. See, for example, James Melvin Washington, ed., *Testament of Hope: The Essential Writings of Martin Luther King, Jr.* (Harper & Row, 1986) and Clayborne Carson, ed., *The Autobiography of Martin Luther King, Jr.* (Warner Books, 1998). It should be remembered, however, that King was not alone in this regard. Most early CORE members came to the cause of civil rights through their commitment to Christian pacifism; many of the early members of the Student Nonviolent Coordinating Committee (SNCC), such as John Lewis, James Bevel, Sandra Cason, and Dorothy Burlage, were drawn to the movement by their religious associations; and all of the members of the Southern Christian Leadership Conference, like King, couched their civil rights commitments within the tenets of their faith.

But what about the vast majority of white southerners for whom religious (especially Christian) faith and practice was a central part of their everyday lives? For some, there is no doubt that their understanding of the Gospels and the teachings of Jesus led them to support efforts by their African American brothers and sisters to gain full citizenship rights, though such sympathies could incur the wrath of their friends and neighbors, leading to physical harassment and social ostracism. Along this interpretational line, historian Paul Harvey, in *Freedom's Coming: Religious Culture and the Shaping of the South from the Civil War through the Civil Rights Era* (University of North Carolina Press, 2007), describes a "folk theology of

segregation" that originated in the postbellum South and explains how black and white religious folk challenged the theologically grounded racism held by most white southerners and ultimately helped to end Jim Crow. For others, religion became a bulwark to thwart attempts to bring down the walls of racial segregation. Charles Marsh, in his *God's Long Summer: Stories of Faith and Civil Rights* (Princeton University Press, 1997) reveals how white leaders as different as Douglas Hudgins, the pastor of First Baptist Church of Jackson, Mississippi, and Sam Bowers, the Imperial Wizard of the White Knights of the Ku Klux Klan, subscribed to a theology that reinforced a commitment to segregation and racial purity.

The essays that follow evaluate how white southerners related to assaults on the Jim Crow system through the prism of their religious faith and practices. Focusing on the state of Mississippi, Carolyn Renée Dupont asserts that segregationists called upon religion to defend the racial status quo by weaving together biblical literalism, political conservatism, and racial segregation. Ordinary pastors and laypersons produced religious tracts and sermon reprints that portrayed segregation as a universal natural law of God, and secular organizations, such as the White Citizens' Councils, recruited clergy to their ranks to help promote a religious defense of segregation.

In contrast, David Chappell notes that while most white southerners held deeply racist beliefs, the ministers of the dominant Protestant denominations (Baptists, Methodists, and Presbyterians) condemned racial prejudice as unbiblical and wrong, and the major organizations representing Southern Presbyterians and Southern Baptists even called for compliance with the *Brown* decision. For most white southern religious authorities, Chappell says, maintaining peace and social order were more important than defying desegregation and prevented them from aligning their interests with segregationist politicians who fomented anti-civil rights efforts in the 1950s and 1960s.

YES ←

Carolyn Renée Dupont

A Strange and Serious Christian Heresy: Massive Resistance and the Religious Defense of Segregation

"**D**uring the past two years there has been a deluge of materials spread over the face of the South in which various Biblical proofs are given for divine sanction of racial segregation . . . not only the ignorant woolhat-hill folk [are] accepting the exegesis of the hate mongers but the more refined as well. . . . The pamphlets, articles, and tracts [are] written by preachers and religious educators well known in the circle of the target audience." Thus observed Will Campbell, the progressive Mississippi Baptist expatriate, in 1957. The writer Lillian Smith confirmed that "[t]here is a great deal of this kind of talk going around these days, quoting chapter and verse, etc." Other religious leaders described how "many segregationists cloak their activities with quotations from the scriptures . . . [and] claims [are] made by certain ministers that the Bible endorse[s] segregation." Indeed, southern Christians seemed so zealous to cite biblical proofs for segregation that Campbell concluded "some of the racial hate being peddled in the name of Jesus Christ" constituted "a strange and serious Christian heresy."

The biblical case for racial segregation enjoyed a renaissance after the *Brown* decision because religion itself seemed a threat to southern apartheid. Religious assaults on segregation included the major denominations' support for *Brown*, the faith-based activism of many black leaders, and the growing conviction in some circles that the Christian faith mandated racial equality. While black activists and their sympathizers wished that white religion would offer a more vigorous call to racial justice, white southerners regarded as dangerous even the limited support religion had conferred on the quest for black equality.

The faith-based indictment of the southern social system, left unchallenged and allowed to grow, could prove disastrous for the project of massive resistance. If Mississippians heeded the voices of their coreligionists outside the Deep South, their energy for the fight against integration might flag. If they heard about the sinfulness of segregation in their churches and religious literature, they might come to doubt the rightness of Mississippi's path of defiance. Surely, they would lack the conviction to resist the Supreme Court, to suffer the closing of public schools, and to visit punishment on their fellows who violated the bonds of white solidarity. Only at great peril could massive resisters forego a religious defense, for the moral challenge to segregation could cost their campaign what it needed most—the enthusiastic and unwavering support of ordinary Mississippians. Because religion now jeopardized segregation, segregationists called on religion to defend it.

The religious case for segregation took a variety of guises and appeared in many places in the form of an influential and pervasive phenomenon Paul Harvey has described as "segregationist folk theology." Though it drew on biblical texts describing the curse of Ham, the tower of Babel, and the example of Israel as a racially exclusive people, segregationist folk theology functioned as an orthodoxy that wove together biblical literalism, political conservatism, and racial segregation, elevating all three to equally revered status. Tugging at any single strand constituted a heretical unraveling of the entire fabric. Those who articulated these ideas took as natural and God-ordained the social world they saw around them, but except for the essential assumption that heaven smiled on the racial hierarchy, the arguments they marshaled displayed little consistency.

Given the thorough blending of its secular and religious aspects, this belief system cropped up in venues outside pulpits, Sunday school classes, radio sermons, and religious literature. Indeed, segregationist folk theology found expression nearly everywhere—in secular newspapers and organizations, at the state's universities and schools, at county rallies, and in legislative chambers. Though it lay dormant much of the time, when segregation seemed imperiled, it erupted with fury through the normally placid surface of life-as-usual. . . .

Segregationist Folk Theology

. . . The multifaceted nature of this religious defense—its reliance on a variety of extra-biblical evidence and claims—displayed the strength, rather than the weakness, of these arguments in the minds of those who espoused them. These expositors believed they had identified a principle so pervasive in its practice and application that it extended beyond the Bible. In a world defined by a God-ordained principle so significant and sacrosanct as they imagined, hierarchies of all sorts revealed themselves throughout the created order.

Layfolk and ministers without powerful denominational connections articulated this theology far more often than religious elites or pastors of large and prominent congregations. The leaders of the Mississippi Baptist Convention, the editors of the *Baptist Record*, and the pastor of Mississippi's largest Baptist church never gave voice to it as such. Neither did the bishop of Mississippi's two white Methodist conferences and the pastors of large Methodist congregations. At the same time, however, Mississippi's most influential Presbyterian leader, Dr. G. T. Gillespie, provides an important exception to this generalization. President of the Mississippi Synod of the Southern Presbyterian Church, Gillespie authored "A Christian View of Segregation," perhaps the best-known and most representative example of the folk theology of segregation. Gillespie and a few others notwithstanding, the folk theology of segregation came far more often from Mississippi's ordinary pastors and from its eager laymen.

Of extant sermons or tracts advertised as "biblical defenses of segregation," few hewed so exclusively to biblical sources as a 1953 sermon preached by Reverend J. C. Wasson, a Methodist minister in the small Delta town of Itta Bena. Wasson offered classic segregationist readings of two texts often employed for this purpose: Genesis 9:18–27, which details the story of Noah's curse on his grandson, "Cursed be Canaan; a slave of slaves shall he be to his brothers," and Deuteronomy 7:1–6, in which God tells the children of Israel, "You shall not make marriages with [surrounding tribes], giving your daughters to their sons or taking their daughters for your sons." In elucidating the Genesis account, Wasson explained that Noah pronounced the curse because Canaan's father, Ham, having found Noah drunk and naked in his tent, had informed his brothers and so "had on this occasion treated his father with contempt or reprehensible levity." Wasson continued: "The word, Ham, means hot and it signifies burnt or

black. Ham's descendants moved southward into Africa, a hot country, without any doubt this was the beginning of the niger [*sic*] race." Wasson preferred the spelling "niger" because, "the words negro and nigger are not in the Bible. In Acts 13:1 is the only place in the Bible where the black race is designated by its proper name: 'And Simeon that was called Niger,' niger the I is a long I, pronounced Ni-ger, the word means black." The Deuteronomy text prescribed "death" as "the penalty for violating the law of segregation," from which Wasson inferred, "No intelligent Bible student can deny that God is the author of segregation." Wasson then proceeded to identify the law of Moses as a command to "be segregated to keep their race pure" and to elucidate other Old Testament stories—the division of Israel into two kingdoms and the Babylonian captivity—as punishment for the sin of miscegenation.

Another Methodist, the prominent attorney John Creighton Satterfield, elaborated the biblical foundations of segregation at a forum at Millsaps College in 1958. While acknowledging that both segregationists and integrationists could find biblical support for their views, Satterfield proceeded to dismember integrationists' favorite passages. Explicating a passage from the apostle Paul's sermon at Mars Hill in Acts 17:26, "God has made of one blood all nations of men to dwell on all the face of the earth," the Methodist layman argued that integrationists who used this verse "imply that there are no differences in men and read into Paul's statement something that he probably did not have in mind." Furthermore, Satterfield maintained, those who favored racial mixing stopped reading the verse too soon. "Paul went on to say 'and hath appointed the bounds of their habitation.'" That last phrase, Satterfield claimed, "justifies the segregation of the races." Satterfield proceeded next to Galatians 3:26–28, another reference favored by religious enemies of segregation: "In Christ Jesus, you are sons of God through faith—there is neither Jew nor Greek, there is neither slave nor free, there is neither male nor female, for you are all one in Christ Jesus." Stripping this verse of its racially egalitarian implications, Satterfield observed: "I am sure neither you nor I believe it is necessary to abolish the differences between male and female in order to live a Christian life." He went on to explain that the "South's system of segregation is not based on 'race prejudice' but on 'race preference.'"

Most biblical defenses of segregation, however, did not stick so closely to biblical texts, and many actually mixed scriptural arguments with other types of evidence. William W. Miller's sermon, "The Bible and Segregation," presented on radio station WTOK in early March, 1956, followed this model. Even though Miller, pastor of the Bible Baptist Church in Meridian, declared that "THE BIBLE DOES CLEARLY AND INDISPUTABLY TEACH SEGREGATION OF THE RACES [emphasis in the original]," only a fraction of his sermon enumerated the classic segregationist texts. He devoted the far greater bulk of his message to assailing the theological credentials of those who advanced a Christian mandate for black equality and elucidating the communist-inspired origins of the movement for racial justice and, especially, of the NAACP. Miller concluded his address with an admonition to the "dear Negro friends and brethren" who might have been in his listening audience: "renounce, the devil inspired, Communist supported and directed NAACP as the slithering serpent that it is. . . . Don't imagine that in following the NAACP segregation line you are walking in the Christian faith. Don't think for a moment that you can pray to God and get His blessing upon a course of action which is antithetical to the Christian faith."

The Hattiesburg Baptist layman, D. B. Red, authored two tracts in the pattern of Miller's sermon. Red's "A Corrupt Tree Bringeth Forth Evil Fruit" took its title from Matthew 7:17, advertising on its cover its purpose as "A plea for RACIAL SEGREGATION Based on Scripture, History and World Conditions." The first half of the tract traced the history of Israel as a people commanded to remain distinct from those around them. Moses, Ezra, Nehemiah, and Hosea had all admonished the Israelites not to intermarry with neighboring tribes. In this rendering, as in Wasson's, the children of Israel failed to obey, sought integration, and reaped dire consequences. Red then turned from biblical texts to world politics, history, and geology. He cited turmoil in Africa and India as a result of integration, explained the role of communism in instigating the movement for racial equality, offered the example of Reconstruction as a moment when the South almost lost its way in the face of forced integration, and finally, detailed the beauty of the created order: "Was it not wise to separate the various minerals instead of pouring them all together?" Mississippi's Senator James O. Eastland endorsed the tract for its "masterful job in marshalling both biblical and secular arguments." Red's other self-published tract, "Race Mixing A Religious Fraud," used much of the same material as an attempt to answer religious "race mixers" who advocated integration. Red admonished in his closing paragraphs: "Is your denomination helping to push us down the Devil's highway of racial integration? If so, remember who is paying the bills and whose civilization is going down the drain. . . . The best way to be heard is to speak through the ballot box and collection plate."

Mississippians contributed to and drank from the stream of tracts and sermon reprints with similar themes,

content, and format that circulated throughout the South. While probably the most famous and well-traveled biblical defense of segregation came from the Mississippi Presbyterian divine, Dr. G. T. Gillespie, his polemic also leaned heavily on secular as well as religious arguments, though its Citizens' Council promoters circulated it under the title "A Christian View on Segregation." The piece began by describing white southerners' abhorrence of racial intermarriage as part of their elevated culture and depicted segregation as a universal law of nature that resulted in improvements wherever it was applied: "The phenomenal development of the race horse, the draft horse, the beef and dairy breeds of cattle furnish impressive evidence that segregation promotes development and progress . . . whereas the intermingling of breeding stock results invariably in the production of 'scrubs' or mongrel types, and the downgrading of the whole herd." When Gillespie turned to the Bible for evidence, he cited many of the same passages and examples as those developed by Wasson and Red, and then finished with a quick tour of American history, calling on statements by Thomas Jefferson, Abraham Lincoln, and Booker T. Washington to argue that segregation "represents the best thinking of representative American leadership." Though the treatise ostensibly qualified itself by asserting that "the Bible contains no clear mandate for or against segregation," Gillespie nonetheless clearly intended to identify segregation as in keeping with the will and plan of God: "[the Bible] does furnish considerable data from which valid inferences may be drawn in support of the general principle of segregation as an important feature of the Divine purpose and Providence throughout the ages."

The fine distinctions of hermeneutics and exegesis that drew fire from Gillespie's theological critics outside the state (and that still invite the musings of scholars) failed to concern the white southern layfolk who served as the pamphlet's primary audience. Gillespie and his promoters likely did not hope to convert integrationists. Rather, they primarily wanted to assure southern segregationists that the Bible did not condemn the practice. Erle Johnston, publicist for Ross Barnett's successful gubernatorial campaign and later director of the state's Sovereignty Commission, understood the goals of Gillespie's sermon and explained that it gave "those segregationists who needed some kind of Biblical inspiration to feel comfortable . . . what they wanted." The address suited the purposes of the racial hierarchy so well that it became one of Governor Barnett's "favorite moral sources" when he cited "pastors and ministers of various faiths [who] supported his position." Indeed, the Brandon, Mississippi, editor who claimed that "Dr. G. T. Gillespie . . . can convince anyone that segregation is neither immoral nor un-Christian and is God's will," demonstrated that legions of Mississippians understood the intent of Gillespie's message.

Such pamphlets, tracts, and sermons represented the formal articulation of the biblical case for segregation, but white Mississippians more often expressed their belief in the divine nature of the racial hierarchy in less structured and formal settings. Segregationist folk theology announced itself in the ordinary operations of life; it wove itself into workday exchanges, peppered private ruminations, and bubbled up in conversation. Charging a grand jury in Scott County, Circuit Judge O. H. Barnett explained: "Segregation is right, it is Christian, and it ought to be taught in the homes and preached from every pulpit in the state and nation." A Presbyterian confided to his diary that "the pure white race and the pure black have been bred naturally and by Divine Providence over a long, long period of time." Similarly, a state highway patrolman demanded that a civil rights worker use his Bible to "[l]ook it up where it says about mongrelizin' of black and white degeneratin' the races." When the activist asked for the exact reference, the patrolman replied, "I don't know, but it's in there.". . .

"God Separated the Races": The Citizens' Councils and the Religious Defense of Segregation

Immediately after the *Brown* decision and in direct response to the threat it posed, leading citizens from the Mississippi Delta organized grass-roots support for segregation. As the South's most avid promoters of the case for segregation, the Citizens' Councils flourished, and the religious argument figured importantly in their program. The organization attracted 25,000 members among the state's middle and upper-middle classes within months after its birth in July 1954. In two years, it grew to 85,000 members in sixty-five chapters in Mississippi alone. In its wild nascent success, the movement spread quickly to other states, reaching a national membership of 250,000 by the end of 1956. By 1960, the Citizens' Councils promoted the gospel of racial purity through annual rallies, a regional paper with a circulation of 40,000, weekly television programs broadcast by twelve stations, and radio shows aired on more than fifty stations. The organization's success owed, in part, to its disavowal of violence, its pledge to maintain segregation by legal methods, its polished and sophisticated use of public media, and a somewhat socially elevated constituency that included senators, lawyers, and prominent businessmen.

In their capacity as self-appointed defenders of "racial integrity and states' rights," the Citizens' Councils recognized that ignoring religious arguments would leave potentially dangerous streams of thought unguarded. Understanding both religion's danger and its possibilities, the group's original mastermind, Robert Patterson, exhorted laymen to "straighten these churches out" and secure their cooperation in the fight against integration. The Mississippi Gulf Coast chapter purposefully solicited "all clergymen occupying pulpits in this community," appealing "for their continued support of racial segregation in our churches." As fellow Christians, the councilors explained, "we . . . feel ourselves entitled to the honest support of our own pastors in this frightening situation." Reverend J. L. Pipkin of Blue Mountain urged the organization to pursue the religious argument more aggressively: "I believe this may be the Christians['] greatest challenge, to get up and tell the truth against these great odds." Indeed, conspicuously Christian councilors, frightened for the future of segregation, militantly advanced an understanding of their faith and segregation as mutually linked.

While the Citizens' Councils deployed an army of Christian spokesmen, they regarded ministers as a prize catch. One chapter proudly boasted "the accession to its ranks of five very fine men of God from the local clergy." Clergyman occupied prominent places in the organization, as did laymen with very public religious commitments. Local pastors commonly offered the invocation at rallies, and prominent ministers served as keynote speakers. Presbyterian ministers who performed these tasks included Dr. G. T. Gillespie, the . . . Reverend [John Reed] Miller of First Presbyterian Church in Jackson, and Reverend William Arnett Gamble, stated clerk of the Central Mississippi Presbytery, who served on the board of the Jackson Citizens' Council. Among Baptists, Dr. David M. Nelson spoke for Council events and wrote literature for the organization; Baptist Reverend Charles C. Jones of Mendenhall, along with the laymen Louis Hollis of First Baptist Church, Jackson, and D. B. Red of Hattiesburg, also occupied a variety of posts in the organization. Methodist pastors who served the organization included Reverend B. K. Hardin of Jackson's Boling Street Methodist Church, and Delmar Dennis, who spoke at rallies and other events. By showcasing this phalanx, the Councils sought to create the impression that they had unanimous support among Mississippi's religious leaders. In 1957 the group claimed that "only two ministers in the state are not with us," an assertion that smacked of hyperbole.

Ministerial participation afforded the Councils a symbolic religious imprimatur and an aura of respectability, but the organization understood that religious *thought* constituted the real battleground for Mississippians' hearts and minds. Thus, to its arsenal of printed segregationist polemics, the Councils added a subset designed specifically for its Bible-reading audience. These Christian defenses of segregation offer prime examples of segregationist folk theology and its multi-faceted foundations. In addition to Dr. Gillespie and his "A Christian View on Segregation," Mississippi College president Dr. Nelson endowed the Citizens' Councils with considerable prestige. Though his pamphlet on "Conflicting Views on Segregation" seemed to suggest a concern with open-mindedness and fair play, the piece aimed primarily to contravene the moral case for integration as a well-intentioned but naïve and unsophisticated perversion of God's divine plan. The text ostensibly reproduced Nelson's correspondence with "Tom," a pseudonymous Mississippi College alumnus. Nelson repeatedly challenged Tom's understanding of segregation as a "moral question" and repudiated his conviction that Christian faith required that "there should be no racial differences." Nelson argued that, in striking down legal segregation, the Supreme Court had attempted "to do what the good Lord in His infinite wisdom did not do. He made the people into races, with racial characteristics, with inherent likes and dislikes, similarities and dissimilarities, and it would be as fallacious for mere man to try to improve upon the work of the Lord as it proved to be in his attempt to build a tower to heaven." When Tom countered that "The promotion of the Missionary Work in the Baptist Church and the teaching [of Christianity] at Mississippi College . . . seemed to be out of line with our practice of excluding Negroes from our colleges and churches," Nelson replied, "Again we demur and call for the chapter and the verse of the Bible. The whole tenor of the Scriptures is against mixed marriages and the pollution of the blood of distinct and separate races."

The Citizens' Councils did not confine their religious defense of segregation to the tract publications and sermon collections that they advertised for sale in their weekly paper. Nearly every issue of the organization's paper, *The Citizens' Council* and its refurbished successor after mid-1961, *The Citizen*, contained an article, op-ed piece, cartoon, letter to the editor, or news item calculated to establish, elucidate, and defend the orthodoxy that God himself had established segregation to spare whites from contamination by blacks and that any attempt "to destroy these God-given distinctions . . . opposes God's plan." A multipart "Manual for Southerners," aimed at school-aged children and printed over several issues in 1957, developed the case for God's blessing on segregation, as indicated by the subheadings "God separated the

Races," "God Doesn't Want Races to Mix," and "Segregation is Christian." Many issues of *The Citizen* included segregationist sermon reprints among its articles. The authors of these included spokesmen from Mississippi's religious communions—the Presbyterian pastor Al Freundt, the Baptist deacon Louis Hollis, and the Methodist Sunday school teacher Dr. Medford Evans. Mississippians, however, represented only part of the team of southern religious spokesmen who made similar arguments in the organization's journal. The paper pulled in the commentary of religious leaders from across the South, including Dr. Bob Jones, Sr., president and founder of Bob Jones University in Greenville, South Carolina, North Carolina Episcopal minister James Dees, and the Texas Episcopalian rector Robert T. Ingram.

Though the Citizens' Councils advanced several different and even contradictory religious arguments for segregation, the organization probably made its most effective faith-based case by tying religious advocacy for racial equality to liberal theology. A corollary line of reasoning maintained that only the proponents of segregation remained loyal to biblical truth and the old-time Gospel of salvation. Council literature repeatedly advanced the trope of liberal ministers as effeminate, deluded, and educated beyond their own capacities to understand or communicate. Such ministers, they argued, were not harmless, over-zealous, do-gooders, but apostates and heretics who flirted dangerously with socialism, if not outright communism, in emphasizing equality and social engagement. The abstruse theology of racial justice preached by such ministers bore little resemblance to the easily understood evangelical Gospel that issued from southern pulpits. Thus, the Council argument made a short leap from advocacy for racial justice to the kind of religious liberalism Mississippians had decried for decades, and the religious defense of segregation remained intimately tied to a defense of conservative, evangelical Christianity. Commitment to segregation became part and parcel of Mississippians' own cherished faith, and they could fear for their own souls if they accepted the argument for racial equality.

Thus, in the religious and racial worlds of white Mississippians, churches and ministers who advocated racial equality dangerously perverted both the Bible and the divine plan, and they constituted an evil worthy of the Christian's most vigorous opposition. As if to confirm the dangerous status of denominations that had endorsed racial equality, the Citizens' Councils included the Episcopal Church and the Methodist Church on a list of organizations under the jarring heading "Here is the enemy." Other Citizens' Council material decried apostasy in the

Catholic Church, the Lutheran Church, and the American Baptist Convention. Almost the entire May 1958 issue of *The Citizens' Council* explored the pernicious "doctrine" of integration in American religious communities. Under the heading "Southern Churches Urge Mixing," the issue featured articles condemning Southern Baptist and Presbyterian literature and documenting the rise of communist influence within the churches. Dr. Nelson closed the issue with a defense of the place of race in the divine plan: "races are different, radically different, and man is not responsible for this difference, but God [is] . . . [to] attempt to merge them in the crucible of miscegenation . . . is the height of blasphemy."

Will Campbell understood the genius of tying the religious defense of segregation to the conservative faith of Mississippians. When he wanted to draft a short series of publications aimed at "Mississippi Cockle Burrs and Georgia Crackers" as a riposte to the Citizens' Council argument, he planned to approach Mississippians with the same kind of chapter and verse method they favored. Though he did "not believe in the Biblical method of proof text," he "want[ed] to encounter them . . . using their own language, own Biblical methods." Wrote Campbell, "If they want to believe a big fish swallowed Jonah, I won't argue with them." Yet he also knew that even "good fundamentalism [c]ould as successfully deny the racist biblical claims" as more modernist or historical critical methods. Such a tract series as Campbell envisioned might have been Mississippi's only prayer for changing its resistant trajectory, for Mississippians who wanted to keep the faith that had been delivered unto them could find no resonance with the idea that God would champion the cause of black equality. . . .

CAROLYN RENÉE DUPONT received her PhD from the University of Kentucky in 2003 and is an associate professor of history at Eastern Kentucky University.

David L. Chappell

 **NO**

Broken Churches, Broken Race: White Southern Religious Leadership and the Decline of White Supremacy

The standard image of the white South in the civil rights struggle is a mob—united in anger against nine black students at Little Rock in 1957 or against James Meredith at the University of Mississippi in 1962. With amazing discipline, southern politicians projected a more organized image of unanimity. . . . But the black minority in the region saw through what turned out to be a veneer of defiance and solidarity. Probably the most important reason they saw through it was that the religious leadership of the white South showed none of the militancy and discipline of the political leadership. . . .

There was a split in the white southern church that never became formalized, though it was conspicuous to those involved in it at the time. The split was over how to deal with the racial crisis of the mid-twentieth century. It was not as neat as the North-South split of the mid-nineteenth century, which is probably why it never became formalized. . . .

Interested observers like Martin Luther King and James Lawson sensed the disarray when they looked at white southern Christians: there was no way these people could measure up to the image of unity and defiance their politicians had created. King and others saw where the weak points were, and they drove in wedges. Scholars, blinded by the abiding racism of most of the white southern clergy, miss this crucial point. The historically significant thing about white religion in the 1950s–60s is not its failure to join the civil rights movement. The significant thing, given that the church was probably as racist as the rest of the white South, is that it failed in any meaningful way to join the anti-civil rights movement. . . .

The historically significant failure of white southern churches was their inability to live up to the militant image that southern politicians had shown. The churches failed to elevate their whiteness—the institutions and customs

that oppressed black folk—above their other concerns. That is what they needed to do to defend those institutions and customs effectively. Members of the churches were a pretty good cross-section of the white South. They loved feeling superior to black folk and they loved segregation; every election and opinion poll makes that clear. But the civil rights militants perceived something that opinion polls and, so far, historians have not examined deeply enough to grasp: that white churches were unwilling to make sacrifices to preserve segregation. They loved other things—peace, social order—more. They could not make defense of segregation the unifying principle of their culture.

Some prominent white southern religious leaders *tried* to achieve unity on the question of segregation—and were for a time confident that they could get it. But they were on the other side. Before the Supreme Court's desegregation decision of 1954, the southern Presbyterians, known as the Presbyterian Church in the United States (PCUS), and, shortly after the decision, the Southern Baptist Convention (SBC) overwhelmingly passed resolutions supporting desegregation and calling on all to comply with it peacefully. People—even historians—are surprised to hear this. The pro-integration resolutions were reiterated later. Both southern denominations elected presidents who were viewed as strong opponents of segregation. Both desegregated their southern seminaries well ahead of most public schools. (By 1958 all SBC seminaries accepted black applicants.) Of course, there was dissent and conflict within the white southern denominations. They were not as unified for compliance with desegregation as their senators were for defiance. Still, it is striking how, initially, the South's religious assemblies sharply opposed the position taken by its elected politicians.

This is not to suggest that the assemblies supported the civil rights movement. They were in their own eyes expressing cautious respect for the duly constituted authority of the Supreme Court. To them, and to us, that may have been a moderate, even conservative, gesture. But the South's political spokesmen believed, at any rate they consistently said, that the high court had abrogated the Constitution and tried to impose a dangerous and insulting revolution on southern society. The battle over forced desegregation in the 1950s began with the white South's religious bodies lined up on one side and its politicians on the other. . . .

Degrees of Segregationism

In opposition to the denominational resolutions, there were occasional fiery statements from southern white clergymen, such as the Rev. Carey Daniel, whose First Baptist Church of West Dallas became a platform for paranoid extremism. Daniel, also executive vice president of the Dallas Citizens' Council, said that Christians had a duty to disobey the Supreme Court, for the Court, in ordering desegregation, had unaccountably contradicted its long established tradition of approving segregation laws. . . .

Another militant segregationist, the Rev. Leon Burns of Columbia, Tennessee, was less interested in the Bible, which he did not get around to until the end of his speech, than he was in sex:

> The average Negro who wants integration is not interested in equal educational and economic advantages with the White race, and when these things are dangled before him by the NAACP he is unmoved, but when they whisper in his ear that someday he will be able to live with a White woman he is very interested. In a survey made among several thousand Negroes a few years ago, it was found that the secret desire of almost every Negro man questioned was to be able to sleep with a White woman. Several flatly stated that they would risk death in the electric chair to do it.

There are other examples of this sort of militant and dishonest rhetoric from clergymen, but they are rare.

Only a few preachers appear in segregationist periodicals and in the widely circulated segregationist pamphlets. Conversely, most secular segregationists avoided discussion of religious themes. Of the small number of southern white ministers who identified themselves with the segregationist cause, most were much less decisive, much less defiant, than Daniel or Burns. . . .

The lack of commitment among white southerners who nominally favored segregation was what made clergymen's statements so important. The most widely published and often-cited segregationist preacher was the Rev. G. T. Gillespie of Jackson, Mississippi. He was known for a single speech in 1954—his only known segregationist statement, much reprinted but apparently never developed. (He died in 1958.) Gillespie said, "While the Bible contains *no clear mandate* for or against segregation as between the white and negro races, it does furnish *considerable data* from which valid *inferences may* be drawn in support of the *general principle* of segregation as *an* important feature of the Divine purpose and Providence throughout the ages" (emphasis added). The most obvious inference to draw from Gillespie's hesitant language was that even committed segregationists were unwilling to claim biblical sanction. Most of them saw no point in trying to be dishonest about that. Gillespie could never articulate a fighting faith for his parishioners. He was hedging segregationists' bets, not exhorting them with a vigorous call to arms.

The most decisive statement Gillespie made was: "Concerning matters of this kind, which in the inscrutable wisdom of God have been left for mankind to work out in the light of reason and experience without the full light of revelation, we dare not be dogmatic." Similarly, in a segregationist collection of essays, the Rev. Edward B. Guerry, an Episcopal priest in Charleston, South Carolina, wrote: "We should endeavor to respect the sincere convictions of those who disagree with us. No one can assume for himself an attitude of infallibility on a matter so complex as this racial question."

Other than careful, respectable, and nearly unassailable arguments like Gillespie's (if they can be called arguments), segregationist publications rarely gave space to clergymen or to religious appeals. Segregationist preachers who deviated from the careful, not very helpful pattern of Gillespie and Guerry tended to be even less useful to the cause. They showed little interest in disciplined strategy or unity behind a party line.

For segregationist leaders who were trying to maintain their authority and respectability, if it was not dangerous to indulge zealots like Carey Daniel and Leon Burns, it was probably not worth the trouble. The Rev. T. Robert Ingram of Houston, a "born-again" Episcopalian, herded Guerry and four other "born-again" southern Episcopalians into a little volume of essays that poured cold water on religious agitation for civil rights in 1960.

But Ingram had a far more ambitious agenda than most segregationists. He seems to have been more interested in the publicity surrounding segregationism than in segregation itself. In August 1960 he laid out his scheme in a letter to Thomas Waring, editor of the influential segregationist newspaper, the *Charleston News and Courier:*

> Briefly, my plan is this: I am in the process of organizing a propaganda drive to explain how the system of law in the United States and all Christian countries . . . is rooted and grounded in the Ten Commandments. Further, to show that each of the Commandments is under attack by an organized movement of liberals and socialists, the spearhead of which is for the abolishment of capital punishment. . . . I am persuaded that my propaganda drive will tie all the loose ends together for Christian people and throw the liberals into [a] position of attacking not [s]imply a series of isolated issues but the whole law of God.

This is the kind of grandiosity that sensible propagandists like Waring eschewed. For all his racism and fear of federal encroachment, Waring was a practical man who knew the importance of concentrating one's fire.

Most segregationist clergymen felt more compelled to act like Waring than like Ingram. The urge to appear moderate and reasonable while proving their segregationism, however, made them unreliable. The Rev. James Dees—an Episcopal priest from South Carolina who would break away from his denomination in 1963 and start his own, the Anglican Orthodox Church—made flexible as well as rigid statements on segregation. In 1955 Dees published a pamphlet, circulated widely in the South, renouncing all gradualism and defeatism and vowing to oppose integration to the bitter end. Yet at the end, Dees admitted:

> There are certain areas where I think that segregation is not practicable [or] sensible. I am glad to note that at the professional level, the races are coming together for what I believe is for good. I observe that the State Medical Society has voted to admit negro doctors. It has long been a practice for ministerial associations to be inter-racial. I think that it behooves the seminaries of our Church to receive negro students, since it would not be practicable to try to provide a separate seminary for the mere handful of negro seminary students that we have.

Most segregationists thought that concessions like these only legitimated the principle of integration.

It is surprising how little southern white clergymen contributed to the record of the segregationist cause, considering how important religion was in the white South in the period. One reason may be that the Bible, which had so much slavery in it, offered so little objective support for postemancipation racism. There was no biblical equivalent of legal segregation or disfranchisement. There were separate nations and tribes in the Bible, but these were not defined the way race was in the modern South: by laws based on biological concepts. The nations and tribes in the Bible were defined by linguistic and cultural divisions. But the two "races" in the modern South both spoke English and practiced evangelical Protestantism.

For whatever reason, the few prominent religious figures associated with segregationism rarely emphasized the Bible, and when they did mention it they betrayed a complete lack of confidence in its usefulness. Generally they aimed to show only that Scripture was ambivalent on equality and brotherhood on this earth, not that it offered any positive warrant for segregation. Dr. Medford Evans ("an active Methodist layman" and former Sunday school teacher), writing in the Citizens' Council organ in January 1963, outlined St. Paul's insistence on certain earthly social distinctions. He thought that these distinctions might be loosely analogous to race, but he was careful to hedge the analogy: "Whether these injunctions of St. Paul are literally binding on Christians today or not, they certainly prove that St. Paul's statement that we are all one in Christ cannot be used to require indiscriminate integration" on earth. Evans cannot have expected such anticlimactic residues of his exegesis to be very useful in rallying apathetic white southerners. Yet his was typical of would-be religious leaders' statements.

A few lay segregationists and occasional clergymen invoked Acts 17:26, where God created the "nations of men" and determined "the bounds of their habitation." But this was selective quotation of a verse that worked better for integrationists: that verse also said (as Fannie Lou Hamer emphasized) that God "made of one blood all the nations of men." It was not a verse that segregationists could rely on or articulate forcefully. Evans avoided it altogether. Gillespie conceded the main point, emphasized not only in Acts but also elsewhere in the Bible: "Paul affirms the unity of the race"—meaning the human race—"based upon a common origin, concerning which there can be no difference of opinion among those who accept the authority of the Bible." He did not mention that popular scientific arguments for racism required a rejection of biblical monogenesis.

Gillespie's position, like that of most literate ministers who supported segregation, was hesitant and inconclusive as to its biblical bona fides. There were references in the Old Testament that he found useful, especially the curse laid on Noah's son Ham after the Flood (Genesis 9:18-29). The point is not that the curse on Ham was universally understood, by anybody literate in biblical studies, to have nothing to do with racial distinctions. Rather, the point is that Gillespie himself could not do much with it. The story of Ham showed that Providence must have been "responsible for the distinct racial characteristics, which seem to have become fixed in prehistoric times, and which are chiefly responsible for the segregation of racial groups across the centuries and in our time." This was not enough to fuel propaganda. In a sense it was not even relevant, since no one was fighting "racial characteristics." Gillespie needed a justification for man-made legal barriers—barriers that applied even to those who had no distinct racial characteristics, who passed for white. Gillespie was on slightly firmer ground in drawing analogies to Old Testament restrictions on intermarriage and cross-breeding of crops. But his qualifications show that he was on the defensive and not entirely confident even there: the permissibility of modern racial laws was "a possible though not necessary inference" from the ancient Hebrew restrictions.

At any rate, when he got to the New Testament, Gillespie nullified what little support he had shaken out of the Old: "There is no question but that the emphasis placed by Our Lord upon the love of God for the whole world (John 3:16 and other passages) was intended in part at least as a rebuke to the bigotry and intolerance of the Jewish leaders, and to counteract the attitude of contempt and indifference which the Jewish people as a whole manifested toward the other peoples of the world." The best Gillespie could do was to argue, with many qualifications, that the New Testament did not *prohibit* segregation and did not positively *require* integration. So, too, Gillespie's colleague at Bellhaven College, Morton Smith, concluded, "We would have to say first of all that the Bible does not condemn segregation. On the other hand it does not necessarily condemn integration. This being the case this whole matter falls into the realm of Christian liberty. Where the Bible is not clearcut . . . the individual must decide . . . on the basis of his own conscience."

On the fringes of the segregation movement, a few clergymen made more out of the curse on Ham, attempting to claim that God created and intended to maintain racial distinctions. But literate ministers either avoided biblical references or, in the manner of Gillespie, qualified them into uselessness. Again, Carey Daniel was exceptional. The *way* Daniel used the Bible seems to make it clear why he was exceptional. Not content with the curse on Ham or God's setting the "bounds of habitation"

of nations, Daniel constructed an obsessive reading of Scripture, entitled "God the Original Segregationist." This took racial segregation to be the central idea of God's plan. Its section titles included "Moses the Segregationist," "Jesus the Segregationist," "Paul the Segregationist," "Nimrod the Original Desegregationist." Christians could be deeply committed to segregation and still not stomach such a distortion of God's sense of priorities. Whatever comfort they might draw from such a reading in private, most were too embarrassed to be associated with anything of the kind in public.

It must be stressed that in public was where it mattered. It is not in dispute that white southerners held deeply racist views (though one might wonder at the strength of a commitment that required such contortions as Daniel's). The question is whether they could organize themselves effectively—publicly—to defend a way of life built on those views.

The Rev. W. A. Criswell, the most celebrated and popular segregationist minister, in a famous address to the South Carolina legislature (again reprinted much but apparently not developed later), mentioned the Bible only once, in passing—not in his actual discussion of segregation, but in the warm-up jokes he told to ingratiate himself with the audience. . . . Criswell made a ringing if somewhat incoherent defense of segregation, drawing on common notions of social traditions, animal breeding, and so forth, but like most segregationist clergymen he contributed little that drew on his expertise. It certainly helped the segregationist cause that men of the cloth lent their authority to commonsensical, pragmatic, traditionalist, or scientific justifications of segregation. But these justifications were not ones that men of the cloth were specially qualified to provide, or were very good at providing.

The question remains whether a significant number of local ministers, especially in the unaffiliated Baptist congregations and independent sects, might have preached segregation more wholeheartedly (and dishonestly) or, when the Word failed them, might have contributed to segregationist militancy by winks and blinks and nods. The printed evidence reveals two things: segregationist organizations and leaders felt a strong need to add religious authority to their cause (else they would not have pulled the tentative ruminations of Gillespie, Evans, and others into their propaganda at all), and they could not find anything more decisive than what these writers offered (else they would naturally have printed it in their periodicals and pamphlets).

On occasion Criswell—and other preachers—may have indulged in some hocus-pocus to show that the Bible sanctioned segregation. Virtually every historian who has touched on the matter assumes that this went on, though no one has produced much evidence. In his published speech on the matter, at any rate, Criswell did not stoop to claim that the Bible sanctioned segregation. Interestingly, it only took him until 1968 to repudiate segregationism altogether, at which time he made a point of admitting that his earlier position had never been justified biblically. Nor did the Rev. Albert Freundt, a prominent segregationist Presbyterian in Mississippi, bother with the Bible in the article he published for the Citizens' Council.

Segregation's biblical sanction was a matter of deep concern that should not be underestimated. The South was the Bible Belt: inerrantist and literalist views ran high. The question of the biblical provenance of their taboos and traditions was, for many white southerners, a subject of great soul-searching. It was not simply propaganda. The soul-searching required honest and literate segregationists to drop any pretensions of conservative views on biblical interpretation: they would have to become radically unbiblical in their derivation of moral support for, let alone commands to maintain, their political institution. It is necessary to read carefully the anguished writings of the moderate segregationists, and would-be segregationists, on the matter.

During the historic struggle in Little Rock in 1957, some of the city's fringe churches had hitherto obscure preachers (Wesley Frank Pruden, for example) making cases for segregation. But two days before the crisis erupted at Central High, the Rev. Dale Cowling, a prominent local minister strongly connected with and supported by the SBC, preached at Second Baptist Church of Little Rock (the church of Congressman Brooks Hays, who later became president of the SBC). Cowling said: "Those who base their extreme opposition to integration upon their interpretation of the Scripture . . . are sincere beyond question. They are simply greatly mistaken in their efforts to prove that God has marked the Negro race and relegated it to the role of servant." Cowling dismissed the segregationist interpretation of Noah's curse on Ham: "A serious study of this section of scripture and History" would reveal that the imputation of Negro descent to Ham's line "is only the conjecture of man. We might as well reason that the Negro is the descendant of any other Old Testament character." Cowling also confined the strictures against intermarriage in Leviticus to the Old Testament dispensation: "Since the coming of the Savior, the clear insistence of the Word of God is that 'in Christ there is neither bond nor free, Greek [n]or Hebrew.'"

The white pastor of First Baptist Church in Poplarville, Mississippi, the Rev. Clyde Gordon, who dissociated himself from "northern agitators" and did not think "immediate" integration was practical, still condemned race prejudice as unbiblical and wrong. "There are some false impressions and conceptions that we need to fight bitterly today. Some of our writers try to take the Bible and prove by it that God is color conscious and, in such an attempt, reveal a staggering ignorance of God and His word." One example sufficed: "Some say that Noah placed a curse on Ham and he became black. That is not truth. It is not so stated in the Bible. . . . The Negro race, along with every one of us, had its beginning back there in Eden." The Negro "is a human being made in the image of God." Gordon did not want to attack segregation; he simply wanted its defenders not to blaspheme themselves.

Such statements infuriated the segregationists but put them on the defensive. Though it is probably impossible to make a complete tally of biblical references, it seems that antisegregationists and moderates refer to Bible stories like the curse on Ham more often than prominent segregationists do. Segregationists' enemies used the curse on Ham story as a foil. It was an opportunity to ridicule the segregationists, to expose their ignorance and failures of reason. Segregationists, in turn, were sensitive to the way people like Carey Daniel exposed their weaknesses, perhaps made segregationist ideology appear weaker than it was. . . .

The Wages of Neutrality

. . . A major variation on the theme of opposition to political preaching is a startling anticlericalism among segregationists. In Chattanooga, a segregationist denounced the PCUS's pro-integration position: "The sad part of this is that just as the rulings of the Supreme Court and their violations of the Constitution have made so many people lose respect for and confidence in the Courts—so the leaders in our churches are forcing many members to lose respect for and confidence in our churches and its leaders." A month after the *Brown* decision, one of the major segregationist leaders of South Carolina, Congressman William Jennings Bryan Dorn, complained to supporters about widespread southern white acquiescence in the decision. He was "alarmed over the tendency exhibited by many of our church leaders, particularly their influence with youth." Another leader of the South Carolina segregationists, state senator Marion Gressette, told the American Legion and other groups during the election campaign of 1956 that his opposition came from two sources: "a few NAACP Mbrs and Church leaders." . . .

Perhaps the ultimate anticlerical statement came from a fan of Strom Thurmond's in 1955: "By now it should be evident to the pro-segregation forces that their real opponent in the fight to provide for the preservation of the white race in America is the so-called christian religion. . . . It should also be evident that segregation in the U.S. is a lost cause unless the prosegregation forces organize across state lines, po[o]l their knowledge and resources, and launch a frontal assault on organized religion by telling all men the truth about themselves and the so-called christian religion." This fan wanted Thurmond to organize all leaders of the southern states to expose falsehood, suggesting that he "notify the heads of the various religious organizations sponsoring integration that they will be exposed as [frauds] and their religion as a myth, just so much modern witchcraft." . . .

The higher segregationists looked in their churches, the worse it got. They blamed preachers more than laymen or laywomen, big-city preachers more than rural and small-town ones, bishops or regional and denominational board members more than preachers. Universities and colleges were, of course, the worst of all. The segregationists spent a lot of time bemoaning the takeover of southern seminaries by integrationists. . . .

In some cases, divinity faculty were indeed disproportionately outspoken in favor of civil rights. In June 1952, when the trustees of the University of the South (Sewanee) rejected a directive of October 1951 from the Synod of Sewanee Province (fifteen southern dioceses) to admit black students, eight of the ten members of the theology faculty protested. The eight maintained that the trustees' position was "untenable in the light of Christian ethics and of the teaching of the Anglican Communion." . . .

Some followed the logic of anticlericalism so far as to dissociate themselves from religion altogether. Roy Harris, the Georgia power broker and sometime officeholder, was one of the most gifted propagandists in the South. When the Methodist hierarchy dared to send his church a new minister who had signed a statement against closing the schools to prevent integration, Harris

boasted, "I ain't been to church since." In June 1954 an Atlanta racist attacked the head of the PCUS, Wade Boggs, who had made forthright statements against segregation. Referring to Boggs's "burning desire to establish a mixed race," the Atlanta racist said, "I *was* a member of your denomination, but left Druid Hills [Presbyterian Church] and the faith along with others when Dr. [Donald] Miller ranted and raved to have the races mixed." He compared clergymen like Boggs with "those Senator Eastland speaks of as 'racial politicians in judicial robes,'" that is, Supreme Court justices, who made "desperate" efforts to force racial mixing by law. "THANK GOD THERE IS NO LAW WHICH REQUIRES CHURCH ATTENDANCE." The best-selling segregationist author Carleton Putnam addressed the southern white clergy with even sterner language: "You watch the federal government take forcibly from the South while you sit with your hands folded in prayer. I'm tired of the sort of combined ignorance and stupidity you have shown. I'm tired of your timid conformity with the popular drift. And finally, I'm tired of your milk and water suggestions that we pass the buck to God while you support a policy which forces the white children of the South against the wishes of their parents into associations they understand better than you do," This sort of rhetoric further divided prominent segregationist spokesmen from the white South's religious authorities, making unity ever more difficult.

DAVID L. CHAPPELL earned his PhD in history from the University of Rochester and is the Rothbaum Professor of Modern American History at the University of Oklahoma. His other books include *Inside Agitators: White Southerners in the Civil Rights Movement* (Johns Hopkins, 1994), which earned the Gustavus Myers Award for Outstanding Book on Human Rights in North America, and *Waking from the Dream: The Struggle for Civil Rights in the Shadow of Martin Luther King, Jr.* (Random House, 2014).

EXPLORING THE ISSUE

Did Southern White Christians Actively Support Efforts to Maintain Racial Segregation?

Critical Thinking and Reflection

1. How did some white southerners employ biblical evidence to support racial segregation in the 1950s and 1960s?
2. Explain the concept of "segregationist folk theology" as it is discussed in Carolyn Dupont's essay.
3. To what extent did religion play a supportive role in the civil rights movement?
4. What distinction does David Chappell make between the racial views of denominational organizations, leading ministers, and segregationist politicians in the South during the civil rights era?
5. Compare and contrast the arguments of Dupont and Chappell in assessing the influence of religion among white southerners with respect to the goals of the civil rights movement.

Is There Common Ground?

Neither Carolyn Dupont nor David Chappell would dispute the fact that religion played a significant role in the civil rights movement of the 1950s and 1960s, but one must be aware of the complexity involved in fully addressing that role. First of all, while this movement for social justice for African Americans possessed a moral and ethical component, it was also primarily a social and political movement. Second, people of various religious backgrounds and affiliations participated in some phase of the movement, but they did not represent a majority of the American people, including those Americans who shared their religious associations. Third, many people from these same religious affiliations actively opposed the goals of the civil rights movement or took a moderate stance that questioned the speed with which racial change seemed to be occurring. The best example of this separation of religious views on civil rights can be seen in Martin Luther King, Jr.'s "Letter from Birmingham Jail," written in 1963 during the Birmingham, Alabama, campaign. Here King is answering an open letter from eight Birmingham religious leaders, both Christian and Jewish, who expressed concern that King and his followers were asking for too much change too fast. King's

irritation with white "moderates" is evident as he insists that a century since emancipation is enough time to have waited for the nation to make good on its promise of equality. Similarly, it is worth pointing out that not all African Americans were comfortable from a religious perspective in taking on the goals of the civil rights campaigns. For them, both ministers and laity, fighting for particular civil rights amounted to political action which fell outside the more essential cause of individual salvation.

The same differences can be found among white southerners. Some carried their religious views directly into the movement; some employed religious arguments to challenge the goals of desegregation; some condemned non-southerners who insisted that their religious faith demanded that they come south to join the struggle; many rejected the linkage between religion and civil rights. As both Dupont and Chappell recognize, the vast majority of white southerners in the 1950s and 1960s were reluctant to turn their backs on what seemed to be the traditional folkways of segregation. Even when the national, regional, or state institutions of particular denominations, such as the Southern Baptist Convention, articulated a position favorable to desegregation, religious followers often failed to follow.

Additional Resources

Joel Alvis, *Religion and Race: Southern Presbyterians, 1946–1983* (University of Alabama Press, 1994)

James F. Findlay, Jr., *Church People in the Struggle: The National Council of Churches and the Black Freedom Movement, 1950–1970* (Oxford University Press, 1993)

Davis W. Houck and David E. Dixon, eds., *Rhetoric, Religion, and the Civil Rights Movement: 1954–1965* (Baylor University Press, 2006)

Charles Marsh, *The Beloved Community: How Faith Shapes Social Justice from the Civil Rights Movement to Today* (Basic Books, 2006)

Mark Newman, *Getting Right with God: Southern Baptists and Race* (University of Alabama Press, 2001)

Internet References . . .

Southern Christian Leadership Conference

nationalsclc.org

The Martin Luther King, Jr. Center

www.thekingcenter.org

The Role of Religion in the Civil Rights Movements

https://www.americanprogress.org/issues/civil
-liberties/news/2004/06/09/861/the-role-of-religion
-in-the-civil-rights-movements/

Selected, Edited, and with Issue Framing Material by:
Larry Madaras, *Howard Community College*
and
James M. SoRelle, *Baylor University*

ISSUE

Did President Nixon Negotiate a "Peace with Honor" in Vietnam in 1973?

YES: Richard Nixon, from *The Vietnam Syndrome* (Warner Books, 1980)

NO: Jeffrey Kimball, from "Debunking Nixon's Myths of Vietnam," *The New England Journal of History* (Winter 1999–Spring 2000)

Learning Outcomes

After reading this issue, you should be able to:

- Describe the major events that led to the United States' involvement in Vietnam from 1954 through 1975.
- Discuss President Nixon's policy of "Vietnamization" of the war.
- Critically analyze the Nixon-Kissinger theory that the U.S. Congress allowed South Vietnam to collapse.
- Critically analyze the "decent interval" theory.
- Critically analyze the shifting "Nixon doctrine" to determine if Nixon negotiated a "peace with honor" with North Vietnam.

ISSUE SUMMARY

YES: Former President Richard Nixon believed that the South Vietnamese government would not have lost the war to North Vietnam in 1975 if Congress had not cut off aid.

NO: Jeffrey Kimball believes that the Nixon-Kissinger versions of the peace negotiations were designed to protect their reputations as diplomatic realists and misrepresented the truth that the failure to bomb North Vietnam into submission had produced a military stalemate by the middle of 1972 and political pressure from liberals and conservatives that forced the two men to negotiate the withdrawal of U.S. troops by early 1973.

At the end of World War II, imperialism was coming to a close in Asia, and anti-imperialist movements emerged all over Asia and Africa, often producing chaos. The United States faced a dilemma. On the one hand, the United States was a nation conceived in revolution and was sympathetic to the struggles of developing nations. On the other hand, the United States was afraid that many of the revolutionary leaders were communists who would place their people under the control of the expanding empire of the Soviet Union. By the late 1940s, the Truman administration decided that it was necessary to stop the spread of communism. The policy that resulted was known as "containment."

The first true military test of the "containment" doctrine came soon. Korea, previously controlled by Japan, had been temporarily divided at the thirty-eighth parallel at the end of World War II. Communists gained control of North Korea, whereas anticommunist revolutionaries established a government in South Korea. When neither side would agree to a unified government, the temporary division became permanent. After North Korea attacked South Korea in late June, 1950, President Truman led the nation into an undeclared war under the auspices of the United Nations. The Korean War lasted three years and was fought to a stalemate.

Vietnam provided the second test of the "containment" doctrine in Asia. Vietnam had been a French protectorate from 1885 until Japan took control during World War II. Shortly before the war ended, the Japanese gave Vietnam its independence, but the French were determined to reestablish their influence in the area. Conflicts emerged between the French-led nationalist forces of South Vietnam and the communist-dominated provisional government of the Democratic Republic of Vietnam established in Hanoi in August 1945. Ho Chi Minh was the president of the DRV. An avowed communist since the 1920s, Ho had also become the major nationalist figure in Vietnam. As the leader of the anti-imperialist movement against French and Japanese colonialism for over 30 years, he managed to tie together the communist and nationalist movements in Vietnam.

A full-scale war broke out in 1946 between the communist government of North Vietnam and the French-dominated country of South Vietnam. The war lasted eight years. After the communist had inflicted a disastrous defeat on the French at the battle of Dienbienphu in May 1954, the latter decided to pull out. At the Geneva Conference the following summer, Vietnam was divided at the 17th parallel pending elections.

The United States involvement in Vietnam came after the French withdrew. In 1955, the Republican President Dwight Eisenhower refused to recognize the Geneva Accords but supported the establishment of the South Vietnamese government whose leader was Ngo Dinh Diem. In 1956 Diem, with United States approval, refused to hold elections which would have provided a unified government for Vietnam in accordance with the Geneva agreement. The Communists in the South responded by again taking up the armed struggle. The war continued unabated for another 19 years.

Both President Eisenhower and his democratic successor, John F. Kennedy, were anxious to prevent South Vietnam from being taken over by the communist. Economic assistance and military aid were given to the South Vietnamese government, which was becoming increasingly unpopular with a majority of the people. Kennedy supported the overthrow of the Diem regime (though not his murder) in October 1963 and hoped that the successor government would establish an alternative to communism. His hopes were unrealized. Kennedy himself was assassinated three weeks later. His successor Lyndon Johnson changed the character of American policy in Vietnam by escalating the air war and increasing the number of ground forces from 21,000 in 1965 to a full fighting force of 550,000 at its peak in 1968.

The next president, Richard Nixon, wanted to get America out of Vietnam but, like former President Lyndon Johnson, he did not want to be the first U.S. President to lose a war. He, therefore, adopted a new policy of "Vietnamization" whereby aid to the Republic of South Vietnam was increased to ensure the defeat of the communists, whereas more responsibility was given to the South Vietnamese military. At the same time, American troops were gradually withdrawn from Vietnam. Guerilla raids into Cambodia in the spring of 1970 to overthrow the left-wing government and destroy the enemy's sanctuaries along the border led to massive antiwar protests at home. In March 1972, American and South Vietnamese troops repelled a massive North Vietnamese invasion. Nixon ordered intensified bombing near Hanoi and mined seven North Vietnamese harbors to stop supplies from China to the Soviet Union.

The Christmas bombings of 1972 probably broke the stalemate in negotiations in Paris between the three sides, which had begun in the spring of 1968 when President Lyndon Johnson had announced he was no longer running for reelection. The Paris Peace Accords of January 1973 were militarily one-sided in favor of Vietnam. Although the remaining 60,000 American troops would be withdrawn within several months, the North Vietnamese would be allowed to keep 150,000 troops in the South. A cease-fire was declared, and several hundred American prisoners of war (POWs) flew home to be greeted warmly by family and friends.

The Paris Peace Accords were barely signed before the terms were broken as North Vietnamese and Vietcong troops started fighting again with the South Vietnamese. President Nixon, embroiled in the Watergate scandal, was unable to come to the aid of President Thieu. Following Nixon's forced resignation on August 9, 1974 (to avoid impeachment proceedings), the problem of Vietnam fell to his successor Gerald Ford. In the spring of 1975, the North Vietnamese army overran South Vietnam. A corrupt, poorly led South Vietnamese army received no help from the United States because Congress refused President Ford's pleas for air power and military assistance. On April 30, the last American helicopter flew out of the American embassy in Saigon onto a ship in the South China Sea. The embarrassingly massive airlift, which left many loyal South Vietnamese behind, was over. So was the Vietnam War. The price was catastrophic. According to Professor Alan Brinkley, "More than 1.2 million Vietnamese soldiers had died in combat, along with countless civilians throughout the region. The United States paid a heavy price as well. The war had cost the nation almost $150 billion in direct costs and much more indirectly. It had resulted in the deaths of over 55,000 young Americans and the injury of 300,000 more. And the nation had suffered a heavy blow to its confidence."

Both Nixon and his Secretary of State, Henry Kissinger, have given their own accounts of the president's handling of the Southeast Asia crisis. See Nixon's *No More Vietnams* (Arbor House, 1985) and his autobiography *RN: The Memoirs of Richard Nixon* (Warner Books, 1978). Kissinger has condensed his two volumes of memoirs pertaining to Vietnam into *Ending the Vietnam War* (Simon and Schuster, 2003) and even further in *Diplomacy* (Simon and Schuster, 1994). Although both men argue that South Vietnam could have been saved, they give different accounts of the peace negotiations leading to the withdrawal of American troops in the winter of 1973. The rivalry between the two is fully explored in Robert Dallek, *Nixon and Kissinger: Partners in Power* (Harper Collins, 2007).

In *No Peace, No Honor: Nixon, Kissinger, and Betrayal in Vietnam* (The Free Press, 2001) Larry Berman, professor of history at the University of California, Davis, has challenged the Nixon-Kissinger version of the ending of the Vietnam War. Through a careful use of declassified notes of key presidential advisers located in the National Archives or presidential libraries, as well as translations of transcript-like narratives of documents from the Hanoi archives, Berman describes a story of "diplomatic deception and public betrayal" regarding the Paris Peace Accords that supposedly brought an honorable end to the Vietnam War in January 1973. Berman accepts the "decent interval" interpretation advanced by CIA agent Frank Snepp in a book of the same title published in 1973 and argues that Kissinger and Nixon realized that once American troops were withdrawn, both sides would violate the cease-fire agreements, and South Vietnam would lose the war within two years. Berman, however, adds a new twist to this view. Both Nixon and Kissinger knew that the South Vietnamese government was doomed to fail, but Nixon expected to resume bombing the North Vietnamese military to prevent

the collapse of South Vietnam, at least until he left office at the end of his second term in January 1977.

In the YES selection, former President Nixon presents his own version of the Vietnam fiasco. His contention is that, despite policy failure by prior presidents, his administration stemmed the tide. When the last U.S. troops were withdrawn and the Paris Peace Accords were signed in January 1973 between the two Vietnams, the South Vietnamese had achieved military victory. Although the victory was short-lived, Nixon argues that South Vietnam would have been saved but for the United States Congress, under the influence of antiwar protesters and the liberal press, which refused to send further aid or to support any U.S. bombing missions in Vietnam.

In the NO selection, Jeffrey Kimball rejects the Nixon-Kissinger version of their foreign affairs that appears in most major college-level survey United States' history textbooks. According to Kimball, the so-called "Nixon doctrine" emerged in the summer of 1969 when the president realized the difficulty of withdrawing troops from South Vietnam without losing the country to communist-controlled North Vietnam. At this juncture, Nixon played the China card against Russia and enlisted their help in ending the war. According to Kimball, the turning point came in the summer of 1972 when both sides realized the war had reached a military stalemate. Nixon was in the middle of a presidential campaign, so the North Vietnamese thought they could get a better deal. With pressure from both liberals and conservatives, the United States would withdraw its troops by early 1973 but the National Liberation Front, which represented the communists in South Vietnam, could maintain their territories. Thieu was no longer guaranteed the withdrawal of the South Vietnamese communist as had been demanded earlier. Now he was given a "decent interval" to win the war or else lose and leave the country.

YES ⬅   Richard Nixon

The Vietnam Syndrome

The final chapters have yet to be written on the war in Vietnam. It was a traumatizing experience for Americans, a brutalizing experience for the Vietnamese, an exploitable opportunity for the Soviets. It was also one of the crucial battles of World War III. . . .

Vietnam was partitioned in 1954, with a communist government in the North under Ho Chi Minh and a noncommunist government in the South with its capital in Saigon. Between the two was a demilitarized buffer zone—the DMZ. Soon Ho's government in Hanoi was infiltrating large numbers of agents into the South, where they worked with guerrilla forces to set up networks of subversion and terrorism designed to undermine the Saigon government.

The interim premier of South Vietnam, Ngo Dinh Diem, became its first president in 1955. He proved to be a strong and effective leader, particularly in containing the communist guerrilla forces that were directly supported by the North in violation of the 1954 Partition Agreement. The Eisenhower administration provided generous economic assistance and some military aid and technical advisers, but Eisenhower rejected proposals to commit American combat forces.

Large-scale infiltration from the North began in 1959, and by 1961 the communists had made substantial gains. Sir Robert Thompson arrived in Vietnam that year to head the British Advisory Mission. Thompson had been Secretary of Defense of the Malayan Federation when the communist insurgency had been defeated there. He and the CIA people on the scene understood the importance of local political realities in guerrilla war. In putting down the rebellion in Malaya over the course of twelve years, from 1948 to 1960, the British had learned that local, low-level aggression was best countered by local, low-level defense. Britain had used only 30,000 troops in Malaya, but had also employed 60,000 police and 250,000 in a home guard.

With the excellent advice he was getting, Diem was able to reverse the momentum of the war and put the communists on the defensive. Just as the war in Malaya

had been won, the war in Vietnam was being won in the early 1960s. But then three critical events occurred that eventually turned the promise of victory into the fact of defeat.

The first took place far from Vietnam, in Cuba, in 1961: the Bay of Pigs invasion. That disastrous failure prompted President John F. Kennedy to order a postmortem, and General Maxwell Taylor was chosen to conduct it. He concluded that the CIA was not equipped to handle large-scale paramilitary operations and decided that the American effort in Vietnam fit into this category. He therefore recommended that control of it be handed over to the Pentagon, a decision that proved to have enormous consequences. The political sophistication and on-the-spot "feel" for local conditions that the CIA possessed went out the window, as people who saw the world through technological lenses took over the main operational responsibility for the war.

Another key turning point came the next year, in 1962, in Laos. At a press conference two months after his inauguration Kennedy had correctly declared that a communist attempt to take over Laos "quite obviously affects the security of the United States." He also said, "We will not be provoked, trapped, or drawn into this or any other situation; but I know that every American will want his country to honor its obligations." At the Geneva Conference in July 1962 fifteen countries signed an agreement in which those with military forces in Laos pledged to withdraw them and all agreed to stop any paramilitary assistance. All the countries complied except one: North Vietnam. North Vietnam never took any serious steps to remove its 7,000-man contingent from Laos—only 40 men were recorded as leaving—and the United States was therefore eventually forced to resume covert aid to Laos to prevent the North Vietnamese from taking over the country.

North Vietnam's obstinacy in keeping its forces in Laos—which had increased to 70,000 by 1972—created an extremely difficult situation for the South Vietnamese. The communists used the sparsely inhabited highlands of eastern Laos, and also of Cambodia, as a route for supplying their forces in South Vietnam. These areas also gave them a privileged sanctuary from which to strike, enabling them to concentrate overwhelmingly superior forces against a single local target and then slip back across the border before reinforcements could be brought in. The "Ho Chi Minh Trail" through Laos enabled the communists to do an end run around the demilitarized zone between North and South and to strike where the defenders were least prepared.

If South Vietnam had only had to contend with invasion and infiltration from the North across the forty-mile-long DMZ, it could have done so without the assistance of American forces. In the Korean War the enemy had to attack directly across the border; North Korea could hardly use the ocean on either side of South Korea as a "privileged sanctuary" from which to launch attacks. But Hanoi was able to use sanctuaries in Laos and Cambodia as staging grounds for its assault on South Vietnam. In addition to making hit-and-run tactics possible, these lengthened the border the South had to defend from 40 to 640 miles, not counting indentations. Along these 640 miles there were few natural boundaries. The North Vietnamese were free to pick and choose their points of attack, always waiting until they had an overwhelming local advantage, in accordance with the strategy of guerrilla warfare. Our failure to prevent North Vietnam from establishing the Ho Chi Minh Trail along Laos' eastern border in 1962 had an enormous effect on the subsequent events in the war.

The third key event that set the course of the war was the assassination of Diem. Diem was a strong leader whose nationalist credentials were as solid as Ho Chi Minh's. He faced the difficult task of forging a nation while waging a war. In the manner of postcolonial leaders, he ran a regime that drew its inspiration partly from European parliamentary models, partly from traditional Asian models, and partly from necessity. It worked for Vietnam, but it offended American purists, those who inspect the world with white gloves and disdain association with any but the spotless. Unfortunately for Diem, the American press corps in Vietnam wore white gloves, and although the North was not open to their inspection, the South was. Diem himself had premonitions of the fatal difference this might make when he told Sir Robert Thompson in 1962, "Only the American press can lose this war."

South Vietnam under Diem was substantially free, but, by American standards, not completely free. Responsible reporting seeks to keep events in proportion. The mark of irresponsible reporting is that it blows them out of proportion. It achieves drama by exaggeration, and its purpose is not truth but drama. The shortcomings of Diem's regime, like other aspects of the war, were blown grossly out of proportion.

"The camera," it has been pointed out, "has a more limited view even than the cameraman and argues always from the particular to the general." On June 11, 1963, the camera provided a very narrow view for the television audience in the United States. On that day, in a ritual carefully arranged for the camera, a Buddhist monk in South Vietnam doused himself with gasoline and set himself on fire. That picture, selectively chosen, seared a single word into the minds of many Americans: repression. The camera's focus on this one monk's act of self-immolation did not reveal the larger reality of South Vietnam; it obscured it. Even more thoroughly obscured from the television audience's view were the conditions inside North Vietnam, where unfriendly newsmen were not allowed.

Recently, in the Soviet Union, a Crimean Tartar set himself on fire to protest the thirty-five-year exile of his people from their ancestral homeland. A picture of this did not make the network news; it did not even make the front pages; I saw a story about it, with no pictures, buried on page twenty-one of the Los Angeles *Times*.

Communist regimes bury their mistakes; we advertise ours. During the war in Vietnam a lot of well-intentioned Americans got taken in by our well-advertised mistakes.

Some Buddhist temples in Vietnam were, in effect, headquarters of political opposition, and some Buddhist sects were more political than religious. The fact that Diem was a devout Catholic made him an ideal candidate to be painted as a repressor of Buddhists. They also played very skillful political theater; the "burning Buddhist" incident was an especially grisly form. But the press played up the Buddhists as oppressed holy people, and the world placed the blame on their target, Diem. The press has a way of focusing on one aspect of a complex situation as "the" story; in Vietnam in 1963 "the" story was "repression."

President Kennedy grew increasingly, unhappy at being allied with what was being portrayed as a brutal, oppressive government. Apparently without seriously considering the long-term consequences, the United States began putting some distance between itself and Diem.

On November 1, 1963, Diem was overthrown in a coup and assassinated. Charges that the U.S. government was directly involved may be untrue and unfair. However, the most charitable interpretation of the Kennedy administration's part in this affair is that it greased the skids for Diem's downfall and did nothing to prevent his murder. It was a sordid episode in American foreign policy. Diem's fall was followed by political instability and chaos in South Vietnam, and the event had repercussions all over Asia as well. President Ayub Khan of Pakistan told me a few months later, "Diem's murder meant three things to many Asian leaders: that it is dangerous to be a friend of the United States; that it pays to be neutral; and that sometimes it helps to be an enemy."

The months of pressure and intrigue preceding the coup had paralyzed the Diem administration and allowed the communists to gain the initiative in the war. Once Diem was disposed of, the gates of the Presidential Palace became a revolving door. Whatever his faults, Diem had represented "legitimacy." With the symbol of legitimacy gone, power in South Vietnam was up for grabs. Coup followed coup for the next two years until Nguyen Van Thieu and Nguyen Cao Ky took over in 1965. The guerrilla forces had taken advantage of this chaotic situation and gained a great deal of strength in the interim.

President Kennedy had sent 16,000 American troops to Vietnam to serve as combat "advisers" to the regular South Vietnam units, but after Diem's assassination the situation continued to deteriorate. In 1964 Hanoi sent in troops in order to be in a position to take over power when the government of South Vietnam fell. By 1965 South Vietnam was on the verge of collapse. In order to prevent the conquest by the North, President Johnson, in February started bombing of the North, and in March the first independent American combat units landed in Danang. As our involvement deepened, reaching a level of 550,000 troops by the time Johnson left office, fatal flaws in the American approach became manifest.

In World War II we won basically by out producing the other side. We built more and better weapons, and we were able to bombard the enemy with so many of them that he was forced to give up. Overwhelming firepower, unparalleled logistical capabilities, and the massive military operations that our talent for organization made possible were the keys to our success. But in World War II we were fighting a conventional war against a conventional enemy. We also were fighting a total war, and therefore, like the enemy, we had no qualms about the carnage we caused. Even before Hiroshima an estimated 35,000 people were killed in the Allied firebombing of Dresden; more than 80,000 perished in the two-day incendiary bombing of Tokyo a month later.

Vietnam, like Korea, was a limited war. The United States plunged in too impulsively in the 1960s, and then behaved too indecisively. We tried to wage a conventional war against an enemy who was fighting an unconventional war. We tried to mold the South Vietnamese Army into a large-scale conventional force while the principal threat was still from guerrilla forces, which called for the sort of smaller-unit, local-force response that had proved so successful in Malaya. American military policy-makers tended to downplay the subtler political and psychological aspects of guerrilla war, trying instead to win by throwing massive quantities of men and arms at the objective. And then, the impact even of this was diluted by increasing American pressure gradually rather than suddenly, thus giving the enemy time to adapt. Eisenhower, who refrained from publicly criticizing the conduct of the war, privately fumed about the gradualism. He once commented to me: "If the enemy holds a hill with a battalion, give me two battalions and I'll take it, but at great cost in casualties. Give me a division and I'll take it without a fight."

In Vietnam during that period we were not subtle enough in waging the guerrilla war; were too subtle in waging the conventional war. We were too patronizing, even contemptuous, toward our ally, and too solicitous of our enemy. Vietnamese morale was sapped by "Americanization" of the war; American morale was sapped by perpetuation of the war.

Democracies are not well equipped to fight prolonged wars. A democracy fights well after its morale is galvanized by an enemy attack and it gears up its war production. A totalitarian power can coerce its population into fighting indefinitely. But a democracy fights well only as long as public opinion supports the war, and public opinion will not continue to support a war that drags on without tangible signs of progress. This is doubly true when the war is being fought half a world away. Twenty-five years ago the ancient Chinese strategist Sun Tzu wrote, "There has never been a protracted war from which a country had benefited. . . . What is essential in war," he went on, "is victory not prolonged operations." Victory was what the American people were not getting.

We Americans are a do-it-yourself people. During that period we failed to understand that we could not win the war for the South Vietnamese: that, in the final analysis, the South Vietnamese would have to win it for themselves. The United States bulled its way into Vietnam and tried to run the war our way instead of recognizing that our mission should have been to help the South Vietnamese build up their forces so that they could win the war.

When I was talking with an Asian leader before I became President, he graphically pointed out the weakness in what was then the American policy toward South Vietnam: "When you are trying to assist another nation in defending its freedom, U.S. policy should be to help them fight the war but not to fight it for them." This was exactly where we had been going wrong in Vietnam. As South Vietnam's Vice President Ky later said, "You captured our war."

When I took office in 1969 it was obvious the American strategy in Vietnam needed drastic revision. My administration was committed to formulating a strategy that would end American involvement in the war and enable South Vietnam to win.

Our goals were to:

—Reverse the "Americanization" of the war that had occurred from 1965 to 1968 and concentrate instead on Vietnamization.

—Give more priority to pacification so that the South Vietnamese could be better able to extend their control over the countryside.

—Reduce the invasion threat by destroying enemy sanctuaries and supply lines in Cambodia and Laos.

—Withdraw the half million American troops from Vietnam in a way that would not bring about a collapse in the South.

—Negotiate a cease-fire and a peace treaty.

—Demonstrate our willingness and determination to stand by our ally if the peace agreement was violated by Hanoi, and assure South Vietnam that it would continue to receive our military aid as Hanoi did from its allies, the Soviet Union and, to a lesser extent, China.

En route to Vietnam for my first visit as President, I held a press conference in Guam on July 25, 1969, at which I enunciated what has become known as the Nixon Doctrine. At the heart of the Nixon Doctrine is the premise that countries threatened by communist aggression must take the primary responsibility for their own defense. This does not mean that U.S. forces have no military role; what it does mean is that threatened countries have to be willing to bear the primary burden of supplying the manpower. We were already putting the Nixon Doctrine into effect in Vietnam by concentrating on Vietnamization. This meant, as Secretary of Defense Melvin Laird put it, helping South Vietnam develop "a stronger administration, a stronger economy, stronger military forces and stronger police for internal security."

The most important aspect of Vietnamization was the development of South Vietnam's army into a strong, independent fighting force capable of holding its own against the communists—both the guerrilla forces and the main-force units from the north that were then waging conventional war.

In October 1969 I sent Sir Robert Thompson to Vietnam as my special adviser, with instructions to give me a candid, first-hand, independent evaluation of the situation. He reported that he was able to walk safely through many villages that had been under Vietcong control for years. He was so impressed with the progress that had been made that he thought we were in "a winning position" to conclude a just peace if we were willing to follow through with the efforts we were making.

After giving sharply increased emphasis to Vietnamization and pacification, the first order of military business was to hit at the enemy sanctuaries and supply lines in Laos and Cambodia. . . .

Cambodia

In March 1969, in response to a major new offensive that the North Vietnamese had launched against our forces in South Vietnam, I ordered the bombing of enemy-occupied base areas in Cambodia. The bombing was not publicly announced because of our concern that if it were, Sihanouk would be forced to object to it. However, even after it was disclosed by leaks to the New York *Times* in April, Sihanouk did not object. On the contrary, in May 1969, two months after the bombing had started, he said, "Cambodia only protests against the destruction of the property and lives of Cambodians. . . . If there is a buffalo or any Cambodian killed, I will be informed immediately. . . (and) I will protest."

In June 1969, Sihanouk said at a press conference that one of Cambodia's northeast provinces was "practically North Vietnamese territory," and the next month he invited me to visit Cambodia to mark the improvement of relations between our two countries. But Sihanouk's tilt toward the United States did not satisfy Cambodian public opinion. The Cambodians strongly objected to North Vietnam's violation of their sovereignty. In a series of rapidly moving events in March 1970, demonstrations against North Vietnamese occupation of Cambodian territory led to the sacking of the North Vietnamese and Vietcong embassies in Phnom Penh. Within a matter of days the North Vietnamese were given forty-eight hours' notice to vacate the country. Tiring of Sihanouk's careful balancing act, the Cambodian Parliament voted unanimously to depose him. . . .

Throughout April we showed restraint while the Vietnamese communist forces ran rampant through Cambodia. Our total military aid delivered to Cambodia consisted of 3,000 rifles provided covertly. The communists did not show similar restraint; they made it clear that their sole objective was domination of Cambodia.

Finally, on April 30, I announced our decision to counter the communist offensive by attacking North Vietnamese-occupied base areas in Cambodia bordering on South Vietnam. Our principal purpose was to under-cut the North Vietnamese invasion of that country so that Vietnamization and plans for the withdrawal of American troops could continue in South Vietnam. A secondary purpose was to relieve the military pressure exerted on Cambodia by the North Vietnamese forces that were rapidly overrunning it. The North Vietnamese had been occupying parts of eastern Cambodia for over five years and returned there after we left; in contrast we limited our stay to two months and advanced only to a depth of twenty-one miles. It is obvious to any unbiased observer who the aggressor was. . . .

The joint operations by the U.S. Army and ARVN wiped out huge stores of North Vietnamese equipment—15 million rounds of ammunition (a full year's supply), 14 million pounds of rice (four months' supply), 23,000 weapons (enough for seventy-four full-strength North Vietnamese battalions), and much more.

Thanks to this and the following year's Lam Son operation in Laos by the South Vietnamese forces, Hanoi was unable to stockpile enough supplies for a full-scale attack on South Vietnam until two years later—in 1972. Valuable time had been won with which to complete the task of Vietnamization. And even when the 1972 offensive came, it was weakest and easiest to contain from the direction of the sanctuaries in Cambodia, a testimony to the effectiveness of our measures. . . .

The 1972 Invasion

The American and South Vietnamese operations in Cambodia and Laos in 1970 and 1971 successfully prevented major North Vietnamese and Vietcong offensives in South Vietnam during those years and made it possible for the United States to continue to withdraw its forces on schedule.

By the spring of 1972 Hanoi recognized that it could not conquer South Vietnam through guerrilla war tactics, even with the help of conventional units, and that it could not win the support of the South Vietnamese people. There was no creditable way for Hanoi to claim any longer that the war in the South was a civil war between the Saigon government and the Vietcong, so North Vietnam dropped the facade of "civil war" and launched a full-scale conventional invasion of the South. Fourteen divisions and twenty-six independent regiments invaded the South. This left only one division and four independent regiments in Laos and no regular ground forces at all in North Vietnam.

As Sir Robert Thompson put it, "It was a sign of the times that this Korean-type communist invasion, which

twenty years before would have prompted united Western action and ten years before a Kennedy crusade, immediately put in doubt American resolve and probably won the Wisconsin primary for Senator George McGovern."

U.S. mining of Haiphong Harbor and the use of our airpower against targets in North Vietnam helped save the day, but the fighting on the ground was done exclusively by South Vietnamese forces. North Vietnam lost an estimated 130,000, killed and disabled. The invasion was a failure. . . .

[Our] actions in 1972 strengthened rather than weakened our new relationship with the Soviets and the Chinese. They both could see that we had power, the will to use it, and the skill to use it effectively. This meant that we were worth talking to. We could be a reliable friend or a dangerous enemy. This did not mean that they could publicly abandon their communist allies in Hanoi. However, their support for Hanoi noticeably cooled, which increased the incentive for Hanoi's leaders to make a peace agreement.

As a result of their decisive defeat in the 1972 offensive and their growing concern about the reliability of their Soviet and Chinese allies, the North Vietnamese finally began to negotiate seriously. But they were as stubborn at the conference table as they were on the battlefield. They wanted victory more than they wanted peace. Despite the overwhelming defeat of the peace-at-any-price candidate in the U.S. November elections, they continued to balk at our minimum terms.

On December 14, I made the decision to renew and increase the bombing of military targets in North Vietnam. The bombing began on December 18. It was a necessary step, and it proved to be the right decision. Although it was a very difficult choice, the realities of war, and not the wishful thinking of the ill-informed, demanded this action. The bombing broke the deadlock in negotiations. The North Vietnamese returned to the negotiating table, and on January 23, 1973, the long-waited peace agreement was finally achieved.

After their decisive defeat on the ground by South Vietnamese forces in the spring offensive and the destruction of their war-making capabilities by the December bombing, the North Vietnamese knew that militarily they were up against almost impossible odds. As the South Vietnamese economy continued to prosper far more than that of the North, Hanoi's communist ideology had less and less appeal. Thieu's Land to the Tiller program, for example, had reduced tenancy from 60 to 7 percent by 1973, a truly revolutionary development that undercut the communists' argument that the government allied itself with the rich and oppressed the people. Also, the North

Vietnamese knew that both the Soviets and the Chinese had a stake in their new relationship with us and might not be willing to endanger that relationship by providing military supplies in excess of those allowed by the Paris peace agreement of January 1973.

From Victory to Defeat

We had won the war militarily and politically in Vietnam. But defeat was snatched from the jaws of victory because we lost the war politically in the United States. The peace that was finally won in January 1973 could have been enforced and South Vietnam could be a free nation today. But in a spasm of shortsightedness and spite, the United States threw away what it had gained at such enormous cost. . . .

On January 2, 1973, the House Democratic Caucus voted 154–75 to cut off all funds for Indochina military operations as soon as arrangements were made for the safe withdrawal of U.S. troops and the return of our prisoners of war. Two days later a similar resolution was passed by the Senate Democratic Caucus, 36–12. This, it should be noted, was before Watergate began to weaken my own position as President, and only three months before withdrawal of American forces was completed, and the last of the 550,000 American troops that were in Vietnam when I took office in 1969 were brought back. . . .

If the peace agreement was to have any chance to be effective, it was essential that Hanoi be deterred from breaking it. In a private letter to Thieu I had stated that "if Hanoi fails to abide by the terms of this agreement, it is my intention to take swift and severe retaliatory action." At a news conference on March 15, with regard to North Vietnamese infiltration into South Vietnam and violation of the agreement, I stated, "I would only suggest that based on my actions over the past four years, the North Vietnamese should not lightly disregard such expressions of concern, when they are made with regard to a violation."

In April, May, and June of 1973, with my authority weakened by the Watergate crisis, retaliatory action was threatened but not taken. Then Congress passed a bill setting August 15 as the date for termination of U.S. bombing in Cambodia and requiring congressional approval for the funding of U.S. military action in any part of Indochina. The effect of this bill was to deny the President the means to enforce the Vietnam peace agreement by retaliating against Hanoi for violations.

Once Congress had removed the possibility of military action against breaches of the peace agreement, I knew I had only words with which to threaten. The communists knew it too. By means of the bombing cutoff

and the War Powers resolution passed in November 1973, Congress denied to me and to my successor, President Ford, the means with which to enforce the Paris agreement at a time when the North Vietnamese were openly and flagrantly violating it. It is truly remarkable that, for two years after the signing of the peace agreement in January 1973, the South Vietnamese held their own against the well-supplied North, without American personnel support either in the air or on the ground and with dwindling supplies.

Throughout 1974 the Russians poured huge amounts of ammunition, weaponry, and military supplies into North Vietnam, and the North in turn poured them into the South. In March 1974 Hanoi was estimated to have 185,000 men, 500 to 700 tanks, and 24 regiments of anti-aircraft troops in the South. With the threat of American air power gone, the North Vietnamese built new roads and pipelines to move their armies and supplies about. At the same time that the Soviet Union was arming Hanoi for the final assault, the United States Congress was sharply curtailing the flow of aid to South Vietnam. U.S. aid to South Vietnam was halved in 1974 and cut by another third in 1975. The United States ambassador to South Vietnam, Graham Martin, warned the Senate Foreign Relations Committee that such cuts in military aid would "seriously tempt the North to gamble on an all-out military offensive." His warning was tragically prophetic.

The original plan of the North Vietnamese was to launch their final offensive in 1976. But then they stepped up their timetable. At the start of 1975 Phuoc Long province fell to the communists, the first province South Vietnam had lost completely since 1954. There was relatively little reaction in the United States. Hanoi decided to make larger attacks in 1975 in preparation for the final offensive in 1926. On March 11, Ban Me Thout fell, and on the same day the U.S. House of Representatives refused to fund a $300 million supplemental military aid package that President Ford had proposed. Together with the earlier cutback of aid, this had a devastating effect on the morale of the South Vietnamese, as well as denying them the means with which to defend themselves; they were desperately short of military supplies and dependent for them on the United States. It also gave a tremendous psychological boost to the North. The North threw all of its remaining troops into the battle. Thieu tried to regroup his undersupplied forces in more defensible perimeters, and the hastily executed maneuver turned into a rout. By the end of April it was all over. Saigon became Ho Chi Minh City.

Hanoi had suffered an overwhelming defeat when it launched a conventional attack on the South in 1972. Then the North Vietnamese had been stopped on the ground by the South Vietnamese, while bombing by our air force and mining by our navy crippled their efforts to resupply their forces in the South. B-52 strikes could have had a devastating effect on the large troop concentrations that Hanoi used in its final offensive, but in 1975 Hanoi did not have to reckon with our air and naval forces, and thanks to ample Soviet military aid they had overwhelming advantages in tanks and artillery over South Vietnam's ground forces. After North Vietnam's victory General Dung, Hanoi's field commander in charge of the final offensive, remarked that "The reduction of U.S. aid made it impossible for the puppet troops to carry out their combat plans and build up their forces. . . . Thieu was then forced to fight a poor man's war. Enemy firepower had decreased by nearly 60 percent because of bomb and ammunition shortages. Its mobility was also reduced by half due to lack of aircraft, vehicles and fuel."

Our defeat in Vietnam can be blamed in part on the Soviets because they provided arms to Hanoi in violation of the peace agreement, giving the North an enormous advantage over the South in the final offensive in the spring of 1975. It can be blamed in part on the tactical and strategic mistakes made by President Thieu and his generals. It is grossly unfair to put the blame on South Vietnam's fighting men, the great majority of whom fought bravely and well against overwhelming odds. A major part of the blame must fall on the shoulders of those members of the Congress who were responsible for denying to the President, first me and then President Ford, the power to enforce the peace agreements, and for refusing to provide the military aid that South Vietnamese needed in order to meet the North Vietnamese offensive on equal terms.

But Congress was in part the prisoner of events. The leaders of the United States in the crucial years of the early and mid-1960s failed to come up with a strategy that would produce victory. Instead, first they undermined a strong regime, and then simply poured more and more U.S. troops and materiel into South Vietnam in an ineffective effort to shore up the weaker regimes that followed. They misled the public by insisting we were winning the war and thereby prepared the way for defeatism and demagoguery later on. The American people could not be expected to continue indefinitely to support a war in which they were told victory was around the corner, but which required greater and greater effort without any obvious signs of improvement.

By following the strategy I initiated in 1969, we and the South Vietnamese were able to win the war militarily by the time of the Paris accords of January 27, 1973. The 550,000 American troops that were in Vietnam when I came into office in 1969 had been withdrawn and South Vietnam was able to defend itself—if we supplied the arms the Paris accords allowed.

But the public had been so misinformed and misled by unwise government actions and the shallow, inflammatory treatment of events by the media that morale within the United States collapsed just when the North was overwhelmingly defeated on the battlefield. We won a victory after a long hard struggle, but then we threw it away. The communists had grasped what strategic analyst Brian Crozier said is the central point of revolutionary war: "that it is won or lost on the home front." The war-making capacity of North Vietnam had been virtually destroyed by the bombings in December of 1972, and we had the means to make and enforce a just peace, a peace with honor. But we were denied these means when Congress prohibited military operations in or over Indochina and cut back drastically on the aid South Vietnam needed to defend itself. In the final analysis, a major part of the blame must be borne by those who encouraged or participated in the fateful decisions that got us into the war in the 1960's, and who then by their later actions sabotaged our efforts to get us out in an acceptable way in the 1970's.

By inaction at the crucial moment, the United States undermined an ally and abandoned him to his fate. The effect on the millions of Cambodians, Laotians, and South Vietnamese who relied on us and have now paid the price of communist reprisals is bad enough. But the cost in terms of raising doubts among our allies as to America's reliability, and in terms of the encouragement it gives to our potential enemies to engage in aggression against our friends in other parts of the world, will be devastating for U.S. policy for decades to come. . . .

RICHARD NIXON was America's 37th president who was twice elected and ended America's participation in the Vietnam War. In August 1974, he resigned the presidency after the Judiciary Committee of the House of Representatives voted to present articles of impeachment against him before the full House. He wrote almost a dozen books in retirement.

Jeffrey Kimball    **NO**

Debunking Nixon's Myths of Vietnam

". . . an account or belief that is demonstrably untrue, in whole or substantial part."

— Thomas A. Bailey

"The time has come to debunk these myths."

— Richard Nixon

Richard Nixon will long be remembered in history textbooks and encyclopedias for having been the first American president to resign his office. It seems almost as likely that he will also be remembered as a president who was uncommonly effective in the arena of foreign policy, because at the turn of the twenty-first century, Nixon's own embattled appraisal of the diplomatic history of his administration—reinforced by Henry A. Kissinger's nuanced variation—occupies a commanding position on the historiographic and public-opinion battlefields. The basic building blocks comprising this intellectual framework are Nixon's claims about his leadership regarding rapprochement with the People's Republic of China, detente with the Soviet Union, and "peace with honor" in Vietnam. Rapprochement and detente are the most celebrated of his policies; his management of the U.S.-Vietnam War is the most controversial and complex.

For many academics, policymakers, journalists, and others among the citizenry, the Nixon-Kissinger paradigm defines in whole or large part their conventional wisdom about the achievements of Nixon-administration foreign policy between the years 1969 and 1974. I venture that it constitutes the canonical perspective of Nixon's diplomatic record. His claim of having opened China has, in particular, achieved the status of historiographic orthodoxy *and* folk legend, which Nixon, a student and practitioner of legend-making, defined as "an artful intertwining of fact and myth, designed to beguile, to impress, to inspire, or sometimes simply to attract attention."

Nixon was ever mindful of Winston Churchill's dictum that history would only treat him well if he wrote his own history. In speeches, interviews, memoirs, and essays during and after his presidency, he portrayed himself as a discerning presidential leader who—possessing a unified conception of global politics—challenged the bureaucracy's narrow-minded, ossified thinking and the public's naive idealism. Maintaining that he had developed a strategy for restoring relations with the PRC even before his election as president, he claimed credit for having initiated rapprochement, and he contended that his motives were noble as well as sensible: bringing China back into the family of nations, reopening trade, ending the U.S.-Vietnam War, and creating an environment for regional peace and stability. Characterizing' his steps toward detente with the Soviet Union as both realistic and imaginative, he claimed successes in advancing nuclear arms control, broadening trade, promoting European stability, and terminating the U.S.-Vietnam War. He lauded the prudent practicality of his Nixon Doctrine, the promising initiatives of his Mideast policies, the righteous realism of linkage diplomacy, and the clever effectiveness of triangular diplomacy in bringing an honorable conclusion to the U.S.-Vietnam War on January 27, J973, through the Paris Agreement on Ending the War and Restoring Peace in Vietnam. Citing his self-styled masterful handling of this intractable conflict—which, he claimed, he had inherited from his Democratic predecessors—he maintained that he had snatched victory from the jaws of defeat, brought American soldiers home, rescued POWs, given the Saigon regime the ability to endure and survive protected the rising capitalist tigers of the Pacific Rim from communism, and preserved American credibility. These putative accomplishments—but especially his claims that he brought an end to the U.S.-Vietnam War, reestablished relations with China, and reduced tensions with the Soviet Union—constituted the key pillars of what Nixon called his "structure of peace."

Kissinger's version of this history was a nuanced variation of Nixon's. As had Nixon, he put a positive spin on the major benchmarks of their joint foreign policy, but he gave himself more credit for having made crucial contributions to the creation of a new international order. He, too, singled out administration opponents for his severest criticism, but he grudgingly acknowledged the dark side of

Nixon's psyche as well as his excessive partisanship, and he noted that these inherent flaws of Nixon's personality had detrimental consequences for his policies and presidency. Kissinger, however, portrayed himself as having been a restraining influence on Nixon and his hardline advisers in the White House.

Nixon, Kissinger, former aides, and some journalists and historians amended the script of this historical drama in the months and years after his resignation from the presidency. They cast the Watergate scandal as the main culprit in causing the breakdown of his administration's foreign policies, particularly regarding South Vietnam, which was ultimately lost, they claimed, because Congress, emboldened by Watergate and in Nixon's absence, failed to provide adequate support to the Saigon regime. Obversely, they portrayed his foreign policy achievements as having redeemed his historical reputation from the embarrassment of Watergate. Appreciated for policies that were seen by many as bold, imaginative, and realistically constructive, Nixon emerged from the ruins of resignation with the prestige of a statesman and peacemaker.

The weakest link in the chain of historical claims that Nixon and his aides and supporters forged in constructing their legend of foreign policy was and is their treatment of the U.S.-Vietnam War. Nevertheless, key elements of their version of history enjoy wide acceptance, in part because they parallel hawkish and pro-war tenets concerning the conflict. For example: North Vietnam (the Democratic Republic of Vietnam; DRV) and South Vietnam (the Republic of Vietnam; RVN) were two separate nations; the military aggression of the Communist North against the potentially democratic South caused the war; it was a just and necessary war; the danger of a regional and global domino effect was real; the key strategic errors were made by liberal Democratic policymakers; the war was militarily winnable; Congress, the press, and the antiwar movement caused U.S. defeat in Vietnam. Even less partisan and more detached historians have not been immune from some of Nixon's claims; for example, that his policies in Vietnam, such as Vietnamization, were guided by a farsighted principle for a new direction in American foreign policy vis-a-vis the third world—the Nixon Doctrine.

Believing that his administration had to seize the moment before antiwar intellectuals and the liberal press preempted the public-relations battlefield, Nixon had begun as early as December 1972 to remold the history of the war. On the nineteenth, the day after the "Christmas bombings" of Hanoi had commenced, he instructed his chief of staff H. R. Haldeman to assemble a spin-control group that would assure him "for all time the coveted title[s] of Peacemaker" and "peace *bringer.*" The strategy

that emerged at the time of the signing of the Paris Agreement in late January 1973 was to build on the emerging "revisionist school" of history, which defended the morality and purpose of the war, "take advantage of the current crest" of public emotion about the return of the POWs, and launch an "all out effort" to "get a lot of people out selling our line" with a few "key points to emphasize."

At another propitious moment twelve years later, Nixon concisely recapitulated his historical "line" on the U.S.-Vietnam War in a small polemical book entitled *No More Vietnams.* Nineteen-eighty-five, its year of publication, marked the tenth anniversary of the fall of Saigon and the first year of President Ronald Reagan's second term. It was also the year in which the movie *Rambo: First Blood, Part-Two* was released—one of several eighties' motion pictures about the war that appealed to those who wanted to believe that Americans could triumph against their old and new enemies around the globe from Vietnam to Iran to Central America. The U.S.-Vietnam War stood as a symbol of victory betrayed, especially to many military veterans of the conflict, but also to those among the larger public who were dismayed about defeat in Vietnam and cynical about politicians after Watergate. How better for Nixon to advance his personal rehabilitation than to reprise his history of the U.S.-Vietnam War in a politically-correct light for the eighties, thereby ingratiating himself with the resurgent new Right and the diplomatically militant administration of President Reagan, who had often proclaimed the war to have been a betrayed noble cause? Although he stressed the triumph of his own policies, Nixon dedicated *No More Vietnams* to "those who served," comparing their competence and bravery to the pernicious naivete and irresponsibility of antiwar demonstrators. As he had previously, Nixon defended his record in Vietnam, arguing once more that his victory had been overturned by the faithlessness of Congress. Now rejecting detente, Nixon issued a call to arms against an expansionist Soviet Union, world Communism, and a revolutionary Third World in the book's last chapter, which was entitled "Third World War."

Because of the U.S.-Vietnam War, the post-World War II cold war consensus on foreign policy had been shattered; yet, by the 1980's the U.S.-Vietnam War had replaced World War II as the most resonant source of historical lessons for citizens and decisionmakers engaged in debate about the best foreign policy course to take in the present and future. Drawing on their interpretation of the history of the U.S.-Vietnam War, noninterventionist opponents of the Reagan administration argued that America's past intervention in Vietnam had been a failed, tragic mistake; therefore, there should be "no more Vietnams."

From the point of view of interventionists like Nixon and Reagan, the U.S.-Vietnam War had been a necessary war that could have been a military and political success had proper strategies been pursued and the war's opponents not undermined the will of the nation to persist. Military intervention in the third world remained in their opinion a viable and necessary option as long as it was properly executed; therefore, there should be more Vietnams—but no more failed Vietnams of the sort allegedly caused by weak-willed liberal politicians, the press, and the antiwar movement.

Nixon intended the title of his little book to be ironic. In an "author's note," he declared that "both during and after the war, as President and private citizen, I found that television and newspaper coverage of the U.S.-Vietnam War described a different war from the one I knew, and that the resulting misimpressions formed in the public's mind were continuing to haunt our foreign policy." He wrote the book, he said, in order to debunk these misimpressions, or myths, as he more often referred to them, thereby correcting the historical record and contributing to the avoidance of more *failed* Vietnams—while encouraging more *successful* Vietnams.

In the course of debunking myths, Nixon created and perpetuated myths through lack of candor about his own management of the war and by misrepresenting accounts that did not correspond with his. An example was his assertion that among the hundreds of "books, thousands of newspaper and magazine articles, and scores of motion pictures and documentaries" about the war, the "great majority" have concluded that "the United States lost the war militarily." It would not have bolstered Nixon's historical image, of course, to have admitted that the war had been lost militarily, since this would have suggested that he had been forced to accept the Paris Agreement, implying in turn that he had settled for something less than victory. Thus, in *No More Vietnams* and elsewhere, he claimed to have won the war militarily by late 1972. In contrast to Nixon, my own sampling of the mountain of books, articles, and movies about the war to which he referred leads me to conclude that the overwhelming majority of authors, producers, directors, and editors have not claimed that the U.S. had been militarily defeated but instead that the U.S. had simply failed to win militarily, with the result that the U.S. government's longstanding policy goals had gone down to defeat.

Several volumes would be required to confute all of Nixon's own myths of the U.S.-Vietnam War, but perhaps it will suffice here to look at two representative issues that illustrate why core elements of Nixon's history of his handling of the war are demonstrably untrue, if not in whole part, at least in substantial part: What was Nixon's plan for the prosecution of the war, and why did it fail?

Straddling the political center of his electoral constituency during the presidential campaign of 1968, Mr. Nixon alternately implied and denied that he had a secret plan to achieve "peace with honor" in Vietnam. As president in 1969, however, he and his assistant for national security affairs, Henry Kissinger, privately assured select groups that they did have a plan and that it would bear fruit before the year was out—but they were secretive in revealing all of its components. Many years later, Nixon explained that before his inauguration he had reviewed strategic options and during "the first months" of his administration had "put together a five-point strategy to . . . end the war and win the peace":

—Vietnamization (the accelerated equipping and training of South Vietnamese armed forces);

—De-Americanization (the gradual withdrawal of U.S. troops and reductions in draft calls);

—Pacification (counter-guerrilla measures);

—Linkage and triangular diplomacy (using rapprochement and detente to lever Beijing and Moscow into pressuring Hanoi);

—Negotiations with Hanoi coupled with "irresistible military pressure" (incursions into Cambodia and Laos and intensified, expanded bombing against North Vietnam, its army in the South, the Southern Vietcong, and the Ho Chi Minh trail).

Nixon's postwar description of his strategy was only superficially accurate. His careful wording obscured complex and dark realities about the details and underlying assumptions of his plan, its contingent, improvised, and evolving nature, and the goals of his strategy.

Regarding his plan's details and assumptions, Nixon neglected to report that his "madman theory" undergirded the conjoined components of negotiations and military pressure. Guided by this theory, he aimed to force concessions from Hanoi not only by damaging their military and logistical capabilities through stepped-up bombing but also by threatening them with the possibility of more drastic escalations, such as invading North Vietnam, mining Northern ports, bombing Hanoi, Haiphong, and Red River dikes, and using nuclear weapons. Threats of this sort were intended to indicate to Hanoi that he was willing to destroy North Vietnam even at the risk of Chinese and Soviet intervention. They were "irrational" in the sense of exceeding the accepted or predictable norms of "rational" statecraft in the circumstances of the time. Because of his past reputation as a zealous anticommunist and his present campaign of bombing in the rest of Indochina, Nixon theorized that the North Vietnamese would soon come to believe that he was indeed a risk-taker who was capable of escalating the war against the DRV out of vengeful anger or unpredictable impulsiveness.

In the anti-detente political climate of the eighties, Nixon was willing to report in *No More Vietnams* that he had also tried to use the carrots of rapprochement and detente to seduce Beijing and Moscow into using sticks of persuasion against Hanoi; that is, that he had attempted to entice them into reducing their shipments of war materiel to North Vietnam, thereby forcing Hanoi to make concessions in its negotiations with Washington. What he did not report or at least make clear in his discussion of triangular diplomacy was that he had additionally sought to play a "China card" against the Soviets by communicating to Moscow that Washington was prepared to improve relations with Beijing in order to facilitate the containment of the Soviet Union. In addition, he incorporated his mad-threat strategy into his dealings with the Soviets, repeatedly hinting to them that dire military measures in Indochina would result from Hanoi's continued "intransigence," with unfortunate consequences for U.S.-USSR relations. Denoting his tilt toward the PRC, he did not, however, employ this approach in his talks with Beijing. Nixon's strategy—developed in private sessions with Kissinger, who also assisted in its tactical implementation—was not only to link other issues to the settlement of the Vietnam War but to link linkage itself to threats designed to induce anxiety in the Soviets and North Vietnamese.

Nixon initiated these strategies of threat, linkage, and triangulation in a series of steps during the first half of 1969. In February, for example, he informed Ambassador Anatolii Dobrynin that the U.S. would link progress in detente to progress in settling the war in Vietnam, and, establishing his credentials as a mad bomber, he escalated bombing raids in South Vietnam and Laos. In March he launched a massive B-52 bombing campaign against Vietnamese Communist forces in Cambodia. At least as early as July 12, Kissinger, on behalf of his boss, cautioned Moscow through Dobrynin that if it failed in persuading Hanoi to negotiate in a way that pleased Washington, Nixon would dramatically expand U.S. bombing against North Vietnam. A few days later, Nixon warned Hanoi in a personal letter that "if by November 1, no major progress was made toward a solution, we will be compelled . . . to take measures of greatest consequence." He subsequently disseminated this threat through other diplomatic channels. By September Kissinger's National Security Council staff and the Joint Chiefs of Staff were finalizing plans to carry out the threat in operation Duck Hook. In mid-October, however, Nixon retreated, abandoning Duck Hook in the face of opposition from Secretary of State William Rogers and Secretary of Defense Melvin Laird, NSC staff criticism of the operation's potential efficacy, North Vietnamese defiance, Soviet noncooperation, and his own anxiety about ongoing antiwar demonstrations and latent negative public reaction.

Duck Hook's cancellation spelled the failure of Nixon's original plan to "end the war and win the peace," and it also exposed the contingent, improvised, and evolving nature of his strategy. In postwar memoirs and histories, Nixon emphasized themes of personal control and farsighted consistency: he described himself as having been on top of things and his plan as having successfully unfolded from beginning to end. The reality was that in the beginning—that is, in 1969—all parts of the plan had not been fully in place, and they had also been unusually subject to the vicissitudes of circumstances and events, which neither Nixon nor Kissinger had adequately anticipated. Secretary Laird, for example, doggedly advocated accelerated de-Americanization, leading Nixon, against Kissinger's opposition, to carry out more rapid troop withdrawals than originally envisioned, which had the effect of eroding his military leverage on the ground in Vietnam. Moreover, the DRV and the USSR proved more impervious to mad threats and linkage diplomacy than Nixon and Kissinger had hoped.

For his part, Nixon was less resistant to home-front pressures than he allowed in his postwar accounts, in which he attempted to portray defeats as victories. He described his televised address to the nation on November 3, 1969, for example, as the most significant and effective of his presidency, because it was well-received by a majority of the public, serving to blunt the impact of the antiwar demonstrations of October and November. What he failed to mention, however, was that the speech was originally intended as his announcement of the commencement of Duck Hook but became instead an attempt to energize the Silent Majority. It was also an acknowledgment that the war was now perceived as "his war."

The November 3 address marked the transition from his original plan to a revised plan. Forced to rearrange strategic priorities, he had decided to place more emphasis than before on Vietnamization and pacification (and to be more aggressive in attacking his opponents on the home front). In addition, he revamped his approach to the Soviets: he would continue to use the lure of detente to induce their assistance with Hanoi, but he would now redouble his efforts to bring about rapprochement with Beijing in order not only to foster its cooperation vis-a-vis Hanoi but also to play the China card against Moscow. (Nixon was encouraged in this direction by the border clashes between Soviet and Chinese forces in 1969 and by the coincidence of Beijing's own diplomatic initiatives to break out of its diplomatic isolation in order to play an "American card" against the Soviets.) As before, Nixon intended to buttress his strategy with forceful threats and military measures: continued bombing in Indochina, threats of expanded bombing against North Vietnam, and, if the opportunity presented itself, decisive ground operations.

Nixon's decision to invade Cambodia in April 1970 was the result of a dynamic process that had begun with his search in the fall of 1969 for a more effective blueprint for victory. It was animated not only by the administration's desire to make a "big play" in 1970 but also by the March 18 military coup against Prince Norodom Sihanouk (which Nixon endorsed), the internecine turmoil that had preceded it, and the administration's concerns about the threat that Communist Vietnamese forces on South Vietnam's Cambodian flank posed to Vietnamization and pacification. The invasion—or incursion, as Nixon called it—produced mixed and tragic consequences. Although it did temporarily disrupt Communist Vietnamese troop deployments and logistics, the operation fell far short of the decisive results for which Nixon had hoped; it brought about a military alliance of convenience between Khmer, Vietnamese, and Chinese Communists; and it helped plunge Cambodia into an abyss of civil war. On the home front, Nixon was unnerved by widespread demonstrations against the incursion, by the killing and wounding of students at Kent State University at the hands of Ohio National Guard troops, and by the intensification of congressional opposition to his direction of the war. The strategic results were that he would not be able to send U.S. troops into Laos or again into Cambodia, he would feel more than before the need to carry out large-scale troop withdrawals from South Vietnam, and his hope of bringing the war to a favorable conclusion by the end of 1970 or the beginning of 1971 had been shattered.

Frustrated by his diminished options, and growing more concerned about citizen impatience with the war and the war's potential impact on his chances for reelection in 1972, Nixon considered yet another revised plan during the fall of 1970. He would placate Americans by rapidly withdrawing all remaining U.S. ground forces except those considered "residual"; he would compensate for that step and also apply pressure on Hanoi by canceling negotiations, issuing an ultimatum, and massively bombing, mining, and blockading North Vietnam. Kissinger successfully argued against this "bug out" strategy, maintaining that a pullout by the end of 1971 would leave them incapable of dealing with setbacks in South Vietnam when the 1972 presidential election took place; it would be better, therefore, to continue with negotiations and extend the timing of troop withdrawals until the end of 1972, "so that we won't have to deliver finally until after the elections."

Implicit in this approach was their acceptance of a stopgap option that Nixon subsequently claimed he had steadfastly rejected; namely, the "decent-interval" solution. The term referred to a scenario in which a somewhat weakened enemy and strengthened Saigon regime would ensure that there would be a sufficiently lengthy period of time between the withdrawal of American forces and the ultimate collapse of the Saigon government, whose preservation had long been the fundamental goal of U. S. policy. For Nixon, such a solution would lend credence to his claim that he had negotiated a satisfactory agreement, thus, in turn, salvaging U.S. credibility and Nixon's honor. Nixon had not abandoned hope of achieving his fundamental goal, but he had come to realize that he might fail.

Nixon's policy goal in South Vietnam was the same as that of Presidents Eisenhower, Kennedy, and Johnson before him. Since the late 1950s, the U.S.-Vietnam War had been a struggle over the political status of South Vietnam. The U.S. was committed to the preservation of a non-Communist, pro-capitalist government in an independent state of South Vietnam. Communist and allied Vietnamese nationalists were committed to the expulsion of U.S. forces and the reunification of North and South, preferably, for the Communists, in the form of a "socialist" nation under a Communist government. Thus, in the secret negotiations held in Paris between the delegations led by Kissinger and Le Duc Tho, which began fitfully in August 1969, Kissinger sought to win agreement primarily on two main issues: the mutual withdrawal from South Vietnam of American and North Vietnamese forces and the continuance of the Saigon regime of Nguyen Van Thieu. Tho sought to win agreement on the unconditional, unilateral withdrawal of U.S. troops and the removal of Thieu from power although, as events proved, this was not quite as important to them as unilateral American withdrawal. There were several other ancillary issues, but these four were fundamental.

Nixon and Kissinger began to abandon the mutual withdrawal formula in principle in September 1970, thereby shifting from a victory strategy—in the sense of ensuring Thieu's survival—to a strategy that allowed for the possibility of a decent-interval solution. Hanoi abandoned its demand for Thieu's removal by the U.S. in October 1972 but received de jure recognition of the Provisional Revolutionary Government (PRG; the government arm of the Southern National Liberation Front) in the territories it controlled.

My interpretation of documentary and secondary evidence leads me to conclude that the two sides agreed to a compromise in which each accepted less than its maximum terms because each had come by mid-1972 to realize that the war was indeed militarily stalemated and that its chances of achieving an acceptable settlement would be better in October, just before Nixon's reelection, than they would be afterward. Moreover, the costs of the war—that is, the monetary, human, political, and international toll—had become unacceptably palpable. Hence, both sides now deemed a compromise solution to be necessary and, therefore, realistic.

Nixon and Kissinger later argued that their triangular policies vis-a-vis Beijing and Moscow had caused Hanoi to accept a diplomatic solution that favored Saigon and Washington. It appears that the PRC and USSR did exert pressure on the DRV in the form of diplomatic advice or admonition, but at the same time, there is no evidence that it was decisive. Instead, it seems that North Vietnam. acted mostly in response to its assessment of the balance of forces on the ground and in the air in South Vietnam, which would favor them after a U.S. withdrawal, and also to its assessment of the American political scene, which limited Nixon's options and exerted pressure on him to compromise. Neither Chinese nor Soviet pressure was the primary contributing cause of Hanoi's decision to negotiate and sign the Paris agreement. Nor is there any compelling evidence that Linebacker I and II, Nixon's two massive bombing campaigns in 1972, forced Hanoi to come to an agreement. Instead, it seems that the military and political consequences of the North Vietnamese Spring Offensive of 1972, which were not favorable to Saigon, were more, significant in bringing about a settlement.

Who won and who lost the war—the U.S. or the DRV? The proof of the pudding is that in the compromise Paris settlement, the U.S., on balance, conceded the most: it withdrew its ground, air, and naval forces; although Thieu remained in power, the PRG was recognized as a legitimate political entity; despite Nixon's Enhance Plus program of military aid for Thieu, his long-term prospects of survival were not good. Thus, the situation in Vietnam

had basically returned to the conditions established in the 1954 Geneva Accords, but with significant improvements for Communist forces: the North Vietnamese Army remained in the South; the PRG and its military arm, the Vietcong, possessed de facto and de jure control of significant portions of Southern territory; the U.S. could not reintroduce troops in the future and not likely re-intervene with air power; and the international community accepted the legitimacy of Vietnam's reunification. It was a cease-fire agreement that might have been achieved in any one of the years before its actual signing in January 1973.

Nixon's argument that the war was won in the Paris Agreement but subsequently lost as the result of Congress's failure to deliver sufficient amounts of aid to Saigon ignored the true terms of the settlement, as well as the demonstrable fact that he and Kissinger had been forced to accept the military realities of the war in 1972 and had yielded to political pressure from congressional liberals and conservatives to get out of Vietnam. What he succeeded in doing, however, was to win, or at least score successes, in the battle for the verdict of history. Through myth-laden accounts of his foreign policies in general and his war policies in particular, as well as his emphasis on Congress's betrayal of the cause, he convinced many that he had forced the other side to accept a peace agreement that favored Saigon. In effect, he and Kissinger succeeded in creating a decent interval—not for Thieu, not for "those who served," not for those on both sides who lost their lives, limbs, or loved ones, and not for the American citizenry or the Indochinese, but for their own reputations. Their's was a message, moreover, that not only helped redeem their prestige but made the war a political football, ill-preparing Americans to understand the meaning and lessons of the war they had just fought.

Jeffrey P. Kimball is professor emeritus at Miami University in Hamilton, Ohio and has written numerous books and articles on American diplomacy. His book on Nixon's Vietnam War won numerous awards, was a History Book Club selection, and was nominated for the Pulitzer Prize.

EXPLORING THE ISSUE

Did President Nixon Negotiate a "Peace with Honor" in Vietnam in 1973?

Critical Thinking and Reflection

1. Trace the events from the Eisenhower years through the Nixon years (1954–1973) leading to the United States' involvement and withdrawal from Vietnam. In your answer, consider the following:
   a. Geneva records (1954)
   b. Diem Regime (1955–1963)
   c. 1956: a year of no elections
   d. Kennedy's policy of counterinsurgency
   e. Johnson's escalation
   f. Nixon Doctrine
   g. Paris Peace Accords (1973)
2. Critically evaluate President Nixon's view of the Vietnam War. Did his policies succeed in bringing a true peace to Vietnam? Could Congress have saved Vietnam in 1973 and 1975? Did Nixon and Kissinger really expect Vietnam to fall after a decent interval?
3. Critically examine the thesis that President Nixon and Secretary of State Kissinger negotiated a peace settlement that was doomed to fail and that U.S. bombing raids should have prevented the collapse of South Vietnam once the cease fire was violated.
4. Compare Nixon's and Kimball's interpretations as to how the Vietnam War ended. Did Nixon withhold evidence that supports Kimball's contention that he and Kissinger expected South Vietnam to collapse after a "decent interval"?
5. What lessons can President Obama learn from the Vietnam War in making policy in Iraq, Iran, and Afghanistan?

Is There Common Ground?

Both today's Republicans and today's Democrats claim to have learned lessons from the Vietnam War. In the presidential election of 2004, the war came back to haunt both candidates. The then President George Bush had to prove he served in the Alabama National Guard during the war, whereas Senator John Kerry had to defend his patriotism as a former leader of the Vietnam Veterans against the War. In the summer of 2009, President Obama was weighing his options in Afghanistan. Should he send troops there? Republicans were reading former CIA agent Lewis Sorley's *A Better War: The Unexamined Victories and Final Tragedy of America's Last Years in Vietnam* (Harcourt Brace, 1999), which argues that Nixons' policymakers, particularly General Creighton Abrams, "dropped General Westmoreland's war of attrition and search-and-destroy missions in favor of a holistic approach aimed at 'pacifying' the population of South Vietnam," for lessons on how to win, whereas Democrats, including Obama, were reading Gordon M.

Goldstein's *Lessons in Disaster: McGeorge Bundy and the Path to War in Vietnam* (Henry Holt, 2008). Bundy was head of the National Security Council under both Presidents Kennedy and Johnson and, like former Secretary of Defense Robert F. McNamara, had second thoughts about escalating the war in 1965. See "A Battle of Two Books Rages," *The Wall Street Journal* (October 7, 2009).

Create Central

www.mhhe.com/createcentral

Additional Resources

David L. Anderson, ed., *Shadow on the White House: Presidents and the Vietnam War 1945–1975* (University Press of Kansas, 1993).

Stephen Cohen, ed., *Vietnam: Anthology and Guide to a Television History* (Alfred A. Knopf, 1983).

George C. Herring, *America's Longest War: The United States and Vietnam, 1950–1975*, 3rd ed. (McGraw Hill, 1996).

Jeffrey Kimball, "The Case of the 'Decent Interval': Do We Now Have a Smoking Gun?" The *SHAFR Newsletter* (September 2001).

James H. Willbanks, *Abandoning Vietnam: How America Left and South Vietnam Lost the War* (University Press of Kansas, 2004).

Internet References . . .

The American Experience: Vietnam Online

www.pbs.org/wgbh/amex/vietnam

Vietnam Center and Archive

http://vietnam.ttu.edu/

White House Tapes: The Presidential Recordings Program

http://millercenter.org/academic/presidentialrecordings/

Selected, Edited, and with Issue Framing Material by:
Larry Madaras, *Howard Community College*
and
James M. SoRelle, *Baylor University*

ISSUE

Has the Women's Movement of the 1970s Failed to Liberate American Women?

YES: F. Carolyn Graglia, from *Domestic Tranquility: A Brief against Feminism*, Spence (1998)

NO: Jo Freeman, from "The Revolution for Women in Law and Public Policy," McGraw-Hill Education (1995)

Learning Outcomes

After reading this issue, you will be able to:

- Identify and explain the significance of the "cult of womanhood" and its major components.
- Summarize the conservative critique of the women's liberation movement.
- Understand the political implications of the women's movement.
- Identify specific changes in the law and public policy pertaining to the status of women in the United States that were products of the women's movement of the 1960s and 1970s.
- Assess the positive and negative consequences of the women's movement of the 1970s.

ISSUE SUMMARY

YES: Writer and lecturer F. Carolyn Graglia argues that women should stay at home and practice the values of "true motherhood" because contemporary feminists have discredited marriage, devalued traditional home-making, and encouraged sexual promiscuity.

NO: Jo Freeman claims that the feminist movement produced a revolution in law and public policy in the 1960s and 1970s that completed a drive to remove discriminatory laws regarding opportunities for women in the United States.

In 1961, President John F. Kennedy established the Commission on the Status of Women to examine "the prejudice and outmoded customs that act as barriers to the full realization of women's basic rights." Two years later, Betty Friedan, a closet leftist from suburban Rockland County, New York, wrote about the growing malaise of the suburban housewife in her best-seller *The Feminist Mystique* (W. W. Norton, 1963).

The roots of Friedan's "feminine mystique" go back much earlier than the post–World War II "baby boom" generation of suburban America. Historians of American women have traced the origins of the modern family to the early nineteenth century. As the nation became more

stable politically, the roles of men, women, and children became segmented in ways that still exist today. Dad went to work, the kids went to school, and mom stayed home. Women's magazines, gift books, and religious literature of the period ascribed to these women a role that Barbara Welter has characterized as the "Cult of True Womanhood," in which the ideal woman upheld four virtues—piety, purity, submissiveness, and domesticity. See Welter's essay in *American Quarterly* (Summer 1996), as well as Barbara Berg's earlier work *The Remembered Gate: Origins of American Feminism: The Woman & the City, 1800–1860* (Oxford University Press, 1978).

In nineteenth-century America, most middle-class white women stayed home. Those who entered the workforce as teachers or became reformers were usually extending the values of the Cult of True Womanhood to the outside world. This was true of the women reformers in the Second Great Awakening and the peace, temperance, and abolitionist movements before the Civil War. The first real challenge to the traditional value system occurred when a handful of women showed up at Seneca Falls, New York, in 1848 to sign the Women's Declaration of Rights.

At the beginning of the twentieth century, a number of middle-class women from elite colleges in the Northeast were in the vanguard of a number of progressive reform movements—temperance, antiprostitution, child labor, and settlement houses. Working in tandem with the daughters of first-generation immigrants employed in the garment industry, the early feminists realized that laws affecting women could be passed only if women had the right to vote. After an intense struggle, the Nineteenth Amendment was ratified on August 26, 1920. The "suffragettes" overcame the arguments of male and female antisuffragists who associated women voters with divorce, promiscuity, and neglect of children and husbands with the ratification of the Nineteenth Amendment. Once the women's movement obtained the vote, however, there was no agreement on future goals. The movement stalled between the two world wars for a variety of reasons: women pursued their own individual freedom in a consumer-oriented society in the 1920s; and the Great Depression of the 1930s placed the economic survival of the nation at the forefront. But World War II had long-range effects on women. Minorities—African Americans and Hispanics, in particular—worked at high wages for over three years in factory jobs traditionally reserved for white males; so did married white females, often in their thirties.

World War II brought about major changes for working women. Six million women entered the labor force for the first time, many of whom were married. "The proportion of women in the labor force," writes Lois Banner, "increased from 25 percent in 1940 to 36 percent in 1945. This increase was greater than that of the previous four decades combined." Many women moved into high-paying, traditionally male jobs as police officers, firefighters, and precision toolmakers. Steel and auto companies that converted over to wartime production made sure that lighter tools were made for women to use on the assembly lines. The federal government also erected federal childcare facilities.

When the war ended in 1945, many of these women lost their nontraditional jobs. The federal daycare program was eliminated, and the government told women to go home, even though a 1944 study by the Women's Bureau concluded that 80 percent of working women wanted to continue in their jobs after the war. Most history texts emphasize that women did return home, moved to the suburbs, and created a baby boom generation, which reversed the downward size of families in the years from 1946 to 1964. What is lost in this description is the fact that after 1947 the number of working women again began to rise, reaching 31 percent in 1951. The consciousness of the changing role of women during World War II would reappear during the 1960s. When Friedan wrote *The Feminine Mystique* in 1963, both working-class and middle-class college-educated women experienced discrimination in the marketplace. When women worked, they were expected to become teachers, nurses, secretaries, and airline stewardesses—the lowest-paying jobs in the workforce. In the turbulent 1960s, this situation was no longer accepted, and by 1973, at the height of the Women's Liberation Movement, women comprised 42 percent of the American workforce. By the beginning of the twenty-first century, middle-class women had made substantial gains in the professions compared with 1960. They represented 43 percent of law school classes as opposed to 2 percent in 1960; 35 percent of students in MBA programs as compared to 4 percent in 1960; 38 percent of all physicians and dentists in contrast to 6 and 1 percent, respectively, in those categories in 1960; and 39 percent in doctoral programs today, up from 11 percent in 1960. Working-class women, on the other hand, have been much less successful in breaking into traditional blue-collar jobs such as truck driving and construction.

One of the consequences of the resurgence of conservatism in the Reagan Era of the 1980s was a blistering criticism of the feminist movement in the United States. Pundit Rush Limbaugh spoke frequently about "feminazis" who were undermining the traditional structures of American society, most particularly the family, and his characterizations were echoed by social critics such as Phyllis Schlafly, Camille Paglia, and others who decried what they viewed as the dangerous excesses of the "radical feminists." The late Elizabeth Fox-Genovese contended that contemporary feminists have not spoken to the concerns of married women, especially women from poor to lower-middle-class families who must work in order to help support the family. Fox-Genovese's *Feminism Is Not the Story of My Life: How Today's Feminist Elite Have Lost Touch with the Real Concerns of Women* (Doubleday, 1996) is peppered with interviews of whites, African Americans, and Hispanic Americans of different classes and gives a more complex picture of the problems women face today. Moderate feminists, such as Cathy Young, author of *Cease Fire! Why Women Must Join Forces to Achieve True*

Equality (Free Press, 1999), challenged the conservatives' arguments that dismissed the real discrimination women had faced in the job market in the 1950s and which seemed to attempt to restore a view of female sexuality as essentially submissive. Historian and feminist Sara M. Evans responded to much of the contemporary criticism of the women's movement by describing a resurgence of feminism in the 1980s and 1990s. Born in large part out of the concern over judicial limitations to abortion rights and highly publicized cases of sexual harassment in the workplace, women's rights advocates rallied to protest against the illusion of equality in the United States that had come to replace acts of more overt discrimination. According to Evans, these conditions resulted in increased membership in the National Organization of Women (NOW) and the National Abortion Rights Action League (NARAL) and mobilized younger women who had taken their improved opportunities in American society for granted. The end result was the emergence of Third Wave feminists who have broken down class, racial, and sexual orientation barriers to achieve a new sense of solidarity and who have joined with women's rights advocates in other countries to globalize their protest. See *Tidal Wave: How Women Changed America at Century's End* (Free Press, 2004).

In the first selection in this issue, F. Carolyn Graglia's critique of contemporary feminism is a throwback to attitudes toward women of the late nineteenth and early twentieth century which applauded the "Cult of True Womanhood" and opposed the women social workers and suffragists who appeared to be intruding upon the man's world. Graglia argues that contemporary feminism ignores women's primary role in raising children and preserving the moral character of the family. She blames "second-wave" feminists, along with the Great Society's social programs, for promoting a sexual revolution that has destroyed the American family by fostering a high divorce rate and sexually transmitted diseases.

In the second selection, Jo Freeman enumerates legislative initiatives championed by activists for women's rights in the 1960s and 1970s—from the Equal Pay Act of 1963 to prohibitions against sex discrimination in employment in 1964 to changes in restrictive abortion laws—and characterizes them as a truly revolutionary shift in American law and public policy. Most notable, according to Freeman, was the introduction of a focus in favor of equality of opportunity and individual choice for women as opposed to an earlier reformist mentality of protective legislation.

YES ↵

F. Carolyn Graglia

Domestic Tranquility

Introduction

Since the late 1960s, feminists have very successfully waged war against the traditional family, in which husbands are the principal breadwinners and wives are primarily homemakers. This war's immediate purpose has been to undermine the homemaker's position within both her family and society in order to drive her into the work force. Its long-term goal is to create a society in which women behave as much like men as possible, devoting as much time and energy to the pursuit of a career as men do, so that women will eventually hold equal political and economic power with men. . . .

Feminists have used a variety of methods to achieve their goal. They have promoted a sexual revolution that encouraged women to mimic male sexual promiscuity. They have supported the enactment of no-fault divorce laws that have undermined housewives' social and economic security. And they obtained the application of affirmative action requirements to women as a class, gaining educational and job preferences for women and undermining the ability of men who are victimized by this discrimination to function as family breadwinners.

A crucial weapon in feminism's arsenal has been the status degradation of the housewife's role. From the journalistic attacks of Betty Friedan and Gloria Steinem to Jessie Bernard's sociological writings, all branches of feminism are united in the conviction that a woman can find identity and fulfillment only in a career. The housewife, feminists agree, was properly characterized by Simone de Beauvoir and Betty Friedan as a "parasite," a being something less than human, living her life without using her adult capabilities or intelligence, and lacking any real purpose in devoting herself to children, husband, and home.

Operating on the twin assumptions that equality means sameness (that is, men and women cannot be equals unless they do the same things) and that most differences between the sexes are culturally imposed, contemporary feminism has undertaken its own cultural impositions. Revealing their totalitarian belief that they

know best how others should live and their totalitarian willingness to force others to conform to their dogma, feminists have sought to modify our social institutions in order to create an androgynous society in which male and female roles are as identical as possible. The results of the feminist juggernaut now engulf us. By almost all indicia of well-being, the institution of the American family has become significantly less healthy than it was thirty years ago.

Certainly, feminism is not alone responsible for our families' sufferings. As Charles Murray details in *Losing Ground,* President Lyndon Johnson's Great Society programs, for example, have often hurt families, particularly black families, and these programs were supported by a large constituency beyond the women's movement. What distinguishes the women's movement, however, is the fact that, despite the pro-family motives it sometimes ascribes to itself, it has actively sought the traditional family's destruction. In its avowed aims and the programs it promotes, the movement has adopted Kate Millett's goal, set forth in her *Sexual Politics,* in which she endorses Friedrich Engels's conclusion that "the family, as that term is presently understood, must go"; "a kind fate," she remarks, in "view of the institution's history." This goal has never changed: feminists view traditional nuclear families as inconsistent with feminism's commitment to women's independence and sexual freedom.

Emerging as a revitalized movement in the 1960s, feminism reflected women's social discontent, which had arisen in response to the decline of the male breadwinner ethic and to the perception—heralded in Philip Wylie's 1940s castigation of the evil "mom"—that Western society does not value highly the roles of wife and mother. Women's dissatisfactions, nevertheless, have often been aggravated rather than alleviated by the feminist reaction. To mitigate their discontent, feminists argued, women should pattern their lives after men's, engaging in casual sexual intercourse on the same terms as sexually predatory males and making the same career commitments as men. In pursuit of these objectives, feminists have fought unceasingly for the ready availability of legal abortion and consistently derogated both motherhood and the worth of full-time homemakers. Feminism's sexual teachings have been less consistent, ranging from its early and enthusiastic embrace of the sexual revolution to a significant backlash against female sexual promiscuity, which has led some feminists to urge women to abandon heterosexual sexual intercourse altogether.

Contemporary feminism has been remarkably successful in bringing about the institutionalization in our society of the two beliefs underlying its offensive: denial of the social worth of traditional homemakers and rejection of traditional sexual morality. The consequences have been pernicious and enduring. General societal assent to these beliefs has profoundly distorted men's perceptions of their relationships with and obligations to women, women's perceptions of their own needs, and the way in which women make decisions about their lives.

Traditional Homemaking Devalued

The first prong of contemporary feminism's offensive has been to convince society that a woman's full-time commitment to cultivating her marriage and rearing her children is an unworthy endeavor. Women, assert feminists, should treat marriage and children as relatively independent appendages to their life of full-time involvement in the workplace. To live what feminists assure her is the only life worthy of respect, a woman must devote the vast bulk of her time and energy to market production, at the expense of marriage and children. Children, she is told, are better cared for by surrogates, and marriage, as these feminists perceive it, neither deserves nor requires much attention; indeed, the very idea of a woman's "cultivating" her marriage seems ludicrous. Thus, spurred on by the women's movement, many women have sought to become male clones.

But some feminists have appeared to modify the feminist message; voices—supposedly of moderation—have argued that women really are different from men. In this they are surely right: there are fundamental differences between the average man and woman, and it is appropriate to take account of these differences when making decisions both in our individual lives and with respect to social issues. Yet the new feminist voices have not conceded that acknowledged differences between the sexes are grounds for reexamining women's flight from home into workplace. Instead, these new voices have argued only that these differences require modification of the terms under which women undertake to reconstruct their lives in accordance with the blueprint designed by

so-called early radicals. The edifice erected by radical feminism is to remain intact, subject only to some redecorating. The foundation of this edifice is still the destruction of the traditional family. Feminism has acquiesced in women's desire to bear children (an activity some of the early radicals discouraged). But it continues steadfast in its assumption that, after some period of maternity leave, daily care of those children is properly the domain of institutions and paid employees. The yearnings manifested in women's palpable desire for children should largely be sated, the new voices tell us, by the act of serving as a birth canal and then spending so-called quality time with the child before and after a full day's work.

Any mother, in this view, may happily consign to surrogates most of the remaining aspects of her role, assured that doing so will impose no hardship or loss on either mother or child. To those women whose natures make them less suited to striving in the workplace than concentrating on husband, children, and home, this feminist diktat denies the happiness and contentment they could have found within the domestic arena. In the world formed by contemporary feminism, these women will have status and respect only if they force themselves to take up roles in the workplace they suspect are not most deserving of their attention. Relegated to the periphery of their lives are the home and personal relationships with husband and children that they sense merit their central concern.

Inherent in the feminist argument is an extraordinary contradiction. Feminists deny, on the one hand, that the dimension of female sexuality which engenders women's yearning for children can also make it appropriate and satisfying for a woman to devote herself to domestic endeavors and provide her children's full-time care. On the other hand, they plead the fact of sexual difference to justify campaigns to modify workplaces in order to correct the effects of male influence and alleged biases. Only after such modifications, claim feminists, can women's nurturing attributes and other female qualities be adequately expressed in and truly influence the workplace. Manifestations of these female qualities, feminists argue, should and can occur in the workplace once it has been modified to blunt the substantial impact of male aggression and competitiveness and take account of women's special requirements.

Having launched its movement claiming the right of women—a right allegedly denied them previously—to enter the workplace on an *equal* basis with men, feminism then escalated its demands by arguing that female differences require numerous changes in the workplace. Women, in this view, are insufficiently feminine to find satisfaction in rearing their own children, but too feminine to compete on an equal basis with men. Thus, having taken women out of their homes and settled them in the workplace, feminists have sought to reconstruct workplaces to create "feminist playpens" that are conducive to female qualities of sensitivity, caring, and empathy. Through this exercise in self-contradiction, contemporary feminism has endeavored to remove the woman from her home and role of providing daily care to her children—the quintessential place and activity for most effectively expressing her feminine, nurturing attributes.

The qualities that are the most likely to make women good mothers are thus redeployed away from their children and into workplaces that must be restructured to accommodate them. The irony is twofold. Children—the ones who could benefit most from the attentions of those mothers who do possess these womanly qualities—are deprived of those attentions and left only with the hope of finding adequate replacement for their loss. Moreover, the occupations in which these qualities are now to find expression either do not require them for optimal job performance (often they are not conducive to professional success) or were long ago recognized as women's occupations—as in the field of nursing, for example—in which nurturing abilities do enhance job performance.

Traditional Sexual Morality Traduced

The second prong of contemporary feminism's offensive has been to encourage women to ape male sexual patterns and engage in promiscuous sexual intercourse as freely as men. Initially, feminists were among the most dedicated supporters of the sexual revolution, viewing female participation in casual sexual activity as an unmistakable declaration of female equality with males. The women in our society who acted upon the teachings of feminist sexual revolutionaries have suffered greatly. They are victims of the highest abortion rate in the Western world. More than one in five Americans are now infected with a viral sexually transmitted disease which at best can be controlled but not cured and is often chronic. Sexually transmitted diseases, both viral and bacterial, disproportionately affect women because, showing fewer symptoms, they often go untreated for a longer time. These diseases also lead to pelvic infections that cause infertility in 100,000 to 150,000 women each year.

The sexual revolution feminists have promoted rests on an assumption that an act of sexual intercourse involves nothing but a pleasurable physical sensation, possessing no symbolic meaning and no moral dimension. This is an understanding of sexuality that bears more than a slight resemblance to sex as depicted in pornography: physical sexual acts without emotional involvement. In addition to the physical harm caused by increased sexual promiscuity, the denial that sexual intercourse has symbolic importance within a framework of moral accountability corrupts the nature of the sex act. Such denial necessarily makes sexual intercourse a trivial event, compromising the act's ability to fulfill its most important function after procreation. This function is to bridge the gap between males and females who often seem separated by so many differences, both biological and emotional, that they feel scarcely capable of understanding or communicating with each other.

Because of the urgency of sexual desire, especially in the male, it is through sexual contact that men and women can most easily come together. Defining the nature of sexual intercourse in terms informed by its procreative potentialities makes the act a spiritually meaningful event of overwhelming importance. A sexual encounter so defined is imbued with the significance conferred by its connection with a promise of immortality through procreation, whether that connection is a present possibility, a remembrance of children already borne, or simply an acknowledgment of the reality and truth of the promise. Such a sex act can serve as the physical meeting ground on which, by accepting and affirming each other through their bodies' physical unity, men and women can begin to construct an enduring emotional unity. The sexual encounter cannot perform its function when it is viewed as a trivial event of moral indifference with no purpose or meaning other than producing a physical sensation through the friction of bodily parts.

The feminist sexual perspective deprives the sex act of the spiritual meaningfulness that can make it the binding force upon which man and woman can construct a lasting marital relationship. The morally indifferent sexuality championed by the sexual revolution substitutes the sex without emotions that characterizes pornography for the sex of a committed, loving relationship that satisfies women's longing for romance and connection. But this is not the only damage to relationships between men and women that follows from feminism's determination to promote an androgynous society by convincing men and women that they are virtually fungible. Sexual equivalency, feminists believe, requires that women not only engage in casual sexual intercourse as freely as men, but also that women mimic male behavior by becoming equally assertive in initiating sexual encounters and in their activity throughout the encounter. With this sexual prescription, feminists mock the essence of conjugal sexuality that is at the foundation of traditional marriage.

Marriage as a Woman's Career Discredited

Even academic feminists who are considered "moderates" endorse doctrines most inimical to the homemaker. Thus, Professor Elizabeth Fox-Genovese, regarded as a moderate in Women's Studies, tells us that marriage can no longer be a viable career for women. But if marriage cannot be a woman's career, then despite feminist avowals of favoring choice in this matter, homemaking cannot be a woman's goal, and surrogate child-rearing must be her child's destiny. Contrary to feminist claims, society's barriers are not strung tightly to inhibit women's career choices. Because of feminism's very successful efforts, society encourages women to pursue careers, while stigmatizing and preventing their devotion to child-rearing and domesticity.

It was precisely upon the conclusion that marriage cannot be a viable career for women that *Time* magazine rested its Fall 1990 special issue on "Women: The Road Ahead," a survey of contemporary women's lives. While noting that the "cozy, limited roles of the past are still clearly remembered, sometimes fondly," during the past thirty years "all that was orthodox has become negotiable." One thing negotiated away has been the economic security of the homemaker, and *Time* advised young women that "the job of full-time homemaker may be the riskiest profession to choose" because "the advent of no-fault and equitable-distribution divorce laws" reflect, in the words of one judge, the fact that "[s]ociety no longer believes that a husband should support his wife."

No-fault divorce laws did not, however, result from an edict of the gods or some force of nature, but from sustained political efforts, particularly by the feminist movement. As a cornerstone of their drive to make women exchange home for workplace, and thereby secure their independence from men, the availability of no-fault divorce (like the availability of abortion) was sacrosanct to the movement. *Time* shed crocodile tears for displaced homemakers, for it made clear that women must canter down the road ahead with the spur of no-fault divorce urging them into the workplace. Of all *Time's* recommendations for ameliorating women's lot, divorce reform—the most crying need in our country today—was not among them. Whatever hardships may be endured by women who would resist a divorce, *Time's* allegiance, like that of most feminists, is clearly to the divorce-seekers who, it was pleased to note, will not be hindered in their pursuit of self-realization by the barriers to divorce that their own mothers had faced.

These barriers to divorce which had impeded their own parents, however, had usually benefited these young women by helping to preserve their parents' marriage. A five-year study of children in divorcing families disclosed that "the overwhelming majority preferred the unhappy marriage to the divorce," and many of them, "despite the unhappiness of their parents, were in fact relatively happy and considered their situation neither better nor worse than that of other families around them." A follow-up study after ten years demonstrated that children experienced the trauma of their parents' divorce as more serious and long-lasting than any researchers had anticipated. *Time* so readily acquiesced in the disadvantaging of homemakers and the disruption of children's lives because the feminist ideological parameters within which it operates have excluded marriage as a *proper* career choice. Removing the obstacles to making it a *viable* choice would, therefore, be an undesirable subversion of feminist goals.

That *Time* would have women trot forward on life's journey constrained by the blinders of feminist ideology is evident from its failure to question any feminist notion, no matter how silly, or to explore solutions incompatible with the ideology's script. One of the silliest notions *Time* left unexamined was that young women want "good careers, good marriages and two or three kids, and they don't want the children to be raised by strangers." The supposed realism of this expectation lay in the new woman's attitude that "I don't want to work 70 hours a week, but I want to be vice president, and *you* have to change." But even if thirty hours were cut from that seventy-hour workweek, the new woman would still be working the normal full-time week, her children would still be raised by surrogates, and the norm would continue to be the feminist version of child-rearing that *Time* itself described unflatteringly as "less a preoccupation than an improvisation."

The illusion that a woman can achieve career success without sacrificing the daily personal care of her children—and except among the very wealthy, most of her leisure as well—went unquestioned by *Time*. It did note, however, the dissatisfaction expressed by Eastern European and Russian women who had experienced, as a matter of government policy, the same liberation from home and children that our feminists have undertaken to bestow upon Western women. In what *Time* described as "a curious reversal of Western feminism's emphasis on careers for women," the new female leaders of Eastern Europe would like "to reverse the communist diktat that all women have to work." Women have "dreamed," said the Polish

Minister of Culture and Arts, "of reaching the point where we have the choice to stay home" that communism had taken away. But blinded by its feminist bias, *Time* could only find it "curious" that women would choose to stay at home; apparently beyond the pale of respectability was any argument that it would serve Western women's interest to retain the choice that contemporary feminism—filling in the West the role of communism in the East—has sought to deny them.

Nor was its feminist bias shaken by the attitudes of Japanese women, most of whom, *Time* noted, reject "equality" with men, choosing to cease work after the birth of a first child and later resuming a part-time career or pursuing hobbies or community work. The picture painted was that of the 1950s American suburban housewife reviled by Betty Friedan, except that the American has enjoyed a higher standard of living (particularly a much larger home) than has the Japanese. In Japan, *Time* observed, being "a housewife is nothing to be ashamed of." Dishonoring the housewife's role was a goal, it might have added, that Japanese feminists can, in time, accomplish if they emulate their American counterparts.

Japanese wives have broad responsibilities, commented *Time,* because most husbands leave their salaries and children entirely in wives' hands; freed from drudgery by modern appliances, housewives can "pursue their interests in a carefree manner, while men have to worry about supporting their wives and children." Typically, a Japanese wife controls household finances, giving her husband a cash allowance, the size of which, apparently, dissatisfies one-half of the men. Acknowledging that Japanese wives take the leadership in most homes, one husband observed that "[t]hings go best when the husband is swimming in the palm of his wife's hand." A home is well-managed, said one wife, "if you make your men feel that they're in control when they are in front of others, while in reality you're in control." It seems like a good arrangement to me.

Instead of inquiring whether a similar carefree existence might appeal to some American women, *Time* looked forward to the day when marriage would no longer be a career for Japanese women, as their men took over household and child-rearing chores, enabling wives to join husbands in the workplace. It was noted, however, that a major impediment to this goal, which would have to be corrected, was the fact that Japanese day-care centers usually run for only eight hours a day. Thus, *Time* made clear that its overriding concern was simply promoting the presence of women in the work force. This presence is seen as a good *per se,* without any *pro forma* talk about the economic necessity of a second income and without any

question raised as to whether it is in children's interest to spend any amount of time—much less in excess of eight hours a day—in communal care. . . .

The Awakened Brünnhilde

. . . Those who would defend anti-feminist traditionalism today are like heretics fighting a regnant Inquisition. To become a homemaker, a woman may need the courage of a heretic. This is one reason that the defense of traditional women is often grounded in religious teachings, for the heretic's courage usually rests on faith. The source of courage I offer is the conviction, based on my own experience, that contemporary feminism's stereotypical caricature of the housewife did not reflect reality when Friedan popularized it, does not reflect reality today, and need not govern reality.

Feminists claimed a woman can find identity and fulfillment only in a career; they are wrong. They claimed a woman can, in that popular expression, "have it all"; they are wrong—she can have only some. The experience of being a mother at home is a different experience from being a full-time market producer who is also a mother. A woman can have one or the other experience, but not both at the same time. Combining a career with motherhood requires a woman to compromise by diminishing her commitment and exertions with respect to one role or the other, or usually, to both. Rarely, if ever, can a woman adequately perform in a full-time career if she diminishes her commitment to it sufficiently to replicate the experience of being a mother at home.

Women were *never* told they could *not* choose to make the compromises required to combine these roles; within the memory of all living today there were always some women who did so choose. But by successfully degrading the housewife's role, contemporary feminism undertook to force this choice upon all women. I declined to make the compromises necessary to combine a career with motherhood because I did not want to become like Andrea Dworkin's spiritual virgin. I did not want to keep my being intact, as Dworkin puts it, so that I could continue to pursue career success. Such pursuit would have required me to hold too much of myself aloof from husband and children: the invisible "wedge-shaped core of darkness" that Virginia Woolf described as being oneself would have to be too large, and not enough of me would have been left over for them.

I feared that if I cultivated that "wedge-shaped core of darkness" within myself enough to maintain a successful career, I would be consumed by that career, and that thus desiccated, too little of me would remain to flesh out my roles as wife and mother. Giving most of myself to the market seemed less appropriate and attractive than reserving myself for my family. Reinforcing this decision was my experience that when a woman lives too much in her mind, she finds it increasingly difficult to live through her body. Her nurturing ties to her children become attenuated; her physical relationship with her husband becomes hollow and perfunctory. Certainly in my case, Dr. James C. Neely spoke the truth in *Gender: The Myth of Equality:* "With too much emphasis on intellect, a woman becomes 'too into her head' to function in a sexual, motherly way, destroying by the process of thought the process of feeling her sexuality."

Virginia Woolf never compromised her market achievements with motherhood; nor did the Brontë sisters, Jane Austen, or George Eliot. Nor did Helen Frankenthaler who, at the time she was acknowledged to be the most prominent living female artist, said in an interview: "We all make different compromises. And, no, I don't regret not having children. Given my painting, children could have suffered. A mother must make her children come first: young children are helpless. Well, paintings are objects but they're also helpless." I agree with her; that is precisely how I felt about the briefs I wrote for clients. Those briefs were, to me, like helpless children; in writing them, I first learned the meaning of complete devotion. I stopped writing them because I believed they would have been masters too jealous of my husband and my children.

Society never rebuked these women for refusing to compromise their literary and artistic achievements. Neither should it rebuke other kinds of women for refusing to compromise their own artistry of motherhood and domesticity. Some women may agree that the reality I depict rings truer to them than the feminist depiction. This conviction may help them find the courage of a heretic. Some others, both men and women, may see enough truth in the reality I depict that they will come to regret society's acquiescence in the status degradation of the housewife. They may then accept the currently unfashionable notion that society should respect and support women who adopt the anti-feminist perspective.

It is in society's interest to begin to pull apart the double-bind web spun by feminism and so order itself as not to inhibit any woman who *could* be an awakened Brünnhilde. Delighted and contented women will certainly do less harm—and probably more good—to society than frenzied and despairing ones. This is not to suggest that society should interfere with a woman's decision to follow the feminist script and adopt any form of spiritual virginity that suits her. But neither should society continue to validate destruction of the women's pact by the contemporary feminists who sought to make us all follow their script. We should now begin to dismantle our regime that discourages and disadvantages the traditional woman who rejects feminist spiritual virginity and seeks instead the very different delight and contentment that she believes best suits her.

F. Carolyn Graglia is a trained lawyer, writer, and lecturer whose articles and books challenge the viewpoint of the modern women's movement.

Abortion

The movement to change restrictive abortion laws began independently of and earlier than the women's liberation movement, but when that movement emerged it quickly captured the abortion issue as its own, energizing and publicizing it along the way. It was the impetus of the feminist movement that led to *Roe v. Wade*, the 1973 Supreme Court decision that eliminated most state abortion laws, after only a few years of public debate and state action on abortion. In some ways the Court was ahead of its time, because public debate had not yet created a consensus. The Court's sweeping removal of a century of legal restriction sparked massive efforts to reduce and reverse its effects. The legal and political controversy has become so polarized that it borders on civil war. It has also tainted many issues that are not obviously related to abortion, with the result that some legislation that might have passed or passed sooner has been stymied. The state battles over ratification of the ERA were infected by opponents' claims that restrictions on abortion would be precluded by it as a denial of equal rights on account of sex. The Court decisions and legislative initiatives that followed *Roe v. Wade* can only be understood within a political context. Rather than reflect changes in legal doctrine that often follow social change, as exemplified by the reinterpretation of the Equal Protection Clause, new decisions and laws are best seen as the victories and defeats of an ongoing political struggle. . . .

In 1967 Colorado became the first state to adopt a law permitting therapeutic abortions if the life or mental health of the mother was threatened, if pregnancy occurred from rape or incest, or if the fetus was deformed. That same year several referral services were set up by nonphysicians to direct women to safer illegal abortions. The public debate over abortion laws became more vociferous, and in the next couple years another ten states adopted therapeutic exceptions. Four states—Alaska, Hawaii, New York, and Washington—went further and repealed virtually all restrictions on abortion. Both of these developments were boosted by the women's movement and the injection into the medical debate of the idea that reproductive freedom was a woman's right. Cases began to reach the lower courts in the late 1960s. Initially these just chipped away at the legal restrictions. Then, in 1969 and 1970, the California Supreme Court and several federal district courts declared their states' laws unconstitutional. In 1971 the Supreme Court granted certiorari to two cases from Texas and Georgia; seven justices heard oral argument in 1971, but the Court asked for a rehearing in 1972 with a full Court. Its decision was announced on January 22, 1973.

Justice Blackmun, writing the majority opinion in *Roe v. Wade* and *Doe v. Bolton*, did not stick to legal analysis. Recognizing the "sensitive and emotional nature of the abortion controversy," he surveyed medical, religious, moral, and historical material before concluding that "this right of privacy, whether it be founded in the Fourteenth Amendment's concept of personal liberty . . . or, . . . in the Ninth Amendment's reservation of rights to the people, is broad enough to encompass a woman's decision whether or not to terminate her pregnancy." While asserting "that the word 'person,'" as used in the Fourteenth Amendment, "does not include the unborn," the Court did recognize that "a State may properly assert important interests in safeguarding health, in maintaining medical standards and in protecting potential life.". . .

Antiabortion forces organized and tested *Roe*'s limits by passing laws and bringing test cases. One group of laws restricted the use of public funds for abortions. Called the "Hyde Amendments" for their most outspoken sponsor, Cong. Henry Hyde (R. Ill.), these attachments to annual appropriations bills deny any federal money authorized by these bills to be used for abortions. Included are restrictions on abortions for military personnel, Peace Corps volunteers, Indians served by federal health programs, health benefits for federal employees, and foreign assistance programs for which abortion is a family planning method. These laws exempt abortions to save the life of the mother; some of them also exempt pregnancies from rape or incest. All of these laws have stimulated acrimonious conflict.

The most controversial have been the restrictions on federal funds for Medicaid recipients—poor people. Several states responded to *Roe* by refusing to pay for Medicaid abortions. In 1977 the Court held that the States did not have to fund abortions for Medicaid-eligible women and could choose to fund only "medically necessary" abortions without violating the Equal Protection clause. The first Hyde Amendment passed Congress in 1976; it reached the Supreme Court in 1980. The Court held that the federal government had no constitutional or statutory obligation to fund abortions even when they were medically necessary. As a result of the Hyde Amendments, the number of federally funded abortions went from 294,600 in 1977 to 165 in 1990. States still have the option of paying for the procedure with state money. In 1990 thirteen states spent sixty-five million dollars for 162,418 abortions. The District of Columbia used to be one of the biggest state funders of abortions, but because much of its budget comes from the federal government, it is subject to Congressional control. Since 1988 Congress has amended the annual appropriations bills to forbid the District to use locally raised funds for abortions.

The other set of cases have tested the extent to which states can regulate the performance of abortion. The success of state restrictions has varied with the composition of the Court, which changed significantly during the Reagan and Bush administrations. Initially the Court affirmed *Roe* and applied strict scrutiny to state regulations. It upheld requirements that a doctor inform a woman about abortion and obtain written consent, but only if the requirements did not interfere with the physician-patient relationship. It found spousal consent statutes unconstitutional but parental notification requirements acceptable if a minor could present her request to a judge when a parent would not agree. Reporting requirements about abortions to the State were constitutional, but mandatory hospitalization and twenty-four-hour waiting periods were not. Advertising could not be restricted, and fetal protection statutes could only apply to viable fetuses.

By 1989 enough conservatives had been added to the Court for the balance of opinions to shift. On July 3, 1989, the Court upheld Missouri's prohibition of abortions on public lands or by public employees and its requirement that viability tests be done on women more than twenty weeks pregnant, by five to four. While it did not overrule *Roe*, the multiple opinions in *Webster* gave the states much more room for regulation than they had had before. Several states quickly passed laws prohibiting or strictly regulating abortion in anticipation that this Court would overrule *Roe* when given the opportunity to do so. The Court agreed to hear only one of the three cases appealed to it and on June 29, 1992, declined to overrule *Roe*, again by five to four. Three of the Reagan appointees, O'Connor, Kennedy, and Souter, wrote the joint opinion in which they opted to follow the judicially conservative tradition of sticking to precedent. "The Constitution serves human values, and while the effect of reliance on *Roe* cannot be exactly measured, neither can the certain cost of overruling *Roe* for people who have ordered their thinking and living around that case be dismissed." However, this decision did away with the trimester framework and dropped strict scrutiny as the standard by which regulations must be judged. Instead it held that the state's interest in protecting human life extends throughout pregnancy; it may regulate at any stage provided that the regulation does not impose an "undue burden" on a woman's right to obtain an abortion. . . .

Legislative Gains

The legislative changes in public policy have been as vast as the judicial changes, but they began earlier. . . .

Although the ERA was not ratified, the two-year battle had some very beneficial side effects. It created a climate in Congress that there was a serious constituent interest in women's rights and established liaisons between feminist organizations and Congressional staff. With this impetus the 92nd Congress, which sent the ERA to the states, passed a bumper crop of women's rights legislation in 1971–72. In addition to the ERA there were laws that (1) expanded the coverage of Title VII and the enforcement powers of the EEOC; (2) prohibited sex discrimination in all federally aided education programs (Title IX); (3) added sex discrimination to the jurisdiction of the U.S. Commission on Civil Rights; (4) prohibited sex discrimination in state programs funded by federal revenue sharing; (5) provided free day care for children of poor families and a sliding fee scale for higher income families (which was vetoed by President Nixon); (6) provided for a child care tax deduction for some parents; (7) added prohibitions against sex discrimination to a plethora of federally funded programs, including health training, Appalachian redevelopment, and water pollution.

Subsequent Congresses have also been active. New laws included the Equal Credit Opportunity Act; the Women's Educational Equity Act, which provides grants to design programs and activities to eliminate stereotyping and achieve educational equity; creation of the National Center for the Control and Prevention of Rape; an amendment to the Foreign Assistance Act requiring particular attention be given to programs, projects, and activities that tend to integrate women into the national economies of foreign countries; prohibitions of discrimination in the sale, rental, or financing of housing; an amendment to Title VII to include pregnancy in employment disability insurance coverage; admission of women to the military academies; and the addition of still more antidiscrimination provisions to federally funded programs such as small business loans.

The States have also been active arenas. Laws have been passed in most states prohibiting sex discrimination in employment, housing, and credit and in some states prohibiting discrimination in insurance, education, and public accommodations. Most states now have no-fault divorce provisions; all but four have equal custody and support laws (two others have equal custody but provide support for only the wife). The changes have been partially a result of pressure from feminist and other public interest groups and partially in response to changes in federal legislation and Supreme Court decisions. Many states have followed the lead of the Federal government in conducting studies to identify gender-based distinctions in their laws and recommend changes. Most of these studies were in response to efforts to adopt a state ERA or ratify the federal amendment.

The Family—Again

Toward the end of the 1980s both the federal and state governments turned their attention toward the family, which had undergone profound changes in the previous two decades. Although family law was traditionally a state prerogative, it had never been completely off limits to the federal government. . . .

In 1990 Congress finally got serious about providing child care to working parents. For decades child care had a negative connotation as something resorted to by poor women who *had* to work. The federal government subsidized some child care during World War II when it wanted women in the factories so the men could go to war, but those funds were eliminated after the war. In 1971 President Nixon vetoed a two-billion-dollar child care bill because of its "family-weakening implications." Presidents Ford and Carter also expressed disapproval of bills in Congress during their Presidencies, though in 1976 some funds were made available to the States that could be used for day care. Finally, in 1988, after four decades of increasing labor force participation by mothers of young children, Congress proposed a major child care bill. It quickly became embroiled in turf battles between committees and conflicts over church and state (e.g., should federal money be used for church-sponsored day care). These were resolved by 1990, and Congress passed a five-year program of tax credits and state grants that President Bush signed into law on November 5, 1990.

The President was not as enthusiastic about signing a bill to mandate unpaid leave for employees on the birth or adoption of a child or illness of a family member. His concern about increasing the costs to business outweighed his commitment to "family values," even though the United States was the only major industrialized country that did not provide such benefits. President Bush vetoed bills passed by Congress in 1990 and 1992 after eight years of wrangling; and said he would support only voluntary leave. However, once a new administration was elected, Congress rushed to pass H.R. 1, the Family and Medical Leave Act, which President Clinton signed on February 5, 1993.

"Family values" also delayed government intervention into family violence. Traditionally, how a family conducted its internal affairs has been considered a private matter. Despite growing evidence of child and spousal abuse, it was many years before legislatures overcame

opposition to mandate action where there was abuse of children, and even more before services were created for spouses—virtually always wives. By 1984, when Congress passed the Family Violence Prevention and Services Act, thirty-two states had domestic violence programs, usually funding for emergency shelters and other programs run by nonprofit organizations. Today virtually all states have such programs, though funding is inadequate. . . .

The Challenges Ahead

The contemporary feminist movement finished the drive to remove discriminatory laws begun after Suffrage. It also altered public perceptions and public policy on the role of women to one that favors equality of opportunity and individual choice. This is reflected in the addition of "sex" to the pantheon of laws that prohibit discrimination in private conduct and in the Court decisions that recognize women's right to equal protection and due process. These changes, which largely occurred during the decade of the 1970s, are nothing less than a revolution in public policy. As late as 1963, the President's Commission on the Status of Women cautioned that "[e]xperience is needed in determining what constitutes *unjustified* discrimination in the treatment of women workers."

As is true of any revolution, the changes that were made created new problems in their wake. Once equal opportunity became a possibility, the fact that it by itself would not lead to equality became clearer. Essentially this policy means that women who are like men should be treated equally with men. It accepts as standard the traditional male life-style, and that standard in turn assumes that one's primary responsibility should and can be one's job, because one has a spouse (or spouse surrogate) whose primary responsibility is the maintenance of house and family obligations. Women whose personal life-style and resources permit them to fit these assumptions could, in the absence of sex discrimination, succeed equally with men.

Most women cannot, however, because our traditional conception of the family, and women's role within the family, make this impossible. Women still bear the primary responsibility for home and child care whether or not they are married and regardless of what their spouse does. The typical woman has more tasks to perform in a typical day than a typical man and thus has less time. Couples who equalize family responsibilities, or singles who take them all on, pay a price for deviancy. And women who spend the greater part of their lives as dependent spouses often find their "career" ended by death or divorce with little to show for it.

What is necessary is a total social reorganization that abolishes institutionalized sex role differences and the concept of adult dependency. It needs to recognize the individual as the principal economic unit, regardless of what combinations individuals do or do not choose to live in, and to provide the necessary services for individuals to support themselves and help support their children. In pursuit of these goals, programs and policies need to make participation by everyone in the labor force to the full extent of their abilities both a right and an obligation. They should also encourage and facilitate the equal assumption of family responsibilities without regard to gender, as well as develop ways to reduce conflict between the conduct of one's professional and private lives. While transition policies are necessary to mitigate the consequences of adult dependency, the goal should be abolition of the sexual division of labor. They should not be ones that permanently transfer dependency from "bread-winners" (male earners) to society in general, nor should they be ones that encourage dependency for a major portion of one's life by extolling its benefits and minimizing its costs. Instead, transitional policies should be ones that educate women to the reality that they are ultimately responsible for their own economic well-being, but are entitled to the opportunities to achieve it.

This too is not enough. Even while the revolution was in process, the feminist movement was generating new public policies to address problems not solved by the mere removal of discriminatory laws and practices. The pervasiveness of violence, the degradation of pornography, and the lack of affordable, available child care are burdens particularly borne by women that equal opportunity programs do not address. As women moved into positions of power, feminist inquiry disclosed new or hidden discriminations, such as the "glass ceiling" and inadequate research into women's health needs. As the family became open to public inspection, a host of problems that more heavily affected women, such as incest, sexual abuse, and domestic violence, became apparent. As science created new ways of reproducing, it compelled reconsideration of the concept of motherhood. And as people diversified their ways of living together, the nature of the family was questioned.

Not all of the new problems can be mitigated by changes in law and public policy. But many can be. As the consequences of the legal revolution ripple throughout society, one task will be to identify where the law can be a useful tool for more social change and to devise appropriate policies to achieve it.

JO FREEMAN earned a PhD in political science from the University of Chicago in 1973 and a J.D. degree in 1982 from the New York University School of Law. She is the author of 11 books on the topics of feminism, social movements, and political parties, including *The Politics of Women's Liberation* (1975), *A Room at a Time: How Women Entered Party Politics* (2000), and *We Will Be Heard: Women's Struggles for Political Power in the United States* (2008).

EXPLORING THE ISSUE

Has the Women's Movement of the 1970s Failed to Liberate American Women?

Critical Thinking and Reflection

1. Discuss the role that women should fulfill in American society in the twenty-first century, according to Graglia. Critically analyze her views of contemporary feminism.
2. List and describe the characteristics of the nineteenth-century "Cult of True Womanhood." Compare the similarities and differences of Graglia's views of what women's roles should be today with the nineteenth-century ideal of womanhood.
3. According to Jo Freeman, in what ways did the women's movement influence changes in laws and public policies concerning the status of women in American society?
4. Compare the analyses of Graglia and Freeman on the impact of the women's movement on American society. Where do they agree, and where do they disagree?

Is There Common Ground?

Both women on the left and women on the right of the political spectrum would deny there is common ground between the two movements. Upon closer inspection, however, an interesting study would be to see how many conservative women active in business and politics took advantage of the Equal Rights Amendment in 1972 and the Higher Education Act (especially Title IX), which opened the doors of collegiate athletics and higher educational opportunities in traditional male fields such as law, medicine, and scientific research. One should also study the number of conservative women politicians, such as Michelle Bachman and Sarah Palin, who have benefited from the expanding political role of women in the past three decades. How much do Bachman, Palin, and other conservative women politicians embody both the liberated woman and the traditional mother?

One of the chief criticisms of the feminist movement of the 1970s stemmed from the fact that the vast majority of its participants were white, middle-class women focused on advancing their own personal goals. Since that time, the women's movement has expanded globally to incorporate women of all classes, races, and ethnicities, including many from developing nations in Africa, Asia, and Latin America. Additionally, in the United States, many women who had never viewed themselves as "feminists" have become more keenly attuned to the debates over women's roles in the public sphere and the workplace, as well as the impact of challenges pertaining to personal decision making tied into the highly charged debate over abortion rights.

Additional Resources

William H. Chafe, *The Paradox of Change: American Women in the Twentieth Century* (Oxford University Press, 1991)

Johnetta B. Cole and Beverly Gray-Sheftall, *Gender Talk: The Struggle for Women's Equality in African American Communities* (Ballantine, 2003)

Sara M. Evans, *Personal Politics: The Roots of Women's Liberation in the Civil Rights Movement and the New Left* (Alfred A. Knopf, 1979)

Estelle B. Freedman, *No Turning Back: The History of Feminism and the Future of Women* (Ballantine, 2001)

Ruth Rosen, *The World Split Open: How the Modern Women's Movement Changed America* (Viking, 2000)

Internet References . . .

Documents from the Women's Liberation Movement

http://library.duke.edu/rubenstein/scriptorium/wlm/

National Women's Liberation

http://www.womensliberation.org/

The 1960–70s American Feminist Movement

https://tavaana.org/en/content/1960s-70s-american
-feminist-movement-breaking-down-barriers-women

Phyllis Schlafly Still Championing the Anti-Feminist Fight

http://www.npr.org/templates/story
/story.php?storyId=134981902

Teach Women's History Project

www.feminist.org/research/teachersguide
/teach1.html

Selected, Edited, and with Issue Framing Material by:
Larry Madaras, *Howard Community College*
and
James M. SoRelle, *Baylor University*

ISSUE

Were the 1980s a Decade of Affluence for the Middle Class?

YES: J. David Woodard, from "A Rising Tide," Praeger (2006)

NO: Thomas Byrne Edsall, from "The Changing Shape of Power: A Realignment in Public Policy," Princeton University Press (1989)

Learning Outcomes
After reading this issue, you will be able to:
• Critically examine "Keynesian" economics.
• Critically examine "supply-side" economics.
• Compare and contrast the strength and weaknesses of both economic philosophies.
• Describe the cultural and economic changes in the United States in the 1980s.
• Describe and critically analyze the political, social, and economic changes that writer Edsall argues took place in the 1980s and after.

ISSUE SUMMARY

YES: According to Professor J. David Woodard, supply-side economics unleashed a wave of entrepreneurial and technological innovation that transformed the economy and restored America's confidence in the Golden Age from 1983 to 1992.

NO: Political journalist Thomas Byrne Edsall argues that the Reagan revolution brought about a policy realignment that reversed the New Deal and redistributed political power and economic wealth to the top 20 percent of Americans.

In 1939, after six years of the New Deal, unemployment in the United States remained at an unacceptably high rate of 17 percent. World War II bailed America out of the Great Depression. When 20 million workers entered the armed forces, married American women, along with African American and Hispanic men and women, filled the void in the high-paying factory jobs. Everyone not only made money but also poured it into war bonds and traditional savings accounts. Government and business cemented their relationship with "cost plus" profits for the defense industries.

By the end of 1945, Americans had stashed away $134 billion in cash, savings accounts, and government

securities. This pent-up demand meant there would be no depression akin to the end of World War I or the 1930s. Following initial shortages before industry completed its conversion to peacetime production, Americans engaged in the greatest spending spree in the country's history. Liberals and conservatives from both political parties had developed a consensus on foreign and domestic policies.

The president's Council of Economic Advisers was composed of Keynesians, who believed that government spending could increase employment even if it meant that budget deficits would be temporarily created. For nearly 25 years, they used fiscal and monetary tools to manipulate the economy so that inflation would remain low while employment would reach close to its maximum capacity. Around 1968, the consensus surrounding domestic and foreign policy broke down for three reasons: (1) the Vietnam imbroglio, (2) the oil cries of 1974 and 1979, and (3) the decline of the smokestack industries.

Lyndon Johnson's presidency was ruined by the Vietnam War. He believed that he could escalate the war and his Great Society programs at the same time. His successor, Richard Nixon, attempted to solve the Vietnam dilemma by bringing the American troops home and letting Asians fight Asians. The process of withdrawal was slow and costly. Also expensive were many of the Great Society programs, such as Social Security, Aid to Families with Dependent Children, environmental legislation, and school desegregation, which Nixon continued to uphold. In August 1971, Nixon acknowledged that he had become a Keynesian when he imposed a 90-day wage and price control freeze and took the international dollar off the gold standard and allowed it to float. With these bold moves, Nixon hoped to stop the dollar from declining in value. He was also faced with a recession that included both high unemployment and high inflation. "Stagflation" resulted, leading to the demise of Keynesian economics.

In early 1974, shortly before Nixon was forced to resign from office, the major oil-producing nations of the world—primarily in the Middle East—agreed to curb oil production and raise oil prices. The OPEC cartel, protesting the pro-Israeli policies of the Western nations, brought these countries to their knees. In the United States, gasoline went from $0.40 to $2.00 per gallon in a matter of days. In the early 1980s, President Jimmy Carter implored the nation to conserve energy, but he appeared helpless as the unemployment rate approached double digits and as the Federal Reserve Board raised interest rates to 18 percent in a desperate attempt to stem inflation.

The Reagan administration introduced a new economic philosophy: supply-side economics. Its proponents, led by economists Martin Anderson and Arthur Laffer, believed that if taxes were cut and spending on frivolous social programs were reduced—even while military spending increases—businesses will use the excess money to expand. More jobs would result, consumers would increase spending, and the multiplying effect would be a period of sustained growth and prosperity. Two books that explain the rise of the post–World War II conservative movement in which Reagan became the major player are Lee Edwards' sympathetic *The Conservative Revolution: The Movement That Remade America* (Free Press, 1999) and Godfrey Hodgson's more critical *The World Turned Right Side Up: A History of the Conservative Ascendancy in America* (Houghton Mifflin, 1996). Gregory L. Schneider's essay

on "Conservative and the Reagan Presidency," in Richard S. Conley, ed., *Reassessing the Reagan Presidency* (University Press of America, 2003) is a sympathetic objective account with a full bibliography.

In the YES selection, Professor J. David Woodard argues that the 1980s was a decade of affluence for all classes. Supply-side economics, he says, unleashed a wave of entrepreneurial and technological innovation that transformed the economy and restored Americans' confidence between 1983 and 1992. He notes with approval the increased participation of the middle class in the stock market. He also points out the risks taken by the new investors, who saw a 22 percent dip in the market in mid-October 1987. While disapproving of the insider trading tactics that landed multimillionaire Wall Street dealers Michael Milken and Ivan Boesky in jail, Woodard approves of the free-market rational actor model espoused by Milton and Rose Friedman in their book *Free to Choose* (Avon Books, 1985), which "effectively" rebutted the government-as-manager thesis.

Although Woodard argues that "a rising tide" raised the income level of 90 percent of Americans, he does not counter the statistical arguments of Edsall, who believes the boat leaked for those blue-collar urban whites and minorities who found themselves in the poverty and lower middle class. Woodard admits that inequalities existed between "the knowledge practitioners" who controlled the new economy and the noneducated blue-collar workers who saw their well-paid union-protected jobs in steel, automobiles, and the oil industry disappear, falling victim to increasing automation and the practice of foreign outsourcing.

Woodard also criticizes the manner in which capitalism has been portrayed by the movie industry in such films as *Wall Street* and *Bonfire of the Vanities*, and he finds distasteful the nonrational "deconstructionist" views of the social science and humanities at America's elite universities. Interestingly, he views President Ronald Reagan as both a premodern and postmodern figure, claiming that while Reagan's convictions were of an earlier time, "his style of image politics, [were] carefully crafted and orchestrated for mass consumption."

Political journalist Thomas B. Edsall disagrees with Woodard's analysis. Yes, there was prosperity in the 1980s, but only for a few groups. The Reagan revolution, Edsall says, brought about a political realignment that redistributed political and economic wealth to the top 20 percent of Americans. His description of the changing landscape of political and economic power in the 1970s and 1980s could just as easily be applied to the present conditions in the United States. Political parties declined in influence;

members of Congress received the bulk of their money from economic interest groups and political action committees (PACS), in spite of reforms to curb their influence; and presidential candidates and presidential office holders operated their campaigns and policy considerations independent of Congress. Edsall believes that the Republican Party attained power because of the defection of the white male working class, both in the South and in the North. He argues that the Wallace third-party movement in 1968 and 1972 capitalized on the consequences of the civil rights and women's movement, which produced affirmative action jobs for women and minorities in areas previously held by white males. The defection of well-paid union jobs in steel, coal, automobiles, and clothing manufacturing to foreign countries also contributed to the income decline of the noncollege-educated white male, who had to settle for low-wage jobs in the service industries.

YES ⤶

J. David Woodard

A Rising Tide

The Reagan Revolution, as the times came to be called, followed the economic growth in real income from 1983 through the end of the president's second term in 1988, to the recession that concluded the Bush presidency in 1992. During this time the gross domestic product (GDP) doubled. In the expansion through the two Reagan terms, "real-after-tax income per person rose by 15.5 percent, [and] the real median income of families, before taxes, went up 12.5 percent." Measured in constant 1990 dollars, the percentage of families earning between $15,000 and $50,000 fell by 5 points, and the percentage earning more than $50,000 in constant dollars rose by 5 points. Millions of families moved up the ladder from the lower class to the middle class. America had gone from "stagflation" and the highest prices in thirty years to galloping capitalism, and everyday citizens were investing in the stock market.

The middle-class market sought the deposits of ordinary savers and young people just beginning to accumulate assets. Wall Street had previously ignored these customers, but now it sought them out. Prudential-Bache, an aggressive firm, was quoted in *Barron's* as saying it "sees its clients as the $40,000-a-year young professional on the fast track." As the market expanded, more individuals placed their money in funds to balance risk and profit. Suddenly the stock market report was of interest to everyone.

Stockbrokers assured investors that their money was safe, but in late 1987 they discovered the real meaning of risk. The market was doing quite well for the first nine months of the year; it was up more than 30 percent and reaching unprecedented heights. Then, in the days between October 14 and October 19, the market fell off a cliff. On October 19, subsequently known as "Black Monday," the Dow Jones Industrial Average plummeted 508 points, losing 22.6 percent of its total value. This was the greatest loss Wall Street had ever suffered on a single day, even worse than the crash of 1929. It took two years for the Dow to recover completely; not until September of 1989 did it regain all the value it lost in the 1987 crash.

One important lesson came out of the crash: investors who sold took a bath. Those who held on and continued a disciplined and systematic program received rewards. The American economy continued as the greatest wealth producer the world had ever seen. The consequence of all this was a standard of living beyond the comprehension of the rest of the world, and a cause for envy by peer nations. While $200,000 was enough to make the top 1 percent of American income in 1980, a family might need well over $300,000 to be in that category a decade later. The Congressional Budget Office estimated that it would take more than $550,000 to be in the top 1 percent in 1992. No sooner had a survivor of the 1970s comprehended what was happening than he became obsolete. Reagan's supply-side ideas unleashed a wave of entrepreneurial and technological innovation that transformed the economy and restored the country's self-confidence. Economic prosperity had been the impossible dream of youth, and now it was everywhere.

The vast majority of the population experienced substantial gains in real income and wealth. With millions of people earning more money, much higher incomes were required to make it to the top 5 percent, or the top 1 percent of the nation's income bracket. At the time, the rising tide of economic prosperity lifted at least 90 percent of the American family boats. For those who lived through it, the 1983–1992 period would be remembered as an uncomplicated golden time, mourned as lost, and remembered as cloudless.

The spending began at home, where people purchased new homes and remodeled older ones. Declining interest rates made mortgages affordable, and the number of single-family homes expanded each year from 1980 to 1988. Consumers also had more cars to drive as the two-income, two-car family became the norm. From 1980 to 1988, the number of new car models increased by half, the most popular being the minivans for suburban families. Lower air fares and discount packages allowed passengers to travel to previously unheard-of places, and the number of people flying overseas rose by 40 percent during the 1980s.

fell apart, and an official examination found that she had never been assaulted and had smeared the excrement and written the epithets herself. Once the truth came out, the two lawyers were subject to legal discipline, but Al Sharpton suffered no repercussions and continued his race-baiting activities. He ran for the New York Senate seat in 1992 and 1994, for mayor of New York City in 1997, and for the Democratic presidential nomination in 2004. Throughout his career he never apologized or explained his activities in the Tawana Brawley case.

The Brawley case showed the power of the new mass media. The "age of publicity," as Louis Kronenberger called it, began in the 1920s when flagpole sitting and goldfish swallowing became ways to get attention. Conspicuous ballyhoo became fashionable after World War II, when couples took their marriage vows on carnival carousels and spent their honeymoons in department store windows. As television grew, so too did the Barnum spirit. World records were set for domino toppling, frankfurter eating, and kazoo playing, and all of it was seen on television. The problem was that no one could predict what was likely to become news or why it would occupy public attention or for how long. More importantly, fame in America not only lasted for just fifteen minutes; it often left devastating results in its wake.

In October of 1987 the country fixated on the rescue of "Baby Jessica" McClure, who fell down an eight-inch-wide, twenty-two-foot-deep hole in her backyard in Midland, Texas. For the next fifty-eight hours the country watched spellbound as rescuers left jobs and worked nonstop to save the baby. On the evening of October 16, paramedics Steve Forbes and Robert O'Donnell wriggled into a passageway drilled through rock to save "Baby Jessica."

When it was over, the gifts sent to her would provide a million-dollar trust fund. Twenty years later, hardened West Texas roughnecks would wipe tears from their cheeks as they talked about the rescue and the media coverage it inspired. The child's parents, Chip and Cissy McClure, subsequently divorced, and one of the rescuers, Robert O'Donnell, killed himself in 1995. His brother, Ricky, said O'Donnell's life fell apart because of the stress of the rescue. In the new media age fame was fleeting and suffocating at the same time.

In 1941 Henry Luce wrote an article for *Life* magazine entitled "The American Century." Luce was the most powerful and innovative mass communications person of his era, and the purpose of his essay was twofold: (1) to urge American involvement in World War II, and (2) to put forth the idea that the American principles of democracy and free enterprise would eventually come to dominate the world. The idea of American preeminence was dangerous in the eyes of some, but the basis of the piece bespoke what most people acknowledged whether they liked Luce's formulation or not.

"We have some things in this country which are infinitely precious and especially American," wrote Luce, "a love of freedom, a feeling for the equality of opportunity, a tradition of self-reliance and independence." Forty-two years later, the editors of *Time* magazine, the sister publication to *Life*, updated Luce's vision with an essay entitled "What Really Mattered." In the essay the *Time* editors evaluated the meaning of America and what values were most precious to its citizens in 1983. They concluded the fundamental idea America represented was freedom, but it was different from what Luce had in mind: "America was merely free: it was freed unshackled. . . . To be free was to be modern: to be modern was to take chances. . . . The American Century was to be the century of unleashing."

During the 1980s the limits of freedom were explored in the political, social, and personal realm. In the 1930s, scientists freed the atom, and fifty years later doctors were trying to free the body from its genetic dictates. Could organ transplants, sex change operations, and genetic manipulation make us immortal? Could the nation be free of superstition, so that Americans could indulge their passions for personal peace and affluence? Freedom was one of the prime conditions of postmodernity, and the cultural preoccupation with it a prelude for change. The advent of a global communications system meant that the world was coming together at one level, and falling apart at another. At the end of the decade the United States was the world's only superpower, yet it would be held captive by countries with only a fraction of its political power, but united by television to worldwide religious followers across the globe.

Postmodernism came of age in this climate in the decade of the 1980s. The election and re-election of ex-actor Ronald Reagan put a new gloss on the possibility of politics shaped by images alone. The convictions of the president were a throwback to an earlier time, but his style of image politics, carefully crafted and orchestrated for mass consumption, was of a newer era. The world was changing, and the older language of genres and forms was becoming obsolete.

J. DAVID WOODARD is Thurmond Professor of Political Science at Clemson University, where he has taught since 1983. He is also the author of *Ronald Reagan: A Biography* (2012) and *The New Southern Politics*, 2nd ed. (2013).

Thomas Byrne Edsall

 **NO**

The Changing Shape of Power: A Realignment in Public Policy

The past twenty years in America have been marked by two central political developments. The first is the continuing erosion of the political representation of the economic interests of those in the bottom half of the income distribution. The second is the growing dominance of the political process by a network of elites that includes fundraisers, the leadership of interest groups, specialists in the technology and manipulation of elections, and an army of Washington lobbyists and law firms—elites that augment and often overshadow political officeholders and the candidates for office themselves.

This shift in the balance of power has not been accompanied by realignment of the electorate, although the shape and relative strength of the Republican and Democratic Parties have changed dramatically.

Twice during the past twenty years, the Republican party has had the opportunity to gain majority status: in the early 1970s, and again after the 1980 election. The first opportunity emerged when the fragile Democratic coalition was fractured by the independent presidential bid of Alabama governor George G. Wallace in 1968. The Democratic party then amplified its own vulnerability four years later with the nomination of Sen. George S. McGovern, Democrat of South Dakota, whose candidacy alienated a spectrum of traditional Democrats from Detroit to Atlanta. This potential Republican opportunity crumbled, however, when the web of scandals known as Watergate produced across-the-board setbacks for the GOP in campaigns ranging from city council contests to the presidency in the elections of 1974 and 1976.

The period from 1978 to 1981 offered even more fertile terrain for the Republican party. Not only had Democratic loyalties dating back to the depression of the 1930s been further weakened during the presidency of Jimmy Carter, with the emergence of simultaneous inflation and high unemployment, but the candidacy

of Ronald Reagan provided the Republican party with its first substantial opportunity to heal the fissures that had relegated the GOP to minority status for two generations. In Reagan, the party long identified with the rich found a leader equipped to bridge divisions between the country club and the fundamentalist church, between the executives of the Fortune 500 and the membership of the National Rifle Association. Just as Watergate halted Republican momentum in the early 1970s, however, the severe recession of 1981–82 put the brakes on what had the earmarks of a potential Republican takeover, for the first time since 1954, of both branches of Congress. In the first two years of the Reagan administration, the Republican party captured the Senate by a six-vote margin and, with a gain of thirty-two House seats, acquired de facto control of the House in an alliance with southern Democratic conservatives. The recession, however, resulted in the return of twenty-six House seats to the Democrats in 1982, and with those seats went the chance to establish Republican dominance of the federal government.

As the two parties have gained and lost strength, the underlying alteration of the balance of political power over the past decade has continued in a shift of power among the rich, the poor, and the middle class; among blacks and whites; among regions in the country; and among such major competitors for the federal dollar as the defense and social services sectors.

The past twenty years have, in effect, produced a policy realignment in the absence of a political realignment. The major beneficiaries of this policy realignment are the affluent, while those in the bottom half of the income distribution, particularly those whose lives are the most economically marginal, have reaped the fewest rewards or have experienced declines in their standard of living.

A major factor contributing to this development is the decline of political parties: In the United States, as well as in most democratic countries, parties perform the function of representing major interests and classes. As parties erode, the groups that suffer most are those with the fewest resources to protect themselves. In other words, the continued collapse of the broad representation role of political parties in the United States has direct consequences for the distribution of income.

As the role of parties in mobilizing voters has declined, much of the control over both election strategy and issue selection—key functions in defining the national agenda—has shifted to a small, often interlocking, network of campaign specialists, fund-raisers, and lobbyists. While this element of politics is among the most difficult to quantify, there are some rough measures. For example, there are approximately thirty Republican and Democratic consultants and pollsters, almost all based in Washington, who at this writing are the principal strategists in almost every presidential and competitive Senate race, in addition to playing significant roles in gubernatorial, House, and local referenda contests.

At another level, the years from 1974 to 1984 show a steady growth in the financial dependence of House and Senate candidates on political action committees (PACS), vehicles through which money is transferred from organized interest groups to elected officeholders. In that decade, the PAC share of the total cost of House campaigns went from 17 percent to 36 percent, while individual contributions fell from 73 percent to 47 percent, with the remainder coming from parties, loans, and other sources. For House Democratic incumbents, 1984 marked the first year in which PACS were the single most important source of cash; they provided 47 percent of the total, compared with 45 percent from individuals.

This shift has, in turn, magnified the influence of a group of lobbyists who organize Washington fund-raisers for House and Senate incumbents, among whom are Thomas Hale Boggs, Jr., whose clients include the Trial Lawyers Association, the Chicago Board of Options Exchange, and Chrysler; Edward H. Forgotson, whose clients include Enserch Corp., the Hospital Corp. of America, and the Texas Oil and Gas Corp.; Robert J. Keefe, whose clients include Westinghouse and the American Medical Association; and J. D. Williams, whose clients include General Electric Co. and the National Realty Committee. The Washington consulting-lobbying firm of Black, Manafort, Stone, Kelly and Atwater provides perhaps the best example of the range of political and special interests one firm can represent. In 1987, one partner, Charles Black, managed the presidential bid of Rep. Jack Kemp (R-N.Y.); another, Lee Atwater, managed

the campaign of Vice-President George Bush; and a third, Peter Kelly, was a principal fund-raiser for the campaign of Sen. Albert Gore (D-Tenn.). At the same time, the firm's clients have included the Dominican Republic, the anti-Communist insurgency in Angola run by Jonas Savimbi, Salomon Brothers, the government of Barbados, the Natural Gas Supply Association, and, briefly, the Marcos government in the Philippines. In addition, the firm has served as principal political consultant to the Senate campaigns of Phil Gramm (R-Tex.), Jesse Helms (R-N.C), and Paula Hawkins (formerly R-Fla.).

A few general indicators of the scope of lobbying and political party bureaucracies point to the sizable influence small elites can exercise over public policy. In 1986, there were almost 10,000 people employed as registered Washington lobbyists, with 3,500 of these serving as officers of 1,800 trade and professional organizations, including labor unions; another 1,300 were employed by individual corporations, and approximately 1,000 represented organizations ranging from the National Right to Life Association to the Sierra Club. The six major political party committees headquartered in Washington now employ roughly 1,200 people. The creation and expansion of such ideological think tanks as the Heritage Foundation, the Center for National policy, the Urban Institute, the American Enterprise Institute, the Cato Institute, and the Hoover Institution have established whole networks of influential public policy entrepreneurs specializing in media relations and in targeted position papers. Within a general framework of increasingly monopolized American mass media—both print and electronic—the growth of the Gannett and Los Angeles Times-Mirror chains are examples of an ever greater concentration of power within the media, just as the acquisition of NBC by General Electric has functioned to submerge a major network within the larger goals of the nation's sixth biggest corporation. Staffers acquiring expertise and influence on Capitol Hill, in the executive branch, and throughout the regulatory apparatus routinely travel to the private sector—and sometimes back again—through the so-called revolving door. In effect, an entire class of public and private specialists in the determination of government policy and political strategy has been created—a process replicated in miniature at the state level.

The rise to authority of elites independent of the electorate at large, empowered to make decisions without taking into direct account the economic interests of voters, is part of a much larger shift in the balance of power involving changed voting patterns, the decline of organized labor, a restructuring of the employment marketplace, and a transformed system of political competition. This power shift, in turn, has produced a policy realignment most apparent in the alteration of both the *pre-tax* distribution of income and the *after-tax* distribution of income. In both cases, the distribution has become increasingly regressive. The alteration of the pre-tax distribution of income is the subject of a broad debate in which there are those, particularly critics on the left, who argue that growing regressivity emerges from government policies encouraging weakened union representation and a proliferation of low-wage service industry jobs. On the other side, more conservative analysts contend that changes in the pre-tax distribution result from natural alterations of the marketplace and the workplace, as the United States adjusts to a changing economic and demographic environment. The figures in table 1, derived from Census Bureau data, indicate changes in the distribution of pretax household income from 1980 through 1985. . . .

The data clearly show a growing disparity in the distribution of income. Of the five quintiles, all but those in the top 20 percent have seen their share of household income decline. In addition, most of the gains of the top 20 percent have, in fact, been concentrated in the top 5 percent of the income distribution. The gain of 1.1 percent for the top 5 percent translates into a total of $38.8 billion (in 1987 dollars) more for this segment of the

Table 1

Shares of Pre-Tax Household Income, by Income Distribution

Income group	Year	
	1980 (%)	1985 (%)
Quintile[a]		
Bottom	4.1	3.9
Second	10.2	9.7
Third	16.8	16.3
Fourth	24.8	24.4
Top	44.2	45.7
Top 5%	16.5	17.6

Sources: Bureau of the Census, *Estimating After-Tax Money Income Distribution,* Series P-23, no. 126, issued August 1983; and ibid., *Household After-Tax Income: 1985,* Series P-23, no. 151, issued June 1987.

[a] A quintile is a block of 20% of the population.

Table 2

Shares of After-Tax Household Income, by Income Distribution

Income group	Year	
	1980 (%)	1985 (%)
Quintile[a]		
Bottom	4.9	4.6
Second	11.6	11.0
Third	17.9	17.2
Fourth	25.1	24.7
Top	40.6	42.6
Top 5%	14.1	15.5

Sources: Bureau of the Census, *Estimating After-Tax Money Income Distribution,* Series P-23, no. 126, issued August 1983; and ibid., *Household After-Tax Income: 1985,* Series P-23, no. 151, issued June 1987.

[a] A quintile is a block of 20% of the population.

population than if the income distribution had remained constant after 1980. These regressive trends were, moreover, intensified by the tax policies enacted between 1980 and 1985, as demonstrated in table 2, based on Census Bureau data.

What had been a $38.8 billion improvement in the status of the top 5 percent in pre-tax income over these six years becomes a $49.5 billion gain in after-tax income, while the bottom 80 percent of the population saw larger losses in its share of after-tax income between 1980 and 1985 than it had seen in the case of pre-tax income. These findings are even more sharply delineated in a November 1987 study by the Congressional Budget Office showing that from 1977 to 1988, 70 percent of the population experienced very modest increases in after-tax income or, for those in the bottom 40 percent, net drops, when changes over that period in the federal income tax, the Social Security tax, corporate tax, and excise taxes are taken into account. In contrast, those in the seventy-first to ninetieth percentiles experienced a modest improvement, and those in the top 10 percent significantly improved their standard of living. For those at the very top, the gains have been enormous. Table 3, developed from Congressional Budget Office data, shows that distribution.

What these tables point to is a major redistribution of economic power in the private marketplace and of political power in the public sector, which, in turn, has been

Table 3

Changes in Estimated Average After-Tax Family Income, by Income Distribution (In 1987 Dollars)

Income group	1977 average income ($)	1988 average income ($)	Percentage change (+ or −)	Dollar change (+ or −)
Decile[a]				
First (poor)	3,528	3,157	−10.5	−371
Second	7,084	6,990	−1.3	−94
Third	10,740	10,614	−1.2	−126
Fourth	14,323	14,266	−0.4	−57
Fifth	18,043	18,076	+0.2	+33
Sixth	22,009	22,259	+1.1	+250
Seventh	26,240	27,038	+3.0	+798
Eighth	31,568	33,282	+5.4	+1,718
Ninth	39,236	42,323	+7.9	+3,087
Tenth (rich)	70,459	89,793	+27.4	+19,324
Top 5%	90,756	124,651	+37.3	+33,895
Top 1%	174,498	303,900	+74.2	+129,402
All groups	22,184	26,494	+9.6	+2,310

Sources: Congressional Budget Offices, *The Changing Distribution of Federal Taxes: 1975–1990,* October 1987.
[a]A decile is a block of 10% of the population.

reflected in very concrete terms in family income patterns. One of the major characteristics, then, of the post–New Deal period in American politics has been a reversal of the progressive redistribution of income that underlay the policies of the administrations of Franklin Roosevelt and Harry Truman.

In the competition between the defense and social welfare sectors, the outcome of a parallel, although more recent, shift in the balance of power can be seen in the years from 1980 through 1987. During this period, the share of the federal budget going to national defense grew from 22.7 percent in 1980 to 28.4 percent in 1987. At the same time, the share of federal dollars collectively going to education, training, employment, social services, health, income security, and housing dropped from 25.5 percent in 1980 to 18.3 percent in 1987.

In many respects, these policy changes reflect the rising strength of the Republican party. In terms of tax policy and the balance of spending between defense and social programs, the Republican party under Ronald Reagan has been the driving force pushing the country to the right. During the past ten years, the Republican party has made substantial gains in the competition for the allegiance of voters, gaining near parity by 1987, reducing what had been a 20- to 25-point Democratic advantage in terms of self-identification to a six- or seven-point edge.

The income distribution trends and the shifts in budget priorities began, however, before the Republican party took over the presidency and the U.S. Senate in 1980. The emergence of a vital, competitive Republican party is less a cause of the changed balance of power in the country than a reflection of the underlying forces at work in the post–New Deal phase of American politics.

Together, these forces—which include the deterioration of organized labor, the continued presence of divisive racial conflict, the shift from manufacturing to service industries, the slowing rates of economic growth, the threat of international competition to domestic production, the replacement of political organization with political technology, and the growing class-skew of voter turnout—have severely undermined the capacity of those in the bottom half of the income distribution to form an effective political coalition.

In tracing the erosion of the left wing of the Democratic party in the United States, it is difficult to overestimate the importance of the collapse of the labor movement. In 1970, the continuing growth in the number of labor union members came to a halt. Unions represented 20.7 million workers that year, or 27.9 percent of the nonagricultural work force. Through 1980, the number of workers represented by unions remained roughly the same, dropping slightly to 20.1 million employees by 1980. At the same time, however, the total work force had grown, so that the percentage of workers who were represented by unions fell to 23 percent in 1980. With the election of Ronald Reagan, however, the decline of organized labor began to accelerate sharply, a process encouraged by Reagan's firing of 11,500 striking patco air traffic controllers, and by the appointment of pro-management officials to the National Labor Relations Board and to the Department of Labor. From 1980 to 1986, not only did the share of the work force represented by unions drop from 23 percent to 17.5 percent, but the number of workers in unions began to fall precipitously for the first time in fifty years, dropping by 3.1 million men and women, from 20.1 million to 17 million, in 1986. During the first half of the 1980s, almost all the decline in union membership was among whites employed in private industry.

The decline of organized labor dovetailed with a continuing shift from traditional manufacturing, mining, and construction employment to work in the technology and service industries. From 1970 to 1986, the number of jobs in goods-producing industries, which lend themselves to unionization, grew only from 23.8 million to 24.9 million, while employment in the service industries, which are much more resistant to labor organizing, shot up from 47.3 million to 75.2 million.

The difficulties of organized labor were compounded by the unexpected decision on the part of many of the major corporations in the early 1970s to abandon what

had been a form of tacit détente between labor and management, in which Fortune 500 companies kept labor peace through agreements amounting to a form of profit sharing by means of automatic cost-of-living pay hikes. Faced with growing competition from foreign producers—in 1968, car imports exceeded exports for the first time in the nation's history, an unmistakable signal that domestic producers of all goods faced serious foreign competition—major American companies dropped the fundamentally cordial relations that had characterized the largest part of postwar union negotiations. Catching the leaders of organized labor entirely unprepared, these corporations adopted a tough, adversarial approach regarding both pay and fringe benefits, willing to break union shops and to relocate facilities either abroad or in nonunion communities in the South and Southwest.

The decline of organized labor was particularly damaging to the Democratic party because unions represent one of the few remaining institutional links between working-class voters and the Democratic party. The decline of political parties has resulted in the end of the clubhouse tie between the party of Franklin Delano Roosevelt and the blue-collar voters of row- and tract-house neighborhoods throughout the Northeast and Midwest. In addition, it is among these white, blue-collar workers that the racial conflicts within the Democratic party have been the most divisive. Interviews with whites in Dearborn, Michigan, the west-side suburbs of Birmingham, Chicago, Atlanta, and New Orleans—all communities that have suffered major industrial layoffs and that are either part of or adjoin cities now run by Democratic black mayors—reveal voters who are disenchanted with the unions that failed to protect their jobs, and with a local Democratic party no longer controlled by whites. Race, which previously severed the tie between the white South and the Democratic party, has, in cities with black mayors, served to produce white Republican voting, not only for president but for local offices that once were unchallenged Democratic bastions.

These developments, in the 1970s, contributed significantly to the creation of a vacuum of power within the Democratic party, allowing the party to be taken over, in part, by its most articulate and procedurally sophisticated wing: affluent, liberal reformers. This faction capitalized first on the public outcry against police violence at the Chicago presidential convention in 1968, and then on the Watergate scandals in the mid-1970s, to force priority consideration of a series of reforms involving campaign finance, the presidential nominating process, the congressional seniority system, the congressional code of ethics—and an expansion of the federal role in regulating the environment, through creation of the Environmental Protection Agency and new water- and air-pollution standards. The strength of this wing of the Democratic party subsided during the 1980s, although its leverage within the party has been institutionalized through the creation of a host of primaries and caucuses in the presidential selection process, giving disproportionate influence to middle- and upper-middle-class voters and interests in a party that claims to represent the nation's working and lower-middle classes. The turnout in primaries and in caucuses is skewed in favor of the affluent and upper-middle class. In addition, these delegate selection processes have been contributing factors in the acceleration of the decline of political organizations in working-class communities.

The Democratic agenda set in the 1970s by the reform wing of the party was, however, more important for what it omitted and neglected than for what was included. The ascendancy of the reformers took place just when the fissures within the Democratic party had become most apparent. In 1968, 9.9 million mostly Democratic voters turned to George C. Wallace, the segregationist-populist governor of Alabama, and they strayed off the Democratic reservation in 1972 when Nixon beat McGovern by a margin of 47.2 million votes to 29.2 million. The cultural and ideological gulf that had steadily widened between these voters and the wings of the Democratic party supporting the antiwar movement, gay rights, women's rights, and civil rights had reached such proportions in the early and mid 1970s that rapprochement between warring factions was difficult, if not impossible.

The rise to prominence within the Democratic party of a well-to-do liberal-reform wing worked in other ways to compound the divisions in the party. Relatively comfortable in their own lives, reformers failed to recognize the growing pressure of marginal tax rates on working- and lower-middle-class voters. The progressive rate system of the federal income tax remained effectively unchanged from the early 1950s through the 1970s, so that the series of sharply rising marginal tax rates that had originally been designed to affect only the upper-middle class and rich, began to directly impinge on regular Democratic voters whose wages had been forced up by inflation. By neglecting to adjust the marginal rate system to account for inflation, in combination with repeated raising of the highly regressive Social Security tax, Democrats effectively encouraged the tax revolt of the 1970s which, in turn, provided a critically important source of support

to the conservative movement and to the rise of the Republican party. . . .

On the Republican side, the same developments that debilitated the Democratic coalition served to strengthen ascendant constituencies of the Right. For a brief period in the late 1970s and early 1980s, the constituencies and interests underpinning the Republican party had the potential to establish a new conservative majority in the electorate. The tax revolt, the rise of the religious right, the mobilization of much of the business community in support of the Republican party, renewed public support for defense spending, the political-financial mobilization of the affluent, and the development of a conservative economic theory promising growth through lower taxes—all combined to empower the political right to a degree unprecedented since the 1920s.

Proposed tax cuts provided an essential common ground for the right-of-center coalition that provided the core of the Reagan revolution. The combination of corporate tax reductions and individual tax cuts embodied in the 1981 tax bill served to unify a divided business community by providing a shared legislative goal, to strengthen the commitment of the affluent to the Republican party, and to attract white working- and lower-middle-class former Democrats who had seen their paychecks eaten away by inflation-driven higher marginal rates. The tax cut theme was adopted as a central element of the speeches of such religious-right figures as the Rev. Jerry Falwell of the Moral Majority, Ed McAteer of the Religious Roundtable, and the Rev. Marion G. (Pat) Robertson of the Christian Broadcast Network. . . .

This growing political tilt in favor of the affluent is further reflected in voting turnout patterns over the past twenty years. During this period, the class-skewing of voting in favor of the affluent has grown significantly. In the presidential election year of 1964, the self-reported turnout among members of professions associated with the middle and upper classes was 83.2 percent, compared with 66.1 percent among those employed in manual jobs, including skilled crafts, a difference of 17.1 points; by 1980, the spread between the two had grown to 25 points, 73 percent to 48 percent. In the off-year election of 1966, the percentage-point spread in terms of voter turnout between middle-to-upper-class job holders and those employed in manual jobs was 18.1 percent; by 1978, this had grown to a 23.8-percent spread. While overall turnout has been declining, the drop has been most severe among those in the bottom third of the income distribution.

For the Republican party, these turnout trends were a political bonanza, accentuated by trends in the correlation between income and both voting and partisan commitment. Through the 1950s, 1960s, and into the early 1970s, the sharp class divisions that characterized the depression-era New Deal coalition structure gave way to diffuse voting patterns with relatively little correlation between income and allegiance to the Democratic or Republican party. By 1980 and 1982, with the election of Reagan and then the enactment of the budget and tax bills of 1981, the correlation between income and voting began to reemerge with a vengeance. By 1982, the single most important determinant of probable voting, aside from membership in either the Republican or Democratic party, became income, with the Democratic margin steadily declining as one moved up the ladder. . . .

In other words, the Reagan years polarized the electorate along sharp income lines. While income made almost no difference in the partisan loyalties of 90 percent of the population in 1956, by 1984 income became one of the sharpest dividing lines between Democrats and Republicans. In 1956, the very poor were only 5 percentage points more likely to be Democratic than the upper-middle class, and 40 points more likely than the affluent top 10 percent of the income distribution. By 1984, however, the spread between the poor and the upper-middle class reached 36 points, and between the poor and affluent, 69 points. . . .

These figures accurately describe an electorate polarized by income, but what they mask are the effects of black and white voter participation on the figures. The civil rights movement, and civil rights legislation enacted in the 1960s, enfranchised millions of blacks who, in 1956, were barred from voting. During the twenty-eight years from 1956 to 1984, roughly 4.2 million blacks entered the electorate. During the same period, blacks' allegiance to the Democratic party, which in 1956 held their loyalty by a 34-percentage-point edge, increased to provide an overwhelming 72-percentage-point Democratic edge in 1984. This infusion of black Democratic support sharply increased the low-income tilt of the party: in 1984, the median family income for whites was $28,674, while for blacks it was $15,982.

The Reagan revolution was, at its core, a revolution led by the affluent. The class polarization of voters . . . cut across the country, but nowhere were the trends stronger than in the South, where a realignment in miniature took place among the white elite. In the 1950s, Democratic allegiance in the South was strongest among the most well-to-do whites, for whom the Democratic party was the vehicle for maintaining the pre-civil rights social structure of the Confederate states. These voters gave the Democratic

party their support by a 5 to 1 margin, higher than that of any other income group in the South. By the 1980s, in the aftermath of a civil rights movement supported by the Democratic party, these same voters had become the most Republican in the South. "The class cleavage had reversed itself," John R. Petrocik, of UCLA, noted. Whites, particularly white men, have become increasingly Republican as blacks have become the most consistent source of Democratic votes. In the five presidential elections from 1968 to 1984, only one Democrat, Jimmy Carter, received more than 40 percent of the white vote, and by 1984, white, male Protestants voted for Reagan over Mondale by a margin of 74 to 26.

The Reagan revolution would, however, have been a political failure if it had not gained extensive support from voters outside the upper-middle class. In addition to the deep inroads made in previously Democratic working-class communities in northern urban areas, perhaps the single most important source of new support for the Republican party has been the religious Right.

In a far shorter period, voters identifying themselves as born-again Christians radically shifted their voting in presidential elections. Between 1976 and 1984, these voters went from casting a 56-to-44 margin for the Democratic candidate, Jimmy Carter, to one of the highest levels of support of any group for the reelection of President Reagan in 1984: 81 to 19, according to *New York Times*/CBS exit polls. This shift represents, in effect, a gain of eight million voters for the GOP.

As a political resource, support among born-again Christians represents not only a loyal core of voters, but a growing core. In contrast with such mainline churches as the United Methodist Church, the United Church of Christ, and the United Presbyterians, which experienced membership losses from 1970 to 1980, the fundamentalist, evangelical, and charismatic churches have seen their congregations grow at an explosive rate: the Southern Baptist Convention by 16 percent, the Assemblies of God by 70 percent, and Seventh Day Adventists by 36 percent.

The Republican party has, in turn, been the major beneficiary of an internal power struggle taking place within the Southern Baptist Convention, now the largest Protestant denomination. During a ten-year fight, the denomination has been taken over by its conservative wing, believers in the "absolute inerrancy" of the Bible. This wing of the denomination, in turn, has been a leading force within the broader religious Right, as such pastors as Adrian Rogers, James T. Draper, Jr., and Charles F. Stanley—all outspoken conservatives—have won the denomination's presidency. The move to the right has been reflected in the ranks of the denomination, producing what amounts to a realignment of the ministry of the Southern Baptist Convention. James L. Guth, of Furman University, found that in just three years, surveys of Southern Baptist ministers showed a remarkable shift from a strong majority in 1981 favoring the Democratic party 41 to 29, to nearly 70 percent in 1984 favoring the GOP, 66 to 26.

The growth of Republican strength is not, however, confined to evangelical and charismatic Christians, and the party appears to be developing a much broader religious base as part of its core constituency. In one of the most interesting recent analyses of voting trends, Frederick T. Steeper, of Market Opinion Research, and John Petrocik, of UCLA, have found that since 1976, one of the sharpest partisan cleavages emerging among white voters in the electorate is between those who attend church regularly and those who never go to church. This represents a major change from past findings. In the period from 1952 to 1960, there was no statistical difference between the Democratic and Republican loyalties of white churchgoers and nonchurchgoers. By the elections of 1972 and 1976, a modest difference began to appear, with nonchurchgoers 7 percentage points more likely to be Democrats than regular churchgoers. By 1986, however, the spread had grown to a striking 35-point difference, with regular churchgoers identifying themselves as Republicans by a 22-point margin, and with nonchurchgoers identifying themselves as Democrats by a 13-point edge. The partisan spread between churchgoers and nonchurchgoers was most extreme among white Northern Protestants (51 points) and Catholics (52 points). These findings dovetail with studies showing that the memberships of such Establishment, nonevangelical denominations as the Methodists, Episcopalians, Lutherans, and Presbyterians were significantly more supportive of the election of Ronald Reagan than the electorate at large. . . .

Cumulatively, developments over the past twenty years—the deterioration of the labor movement; economically polarized partisanship; the skewing of turnout patterns by income; stagnation of the median family income; the rising importance of political money; the emergence of a Republican core composed of the well-to-do and the religious; the globalization of the economy; and competition from foreign producers—have combined to disperse constituencies and groups seeking to push the country to the left, and to consolidate those on the right. The consequences of that shift are most readily seen in the figures in table 3, which show that 80 percent of the population

has experienced a net loss in after-tax income between 1977 and 1988, while the top 5 percent has seen average family income grow by $26,134, and the top 1 percent, by $117,222.

In the long run the prospects are for the maintenance of a strong, conservative Republican party, continuing to set the national agenda on basic distributional issues, no matter which party holds the White House. Barring a major economic catastrophe, or a large-scale international conflict, the basic shift from manufacturing to service industry jobs is likely to continue to undermine the political left in this country, not only for the reasons outlined earlier in this essay, but also by weakening economically—and therefore politically—those in the bottom 40 percent of the income distribution.

In the thirty-year period spanning 1949 to 1979, the number of manufacturing jobs grew by an average of three million a decade, from 17.6 million in 1949, to 20.4 million in 1959, to 24.4 million in 1969, and finally to a high of 26.5 million in 1979. This growth in no way kept pace with the increase in service industry jobs, which shot up from 26.2 million in 1949 to 63.4 million in 1979, but the continuing, if modest, manufacturing expansion provided a partial cushion in an economy going through a major restructuring—a restructuring involving the loss of 950,000 jobs in steel and other metals industries, automobiles, food production, and textiles from 1972 to 1986. From 1979 to 1986, however, the absolute number of manufacturing jobs began to decline, dropping from 26.5 million to 24.9 million, a loss of 1.6 million jobs.

These employment shifts have been particularly damaging to blacks and Hispanics. From 1970 to 1984, in major northern cities, there has been a massive decline in the number of jobs requiring relatively little education—the kind of jobs that provide entry into the employment marketplace for the poor—and a sharp increase in the number of jobs requiring at least some higher education: "Demographic and employment trends have produced a serious mismatch between the skills of inner-city blacks and the opportunities available to them . . . substantial job losses have occurred in the very industries in which urban minorities have the greatest access, and substantial employment gains have occurred in the higher-education-requisite industries that are beyond the reach of most minority workers," according to William Julius Wilson, of the University of Chicago (see table 4).

While blacks and Hispanics will, at least for the time being, disproportionately bear the burden of this shift in job requirements, the altered structure of the marketplace will work to the disadvantage of the poorly educated of

Table 4

Changes in the Combined Number of Jobs, by Employee Education Level, in New York, Philadelphia, Boston, Baltimore, St. Louis, Atlanta, Houston, Denver, and San Francisco, 1970 and 1984

	Number of Jobs		
Mean level of employee education	1970	1984	Change, 1970–84
Less than high school	3,068,000	2,385,000	−683,000
Some higher education	2,023,000	2,745,000	+722,000

Sources: Computed from William Julius Wilson, *The Truly Disadvantaged: The Inner City, the Underclass, and Public Policy* (Chicago: University of Chicago Press, 1987), table 2.6, p. 40. The table, in turn, is taken from John D. Kasarda, "The Regional and Urban Redistribution of People and Jobs in the U.S." (Paper presented to the National Research Council Committee on National Urban Policy, National Academy of Sciences, 1986).

all races. In 1985, there were 30.6 million whites over the age of twenty-five without a high school education—five times the number of blacks without high school degrees (5.9 million) and seven times the number of poorly educated Hispanics (4.4 million). These job market trends will intensify throughout the rest of this century. According to estimates by the Department of Labor, 21.4 million jobs will be created between 1986 and the year 2000, all of which will be in service industries or government, as losses in traditional goods manufacturing industries are unlikely to be fully offset by gains in the technology manufacturing sector. In terms of educational requirements, there will be a significant increase in the proportion of jobs requiring at least one year of college education, no change in the proportion of jobs requiring a high school degree, and a sharp decline in the percentage of jobs requiring no high school education.

In effect, trends in the job market through the next ten years will in all likelihood exacerbate the regressive distribution of income that has taken place over the past decade. Under American democracy, those who are unemployed or marginally employed are weakest politically. The decline of traditional political organizations and unions has made significantly more difficult the political mobilization of the working poor, the working class, and the legions of white-collar workers making from $10,000 to $25,000 a year—a universe roughly containing 24.6 million white households, 3.4 million black households, and 2 million Hispanic households. Within this group, providing a political voice becomes even more difficult for those workers with poor educations who have been dispersed from manufacturing employment into cycles of marginal work. While most of those who have lost manufacturing jobs have found full-time

employment, such workers have, in the main, seen wages fall and fringe benefits, often including medical coverage, decline or disappear, leaving them even further outside of the American mainstream and even less well equipped to ensure adequate educational levels for their children. When combined with the declining voter turnout rates associated with falling income, these workers have fallen into what amounts to a new political underclass.

The major forces at work in the last two decades of the post–New Deal period are, then, cumulatively functioning to weaken the influence and power of those in the bottom half of the income distribution, while strengthening the authority of those in the upper half, and particularly the authority of those at elite levels. Trends in political competition and pressures in the private marketplace have combined to create a whipsaw action, reversing New Deal policies that empowered the labor movement and reduced disparities between rich and poor. Recent forces, both in the marketplace and in the political arena, have not produced a realignment of the electorate, but, in terms of outcomes, there has been a realignment in public policy—with few forces, short of a downturn in the business cycle, working against the continuing development of a political and economic system in which the dominant pressures will be toward increased regressively in the distribution of money and in the ability to influence the outcome of political decisions.

Thomas Byrne Edsall is a widely respected political journalist who has been a frequent contributor to *Atlantic Monthly*, *New Republic*, *Washington Post*, and the *New York Times*. He is the author of *The Politics of Inequality* (1984) and *Power and Money: Writings about Politics, 1971–1988* (1988).

EXPLORING THE ISSUE

Were the 1980s a Decade of Affluence for the Middle Class?

Critical Thinking and Reflection

1. Discuss and critically evaluate the following statement by political journalist Thomas B. Edsall:

   Together; these forces—which include the deterioration of organized labor, the continued presence of divisive racial conflict, the shift from manufacturing to service industries, the slowing rates of economic growth, the threat of international competition to domestic production, the replacement of political organization with political technology, and the growing class-skew of voter turnout—have severely undermined the capacity of those in the bottom half of the income distribution to form an effective political coalition.

2. Critically evaluate the reasons why white males defected from the Democratic Party. How much can be attributed to job replacement from companies outside the United States or from competition from women and African American and Hispanics?

3. The Republican Party has increased its membership and influence equal to the Democratic Party since the 1970s. Critically analyze and discuss the importance of economic, cultural, and religious factors in this shift. In your discussion evaluate whether cultural or economic issues are more important in explaining the transformation.

4. Professor Woodard entitles his chapter on the 1980s "A Rising Tide." Explain what he means by this. Woodard argues that the values of reason, order, and science conflicted with the criticisms of postindustrial society under the labels of "deconstruction or postmodernism." Critically analyze what he means by this contradiction.

5. Critically analyze the following two statements by Professor Woodard: "The vast majority of the population experienced substantial gains in real income of wealth"; and "The rising tide of economic prosperity lifted at least 90 percent of the American family boats." Is it possible to reconcile these statements with Edsall's view that the lower-middle class and the poor were hurt by Reaganomics?

6. Explain who the "knowledge workers" are. How did they attain economic power in America? Define the following terms:

   a. Me decade
   b. My decade
   c. Yuppie
   d. Leveraged buyout
   e. Greenmail

Is There Common Ground?

It's difficult to find common ground between the critics of "supply-side" economics who believe the 1980s widened the income gap between the rich and the middle class while supporters of economics maintained all classes benefited from the prosperity of the era. Edsall's major thesis is that in the 1980s, a policy rather than a political alignment was led by the upper-middle and upper classes. This view is supported by Frederick Strobel, a former senior business economist at the Federal Reserve, Bank of Atlanta, in *Upward Dreams, Downward Mobility: The Economic Decline of the American Middle Class* (Rowman &

Littlefield, 1993). The reasons that Strobel gives for the economic decline include an increased supply of workers (baby boomers, housewives, and immigrants), a decline in union membership, a strong dollar, an open import dollar that destroyed many U.S. manufacturing jobs, corporate merger mania, declining government jobs, energy inflation, high interest rates, and the corporate escape for federal, state, and local taxes.

Unexpected criticism also comes from President Reagan's own director of the Office of Management and Budget, David A. Stockman. His *Triumph of Politics: Why the Revolution Failed* (Harper & Row, 1986) details the "ideological hubris" that surrounded Reagan's advisers, who, in conjunction with a spendthrift Congress beholden to outside interest groups, ran up massive budget deficits by implementing a theory known as supply-side economics. More critical from the left are a series of academic articles in *Understanding America's Economic Decline*, edited by Michael A. Bernstein and David E. Adler (Cambridge University Press, 1994). Also critical are the writings of Kevin Phillips, especially *The Politics of Rich and Poor: Wealth and the American Electorate in the Reagan Aftermath* (Random House, 1990) and Joseph J. Hogan, "Reaganomics and Economic Policy," in Dilys M. Hill et al., eds., *The Reagan Presidency: An Incomplete Revolution?* (St. Martin's Press, 1990), which argues, "while constantly disavowing government interventionism and proclaiming the virtues of a free market economy, the Reagan administration continually pursued economic expansionist policies based upon massive government deficits, periods of maintained monetary expansionism and unprecedented high levels of international borrowing."

For dissenting views that support supply-side economics as the key policy leading to America's economy since the early 1980s, see almost any issue of *Commentary, the National Review, The Weekly Standard, Barron's,* and editorial pages of *The Wall Street Journal*. For example, see "The Real Reagan Record," *The National Review* (August 31, 1992, pp. 25–62); in particular, the essays by Alan Reynolds in "Upstarts and Downstarts," who asserts that all income groups experienced significant gains in income during the 1980s; and Paul Craig Roberts, "What Everyone 'Knows' about Reaganomics," *Commentary* (February 1992), which is critical of the Keynesian explanation for the economic downturn in the early 1990s. Two books that fully support Reagan's positive contribution to the prosperity of the 1980s (in addition to Woodard) are John Ehrman, *The Eighties: America in the Age of Reagan* (Yale University Press, 2005) and Cato Institute economist Richard B. McKenzie, *What Went Right in the 1980s* (Pacific Research Institute for Public Policy, 1994). Karl Zinsmeister, "Summing Up the Reagan Era," *Wilson Quarterly* (Winter 1990) is similar to

Woodard and Ehrman in its interpretation. James D. Torr, editor, provides balanced treatments in *Ronald Reagan* (Thomson Gale, 2001) and *The 1980s: America's Decades* (Greenhaven Press, 2000). The two most recent and important collection of essays by historians and political scientists are Richard S. Conley, ed., *Reassessing the Reagan Presidency* (University Press of America, 2003) and W. Eliot Brownlee and Hugh Davis Graham, eds., *The Reagan Presidency: Pragmatic Conservatism and Legacies* (University Press of Kansas, 2003), which lives up to its title. In the essay on taxation, authors Brownlee and C. Eurgene Steurerle argue that Reagan's commitment to the extreme version of the Laffer curve came in 1977, two or three years earlier than the version given by David Stockman, just before his victory in the 1980 New Hampshire primaries where supposedly Laffer drew his famous curve on a dinner napkin. The two authors claim that Reagan had been reading economist Jude Wanniski's *Wall Street Journal* editorials supporting Laffer's ideas. Finally worth consulting for the worldwide perspective is Bruce J. Schulman, "The Reagan Revolution in International Perspective: Conservative Assaults on the Welfare State across the Industrialized World in the 1980s," in Richard Steven Conley, ed., *Reassessing the Reagan Presidency*. For Reagan's impact on the 2008 presidential race, see Karen Tumulty, "How the Right Went Wrong: What Would Ronnie Do? And Why the Republican Candidates Need to Reclaim the Reagan Legacy," *Time* (March 26, 2007).

Additional Resources

Samuel G. Freedman, *The Inheritance: How Three Families and America Moved from Roosevelt to Reagan and Beyond* (Simon & Schuster, 1996)

Doug Rossinow, "Talking Points Memo (A Critical Review of Three Books on the Reagan Years)," *American Quarterly*, 59/4 (2007)

Sean Wilentz, *The Age of Reagan: A History 1974–2008* (Harper Collins, 2008)

Internet References . . .

American Experience - Reagan

http://www.pbs.org/wgbh/americanexperience
/films/reagan/player/

National Center for Policy Analysis

www.public-policy.org/web.public-policy.org
/index.php

Time Line for Silicon Valley, 1885–1916

http://www.scaruffi.com/politics/silicon.html